Chartered Institute for Securities & Investment Diploma

CW01660241

STUDY TEXT

Bond and Fixed Interest Markets

2010

In this 2010 edition

- A **user-friendly format** for easy navigation
- **Exam tips** to put you on the right track
- A **Test your knowledge** quiz at the end of each chapter
- A full **index**

APPROVED WORKBOOK

LEARNING MEDIA

Published February 2010

ISBN 9780 7517 8199 1

British Library Cataloguing-in-Publication Data
A catalogue record for this book
is available from the British Library

Published by

BPP Learning Media Ltd
BPP House, Aldine Place
London W12 8AA

www.bpp.com/learningmedia

Printed in Great Britain

Your learning materials, published by BPP Learning Media Ltd, are printed on paper sourced from sustainable, managed forests.

£195.00

Contents

1 Introduction to Bonds and Fixed Interest Investment and Management

INTRODUCTION

This section is primarily intended to provide you with an overview of the fixed income instruments we need to consider and principles of fixed income fund management, most of which is then expanded upon in later chapters.

The key area that is covered in some depth here, however, details the various types of investor that we may be interested in bonds and fixed interest investments along with details regarding their tax status, regulation and designated professional bodies.

CHAPTER CONTENTS

Chapter Learning Objectives

The syllabus areas covered by this section are

Investors

Students should be able to demonstrate the suitability of specific securities to specific requirements of domestic and international investor classes.

- Pension Funds
- Mutual Funds/Unit Trusts/OEICs
- Life & General Insurance Companies
- Hedge Funds/Speculators
- Individuals
- Market makers

Students should possess a broad understanding of the preferences of and constraints on, these types of investor and any implications for their investment policy.

1 What is a Bond?

1.1 Definition and development

A bond may be defined as a negotiable debt instrument for a fixed principal amount issued by a borrower for a specific period of time, making a regular payment of interest/coupon to the holder until it is redeemed at maturity, when the principal amount is repaid.

Bond

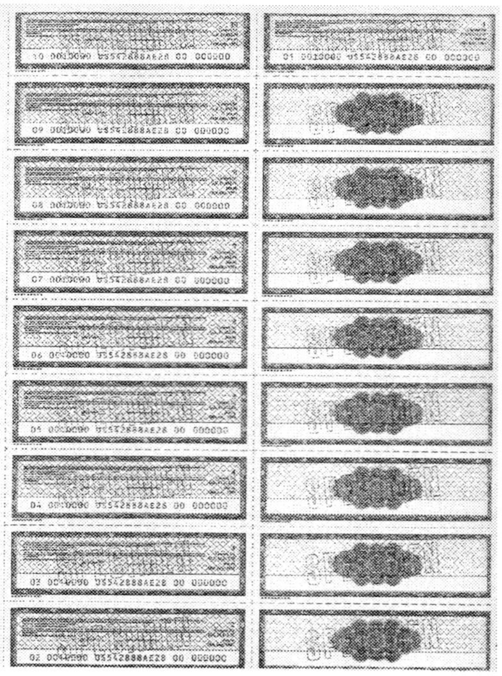

Coupon

Historically, bonds began as very simple negotiable debt instruments, paying a fixed coupon for a specified period, then being redeemed at face value – a 'straight bond'. In the 1960s and 1970s, bond markets were seen as being investment vehicles for 'widows and orphans'. They were thought to be dull markets with predictable returns and very little in the way of gains to be made from trading.

The bond markets emerged from this shadow during the mid-1970s when both interest rates and currencies became substantially more volatile. Bonds have emerged over the past few decades to be much more complex investments, and there are now a significant number of variations on the basic theme.

While it is perhaps easy to be confused by the variety of 'bells and whistles' that have been introduced into the market in recent years, one should always bear in mind that the vast majority of issues are still straight bonds. The reason for this is that investors are wary of buying investments that they do not fully understand. If an issue is too complex, it will be difficult to market.

1.2 Who issues bonds and why

Bonds are used by a number of issuers as a means of raising finance. Major bond issuers include the following.

- **Sovereign governments** – governments of national sovereign states who need to raise finance to help them cover any national debt or budget shortfall.
- **Supranational institutions** – such as the ECB.
- **Official institutions** – such as local authorities who need to raise finance to help them cover any local budget shortfall.
- **Banks** – who need to raise finance for their lending activities.
- **Savings Banks** – or building societies who need to raise finance for their business purposes.
- **Companies** – who need to raise cash to help them finance business requirements.

Regardless of who the issuer is, there are a number of general characteristics that any bond is likely to have which we will examine next.

1.3 General characteristics

Examining the above definition in a little more detail reveals the general characteristics that a bond may have.

1.3.1 Negotiable instrument

Negotiability means that it is a piece of paper that can be bought and sold. For certain types of bonds, this is easier than for others. Government bonds tend to be highly liquid, i.e. very easy to buy or sell, whereas certain corporate bonds are almost illiquid and are usually held to maturity by the initial buyer.

1.3.2 Nominal value

As we noted above, all bonds are issued for a fixed principal amount or nominal value, which historically represented the amount invested. On UK bonds, it is normal to have a bond nominal value of £100, and bond prices are quoted on this basis. Similarly, European and US bonds prices are typically quoted per €100 or $100 nominal respectively. This nominal value serves two important purposes.

- Determining the scale of the coupon payments.
- Determining the value of the redemption proceeds.

We will discuss both purposes below.

1.3.3 Maturity

Initially, all bonds were redeemable after a specific maturity date, which determined when the principal is due for repayment. However, there are now a number of variations we will need to consider. We can subcategorise bonds between

- Redeemable bonds.
- Irredeemable/perpetual bonds.

Redeemable bonds

The majority of bonds fall into this category, though there are some subsets that we will need to consider, as follows.

- **Single-dated bonds** – bonds which mature at a pre-set date only, by far the most common form.
- **Double-dated bonds** – bonds that can be redeemed by the issuer between specified dates. On a double-dated bond, the earlier date specifies when the issuer may redeem, the later date specifies when the bond must be redeemed.
- **Callable bonds** – where the issuer of the bond is able to redeem the bond at an earlier date, should they wish to do so. Double-dated bonds may be considered as a subset of callable bonds, though callable bonds may have many other features (e.g. call premiums) and may be callable throughout their lives.
- **Putable bonds** – a more recent innovation, which gives the holder the ability to sell the bond back to the issuer at a premium over the face value.

Irredeemable bonds

On irredeemable or perpetual or undated bonds, there is no maturity date and the issuer is under no obligation to redeem the principal sum, though he may have the right to do so if he wishes. On these bonds, the coupon will be paid into perpetuity unless the users chooses to redeem them.

1.3.4 Coupon

The basis for the determination of the bond coupon is set before issue, though this does not mean that the value is known at that date. Whilst the vast majority of bonds issued are straights (i.e. a fixed coupon), there are a number of variants on this theme. In addition, there are bonds whose coupons vary with economic factors. We may, therefore, categorise bond coupons between

- Pre-determined.
- Variable.

However the amount is calculated, the full coupon for the period will be paid to the holder of the bond on the ex-div date.

Pre-determined coupons

As we have already stated, this category would include the vast majority of bonds. On these bonds, the gross annual coupon (i.e. the amount due to be paid in a one-year period, irrespective of the frequency of payment) is specified as a percentage of the nominal value of the bond. Sub-classes here would include

- **Straight/fixed coupon bonds** – where the coupon is at a set level for the entire life of the bond.
- **Stepped coupon bonds** – where the coupon increases in steps to pre-specified amounts as the bond moves through its life.
- **Zero-coupon bonds** – bonds that carry no coupon and simply redeem at face value at maturity. On such bonds, the investors realise a return by paying only a fraction of the face value.

Variable coupons

This category would include

- **Floating rate bonds** – where the coupon varies as interest rates vary.
- **Index-linked bonds** – where the coupon and redemption proceeds figures get scaled for the effects of inflation.

1.3.5 Coupon frequency

The coupon frequency, i.e. the frequency of the payment of the coupons is predetermined before issue, normally following the local market conventions. As a result, all investors will (or should) be aware of those dates.

Conventions regarding the frequency of payment differ between the various bond markets. Some markets have a convention of paying semi-annual coupons, as is the case in the UK and the US, whereas other markets, in particular the Eurobond market, France and Germany, pay coupons on an annual basis.

1.3.6 Recipient

The norm is that the holder of the bond receives all of the asset flows from that bond throughout its life to the maturity date. There are, however, some markets where it is possible to strip the coupons and the bond apart so that the holder of the underlying bond may receive the redemption proceeds, whilst the coupons (the 'tint') are paid to another party.

1.3.7 Redemption at maturity

As we noted above, it is possible for bonds to be issued that will not redeem at maturity, namely irredeemables. Most bonds are, however, redeemed though (once again) there are a few variations to be aware of. The primary consideration here is the form that the redemption proceeds takes, which may be either

- Cash.
- Other assets.

Cash redemption proceeds

Once more, the vast majority of bonds fall into this category whereby the bonds are redeemed in cash at maturity. This redemption may be

- **At par value** – redeemed at the nominal value of the bond at the redemption date.
- **At a premium** – redeemed at a specified premium above the nominal value of the bond at the redemption date.

The first is by far the most common.

Other assets

Instead of obliging the issuer to repay cash at maturity, the bond may offer the holder the choice between normal cash redemption proceeds and some other asset, such as

- An alternative bond of a later maturity.
- Shares issued by a corporation.

1.3.8 Usual form

By far the most common form taken by a bond is that it:

- pays a fixed coupon
- matures at a single date
- redeems in cash at par

So our examination on bonds concentrates on these. Other bonds can be viewed as a variant on this normal form.

2 WHAT ARE FIXED INTEREST MARKETS

2.1 Introduction

Bonds must be considered the primary fixed income asset class and the majority of this course concentrates on this area. They are, however, by no means the only fixed income instrument. In considering the bonds and fixed interest markets we must examine

- **Bonds** – as outlined above
- **Money Market Instruments** – short term instruments having very similar characteristice to either zero coupon bonds or to straight bonds whose values and returns are very much driven by interest rates
- **Preference Shares** – shares that pay a fixed dividend either
  - Until a set maturity date at which time they are redeemed – like a straight bond
  - Into perpetuity, perpetual shares – like an irredeemable bond
- **Convertibles** – either convertible bonds or convertible preference shares
- **Collective Investments** – in respect of such instruments
- **Derivatives** – based on the above instruments, i.e.
  - Bond futures/options
  - Interest rate futures/options
  - Interest rate swaps

In addition to the above, we must also examine the areas of

- **Foreign Currency** – the impact of exchange rates on investment in overseas bonds
- **Fund Management** – the techniques and considerations for managing a portfolio of fixed income instruments
- **Performance Measurement** – measuring and appraising any resultant investment performance.

3 Investment Management – An Overview

3.1 Definition

Investment management is the management of an investment portfolio on behalf of a private client or an institution, the receipt and distribution of dividends, and all other administrative work in connection with the portfolio.

This management may be conducted on either

- A discretionary basis, in which case the investment manager acts at his own discretion in the management of the portfolio, without referring to the client; or
- A non-discretionary basis, in which case the manager recommends investment sales and purchases to the client and awaits the latter's approval.

3.2 Purpose and considerations of investment management

Investment management involves the investment of a client's assets in order to meet a number of key objectives. The objectives will vary from investor to investor and consequently the process of investment management must start with a detailed consideration of the fund's objectives in order to determine the appropriate investment policies.

Broadly speaking, the fund objectives fall into one of two categories.

- To maximise their returns, i.e. positive net worth individuals looking for a portfolio to match their risk/return preferences.
- To match liabilities, e.g. pension funds where the aim is to match asset and liabilities or minimise any mismatch.

To satisfy these funds' objectives, the investment manager needs to know the fund constraints he must operate within based on the requirements of the client, i.e.

- Time horizons.
- Liabilities to be met.
- Liquidity needs.
- Risk aversion/risk tolerances.
- Tax status.
- Other preferences and legal constraints, e.g. ethical considerations.

This is needed for at least three reasons.

- It is a prerequisite to the initial portfolio structure.
- It influences the kinds of portfolio adjustment that can be made.
- It consequently influences portfolio performance.

3.3 The regulatory framework for the investment manager

The regulation of the UK financial services industry continues to evolve. Prior to the advent of the Financial Services Act 1986, the industry was almost completely self-regulating.

The Financial Services Act 1986 was not a detailed legal code as one might anticipate, but rather a statutory framework that made provision for the recognition of detailed rules produced by the investment industry itself – the self-regulatory aspect of the regulatory structure.

A key element of the system was the Financial Services Act 1986, which contained the basic premise that those conducting investment business in the UK obtain authorisation. On 30 November 2001, **the Financial Services and Markets Act 2000** (FSMA), came into force replacing the Financial Services Act 1986. Whilst practitioners and consumers are actively consulted, it is the FSA, a statutory body, that co-ordinates the regulation of the industry.

The provision of investment management services constitutes a **regulated** activity as defined by FSMA. Thus, any firm providing these services will require **authorisation**.

3.4 The role of the fund manager

Individual investors or organisations may choose to manage their own funds, though frequently the services of an external fund manager may be called on. The advantages and disadvantages of in-house management and external fund management can be summarised as follows.

	Advantages	Disadvantages
In-House	▪ Efforts entirely devoted to interests of fund. ▪ Fund trustees can remain in very close contact with what is happening to the fund. ▪ Funds should be more secure, since no third party is involved.	▪ Expensive, only appropriate for large funds. ▪ Fund managers may become complacent due to lack of competition resulting in poorer performance. ▪ Difficulty of attracting and retaining a highly paid investment specialist.
External	▪ Under constant pressure to perform. ▪ Suitable for all sizes of fund. ▪ Benefit from economies of scale in connection with transaction costs. ▪ Easier to keep up to date with the rapid pace of organisational and technological changes creating the need for continual updating and retraining.	▪ Fund will be just one amongst many managed. ▪ Small but definite increase in security risk, even with all the regulatory checks and safeguards in place. ▪ Fund's trustees more removed from the day-to-day fund management and may receive less comprehensive and less timely information.

Regardless of whether funds are managed internally or externally, the role of the fund manager is to act on behalf of its clients, managing the money in his charge.

These funds may be lodged with a fund manager either through collective investment schemes such as unit trusts or investment trusts, which may have a specific trust deed directing their investment strategy, or through discretionary arrangements with individual customers.

To safeguard the assets of the individual investors, funds are frequently managed under trust. This means that **all** of the funds' assets are registered in the name of the trustees rather than the managers, with the managers only having the authority to undertake particular transactions (e.g. buying or selling securities) on behalf of trustees.

3.5 The role of the trustees

The role of the **trustee** is to protect and control the trust property. It is the responsibility of the trustee to invest the trust property, though this role is frequently delegated to a fund manager.

If the fund is managed under trust and there are no specific instructions for its investment in the trust deed, the trustee must invest the funds in accordance with the Trustee Act 2000. Where there are specific investment criteria laid out in the trust deed, the trustee must ensure that these are not breached by the fund manager.

3.6 Overview of the fund management process

The process of fund management involves the investment of an investors' assets in order to meet a number of key objectives. The objectives will vary from investor to investor and consequently the process of fund management must start with a detailed consideration of the fund's objectives and associated constraints.

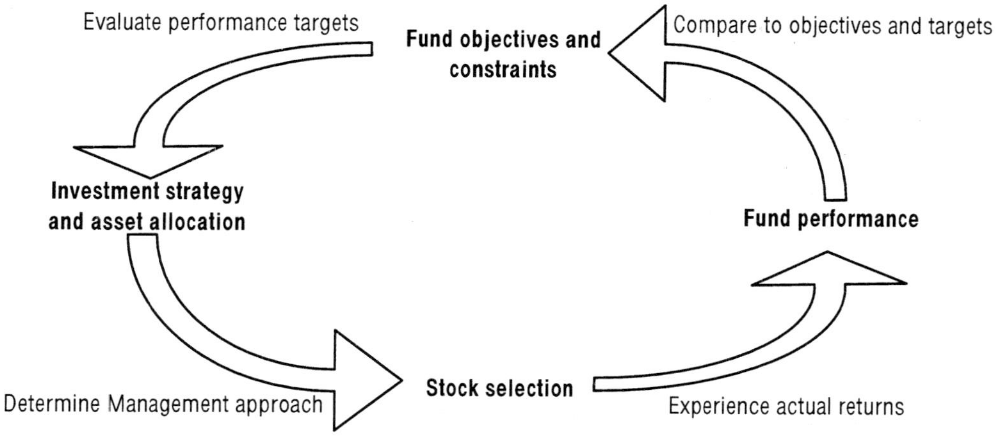

Once the objectives and constraints of the particular fund have been established, the next stage is to develop the investment policy/strategies that will be used in order to achieve these objectives. All these considerations will be detailed as recommended investment policy/strategy options.

These recommendations must then be submitted to the client for approval. In simple situations there may be one obvious approach for the manager to adopt, in more complex situations, several alternatives may be presented to the client forming the basis of a discussion leading to the finally agreed investment policy/strategy statement.

The resultant investment policy/strategy statement forms the basis of the management approach. This strategy will determone the long term strategic asset allocation options selected to achieve the client's objectives. Asset allocations should not, however, be set in stone. Different asset categories perform better in different economic situations and the fund manager must be ready to respond to such circumstances.

Along with the long term strategic asset allocation, the strategy may also detail market timing/tactical asset allocation options that may be adopted by the fund in those differing circumstances. The strategy details asset allocations and limits but will not detail stock or product recommendations.

Finally, the investment strategy will probably detail any performance benchmarks against which the fund performance is to be assessed.

When the overall strategy and policy of the fund have been determined, the final stage is to select the stock that will make up the portfolio and approaches to this are discussed later.

The final stage of the investment process is to evaluate whether the fund is achieving its objectives through a consideration of its performance. Fund performance should be reviewed no less than once a year, certainly more regularly for short term funds, and will look to achieve a number of objectives.

- **Client circumstances** – we should firstly look to determine whether any client circumstances have altered as this may result in an alteration of the client's objectives. Any significant changes may require a modification to the investment strategy.
- **Performance review** – we need to monitor the performance of the fund against the selected benchmark to ensure that it is achieving its objectives.
- **Portfolio rebalancing** – following on from the performance review we should consider whether there is any need to update the agreed asset allocations. Care needs to be taken here in respect of the tax liabilities that may arise from the effects of any rebalancing.

The fund management process cannot, however, be thought of as a step by step process that finishes at this stage, rather it is an ongoing process. This review will establish the strategy for the next period and the process will continue.

3.7 Risk reward profile

3.7.1 Introduction

Fundamental to an understanding of fund management is an appreciation of the relationship between risk and return, that is

High Risk = High Expected Return

Investments offer a range of risk and return which can be summarised as follows.

Risk	Investments
Low Risk	▪ National Savings Certificates
	▪ Bank and Building Society Accounts (Including money market deposits)
	▪ Gilts Held to Redemption
↑	▪ Gilts Sold Before Redemption (Here, there is the risk of a fall in the value of the stock)
	▪ Local Authority Issues
	▪ Corporate Bonds (Dependent on the credit rating)
Medium Risk	▪ Life Assurance Policies
	▪ Unit and Investment Trusts in equities and low quality corporate bands
↓	▪ Shares, Property and junk bonds
High Risk	▪ Warrants, Futures and Options, Bonds in default (However, there is only a limited risk in purchasing an option or a warrant since, here, only the premium can be lost)

Before offering any investment advice, it is vital to ensure that the risk and returns match the customer's criteria.

3.7.2 Diversification

One of the key benefits of employing a fund manager or using investment funds is that the investor's funds may be being pooled with those of other investors. This pooling allows the investor's money to be spread over a range of assets.

In any investment there are two types of risk: the general market risk of investing in bonds or shares, and the specific risk of any individual investment. For example, if an investor were to put all his money into the bonds of one company, there would first be the risk that the market in all bonds would fall, causing the value of the investment to fall and secondly, the risk that the bonds of this company itself may suffer from a specific incident causing the bond price to fall.

If an investor is able to buy more investments, he will be taking on board specific risks of different companies. Eventually, there will be a situation where, because of specific risks, some of the investments will fall, but others will rise. Overall, through this process of diversification, investors are able to rid themselves of the specific risk of a stock. It is however impossible to remove the market risk.

4 Institutional Investment Management

4.1 Introduction

4.1.1 Changes in ownership

While an individual investor may choose to manage his own money, the majority of investors in the UK are turning towards fund managers to manage their assets. The proportion of funds directly held by individuals has fallen rapidly over the last 40 years while the proportion managed by institutions has correspondingly risen. There are several reasons for this shift.

A major factor here is that investment by individuals in the financial markets is now more likely to be indirect rather than direct. A large proportion of individual investors are likely to invest via pension funds or collective investment schemes. Ultimately, institutions represent individuals' collective involvement in the market, but why this shift to indirect investments?

One of the reasons for this shift is that commissions have come down for institutional investors, but commissions for private customers still remain high unless customers are undertaking large transactions, this may limit their access to the market place.

Equally, it is important for an investor to buy a range of assets. This restricts the level of risk he may face but, with only a limited amount of capital, it may be impossible at today's commission rate for an investor to spread his money over a wide enough portfolio to minimise risk. Consequently, it makes sense for small investors to pool their money into large funds, which can be invested on their behalf by professional fund managers. The growth of investment advisors servicing the individual investor has probably also contributed here. Investment advisors have tended to focus mainly on packaged products rather than individual securities. An increased awareness of the benefits of diversification has led advisors to only recommend individual securities to those with considerable funds to invest.

A further advantage of using a managed fund is that it provides the private customer with easier access to overseas markets and, therefore, exposure to new industries and economic conditions.

In addition to these points, social changes have occurred such that in the 1960s and 1970s individuals were less likely to invest funds directly in the market. The movement away from individual share and bond ownership was accelerated by the increasing burden of taxation on investment income. This was particularly the case in the 1970s.

One final reason can be found in marketing – a company is not allowed to advertise or promote its existing securities directly to the public. By contrast, the public has been besieged with adverts from providers of insurance, pension and collective investment products. The effect of this is hard to ascertain but likely to have encouraged individuals into packaged products and away from individual securities.

4.1.2 Implications

With the majority of funds under the control of professional fund managers, it is likely to lead to greater market efficiency. Thus, it is harder for the active fund manager to add significant value. The difficulty that active fund managers are experiencing in beating benchmarks has led to an increase in tracker funds.

Individual funds have grown in size. Such large institutional funds experience difficulties as the liquidity in the market for many instruments may be insufficient for them to efficiently achieve their investment objectives.

With such large quantities of funds in the hands of institutional fund managers, the competition for new issues will be considerable, particularly for any large new issues that managers are anxious to include within their portfolios. Individual managers may find applications scaled down or fail to secure stock.

The greater proportion of institutional shareholders gives fund managers far more influence in company affairs. It would not be uncommon for a company meeting to be effectively controlled by a small number of fund managers. This has allowed fund managers to be far more involved in corporate affairs, for instance removing a board if they do not feel shareholder value is being created. It is institutional shareholders who will generally determine the success or failure of a takeover bid. Thus, fund managers may be required to take a more active role in the governance of companies in which they have a significant stake.

4.2 Types of fund

Exam tip

> Optional 15 mark Section C questions have asked what investments are suitable for certain clients, most recently in Summer 2006, Winter 2002 and Winter 2001.

There are a variety of different types of funds that exist, each with its own particular risk/reward profile, as a result of

- Their initial objectives – return maximising/liability matching.
- The value and time horizons of the liabilities they have to meet (if any).
- The assets they can invest in.
- The liquidity they require in the fund.
- The risk they can tolerate in the fund.
- Their tax status.
- Legislation governing their powers.

4.2.1 Pension funds

Assets and liabilities

A pension fund is an example of a liability-matching fund. It represents a pool of money to be invested now to achieve either

- A specific return based on the employee's salary and number of years' service with the company – a **defined benefit/final salary scheme**; or
- A general increase in value over the contributions paid on behalf of the employee – a **defined contribution/money purchase scheme**.

Generally speaking, pension funds have fairly **long-term** time horizons and, as such, are prepared to take on board a higher degree of risk, since any shortfall in the fund can be made up in future investment performance. That is, the **investment policy** depends on the **maturity** of the fund. If the fund beneficiaries are close to retirement, then it would be more appropriate to select shorter term, safer investments. However, in general, the above comment is applicable.

Pension funds must also keep control over the real rate of return that they earn, since their liabilities, the potential pension payments calculated by the fund actuaries, will be expanding in line with inflation. As a consequence, pension funds tend to invest in slightly more speculative assets, often referred to as **real assets**, such as **equities and property**, since these offer a degree of protection against the impact of inflation.

In addition, they tend to keep a proportion of the fund in fixed interest instruments. In particular, they will tend to be substantial holders of index-linked stocks, partly because these guarantee real returns over a period of time, but also because the bonds themselves tend to have fairly high durations and therefore are sensitive to movement in real interest rates.

Equally, however, the pension fund will need to keep some assets in a liquid form and the government bond market represents a highly liquid market place in which to invest money, gaining a moderate but close to **risk-free** return.

BPP LEARNING MEDIA

Tax status

All contributions paid to pension funds are tax free, i.e. no income tax burden is suffered by individuals on contributions paid on their behalf, and tax relief can be claimed on contributions that they pay themselves (within limits).

In addition, pension funds approved by Her Majesty's Revenue and Customs (HMRC) are **gross funds**, i.e. they pay no UK tax on either fund income or capital gains.

However, pension funds are not able to reclaim the 10% income tax which is assumed to have been paid on UK dividends received. In addition, there may be withholding tax on overseas investments, which may not be recoverable.

The only occurrence of tax in relation to pension funds occurs (in the form of income tax) on receipt of pensions in retirement.

Legislation

Pension rules are derived from a number of sources, specifically

- Pensions Act 1995, 2004, 2007, 2008
- The Occupational Pensions Regulatory Authority (OPRA)
- Finance Act 2004
- Myner's Review

Designated professional bodies

The National Association of Pension Funds (NAPF) was formed in 1923 to provide representation and other services to those involved in designing, operating, investing and advising occupational pension schemes in the UK. The NAPF represents the voice for such individuals by keeping them informed of, and asking them to express their views/vote upon, relevant issues.

In 1947, the NAPF set up an Investment Committee to provide asset management help and advice to NAPF members. In March 2000, following the introduction of UK Investment Performance Standards (UKIPS), the committee changed its title to the UK Investment Performance Committee (UKIPC) which formally approved UKIPS as the local version of GIPS (Global Investment Performance Standards).

UKIPC now represents the prime consultative body in the UK, being sponsored by the NAPF, the Association of British Insurers (ABI) – see life assurance and general insurance companies below – and the Investment Management Association (IMA) – see collective investments below.

The Investment Performance Committee has the following seven sub-committees.

- **Shareholder Affairs** – concerned to protect the interests of pension funds as shareholders. Topics of interest include corporate governance, director's remuneration, long-term incentive and share schemes and any proposals in these areas.
- **Markets** – concerned to ensure that pension funds have access to efficient, liquid and well-managed markets. Topics of interest to this sub-committee include stock exchange strategy and developments, and takeovers.
- **Law, Accounts and Tax** – deals with legal issues affecting trustees, such as custody, investment responsibilities and investment management agreements. Liaises with the Accounting Standards Board (ASB) to support improvements in UK reporting. Tries to ensure that the UK fiscal regime remains favourable for pension funds.
- **External Affairs** – responsible for the issue of Investment Committee Bulletins and Briefings.
- **Performance Measurement** – addresses the performance track records of investment managers and has issued codes for their disclosure.

- **Property** – ensures that Investment Service participants are briefed on circumstances particular to this asset class, such as valuation and liquidity.
- **Voting Issues** – helps pension funds and investment managers exercise votes on a well-informed basis.

In addition, the Investment Performance Committee undertakes special projects covering such areas as self-investment and the visibility of investment management fees.

4.2.2 Life assurance companies

Assets and liabilities

Life assurance is a form of insurance against an eventuality that is **assured** (hence, the name) to arise, i.e. that people will die. As such, it is another form of liability-matching fund. Life assurance policies take a number of forms.

- **Term assurance policies** – where an individual's life is insured for a specific period or term in a similar way to normal car or household insurance.
- **Whole of life policies** – where a capital sum will be paid upon the death of the policyholder, whenever that may be.
- **Endowment policies** – which combine life insurance and savings. These policies are generally associated with mortgages where the savings element is designed to pay off the capital borrowed at the end of the term of the policy, and the life insurance will repay the mortgage should the policyholder die before the end of that term.

In common with pension funds, life assurance companies tend to have reasonably **long-term** liabilities and, as such, are able to take on board a higher degree of risk. Once again, this tends to involve a high proportion of their assets being invested into equities and property, with only a smaller proportion being invested into the fixed interest markets.

As a long-term fund, life assurance companies are able to take reasonably high degrees of risk and again may be tempted towards the higher duration stocks in the bond markets.

Within the industry, there are a variety of policies available ranging from with profits policies, which share in the profits of the fund but attract higher premiums, to without profits policies, where the premiums are lower but the profits go to the insurance company.

Tax status

There is no tax relief on the payment of life assurance premiums on new policies (though there is on certain older policies).

All fund income and capital gains are taxable, which will result in the investment manager selecting investment vehicles that are more tax efficient.

Proceeds paid from life policies are taxable unless the policy is a **qualifying** policy, in which case the proceeds are tax free.

Legislation

In terms of regulation, the key regulator is the FSA which, under the FSMA 2000, is given a wide range of interventionist powers.

Both life assurance funds and general insurance funds are closely monitored to ensure that the solvency of the company is in no way called into question. Overall, this tends to make both of them more risk adverse than pension funds, but there is a marked difference between life assurance companies and general insurance companies in relation to the risk/reward profile they adopt.

The basic measure of solvency is that the assets of the fund must exceed the liabilities of the fund, both derived using prudent measures. Where there are concerns about the solvency of a fund, then they may intervene in order to guarantee the policyholders' rights.

The FSA operates a compensation scheme for UK investment, banking and insurance firms who become insolvent and unable to meet their obligations. Claims under the scheme are subject to limits set out in the FSA Handbook.

Designated professional bodies

The designated professional body covering the life assurance industry is the Association of British Insurers (ABI). The ABI has the following main aims.

- **Representation** – to represent members' interests to government, regulators, and other political and trade bodies, and to help them develop international activities.
- **Monitoring** – of proposed legislation, regulation, tax and other policy measures.
- **Promotion** – of the concept of insurance to the media and consumer organisations.
- **Information and guidance** – through its Investment Committee, the ABI provides technical guidance, statistical information, investment information and standards in all relevant areas.
- **Codes of conduct** – the ABI has developed codes of conduct governing insurance practice with which members must comply.

The ABI considers the current issues of investment that affects one of the roughly 400 companies it represents such as

- Corporate governance
- Auditor independence
- Socially responsible investment
- Executive remuneration
- European shareholder rights
- UK listing rules

4.2.3 General insurance companies

Assets and liabilities

General insurance companies clearly aim to be able to match their liabilities. They have a much shorter liability profile than life funds. In essence, insurance is like taking a bet. The insured person pays the company the premium. The insurance company makes money if they are able to take in this premium and earn investment income on it which exceeds the amounts of any claims arising on the policy.

Since claims are likely to arise in the immediate future, for example let us say in the next year, they are unable to take substantial risks forcing them to invest a greater proportion of their fund into **short-term** 'risk-free' government securities. Whilst the returns may not be as high, the fund simply cannot take any risk.

Both life assurance funds and general insurance funds are closely monitored by the FSA to ensure that the solvency of the company is in no way called into question. Overall, this tends to make both of them more risk adverse than pension funds, but there is a marked difference between life assurance companies and general insurance companies in the risk/reward profile they adopt.

Tax status

General insurance business profits are subject to normal corporate tax rates.

Legislation

General insurance business is governed by the same rules and regulations as life insurance business covered above.

Designated professional bodies

As with life assurance, the relevant professional body covering the general insurance industry is the ABI.

4.2.4 Collective investment schemes

Assets and liabilities

Collective investment schemes are return-maximising funds. They are vehicles through which a large number of small investors pool their money together to achieve a large fund, which is placed under professional investment management. UK funds can be in the form of

- Investment trusts
- Venture capital trusts
- Unit trusts
- Open-ended investment companies (OEICs)

These all have slightly differing forms.

Investment trusts

The name investment trust is, to an extent, a misnomer. Investment trusts are not trusts in law, rather they are public limited companies whose shares are listed on the Stock Exchange.

Investment trusts initially raise money by issuing shares. If an individual wishes to realise his investment/(make a new investment), he needs to sell the shares to/(buy some shares from) someone else. If someone wishes to invest they must buy some of the already existing shares.

As a result, investment trusts are not faced by inflows and outflows of funds. An investment trust is therefore referred to as a **closed-ended fund**, in that the size of the fund itself is independent of the buying or selling of shares; it is a function of the initial capital subscribed and the gains generated on that capital.

The objectives of the investment manager is to maximise the value of the shares of the investment trust which, if the fund has a **split capital structure**, may be

- **Income Shares** – This class of capital is entitled to all the income from the underlying portfolio and a fixed entitlement of capital. Their value is therefore a function of the level of dividend payments, the timescales over which these will be received and the ultimate capital value.
- **Capital Shares** – At the end of the company's life (set as a fixed period at the inception of the investment trust), the capital shares are entitled to the value of the underlying portfolio, less the income and preference share's fixed right to capital represented by their nominal value. The typical life of an investment trust with such a class of capital is seven to ten years. Capital shares tend to be volatile as they accept the majority of the underlying portfolio's capital risk.
- **Preference Shares** – These provide a constant dividend which is paid in any year in which dividends are paid. They also have an entitlement to a fixed nominal value on the winding up of the company. With some of the more recent preference share issues this has been as low as 1p per share. These are sometimes referred to as Annuity Income Shares as, like an annuity, they provide a high level of income in return for an initial capital investment. Indeed, since the initial investment is eroded over the life of the investment trust, the dividend yield will be very high.
- **Zero Dividend Preference Shares** – These offer a predetermined capital growth over the life of the investment trust, receiving only a fixed capital sum on winding up, before any capital is returned to other shareholders. This capital return is not certain, however, as the assets of the investment trust could be insufficient to cover this sum on a winding up if the trust performs particularly badly.

Venture capital trusts

These are a type of investment trust company with tax advantages for investors. They invest in new and growing small businesses and allow investors to get direct exposure to this sector of the market by buying a share in the Venture Capital Trust.

Unit trusts

Unit trusts are, in legal terms, the same as trusts and as such their activities are monitored by trustees.

Unlike investment trusts, unit trusts may suffer significant inflows and outflows of cash, and as such are referred to as **open-ended** funds. As a result, unit trusts need to maintain a reasonable degree of liquidity.

This situation arises from the way in which unit trusts operate. Unit trusts raise money by issuing **units**, which are **created** by the fund manager when cash is subscribed. This cash forms the initial pool of funds invested by the manager for the unit holders.

The manager must then act as a market maker for the units, quoting **bid** and **offer** prices based on the bid and offer values of the underlying investments and the level of his initial charge. If an individual wishes to buy/(sell) units, then the fund manager must accommodate him. The manager will attempt to match buys and sells, though this may not always be possible. If the buys exceed the sells, the fund manager will have to create new units and invest, as part of the trust property, the excess cash received. If, however, the sells exceed the buys, the fund manager will have to liquidate some units, i.e. sell some of the underlying investments of the fund and cancel the units.

Consequently, the number of units in issue and the capital value of the fund may vary considerably.

The overall objectives of each fund are determined in advance in the trust deed. This states the objective in terms of risk/reward profile and may indicate the appropriate markets in which to invest. For example, it may be felt worthwhile for a fund manager to establish a unit trust investing in highly speculative emerging market bonds in order to maximise returns for its investors.

On the other hand, other groups of investors may wish to have their money placed into reasonably secure short-term liquid issues (e.g. short-dated gilts) generating a reasonable income flow. Each scheme will have its own particular emphasis and a selection of stocks and a strategy will be determined by this emphasis.

Open-ended investment companies (OEICs)

The Treasury introduced regulations in connection with open-ended investment companies in early 1997. These created a third type of investment product with many of (the best) features of both unit and investment trusts. However, it was envisaged within the regulations that many existing unit trusts would wish to convert into this new more flexible format. This is possible without any tax implications on transfer.

In order to accommodate the OEICs into the system, a special company structure was introduced in order to allow a company to continually issue and redeem its own shares, making it **open ended**. The end result is an investment product that is more flexible and more appealing to the Continental European market.

OEICs are able to issue both bearer and registered shares. Several classes of shares are possible and within each class, it is possible to have both large and small denomination shares.

Tax status

Investment trusts

The regulation of investment trusts by HMRC is through the Income and Corporation Taxes Act of 1988. The main requirement here is for the investment trust to qualify for approved status. As a result of gaining such status, the fund will not be subject to income taxes, although it will of course be subject to corporation tax as a company.

Unit trusts

Unit trusts may be either authorised or unauthorised. Authorised unit trusts are subject to corporation tax on any income generated and are exempt from tax on any capital gains.

Unauthorised unit trusts are subject to income tax on their income and capital gains tax on capital gains.

Open-ended investment companies (OEICs)

The tax status for OEICs is as for authorised unit trusts, in that income is taxed whereas gains are not.

Legislation

Investment trusts

Investment trusts are controlled by a variety of regulators. The UK Listing Authority puts restraints on the level of investments that can be undertaken; HMRC controls regulations with regard to the tax status of the funds.

Unit trusts

The operation of unit trusts is governed by the Financial Services and Markets Act 2000 which is enforced by the FSA.

Open-ended investment companies (OEICs)

OEICs are regulated predominantly by the FSA from whom they will require authorisation in a similar way to unit trusts. Significant differences exist, however, in the corporate rather than trust structure and also the provision for single pricing.

Designated professional bodies

The designated professional body covering collective investments is the Investment Management Association (IMA), which was formed in 2002 through the merger of the Association of Unit Trusts and Investment Funds (AUTIF) and the Fund Management Association (FMA). The key aims of IMA are as follows.

- **Representation** – IMA acts as the industry representative in relation to legislative, regulatory and tax issues.
- **Liaison** – with the FSA and other organisations in the UK and Europe on regulatory matters.
- **Awareness** – to increase public awareness and understanding of investment funds.
- **Training and education** – to improve training standards in the industry and seek to integrate personal finance education into the school curriculum.
- **Information service** – to members and non-members on relevant matters.

4.2.5 Offshore funds

As well as UK funds, many offshore funds exist which may be either

- **Regulated** – in which case they may be marketable in the UK. Typically Exchange Traded Funds (ETFs) are regulated offshore funds that can be marketed in the UK and have a structure not dissimilar to OEICs.
- **Unregulated** – in which case they cannot be marketed in the UK. Typically hedge funds fall into this category.

4.2.6 Banks

Assets and liabilities

London has a highly developed banking market ranging from the high-street banks to the large international banks that have a presence in the London market. The range of services is considerable, from the straightforward deposit-taking and lending to the more sophisticated corporate finance and money market activities run of the merchant banks and capital markets divisions. In general, however, bank liabilities are **short term**, since the bulk of their assets are derived from deposit taking, most of which is repayable on demand.

In recent years, the commercial pressure on the conventional banking activities through the process of diversification has forced the banks to expand their activities into the areas of financial services and, in particular, the provision of investment advice to the individual customer.

Taxation

All income and capital profits from investments are taxed as if they were part of trading profit and, as such, bear corporation tax at the relevant rates.

Legislation

Introduction

To the extent that the banks conduct regulated activities, e.g. accept deposits, they will be brought under the scope of FSMA 2000 and therefore be obliged to seek authorisation.

The role of the Bank of England

The Bank of England's responsibility for banking supervision was transferred to the FSA as part of the Bank of England Act 1998. Despite losing responsibility for banking supervision, the Bank of England gained the freedom in 1998 to set official UK interest rates.

Interest rates decisions are taken by the **Bank's Monetary Policy Committee (MPC)**. The MPC is made up of representatives of the governing body of the Bank of England and industry experts appointed by the Chancellor, and sets interest rates to meet the target for overall inflation in the economy. The inflation target is set each year by the Chancellor of the Exchequer, not by the Bank. This is part of the Bank's responsibility to achieve price stability in the economy. The Bank implements the interest rate decisions through its activities in the financial market, in particular by setting the interest rate at which the Bank lends to banks and other financial institutions.

The Bank is also responsible for maintaining stability in the financial system by analysing and promoting initiatives to strengthen the financial system, and by monitoring financial developments, to try to identify potential threats to financial stability. It is also known as the financial system's 'lender of last resort', providing funds in exceptional circumstances. In this work, the Bank co-operates closely with HM Treasury and the FSA. The Governor of the Bank also appoints the chairman of the Panel on Takeovers and Mergers.

Designated professional bodies

The designated professional body governing banking is the *ifs* School of Finance, formerly the Institute of Financial Services (IFS), the official brand of the Chartered Institute of Bankers (CIB). The primary aim of the *ifs* School of Finance is to ensure the thorough training and ongoing development of individuals in the banking, and broader financial services, sector.

4.2.7 Building societies

Assets and liabilities

In the past, building societies have provided an extremely limited range of services mainly linked to long-term lending on property. The Building Societies Act 1986 considerably expanded the range of services that societies are able to provide.

Under the legislation governing building societies, they are able to

- Transact business in the **forex** market.
- Operate estate agencies.
- Establish and manage **ISAs**.
- Provide **investment services**, however, this will bring the society under the auspices of the FSA. In practical terms, many societies avoid their obligation to this end by becoming appointed representatives of a specific firm.
- Make **unsecured loans**. As with many of the other changes introduced in the Building Societies Act 1986, this makes the societies much more like retail banks.
- In a further relaxation of the controls, societies are now able to obtain up to 20% of their finance from beyond the depositor base by accessing the capital markets. Indeed, with the permission of the regulator, this limit can be extended to a level of 40%.

Taxation

Building societies deduct basic rate tax from interest paid to investors, which may be reclaimed by non-taxpayers.

Legislation

Under the Building Societies Act of 1986, building societies were regulated by the Building Society Commission (BSC). With the advent of the FSMA, the powers of the BSC have been passed to the FSA, who now regulate building societies in the UK.

Designated professional bodies

The Building Societies Association (BSA) is the trade association for the UK's building societies. The BSA was established in 1869 and has two principal functions.

- **Representation** – the BSA puts forward the industry view to government, the media and other interested bodies.
- **Information and advice** – provided to members on a range of relevant subjects.

4.2.8 Charities

Assets and liabilities

Charities are formed when individuals or groups of individuals perceive a specific need and make donations or raise funds to help alleviate that need. In this context, the liabilities a charity faces are the costs of alleviating the need, and their assets are funds and donations received.

Taxation

The importance of charities is indicated by the very favourable tax treatment they receive. Charities are exempt of all forms of taxation on income and capital. In addition, they may claim back income tax at the basic rate on donations made under deed of covenant.

This tax exemption may be restricted, however, if some of its income is used for non-charitable purposes.

Legislation

In order to take advantage of the preferential status afforded to charities, an organisation must qualify as one. An organisation may qualify as a charity if it has as its aims

- The relief of poverty.
- The advancement of education.
- The advancement of religion.
- The pursuit of other aims that are deemed to be beneficial to the community.

Charities are subject to the regulation of the Charities Act 1993, as updated by the Charities Act 2006. The Act governs such factors as

- Registration of charities.
- Supervision and control of charities.
- Accounting and reporting requirements.
- Charity property and investment powers.
- Persons who may act as trustees.
- Controls on fundraising.

and it also enhanced the powers of the Charity Commission.

The Charity Commission is a government department whose role is

- To promote the effective use of charitable resources by encouraging the development of better methods of administration, by providing information or advice to trustees and by investigating any abuses.
- To maintain the register of charities.
- To enquire into the operation of charities to ensure that there is no misconduct or mismanagement.

5 Individual Investment Management

5.1 Fundamental criteria for providing investment advice

One of the Conduct of Business rules issued by the FSA requires that the firm obtain information about its customer. This ties in with the specific rule on suitability, which requires the firm to give suitable advice based on the information it knows or might reasonably infer about an individual customer.

This information will normally be obtained through the use of a customer questionnaire. If the customer does not respond to the questionnaire, it will not necessarily prevent the firm from acting on his or her behalf. If the firm warns the customer of the adverse effect of not responding, suitability is considered and any other client or money laundering documents required are in place. However, it will limit the protection that the customer receives.

5.1.1 Key information

- **The Customer's Income**
- **Present Net Assets**
  - Is the customer a home owner?
  - What other investments does the customer have?

- **Tax Position**

  Is the customer a higher rate taxpayer? If so, only certain instruments will have the appropriate features. One of the most effective investments for a higher rate taxpayer is short-dated low-coupon gilts. The advantages of these stocks are that as low-coupon stocks they trade below par, and will be redeemed at par within the next seven years, generating a tax-free gain.

- **Their Investment Objectives**

  Some investors may be prepared to take on substantial levels of risk. Others may require that their capital remains safe whilst producing a steady flow of income. An investment which lends itself to the latter objective is an FRN. Since it carries a regular coupon and as the coupon varies with the market return, it tends to retain its par value.

  Other investors will not be concerned with the income flows from an investment, but will wish their portfolio to be biased towards capital growth.

6 SELECTING A FUND MANAGER

The factors considered by sponsors in selecting a fund manager include the following.

Past performance

Past performance should be considered in relation to the risk profile of the assets under management. It should also be considered over a long period to assess the variability in performance rather than simply contemplating short-term absolute performance. Absolute performance should also be considered against an appropriate benchmark for the industry peer group or the markets invested in. It could also be argued that for funds, such as pension funds, it is the generation of a real return, rather than nominal return, that is of consequence.

Consistency of management

Sponsors need to take care that they do not select a fund manager on the basis of a performance history that relates to a particular fund manager or methodology that is no longer a feature of that firm. Certain skill-based investment approaches will be very dependent on the individual fund manager.

Internal controls and regulation

In the wake of regulatory problems that have been well publicised, sponsors are likely to be increasingly concerned as to the effectiveness of regulatory controls within any fund manager. Particular areas of concern might include investment restrictions, custody and segregation.

Management style

An assessment of the approach is critical to the needs of the fund itself. The fund sponsor must select a style that is compatible with the fund's objectives. This would necessitate a consideration of active or passive management and their respective risks and returns.

Fees

The level of management fees will obviously be an issue. The adverse publicity surrounding the performance failures of active managers has led to increasing focus on performance fees. Active management will increasingly need to prove its worth by achieving good performance to justify its charging structure.

Chapter Roundup

- A bond is a negotiable debt instrument for a fixed principal amount issued by a borrower for a specific period of time and typically making a regular payment of interest.
- The interest payment is known as the coupon and it is based on the nominal value of the bond. The nominal value also refers to how much capital shall be paid on maturity.
- Investment management is the management of an investment portfolio on behalf of a private client or an institution.
- The objective of the fund/investors will either be to match future liabilities or to maximise returns within given risk parameters.
- Whilst the investment manager will take primary responsibility for managing the money, the role of protecting the assets is often passed over to a trustee.
- There are two main types of pension scheme: defined benefits schemes which pay a proportion of final salary at retirement; and defined contribution schemes which pay a pension based on the amount of contributions and investment performance up to retirement.
- Life assurance and general insurance companies also invest the premiums they receive to generate returns.
- Collective investment schemes include unit trusts, investment trusts, open-ended investment companies (OEIC) and exchange traded funds (ETF). All offer investors benefits of diversification, professional fund management and the opportunity to invest in worldwide assets.
- Hedge funds are a form of unregulated fund able to take on any one of many different strategies and approaches.

Test Your Knowledge

Check your knowledge of the Chapter here, without referring back to the text.

1. What is the tax status of UK pension funds?

2. Who is the designated professional body for life assurance?

3. Unit trusts are open-ended, investment trust are closed ended. What do these terms mean?

4. Who regulates building societies?

5. Whast is the tax position of a charity?

6. How would you describe the liabilities of a young pension fund and how would it alter if it was mature?

7. Who are unit trusts regulated by?

Test Your Knowledge: Answers

1. They are gross funds i.e. they do not pay tax on either income or gains.
2. Association of British Insurers whose aims are
   - Representation of members interests.
   - Monitoring proposed legislation.
   - Promotion of insurance.
   - Information and guidance provision to the industry.
   - Codes of conduct monitoring.
3. An open ended fund is one where money flows in and out as people invest or divest. As a result the funds under management may change considerably from day to day.

   A closed ended fund is one where the funds under management remain stable irrespective of investment or divestment. In a closed ended fund new investors must buy shares from old investors rather than passing it to the fund manager.
4. The FSA.
5. Charities pay no tax on either income or gains. In addition they can claim back income tax at the basic rate on any donations received.
6. A young pension fund has long-term time horizons with real liabilities affected by inflation. In a mature fund the time horizons are short.
7. Unit trusts are regulated by the FSA.

2 Discounted Cash Flow

INTRODUCTION

Discounted cash flow is a basic, but very important, evaluative technique. Whenever we are asked to value a bond or money market instrument, in all probability we will be applying DCF techniques.

Pure DCF questions are rarely directly asked in the exam, it is more likely that you will be applying these ideas in the context of bond pricing that we examine in the following section. An understanding of DCF is, therefore, core to many of the ideas considered in later sections and you should not proceed past this chapter without mastering all of the techniques within it.

CHAPTER CONTENTS

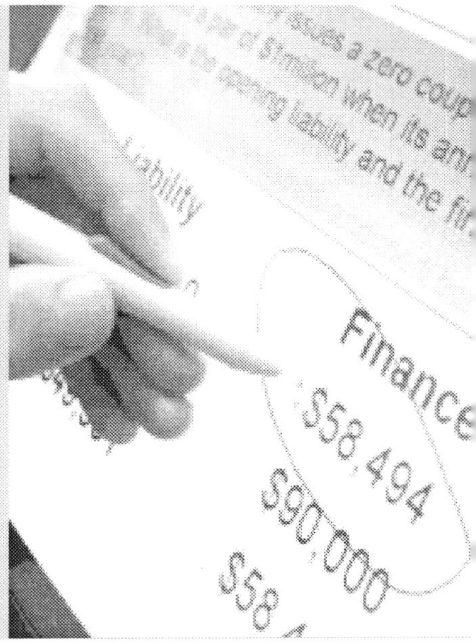

Chapter Learning Objectives

The syllabus areas covered by this section are

Analysis

Students should possess a broad understanding of both static and dynamic methods for the analysis and construction of fixed income securities containing both certain and contingent cashflows. Variable rate securities will be included. Students should be aware of the limitations of assumptions and mathematical techniques upon results. Although analysis will be concerned principally with 'risk–free' securities, students should be aware of the further considerations for 'risky' securities and the effect they may have on expected return. Students should possess a thorough comprehension of single–period and multi–period, single currency and multi–currency portfolio management theory.

Present and Future Value

- Certain & Contingent

1 Introduction

Central to all our theories regarding the valuation of securities is discounted cash flow (DCF) and the time value of money. It is therefore essential that we understand this topic thoroughly and the relevance of the measures that we derive.

The various valuation ideas are based on the Dividend Valuation Model (DVM) which states that

"The market value of a security is the present value of the future expected receipts discounted at the investors' required rate of return."

The market value of a security is equal to the present value of a security's cash flow.

We will see this idea again when calculating bond prices, yields and durations, hence the importance placed on the basics.

However, before we can go on to use this idea, we need to consider how an investor may establish their required rate of return.

Suppose a bank lends you £100 to be repaid with interest in one year's time with inflation running at 3%.

For the bank to be just as well off in real terms, it will need to receive £103 in one year to cover inflation, i.e. the minimum interest it can charge would equate to the rate of inflation.

However, banks are in business to make profits (being better off), not be just as well off, so the bank will charge more than this.

The rate the bank will charge is given by the Fisher equation.

Formula to learn

$$(1 + r) = (1 + i)(1 + R)$$

where

r = nominal rate (total annual rate)
i = inflation rate
R = real rate of return

The real rate being the excess return required by the bank to compensate for

- Its loss of flexibility (you have its cash).
- The risk it is taking (you may default).

2 The Time Value of Money and Interest Rates

2.1 Introduction

A starting point is the realisation and appreciation of the time value of money, which we will all be aware of as a result of the payment (or possibly the receipt) of bank interest.

Bank interest can take one of two forms.

- Simple interest.
- Compound interest.

Each of which are illustrated below with the aid of the following example.

Example

£100 is deposited in an account paying interest at 10% per annum (simple or compound as applicable). How much interest will be earned during the year, and what will be the value of the deposit at the end of

- The first year?
- The nth year (say 5th)?

2.2 Simple interest

If a bank account were to offer a simple interest rate, then the interest received each year would be based on the original capital invested only. Hence, in relation to the above example, we would have the following solution.

Solution

First year

The interest earned in this year would be based on the capital originally invested (£100) and the simple rate of interest (10%). The interest could be calculated using the formula

Formula to learn

$$i_1 = D_0 \times r$$

where

i_1 = interest earned by the end of the first year (time = 1)
D_0 = original capital invested at the start of the first year (time = 0)
r = interest rate stated as a decimal, here 10% or 0.10

Giving

$i_1 = £100 \times 0.10 = £10$

At that date, the deposit will be worth £110.

N^{th} Year

With simple interest, the interest generated each subsequent year will be exactly the same, since it is only based on the original capital invested. Hence, we can apply the same formula to calculate this year's interest as

$i_n = D_0 \times r$

giving for the fifth year

$i_5 = £100 \times 0.10 = £10$

We can see that the value of our deposit is growing by £10 each year.

In conclusion, with simple interest, we earn the same amount of interest each year. At the end of n years, the total interest we will have earned will be

$n \times$ annual interest

or

$i_{tot} = n \times (D_0 \times r)$

which, when added to our starting capital of D_0, gives the value of our deposit as

$D_n = D_0 + n \times (D_0 \times r)$

Applying this to the above example gives

$D_5 = D_0 + n \times (D_0 \times r) = £100 + 5 \times (£100 \times 0.10) = £150$

which is perhaps the result we expected. Five years' interest at 10% per annum should add a total of 50% to the value of the deposit with flat rate interest.

2.3 Compound interest

2.3.1 Annual compounding

Interest rates are described as compound interest if, in each year, interest is earned on the total value of the deposit at the start of the year, i.e. original capital plus any interest previously earned. With compound interest, we receive interest on our previous interest.

Solution

First year

The interest earned in this year would be based on the value of the deposit at the start of the year, i.e. the capital originally invested (£100) and the compound rate of interest (10%). The interest could again be calculated using the formula

Formula to learn

$i_1 = D_0 \times r$

where

i_1 = interest earned by the end of the first year (time = 1)
r = interest rate stated as a decimal, here 10% or 0.10
D_0 = original capital invested at the outset (time = 0)

Giving

$i_1 = £100 \times 0.10 = £10$

At that date, the deposit will be worth £110, which we could have calculated directly using the formula

$D_1 = D_0(1 + r) = £100 \times (1 + 0.10) = £100 \times 1.10 = £110$

where D_1 = the value of the deposit at time 1. We can see that, so far, this is identical to the simple interest example above, however this is only true for the first year.

N^{th} year

With compound interest, the interest generated each subsequent year will be based on the value of the deposit at the start of each year. We could state this in a formula as

$i_n = D_{n-1} \times r$

In order to calculate the interest for the fifth year, we would need to know the value of the deposit at the start of the fifth year/end of the fourth year. From our Year 1 illustration above, we noted that the value of the deposit at the end of the first year/start of the second was given by

$D_1 = D_0(1 + r)$

This amount would then grow by the end of the second year/start of the third year to

$D_2 = D_1(1 + r) = D_0(1 + r)^2$

In a similar way, we could calculate the value of the deposit at the end of each subsequent year as

$D_3 = D_2(1 + r) = D_0(1 + r)^3$ – end of third/start of fourth
$D_4 = D_3(1 + r) = D_0(1 + r)^4$ – end of fourth/start of fifth
$D_5 = D_4(1 + r) = D_0(1 + r)^5$ – end of fifth/start of sixth

which could be described generally as

$D_n = D_0(1 + r)^n$ – end of nth/start of $n + 1^{th}$

Hence, at the end of the fourth year/start of the fifth the value of the deposit would be

$D_4 = D_0(1 + r)^4 = £100\ (1 + 0.10)^4 = £100 \times 1.1^4 = £146.41$

and, hence, the interest generated in the fifth year would be

$i_5 = D_4 \times r = £146.41 \times 0.10 = £14.641$

taking the value of the total deposit up to £161.051 (£146.41 + £14.641) by the end of the fifth year, which we can confirm with the formula

$D_5 = D_0(1 + r)^5 = £100\ (1 + 0.10)^5 = £100 \times 1.1^5 = £161.051$

This is a larger sum than under simple interest, since we are receiving interest on our previously earned interest.

2.3.2 Non-annual compounding

Generally, bank and building society accounts quote an annual interest rate that is liable to be compounded, though the compounding may be more regular than once per annum. There is no standard in relation to the frequency of compounding. Bank accounts regularly compound monthly, instant access building society accounts are frequently compounded quarterly, though many are six monthly or annually.

Generally, two rates are quoted.

- A flat rate.
- An Annual Percentage Rate (APR).

What are these quotes and what difference does this make to our deposit?

Flat Rate

Example

£100 is deposited in an account quoting an annual flat rate of 10% compounding quarterly, calculate the interest earned and value of the deposit by the end of the first year.

Solution

A flat rate of r per annum which compounds m times a year would generate interest of $\frac{r}{m}$ each period, i.e. with a flat rate of 10% compounding quarterly (four times per annum), the interest generated each period would be $\frac{10\%}{4} = 2.5\%$.

We can now see that we are generating an interest rate of 2.5% per period, hence at the end of four periods (one year), the value of our deposit will have grown to

$£100\ (1 + 0.025)^4 = £100 \times 1.025^4 = £110.38$

which is slightly more than when interest is compounded annually.

Example

£100 is deposited in an account quoting an annual flat rate of 10% compounding monthly. What is the value of the deposit at the end of one year?

Solution

The rate per month would be $\frac{10\%}{12} = 0.83333\%$.

Hence at the end of 12 months (one year), the value of our deposit will have grown to

$£100\ (1 + 0.0083333)^{12} = £100 \times 1.0083333^{12} = £110.47$

which is slightly more than when interest is compounded both annually and quarterly.

What we can conclude is

- The more frequent the compounding, the better.
- The higher the interest rate, the greater the benefit of frequent compounding.

Annual percentage rate

We can see from the above that if the interest compounds monthly we have generated interest of £10.47 over the first year based on our initial £100 deposit – an effective rate of 10.47%. This effective rate is the APR. It tells you exactly how much you will earn over a year (or pay if you are borrowing) based on the flat rate and the frequency of compounding.

Relevance

The relevance of the above distinction between simple and compound interest is that different instruments apply different bases. It is most common to find ourselves using the ideas of compound interest, however money market instruments apply simple interest ideas when considering terms less than one year.

We could summarise the application of these ideas as follows.

	Bonds	Money Market Instruments
Period < 12 months	Compound rates	Simple rates
Period > 12 months	Compound rates	Compound rates

We will see these ideas again when pricing bonds and money market instruments.

3 Terminal Values and Net Terminal Values

3.1 Introduction

Using the above ideas, we can calculate how the value of an investment may change over time given its rate of return, or what value it may have at the end of a given period – its terminal value.

3.1.1 Illustration

We will use the following example throughout to illustrate the ideas.

Example

A company will receive income net of direct costs of £100,000 p.a. over the three-year life of Investment A, a total of £300,000.

An alternative three-year investment, B, will generate £324,000 at the end of the third year.

The initial capital required for either investment is £240,000, resulting in a potential profit of £60,000 from Investment A or £84,000 from Investment B.

Which investment, if either, should be undertaken on the basis that the alternative use for this cash is to place it on deposit for three years, earning compound interest at 10% p.a.?

Looking at the cash flow returns we have

Time	Investment A (£)	Investment B (£)
1	100,000	–
2	100,000	–
3	100,000	324,000

Certainly Investment B will generate more cash, but Investment A will enable us to receive cash sooner. This would allow us to do one of the following.

- Invest the cash received and earn additional interest.
- Use the receipts from Investment A to reduce our borrowings and hence save costs.

Either way there is a hidden cost attached to selecting Investment B in that we would lose interest that could have been received/saved by selecting Investment A. Our decision would, therefore, depend on that rate of interest.

3.2 Terminal values

3.2.1 Introduction

Terminal value calculations consider

- Each cash flow generated by an investment.
- The timing of the cash flow.

And calculate how much cash could be generated to the end of an investment if the returns were banked each year to generate interest.

If the returns plus the interest they generate exceeds the total that could be generated had we simply banked the cash at the outset rather than investing it, then we accept the investment. The decision criterion could be stated as

An investment should be accepted if it produces a surplus in cash terms after accounting for interest.

Solution

Since we can receive 10% p.a. on any cash generated, then the effects of selecting A or B would be as follows.

Investment A

Time	Balance B/F (£)	Interest for Year (£)	Receipt at Year-end (£)	Balance C/F (£)
1	–	–	100,000	100,000
2	100,000	10,000	100,000	210,000
3	210,000	21,000	100,000	331,000

Thus, undertaking Investment A will result in cash in the bank of £331,000 at the end of the three years.

Investment B

Investment B will result in a receipt of £324,000 at the same time, hence this is its terminal value.

Bank Account

Time	Balance B/F (£)	Interest for Year (£)	Receipt at Year-End (£)	Balance C/F (£)
1	240,000	24,000	–	264,000
2	264,000	26,400	–	290,400
3	290,400	29,040	–	319,440

Conclusion

Both investments produce a better end position than the simple investment in the bank. Investment A will result in £11,560 more cash (£331,000 – £319,440) and Investment B £4,560 more (£324,000 – £319,440). Comparing the two, Investment A now appears preferable to Investment B.

It would certainly seem that it is in the investor's interest to pay more attention to the cash flows expected from an investment and to the timing of these cash flows, than to consider solely the level of profit.

Alternative Solution

An alternative way of dealing with the example would be by compounding the interest on each flow individually.

Investment A

Time	Cash Flow (£)	Compound Factor (10%)	Terminal Value (£)
1	100,000	1.10^2	121,000
2	100,000	1.10	110,000
3	100,000	1	100,000
Terminal value			331,000

Investment B

Time	Cash Flow (£)	Compound Factor (10%)	Terminal Value (£)
1	0	1.10^2	0
2	0	1.10	0
3	324,000	1	324,000
Terminal value			324,000

Here, we have compounded each flow by adding on interest at 10% p.a. for the number of years remaining until the end of the lives of the investments. To achieve this, we have multiplied the cash flow in each year by the compound factor which, in general terms, may be written as

Formula to learn

Compound factor with n years to run = $(1 + r)^n$

where r is the rate of interest expressed as a decimal (here, r = 0.10) and n is the number of years' compounding required.

Clearly, the calculations have produced the same result, but the method used is somewhat neater. We have compounded the flows to produce what is termed the terminal value of each cash flow.

Again, this can be compared to the £319,440 terminal value from the bank account to show that the investments are worthwhile.

The following example illustrates the use to which these ideas have been put in the exam.

Example

A 4 year bond pays an annual coupon of 8%. Calculate the terminal value if the future coupons received can be reinvested at 6%.

Solution

Time	Cash Flow (£)	Compound Factor (6%)	Terminal Value (£)
1	8	1.06^3	9.53
2	8	1.06^2	8.99
3	8	1.06	8.48
4	108	1	108.00

3.3 Net terminal value

The net surplus or deficit from the investment (£11,560 for Investment A, £4,560 for Investment B as calculated above) is known as the net terminal value (NTV). Since it is positive, indicating a surplus, the investments are worthwhile and should be accepted. Had it been negative, indicating a deficit, we would have rejected the investments.

Rather than calculating separately the terminal values of the investment and the bank account, we can combine them in one net terminal value calculation as follows.

Investment A

Time	Cash Flow (£)	Compound Factor (10%)	Terminal Value (£)
0	(240,000)	1.10^3	(319,440)
1	100,000	1.10^2	121,000
2	100,000	1.10	110,000
3	100,000	1	100,000
Net terminal value			11,560

Here, we are considering the £240,000 invested initially as a cash outflow on which we will lose interest. In turn, we get the investment inflows that generate interest, but it is the net difference we are interested in.

Investment B

Time	Cash Flow (£)	Compound Factor (10%)	Terminal Value (£)
0	(240,000)	1.10^3	(319,440)
1	0	1.10^2	0
2	0	1.10	0
3	324,000	1	324,000
Net terminal value			4,560

3.4 Conclusion

Net terminal values are useful for evaluating individual investments or investments with the same end date. If, however, we are trying to evaluate investments with different end dates, then we cannot compare the terminal value of one directly to that of the other. For example, how could we compare the terminal value of Investment A of £331,000 at the end of three years to the terminal value of a third investment of £350,000 at the end of six years? In order to make this comparison, we must compound the interest out to a common date. In this instance, six years would be sensible. However, this method may become very cumbersome, especially if we have some investments that will continue forever and never terminate!

4 Present Values and Net Present Values

4.1 Introduction

As we have just seen, one way of accounting for the interest is by compounding the flows and calculating the terminal values. However, as we stated, if we are to compare investments, we will have to calculate to a common date, say the end of the longest investment time. An alternative approach is to use present values where we take the common date as the present (today).

4.2 Present Values

Present value calculations consider for any investment

- Each relevant cash flow.
- The timing of the cash flow.

And calculate how much cash would need to be invested now to generate these same amounts of cash at these same future dates.

If we can get the same cash at the same dates by investing less upfront now, then we should accept the investment.

Solution

Investment A

Investment A generates the following cash flows.

Time	Cash Flow (£)
1	100,000
2	100,000
3	100,000

Looking at each of these in turn, how much cash would we need to invest now at our 10% rate of return to have £100,000 in each year?

Year 1

If we invest x now, then in one year it will grow to $x \times 1.10 = 1.10x$. Since we know that this is £100,000, then we can calculate x as

$1.10x = £100{,}000$

or

$$x = \frac{1}{1.10} \times £100{,}000$$

x = £90,909

Year 2

Similarly, x invested now will grow to $x \times 1.10^2 = 1.21x$ after two years, hence

1.21x = £100,000

or

$$x = \frac{1}{1.21} \times £100{,}000$$

x = £82,645

Year 3

And x invested now will grow to $x \times 1.10^3 = 1.331x$ after three years, hence

1.331x = £100,000

or

$$x = \frac{1}{1.331} \times £100{,}000$$

x = £75,131

Conclusion

Putting these all together, we have

Time	Cash Flow (£)	Discount Factor (10%)	Present Value (£)
1	100,000	$\frac{1}{1.10}$	90,909
2	100,000	$\frac{1}{1.10^2}$	82,645
3	100,000	$\frac{1}{1.10^3}$	75,131
Present value			248,685

In total, the present value of these receipts is £248,685. What this means is that given this 10% rate of return, we would be indifferent between £100,000 each year for three years and £248,685 now.

Rather than compounding up the cash values for interest generated to the end of the investment, we are **discounting down**, i.e. reducing future cash values to their equivalent value today.

Discounting is effectively the reverse of the compounding process and in a similar way, we could apply a general formula for any time of

Formula to learn

$$\text{Discount factor at Time n} = \frac{1}{(1+r)^n}$$

where r is the rate of interest expressed as a decimal (here r = 0.10) and n is the number of years' discounting required.

Investment B

Calculating the present value for Investment B gives

Time	Cash Flow (£)	Discount Factor (10%)	Present Value (£)
3	324,000	$\frac{1}{1.10^3}$	243,426
Present value			243,426

What this means is that, given the 10% rate of return, we would be indifferent between £324,000 in three years and £243,426 now.

Bank

What is the present value of our option of banking the cash for a comparison? Under this option we left the cash in the bank until Year 3, when it had grown to £319,440. This is then the cash flow to discount giving

Time	Cash Flow (£)	Discount Factor (10%)	Present Value (£)
3	319,440	$\frac{1}{1.10^3}$	240,000
Present value			240,000

This one really proves the idea, as what it shows is that we are indifferent between £319,440 in three years and £240,000 now, which stands to reason as to get £319,440 in three years will require us to invest £240,000 in the bank now.

Conclusion

Of our three alternatives, Investment A again gives the best return – the highest present value.

4.3 Changing rates

In the above calculations we have assumed that the rate will remain constant throughout. For example, the discount factor applied to establish the present value of investment B was $\frac{1}{1.10^3}$, taking in three years' compound interest at 10%p.a. each year.

What if the rates in each of the three years were not the same and we faced changing rates across the period? To appreciate the approach here we must recognise that

$$\frac{1}{1.10^3} = \frac{1}{1.10} \times \frac{1}{1.10} \times \frac{1}{1.10}$$

10% across the first year	10% across the second year	10% across the third year

If rates vary across the years we will simply need to incorporate the relevant rates into the discount factor.

Example

Value investment A if rates are 10% across the first year, 9% across the second and 8% across the third.

Solution

Time	Cash Flow (£)	Discount Factor	Present Value (£)
1	100,000	$\frac{1}{1.10}$	90,909
2	100,000	$\frac{1}{1.10} \times \frac{1}{1.09}$	83,403
3	100,000	$\frac{1}{1.10} \times \frac{1}{1.09} \times \frac{1}{1.08}$	75,225
			251,537

We will see an application of this idea when we deal with pricing money market instruments.

4.4 Net present value

The present value of Investment A is £8,685 higher than could be expected from the bank. Investment B has a present value that is £3,426 higher than that from the bank. These represent the net present values of these investments.

In a similar way to terminal values, we could calculate a net present value in one go rather than calculating separately the present value of the investment and the banking option, as follows.

Solution

Investment A

Time	Cash Flow (£)	Discount Factor (10%)	Present Value (£)
0	(240,000)	1	(240,000)
1	100,000	$\frac{1}{1.10}$	90,909
2	100,000	$\frac{1}{1.10^2}$	82,645
3	100,000	$\frac{1}{1.10^3}$	75,131
Net present value			8,685

You will note that the cash flow at Time 0 (now) is not discounted. £240,000 now is worth £240,000 now. Discounting takes account of the time value of money.

Investment B

Similarly for Investment B, we get

Time	Cash Flow (£)	Discount Factor (10%)	Present Value (£)
0	(240,000)	1	(240,000)
3	324,000	$\frac{1}{1.10^3}$	243,426
Net present value			3,426

Conclusion

For an accept or reject decision, the criterion is as before – a positive net present value (NPV) indicates a cash surplus after accounting for interest and we should therefore accept. A negative NPV indicates a cash deficit and we should therefore reject.

If we were to choose between various investments, we would now simply select the investment with the highest NPV.

4.4.1 Relationship between present and terminal values

One final point to note is that there is a direct relationship between present and terminal values, either gross or net. If we take the present or net present value of any investment and compound it up for the appropriate number of years, we will get the corresponding terminal or net terminal value as we can see from our sample investments.

Solution

	Net Present Value (£)	Compound Factor	Net Terminal Value (£)
Investment A	8,685	1.10^3	11,560
Investment B	3,426	1.10^3	4,560

5 Timing of Flows

It is vital to appreciate that when we discount for one year, we are eliminating **exactly** one year's interest, implying that exactly one year had elapsed before the relevant flow occurred.

We must carefully distinguish between a year and a point in time. Year 1 of an investment will run for 365 days from day 1. It will cover a number of points in time. Day 1, we would call Time 0. Three months later would be Time ¼. Six months later is Time ½. Nine months later is Time ¾ and 12 months later is Time 1. Hence, Year 1 runs from Time 0 to Time 1. Diagrammatically

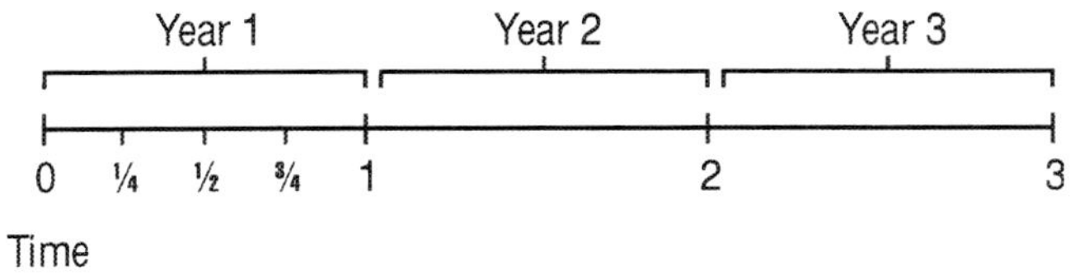

When establishing our discount factors, the important point is the exact timing of the cash flows that have occurred, not the year in which it occurred.

Example

We buy a production machine on 1 January 2008 for £240,000 and the first sales receipt of £100,000 occurs on 31 December 2011. How much time has elapsed to that date?

Solution

2011 is obviously three years after 2008, however, it is four years from the start of 2008 to the end of 2011 – think how old you would call yourself, had you been born on 1 January 2008.

Strictly speaking, $3\frac{364}{365}$ years have elapsed between the two dates, hence we would need to discount the £100,000 for four years as we would if the £100,000 had, in fact, been receivable on 1 January 2012 (just one day later).

Of course, in practice, the above is unlikely in that cash flows do not normally occur at yearly intervals. However, we may need to make this assumption in order to be able to do the calculations. It is quite common to assume that all capital flows will be incurred at the start of an investment and that all future flows will arise at the ends of years, though we can cope with other time periods as we will see.

We now need to develop our analysis to cover three real-world complications.

- Annuities and perpetuities.
- Non-annual receipts and payments.

6 Discount Factors

6.1 Introduction

We established above that the general term for a discount factor to be applied to cash flows at time n is

$$\text{Discount factor at Time n} = \frac{1}{(1+r)^n}$$

This is fine if we are only dealing with a few cash flows or have a spreadsheet model to cope with a large number, but what if this is not the case? There are some other situations for which we can establish discount factor formulae to make manual calculations simpler, specifically

- Level annuities.
- Level perpetuities.

6.2 Annuities

An annuity describes the situation where we have equal annual cash flows for a set period, such as in Investment A. Here, we have £100,000 received at the end of each of the next three years and so far, we have appraised each flow separately.

However, since for all the receipts, we are multiplying the discount factor by £100,000 each time, we can simplify the calculation by multiplying £100,000 by the total of the discount factors, i.e.

$$£100{,}000 \times \left(\frac{1}{1.10}+\frac{1}{1.10^2}+\frac{1}{1.10^3}\right) = £100{,}000 \times 2.48685$$

$$= £248{,}685 \text{ as before}$$

The discount factor of 2.48685 is termed the three-year annuity factor at 10%. This annuity factor can be calculated using the following formula.

Formula to learn

$$\text{Annuity discount factor for Times 1 to n} = \frac{1}{r}\left(1-\frac{1}{(1+r)^n}\right)$$

where r is the rate of interest p.a. expressed as a decimal.

Using this formula to calculate the three-year annuity factor at 10% gives

$$\text{Annuity discount factor for Times 1 to n} = \frac{1}{0.10}\left(1-\frac{1}{1.10^3}\right)$$

$$= \frac{1}{0.10}(1-0.751315)$$

$$= \frac{1}{0.10}(0.248685)$$

$$= 2.48685$$

6.3 Perpetuities

A perpetuity refers to an equal annual flow that will continue indefinitely.

Any series of flows that continue beyond 50 years could be approximated to a perpetuity without much impact or loss of accuracy.

Clearly, it will be impossible for us to evaluate each individual cash flow going on forever. For this situation, we must have a shortcut.

Example

We are going to receive £10,000 p.a. in perpetuity and the interest rate (which we will now start to refer to as a cost of capital) is 10% p.a. How would we value this series of flows?

To get a present value, we need to know how much cash invested now at 10% p.a. would provide £10,000 p.a. in perpetuity. We would be indifferent between these two things which, by definition, means that it is the present value.

Solution

If we are to receive exactly the same amount in perpetuity, then we must never add to or eat into our capital invested. We are looking for an income of exactly £10,000 p.a.

Since our interest rate is 10% p.a., we can achieve this level of income by investing £100,000, which will generate the required income level.

The relationship being £100,000 × 10% = £10,000.

Now we know that £10,000 × Perpetuity discount factor = £100,000 (the present value), hence the perpetuity discount factor in this case is $\frac{1}{0.10}$.

Note. What we have found is the discount factor for a stream of cash flows starting in one year, i.e. at Time 1.

6.3.1 Discount factor

The general discount factor formula for a level perpetuity stream of cash flows starting at Time 1 for this is

Formula to learn

$$\text{Perpetuity discount factor} = \frac{1}{r}$$

where r is the rate of interest p.a. expressed as a decimal.

6.4 Non-annual time periods

6.4.1 Introduction

So far, we have only considered examples with cash flows occurring at precisely annual intervals. This is clearly an oversimplification and was done to make the calculations easier. In practice, we are liable to have investment opportunities that offer either more or less regular returns. How can we deal with these non-annual time periods in our calculations?

To incorporate any factor, we need to establish three things.

- The cash flow value.
- The timing of the flow.
- The discount rate for that time.

Our problem here is to achieve the latter for say six-monthly or quarterly or even monthly periods and the first factor to consider is whether we are considering an instrument that uses a simple interest basis or compound interest.

6.4.2 Simple interest

As we noted earlier, money markets have a convention of applying a simple interest basis. If we were quoted a rate of, say, 10% p.a. then this would equate to

- 3 months 2.5% (10% $\times$ $^{3}/_{12}$)
- 6 months 5% (10% $\times$ $^{6}/_{12}$)
- 9 months 7.5% (10% $\times$ $^{9}/_{12}$)
- 12 months 10%

Example

A money market instrument will return £10,000 at the end of each quarter for the next year. Money market rates are quoted as 10% p.a. calculate the price of the instrument.

Time	Cash Flow (£)	Discount Factor (10%)	Present Value (£)
¼	10,000	$\frac{1}{1.025}$	9,756
½	10,000	$\frac{1}{1.050}$	9,524
¾	10,000	$\frac{1}{1.075}$	9,302
1	10,000	$\frac{1}{1.100}$	9,041
Present value			37,673

6.4.3 Compound interest

We have already been dealing with non-annual time periods to an extent, specifically those longer than one year. We know that the general discount factor for an individual cash flow is given by the formula

$$\text{Discount factor at time n} = \frac{1}{(1+r)^n}$$

This enables us to calculate the discount factor for a longer period, say two or three years, given the annual rate, r. The point to note is that this does not just work for whole years, it also works for partial periods, e.g. 1½ years or ¼ of a year.

Example

A bond will generate £10,000 at the end of each quarter for the next year. Our required return is 10% p.a. Establish the price of the bond.

Solution

Laying out the cash flows as normal, we can calculate the NPV as follows.

Time	Cash Flow (£)	Discount Factor (10%)	Present Value (£)
¼	10,000	$\frac{1}{1.10^{1/4}}$	9,764
½	10,000	$\frac{1}{1.10^{1/2}}$	9,535
¾	10,000	$\frac{1}{1.10^{3/4}}$	9,310
1	10,000	$\frac{1}{1.10}$	9,091
Present value			37,700

6.4.4 Equivalent rates

Introduction

In the above, we resorted to first principles in order to solve the problem. This proved to be practical with only five cash flows, but what if we had a longer annuity or a perpetuity? Both of these examples have something in common, i.e. both represent four-period non-annual annuities. Could we establish an equivalent rate that would allow us to use these annuity and perpetuity formulae?

The answer is, of course, yes.

If r was this equivalent discount rate for the non-annual period, then the normal discount factor for that period would be of the form

$$\text{Discount factor} = \frac{1}{(1+r)^n}$$

Hence, to get the equivalent discount factor, we need to equate this to the matching factor based on an annual rate and solve for r, i.e.

Based on the compound interest example above, our non-annual period is a quarter of a year. Therefore, we will equate the one period equivalent discount factor to the ¼ year factor we used above, i.e.

$$\frac{1}{1+r} = \frac{1}{1.10^{1/4}}$$

$$1+r = 1.10^{1/4}$$

$$1+r = 1.0241137$$

$$r = 0.0241137 \text{ or } 2.41137\%$$

What this is saying is that 2.41137% compounding each quarter is the equivalent of 10% p.a. This sounds fairly close to what we would expect, since at a flat rate of interest, we would calculate the quarterly rate at 2.5% (10% ÷ 4).

The 'proof of the pudding' is to use this in our annuity formula that gives the following.

$$\text{The annuity discount factor for Times 1 to n} = \frac{1}{r}\left(1-\frac{1}{(1+r)^n}\right).$$

Hence, with r = 2.41137%, we get for a four-period annuity

$$\text{Annuity discount factor} = \frac{1}{0.0241137}\left(1-\frac{1}{1.0241137^4}\right)$$

$$= \frac{1}{0.0241137}(1-0.9090909)$$

$$= \frac{1}{0.0241137}(0.0909091)$$

$$= 3.7700$$

Thus, we can evaluate the NPV as

Time	Cash Flow (£)	DF (2.41137%)	Present Value (£)
0	(32,000)	1	(32,000)
1–4	10,000	3.7700	37,700
Net present value			5,700

As we can see, this is exactly the same as the result above.

Calculation

Expressing what we have done here as a formula, we could state that the equivalent period interest rate for a non-annual period could be calculated from the annual rate as follows.

Formula to learn

$$\text{Equivalent rate} \Rightarrow \frac{1}{1+r} = \frac{1}{(1+R)^n}$$

or

Formula to learn

$$1 + r = (1 + R)^n$$

where

r = rate for the non-annual period that we are solving for
R = annual rate
n = number of years in one non-annual period

Example

Calculate the present values of the following flows at the noted discount rates.

£10,000 receivable in nine months' time with a cost of capital of 20% p.a.

£20,000 receivable each 15 months in perpetuity with a cost of capital of 15% p.a.

Solution

£10,000 @ 20% p.a.

Using the equivalent period interest rate formula, we get

$$\begin{aligned} 1 + r &= (1 + R)^n \\ 1 + r &= 1.20^{3/4} \\ 1 + r &= 1.14653 \\ r &= 0.14653 \text{ or } 14.653\% \end{aligned}$$

$$\text{Present value, therefore} = £10{,}000 \times \frac{1}{1.14653} = £8{,}722$$

£20,000 in perpetuity @ 15% p.a.

Using the equivalent period interest rate formula, we get

$$\begin{aligned} 1 + r &= (1 + R)^n \\ 1 + r &= 1.151^{3/4} \\ 1 + r &= 1.19089 \\ r &= 0.19089 \text{ or } 19.089\% \end{aligned}$$

$$\text{Present value in perpetuity} = £20{,}000 \times \frac{1}{0.19089} = £104{,}771$$

6.4.5 Conclusion

In understanding any DCF exercise there are three primary factors to determine, time, cash flow value, rate. The important fact here is that DCF can be applied to any frequency of cash flows so long as we are consistent with these factors.

The unit of time used should always be based on the frequency of the cash flows, and the cash flow value and rate to apply should match with this. For example considering these three factors for different cash flow frequencies we need to apply the following.

	Cash flow frequency			
	Monthly	Quarterly	Semi-annual	Annual
Unit of time	Month	Quarter	½ year	Year
Cash flow	Month	Quarterly	Semi-annual	Annual
Rate	Per month	Per quarter	Per half-year	Per annum

We will see these ideas later when considering bond pricing and we will need to be aware of how to determine the relevant periodic cash flow value and periodic rate.

6.5 Continuous compounding and exponential growth

6.5.1 Introduction

Interest rates tend to be quoted in annual terms, i.e. the interest rate is per annum regardless of the frequency of the payments. If we are quoted such a rate of interest, then the actual annual return we receive will depend on how frequently it is compounded.

Example

We are quoted a rate of 32% p.a., this may be 16% each half year or 8% per quarter or 2.667% per month or 0.0877% per day. If we compound these up to get the actual annual rate that we will earn we get

Compound Period	Calculation	Actual Rate %
Annual	$1.32^1 - 1$	32.00
Half yearly	$1.16^2 - 1$	34.56
Quarterly	$1.08^4 - 1$	36.05
Monthly	$1.02667^{12} - 1$	37.14
Daily	$1.000877^{365} - 1$	37.69

As we can see, the actual rate is increasing, but tending towards a limit. This continuous compounding limit is given by

Formula to learn

$$R = e^{rt} - 1$$

where

e = exponential constant (2.7182818)
r = quoted annual rate as a decimal
t = time period being considered as a proportion of a year

Thus, over one year, converting the 32% rate to a continuously compounding rate gives a return of

$$\begin{aligned} R &= e^{rt} - 1 \\ &= 2.7182818^{0.32 \times 1} - 1 \\ &= 1.3771 - 1 \\ &= 0.3771 \text{ or } 37.71\% \end{aligned}$$

a slightly higher rate than the daily one, as it compounds continuously.

6.5.2 Natural log returns

Above we saw how if you had a quoted annual rate and wanted to see what the actual annual return was if the annual rate was continuously compounded, we applied

Formula to learn

$$R = e^{rt} - 1$$

What happens if we know the actual annual return from an investment that was continuously compounded but we wanted to know the quoted annual rate? Here we would need to determine the natural log return.

Example

A security rises from 100 to 110 over half a year. What is the annual continuously compounded rate of return?

Solution

$R = e^{rt} - 1$

Or

$1 + R = e^{rt}$

Now

$$1 + R = \frac{110}{100} = 1.10$$

giving

$e^{rt} = 1.10$

Now for a half a year, t = 0.5, and so to get the annual return r, we need to solve

$e^{r \times 0.5} = 1.10$

We can do this by taking the natural log of both sides, i.e.

$\ln(e^{r \times 0.5}) = \ln(1.10) = 0.0953$

Now by definition, $\ln(e^{x}) = x$, and so we have

$$\begin{aligned} r \times 0.5 &= 0.09531 \\ r &= 0.1906 \text{ or } 19.06\% \text{ p.a.} \end{aligned}$$

6.5.3 Benefits of natural log returns

Natural log returns more accurately model the continuous/experimental growth exhibited by companies (market value movements) and economies (GDP growth).

Natural log (continuously compounded) returns have the advantages of being additive, i.e. in order to calculate the annual return from, say, quarterly returns, the four quarters figures simply need to be added (instead of compounded). A natural log measurement is, therefore, more convenient when assessing returns over several time periods.

Natural log returns will be lower than their equivalent arithmetic returns, though there is little benefit in this as such. Risk and return information is useless in isolation, its relevance becomes clear when compared to alternatives (i.e. all returns have been calculated on a natural log basis or all on an arithmetic basis).

A log-normal distribution of prices has the advantage that share volatility in absolute terms varies with the underlying price (e.g. a share that has 10× the value than another is likely to exhibit price variations that are 10× larger than the other). It also has the advantage that share prices can never be negative.

6.5.4 Continuous Discount Factor

This method of establishing a discount rate is used in options valuation. The discount factor that results from its use is

$$\frac{1}{1+r} = \frac{1}{1+\left(e^{rt}-1\right)} = \frac{1}{e^{rt}} = e^{-rt}$$

7 Returns

7.1 Introduction

We may need to calculate either the total return achieved on an investment or the annual return in percentage terms.

7.2 Total Return

To an extent, the total return calculation is quite intuitive

Example

An investment is bought for £100 and sold for £109 3 years later. What is the total return?

Solution

Gain = £9 (£109 – £100)

$$\text{Return} = \frac{9}{100} = 0.09 \text{ or } 9\%$$

Though it may not be apparent, this is actually a terminal value exercise. If we measure time in 3 year periods and we use the rate R as the rate for a 3 year period then we have

Time	Cash Flow (£)	Compound Factor	Terminal Value (£)
0	100	(1 + R)	109

So we have

$100 \times (1 + R) = 109$

or

$(1 + R) = \frac{109}{100} = 1.09$

R = 0.09 or 9%

More generally we could say that in calculating the total return

Formula to learn

$$(1 + R) = \frac{\text{Terminal Value}}{\text{Cost}}$$

7.3 Annual Return

If we wished to calculate the annual return we would need to solve for r in the terminal value table.

Time	Cash Flow (£)	Compound Factor	Terminal Value (£)
0	100	$(1 + r)^3$	109

Which gives

$100 \times (1 + r)^3 = 109$

or

$(1 + r)^3 = \frac{109}{100}$

$1 + r = \sqrt[3]{\frac{109}{100}} = 1.02915$

r = 0.02915 or 2.915%

This relationship could, more generally, be expressed as

Formula to learn

$$(1 + r)^n = \frac{\text{Terminal Value}}{\text{Cost}}$$

Where n = number of years to the terminal date.

This is known as the holding period return and we will see this again later in the section on bond yields.

Example

Earlier on in this section we calculated the terminal value of a 4 year band paying an annual coupon of 8% where the reinvestment rate was 6% as £135. If the bond cost £103.39 calculate

(a) total return
(b) annual return

Solution

(a) Total Return

$$1 + R = \frac{135.00}{103.39} = 1.3057$$

$$R = 0.3057 \text{ or } 30.57\%$$

(b) Annual Return

$$(1 + r)^4 = \frac{135.00}{103.39} = 1.3057$$

$$(1 + r) = \sqrt[4]{1.3057} = 1.069$$

$$r = 0.069 \text{ or } 6.9\%$$

7.4 Problem with these calculations

The problem with these calculations is that they can only be undertaken if we know the terminal value, which can only be assessed if we know the reinvestment rate as we had in this example.

What if we did not know the reinvestment rate?

In the example above, the annual return of 6.9% was greater than the reinvestment rate of 6%. Rather than reinvesting at 6%, perhaps we should have reinvested in more of this bond and achieved a higher overall return. In this situations the return and reinvestment rate would be one and the same, but how would we calculate the return in this circumstance?

However, this is a 'chicken and egg' question. We cannot calculate the terminal value, hence the return, without the reinvestment rate, and we cannot calculate the reinvestment rate without the return.

The approach that achieves this objective is the internal rate of return.

8 INTERNAL RATE OF RETURN/YIELD

8.1 Definition

The **internal rate of return** (IRR), can be defined as follows.

IRR = the rate of interest that discounts the investment flows to a net present value of zero

This can only be properly assessed through trial and error, though it is possible to approximate by the following method.

8.2 Calculation

The method we use is called interpolation. We evaluate the NPV at two different rates and then, by assuming a straight-line relationship, estimate where it becomes zero. The IRR formula for this is as follows.

Formula to learn

$$IRR = R_1 + \left(\frac{N_1}{N_1 - N_2} \times (R_2 - R_1) \right)$$

where

R_1 = first selected cost of capital
R_2 = second selected cost of capital
N_1 = NPV of the investment when discounted at R_1
N_2 = NPV of the investment when discounted at R_2

Interpolation means finding a result between the two figures that we have chosen, i.e. selecting R_1 and R_2 such that the IRR falls in between.

Extrapolation means estimating a figure outside of that range, i.e. selecting values for R_1 and R_2 such that the IRR does not fall in between.

Interpolation will give the more accurate solution, hence we should always try to achieve this if possible.

Example

Earlier on in this session we considered investment A that cost £240,000 and returned £100,000 p.a. for 3 years. We calculated its net present value at 10% to be £8,685. If we calculated at 15% we would get a net present value of £(11,877). What is the IRR?

Solution

We now know that the IRR lies somewhere between 10% and 15% since it is the rate that corresponds to a zero NPV. We need to estimate the rate that will yield zero, but how?

Over a range of 5% (between 10% to 15%) the net present value has fallen by £20,362 (from £8,685 to £(11,677)). We therefore assume that the £20,362 fall in the NPV equates to the 5% increase in the rate.

If we take 10% as our starting point (for which the NPV is £8,685) we need a change of £(8,685) to get the NPV down to zero. This will require a change in the rate of interest of

$$\text{Change in rate} = \frac{£8,685}{£20,362} \times 5\% = 2.133\%$$

Hence, the internal rate of return is

$$IRR = 10\% + \left(\frac{£8,685}{£8,685 - £(11,677)} \times (15\% - 10\%) \right)$$

IRR = 12.133%

As we can see, this corresponds fairly closely to the true IRR of 12.0444%. However, it is important to appreciate that this is only an approximation to the IRR, since we have assumed that the NPV changes linearly with the rate of interest, which is not, in fact, the case.

This can be seen graphically as follows.

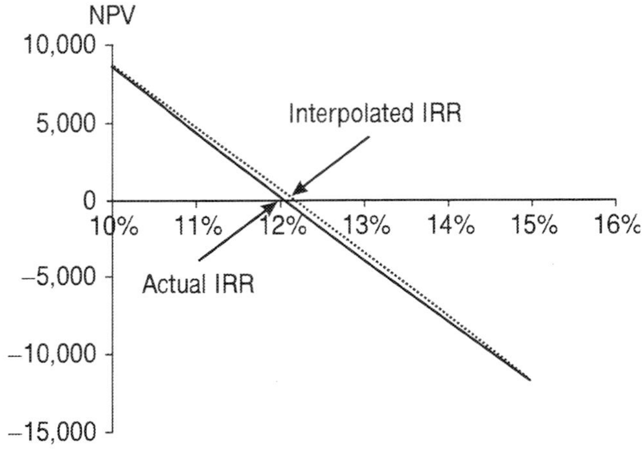

In addition, a different pair of rates from the 10% and 15% we used would yield a different IRR.

If we had used rates of 5% and 20%, we would estimate the IRR as

$$\text{IRR} = 5\% + \left(\frac{£32,325}{£32,325 - £(29,352)}\right) \times (20\% - 5\%)$$

IRR = 12.862%

What we can see from this is the closer the rates to the actual IRR, the more accurate the result.

Example

Applying these ideas to our 4 year 8% bond, what is the IRR, the rate of return achieved if we reinvest all future coupons received at the same rate.

Solution

At a reinvestment rate of 6% we calculated a return of 6.9%. If we could invest at a higher rate we would get a higher total return, so the IRR should be above 6.9%.

To undertake an IRR we must choose 2 rates, calculate the NPV at those rate and apply the above interpolation formula. The two rates we will try are 6.9% and 8%.

Time	Cash flow (£)	DF (6.9%)	PV (6.9%) (£)	DF (8%)	PV (8%) (£)
0	(103.39)	1	(103.39)	1	(103.39)
1	8.00	$\frac{1}{1.069}$	7.48	$\frac{1}{1.08}$	7.41
2	8.00	$\frac{1}{1.069^2}$	7.00	$\frac{1}{1.08^2}$	6.86
3	8.00	$\frac{1}{1.069^3}$	6.55	$\frac{1}{1.08^3}$	6.35
4	108.00	$\frac{1}{1.069^4}$	82.70	$\frac{1}{1.08^4}$	79.38
			0.34		(3.39)

So we have

$R_1 = 6.9\%$

$R_2 = 8.0\%$

$N_1 = 0.34$

$N_2 = (3.39)$

and so

$$IRR = 6.9\% + \frac{0.34}{0.34-(3.39)} \times (8.0\% - 6.9\%) = 7.0\%$$

So if the future coupons can be reinvested at 7% we will get a 7% return.

9 Securities Evaluation and DCF

9.1 Introduction

The Dividend Valuation Model (DVM) is the basis for all our calculations relating to the market value of any investment.

In order to raise finance, a company must attract investors, i.e. the investors must believe that they will receive a return sufficient to match their requirements. If they do not believe this, they will not invest.

As a result, the market value of a security at any point in time is determined by two factors.

- The returns (dividends/interest/capital growth) that the investors expect.
- The rate of return that the investors require.

The DVM states that the

Market value = Present value of the future expected receipts discounted at the investor's required rate of return

That is we assume investors rationally evaluate the returns in order to determine what they are willing to pay. Though we may be cynical about particular investors, in the UK we can be fairly sure that the majority of dealing is rationally assessed.

Alternatively, the investor's required rate of return can be calculated as the IRR of the current market value and subsequent repayments (dividends, interest, capital, etc.). **Note.** These comments relate equally to **all** investments.

9.2 Illustration

We will see the application of this idea to various types of securities in the following sections, but the following is included for illustration.

Example

A bond pays an annual coupon of £9 and is to be redeemed at £100 in three years. The required return on these bonds (prevailing interest rate) is 8%. What will be their market value?

Solution

Their market value can be established by calculating the present value of the associated cash flows at the required rate of 8%. The cash flows from the bond will be £9 coupon at the end of each year, and £100 capital redemption at the end of the third year, i.e. £109 is received in total at that time.

The market value can, therefore, be calculated as follows.

Time	Cash Flow (£)	Discount Factor (8%)	Present value (£)
1	9.00	$\frac{1}{1.08}$	8.33
2	9.00	$\frac{1}{1.08^2}$	7.72
3	109.00	$\frac{1}{1.08^3}$	86.53
Market value			102.58

10 Assumptions Underlying DCF

10.1 Introduction

At this stage, it is worthwhile considering the assumptions we have implicitly been making in all of the NPV and IRR calculations made to date.

10.1.1 The basic assumptions

- The cash flows expected to accrue from any investment can be considered in isolation, and are independent of decisions relating to any other investment.
- The cash flows are known with certainty.
- No firm or individual has sufficient funds to affect the price of funds.
- Investors have a time preference for money and make rational decisions accordingly.

10.1.2 The assumptions as to reinvestment rates

The fundamental difference between NPV and IRR is the assumption made about reinvestment rates. Under NPV we are implicitly assuming that any surplus funds generated can be reinvested to earn a return equal to the discount rate.

However, the IRR calculation assumes that surplus funds will be reinvested to earn a return equal to the IRR, that the time value placed on money is this rate.

Conceptually, NPV is better because regardless of the actual investment that is generating the cash flows, we always assume the flows can be reinvested at the same rate.

There is no real justification for saying that returns from one investment can be reinvested to earn a return in excess of the returns earned from any other investment, as with the IRR.

Chapter Roundup

- To calculate a present or terminal value there are three relevant factors.
  - Cash flow – value to be multiplied by the relevant compound or discount factor.
  - Timing – determines which factor to use, basic, annuity, perpetuity.
  - Rate – determines the rate r for that factor.
- Fisher equation

  $(1+r)=(1+i)(1+R)$
- Compound factor

  Basic – Compound factor with n years to run = $(1 + r)^n$
- Discount factors
  - Basic

    $$\frac{1}{(1+r)^n}$$
  - Basic continuous

    $$\frac{1}{e^{rt}}$$
  - Annuity

    $$\frac{1}{r}\left(1-\frac{1}{(1+r)^n}\right)$$
  - Perpetuity

    $$\frac{1}{r}$$
  - Equivalent rates

    $1 + r = (1 + R)^n$

    where r = rate for the non-annual period that we are solving for
    R = annual rate
    n = number of years in one non-annual period
  - Continuous

    $$\frac{1}{1+r}=\frac{1}{1+\left(e^{rt}-1\right)}=\frac{1}{e^{rt}}=e^{-rt}$$

- Returns
  - Total returns

    $$(1 + r)^n = \frac{\text{Terminal Value}}{\text{Cost}}$$

  - IRR

    Calculated by estimating two rates then interpolating using

    $$IRR = R_1 + \left(\frac{N_1}{N_1 - N_2} \times (R_2 - R_1)\right)$$

Test Your Knowledge

Check your knowledge of the Chapter here, without referring back to the text.

1. What is the terminal value of £1,000 invested now for six years at 8% p.a.?

2. An asset is purchased for £50. Over the next four quarters, it has returns of 4%, 5%, 2% and –3%. what will be the value of the asset at the end of the year?

3. You invest £7,000 at 7% for four years and 8% thereafter. What is the terminal value at the end of nine years?

4. An investment rises in value from £5,000 to £6,742 over four years. What is its constant annual rate of appreciation?

5. What is the present value of £1,000 received in eight years' time at 10% p.a.?

6. What is the present value of receiving £1,000 p.a. for six years starting in one year's time at 8% p.a.?

7. What is the value of a bond with an infinite life that pays £100 per annum when the required rate of return is 8%?

8. What is the terminal value of £10,000 invested at 8% for 150 days continuously compounded?

9. What is the present value of £10,000 received in 200 days at 9% p.a. continuously compounded?

10. An investor bought 1,000 shares in Megagrowth plc at 74 pence each, received net dividends of 3 pence per share and 6 pence per share at the end of each of the first two years respectively, and then sold them at the end of the second year for 80 pence each.

Test Your Knowledge: Answers

1.

Time	Cash Flow (£)	Compound Factor (8%)	Terminal Value (£)
0	1,000	1.08^6	1,587

2.

Time	Cash Flow (£)	Compound Factor	Terminal Value (£)
0	50	$1.04 \times 1.05 \times 1.02 \times 0.97$	54.02

3.

Time	Cash Flow (£)	Compound Factor	Terminal Value (£)
0	7,000	$1.07^4 \times 1.08^5$	13,482

4.

Time	Cash Flow (£)	Compound Factor	Terminal Value (£)
0	5,000	$(1 + r)^4$	6,742

$$5{,}000 \times (1 + r)^4 = 6{,}742$$

$$(1 + r)^4 = \frac{6{,}742}{5{,}000}$$

$$1 + r = \sqrt[4]{\frac{6{,}742}{5{,}000}} = 1.0776$$

r = 0.0776 or 7.76%

5.

Time	Cash flow (£)	Discount Factor (8%)	Present Value (£)
8	1,000	$\frac{1}{1.1^8}$	467

6.

Time	Cash Flow (£)	Discount Factor (8%)	Present Value (£)
1	1,000	$\frac{1}{1.08}$	926
2	1,000	$\frac{1}{1.08^2}$	857
3	1,000	$\frac{1}{1.08^3}$	794
4	1,000	$\frac{1}{1.08^4}$	735
5	1,000	$\frac{1}{1.08^5}$	681
6	1,000	$\frac{1}{1.08^6}$	630
Present value			4,623

Alternative

Using the annuity formula gives

$$1{,}000 \times \frac{1}{0.08}\left(1 - \frac{1}{1.08^6}\right) = 4{,}623$$

7.

Time	Cash flow (£)	Discount Factor (8%)	Present Value (£)
1–∞	100	$\frac{1}{0.08}$	1,250

8. r = 0.08 t = 150/365 = 0.411

Your terminal wealth equals

$£10{,}000 \times e^{rt} = £10{,}000 \times e^{0.08 \times 0.411} = £10{,}000 \times 1.0334 = £10{,}334$

9. r = 0.09 t = 200/365 = 0.548

The present value equals

$£2{,}000 \times e^{-rt} = £10{,}000 \times e^{-0.09 \times 0.548} = £10{,}000 \times 0.9519 = £9{,}519$

10. Using the interpolation approach

Amount invested = 74p

Total return = 89p (3p + 6p + 80p)

Approx total return = 89/74 = 1.20 or 20% over 2 years or 10% p.a.

Trying 5% and 10% gives

Time	Cash Flow (£)	DF (5%)	PV (5%) (£)	DF (10%)	PV (10%) (£)
0	(74)	1	(74.00)	1	(74.00)
1	3	$\frac{1}{1.05}$	2.86	$\frac{1}{1.10}$	2.73
2	6	$\frac{1}{1.05^2}$	5.44	$\frac{1}{1.10^2}$	4.96
2	80	$\frac{1}{1.05^2}$	72.56	$\frac{1}{1.10^2}$	66.12
			6.86		(0.19)

$$\text{IRR} = 5\% + \frac{6.86}{6.86-(0.19)} - (0.19) \times (10\% - 5\%) = 9.87\%$$

3 Pricing Fixed Income Investments

INTRODUCTION

This section follows on from the DCF section applying the ideas covered there to the evaluation of bonds and money market instruments, building in along the way certain practical characteristics of those markets.

What we consider here is the pricing of straight bonds, zero coupon bonds, floating rate bonds, index-linked bonds and money market instruments both at coupon payment dates and between coupon payment dates.

The ideas in this section are regularly examined.

CHAPTER CONTENTS

CHAPTER LEARNING OBJECTIVES

The syllabus areas covered by this section are

Analysis

Students should possess a broad understanding of both static and dynamic methods for the analysis and construction of fixed income securities containing both certain and contingent cashflows. Variable rate securities will be included. Students should be aware of the limitations of assumptions and mathematical techniques upon results. Although analysis will be concerned principally with 'risk–free' securities, students should be aware of the further considerations for 'risky' securities and the effect they may have on expected return. Students should possess a thorough comprehension of single–period and multi–period, single currency and multi–currency portfolio management theory.

Present and Future Value

- Certain & Contingent

1 PRICING BONDS

1.1 Introduction

Since the cash flow values and timings from a bond are known with such certainty, at least for a straight bond, the application of DCF evaluation techniques is clearly appropriate.

There are, however, two bond pricing aspects to consider.

- DCF evaluation.
- Clean and dirty bond pricing.

The first of these ideas is the method that we will primarily use to evaluate a bond, the second of these is relevant for determining the correct tax treatment.

2 DISCOUNTED CASH FLOW EVALUATION

Exam tip

> Questions in this area have become increasingly complex over the last few years. Before 2000 it was rare to be asked to price anything other than a single gilt strip. More recently the exam has required the pricing of index linked gilts. The exam tips in the remainder of this session simply refer you to relevant exam questions. See Summer 2008 Question 1, Winter 2006 Question 2.

2.1 Fixed coupon bonds

2.1.1 Annual coupon redeemables

A straight redeemable fixed coupon bond pays a coupon to the maturity date, then pays the redemption proceeds at that date. If we know the required return to the bondholders, we can, evaluate this bond using DCF. If the bond is of a fairly short maturity, we may consider each cash flow separately. If, however, the bond is longer dated, it would be more convenient to apply the idea in the calculation of an annuity.

Example

A bond pays an annual coupon of 9% and is redeemable at par in three years. Evaluate this bond if interest rates are

- 8%
- 9%
- 10%

Solution

Interest rate at 8%

Time	Cash Flow (£)	DF (8%)	Present Value (£)
1	9.00	$\frac{1}{1.08}$	8.33
2	9.00	$\frac{1}{1.08^2}$	7.72
3	109.00	$\frac{1}{1.08^3}$	86.53
	(100.00 + 9.00)		102.58

Interest rate at 9%

Time	Cash Flow (£)	DF (9%)	Present Value (£)
1	9.00	$\frac{1}{1.09}$	8.26
2	9.00	$\frac{1}{1.09^2}$	7.57
3	109.00	$\frac{1}{1.09^3}$	89.17
			100.00

Interest rate at 10%

Time	Cash Flow (£)	DF (10%)	Present Value (£)
1	9.00	$\frac{1}{1.10}$	8.18
2	9.00	$\frac{1}{1.10^2}$	7.44
3	109.00	$\frac{1}{1.10^3}$	89.89
			97.51

Conclusion

This example illustrates two important features about bonds, specifically

- There is an **inverse relationship between bond prices and interest rates**, i.e. as interest rates rise, market values fall (and vice versa).
- When the **coupon rate on the bond is equal to the prevailing interest rate, the bond will be valued at par**, as illustrated above when interest rates are 9%.

It is vital that you are aware of, and comfortable with, these two conclusions. Their appreciation is essential for the effective appraisal of a bond investment or the management of a bond portfolio.

This calculation may be expressed mathematically as follows.

Formula to learn

$$\text{Straight bond price} = \frac{C_1}{(1+r)} + \frac{C_2}{(1+r)^2} + \frac{C_3}{(1+r)^3} + \cdots + \frac{C_n + R}{(1+r)^n}$$

where

r = investor's required return

We shall refer to this formula from time to time, however, the above tabular approach to the calculation is probably most convenient.

Example

Calculate the value of the above bond at 10%, assuming it matures in eight years.

Solution

This bond will pay its coupon for the next eight years, an eight year annuity, and then be redeemed, a one off par payment. Its value will, therefore, be as follows.

Time	Cash Flow (£)	Discount Factor (10%)	Present Value (£)
1–8	9.00	$\frac{1}{0.10}\left(1-\frac{1}{1.10^8}\right)$	48.01
8	100.00	$\frac{1}{1.10^8}$	46.65
			94.66

We can clearly see from this that the price of a bond is

Price of bond = PV of coupons + PV of redemption proceeds

and we may need to disaggregate the price in this way.

2.1.2 Semi-annual coupon redeemables

Exam tip

Summer 2004 Question 2, Summer 2002 Question 1

When we have a semi-annual coupon (e.g. gilts), we should discount the semi-annual cash flows at the semi-annual rate. **Note.** the market convention for gilts is to quote the annual yield by simply doubling the semi-annual figure, and prices are in £s rounded to the nearest 6 decimal places (though for exam purposes two decimal places will suffice).

Example

Evaluate a five-year 10% gilt on a quoted GRY of 8%.

Solution

This bond will pay a £5 coupon every six months for the next five years and then be redeemed at par. The appropriate rate for discounting these semi-annual flows is 4% (the semi-annual rate based on the above market convention). Its value will therefore be

Time ($^1/_2$ years)	**Cash Flow (£)**	**Discount Factor (4%)**	**Present Value (£)**
1–10	5.00	$\frac{1}{0.04}\left(1-\frac{1}{1.04^{10}}\right)$	40.55
10	100.00	$\frac{1}{1.04^{10}}$	67.56
			108.11

2.1.3 Double dated bonds

We can adopt the same approach for double dated bonds. The only issue to resolve here would be the bond term, i.e. will it be redeemed early or left to mature at the end date? The answer to this is given by reference to the bond coupon and prevailing interest/discount rates

- If coupon > interest rate then the debt is quite expensive and the bond will be redeemed early, if necessary being refinanced at this new lower rate.
- If coupon < interest rate the bond represents a cheap source of finance and should be run at the end of its term.

Example

A Treasury 8% may be redeemed in 5 years but must be redeemed no later than 7 years from now. Calculate its price if rates are 6%.

Solution

Since coupon (8%) > prevailing rates (6%) the bond will be redeemed early, hence its price will be

Time	**Cash Flow (£)**	**Discount Factor (6%)**	**Present Value (£)**
1–5	8	$\frac{1}{1.06}\left(1-\frac{1}{1.06^{5}}\right)$	33.70
5	100	$\frac{1}{1.06^{5}}$	74.73
			108.43

2.1.4 Irredeemables

When we have an irredeemable bond, we are evaluating a perpetuity stream of cash flows.

Example

Evaluate a 9% irredeemable, assuming interest rates are 10%.

Solution

Time ($^1/_2$ years)	Cash Flow (£)	DF (4%)	Present Value (£)
1–∞	9.00	$\frac{1}{0.10}$	90.00
			90.00

2.1.5 Strips and zero coupon bonds

Exam tip

Winter 1999 Question 2

The price of a strip is calculated using the above ideas (adjusted to reflect the semi-annual convention in the gilts market) as for a zero-coupon bond.

Formula to learn

$$\text{Price} = \frac{£100}{(1+r)^n}$$

where

r = semi-annual GRY
n = number of $^1/_2$ years (and fractions thereof) to redemption

Example

A strip matures in four years two months time. Price it on the basis that the quoted yield is 6%.

Solution

The quoted yield = 6%, therefore the semi-annual rate

r = 3%

The time to maturity is 4 years 2 months, so

$n = 8^{2/6}$ half years

so

$$\text{Price} = \frac{£100}{1.03^{8^{2/6}}} = £78.17$$

2.2 Variable coupon bonds

2.2.1 Floating rate note (FRN)

Exam tip

Examined in Summer 2007 Question 4, Summer 2001 Question 1, Summer 2000 Question 1

With a floating rate bond, the coupon rate is reset at each payment date (or possibly even more regularly) to prevailing interest rates. The implication of this is that at a reset date the bond will be valued at par based on the relationship that we established above. In addition, the cash value of the next coupon has now been set. Though all subsequent coupons will still be reset at the next reset date if interest rates move, the next coupon will not be.

This resetting of the coupon at each payment date ensures that the clean price of an FRN is always close to par.

FRNs therefore safeguard the par value of the investment rather than showing great swings in value as interest rates fluctuate (as is demonstrated by normal bonds).

To evaluate a FRN, we have a choice of methods, specifically

- First principles.
- A more practical alternative.

FRNs tend to be reset by reference to LIBOR or LIBID, money market rates. As a result, FRN pricing follows money market conventions, applying simple rates over periods less than one year.

First principles

From first principles, we can evaluate the FRN using the relationship

$$\text{Price} = \frac{C_1}{(1+r)} + \frac{C_2}{(1+r)^2} + \frac{C_3}{(1+r)^3} + \cdots + \frac{C_n + R}{(1+r)^n}$$

The difficulty with this approach is that we do not know what the future coupons will be.

Example

The current interest rate is at 10% and expected to remain at that level for the foreseeable future. A floating rate note (FRN) has just paid its most recent annual coupon, and future coupons have been reset to 10%. Calculate the current market value of the FRN.

Solution

$$\text{Price} = \frac{10}{1.10} + \frac{10}{1.10^2} + \frac{10}{1.10^3} + \cdots + \frac{110}{1.10^n} = £100.00$$

Practical alternative

A more flexible alternative is to imagine that the bond may be sold at the next reset date at its par value. Though it is not necessary that the holder intends to sell at this date, it is always an option open to him and hence can validly be used to determine the current price. Based on this idea, we could establish the market value of this FRN as follows.

Formula to learn

$$\text{FRN Price} = \frac{\text{Next coupon} + \text{Par value}}{(1+R)}$$

Where R = rate for the period to the next coupon, ie $R = r \times {}^{Days}\!/_{365}$ (assuming UK convention)

so more generally

Formula to learn

$$\text{FRN Price} = \frac{\text{Next coupon} + \text{Par value}}{1 + r \times {}^{Days}\!/_{365}}$$

where Days = time to the next coupon

Example

Calculate the current market value of the above FRN, if

- Interest rates stay at 10%.
- Interest rates suddenly leap to 11% and are expected to remain at that level.

Solution

Interest at 10%

$$\text{Price} = \frac{10+100}{1.10} = £100.00$$

Interest at 11%

In this situation, the next coupon in one year's time will remain at £10, its value determined at the last reset date. All further coupons will, however, be reset to £11 at the next date (assuming no further interest rate changes), giving rise to a par value at that time. The current market value is therefore

$$\text{Price} = \frac{10+100}{1.11} = £99.10$$

As we indicated above, however, the advantage of this method comes when we are evaluating the FRN between coupon payment dates.

Example

Calculate the market value of the above FRN if we are 91 days into the annual coupon (non-leap year) payment period and interest rates have moved to 11%.

Solution

Days to next coupon = 274

$$\text{Price} = \frac{10+100}{1+0.11 \times {}^{274}\!/_{365}} = £101.75$$

You will note that the bond is valued above par even though the interest rate exceeds the value of the next coupon. That is as a result of the three months' accrued interest in this FRN at that date (see clean and dirty pricing later).

Conclusion

FRN prices vary with

- Accrued interest.
- Interest rates.

Although the resetting of the coupon at each repayment date ensures that the clean price is always close to par.

As we noted above, FRNs safeguard the par value of the investment rather than showing great swings in value as interest rates fluctuate (as is demonstrated by normal bonds). What they do not do, however, is safeguard against any loss of real value due to the effects of inflation.

2.2.2 Index-linked issues

Exam tip

Winter 2006 Question 2, Winter 2005 Question 10

Effect of index-linking

With an **index-linked gilt** (ILG), all the cash returns, both coupon and redemption proceeds, vary with inflation since the issue reference date.

Example

A 3% semi-annual ILG was issued some years ago and has just paid a coupon. The RPI at the issue reference date stood at 100. The RPI at the reference date for the coupon just paid stood at 140. What was the cash value of the coupon just paid and the redemption value if redemption was due on that date?

Solution

In the absence of inflation, the coupon and redemption proceeds would be

- Coupon £1.50 (£100 × 3% × $^1/_2$)
- Redemption proceeds £100.00

Since we have suffered 40% inflation since issue, based on the increase in the RPI, the figures at that date would now be

- Coupon $£1.50 \times \frac{140}{100} = £2.10$
- Redemption proceeds $£100.00 \times \frac{140}{100} = £140.00$

Reference dates and the effectiveness of the inflation proofing

You may have noted the term **reference date** and may well be wondering what this is. For all ILGs there needs to be a reference date for measuring the RPIs used in this calculation. That reference date was historically eight months prior to the related cash flow but for issues since September 2005 this has been reduced to three months, i.e. dependent on the issue date

- The issue reference date is three/eight months prior to issue.
- The reference date for any coupon is three/eight months prior to its payment date.
- The reference date for the redemption proceeds is three/eight months prior to redemption.

This can be represented as follows.

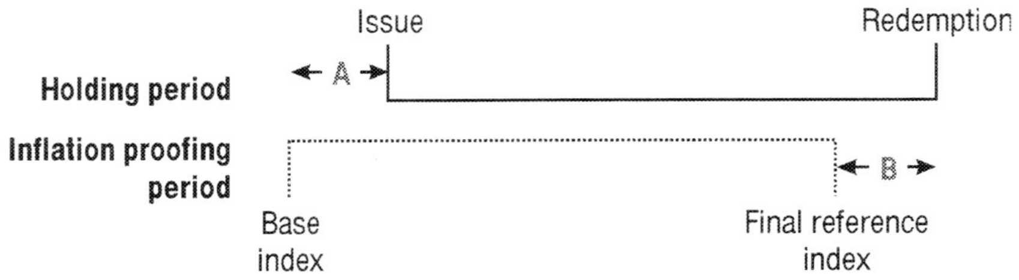

As the base index figure is the one three/eight months prior to the issue date, and the final reference rate is the index value three/eight months prior to redemption, the holder is compensated for inflation for the three/eight months prior to the issue (A), but exposed to inflation for the last three/eight months (B).

It is therefore true to say that we are not guaranteed a real rate of return in any period due to the time lag involved.

Determining ILG cash flows

The 3% ILG example above illustrates the idea underlying the impact of inflation on ILG cash flows, however we now need to examine this in a little more detail before we can go on to consider the pricing of such bonds.

8 month ILGs

With the 8 month ILGs, the reference RPI is the figure for the month eight months prior to the relevant cash flow. Hence for a cash flow on, say, 20 November, the reference RPI would be the one for the previous March.

Example

A 3% semi-annual ILG was issued on 20/11/1988, calculate the coupon and redemption proceeds due on 20 November this year based on the following RPI statistics.

	Jan	Feb	Mar	Apr	May	Jun	Jul	Aug	Sep	Oct	Nov	Dec
1988	103.3	103.7	104.1	105.8	106.2	106.6	106.7	107.9	108.4	109.5	110.0	110.3
Current year	193.4	194.2	195.0	196.5	197.7	198.5	198.5	199.2	200.1	200.4	201.1	202.7

Solution

As before, the real (pre-inflation) coupon and redemption proceeds would be

- Coupon — £1.50 (£100 × 3% × $^1/_2$)
- Redemption proceeds — £100.00

Based on the above RPI statistics, the issue reference date RPI is 104.1 (March 1988 – 8 months prior to the issue), and the RPI for the cash flow reference date is 195.0 (March of current year – 8 months prior to the relevant cash flow), giving

- Coupon — $£1.50 \times \frac{195.0}{104.1} = £2.8097$
- Redemption proceeds — $£100.00 \times \frac{195.0}{104.1} = £187.3198$

Note. With 8 month ILGs, cash flows are rounded down to 4 decimal places except for

- $2^1/_2$% 2011 – rounded down to 2 DPs
- 2% 2035 – rounded to the nearest 6 DPs

3 month ILGs

With the 3 month ILGs, the reference RPI is calculated by interpolation for the exact date in question. In undertaking this assessment we take the reference RPI for the first of any month as the RPI for the month three months earlier. For example, the reference RPI for 1 November is the RPI for the previous August, the reference RPI for 1st December is the RPI for the previous September etc.

The interpolation formula to then apply to calculate the RPI for the specific date (rounded to the nearest 5 decimal places) is

$$\text{Ref RPI}_{\text{Day}} = \text{Ref RPI}_{\text{C}} + \frac{\text{Day} - 1}{\text{Days in coupon month}}(\text{Ref RPI}_{\text{C+1}} - \text{Ref RPI}_{\text{C}})$$

Where

Day = cash flow day in the coupon month
$\text{Ref RPI}_{\text{Day}}$ = reference RPI for the specific date in question
$\text{Ref RPI}_{\text{C}}$ = RPI for the 1st of the coupon payment month
$\text{Ref RPI}_{\text{C+1}}$ = RPI for the 1st of the following month

The Days – 1 on the numerator is to account for the fact that the reference RPIs are taken as being those related to the 1st of the month. Hence for a cash flow on the 1st of the month, zero interpolation would be required, for a cash flow on the 2nd, one days interpolation would be required, etc.

Example

A 3% semi-annual ILG was issued on 20/11/2005, calculate the coupon and redemption proceeds due on 20 November this year based on the following RPI statistics.

	Jan	Feb	Mar	Apr	May	Jun	Jul	Aug	Sep	Oct	Nov	Dec
2005	188.9	189.6	190.5	191.6	192.0	192.2	192.2	192.6	193.1	193.3	193.6	194.1
Current year	193.4	194.2	195.0	196.5	197.7	198.5	198.5	199.2	200.1	200.4	201.1	202.7

Solution

Once again, the real (pre-inflation) coupon and redemption proceeds would be

- Coupon £1.50 (£100 × 3% × $^1/_2$)
- Redemption proceeds £100.00

Based on the above RPI statistics,

- Reference RPI for 1 November 2005 = 192.6
- Reference RPI for 1 December 2005 = 193.1
- Reference RPI for 1 November of the current year = 199.2
- Reference RPI for 1 December of the current year = 200.1

From which we can calculate the issue reference date RPI (20 November 2005) as

$$\text{Ref RPI}_{20/11/05} = 192.6 + \frac{20-1}{30}(193.1 - 192.6) = 192.91667$$

And the reference RPI for the coupon in question (20 November of the current year) as

$$\text{Ref RPI}_{20/11/\text{Current}} = 199.2 + \frac{20-1}{30}(200.1 - 199.2) = 199.77000$$

Applying these figures assuming the ILG is due for redemption gives

- Coupon $£1.50 \times \frac{199.77000}{192.91667} = £1.553287$
- Redemption proceeds $£100.00 \times \frac{199.77000}{192.91667} = £103.552482$

Note. With 3 month ILGs cash flows are rounded to the nearest 6 decimal places

Evaluation

Having established the specific cash flows we can now consider the issue of pricing which brings with it a number of further problems. The principal problem is that the returns in the future (in money terms) are not constant, but will vary in line with the rate of inflation, and are thus unknown.

Any valuation will, therefore, be heavily dependent upon assumptions made regarding future inflation. We will illustrate the alternative methods of evaluation by way of an example.

Example

A 3% index-linked gilt issued several years ago is redeemable in 2½ years.

The RPI for the issue reference date was 100, and the RPI for the last coupon (just paid) was 140.

Inflation has recently been running at 2% every six months and is expected to continue at this level. Bondholders require a return of 5% every six months. Calculate the price of the gilt.

Solution

Establish the cash flows

Assuming zero future inflation from the last coupon reference date, all future coupons and the redemption proceeds would be

- Future semi-annual coupons $£1.50 \times \frac{140}{100} = £2.10$
- Redemption proceeds $£100.00 \times \frac{140}{100} = £140.00$

Most of these flows will, however, be uplifted by future inflation and this needs to be incorporated into the evaluation. This may be achieved in one of three ways.

Alternative 1 – Discount the nominal flows at nominal rates

Time ($^1/_2$ years)	Cash Flow (£)		DF (5%)	Present Value (£)
1	$2.10 \times 1.02 =$	2.142	$\frac{1}{1.05}$	2.040
2	$2.10 \times 1.02^2 =$	2.185	$\frac{1}{1.05^2}$	1.982
3	$2.10 \times 1.02^3 =$	2.229	$\frac{1}{1.05^3}$	1.925
4	$2.10 \times 1.02^4 =$	2.273	$\frac{1}{1.05^4}$	1.870
5	$142.10 \times 1.02^5 =$	156.890	$\frac{1}{1.05^5}$	122.927
				130.744

Alternative 2 – Discount the Real (Pre-Inflation) Flows at Real Rates

The required nominal return every six months is 5%, though 2% of this will be satisfied by appreciation in the cash flow values due to inflation. The real required return beyond this, therefore, will be given by the Fisher relationship.

Formula to learn

$$(1+r) = (1+i)(1+R)$$

where

r = the monetary or nominal rate (5% here)
i = inflation rate (2% here)
R = real rate of return

Therefore

$1.05 = 1.02(1 + R)$

Giving

$$1 + R = \frac{1.05}{1.02} = 1.02941$$

Hence

$R = 0.02941$ or 2.941%

Applying this to the real (pre-inflation) future cash flow values gives

Time	Cash Flow (£)	Discount Factor (2.941%)	Present Value (£)
1–5	2.10	$\frac{1}{1.02941}\left(1-\frac{1}{1.02941^5}\right)$	9.633
5	140.00	$\frac{1}{1.02941^5}$	121.111
			130.744

Alternative 3 – Discount the original real (pre-inflation) flows at real rates then adjust for past inflation

Using the above real required return of 2.941% and applying this to the original cash flows gives

Time	Cash Flow (£)	Discount Factor (2.941%)	Present Value (£)
1–5	1.50	$\frac{1}{1.02941}\left(1-\frac{1}{1.02941^5}\right)$	6.881
5	100.00	$\frac{1}{1.02941^5}$	86.508
Real price (ignoring past inflation)			93.389
Adjusting for cumulative past inflation			× 1.400
Nominal price paid			130.744

This latter method, though strange, is substantially the most convenient as it causes no difficulties in establishing the cash flows.

Price Quoted

Hence, for an index-linked gilt, we could state

Formula to learn

Real price = PV of the original cash flows at real rates	– the price quoted for 3 month ILGs
Nominal price = Real price × (1 + i)	– the price quoted for 8 month ILGs

where

i = cumulative inflation to be incorporated into the price by reference to the relevant RPI.

Price Paid

Despite the difference in how they are quoted, it is the nominal price that is paid on all ILGs (8 month and 3 month), hence the only final issue is how we establish (1 + i).

8 month ILGs

For 8 month ILGs

(1 + i) = cumulative inflation in the current coupon just paid.

Given that coupons are paid every six months and the 8 month time lag in the measurement of the RPIs, we will already know the RPI for the next coupon which will be the RPI from two months ago (eight months before the next coupon). We may, therefore, establish (1 + i) as follows

$$(1 + i) = \frac{(1 + i_1)}{(1 + i_2)}$$

where

i_1 = cumulative inflation in the **next** coupon calculated by reference to the relevant RPIs

i_2 = estimated future semi-annual inflation rate (**Note.** semi-annual inflation compounds to give an annual figure, it is not simply doubled)

3 month ILGs

For 3 month ILGs, we simply have

(1 + i) = cumulative inflation in the current coupon just paid.

2.3 Calculation between coupon dates

The calculations so far have been based on the evaluation of the bond immediately after a coupon payment date. If the bond was to be valued between coupon payment dates, one of two alternative approaches could be adopted

- First Principles
- A more practical alternative

The first principles approach would be to discount each flow based on the exact time to its receipt, e.g. if a bond is one quarter of the way into its coupon payment period and the next coupon will not be received for another three quarters of that period, then

Formula to learn

$$\text{Price} = \frac{C_1}{(1+r)^{3/4}} + \frac{C_2}{(1+r)^{1 3/4}} + \frac{C_3}{(1+r)^{2 3/4}} + \cdots + \frac{C_n + R}{(1+r)^{(n-1/4)}}$$

Example

We hold 10% Loan stock (annual coupon) redeemable at par in three and three quarter years. The Calculate the current price if the GRY is 11%.

Solution

Time	Cash Flow (£)	DF (11%)	Present Value (£)
$^3/_4$	10.00	$\frac{1}{1.11^{3/4}}$	9.25
$1^3/_4$	10.00	$\frac{1}{1.11^{1\,3/4}}$	8.33
$2^3/_4$	10.00	$\frac{1}{1.11^{2\,3/4}}$	7.50
$3^3/_4$	110.00	$\frac{1}{1.11^{3\,3/4}}$	74.38
			99.46

Conclusion

The calculations can be undertaken in this way, though working in quarter periods is far from convenient and removes the possibility of utilising annuity or perpetuity discount factors which would be preferable for longer dated or irredeemable bonds. Some alternative would, therefore, be preferable.

Practical alternative

A practical alternative that can be applied for both bonds and for money market instruments is to say that the price now, three quarters away from the next coupon, will be the cum-interest price the bond would have were we at the next coupon payment date, discounted back to reflect the fact that all actual cash flows will arise three quarters of a period later than this assessment assumes. That is

Formula to learn

$$\text{Price} = \left(C_1 + \frac{C_2}{(1+r)} + \frac{C_3}{(1+r)^2} + \cdots + \frac{C_n + R}{(1+r)^{n-1}} \right) \times \frac{1}{(1+r)^{3/4}}$$

The last term in this relationship accounts for the fact that we are ¾ of a period away from the next coupon being paid, the earlier part is the cum interest bond pricing relationship which enables us to use the annuity or perpetuity formula where relevant.

Notes

- Here we have used $^3/_4$ as the period for discounting, what we should use is the appropriate fraction of the coupon period using the day-count convention relevant to that bond issue (see day count conventions later).
- An alternative for bonds would be to value at the start of this coupon period then compound up by $^1/_4$ of a period, however this method does not work for money market instruments and so is not recommended, We consider it better to have a single approach that works for all instruments.

Example

Using the above example, i.e. we hold 10% Loan stock (annual coupon) redeemable at par in three and three quarter years on a GRY of 11%.

Solution

Time	Cash Flow (£)	Discount Factor (11%)	Present Value (£)
0	10.00	1	10.00
1–3	10.00	$\frac{1}{0.11}\left(1-\frac{1}{1.11^3}\right)$	24.44
3	100.00	$\frac{1}{1.11^3}$	73.12
Value Cum-Interest at Next Coupon Date			107.56
Discounted back for three quarters of a period			$\times \frac{1}{1.11^{3/4}}$
Value one quarter of the way through period			99.46

Index linked gilts

Very much the same approach needs to be applied for ILGs but the approach needs to differ between the two classes of 8 month and 3 month ILGs.

8 month ILGs

For 8 month ILGs the calculations will need to be done in exactly the same way as above, i.e. calculate the nominal cum-interest value at the next coupon payment date then discount it back over the appropriate period using nominal rates.

3 month ILGs

For 3 month ILGs the calculations will need to be done based on real rates (giving the quoted real price for the specific date) and then adjusted for inflation to give the nominal price paid.

That is, calculate the real cum-interest value at the next coupon payment date then discount it back over the appropriate period using real rates to give a real price at the relevant date. To get the nominal price paid we then need to adjust for inflation as we did earlier, ie

Nominal price = Real price × (1 + i)

Where

(1 + i) = cumulative inflation to the transaction cash flow date using the PRI interpolation formula introduced earlier.

3 Clean and Dirty Prices

Exam tip

> Regularly examined, see Winter 2009 Question 1, Winter 2007 Question 4, Summer 2006 Question 7, Winter 2005 Question 1, Summer 2005 Question 1, Winter 2003 Question 1

3.1 Introduction

A further pricing aspect is clean and dirty pricing, the distinction being made for tax purposes as income and capital gains may be taxed differently on bonds.

The value of a bond has two elements, the underlying capital value of the bond itself (the **clean price** which is quoted) and the coupon that it is accruing over time (**accrued interest**). Periodically, this coupon is distributed as income to the holders or, more specifically, the individual who was the registered holder on the ex-div date (which for gilts is normally, **seven business days** prior to payment date).

The **dirty price** calculated above using DCF is the price that is paid for a bond, which combines these two elements. Consequently, ignoring all other factors that might affect the price, a dirty price will rise gradually as the coupon builds up and then falls back as the stock is either marked ex-div or pays the dividend.

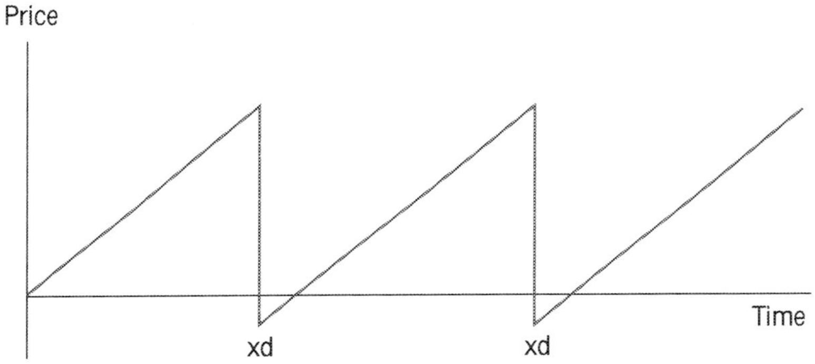

The advantage that this offered investors in the past was that rather than claiming the dividend, they could sell the bond at the high price just prior to the payment of the dividend, and this gain would be free of tax. This process was known as **bond washing**. In February 1986, the UK moved to a system of clean pricing that separates the two elements.

Under clean pricing, whenever an investor purchases a bond, they pay the quoted price (the **clean price**), which represents the capital value of the underlying bond with an allowance made for the interest element, allowing the two elements (income and gain) to be taxed separately.

We will illustrate the application of clean and dirty pricing below in the context of UK Gilts, applying gilt market conventions in order to establish the ideas. The only variation we may experience with other bonds is the specific day count convention that is applied in that market (which is covered next).

3.1.1 Cum dividend bargains

A purchase made before the ex-div date is referred to as a cum div bargain. In this situation, the buyer of the bond will be the holder on the next ex-div date and will, therefore, receive the full coupon for the period. The seller, however, has held the bond for part of this period and is therefore entitled to a part of that coupon. To account for this, the purchaser of the bond must compensate the seller for the dividend which he has earned.

Example

As a result, the purchaser will pay the clean price plus the interest from the last payment date up to the purchase. On the next payment date, the holder will receive the whole of the interest for the six months. However, on a net basis, they will only have received the interest for the period of ownership.

The formula used by the Debt Management Office in the gilts market is

$$\text{Dirty price} = \text{Clean price} + \text{Periods coupon} \times \frac{\text{Days}}{\text{Days in period}}$$

Where

Days = number of days from the last coupon payment date up to and including the calendar day before the settlement day (next business day following the trade for Gilts)

Days in period = number of days from the last coupon payment date up to and including the calendar day before the next coupon

Thus, the periods coupon is spread over the number of days in the period, giving a coupon per day, then allocated to the relevant holder on a daily basis.

Example

Coupons are paid on 1 April and 1 October. On 10 July, an investor buys £10,000 nominal of Treasury 8% @ 101.50 for settlement on 11 July. How much is paid?

Solution

		(£)
Clean Price	£10,000 @ 101.50	10,150.00
Accrued Interest	$(£10,000 \times 4\% = £400) \times \frac{101}{183}$	220.77
Dirty Price		10,370.77

The number of days having been calculated as follows.

Month		Days	Days in Period
April	**From last coupon (inclusive)**	30	30
May		31	31
June		30	30
July	**To day before settlement**	10	31
August			31
September			30
		101	183

3.1.2 Ex-dividend bargains

An ex-div bargain is one occurring after the ex-div date, but before the coupon is paid. Gilt-edged stocks, for example, are usually marked ex-div seven business days prior to the payment day in order to allow the DMO to ensure that the dividend is paid to the appropriate party. Any person buying the stock after it has been marked Ex will not, therefore, be entitled to the interest. Consequently, the pricing must reflect this.

Example

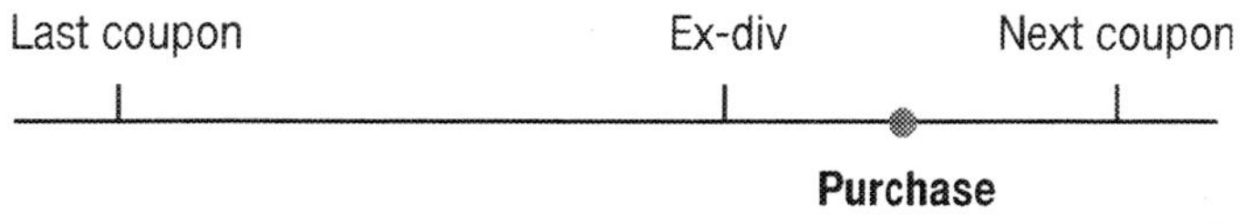

In this situation, the buyer of the bond will be entitled to the coupon for the last few days of the period, but will receive nothing, as this will all go to the seller who held at the ex-div date. He will, therefore, require this to be adjusted in the price.

Accordingly, he pays the clean price as determined by the market less the number of days worth of interest that he is not receiving.

The formula used in this situation by the Debt Management Office in the gilts market is

Formula to learn

$$\text{Dirty price} = \text{Clean price} - \text{Periods coupon} \times \frac{\text{Days}}{\text{Days in period}}$$

Where

Days = number of days from the settlement day (next business day) to the calendar day before the next coupon payment date (inclusive)

Days in period = number of days from the last coupon payment date up to and including the calendar day before the next coupon

4 Day Count Conventions

Exam tip

Questions on this area have historically been asked in isolation. This area is now more commonly covered with a clean/dirty pricing question such as Winter 2005 Question 1, Summer 2005 Question 1 and in company bonds from differing markets, eg Summer 2009 Question 7.

4.1 Conventions

In the preceding two sections we needed to be able to deal with the practicality of being part way through a coupon period, and to achieve that we needed to establish what fraction of that period we are either from the start of the period or from the end of the period.

- For our between coupon dates DCF evaluation we needed to know what fraction of the period we were away from the next coupon.
- For our clean and dirty pricing calculations we needed to know
  - Cum div bargain – what fraction we are from the start of the period
  - Ex-div bargain – what fraction we are from the end of the period

And so the question is, how do we establish the appropriate fraction of the period.

In all of the assessments that we do we will use

Formula to learn

$$\text{Fraction of period} = \frac{\text{Days}}{\text{Days in Period}}$$

Where either

- Days = number of days from the start of the period
- Days = number of days to the end of the period

as appropriate.

But the question is, how do we count the number of days for the top and bottom lines of this fraction?

Unfortunately there is no single universally applied answer to this question and there are a number of day count conventions that we need to be aware of. What is universally applied, however, is that the reference dates that we count from and to are cash flow dates, i.e. coupon payment dates, maturity dates or transaction settlement dates. We will always be measuring between cash flow dates.

4.2 Actual/Actual

Actual/Actual is the basis used for UK Gilts that we illustrated above under clean and dirty pricing. It is the basis for all Euro and US government bonds and for Eurobonds issued after January 1999.

Under this basis, as we saw above,

- Days = either
  - number of days from the last coupon payment date up to and including the calendar day before the settlement day (Cum Div).
  - number of days from the settlement date up to and including the calendar day before the next coupon. (Ex Div)
- Days in Period = number of days from the last coupon payment date up to and including the calendar day before the next coupon.

These calculations must be done based on exact calendar dates, taking account of leap years where necessary.

4.3 Actual/365 and actual/360

Actual/365 is the convention applied to Japanese Government bonds and to the floating rate notes (FRNs) and money market instruments of the UK, Australia, Canada, New Zealand and some other commonwealth countries. Actual/360 is the convention applied to most other countries money markets and FRNs.

On these bases the top line, Days, is counted as above based on specific calendar dates taking account of leap years. However the Days in Period is set at 365 or 360 irrespective of the actual length of the year.

It should be noted that in such markets, the quoted coupons and yields are those applicable to a 365 or a 360 day period and so, for example, the actual coupon paid for a year may not simply be that expected from the coupon rate.

For example, if we hold $100,000 nominal US money market instrument quoting a 6% coupon, the actual coupon paid in a year would not simply be $6,000, rather it would be

- Normal year = $\$100,000 \times 6\% \times {}^{365}/_{360} = \$6,083.33$
- Leap year = $\$100,000 \times 6\% \times {}^{366}/_{360} = \$6,100.00$

4.4 30/360 and 30E/360

30/360 is the basis used for domestic US bonds (Yankee bonds, federal agencies, corporate and municipal bonds).

30E/360 is the basis applied to Eurobonds issued before January 1999, sometimes referred to as legacy bonds.

Under each of these bases each full month, including February, is assumed to have 30 days, giving 360 for the full year, the Days in Period.

The Days figure for the top line is, as for all such calculations, assessed by reference to cash flow dates. If the cash flow date that starts the period in question is D1/M1/Y1, and the cash flow date that ends the period in question is D2/M2/Y2, then

Formula to learn

$$\text{Days} = 360 \times (Y2 - Y1) + 30 \times (M2 - M1) + (D2 - D1)$$

In undertaking these calculations, however, we must bear in mind the following

30/360 — If D1 = 31, change to 30
If D2 = 31, change to 30 but *only* if D1 = 30 or 31

30E/360 — If D1 = 31, change to 30
If D2 = 31, change to 30

Once again, the last day in February is always regarded as day 30.

4.5 Others

There are other bases applied in certain markets but there are the main ones that we need to be aware of.

Example

A bond has a coupon payment date of 31 December, the number of Days for pricing calculations will be as follows.

Settlement Date	Days Convention		
	Actual	30	30E
27 February	58(58)	57(57)	57(57)
28 February	59(59)	60(58)	60(58)
29 February	NA(60)	NA(60)	NA(60)
1 March	60(61)	61(61)	61(61)
24 March	83(84)	84(84)	84(84)

Figures in brackets refer to leap years.

Example

A bond has a coupon payment date of 28 April, the number of Days for pricing calculations will be as follows.

Settlement Date	Days Convention		
	Actual	30	30E
31 July	94	93	92
1 August	95	93	93
31 August	125	123	122
1 September	126	123	123

4.6 Applications

The application of the above day count conventions in the major bond and money markets is as follows.

Country	Bonds	Money Markets
UK	Actual/Actual	Actual/365
US – Government – Yankee, federal, corporate, municipal	Actual/Actual 30/360	Actual/360 –
Eurozone – Government – Eurobonds issued after January 1999 – Eurobonds issued pre January 1999 – Sterling Eurodeposits	Actual/Actual Actual/Actual 30E/360 –	Actual/360 – – Actual/365
Japan	Actual/365	Actual/360
Australia	Actual/Actual	Actual/365
Canada	Actual/Actual	Actual/365
New Zealand	Actual/Actual	Actual/365

5 Pricing Money Market Instrument

5.1 Introduction

Money market instruments have many similar characteristics to bonds. Many money market instruments are pure discount instruments like zero coupon bonds, others pay regular coupons and are redeemed at pre-set dates like straight bonds. In addition, all quoted rates on money market instruments are annualised, as for bonds. As a result, the approach to pricing money market instruments is essentially the same as that of pricing such bonds.

The important difference, however, is that money markets use the simple interest convention for periods of less than 12 months applying the day count conventions discussed above to establish the rate for the relevant period. Therefore if the quoted annual rate is r, then the rate for a specific period is

Discount rate = $r \times {}^{Days}/_{365}$ for Sterling instruments (plus others noted above)

or

Discount rate = $r \times {}^{Days}/_{360}$ for Dollar, Euro and Yen instruments

The corresponding discount factor (DF) for such a period will, therefore, be

$$DF = \frac{1}{1+(r \times {}^{Days}\!/_{365})}$$ for Sterling instruments (plus others noted above)

or

$$DF = \frac{1}{1+(r \times {}^{Days}\!/_{360})}$$ for Dollar, Euro and Yen instruments

Example

The quoted rate on a money market instrument is 9%, what is the discount rate and discount factor for a 120 day period?

Solution

Sterling

Discount rate = 9% × $^{120}/_{365}$ = 2.9589%

$$DF = \frac{1}{1+(r \times {}^{Days}\!/_{365})} = \frac{1}{1.029589}$$

Dollar/Euro/Yen

Discount rate = 9% × $^{120}/_{360}$ = 3.0000%

$$DF = \frac{1}{1+(r \times {}^{Days}\!/_{360})} = \frac{1}{1.03}$$

5.2 Discount Instruments

Pure discount instruments such as Treasury Bills are issued for periods that are typically less than three months. They are issued at a discount and mature at par.

We can, therefore, establish the price of such an instrument by discounting the par value back using the discount factors established above giving

$$Price = \frac{\text{Maturity Value}}{1+(r \times {}^{Days}\!/_{365})}$$ for Sterling instruments (plus others noted above)

or

$$Price = \frac{\text{Maturity Value}}{1+(r \times {}^{Days}\!/_{360})}$$ for Dollar, Euro and Yen instruments

Where

Days = number of days to maturity.

Example

Price a Treasury Bill with a par value of

- £1,000
- $1,000

maturing in 38 days when the quoted rate is 5%

Solution

£1,000 Treasury

Here we will need to apply the Sterling basis of

$$\text{Price} = \frac{\text{MaturityValue}}{1+(r\times {}^{\text{Days}}\!/_{365})}$$

giving

$$\text{Price} = \frac{£1{,}000}{1+(0.05\times {}^{38}\!/_{365})} = \frac{£1{,}000}{1.0052055} = £994.82$$

$1,000 Treasury

Here we will need to apply the Dollar basis of

$$\text{Price} = \frac{\text{Maturity Value}}{1+(r\times {}^{\text{Days}}\!/_{360})}$$

giving

$$\text{Price} = \frac{\$1{,}000}{1+(0.05\times {}^{38}\!/_{360})} = \frac{\$1{,}000}{1.0052778} = \$994.75$$

5.3 Coupon Paying Instruments

We will approach the pricing of a coupon paying money market instrument such as a certificate of deposit (CD) in a similar manner to that of a straight bond. That is, we will look to schedule out the cash flow values, their timings, and the relevant rates in order to undertake a standard DCF tabular calculation.

Valuation of CDs

The simplest case is that of a CD where the maturity is in less than one year, therefore there is only one cash flow at the point of maturity being the principal + interest.

Formula to learn

$$\text{Interest} = \text{Principal} \times \text{Stated yield} \times \frac{\text{Life(Tenor)}}{365\,*}$$

* or 360 as relevant giving

Formula to learn

$$\text{Maturity value} = \text{Principal} + \left[\text{Principal} \times \text{Stated yield} \times \frac{\text{Life(Tenor)}}{365\,*}\right]$$

Such instruments can then be priced by discounting this maturity value back to a present value as for discount instruments above, i.e.,

$$\text{Price} = \frac{\text{MaturityValue}}{1+(r\times {}^{\text{Days}}\!/_{365})}$$ for Sterling instruments (plus others noted above)

or

$$\text{Price} = \frac{\text{MaturityValue}}{1+(r\times {}^{\text{Days}}\!/_{360})}$$ for Dollar, Euro and Yen instruments

Where

Days = number of days to maturity.

Example

A £1,000,000 three-month (91-day) CD is issued with a stated yield or coupon of 8%.

$$\text{Maturity value} = £1{,}000{,}000 + \left[£1{,}000{,}000 \times 0.08 \times \frac{91}{365}\right]$$

$$= £1{,}019{,}945.21$$

After 35 days, the CD is traded at a yield of 7¼%. The seller will receive the maturity proceeds discounted by the required yield over the remaining 56 days (91 – 35). Hence

$$\text{Price} = \frac{£1{,}019{,}945.21}{1+(0.0725 \times {}^{56}\!/_{365})} = \frac{£1{,}019{,}945.21}{1.011123288} = £1{,}008{,}724.87$$

The proof of this is that £1,008,724.87 invested at 7¼% for 56 days will generate a settlement value of £1,019,945.21, the maturity value of the CD.

With CDs with a maturity of over one year, the position is complicated by the payment of coupons during the life of the certificate. However, in essence, the process is the same with the flows arising from the CD being discounted back to their present value at the required yield.

A similar approach to this can be used for evaluating repos as we will see later.

Example

A CD for £2,000,000 is issued for four years at a rate of 7% and after one year and 65 days it is sold at a yield of 6½%. The third year of the life of the CD is a leap year. Calculate its sale price.

We firstly need to establish the cash flow values, timings and rates involved which, when the CD was issued, will have been

Time	Cash Flow	Discount Rate for Year
1	£2m × 7% × 365/365 = £140,000.00	6.5% × 365/365 = 6.5%
2	£2m × 7% × 365/365 = £140,000.00	6.5% × 365/365 = 6.5%
3	£2m × 7% × 366/365 = £140,383.56	6.5% × 366/365 = 6.517808%
4	£2m × 7% × 365/365 = £140,000.00	6.5% × 365/365 = 6.5%

After 1 year 65 days, the remaining cash flows arising from the CD

£140,000	£140,383.56	£2,140,000
300 days	1 leap year	1 year

The value of the CD at the point of sale is the present value of these future cash flows discounted by the required yield of 6½%.

Solution

Alternative 1

Then using the idea we had above for pricing bonds between coupon dates we have

Time	Cash Flow (£)	Discount Factor (6.5%)	Present Value (£)
0	140,000.00	1	140,000.00
1	140,383.56	$\frac{1}{1.06517808}$	131,793.51
2	2,140,000.00	$\frac{1}{1.06517808 \times 1.065}$	1,886,435.43
Value Cum-Interest at Next Coupon Date			2,158,228.94
Discounted back for 300 days		×	$\frac{1}{1+0.065 \times {}^{300}\!/_{365}}$
Value 65 days into the second year			£2,048,773.90

Alternative 2

An alternative approach is as follows.

The first step is to take the value of the final flow and discount it back to the previous payment date.

$$£2,140,000 \times \frac{1}{(1+0.065)} = £2,009,389.67$$

This value represents the value of the flows at the end of the third year. The dividend at the end of Year 3 must be added to this and the total discounted back to the end of the second year.

$$(£2,009,389.67 + £140,383.56) \times \frac{1}{\left[1+(0.065 \times 366/365)\right]} = £2,018,228.94$$

The final stage discounts the cumulative flows back to today's date. The overall effect of this process is to bring all of the flows that are occurring in the future back to today's value as determined by the required yield.

$$(£2,018,228.94 + £140,000) \times \frac{1}{\left[1+(0.065 \times 300/365)\right]} = £2,048,773.90$$

In summary

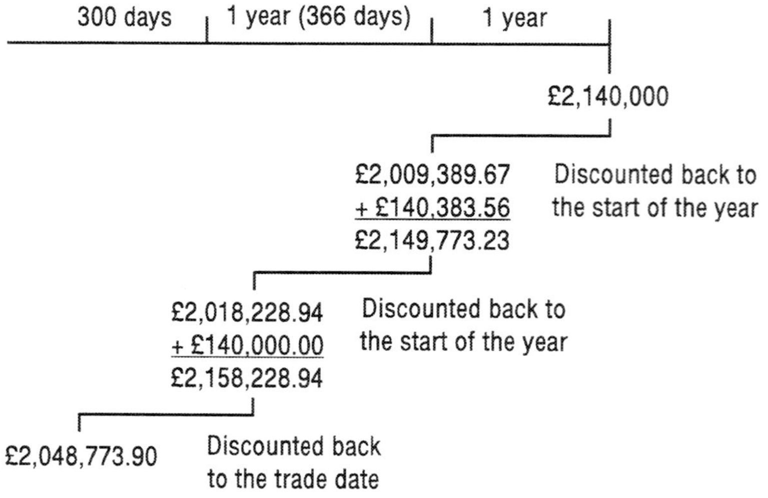

As you can see this alternative approach gives the same result and you can decide which of these two alternatives you prefer.

Chapter Roundup

- **Pricing of bonds**

  Market convention for gilts

  – Quoted yield = 2× semi-annual yield
  – Quoted price = clean price

  You must be able to price a bond using DCF

  You must be able to undertake clean/dirty pricing calculations

  – Fixed coupon

    Price = PV of nominal flows

  – FRN

    $$\text{FRN Price} = \frac{\text{Next coupon} + \text{Par value}}{1 + r \times {}^{\text{Days}}\!/_{365}}$$

  – ILGs

    Real price = PV of the original cash flows at real rates – the price quoted for 3 month ILGs
    Nominal price = Real price × (1 + i) – the price quoted for 8 month ILGs

    3 month:

    (1 + i) = cumulative inflation in the current coupon just paid

    8 months:

    $$(1 + i) = \frac{(1 + i_1)}{(1 + i_2)}$$

    Where

    i_1 = cumulative inflation in the **next** coupon calculated by reference to the relevant RPIs

    i_2 = estimated future semi-annual inflation rate (**Note.** semi-annual inflation compounds to give an annual figure, it is not simply doubled)

  – Cum div

    $$\text{Dirty price} = \text{Clean price} + \text{Periods coupon} \times \frac{\text{Days}}{\text{Days in period}}$$

  – Ex div

    $$\text{Dirty price} = \text{Clean price} - \text{Periods coupon} \times \frac{\text{Days}}{\text{Days in period}}$$

- **Day count conventions**

  You need to be familiar with the main day count conventions and the markets they are applied to.

- **Pricing of money market instruments**
  - Treasury Bills

$$\text{Price} = \frac{\text{Maturity Value}}{1 + (r \times \text{Days}/365)}$$ for Sterling instruments (plus others noted above)

or

$$\text{Price} = \frac{\text{Maturity Value}}{1 + (r \times \text{Days}/360)}$$ for Dollar, Euro and Yen instruments

  - CDs maturing in less than one year

$$\text{Interest} = \text{Principal} \times \text{Stated yield} \times \frac{\text{Life (Tenor)}}{365\,*}$$

$$\text{Maturity value} = \text{Principal} + \left(\text{Principal} \times \text{Stated yield} \times \frac{\text{Life (Tenor)}}{365\,*}\right)$$

$$\text{Proceeds of sale} = \text{Maturity value} \times \frac{1}{1 + \left(\text{Required yield} \times \text{No. of days remaining}/365*\right)}$$

* or 360 as applicable

Test Your Knowledge

Check your knowledge of the Chapter here, without referring back to the text.

1. (a) Price a 5 year 6% gilt with a quoted GRY of 7%.

   (b) Calculate the price if this were a 5% a gilt or a 7% gilt.

2. A floating rate note is in issue. It is due to pay its 5% annual coupon in 73 days, calculate its price if rates are currently 6%.

3. A 2% index linking gilt that was issued in 2002 and has just paid a coupon is due to be redeemed in 4 years. The RPI for the issue reference date was 160. Inflation is running at 1% every six months, index linked gilts have a quoted nominal GRY of 5% p.a.

   (a) Calculate the price of this ILG given the following:

RPI eight months ago	192
RPI three months	196
RPI now	198

   (b) Calculate the price if the gilt had been issued in 2006.

4. Conversion 10¼% stock was quoted at £104.91 on Tuesday 23 February. Interest payment dates are 22 May and 22 November. What would a purchaser on 23 February pay for £100 nominal?

5. You buy £10,000 nominal of 3½% War Loan on Tuesday 2 September cum div and pay £3,915.10 excluding transaction costs. Interest payment dates are 1 June and 1 December. Calculate quoted price per £100 nominal on 2 September.

6. A $500,000 two year CD was issued to Y on 1 January with interest payable annually in arrears. The issue rate was 11%.

   On 20 October of the first year, Y sells the certificate to Z when interest rates have dropped to 10%. Assuming Z accepts this rate, calculate the amount Z would pay for the CD.

7. $100,000 of 181 day commercial paper is issued at a discount to yield 8%. What is the price paid?

TEST YOUR KNOWLEDGE: ANSWERS

1. (a) 5 year 6% gilt will pay ten £3 semi-annual coupons to maturity. The quoted GRY of 7% implies a semi-annual yield of 3.5% ($^{7\%}/_{2}$). Hence the price will be

Time (Half-years)	Cash flow (Semi-annual)	DF (3.5%) (Semi-annual)	PV
1–10	3.00	$\frac{1}{0.035}\left(1-\frac{1}{1.035^{10}}\right)$	24.95
10	100.00	$\frac{1}{1.035^{10}}$	70.89
Price for 6% gilt			95.84

(b) A 5% gilt will pay a £0.50 lower coupon every six months, a 7% gilt will pay a £0.50 higher coupon every six months. The present value of this coupon difference is

Time (Half-years)	Cash flow (Semi-annual)	DF (3.5%) (Semi-annual)	PV
1–10	0.50	$\frac{1}{0.035}\left(1-\frac{1}{1.035^{10}}\right)$	4.16

Giving

Price of 5% gilt

Price of 6% gilt	95.84
PV of coupon difference	(4.16)
	91.68

Price of 7% gilt

Price of 6% gilt	95.84
PV of coupon difference	4.16
	100.00

2. $$\text{FRN Price} = \frac{\text{Next coupon} + \text{Par value}}{1 + r \times {}^{\text{Days}}/_{365}}$$

$$\text{FRN Price} = \frac{5 + 100}{1 + 0.06 \times {}^{73}/_{365}} = £103.75$$

3. (a) Since the gilt was issued in 2002, the RPI reference dates would be those 8 months before the relevant coupon. Hence the RPI for the last coupon just paid would be 192.

The quoted nominal GRY is 5%, hence the semi-annual nominal GRY is 2.5%. With semi-annual inflation at 1%, the real semi-annual yield (r) can be calculated as

$$1.025 = 1.01 \times (1 + r)$$

$$1 + r = \frac{1.025}{1.01} = 1.01485$$

$$r = 0.01485 \text{ or } 1.485\%$$

Now, the price of an ILG is

$$\text{Price} = \text{PV of the original cash flows at real rates} \times (1+i)$$

Where i = cumulative inflation in the last coupon

$$(1 + i) = \frac{192}{160} = 1.20$$

i = 0.20 or 20%

PV of the original cash flows at real rates is

Time (Half-years)	Cash flow (Semi-annual)	DF (1.485%) (Semi-annual)	PV
1–8	1.00	$\frac{1}{0.01485}\left(1-\frac{1}{1.01485^8}\right)$	7.49
10	100.00	$\frac{1}{1.01485^8}$	88.88
			96.37

Price = £96.37 × 1.20 = £115.64

(b) If the gilt had been issued in 2006, the RPI reference date would be that 3 months prior to the relevant cash flow date. The only difference this would make to the above calculation is

$$(1 + i) = \frac{196}{160} = 1.225$$

giving

Price = £96.37 × 1.225 = £118.05

4. Accrued interest is from 22 November (last coupon date) to 23 February (day before settlement day) inclusive, i.e.

		Accrued	Coupon
Days	November	9	9
	December	31	31
	January	31	31
	February	23	28
	March		31
	April		30
	May		21
Dirty price paid		94	181

	(£)
Quoted clean price	104.91
Add: accrued interest $\frac{94}{181} \times 5.125$	2.66
Dirty price paid	107.57

A purchaser on 23 February would pay £107.57 for £100 nominal.

5. Accrued interest is for the period 1 June (last coupon date) to 2 September (day before settlement date) inclusive, hence

	Accrued	Coupon
June	30	30
July	31	31
August	31	31
September	2	30
October		31
November		30
	94	183

Accrued interest equals $\frac{94}{183} \times 1.75 = £0.899$

	(£)
Price paid (dirty price) per £100 nominal = £3,915.10 ÷ 100	39.151
Less: Accrued interest	(0.899)
Quoted (clean) price	38.252

6. Annual interest payable equals

$\$500,000 \times 11\% \times 365/360 = \$55,763.89$, i.e. $55,763.89 will be paid on 31 December this year and $555,763.89 at maturity next year.

At 10% the value at 31 December this year is

$$\frac{\$555,763.89}{1+\frac{0.10\times365}{360}} + 55,763.89 = £560,366.67$$

The number of days between 20 October and 31 December

	Days
October	12
November	30
December	31
	73

Payment by Z equals $\frac{\$560,366.67}{1+\frac{0.10\times73}{360}} = \$549,229.51$

7. Price paid = $\frac{\$100,000}{1+\frac{0.08\times181}{360}} = \$96,133.31$

4 Gilts and UK Government Debt

INTRODUCTION

Gilts are the primary sterling fixed interest investment. They are issued to raise finance for the government in order to finance its chosen policies, and the returns they pay are guaranteed by the government.

This section introduces the various characteristics that gilts may be observed to have, how they may be issued, traded and ultimately redeemed.

As the primary sterling fixed interest investment, a knowledge of this area is key to the whole course.

CHAPTER CONTENTS

Chapter Learning Objectives

The syllabus areas covered by this section are

Form and Structure of Securities

Students should be familiar with the form and structure of fixed income securities.

- Straights
- Index–linked
- Zero coupon
- Convertible
- Floating rate
- Synthetic e.g. strips

Investors

Students should be able to demonstrate the suitability of specific securities to specific requirements of domestic and international investor classes.

- Central banks

Government Securities Markets

Students should possess a detailed knowledge of the government securities markets of the UK, US, Japan and Euro and knowledge of the practices and conventions in the Australian and Canadian government securities markets. Beyond a knowledge of their existence and relative size this need not extend to agency, government sponsored enterprise, mortgage or corporate bond markets outside the UK. Students should be familiar with:

- Regulatory authorities
- Methods and types of issuance
- Withholding taxation
- Secondary market
- Structure
- Dealing practices
- Price transparency
- Transaction publication
- Settlement and custody practices
- Funding
- Repo/stock borrowing

For the four detailed markets, knowledge should extend to securities which are anomalous for specific reasons e.g. FOTRA or strippability. Students should be aware of the procedures for stripping securities and the implications for rump issues. Students should be aware of the existence of cash – derivative arbitrages and their potential impact upon market price behaviour. Students should be able to calculate the cash/futures price relationship. Students should be familiar with the taxation of UK residents and the taxation of non–residents in the other three detailed markets.

UK Fixed Interest Market

Students should be familiar with the UK fixed interest market including 'eurosterling' (see 7. below). Students should be familiar with the common issuance forms and structures in this market.

Role of the Authorities

- Bank of England and London Stock Exchange
- Listing Rules
- Primary Market
- Methods of Issuance

Secondary Market

- Structure and Methods of Dealing
- Code of Practice

Settlement

- Stock Borrowing/Lending

1 UK Government Bonds – Gilts

Exam tip

> Questions from this section are basic definitions or discussions of characteristics which mainly arise as sub-components of compulsory Section A questions.

1.1 Characteristics

Governments, as a rule, spend more money in a year than they raise in revenue. Consequently, they are obliged to borrow money to cover the deficit. Due to their generally high credit rating, they are able to borrow substantial sums with a wide range of maturities. The combination of this high credit rating and the size of the issues attracts investors. Government debt markets are the largest markets in the world in terms of activity.

1.2 Gilts

Gilts are UK government bonds. Historically, they were issued and managed by the Bank of England on behalf of the government; however, this role is now undertaken by the Debt Management Office (DMO).

Let us take a typical issue and use it to examine the key characteristics of gilts.

Treasury	$7\frac{3}{4}$%	2012–15	@	126.56
|	|	|		|
Name	**Coupon**	**Maturity**		**Price**

1.2.1 Name

Each stock bears a title. Treasury, Exchequer, Funding, Conversion, Consolidated (Consols), and War Loan are gilt names used to indicate the government department that issued the debt. These names mean nothing in themselves and are simply used to indicate the government department that issues them, or, in the case of Conversion, the fact that they had resulted from a conversion of an existing stock. All are equal in ranking as government bonds and carry the full backing of the UK government.

1.2.2 Coupon

The gilt coupon is the rate of interest that will be paid each year based on the nominal value of the stock. In the UK, the convention is for this coupon to be paid on a semi-annual basis, in equal instalments. However, the 2½% consolidated stock pays on a quarterly basis.

The coupon is paid to the investor who is holding the gilt on the ex-div date. Gilts go ex-div seven business days before the coupon is paid. The one exception here is the 3½% War Loan which goes ex-div 10 business days before the coupon is paid.

Since April 1998, gilts have paid their coupons gross. Prior to that date, they were paid net of lower rate tax. Note that this does not exempt holders from paying tax. It simply means that none has been paid yet. Indeed, if investors consider it most appropriate to do so for administrative reasons, they can elect to continue to receive the coupons net on any gilt.

1.2.3 Maturity

The maturity date is the date on which the government has agreed to repay the debt. In this case, the government has issued debt with two dates – a double-dated stock. The government has reserved its right to redeem the debt from 2012, but must redeem the stock by 2015. The decision on redemption will be taken with reference to the coupon. If the government is able to replace the borrowing at a cheaper rate, then it will redeem the stock on the earlier of the two dates. Gilt-edged stocks are classified with respect to their maturity dates. The official Debt Management Office definitions are as follows.

- **Shorts** – gilts with **7 years or less** to run.
- **Mediums** – gilts with **between 7 and 15 years** until redemption.
- **Longs** – gilts with **over 15 years** until redemption.

Note, the financial press use a different categorisation for short gilts, referring to gilts with less than five years to maturity as short.

Double-dated stocks are normally classified using the later of the two dates, since this is the point on which redemption has to take place.

In the past, the government has been able to issue some bonds without specifying a date on which redemption will take place. These **undated stocks** are all redeemable from a certain date. For example, the Treasury 3% 66 **Aft** has been redeemable since (**or after**) 1966, however, unlike double-dated stocks, there is no date by which the issue must be redeemed. Since there are no undated stocks with coupons in excess of 4%, it seems unlikely that the government will willingly buy them back in the near future.

Most of the undated stocks are very small issues with very limited liquidity. The largest issue is the 3½% War Loan with approximately 2 billion nominal in issue.

Whilst there are no set dates for redemption, one stock – the 3½% Conversion Loan 61 Aft (where Aft represents after the date from which the stock can be repurchased) – is subject to a redemption fund. Under the terms of its issue, 1% of the nominal value of this stock must be repurchased in each year after 1961 whenever the nominal price is below 90. As a consequence, given the low coupon rate, the government is committed each year to redeeming 1% of the nominal value of this stock and this in part accounts for its anomalous price compared to the other undated issues.

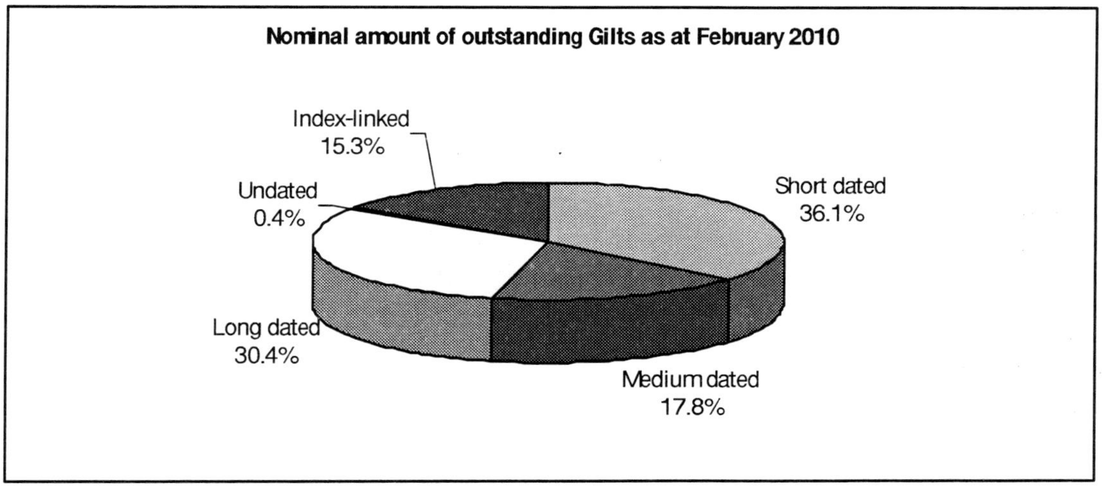

Overall market size £886.61 billion

Source: DMO

1.2.4 Price

The gilt price is quoted in terms of the amount that an investor would have to pay in order to buy £100 nominal of the stock. Technically, an investor can buy as much as they want of a gilt. The market simply adopts this as a convention for the quote. The price is quoted in pounds and pence (decimal terms).

1.2.5 Yield

In the *Financial Times*, both the Flat and Gross Redemption Yield (GRY) are published. By convention, the yield figures shown for gilts is twice the six-monthly yield, **not** the six-monthly yield compounded.

1.3 Types of gilts

1.3.1 Straight or conventional gilts

Our example above represents a straight gilt paying a fixed coupon at 7¾% p.a. until maturity. The market value of such straight bonds may vary significantly as interest rates vary, as we will see later. This may however be expected since, as interest rates rise and fall, this coupon rate will become less or more attractive.

1.3.2 Floating rate gilts

The government has also issued floating rate gilts. These bonds paid a quarterly coupon gross of tax. The coupon rate was refixed on a quarterly basis at LIBID minus $^1/_8$. Once again, this enabled the government to raise low-cost, medium-term finance and fill a demand in the market.

The advantage of a floating rate bond is that the coupon rate is always at a fair level regardless of interest rate movements, hence the price remains at or around par. Thus, a floating rate bond protects the nominal value of the investment. There are currently no variable coupon gilts in issue.

1.3.3 Index-linked stocks

Whilst a floating rate gilt may protect the nominal value of the investment, it cannot protect against the effects of inflation which, over time, eats into this value in real terms. This protection can, however, be achieved with index-linked bonds.

As inflation increases, the return demanded by investors, the yield, will also increase in order to maintain the real rate of return. Because inflation in the UK has been an issue over the past 40 years, successive governments have issued a number of index-linked gilts which automatically compensate the investor for the impact of inflation. **This compensation for inflation is applied to both the coupon and the capital repayment and cash flows**.

These cash flows are scaled up by the increase in the **Retail Prices Index (RPI)** from the issue reference date to the payment reference date and the **DMO** now uses as a reference the RPI **three months** prior to the relevant cash flow date. Note that this 3 month lag is a recent development, having always been eight months up to September 2005. As a result, the bulk of existing I/L stock has an 8 month lag, even though index-linked gilt issues from September 2005 onwards have a 3 month lag.

When index-linked gilts were first issued in 1981, they were open only to institutional investors such as pension funds. In 1982, the Government opened the market to all investors and since then, a substantial number of individuals have purchased index-linked stocks. However, the market itself is limited, representing only 15.3% of the outstanding gilts in issue. Much of the stock is locked away in institutional portfolios and, consequently, liquidity in this market can be very low, resulting in wide spreads between bid and offer prices and large fluctuations.

1.3.4 Convertible gilts

Convertible gilts are issued with an option to convert at a future date (or dates) into longer dated issues. The alternative course of action open to the holder is to allow the bond to mature and receive the redemption proceeds.

In April 1994, the government issued a convertible bond. At each of the coupon dates up until February 1996, the holders had the right to convert the bond into a specified longer dated issue. However, the longer the delay in converting, the lower the value of the longer bond that the holder received.

Feb 95	£88 nominal of Treasury 9% 2012
Aug 95	£87
Feb 96	£86

The rationale behind this was that the government was unwilling to issue longer dated stocks at the time of the issue since this would lock them into 'unrealistically high' yields (the issue took place just after the bond crash in 1994).

Consequently, by issuing a shorter dated stock with ability to convert into a longer issue, the government was able to signal to the market its view on yields whilst raising cost-effective finance. The difficulties in valuing this type of product have discouraged the Bank/DMO from further issuance.

There are currently no outstanding issues of convertible gilts.

1.3.5 Foreign currency debt issues

Under the full funding rule, the government will not raise any of its normal finance in a foreign currency.

Historically, however, the government has been obliged to issue some foreign currency gilts in order to finance the foreign currency reserves at the Bank of England. There are no such outstanding bonds at present.

2 Government Funding and the Gilt Market

2.1 Introduction

The UK gilt-edged market is one of the largest government bond markets in the world. It offers the investor a wide diversity of stocks, all carrying the full guarantee of the UK government (and an AAA rating).

2.2 The role of the Bank of England

In the past, the key player in the gilt-edged market has been the UK's Central Bank – the Bank of England. Historically, its role has been all-embracing, covering all elements of the government's finances.

- **The government's bank**

  The Exchequer maintains its bank accounts at the Bank of England.

- **Manager of the UK's reserves**

  The government holds assets in both sterling and foreign currency and these monies must be managed. Here the Bank operates very much like a conventional fund manager. The priorities would be accessibility and matching to their needs/exposure. A significant proportion of the reserves will be held in gold and dollar denominated products. These reserves are used for intervention in the Forex markets to manage the currency.

- **Manager of the National Debt**

  The Bank was responsible for the issuance of gilt-edged securities and smooth functioning of the primary and secondary markets in gilts.

- **The implementer of monetary policy**

  The Treasury maintained control of economic policy and used the Bank to implement its monetary policy through the money markets.

- **The regulator of the banking sector**

  Acting as lender of last resort to the banking system and as lead regulator. This formed part of an implicit and wider brief with regard to the stability of the UK capital markets.

2.3 Bank of England reform

However, in May 1997 the government announced a major reform of the structure of responsibilities within the financial markets, and the gilt-edged market in particular. As a result of this new structure, the Bank has won operational independence and took full responsibility for the establishment of monetary policy in the UK, although the overall target for inflation and the divergence bands around this are set by the government. The current target is 2% inflation with an allowable range of 1% to 3%. These bands allow the government to set the broad tone of policy and, by requiring the Bank to justify either over or underperformance, ensure that there is no deflationary bias built into the system.

The argument behind this move to independence is that it allows the Bank to take key long-term decisions rather than seeking 'pragmatic' political short-term solutions. The idea is that stability of monetary policy should create a stable economic environment and therefore encourage growth.

However, against this new found independence, the Bank lost its regulatory role in the market. Equally, the practicalities of gilt issuance and administration of the dealing system have now passed to the Treasury, in the form of the Debt Management Office (DMO).

The 'Old' Bank of England

The Bank of England	The Debt Management Office (DMO)	Banking Regulation
This is the part of the Bank which is given independent responsibility for monetary policy. It will also take responsibility for the management of the Forex reserves and intervention in the Forex market on behalf of the government.	This organisation has responsibility for the government's borrowing requirement and the functioning of the gilts market. It also manages the government's sterling assets and accounts.	These responsibilities were transferred from the Bank to the Financial Services Authority (FSA) under the terms of the Bank of England Act 1998. This took effect on 1 June 1998.

Part of the logic behind the splitting of the other functions of the Bank was to separate the daily financing of the government from the Central Bank for fear of any confusion that might be created by the interplay of the two operations. For example, the Bank raising finance at certain key points in time might be interpreted as signals with regard to the direction of monetary policy.

The National Debt

Whilst the issuance of bonds represents the primary method by which the government satisfies its annual borrowing requirement, it should be appreciated that there are other sources, such as National Savings products. The rest of this chapter considers the issue of government debt.

2.4 The structure of the gilts market

Over the past 20 years, the gilt-edged market has undergone a substantial change. The Bank of England's objective in introducing change from the mid-1980s onward was to ensure that the government had access to a gilt-edged market that was

- Liquid.
- Competitive.
- International.
- Safe.
- Technologically advanced.

As mentioned above, the structural integrity of the market is now the responsibility of the DMO.

3 New Issues of Gilts

Exam tip

> This area has been examined in Section A, e.g. Summer 1999 Question 5, but more frequently arises in a larger Section C discussion, e.g. Winter 2002 Questions 16, Summer 2001 Question 10.

3.1 The DMO

3.1.1 Role of the DMO

The prime responsibility of the DMO is to ensure that the government is able to borrow the money it requires to fund the **Public Sector Net Cash Requirement (PSNCR)**. The most important source of financing open to the government is the gilts market.

The DMO is in charge of the issuance of new government stock into the market. There are a variety of methods of issue the DMO can use. Its choice of method depends very much on the amount of debt it has to issue in the fiscal year, and the current market conditions.

3.1.2 The funding remit

The Bank/DMO has great flexibility with regard to issuance through the Treasury funding remit. This remit details the volume of issuance the government needs during the year to fund the public sector borrowing requirement, but does not specify either the stocks or the times at which this borrowing must be raised. The detail of when the money is to be raised from the market will be left to the DMO.

3.1.3 The issuance timetable

The DMO has a structured issuance timetable of running auctions at the end of each month, announcing the dates of all auctions for the following 12 months in March (alongside the Budget). The only flexibility within this is with regard to the auction which normally would take place at the end of November. Subject to the timing of the pre-Budget announcement, this auction may well take place in early December.

The DMO envisages that each auction will be for at least £2bn nominal and will tend to be issued into one of the existing benchmark stocks. Prior to the beginning of each calendar quarter, the DMO will announce the specific gilts for each of the auctions taking place in that quarter and in the week before the auction it announces the size of the auction.

Unlike most other government bond markets, the DMO possesses the ability to issue stock directly into the secondary market via the creation of tap stocks without having any pre-announced schedule. However, in the July 1995 Debt Management Report, the Bank committed itself to limiting tap issues on conventional issues to around 10% of issuance. Furthermore, these taps will be used for exceptional market management, eg to support the market's liquidity rather than exploit timing advantages.

3.2 Methods of Issue

3.2.1 Tenders (Uniform Price Auctions)

In 1979, the Bank/DMO switched from a fixed price system of offering debt to the public to a tender (Dutch auction) system. Under the tender system, the Bank/DMO announces its intention to issue a volume of stock and a minimum price at which it is prepared to accept bids.

Those investors who wish to participate in the tender submit their bids to the Bank/DMO. The allocation process is best seen by way of an example.

Example

The DMO wishes to issue £700m of the Treasury 9¾% 2010s and set a minimum price of 99 (most new issues of gilts in the UK are issued at below par value). The following bids are received.

£100m @ 101.5
£200m @ 101
£200m @ 100.5
£400m @ 100
£400m @ 99.5
£500m @ 99

Under the tender system, those investors who bid the highest price will be allocated first. However, the price they pay will be one common strike price for the whole issue. In this case, the £100m of stock bid for at 101.5 will be allocated first, then the £200m at 101, £200m at 100.5 and then £200m of the £400m bid at 100. All investors who have been allocated the stock will pay the common strike price of 100.

In the event that the bid fails, any stock surplus will be taken on to the books of the DMO and is referred to as tap stock. When the market conditions are right, the DMO will then release the tap stock through the secondary market.

3.2.2 Auctions

In 1987, the Bank/DMO started to experiment with a series of competitive auction issues. The competitive auction is the prime mechanism for issuing new stocks in the American T-bond market. The auction has been so successful that the DMO now very rarely uses the tender method. It is now only with index-linked auctions that the uniform price method is used.

Competitive auctions function in much the same way as tenders. The DMO announces an issue and then accepts bids from investors who wish to participate in the issue. The principal difference here is that, whilst investors are allocated on a highest price first basis, the investors actually pay the price at which they bid, rather than a common strike price.

Using the tender example above, the first investor to be allocated would be the £100m bid at 101.5, but rather than a common strike price of 100, the investor would pay 101.5. In order to help the market gauge the appropriate level at which to pitch its bids, gilts issued by way of an auction are traded in **when-issued form** for a week before the issue date. The when-issued form is a grey market in gilts and trades on an if, as and when-issued basis. If for any reason the auction is withdrawn, then the grey market deals disappear.

In order to encourage participation in competitive auctions, the DMO allows non-competitive bids. These are bids where the investors do not attempt to estimate the appropriate price for the gilt, but merely indicate that they would wish to be buyers at an average price. The ability to make non-competitive bids is restricted to individuals at up to a value of £0.5m nominal for conventional gilts, and £0.25m for ILGs. Market makers are limited to ½% of the auction for their non-competitive bids.

Once all the bids have been received, the non-competitive bids are allocated stock and then the competitive bids are allocated on a highest price first basis. Once the entire issue has been allocated, the non-competitive bids are priced at the average of the accepted competitive bids.

Once the auction is complete, the DMO undertakes to maintain a fallow period for a reasonable time after the end of the auction during which it will not issue stocks of a similar maturity. However, given the structuring of monthly auctions, this term is now reasonably irrelevant.

One issue that exists with the competitive auction approach is the 'winner's curse'. Those applicants who bid at a high price will win, but will also pay the price they bid.

In conventional auctions, this is seen as an acceptable risk. To encourage the expansion of the index-linked market, it is normal to use the tender or uniform price methodology.

3.2.3 Tap issues

The two methods of issue that have been discussed so far represent the normal scheduled ways in which government bonds are released to the market. The third tap issue method is much less conventional. Here the DMO sells bonds into the secondary market rather than organising the formal primary market.

Tap stocks arise in one of two ways. Firstly, they may be the result of a failed public issue, either tender or auction, where the bids received failed to meet the minimum required by the DMO – this is rare. Secondly, the DMO may simply open up an existing issue and issue a new tranche of a stock.

In the past, this used to be a formal method of issuance and in the early 1990s represented at least half of the total issuance by the Bank. The DMO is now committed to using the tap facility to stabilise the market.

Taps themselves were, as mentioned above, conventionally used for small amounts of funding where the DMO perceived there to be a window of opportunity in the market place. At this point, the Bank simply started dealing into the secondary market, selling what are new gilts as if they were existing stocks.

However, under the new regime it is more conventional for the approach to come from the market makers, who are experiencing a shortage of stock, to the DMO. If there are several approaches, the DMO may hold a '**mini tender**'. The DMO will announce the creation of a tap at 10:15 and ask for bids from the GEMM half an hour later at 10:45. The DMO will announce when the issue is filled. Many of the taps will come from the more illiquid issues such as the index-linked stocks.

In response to the credit crisis in 2008, the DMO used a series of mini-tenders to supplement the pre-announced auctions. The use of mini-tenders was extended to the first quarter of 2009.

The DMO is very keen on the idea of opening up existing stocks rather than creating new stocks, and the gilts market is justly criticised at present for having such a diversity of coupons and maturities, which is confusing to overseas investors. Consequently, the DMO is consciously attempting to focus liquidity into key benchmark stocks and wherever possible, the DMO will issue new tranches of the main benchmarks.

If a tranche of a stock is opened up during a coupon period, the new stock issued will not rank for a full coupon. Consequently, it needs to be identified from the existing stock which ranks for its full six-monthly coupon. These tranche stocks are identified by the letter 'A' after the name of the stock. For example, 9% Conversion 2011 pays its coupon on 12 July and 12 January each year. A new tranche is opened up in May and this stock will pay a coupon on 12 July, but this coupon will only be for two and a half months. Up until the payment of its first coupon, the new tranche of the stock will be known as 9% Conversion 2011 A stock. From the date of the next coupon, the two stocks are completely fungible, since they will both now be ranking for a full dividend on 12 January. It is possible for there to be more than one tranche open in a particular stock, in which case there will be not only 'A' stocks, but also Bs and Cs.

Since the mid-1990s, the DMO has chosen to issue fully fungible tranches which will rank for a full coupon from the start.

4 Dealing

The market structure for dealing in UK gilts has changed substantially over the years. For the most part, it has been brought into line with the American system although there are some peculiarities of UK markets that still persist.

Overview of the Gilts Market

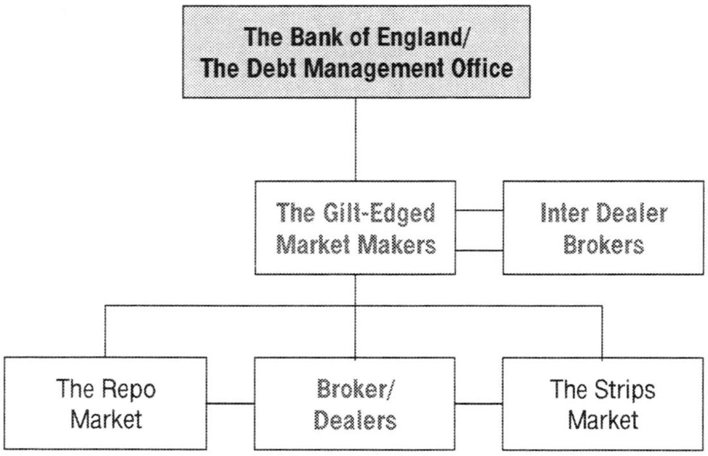

4.1 Gilt-Edged Market Makers (GEMMs)

4.1.1 Introduction

The Gilt-Edged Market Makers (GEMMs) are the primary dealers in this market place, and they are, in effect, the central focus for activity. Gilt-edged market maker status is awarded to firms who apply directly to the DMO.

The DMO will not allow any firm to become a market maker – it must be happy that the firm in question is prepared to uphold the standards of the market and that its addition to the list of existing market makers will not in any way render the market unprofitable.

GEMMs were originally required to be separately capitalised companies. The reason for this was to isolate the gilt-edged market making firm from the other aspects of the business, therefore limiting the risks faced by the GEMM to those of the market making business alone. However, with opening up of the gilt repo market and the introduction of the **Capital Requirement Directive**, this requirement has now been dropped. Each firm must, however, have sufficient capital for the level of business the DMO anticipates it taking on, and the management must be of sufficiently high calibre.

The DMO's role within the regulatory framework in the gilts market is to ensure that the market is solvent and efficient. It does not wish to be involved with much of the day-to-day regulation of dealing practices. Consequently, all GEMMs are required to be members of the Stock Exchange, which has rules governing dealing in the gilt-edged markets.

Once admitted to the market place, the GEMM's obligation is to make a continuous two-way price in all gilt-edged securities. This price is firm up to a quantity agreed with the DMO. In return for their obligation to make a continuous market place and therefore putting their capital backing behind the market, GEMMs have a number of important advantages.

- A direct dealing relationship with the DMO.
- Sole access to the inter dealer broker (IDB) network (see below), enabling them to take and unwind large positions.
- Access to borrowing facilities at the DMO.

As mentioned above, the DMO does not want to encourage too many market makers since this will undermine the profitability of existing companies. At present, there are 15 market makers operating in the gilts market and the DMO does not envisage a rapid change in this number.

Gilt-edged market makers are able to quote their prices through the Stock Exchange's SEAQ system. However, most price information is quoted through other systems such as Reuters and Telerate. Dealing is conducted by telephone, there being no physical market place.

4.1.2 The market in index-linked stocks

At present the market in ILGs is relatively limited. Whilst ILGs represent around 15.3% of the outstanding gilt market, they only account for around 1% of daily turnover. However, the government is keen to maintain and, if possible, increase the current level of issuance.

Part of the motivation behind the desire to increase the level of ILG issuance is to maintain the pressure on themselves to control the level of inflation. If inflation is low then the finance cost, in nominal terms, will likewise be low which will benefit the government. Conversely, if inflation is allowed to accelerate, then the government will suffer cash flow problems.

Equally, conventional debt, because it is fixed in terms of its return, is subject to a degree of inflation risk. This risk is undoubtedly priced into the yield on conventional bonds. Estimates vary as to the extent of the inflation risk premium, however, measures based on the difference between the breakeven rate of inflation and the consensus of City forecasts suggest that it has been of the order of 50 to 100bp. As such, ILGs represent a cheaper form of finance.

The problem for the Bank/DMO was how to increase the issuance into this market. The market in ILGs has traditionally been a 'buy and hold' market. As such, simply increasing the volume of issuance would not be enough. Excess supply would force the yield up and the price down. However, the demographic drift of society towards an older population will require pension funds to hold more assets in the form of bonds.

This increase in the holdings of gilts by pension funds, which currently represent around 9% of the average fund, will undoubtedly increase buying pressure. Given the nature of the liabilities of many pension funds which are linked to final salaries, this will tend to focus the increased demand for ILGs. Whilst this increase in the level of demand will increase the ability of government to issue, it will do nothing for the liquidity of the market.

4.2 Inter Dealer Brokers (IDBs)

An inter dealer broker is an intermediary between market makers. They enable market makers to take and unwind large positions without revealing this to other market makers and participants in the market place.

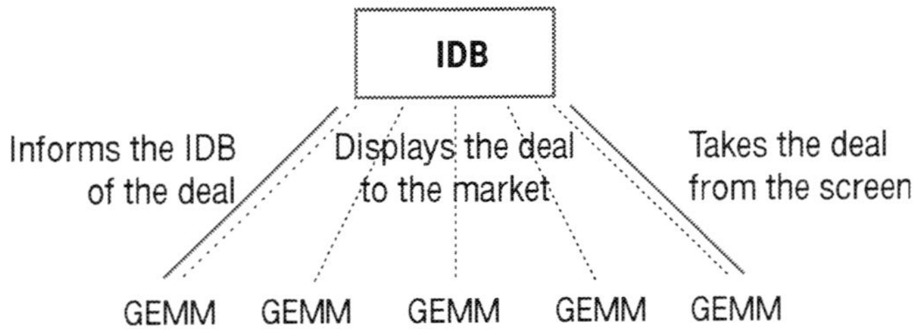

The system works by each inter dealer broker (there are presently five firms acting as IDBs) operating a screen system which has a screen in each of the market makers' offices. A market maker who is particularly long or short of a stock contacts one of the IDBs and places a bid or offer on the screen. This appears simultaneously in all other market makers' offices, but does not indicate the market maker who is placing the bid or offer.

Another market maker who may wish to take the opposite position to the first market making firm then contacts the IDB and 'hits' (or 'takes' or 'lifts') the IDB quote. It is this market maker who pays commission to the IDBs of $^1/_{128}$ of 1%. The commission is low, but the trades are all principal trades matched against two market makers guaranteed by the DMO and so contain minimal risk and are of considerable size.

The IDBs are again regulated by the DMO, which ensures that they do not expose themselves to undue risk. The IDBs must undertake each trade as a matched agency cross and may under no circumstances take positions on to their own books.

In addition to being regulated by the DMO, IDBs are regulated in the conduct of their business by the Stock Exchange, which insists on strict principles and procedures to ensure that bids between rival market makers are allocated in an efficient and fair fashion.

IDBs are one of the innovations introduced in the mid-1980s and were modelled on the US market where IDBs have existed for many years.

4.3 Broker dealers

The GEMMs are primarily concerned with an inter-professional market and rarely deal themselves with individual investors other than the large institutions. Below the gilt-edged market makers there exists a secondary chain of dealers – the ordinary broker dealers. These are all member firms of the Stock Exchange and are governed by the Stock Exchange code on dealing in the gilt-edged market.

As mentioned above, market makers are obliged to make a firm two-way price quote during normal market hours. The price quoted is firm to these broker dealers (and not to the other market makers). Individual investors who wish to purchase gilts, normally approach the market through a broker dealer, who will then access one of the market makers on the client's behalf.

4.4 The strips market

On 8 December 1997, a fully functional strips market was launched in the UK.

4.4.1 What is strips?

The term strips stands for Separately Traded and Registered Interest and Principal Securities. Put simply, a strips market allows for the trading of a bond, not simply as a package of flows, but as individual flows.

The system takes an ordinary bond and breaks it down into its component parts. Each flow from a bond is converted into a zero-coupon bond.

For example, a five-year Gilt with a semi-annual coupon of 6% would become 11 zero-coupon bonds, one for each of the 10 individual coupon flows of £3 and one final zero-coupon bond formed out of the principal. These zero-coupon bonds range in maturity from six months to five years.

Given that the strips market is derived from the same market as the underlying bonds, then the possibility of arbitrage exists between the two to ensure that prices are consistent.

4.4.2 Which bonds are strippable?

At the outset of the market, only the main benchmark issues were designated as strippable. The current benchmarks are all on one of two coupon payment cycles:

- 7 March, 7 September
- 7 June, 7 December

Creating a fungible market in coupon strips, since the six-month strips from all of the bonds will be indistinguishable. It is vital that there is a liquid market in both the bonds and the strips in order to ensure fair pricing and efficient arbitrage.

The Current Benchmark Issues
4¾% Treasury 2010
3¼% Treasury 2011
4¼% Treasury 2011
5% Treasury 2012
5¼% Treasury 2012
4½% Treasury 2013
2¼% Treasury 2014
5% Treasury 2014
4¾% Treasury 2015
8% Treasury 2015
4% Treasury 2016
5% Treasury 2018
3¾% Treasury 2019
4½% Treasury 2019
4¾% Treasury 2020
8% Treasury 2021
4% Treasury 2022
5% Treasury 2025
4¼% Treasury 2027
6% Treasury 2028
4¾% Treasury 2030
4¼% Treasury 2032
4½% Treasury 2034
4¼% Treasury 2036
4¾% Treasury 2038
4¼% Treasury 2039
4½% Treasury 2042
4¼% Treasury 2046
4¼% Treasury 2049
4¼% Treasury 2055

Details correct as at 10 February 2010, Source: DMO.

Both coupon and principal strips are fully fledged gilts and liabilities of Her Majesty's Government.

Gilts are stripped and reconstituted via facilities through the UCGO (Upgraded CGO) system. It is not possible to remove a strip from the CGO and hold it in paper form. Strips are not available from the National Savings Stock Register.

Index-linked gilts

The strips market began with conventional gilts. Stripping index-linked gilts continues to be considered in the light of experience gained with conventional gilt strips. At present, the fear is that stripping ILGs will fragment an already thin market.

The features of strippable stocks

Stripped coupons from different strippable gilts with the same coupon dates are fully fungible in order to increase liquidity.

Strippable gilts are gross paying whether held in stripped form or not. This means they are not subject to associated withholding tax or to the quarterly accounting arrangements introduced in connection with the gilt repos.

The mechanics of stripping facility

There is no limit to the amount or proportion of any eligible issue that can be stripped or reconstituted, however the minimum strippable amount for all gilts is £10,000 nominal going up in steps of £10,000.

As already mentioned, the pool of strippable bonds should ensure that there is no undue fragmentation of the market.

4.4.3 Why trade strips?

Strips provide the perfect instrument for liability matching (giving the investor a direct match) and carry no reinvestment risk.

As mentioned above, the strips market creates a far wider spectrum of available durations. In addition to the duration enhancement, the convexity of the strips is also be greater, reflecting the greater dispersion of the cash flow. For example, considering the 8% Treasury 2021 we have at present.

	Modified Duration	Convexity
Conventional Gilt		
8% TRS 2021	10.99	1.88
STRIPS		
2021 Principal	23.06	5.43
2008 Coupon	10.99	1.26

In addition to the uses above, those houses offering products with guaranteed returns will be able to collateralise their obligations through the strips market.

4.4.4 Tax treatment

Corporate investors

From the perspective of the corporate investor, income and capital gains are deemed to be the same for tax purposes. In addition, all strippable gilts are gross paying and exempt from the quarterly accounting requirements. Consequently, there will be no difference between the bond and the stripped form allowing for perfect arbitrage.

Individual investors

For individuals, coupon flows on gilts are subject to income tax, however, any gains are not at present subject to capital gains tax. When in stripped form all flows are deemed to be income taxable. Consequently, there is a potential tax disadvantage in entering the strips market in the loss of the tax-free gain.

Where an individual holds a strip, it will be marked to market on an annual basis and the difference taxed as income, as opposed to the existing rules where the difference in value would only be taxed at maturity or on disposal.

4.4.5 Market structure

Gilt-edged market makers make a market in strips as part of their general market-making obligations. Consequently, strips seem no different from the existing bonds in issue, with the exception that strips are quoted on a yield basis.

5 SETTLEMENT

5.1 Introduction

The normal convention for gilt settlement is that bargains settle on the business day following the trade.

Delayed or advanced

For gilt-edged securities, it is possible to advance settlement. For deals struck before noon, it is possible to elect for **same day** settlement, marked **'for cash'** and referred to as 'cash cash'.

Equally, it is possible to delay settlement.

By agreement, the parties may settle a transaction within **such a period as may be agreed**. This delay is designed to enable a reasonable time for the participants either to deliver the securities or raise the funding.

With **gilt-edged switches,** investors may wish to switch from long-dated stock into short-dated stock. Under the terms of this trade, the investor will swap one gilt in exchange for another. In order to avoid a flow of funds between the two parties to the trade, provided that the settlement values of the trades are broadly in line (10% variation allowed) with each other, the bargain may be marked **CN** for **contingent**.

This means that no settlement moneys will change hands, only the nominal values, and any difference will pass between the two investors. A bargain marked CN may not settle immediately. However, if the bargain has not been settled within a maximum of **ten business days**, the investor who is ready to settle may enforce settlement.

In these circumstances, it will of course be an ordinary bargain and settle for cash. The second half of the deal will then settle when the other party is able to deliver the gilt.

5.2 CREST

The normal settlement function is undertaken by CREST, part of Euroclear, which operates an electronic book entry system for gilts.

In March 1996, the Bank allowed gilts to settle through external systems. It is now possible to settle transactions in UK gilts through Clearstream, Euroclear and the Republic Bank of New York. This reform further enhanced the appeal of the UK market to overseas investors who are likely to be familiar with these settlement regimes.

6 Taxation

6.1 Domestic taxation issues

As a result of the tax reforms to facilitate the repo market, there have been substantial changes in the way in which both income and capital gains taxes apply to gilt-edged securities.

Income taxes

As of 6 April 1998 all gilt interest is paid gross, except where the holders choose otherwise.

Capital gains tax

Prior to 6 April 1996, all gains on UK government stock and qualifying corporate bonds (issued in sterling and non-convertible) were free of capital gains tax. To link in with the introduction of a strips market, the government felt obliged to ensure that the treatment of zero-coupon bonds and coupon bonds was consistent, otherwise there would exist a tax block to the creation of a strips market. At present, the discount on a zero-coupon bond is deemed to be income and, therefore, income taxable.

As a consequence of this disparity in tax treatment, all gains by non-individuals are now treated as income and subject to tax. Equally, all interest flows are deemed to accrue over the life of the instrument concerned as opposed to the existing treatment of taxation upon receipt.

For those persons who are caught by the new change there is, however, one benefit they will derive. Any losses incurred on their gilt-edged positions are now deemed to be a loss relievable against income tax.

Whilst initially it was the intention to include individuals with this reform, the political issues behind the decision to remove the capital gains tax exemption mean that the alteration does not apply to individuals who continue to be taxed as they have been in the past. This means that some of the advantages of the strips market did not accrue to individuals.

7 Local Authority Debt

Unlike certain Federal securities in the US market, local authority debt carry a far less implicit guarantee. If the authority defaults there is only a moral obligation on the part of the government to support them.

The local authorities are able to issue a variety of stocks.

7.1 Fixed loans

A fixed loan is in effect a mortgage and indeed, these instruments may be known as Local Authority Bonds or Mortgages. It is a loan that is arranged for a set maturity. During the period of that loan, interest is paid to the lender. **There is no secondary market** in this type of security. It is very much like a mortgage on a house.

7.2 Local Authority Negotiable Bonds (Yearlings)

This is short-term local authority debt. In essence, it is a bond like a gilt, carrying a coupon. The maturity of this bond will be either one or two years. The market in these bonds trades in set blocks, the size of a block being **£1,000 nominal**. Unlike fixed loans, there is a full secondary market in yearlings.

It is possible for yearlings to be issued with maturities of up to five years. However, the normal form was for one-year and six-day maturity.

7.3 Local Authority Stocks

In essence, a Local Authority Stock is the same as a gilt. It is a longer term bond carrying a coupon that pays semi-annually and there is a full secondary market in Local Authority Stocks. The yield on Local Authority Stocks will be slightly above the yield on gilts, reflecting the slight risk of default.

7.4 Current state of the market

Over the past decade, issuance in the market has dried up. Rather than allow the authorities to raise their own finance, the Local Authority Borrowing Requirement (LABR) has been subsumed into the PSNCR. The government has then made some of the finance raised through the PSNCR available via the Public Works Loan Board (PWLB). This constraint has now been relaxed and Local Authorities are allowed to borrow again in their own right.

The **Private Finance Initiative** (PFI) was launched by the government in order to encourage the use of private finance for major projects such as building bridges and hospitals. The logic behind this is that it will be more efficient than the current government funding structure and will potentially tap new areas of the investment community. This should particularly encourage the local community to invest in projects that have a direct bearing on their environment and welfare. This may represent an additional drain on the banking sector or alternatively may act as the catalyst for the development of a non-government debt market. These bonds will not carry the formal backing of the government.

The government has pledged to make it easier for projects to use the PFI and in time this should lead to far greater issuance in the UK non-government bond market.

Chapter Roundup

- You need to be familiar with and able to describe gilt characteristics
  - Coupons
  - Maturity
  - Types
  - Redemption
- You need to be aware of the roles of the Bank of England and the DMO.
- You need to be able to describe issuance methods
  - Tender
  - Auction
  - Tap issues
- You need to be able to describe secondary market dealing and the participants.
  - GEMMs
  - IDBs
  - Broker dealers
  - Strips
- You need to be able to describe settlement and taxation issues

Test Your Knowledge

Check your knowledge of the Chapter here, without referring back to the text.

1. Describe the role of the DMO.

2. Describe the types of gilt that may be issued.

3. Describe the issuance methods currently used by the DMO and the circumstances when they may be used.

4. Describe the role of the secondary market participants.

5. Describe gilt settlement arrangements and alternatives.

Test Your Knowledge: Answers

1. See Section 3.1

2. See Section 1.3

3. Discuss:

   - Auction – regular pre-scheduled primary market financing issues
   - Tap – unscheduled secondary market issues in exceptional circumstances

   See Section 3.2

4. Discuss:

   - GEMMs
   - IDBs
   - Broker dealers

   See Section 4

5. Discuss:

   - Settlement timing
   - Crest

   See Section 5

5 Domestic Corporate Bonds

INTRODUCTION

In this section we extend our knowledge of bonds to cover bonds issued by companies.

We need to be aware of the similarities and differences between gilts and corporate bonds in order to understand their use as investments. We also need to be aware of the major issuers of corporate bonds, why they may issue bonds and what regulations they may be subject to.

CHAPTER CONTENTS

Chapter Learning Objectives

The syllabus areas covered by this section are

Form and Structure of Securities

Students should be familiar with the form and structure of fixed income securities.

- Convertible
- Asset–backed
- Security
- Covenants
- Negative pledge
- Charges and liens
- Events of default
- Governing law
- Sinking funds
- Purchase funds
- Call features
- Embedded options
- Bearer/Registered
- Type of documentation
- Listing

Investors

Students should be able to demonstrate the suitability of specific securities to specific requirements of domestic and international investor classes.

- Banks
- Savings Banks – Building Societies
- Corporations

Students should possess a broad understanding of the preferences of and constraints on, these types of investor and any implications for their investment policy

International Securities (Eurobonds)

Students should be thoroughly familiar with the International (or Eurobond) Markets. Students should be familiar with the various types of issue and, in particular, with common issuance forms and structures in the Eurosterling market.

Regulatory bodies

- ICMA

Listing arrangements

- Bank of England and Sterling Issues

Primary markets

- Methods of issuance

Secondary market

- Methods of dealing

Settlement and custody

- CEDEL and Euroclear

1 Introduction to Corporate Bonds

Exam tip

Basic definition questions often arise in Section A from topics in this Chapter, eg Winter 2008 Question 8.

1.1 Distinguishing characteristics

An understanding of Gilts provides a good basis for the understanding of corporate bonds and, indeed, any bonds, since they all share many common characteristics. What we primarily need to concentrate on are the differences between the various types of bonds we experience.

The main difference between corporate bonds and gilts is that gilts are guaranteed by the UK government, whereas corporate bonds are only guaranteed by the company that issued them. As a result, an investor in corporate bonds will experience some risks that are not experienced by an investor in gilts.

Clearly, if an investor is facing a higher risk he will demand a higher return in compensation, so we may anticipate that companies must consequently borrow at higher rates than the government.

In common with all borrowers, however, companies look to minimise the cost of any borrowings that they make, and much of what follows is a discussion of those additional risks and efforts made by companies to limit, or compensate for, those risks in order to reduce their borrowing costs.

Whilst it is easy to get confused by all of the 'bells and whistles' of the variations available, we should bear in mind that the majority of issues are straight bonds with a fixed coupon and redemption date.

1.2 Additional risks of corporate bonds

The additional risks faced by investors in corporate bonds include the following.

1.2.1 Credit and default risk

Credit and default risk is the risk of the issuer defaulting on its obligations to pay coupons and repay the principal. The ratings by commercial rating companies can be used to help assess this risk.

1.2.2 Liquidity and marketability risk

Liquidity risk has to do with the ease with which an issue can be sold in the market. Smaller issues are especially subject to this risk. In certain markets the volume of trading tends to concentrate into the 'benchmark' stocks thereby rendering most other issues illiquid. Other bonds become subject to 'seasoning' as the initial liquidity dries up and the bonds are purchased by investors who wish to hold them to maturity.

1.2.3 Issue specific risk

There may be issue specific risk factors which tend to either increase or decrease the risk, e.g. issuer options such as the right to call for early redemption or, possibly, holder options.

1.2.4 Fiscal risk

Fiscal risk represents risk that withholding taxes will be increased. For foreign bonds there would also be the risk of the imposition of capital controls locking your money into the market.

1.2.5 Currency risk

For any investor purchasing overseas or international bonds then there is obviously also the risk of currency movements.

2 The Corporate Debt of Markets

The corporate bond markets are made up of three elements as follows.

- Domestic corporate issues.
- Overseas issuers of sterling debt – 'bulldogs'.
- Eurosterling issues.

Progressively the first two of these three areas have declined in relative importance since the 1970s. With both domestic corporates and bulldogs, the growth of the Eurosterling market has fundamentally undermined their issuer base. In the case of the domestic debt market, the issuance level was never strong given the 'cult of the equity' that has dominated the UK markets since the 1950s and led to one of the largest equity markets, by number of stocks, in the world.

A further inhibitor of the growth of the market has been that once a borrower has 'tapped' the Euromarket then it is unlikely to be able to re-enter the domestic market, given the normal covenants included in the issues. Eurobonds are generally unsecured debt and most issues carry with them a negative pledge assuring the lenders that no debt with a higher level of security will be issued. In the domestic markets, it is conventional for debt to carry security.

Much of the paper currently traded in the market is stock that was issued during the 1960s and 1970s when the market was reasonably liquid. As these issues reach maturity, the market will contract even further.

3 Corporate Bond Characteristics

Though in principle, there are many similarities between corporate bonds and gilts, there are a number of distinguishing corporate bond characteristics that we must be familiar with.

3.1 Debentures/loan stock

Debentures and loan stock are written acknowledgement of debt which, as such, can often be traded. The word debenture is used when the lender is being furnished with some security by the borrower. When no security is being provided, the stock is referred to as loan stock or unsecured loan stock (ULS).

There is no obligation for a company to give security on any loan. However, the consequence of not giving security will be that the coupon it is obliged to pay will be higher. Many companies have issued unsecured loan stock in the UK markets, but they tend to be only those companies with, in general, a high credit rating or status.

3.2 Eurobonds

The corporate borrower has a choice as to which market to issue into. Large multinational firms with high credit ratings are able to access the Eurobond or international market. Smaller companies will be constrained to use the less active domestic corporate bond market.

A Eurobond could be defined as an international bond issue, underwritten by a syndicate of banks, and sold principally in countries other than that of the currency of denomination.

However, the instruments are essentially the same, the only difference being that the pace of innovation is greater in the Euromarkets. The basic terms of any issue will be contained in the **indenture**.

3.3 Legal form

Most Eurobonds issued are in bearer form, whereas domestic issues are obliged to be in registered form.

3.4 Coupons

Exam tip

> Questions in this area tend to be small definitions as part of compulsory Section A questions, e.g. Winter 2004, Question 4.

Most bonds are issued with a fixed coupon. However, a number of variations are possible.

3.4.1 Zero coupon

Bonds may be issued with zero coupon or a very small coupon. Such bonds would be issued at a discount to their redemption value to provide an acceptable gross redemption yield.

In the UK, discounted bonds will be subject to a specific tax regime if their discount exceeds either 0.5% for each year of life or 15% in total. Bonds that exceed these criteria may be referred to as deep discount bonds and the owner will pay income tax on the excess received over cost when realised by sale or redemption.

3.4.2 Stepped coupons

A stepped coupon rises over the life of the bond.

Year	**(%)**
1	4
2	6
3	8
4–10	10

The advantage to the issuer is that it will not be burdened by the full interest cost in the early years of the debt. However, overall the issuer will be paying a higher coupon rate. It is also possible to issue a reversed stepped coupon with the coupon rate declining progressively over the life of the bond.

3.4.3 Step-up clauses

As a result of some significant downgrades, it is not uncommon to build step-up clauses into debt documentation. A typical clause might say "If the borrower's rating falls below investment grade then the coupon rises by 50bp". In this way, lenders can at least partially protect themselves against downgrades.

3.4.4 Floating rate notes (FRNs)

Floating rate notes are ordinary bonds where the coupon level varies in line with some measure of the market rate of interest (commonly LIBOR – London Inter Bank Offered Rates or LIMEAN – the average of the offered and bid rates). The coupon on these bonds comprises two elements. Firstly, the reference or **index rate**, for example LIBOR, and secondly, a **quoted margin**, the rate above LIBOR that must be paid. An example might be a five-year bond with a coupon of LIBOR (the index rate) plus 25bp (the quoted margin).

Initially, in this market, the quoted margins were measured in half and a quarter per cent but, with competitive pricing, these have come down to a matter of mere basis points.

The quoted margin is established at the outset of the deal and reflects the borrower's credit rating and the size of the issue, along with the market conditions at the time.

Other conditions may be included. A bond may be a **drop lock** where the coupon is allowed to float but once it reaches its set minimum, the bond locks into being a fixed coupon bond at that minimum interest rate.

These are obviously fairly rigid structures and have been replaced frequently by floors where the bond's coupon level cannot fall below a certain point. For example, the floor of a bond might be 5%. If the index rate and the quoted margin gradually floated down to this level then, at the point of 5%, the coupon will be locked. However, as the index rate began to pick up, then the coupon could increase beyond 5% unlike with a drop lock where, of course, once it touches the floor, the bond is locked until redemption.

The minimum rate or floor is obviously a protection for the investor purchasing the floating rate note. It is possible for the issuer also to take up protection in the form of a ceiling or a cap whereby as interest rates rise, the coupon on the FRN also rises, but not beyond this pre-set ceiling.

It has been common for issuers to offset the costs of establishing a ceiling by including a floor value (**minimax bonds**), which in effect collars the interest rate available on the floating rate note. It cannot exceed a pre-set ceiling nor can it fall beneath a pre-set floor. Within these basic market conventions a number of variants have been introduced.

A further issue to consider is the frequency of refixing of the coupon. Most Eurobonds pay annual coupons, however, with floating rate notes the convention is normally to refix the coupon rate on a six-monthly basis. Depending on the nature of the market, it may even be that the refixing frequency is greater, perhaps refixing on a six-weekly basis.

By refixing more rapidly than the coupon is paid (**mismatch floaters**) the bond closely tracks markets' rates. As a consequence, one would normally expect floating rate notes to trade around the par level, since any interest rate movements are reflected in the coupon and not in the capital value of the bond. FRNs that refix more frequently than they pay coupons are referred to as mismatched floating rate notes.

A number of variants on the theme of the FRN have emerged. An example of this is the issuance of 'inverse FRNs'. With an inverse FRN, the coupon rate is given by the formula

(Fixed rate – LIBOR) + Quoted margin

For example

$(17\tfrac{1}{2}\% - 2 \times \text{LIBOR}) + 25\text{bp}$

In most instances the quoted margin is ignored. The advantage in issuing this type of stock is that the investor is in effect taking an option on the direction of interest rates and this may increase the level of demand.

3.5 Redemption

Exam tip

> Again, questions in this area tend to be small definitions as part of a compulsory Section A question, e.g. Summer 2003 Question 8, Winter 2002 Question 10.

Corporate bonds can have a variety of redemption terms.

3.5.1 Bullets

The vast majority of bonds issued are still in the form of bullets. A bullet issue has a single redemption date. There has been a tendency to issue callable bonds, or indeed putable bonds, where the holder has the right to call for early redemption, but the complications involved in analysing these issues often dissuade investors from purchasing them. This shift away from unorthodox redemption patterns is particularly true for the next two potential repayment schemes that are now rarely used.

3.5.2 Sinking funds or sinkers

A sinking fund is a process whereby a proportion of the bonds in issue are redeemed each year.

$250 issue to be redeemed in four instalments

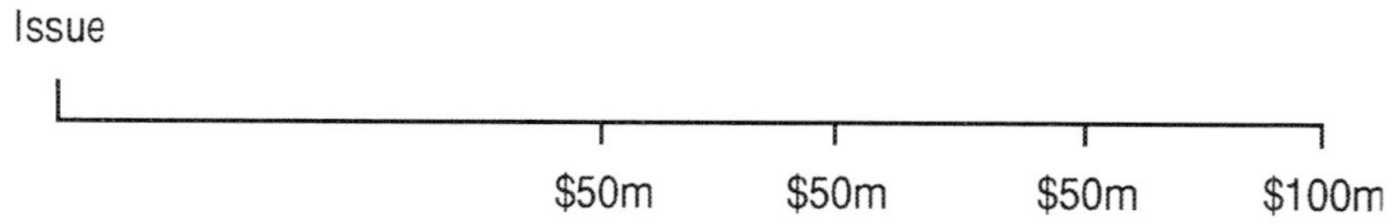

The bonds to be redeemed in each year are selected by the process of 'drawing' the serial numbers. The serial numbers of the bonds drawn in this way are then published and the holders submit the bonds to the paying agent for redemption at par. The final repayment is normally larger than the others and is referred to as the balance or balloon repayment.

Sinking funds tend to come into operation towards the end of the bond's life and rarely start to redeem from the first coupon date.

3.5.3 Purchase fund

A purchase fund buys back the bonds in the secondary market, and not at par. The obligation to repay is triggered by a condition specified in the offer document, normally the bond trading below par.

Purchase funds are found outside the Euromarkets. In the UK gilt-edged market, the 3½% Conversion 62 Aft has a purchase fund whereby 1% of the nominal is repurchased each year that the nominal value lies below 90.

3.5.4 Serial notes

A serial note is one where a proportion of the capital is repaid each year along with the interest. An example outside the Euromarkets would be the Federal Agency stocks ('Fannie Maes') in the US.

3.5.5 Optional redemption

The option to redeem a bond can be given to either side of the deal. An issuer call right would give the issuer the right to seek an earlier redemption; for example, the double-dated gilts in the UK market, where the government has the right to redeem from the earlier of the two dates, but must redeem by the later date.

A second form of option may be given to the bond holder in the form of a holder put right giving the holder the right to require the board to be redeemed at a specific price.

3.6 Currency

There is no need for the currency of the coupon and that of redemption to be the same; it is entirely possible for the two to be different (**dual currency bonds**). For example, a bond may pay coupons in dollars and be redeemed in sterling. The rate of exchange can either be established at the outset or be the spot rate at the time of the transaction.

Bonds have also been issued, which contain an option to use a variety of currencies, either at the issuer or holder's choice.

3.6.1 Duet bonds

These issues pay coupons that are themselves the difference between two rates. An example of this was a 10% Kgdm of Denmark issue (based in $ and yen) where the coupon was 16½% of the $ amount minus 6½% on the yen base.

3.6.2 Heaven and hell

Redemption on these bonds takes place in the base currency, using a formula based on changing rates. For example

$$\left(1-\frac{\text{Maturity yen spot}-169}{\text{Maturity yen spot}}\right)\times \text{Face value}$$

In this case, the redemption value of the bond is closely tied to the yen spot rate. If the rate were to fall to 84½, then the redemption value would be

$$\left(1-\frac{84\frac{1}{2}-169}{84\frac{1}{2}}\right)\times \text{Face value}$$

$$\left(1-\frac{84\frac{1}{2}}{84\frac{1}{2}}\right)\times \text{Face value} = 0$$

Alternatively, if the rates rose, then the bondholder would receive redemption in excess of the par value. A variant on this theme has been the 'purgatory and hell' bond, which has a cap on the upside value.

This concept of linking the redemption value to external indicators has also used the interest rate. By linking the redemption value to the change in the interest rate over a specified period, a bond with a longer duration than its maturity can be created.

For example, a two-year MTN where the redemption proceeds are calculated using the following formula.

Face value + [10 × (Current 3-year rate – 3-year rate @ Maturity)%]

If rates were to rise by 30bp over the next two years, then the redemption value would be

100 + [10 × (–0.3%)] = 97

The end result is a two-year bond with a modified duration of ten years. In a market where there may be a shortage of stocks with high durations, then this issue may appeal to investors.

Obviously, care has to be taken with all of these variants to the straight issues, since if they were incorrectly structured, then they could result in huge potential problems for the issuer. Equally, bonds with special terms tend to be highly targeted towards specific investors with specific objectives. The general investor would understandably be confused by all the 'bells and whistles'.

3.7 Equity sweeteners

3.7.1 Introduction

As with domestic corporate stocks, it is possible for the issuer to include equity sweeteners or kickers with the issue to make up for a low-coupon rate by way of convertibles in issue or attached warrants.

3.7.2 Convertibles

A conversion right gives the bondholder the right, at a specified date or dates in the future, to convert their bond into shares of the company. The rate of conversion will be fixed at the time of issue and represents an option to purchase the shares at a given price.

Depending on the movement in the underlying share price, this conversion right or option may be very valuable indeed. The trade-off in this sort of issue is that the coupon will often be much lower than the market would otherwise expect on a bond from that particular company.

3.7.3 Warrants

A warrant is similar in many ways to a conversion right. The principal difference is that rather than converting a bond into shares, a bond is issued with a warrant attached to it and that warrant gives the holder the right to buy new shares at a specified price from the company at specified dates in the future. A warrant is effectively **a call option** to subscribe for new shares in the company.

The advantage to the company of issuing warrants rather than convertible bonds is that the holder of the bond may **split** the warrant off and trade both aspects of the security separately.

3.8 Security

Exam tip

> Questions are often asked about debt security, especially in the context of liquidation priority, see Summer 2005 Question 3 and Summer 2004 Question 6.

Companies have the ability to issue debt which is secured against the company's assets. There are two types of legal charge that a company can issue over its assets.

3.8.1 Fixed charge

A fixed charge is a charge over an identifiable asset of the company; the debenture deed will note the specific asset in question. Typically, a specific non-current asset such as land or a freehold building will be used for this purpose, as it can be readily identified and should not deteriorate substantially in value over the term of the debenture.

The commercial impact of having a fixed charge is that the company cannot sell the asset in question unless the debenture holder releases the charge. The debenture holder is unlikely to do this unless he is offered some equally good asset over which he can have an alternative charge.

If the company falls into arrears with its interest payment or defaults on its capital repayment, then the debenture holder can either

- Appoint a receiver and obtain income from the assets held under charge; or
- Take possession of the asset and sell it, using the proceeds to repay the debentures in full. Any excess proceeds will be returned to the company; any shortfall will become an unsecured liability of the company.

3.8.2 Floating charge

A floating charge is secured against the assets in general rather than against specific assets. A floating charge has no effect until the company defaults on a loan. At this stage, the holder of a floating charge has the right to appoint a receiver to take over the running of the company. The receiver will then manage the company and any money coming in will be used to repay the bondholder's debt.

Unlike a fixed charge, where the company loses the right to dispose of an asset covered by a charge, here the company has full rights over the assets of the business until there is an event of default. At that stage, and at that stage only, does the charge crystallise.

3.8.3 Relevance – priority on liquidation of a company

Fixed charges are legally superior to floating charges. This is demonstrated by looking at the order of payout on the liquidation of a company. The process of liquidation is one in which the company is wound up by a liquidator. The company is turned into its liquid asset – cash. Assets are sold, money is collected and then used to pay out, in a specific order, the obligations of the company.

The liquidator's task is to convert the company into cash as quickly and efficiently as possible. In the UK, the order of payout is determined by the Insolvency Act 1986 (as amended by the Enterprise Act 2002), and is as follows.

Priority on Liquidation
1. The Liquidator's Fees
2. Fixed Charge Holders
3. Preferential Creditors
4. Floating Charge Holders
5. Unsecured Creditors
6. Subordinated Creditors
7. Preference Shareholders
8. Ordinary Shareholders

The liquidator will pay out each category in full before moving on to the next. Since most liquidations may be the result of insolvency, there may be insufficient funds left to pay out all debts. The order of liquidation is an attempt to reward those who have some form of security first before moving on to the unsecured creditors.

The Preferential Creditors category includes contributions to occupational pension schemes and, to a very limited extent, the employees of the firm. When the liquidator runs out of money the category being dealt with at that stage will receive, on a pro rata basis, the proportion of its debt that can be covered by available funds. For example, the unsecured creditors in a liquidation may receive only 14p in the pound. The important point to note is that shareholders receive their money last. They are the owners of the company who must take the risks as well as reap the rewards. Should the company be wound up and there be a surplus on liquidation, the ordinary shareholders would receive that surplus.

The Enterprise Act 2002 (EA 2002) attempts to reduce the number of liquidations that take place in the UK. Under the terms of the Act, there is greater use of administration. Administration is a sort of protective state into which the company is put when it experiences difficulties. The job of the administrator is to find a way through the current difficulties and to, hopefully, bring the company back to stability. It is analogous to Chapter 11, Protection in the USA.

Another change brought in by the EA 2002 was an attempt to protect the unsecured creditors. Firstly, the State, which had been a preferred creditor, lost its advantage and now ranks with the unsecured creditors. In addition, for floating charges issued after September 2003, a prescribed portion of the pool of assets available to them in liquidation is put aside to meet the claims of the unsecured creditors.

It will again be noted from order of priority on liquidation that subordinated loan stock can be issued. A subordinated loan is one which on liquidation ranks below the unsecured creditors for payout. As such, subordinated creditors take on board a higher degree of risk and obviously require a higher degree of return to compensate them.

One of the prime reasons for issuing subordinated stock in the past has been that it has a fairly beneficial impact on the capital adequacy calculation for any securities house or bank. Subordinated loans subject to exemptions and controls will be treated as primary capital in the same way as issued share capital.

Finally, the value of a company is irrelevant if the stock itself has been guaranteed by another company. Often within groups of companies the subsidiaries may borrow money directly from the market. The loan may carry its own security or be guaranteed by the holding company. This debt is then referred to as guarantee stock. The value of this guarantee obviously depends upon the stability of the holding company.

Alternatively, rather than the guarantee coming from the holding company, it may come from a subsidiary which has been established with strong capital security.

Group structures and liquidation

Where a group of companies goes into insolvency, the situation is more complex. We will demonstrate the issues of group structure and liquidation with the following example.

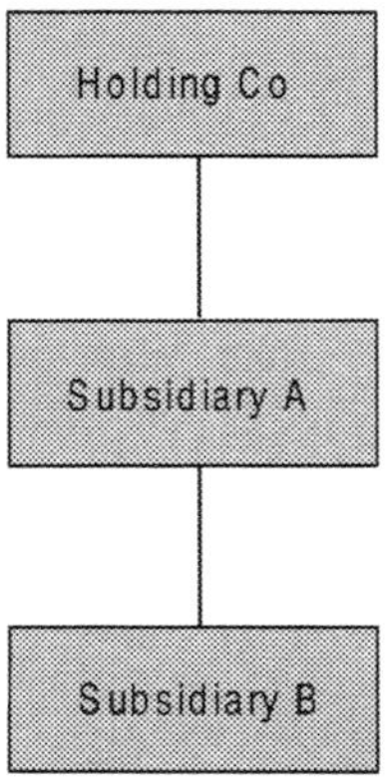

In this situation the affairs of B must be dealt with first. Once this company has been liquidated and any surplus has been transferred to its owner (A), then the process can continue.

Subsidiary A can now be wound up. Once again, any surplus is transferred to the owner, in this case the holding company. Only once this has been done can we deal with the affairs of the holding company this is known as structural subordination.

This clearly has an important impact on the priority of various obligations. Any debt issued by B will be dealt with before the obligations of A are considered. Consequently, if subsidiary B holds most of the assets of the group and has unsecured debt, whilst the holding company has debt secured by a floating charge, then it is the unsecured debts of B that will be discharged first. Only if there is any excess will this be passed up the chain to the holding company.

Therefore, despite the priority that they possess, the floating chargeholders have been structurally subordinated to the unsecured debt in subsidiary B.

This situation can either be exacerbated or diminished through the use of inter-group guarantees. Where the holding company guarantees the debt of the subsidiary, once again they prioritise the obligations of the subsidiary over those of the holding company. This is referred to as contractual subordination. Alternatively, the subordination effect can be reduced if the subsidiaries guarantee the debt of the holding company. In this situation the guaranteed holding company debt will be treated as a debt of the subsidiary in determining the liquidation priority, the subsidiary guarantor effectively taking the debt on as its own.

3.8.4 Unsecured debt

There is no obligation for a company to give security on any loan. However, the consequence of not giving security will be that the coupon it is obliged to pay will be higher. Many companies have issued unsecured loan stock in the UK markets, but they tend to be only those companies with in general, a high credit rating or status.

3.9 Covenants

3.9.1 Normal debt covenants

Covenants are terms and conditions attached to a bond issue.

Exam tip

Once again, questions in this area tend to be small definitions as part of compulsory Section A questions, e.g. Summer 2008 Question 7, Winter 2006 Question 6, Winter 2004 Question 5, Summer 2004 Question 6, although occasional optional Section C questions do arise, e.g. Winter 2008 Question 10.

The negative pledge

The negative pledge clause specifically relates to Euromarkets. Most Eurobonds are not secured in any way against the underlying assets of the borrower. A negative pledge clause is where the borrower undertakes to refrain from raising other finance on which it grants a better security. In effect, this means that any borrower who raises funds through the Euromarkets is normally then prevented from raising money through the domestic markets since, in general, domestic investors will require some form of security.

This limitation can be waived within a bond agreement to allow for modest amounts of secured or prioritised borrowings. This may be referred to as priority borrowing limits.

Cross default clause

A cross default clause is included in most loan agreements and states that if the borrower defaults on any one of its loans, then this will constitute a default of this borrowing as well.

The important consequence of this is that the borrower may default on one loan due to, perhaps, overly strenuous covenants which the lender is prepared to waive, but that will still constitute a default for any other borrowing which has a cross default clause in existence.

Pari passu clause

A pari passu clause ensures that any lender is granted the same level of security as given to any new lenders.

Restrictive financial covenants

It is possible to include within the loan documentation a number of key financial ratios, which the borrower must not exceed, known as restrictive financial covenants. These normally include some measure of the ability to pay interest and may state an express limit on the overall level of borrowing that can be undertaken. These forms of covenant are notoriously difficult to enforce and are frequently strongly resisted by the borrower.

New owner clause

A new owner clause is included to allow the lender the right of repayment, should the ownership of the corporate borrower change.

Nature of business

This is linked to the new owner clause. Should the nature of business undertaken by the company change dramatically, this will again affect the rights of the holders of the bonds, and may give the right to request a redemption of the bond.

Material adverse change

Under a Material adverse change (MAC) clause, a loan becomes repayable (or a facility is withdrawn) if a major adverse event takes place. The principal problem with these clauses is that they are, by their nature, relatively vague as to what constitutes a material adverse change. For example, no MACs were activated by virtue of the events of 11 September 2001. They are often argued to be too vague to enforce.

3.9.2 Covenants relevant to riskier debt

These covenants create more detailed and more onerous requirements on companies which are subject to a higher degree of risk.

Limitation on additional indebtedness

A restriction on the company that limits the ability to take on further indebtedness unless it meets certain conditions. These conditions are normally linked to key ratios such as interest cover.

Limitation on restricted payments

This covenant limits the company's ability to pay dividends or repurchase its own capital. Once again, these limits are often linked to key ratio cut-off points, such as interest or asset cover.

Limitations on transactions with affiliates

This limits the ability of the company to enter into transactions with an affiliate unless they are on normal commercial terms.

Limitation on dividend and other payment streams from subsidiaries

A general covenant prohibiting any subsidiary from entering into an agreement which limits its ability to remit dividends up to the holding company.

Disposal proceeds of asset sales

This ensures that the company cannot sell assets unless they receive a fair market value and unless a specified percentage of the consideration is received in cash. A further extension to this clause is often that the monies received are used to

- Repay senior debt; or
- Reinvest within the business within one year; or
- Repay the debt.

These are just examples of the type and range of covenants that are normal in the higher yielding markets.

In all loan negotiations there is an element of haggling. The borrower will seek to diminish the restrictions caused by covenant, whereas the lender wishes to obtain the greatest degree of coverage possible. In the end, the result is often a reflection of general credit availability. During periods where credit is relatively scarce, borrowers will be obliged to accept relatively intrusive covenants.

3.9.3 Events of default

A breach of the covenants or the failure to pay the coupon or principal on the due dates are events of default. Whilst within the agreement there may be allowance for 'grace periods', if the borrower remains in default, the loan is immediately repayable. One obvious question that arises is how this may be achieved, and possible alternatives include:

- Equity swap – where the borrowers agree to exchange their bonds for new shares in the company. This may well result in the almost complete dilution of the interest of the current shareholders.
- Pre-packs – where a deal to sell the assets of a failed company is agreed prior to insolvency and is then completed immediately after the appointment of administrators or receivers.
- Administration – where an administrator is appointed to take over the company and determine the best course of action in respect of the bondholders. This may be to allow the company to continue to trade or to liquidate the company and realise its assets.

If the directors of a company anticipate that it will default through a breach of covenant they should take immediate action, especially where there are cross default clauses that will require them to deal with the likelihood of defaulting on several borrowing obligations.

In such circumstances, the Director would be best advised to contact all lenders to discuss the situation in order to determine whether they would be willing to ease the covenant. Lenders may prefer to ease the covenants and permit the company to continue if it can show that it has a viable future. At the same time, the Director should contact the LSE to notify them of the situation in order to avoid a false market in the company's shares.

If an agreement cannot be made, however, it is most likely that the company will default.

Most bonds are constituted in such a way that there is a trustee who is responsible for ensuring that the bondholder's interests are protected. Where there is no trustee, the bondholder is obliged to seek redress directly from the company.

4 Bond Credit Ratings

Exam tip

> Definitional Section A questions arise from this section, e.g. Winter 2003 Question 4 along with scenario style questions in Section C, eg Summer 2009 Question 12.

4.1 Introduction

All issues except those companies or corporations with high name recognition (household names) require a credit rating from one of the agencies. The three main agencies offering credit ratings at present are

Moody's, Standard & Poor's and Fitch Ratings. The credit rating itself gives an indication to potential investors of the level of security that they can find in a particular issue.

Investment Grade (Prime)		
Moody's	**Standard, Poor's & Fitch**	**Meaning**
Aaa	AAA	Highest quality
Aa1 Aa2 Aa3	AA+ AA AA–	High quality
A1 A2 A3	A+ A A–	Strong capacity to pay
Baa1 Baa2 Baa3	BBB+ BBB BBB–	Adequate capacity to pay
Non-Investment Grade (Non-Prime or Junk)		
Moody's	**Standard, Poor's & Fitch**	
Ba1 Ba2 Ba3	BB+ BB BB–	Capacity to pay uncertain
B1 B2 B3 Caa	B+ B B– CCC	High risk
Ca C	CC C	Vulnerable to default
Ba1	D	Already in default

4.2 Investment grade – Standard & Poor's

AAA

Debt rated AAA has the highest rating assigned by Standard & Poor's and has the capacity to pay interest and repay principal which is extremely strong.

AA

Debt rated AA has a very strong capacity to pay interest and repay principal and differs from highest rated issues only in a small degree.

A

Debt rated A has a strong capacity to pay interest and repay principal, although it is somewhat more susceptible to the adverse effect of changes in circumstances or the economic conditions facing the company than debt in higher rated categories.

BBB

Debt rated BBB is regarded as having an adequate capacity to pay interest and repay principal. Whereas it normally exhibits adequate protection, adverse economic conditions or changes in circumstances are more likely to lead to a weakened capacity to pay interest and repay principal for debt in this category than in higher rated categories.

4.3 Non-investment grade – Standard & Poor's

Non-investment grade securities sometimes referred to as speculative securities. Prior to the advent of 'junk bonds', companies could not issue into these captions, and any companies categorised with ratings below BBB were companies who had been downgraded from higher ratings; these were referred to as 'fallen angels'. However, the junk bond market, which started in the 1980s, now enables corporates with speculative credit ratings to issue debt.

BB

Debt rated BB has less near-term vulnerability to default than other speculative issues. However, it faces major ongoing uncertainties or exposure to adverse business, financial or economic conditions which could lead to inadequate capacity to meet timely interest and principal payments. The BB rating category is also used for debts that are subordinated to senior debt that is assigned an actual or implied BBB rating.

B

Debt rated B has a greater vulnerability to default, but currently has the capacity to meet interest payments and principal repayments. Adverse business, financial or economic conditions will be likely to impair capacity or willingness to pay interest and repay principal.

CCC

Debt rated CCC has a currently identifiable vulnerability to default and is dependant upon favourable business, financial and economic conditions to meet timely payment of interest and repayment of principal. In the event of adverse business, financial or economic conditions, it is not likely to have the capacity to pay interest and repay principal. The CCC rating category is also used for debts subordinated to senior debt assigned an actual or implied B or B minus rating.

CC

The rating CC is applied to debts subordinated to senior debts that are assigned an actual or implied CCC rating.

C

The C rating is typically assigned to debts subordinated more in relation to senior debt with a higher rating. The C rating may be used in certain circumstances to cover a situation where a bankruptcy petition has been filed but debt service payments are still being made.

D

Debt rated D is in payment default. The D rating category is used when interest payments or principal payments are not made on the date due, even if the applicable grace period has not expired.

Other points

Within Standard & Poor's weighting system, the plus and minus sign indicates the relative standing of the debt within one of the major captions. The letter I indicates that the rating is implied. An implied rating will be given to a sovereign borrower who has not expressly asked for a rating to be produced.

4.4 Implications of a rating

4.4.1 Low rating

As mentioned above, it would be very difficult for any company without a credit rating to raise money in bond markets, and the market itself is confined to dealing with high credit-worthy stocks exclusively in the investment grade.

4.4.2 Downgrade

A bond may be placed on **credit watch** as a prelude to a potential **downgrade**. If a bond is placed on credit watch then it is likely that its credit spread will widen with the consequence of a fall in price. This impact is less pronounced for the higher rated (investment grade) bonds but becomes quite significant for non-investment grade bonds or those falling from investment grade to non-investment grade.

The more a bond get downgraded, the fewer investors will find it to be of interest. There are, of course, specialist high yield funds, however as a general rule the major investors prefer the higher rated bonds.

One big step is when a bond falls from investment grade to non-investment grade, or high yield. At this stage there tends to be many forced sellers and prices can be expected to decline dramatically. For example, all UCITS compliant investment grade bond funds will no longer be able to hold the bond and will be required to sell it. Whilst a non-UCITS fund may have more leeway and a fund that is not promoted as investment grade would not be bound by this rule, a UCITS fund managed as investment grade must strictly apply that criteria.

Where a fund holds a bond that is expected to be placed on credit watch, the issue that arises for fund manager is whether the holding should be retained until the situation is clarified or whether the manager would be best advised to dispose of the holding now in anticipation of the potential downgrade.

The practical reality is that the market invariably anticipates any credit changes and prices tend to move prior to the formal upgrade or downgrade. If any potential downgrade has not yet been factored in by the market in general and the manager's expectation is in advance of market views then he should sell the bond now to avoid the potential adverse consequences that he is anticipating. If, however, the potential for a downgrade has already been factored in to the current bond price, the fund manager may be better advised to retain the bond until its status is formally announced since markets often overreact to potential falls.

4.5 Insured or 'credit enhanced' bonds

A feature of many smaller US corporate issues and of the emerging markets has been the insured bond in which a third party guarantees a smaller issuer against default, in return for a fee.

This third part guarantee is normally give by a **monoline insurer**. A monoline insurer is one who can only write a single line of insurance contract, in this case a **credit insurance**.

Monoline credit insurance is irrevocable and unconditional with the result that if the issuer fails to pay the coupon/principal on a timely basis then guarantor must do so. As a result, the risk to bond investors becomes a function of the monoline insurers credit rating rather than that of the issuer. Through this credit wrap, the bond is credit enhanced.

The established primary financial guarantors are rated AAA with the result that any issuer's guaranteed debt is also rated AAA. This enhanced rating both reduced the issuers borrowing costs and increases marketability of their debt. It also enhances security and liquidity for investors. Investors also benefit from the credit monitoring expertise of the guarantor.

The cost of insurance to the issuer is a substantial proportion (typically $\frac{2}{3}$) of the credit spread, though the issuer still benefits from the remainder of the spread and the enhanced marketability.

So far, only a small number of UK domestic issues (normally by housing associations) have built in some degree of credit enhancement.

5 Asset-Backed Securities and Structured Debt Products

Exam tip

> Questions in this area are normally sub-components to Section A questions involving basic definitions or comparisons to other bonds (especially FRNs), e.g. Summer 2008 Question 3, Winter 2004 Question 4 and Summer 2004 Question 7. They may, however, involve more in-depth discussion of collateralisation and structured products in 15 mark optional section C questions, e.g. Summer 2004 Question 13, Summer 2003 Question 13.

5.1 Asset securitisation

The process of asset securitisation has created a very deep market in the US though less so in continental Europe. The UK market is relatively small but is growing fast.

The logic of the process is that a company which has financial assets on its balance sheet will be able to convert these into cash. In essence, the operation is simple.

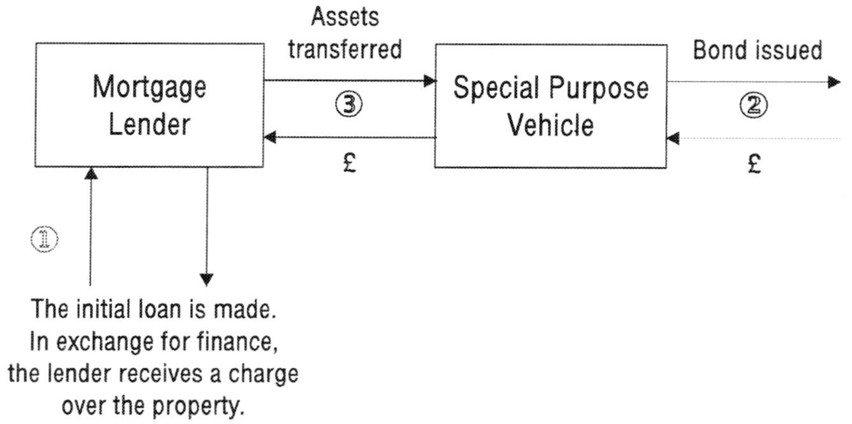

The initial transaction (1) is a straightforward secured loan as the mortgage lender advances funds secured against the property of the borrower. Traditionally, the lender would then simply hold this asset (the loan) until the mortgage was redeemed. During the life of the loan the lender earns the interest on the loan.

However, the problem with this is that it ties up the lender's resources. In more competitive lending markets this can represent a serious commercial constraint on the operation of the lender.

Asset securitisation allows the lender to release the locked-in capital. The loans to be securitised are transferred (3) to a special purpose vehicle (a trust company). The purchase of these financial assets is funded by the issue of bond by the SPV (2). The rationale behind this is that this '**ring-fences**' the assets and protects them from the credit risk of the initial borrower. Credit risk is an issue for an ordinary corporate who is securitising, for example, their credit card receivables.

One of the main problems surrounding the evaluation of mortgage-backed securities is the innate variability of the cash flows. The normal variable is the rate of prepayment (early redemption of the mortgage). This will vary in line with interest rate conditions and may result in the capital being paid back early. Obviously, all payments within mortgage streams (on straightforward repayment mortgages) contain some element of redemption payment. The prepayment risk is not concerned with this predictable redemption, but with the lump sum redemptions prior to the expiry of the mortgage's term. In the UK, this feature is exacerbated by a tendency for most mortgages to carry floating interest rates which will, of course, create another dimension of uncertainty.

This variability will be most obvious in the context of simple **pass-through** products where the cash flows to the bondholders match the inflows from the underlying portfolio of mortgages. In this case, the exposure of the bondholders is both to interest rate and prepayment risk.

5.2 Debt and mortgage passthrough certificates

Debt and mortgage passthrough certificates are securities which enable an investor to receive a pro rata share of the cash flows coming from a pool of bonds, loans, mortgages etc, i.e. debt. As such, they are fairly simple instruments. It is possible to create more complex derivative structures for pools of mortgages, such that an investor need not receive a pro rata share of the cash flows. The benefit of this is that each mortgage derivative security can be more precisely tailored to individual investor requirements.

Two forms of debt derivatives are as follows.

- Collateralised Debt Obligations (CDOs)
- Stripped Mortgage-Backed Securities.

5.3 Collateralised debt obligations

5.3.1 The purpose and structure of CDOs

In the US, a number of specialised products have developed around the generic heading of collateralised debt obligations (CDOs). Where underlying collateral is mortgages this maybe referred to as a collateralised mortgage obligation (CMO), where the underlying collateral is a portfolio of financial assets such as high yield bonds it maybe referred to as a collateralised bond obligation (CBO) and where it refers to bank loans it may be referred to as a collateralised loan obligation (CLO) .

A CDO is an asset-backed investment vehicle designed to redistribute the risk and return from a pool of bonds to meet the needs of both the issuer and the investors. CDOs rely on the principle of diversification, CDO issues typically being investment grade bonds that are backed by a portfolio of non-investment grade assets which, through the spread of investment quality and through low return correlation, provide investment grade performance.

Balance sheet CDO

A balance sheet CDO will be issued by a bank or financial institution that has a portfolio of risky assets in its accounts that it would like removed. The primary purpose of the CDO is to remove these assets and their associated credit risk from the issuer's balance sheet through a CDO (an SPV). The bank sells the assets to the CDO for cash, replacing the asset on its balance sheet with a cash asset.

The CDOs raises finance to purchase the assets by issuing a range of securities (tranches or tiers) to investors, each security having different interest rate risk, credit risk and return and repayment priority. As such, the CDO is a single pool of assets that is used to back several securities. The typical structure of a CDO would include:

- A senior tranche usually paying a floating rate coupon and representing 70%-80% of the fund
- Tranches of more junior and subordinated debt with decreasing credit quality paying fixed coupons and representing 10%-15% of the fund
- An equity tranche offering a variable geared equity return, representing 10%-15% of the fund.

A CDO will usually be a trust, ie run by trustees for the benefit of the investors, with the different CDO tranches having differing liquidation priority rights – the senior tranche having an absolute priority to income and principal.

Though run as a trust, the CDO has a corporate style structure in which the equity tranche holds the voting rights, though these equity voting rights are somewhat notional since the sole purpose of the entity is to collect asset income and distribute it in a pre-defined order to the various bond and equity holders.

The basic principle of a CDO is that the further down the tranche structure the greater the risk. The junior subordinated debt will carry a higher coupon than the senior tranche to reflect this additional risk, though the equity tranche suffers the greatest risk, facing the first of any losses that may arise. Typically part of the equity tranche will be retained by the issuer to ensure it only repackages good debt with a low default correlation.

In the event of a default, however, the senior CDO bond holders can usually take control of the CDO, accelerating payments to themselves or liquidating assets to achieve their anticipated return. The lower tranches and equity holders will have no influence at this stage and experience significant risks under these circumstances.

As a result, the lower rated tranches are the least likely to provide the returns expected from their initial redemption yields, whereas the higher tranches are most likely to realise these yields. That having been said, the redemption yields are not guaranteed for any tranche, and a significant asset default will have an adverse impact on the yield of even the highest tranche.

Most CDOs are actively managed and may hold a portfolio of say, 100 corporate bonds with an average credit rating of B+. When trading, the CDO manager would be required to maintain this average credit rating.

If the total size of the portfolio is, say, $250m then it may have six classes of security as follows.

Class	Amount $	Proportion of deal %	Subordination %	Class rating
A	200.0	80.00	20.00	AAA
B	12.5	5.00	15.00	AA
C	10.0	4.00	11.00	A
D	7.5	3.00	8.00	BBB
E	7.5	3.00	5.00	BB
Equity	12.5	5.00	0.00	N/A

Though the highest class tranche, A, amounts to 80% of the CDO value, they carry the lowest risk as they have 20% subordination. If there is, say, a 5% default, this will initially be borne by the Equity holders and hence have no direct impact on the other tranches. This does not, however, mean that the other tranches will be unaffected. If equity has lost 5% then we will now have the following situation.

Class	Amount $	Proportion of deal %	Subordination %	Class rating
A	200.0	81.64	18.36	AAA
B	12.5	5.10	13.26	AA
C	10.0	4.08	9.18	A
D	7.5	3.06	6.12	BBB
E	7.5	3.06	3.06	BB
Equity	7.5	3.06	0.00	N/A

As we can see, the level of subordination has been reduced for all the higher tranches, most significantly for the lower levels. As a result, all the tranches are exposed to a greater risk and their rating may, therefore, fall.

Synthetic CDO

Banks and financial institutions may be able to sell certain assets where they face a credit risk, however they may have other assets on which they face credit risk that they either cannot or do not wish to sell. For example, there may be adverse tax consequences from selling certain assets, or legal restrictions on their sale, especially on certain foreign debt. In addition, a bank may not wish to sell a particular loan as it wishes to maintain a relationship with the client concerned. A synthetic CDO allows the institution to avoid the credit risk on such debt without selling the asset.

In a synthetic CDO, the CDO raises finance by issuing a range of securities, as with a balance sheet CDO, and these funds are then invested in a high quality bond portfolio. The CDO then sells a credit default swap (CDS) to the institution based on its risky asset. By this route,

- the bank avoids the credit risk it would otherwise face on the relevant debt
- the CDO takes on the credit risk with the CDS premium received providing the additional income to compensate for this risk

The total income of the synthetic CDO is, therefore, the return from the high quality bond portfolio plus the CDS premium, and this will be distributed to the various investment tranches as appropriate.

As with a balance sheet CDO, the institution may retain a share of the equity tranche to provide an incentive to ensure that the debt is properly managed.

Additionally, a synthetic CDO may be fully funded, ie provide cover for all of the institutions debt, or partly funded, only covering part of the debt.

5.3.2 Sequential pay trances

The original CMOs were fairly simple in structure and took the form of sequential pay tranches or bonds. The CMO is split into several tranches, identified as A, B, C, etc. Interest from the mortgages is paid to all tranches in proportion to their principal investment. However, principal repayments are first used to repay Tranche A. When all of Tranche A has been repaid, the next principal repayments are used to repay Tranche B and so on.

Although the priority for repayment of principal is known, the timing of principal repayments is not, although it can be forecast with a prepayment speed assumption (PSA).

The sequential order of repayment means that the first tranches will have average lives shorter than the underlying mortgage collateral, while the later tranches will have average lives longer than the underlying collateral.

However, the volatility of the average life for each tranche is still significantly affected by the prepayment speed.

The simple sequential pay CMOs are sometimes referred to as plain vanilla CMOs.

5.3.3 Accrual bonds

Accrual bonds are sometimes referred to as Z bonds. They are so called because they are similar to zero-coupon bonds. In addition to the usual tranches in a sequential pay CMO, a Z bond may be added. The Z bond does not receive any cash interest in the early years, receiving instead additional Z bonds. The cash interest so released is then used to pay down the principal balances on the other tranches.

Effectively, the Z bond investors are using their interest to buy principal from investors in the other tranches.

Some bonds are partial accrual bonds, which receive part accrual of interest and part cash interest.

The impact of Z bonds is to shorten the average life of the other tranches, while the Z bonds have a very long average life.

Investors who wish to avoid reinvestment risk will find Z bonds attractive, since they receive no intermediate cash flows.

For example a Real Estate Mortgage Investment Conduit (REMIC), creates a number of sub-bonds within the issue A, B, C and Z. The A (1st class), B (2nd class) and C (3rd class) bonds all carry coupons which have normally been fixed (particularly in the US). Any redemption/prepayment monies are used firstly to pay the A class bonds and subsequently, the Bs and Cs. Eventually, any remaining monies are paid to the Z class (companion bond).

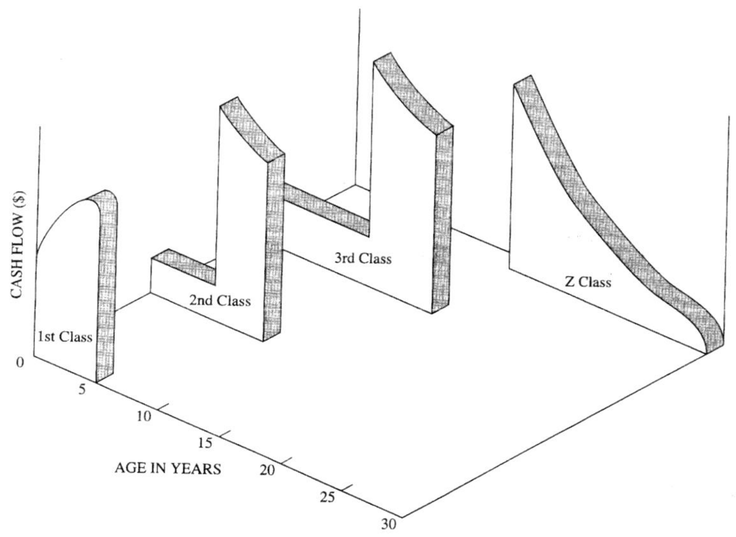

Source: Financial Market Rates and Flows, 5th Edition – Van Horne

5.3.4 Planned Amortisation Class tranches

A planned amortisation class (PAC) tranche is one that is expected to amortise at a rate fixed in advance. If the actual prepayment speed lies within a particular range, the amortisation rate will be achieved. However, if the prepayment speed is significantly different from that expected, the amortisation rate may be faster or slower than expected. Hence, it is not guaranteed.

If the actual prepayment speed is uncertain but one tranche is given a planned amortisation rate within a particular range of prepayment speeds, the amortisation of another tranche must become more uncertain as a result. This is known as the **companion bond**. Other names for it are 'non-PAC' or 'support'.

An alternative to the REMIC is the Planned Amortisation Class bond where profiles are established based upon conservative estimates of prepayment risk capital redemption.

The actual prepayment speed is uncertain, but one tranche is given a planned amortisation rate within a particular range of prepayment speeds; the amortisation of another tranche must become more uncertain as a result. This is known as the **companion bond**. Other names for it are 'non-PAC' or 'support'.

Principal Cash Flows for a PAC and Companion Bond

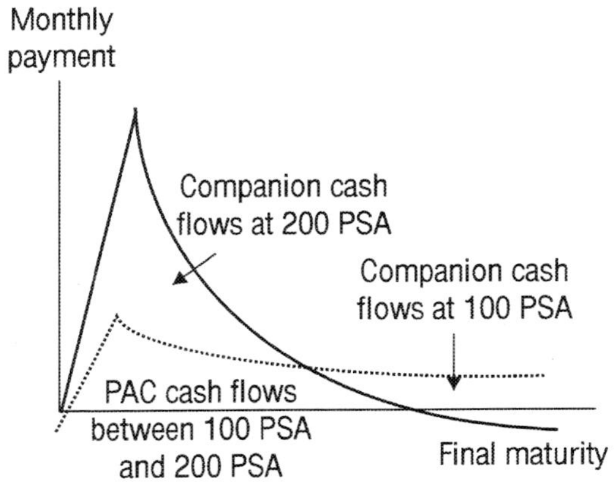

Source: A S Carron

The dotted line shows the total principal repayments with a prepayment speed of 100% PSA. In this case, all of the early principal repayments are used to satisfy the planned amortisation of the PAC. The companion bond has to wait until the end to receive any principal repayments.

The unbroken line indicates the total principal repayments with a prepayment speed of 200% PAC. In this case, more principal is being received in the early years than is required to meet the planned amortisation of the PAC. Any excess is repaid to the companion bond.

Anywhere between 100% PSA and 200% PSA, the planned amortisation can be met. If the speed moves outside this range, however, the PAC investor will not receive the exact amortisation rate desired. The PAC creates more certain cash flows than a sequential pay tranche. The PAC has good average life predictability, while the companion bond has a highly volatile average life.

The certainty of the cash flows to the PAC may vary through the CMO's life. If there are substantial repayments in earlier years, this will mean that all of the companion bond may be paid off. If this happens, then the PAC is exposed to changing prepayment speeds in the future. However, if the level of prepayments is at the low end of the range, this will mean that very little, if any, of the companion bond is paid off. This will build up a cushion for later years, meaning that the range of speeds within which the PAC amortisation can be achieved will widen.

Period	Expected Amortisation of Principal	Amortisation with Slow Prepayment Speed	Amortisation with High Prepayment Speed
1	$5,000	$4,000	$6,000
2	$5,000	$4,000	$6,000
3	$5,000	$6,000	$4,000
4	$5,000	$6,000	$4,000

5.3.5 Targeted Amortisation Class (TAC)

A targeted amortisation class (TAC) is similar to a PAC, except that its targeted amortisation schedule will only be met at one prepayment speed. If the actual prepayment speed is higher than expected, then the TAC will be repaid earlier than targeted. If the actual prepayment speed is lower than expected, the TAC will be repaid later than targeted.

The certainty of cash flows for a TAC is less than for a PAC and it has a more volatile average life. As a result, yields on TACs will exceed yields on PACs.

5.3.6 Security

Investors holding asset-backed securities such as MBS are not protected with any **fixed or floating charge** on the issue's assets, unlike a typical debenture. Instead of offering security, credit risk can be reduced by using a third party to insure against default. In the case of 'Ginnie Mae' – Government National Mortgage Association – the third party is the US government. Alternatively, the MBS may be **overcollateralised**. In other words, the underlying collateral may represent $100m, but the MBS issued may only represent $90m, thus allowing a $10m buffer to guard against default.

5.3.7 Average life

For securities that have a planned amortisation (payment of principal), the **actual** maturity is practically irrelevant to the investor. Instead, the average life (or weighted average life – WAL) is more useful. This measure represents the average time to return a dollar of **principal**. It is calculated by multiplying each portion of principal received by the time at which it is received, and then summing and dividing by the total amount of principal.

Example

Calculation of average life

Time (t)	Principal (P)	T × P
1	40	40
2	30	60
3	20	60
4	10	40
	100	200

$$\text{Average life} = \frac{200}{100} = 2$$

This measure is similar to the Macaulay duration. Duration is calculated in a slightly different way and represents the average time to return a dollar of price, i.e. it incorporates all of the bond's cash flow, whereas WAL only considers principal. Many would argue that duration is a more appropriate measure than 'just' average life.

5.4 Structured debt

Exam tip

Last examined in Summer 2007 Question 11

Structured debt does not have one simple and easy definition, it embraces a wide diversity of structures and instruments.

The asset-backed solutions link the cash flows on the bond to underlying asset/income flows within the borrower. In this ways, they offer a way of significantly reducing the risks faced by the bond holders. For smaller borrowers this issues is particularly problematic and without structured bonds it is unlikely that they would be able to access the market at all, thus condemning them to raise their finance through the banking sector.

Asset-backed bonds began in the mortgage sector but it soon became clear that any stream of cash flow could, as long as it is reasonably reliable, be used to back a bond. The market has expended considerably in recent years to embrace credit cards, car loans and many more diverse income streams (even music royalties).

The traditional securitisation structure allows for different sub classes on bonds to be created. The senior tranches will carry very low variability/risk and will therefore be attractive to conservative investors who are normally active in providing finance to this size of company. The risk is normally borne by the companion or first loss category of bonds. In many instances these will be retained by the borrower. Failing this then the legal structure surrounding the securitisation will also allow for the risk to be retained within the company through the inclusion of guarantees.

Credit-linked notes will conventionally embed some form of credit protection within the bond. This can be by way of a traditional credit enhancement through an insurance contract. Alternatively it can be provided by the inclusion of a credit derivative such as accredit default swap. Once again as with securitisation this has the effect of changing the nature of the exposure and attracting a far wider range of potential investors than would otherwise have been the case.

Traditionally, the analysis of the risk within these small to medium sized entities would have limited the borrowing that they could undertake and constrained their gearing. By structuring the exposure it has enabled borrowers to raise more in the form of debt finance than would otherwise have been the case.

5.5 Hybrid bonds

A hybrid bond is a security that combines characteristics of both debt and equity. Fixed rate hybrids pay a predictable return or dividend until a certain date, at which point the holder has a number of options, possibly including converting the securities into the underlying share. The most common examples of hybrids are convertible bonds and convertible preference shares.

Though hybrids pay a fixed return like bonds, the payments are voluntary. A missed payment does not constitute a default and payments do not normally accumulate if deferred. Like equities, they tend to be irredeemable or very long dated and they rank behind other debt if the company becomes insolvent.

Banks and financial institutions have been using hybrids since the early 1990s for regulatory capital purposes. Issuance, predominantly from banks (in the form of tier one capital – see below), has grown significantly, however the rating agencies' revision of the treatment of Hybrids in 2005 triggered a new wave of interest amongst non-financial issuers.

The motives behind corporate hybrid issues include the following

- Consolidating credit ratings by buying back senior debt.
- Refinancing pension deficits by using the proceeds of the issue to increase the pension fund. This reduces the deficit and, if the hybrid is assessed as partly equity, replacing the pension liability debt will also have a positive impact on the company's credit rating.
- Financing corporate activity such as M&A, share buybacks or LBOs (leverage buy-outs), providing non-dilutive capital and flexibility.

For bond investors investor, hybrids offer higher yields than conventional debt but are not without risk. For equity investors, hybrids provide a tax efficient, long-term source of finance to the company without either the diluting effect of an equity issue or the risk of extra gearing from a debt issue where the coupons cannot be deferred if circumstances dictate. Investors in the equity still enjoy the benefits associated with any improvement in company performance.

6 Corporate Bond Issuers

6.1 Introduction

Corporate bond issuers can be spilt into two broad categories

- Non-Financial Businesses
  - Commercial companies
  - Investment trusts
- Regulated Financial Businesses
  - Banks
  - Building societies/savings banks
  - Life assurers

Irrespective of which category an issuer falls in, the purpose of issuing corporate debt is to raise finance in order to finance the activities of the business without issuing shares. There are a number of advantages to a company of raising finance by issuing debt rather than equity, specifically

- Debt finance, at least at lower debt levels, tends to have a lower cost than equity finance for two reasons
  - Equity represents a higher risk class and hence demands higher returns
  - Debt costs (interest payments) are allowable for tax purposes whereas equity costs are not.

- Issuing debt does not dilute the current shareholders' interests, which may be very important especially in a group situation.
- Issuing debt avoids the legal constraints contained within the Companies Acts on the issue of shares by companies.
- The practical formalities and associated costs of share issues are more onerous than those of bond issues.

6.2 Non-financial businesses

Non-financial corporate issuers that, in the UK, are not subject to the regulation of the FSA are free to raise finance to any level and in any form that they wish subject to satisfying any Stock Exchange listing requirements.

Typically, these entities will look to match the term of any finance to the term of the project that they are raising the finance for. They will tend to finance short-term requirements through bank borrowings, finance longer-term projects through debt (20 year projects through 20 year debt) and finance ongoing business expansion through either long-term debt or equity issues.

In matching the debt to the project being financed, companies will also consider the cash generation from the project and its ability to service the debt finance. For example, if it is anticipated that the initial project returns will be low but will rise later then the issuer may consider a stepped coupon bond.

Companies must, therefore, look to ensure that the cash inflows from any projects financed are of the right scale and timing to service the cash outflows from servicing their finance. Companies that achieve this easily will tend to have a good credit rating and correspondingly low borrowing costs. Companies that struggle to achieve this will have a poorer credit rating and correspondingly high borrowing cost.

6.3 Regulated financial issuers

6.3.1 Introduction

Regulated financial corporate issuers such as banks and building societies tend to be very big issuers of corporate bonds.

The basic business of banking is that banks raises finance as cheaply as possible through the issue of bonds and then lend this money at higher rates to their customers making money on the difference or margin. The profit that banks achieve is, to a very great extent, determined by the size of its loan book and the margin that it is making on those loans.

Banks are, therefore, always looking for ways to expend their loan book and widen their margins. However increasing gearing (the balance between debt and equity) increases the risk of insolvency if, for some reason such as the default of customers, the debt cannot be serviced. A bank collapse would not be in the best interest of either its customers or the economy as a whole.

In the interests of protecting the consumer and the economy as a whole, it is essential to place some constraints on the ability of banks to borrow by issuing debt, and one aspect of FSA regulations is to ensure that banks do this by satisfy the capital adequacy directive as specified now in the Basel II banking agreement.

These capital requirements are very much tied in with the liquidation priority order discussed earlier. Customers who have money deposited with a bank will be regarded as unsecured creditors who will therefore rank at best beside and very possibly below bond holders in the event of liquidation. The greater the debt in issue, the greater this risk to customers (and the economy) becomes.

In outline, what the capital adequacy rules require is a certain balance between the finance and creditors at or above the unsecured level and the finance at lower levels – what may be regarded as a healthy level of gearing.

6.3.2 Basel and the Capital Requirements Directive

Exam tip

> Most recently examined as a Section C question in Summer 2009 Question 9, Summer 2008 Question 13, and a Section A question in Summer 2005 Question 6.

The Basel Committee on banking supervision is a committee of the Bank for International Settlements. The bank's name dates from its original role dealing with war reparations after World War I. Its current role is to encourage co-operation between central banks such as the Bank of England and increasingly other agencies such as our own Financial Services Authority in order to promote international monetary and financial stability.

The Basel committee members are from the G10 countries and in 1988 the committee produced the Basel Accord in response to concerns that banks operating internationally were not always adequately capitalised. The Accord was a voluntary agreement that aimed to strengthen the stability of the international banking system and introduce consistency of regulatory treatment around the world.

The committee issued Basel II, the successor to the Basel Accord in June 2004. This aims to create an even better regulatory capital regime by making risk measurement more sensitive and precise. This will apply in part from 31 December 2006 with some rules following from 31 December 2007

The original **Basel Accord** was legislated by directives issued by the EU. The most important of these, the **Capital Adequacy Directive (CAD)** was introduced in 1993 and amended in 1998 (CAD2). The new version of this directive known as the **Capital Requirements Directive (CRD)** was adopted by the EU in 2006 to deal with Basel II and is due to come in to force in January 2007.

Under the rules of Basel II, banks are required to keep sufficient reserves of capital (capital adequacy) to soak up losses so that depositors can always get their money back and this is subject to regulation by the Financial Services Authority (FSA).

There are a number of key requirements for the capital of banks.

- A bank's capital should be capable of absorbing losses. This means in practice that holders of capital are the last creditors to be paid in the event of a liquidation.
- The capital should have no fixed costs so there should be no contractual obligation to pay dividends. Similarly where certain capital is in the form of debt, interest payments must be capable of being deferred.
- The capital should be fully paid up so that the bank has the funds.

Regulatory capital is defined in the UK in terms of Tier 1, 2 and 3 capital, moving from equity through to various kinds of debt, and it is these levels that the FSA monitors. The FSA also monitors large credit exposures. The bigger the exposure, the more likely it is to threaten the solvency of the bank in the event of default. A bank must notify the FSA if it proposes to enter into a transaction or transactions which would lead to an exposure of 25% of the bank's capital.

Tier 1 capital

Core Tier 1 capital

Tier 1 capital is the highest form of capital of a bank and is regarded by the FSA as broadly equivalent to equity. This means it must be capable of absorbing losses so that the bank can continue trading even if it makes losses up to the value of that capital. The majority of this capital is made up of

- fully paid-up ordinary shares
- irredeemable or perpetual non-cumulative preference shares
- retained earnings (profits taken to reserves after payment of dividends and tax)
- share premium reserve and other disclosed reserves
- minority interest

That is, the capital must be permanent and fully paid so that the bank has the funds indefinitely. In addition, any dividends on this capital must be discretionary so that they can be waived in the absence of distributable profits. This capital is known as core Tier 1 capital.

Innovative tier 1 capital – Preferred securities

Basel II allows banks to hold 15% of total Tier 1 capital in the form of a special kind of debt, and this is known as innovative Tier 1 capital or preferred securities. As it is debt, the bank gets tax relief on the interest payments. This debt will be more attractive than issuing additional shares because dividends paid on share capital are not an allowable tax deduction and increasing share capital decreases earnings per share.

The way preferred securities work for UK banks is as follows

- The bank establishes a limited partnership in, probably, Jersey
- This limited partnership issues the preferred securities to investors, wealthy investors or companies
- The limited partnership then uses all of the proceeds to finance inter-company debt securities issued by the bank.
- The bank pays interest to the limited partnership which services the payments due on the preferred securities.

Using this limited partnership results in the preferred securities being treated as minority interest in the group accounts of the bank which then counts as Tier 1 capital. In addition, the interest paid by the bank can be deducted for tax purposes in the UK.

Tier 2 capital

Tier 2 capital is debt that is other forms of equity not falling within Tier 1 and subordinated debt and includes

- cumulative preference shares
- revaluation reserves (made up of either asset revaluation or unrealised gains/losses on securities)
- subordinated debt
- undisclosed or hidden reserves
- any hybrid (debt/equity) capital instruments

Tier 2 capital is divided into Upper Tier 2 and Lower Tier 2. Upper Tier 2 is any of the above that are irredeemable or undated. Lower Tier 2 capital is redeemable or dated, normally with a maturity date of more than 5 years.

The requirements are that

- Tier 2 capital as a whole cannot exceed Tier 1 capital
- Lower Tier 2 capital cannot exceed 50% of Tier 1

Tier 3 capital

This is the capital that supports trading book activity or foreign currency risk. Broadly it is short- term subordinated debt with a minimum maturity of 2 years. To date, most UK banks do not have Tier 3 capital.

Contingent capital

Following the difficulties of the credit crunch in 2008 the idea of banks issuing contingent capital emerged with some support.

Contingent capital would allow banks to convert debt instruments into equity in an emergency, making it far easier for them to boost their capital holdings during a time when capital markets might have frozen. The idea is that this is much better to convert the debt than let the company collapse. Supporters of this idea believe that with debt holders aware of the possibility debt could be converted into equity would force more market discipline on the major banks.

7 Domestic Corporate Debt Markets

7.1 Introduction

As we noted at the outset, the domestic corporate debt market has been eclipsed by the growth in the issuance of the Eurosterling market. The only borrowers who regularly issue in this market are smaller corporates who do not (for the most part) possess a credit rating or property-based companies who are able to offer security through charges over their property. However, there are signs of a resurgence in interest in domestic debt. Individual Savings Accounts (ISAs) allow the creation of tax-free collective investment vehicles offering the enhanced returns that bonds offer over bank accounts without the risks of equity.

There are also some quasi-debt issues in the UK.

7.1.1 Permanent interest bearing shares/Perpetual subordinated bonds

Permanent interest bearing shares (PIBS) are a form of debt issued by mutual building societies. PIBS from demutualised building societies are known as perpetual subordinated bonds (PSB). As the name suggests, they are perpetual issues with no date for redemption and carry a fixed (or floating) coupon.

7.1.2 Preference shares

Preference shares are a hybrid instrument representing a combination between debt and equity finance.

Preference shares have many of the features of ordinary share capital.

- They are not redeemable, however many stocks have been issued over the last few years which specify either a conversion right, allowing conversion into equity shares, ordinary shares, or have specified a redemption date on which the shares will be redeemed.
- In the event of a liquidation, they rank just above the ordinary shares at the bottom of the list.

However, there are a number of features that make them less like ordinary shares.

- In general, preference shares will not carry a vote, although most company constitutions allow for preference shares being given the vote if dividends are not paid for five years.
- They are preferred over ordinary shares in two important ways.
  - Firstly, the dividend on the preference share must be paid, before any ordinary dividend is distributed. In the event that in a year neither preference nor ordinary dividend is paid then before any ordinary dividend is paid in the future, the preference dividend and any arrears must firstly be paid.
  - In terms of the preference on winding up, once again the preference shares will be preferred over ordinary shares. However, they will only receive the nominal value of each share. Any surplus left after this will go to the ordinary shareholders.

In addition, preference shares have other features that are fundamentally debt driven.

As a rule, the dividend on a preference share is a fixed coupon, for example 7.5 preference stock. This means that the company will pay 7.5% of the face value of the share each year to the holder and that this coupon will be regardless of the level of profits. However, there are certain preference shares that have been issued with a participation right. Under these shares' constitution, any profits over a specified level will be available for distribution amongst all the shareholders of the company – ordinary and preference.

To conclude, preference shares have many of the features of debt and yet carry with them most of the risks of equity. As such they represent a reasonably poor investment.

The saving grace of many preference shares are conversion rights. Many preference shares are issued in convertible form, allowing the holder on specified dates to convert preference shares into ordinary shares which will rank in full for a dividend. As with convertibles, evaluation of convertible preference shares presents a number of difficulties. The simplest, and the most effective, measure will be to treat the conversion right as an option into the equity and evaluate using the normal options models.

As can be seen from the above, preference shares carry the risks of equity with the returns of debt and as such do not represent attractive investment opportunities for individual investors.

However, investors may be drawn to preference shares by virtue of the stability of the earnings pattern that they offer and the potential conversion rights that may be given.

In thinking about preference shares and bonds, though they may have some similar characteristics two important differences are

- preference shares are quoted dirty (bonds use clean prices)
- the quoted preference share dividend is the net dividend, ie. Net of lower rate tax.

7.2 The Bulldog sector

A bulldog bond is a sterling denominated issue made into the UK markets by an overseas borrower. The equivalent market in the US is the Yankee bond market and in Japan the samurai bond market.

The market developed during the era of exchange controls. Under this policy of exchange control, money was in effect locked within an economy, and only limited amounts of currency could flow outside the control of the government. In this environment, if a borrower wished to raise sterling debt then the only option was to issue into the UK domestic market.

The principal issuers in the market place were governments. In particular, the Scandinavian governments raised a considerable portion of their debt through the bulldog market.

7.3 The growth of Eurosterling

The bulldog market, however, became gradually undermined by the growth of Eurosterling. Eurosterling is sterling outside of the control of the UK government. Gradually, during the 1950s and 1960s, pools of sterling began to be held outside the UK and these became the Eurosterling sector, enabling issuers to raise money through the Euromarkets without having to concern themselves about domestic regulation.

The growth of the Eurosterling sector was increased rapidly in 1979 when the government abolished all exchange controls on flows of sterling. At that point, large pools of sterling moved outside the UK into the international market place giving the Eurosterling market a liquidity it had previously lacked. Bulldog bonds have all of the characteristics of Eurobonds. By convention they are bearer and have no withholding tax, paying coupons gross and consequently there is no difference between the two issue styles.

Given the choice after the opening of the exchange controls in 1979, most issuers would choose to use the more liquid, efficient and larger Eurosterling market, than constrain themselves by bulldog bond issues. As a result, issuance in the market has fallen substantially and seems unlikely to rise again. However, there are a number of constraints imposed upon the Eurosterling market by the Bank of England.

Amongst these, an important constraint is that the Bank regards any issuer issuing more than four bonds in a 12-month period as a deposit taker (bank). As such, they need to seek authority from the Bank. One potential solution to this would be for a regular corporate borrower to issue notes under a Medium Term Note programme. However, the Bank initially placed a restriction that the maximum life of paper issued under an MTN be five years. In January 1997, this control was relaxed and now MTNs, in line with the US, are fully flexible with regard to maturity.

Potentially barred from the Eurosterling market, borrowers choose to issue into the other Euromarkets rather than re-enter the domestic markets. Thus, large corporates who may wish to borrow in sterling are often forced to issue in other currencies, and then swap into sterling, in order to circumvent the controls.

7.3.1 Residual bulldog market

There are still Bulldog stocks being actively managed in the market place due to the size and the maturity of the original issues. By convention, UK institutional investors have always tended to prefer longer-dated issues and most of the bulldogs were issued into the 15 to 30-year range. Therefore, many of the issues still have reasonably long maturities and are still traded. This is also a feature of the Yankee market in the US where the investor base remains willing to invest in longer issues than the Euromarket.

7.4 The growth of corporate debt

The past few years have seen a significant change in the usage of the corporate debt markets.

As government bond markets have declined, corporate issuance has risen. In the UK, the size of the corporate bond market is now greater than the size of the gilt-edged market. There are a number of reasons for this change.

- Banks have come under increasing regulation and consequently have been less able to lend from their own balance sheets. It therefore makes sense for them to arrange debt issuance.
- Companies have become increasingly concerned about the efficiency of their capital structure. Much is made now about the Weighted Average Cost of Capital (WACC). In effect, this is an average of the cost of equity and the cheaper cost of debt. Modern valuation theory suggests that companies should endeavour to maximise their return over their cost of capital. Many firms have historically restructured their balance sheets by reducing the equity and increasing their debt.
- Mergers and acquisition activity is further fuelling this need for new debt capital.
- As government bond markets contract, the investment opportunities shrink. Investors are therefore compelled to take an interest in corporate debt. This also fits into the demographic trends currently affecting the pension industry. As the population gets older, pension funds will tend to move towards safer investment categories such as debt.
- Within the Euroland bloc, the advent of the single currency has removed an element of risk (forex risk arising from cross-border investment) and therefore reduced reward. Consequently, investors are seeking extra reward by moving down the credit curve.

These factors have all come together in order to stimulate the increase in issuance that we have witnessed.

7.5 The issuance process

7.5.1 Introduction

If a company wishes to issue its securities to the public it must conform to some basic rules and procedures. Initially, all securities issues are governed by the Public Offers of Securities Regulations (POSRs). However, if a borrower wishes to attract a high level of interest in their issue then they may elect to face a more onerous set of regulations called the **Listing Rules**. These rules were administered by the London Stock Exchange on behalf of the Government. However, given the nature of this responsibility it was felt appropriate to transfer this role (the **UK Listing Authority**) to the FSA. Accordingly, in 2000 the FSA assumed the role of the UKLA and adopted the old listing rules (the "Yellow Book"), now referred to as the "Purple Book".

The style of regulation has switched to a much more informal mode now and issues in excess of twenty million are reported to the British Merchant Bankers Association (BMBA), who operate an unofficial queuing system that endeavours to ensure that two large issues do not hit the market at the same time, since this would obviously impair their ability to place the full value of the stock.

The Bank of England does, however, insist that the lead manager is effective for each issue and this requires them to be organised and managed in the UK or from a country outside, which has reciprocal agreements with UK brokers. The Bank of England also likes to be informed of any unusual features to the issue, so they can ensure these do not in any way imperil the quality of the markets in the UK.

However, as mentioned above, the prime regulatory work rests with the UKLA and their issuance procedures.

The Issuance Timetable

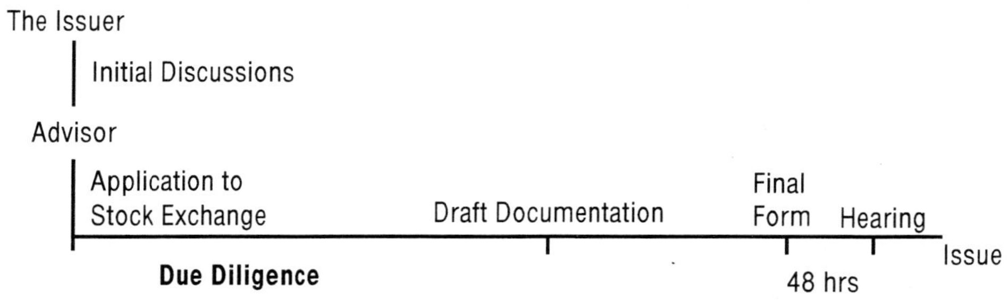

The first step in the process is for the issuer to identify an advisor. This advisor is responsible for ensuring that the obligations of the Listing Rules are complied with and for undertaking the process of due diligence, which means ensuring that the company is fit and proper to enter the market place.

The advisor applies for a hearing date for the issuance of the securities. Fourteen days prior to that hearing, draft documentation is produced, and 48 hours prior to the hearing final form documentation, including any adverts to be published, must be given to the UKLA. The hearing determines whether the company has complied with the obligations of the Listing Rules, and in general terms whether the UKLA believes the company is fit and proper to be part of the market place.

One of the key elements in the listing process is the production of a listing prospectus. This document contains all the information an investor would require in order to make an informed investment decision.

7.5.2 Contents of a Listing Prospectus

- Those responsible for the issuance of the particulars including the directors and, potentially, the Listing Agent. The importance of this is that these parties may be sued as a result of any misleading information within the document.
- The details of the securities that are to be issued.
- Information about the issuer and its current capital structure.
- Recent financial information about the company.
- Information about the activities of the company and the outlook for the future.

In addition to the detailed requirements laid down in the Listing Rules, there is also the obligation to disclose any other information which is relevant to the potential investor.

These contents requirements also apply to Eurosterling issues where a listing is sought on the London Stock Exchange.

Even if a company has complied with the obligations of the Listing Rules in full, it may still be refused admittance on one of two grounds.

- If it is not deemed to be fit and proper by the exchange.
- If it has failed to comply with the rules of another exchange inside the European Community.

If a company is not seeking a listing then they are governed not by the Listing Rules but by the Public Offers of Securities Regulations. These rules are, however, very similar in nature to the Listing Rules and call for the production of a prospectus, which is a document similar in structure to a listing prospectus but contains slightly less detail.

With regard to both a listing prospectus and prospectuses, there are exemptions with regard to the need to produce these relatively expensive documents.

The primary exemption is for the issuance of securities to professionals. This exemption is widely used in bond markets and in many cases no prospectus is produced.

Once permission has been granted for the issue to take place, then the normal issuance form used in the market is that of placement. Under a placing or selective marketing the company's broker undertakes to sell the issue down to underlying clients. This may be exclusively through the company's own sales team or, as in the form of the Euromarkets, it may create a syndicate that will undertake to place the issue.

In common with the equity markets, it may be possible to ensure that the issue is a complete success as far as the issuer is concerned, by obtaining underwriting. With an underwriting agreement, a number of firms agree to subscribe for the debt in the event that the public fails to meet the full allocation. In return for this they receive a fee which is payable whether their services are used or not. There is no obligation on the part of the issuer to elect for underwriting, but if there is no underwriting agreement then the issuer will have to ensure that the issue is priced generously to encourage individuals to purchase the bonds.

7.6 Dealing and settlement

As listed securities, all stocks are available for trading through the Stock Exchange's systems. Any member firm of the exchange may decide it wishes to act as a market maker in any of the stocks. If this is the case, it will then be able to display its prices through the SEAQ Screen Systems. Any firm that elects to become a market maker in this way is obliged to quote a firm two-way price to the market place throughout the trading day, which commences at 08:00 and ends at 16:30.

Due to lack of liquidity in the market place, very few firms are prepared to commit themselves as market makers in sterling corporate debt. However, a number of issues do possess a level of liquidity and therefore have market making interests.

In terms of the investors in the market place, very few individuals venture into this market unless perhaps attracted by the conversion rights given by certain issues. The major investors are the pension funds, insurance companies, building societies, collective investment schemes and financial institutions.

The settlement of bulldog bonds and local authority stocks takes place on the next business day. Domestic corporate bonds are settled using a three-day rolling cycle.

In addition, bulldog bonds may settle through the Eurobond clearing houses (Euroclear and Clearstream) on the three-business-day cycle.

7.7 Taxation

Both local authority issues and domestic corporate issues will pay income net of 20% lower rate income tax. Bulldog bonds, on the other hand, are able to pay coupons gross.

Any overseas investor has the possibility of reclaiming any tax suffered in the UK and pension funds and charities are able to request the payment to income gross.

With respect to capital gains tax, qualifying sterling bonds are exempt from capital gains tax in the same way as gilts. The requirements for qualification are that the bond is issued in sterling and is not redeemable in any other currency and that the bond carries no conversion rights.

There was an attempt to exploit this taxation treatment of the capital gains through the issue of zero-coupon bonds. Zero-coupon bonds carry no coupon right and merely trade at a discount to the final redemption value. This discount in effect is the coupon stream for the bond, but can be seen as a capital gain. Consequently, following basic tax rules, the entire income flow will be seen as a capital gain and therefore free of tax.

HMRC has changed the tax rules to ensure that any income derived in this way is deemed as taxable income and indeed have extended the treatment to deep-discount and deep-gain securities.

A deep-discount security is one where the discount is effectively 0.5% per annum over the life of the bond or 15% of the value in total. Here, this element of a discount is taxed as income in the year in which it is received. Deep-gain securities are redeemable at a premium over the issue price. To qualify as a deep-gain security, the premium must be 0.5% per annum or 15% in total of the value of the bond. As with deep-discount securities, this gain element is treated as income in the year in which it is received.

8 The Euromarkets

8.1 The nature of the market

In essence, the Eurobond market is like any other fixed interest market place. The only real difference is that it is not constrained by any national barriers and is perhaps the only truly global market. The term 'Euro' in this sense is then somewhat misleading and should be replaced perhaps by 'international bonds'.

The market itself is dominated by supranational organisations, governments and highly rated corporate borrowers. The nature of the borrowers and the size of the market have encouraged innovation in the Euromarkets which then filters down into the domestic fixed interest markets.

8.2 The historical development of the market

The Euromarket was formed in the 1960s because of the then pressures in the world capital markets. Since then, many commentators have predicted the demise of the market but this has, so far, failed to materialise.

In the immediate post-war period, the dollar became established as a quasi-international currency, due to its central position within the Bretton Woods system. Investors were keen to hold the dollar and large overseas holdings of dollars started to build up outside the US. This process was accelerated by the start of the Cold War when the Eastern European countries repatriated their dollar assets.

At that time, when most countries had strict currency controls, the American market remained open to overseas investors and borrowers. Given the attractiveness of the dollar, the US Yankee market became an important source of finance to non-US borrowers. However, given the lack of familiarity of the borrowers to the US market, they were obliged to offer slightly higher coupons in order to attract investors.

In 1961, President Kennedy introduced the Interest Equalisation Tax (IET) and exchange controls to stop this huge outflow of dollars from the US. At this point, the conditions for the Euromarket were formed.

- Large pools of dollars held outside the US and therefore beyond the control of the US authorities.
- Borrowers who had been used to borrowing in dollars finding that the conventional market was closed to them.
- The existence in London of a centre where most of the international banks had operations, in a market place which was, at that stage, free of regulatory control.

In these conditions, the IET was simply the catalyst that ignited the market. Since then, despite the removal of the IET, the market has continued to develop. The widespread removal of exchange controls has done nothing to limit this development. Indeed, the removal of exchange controls in the UK, which makes bulldog bonds in effect equivalent to Eurosterling issues, has done nothing to alleviate the decline in that market.

The market that developed in the 1970s and 1980s was primarily driven by the new issue side or the primary market. In recent years, however, the secondary market has become increasingly sophisticated and liquid.

8.3 The primary market

The primary market is the market in which new issues are brought to the public for the first time. As mentioned above, in the Euromarkets it was initially the primary market that was almost the sole concern, with the bulk of issues being traded out in the primary market and very rarely surfacing thereafter. After a number of unorthodox issuance techniques developed in the 1980s, order was brought by the International Primary Markets Association (IPMA), now part of the **International Capital Market Association (ICMA)**.

8.3.1 The International Capital Markets Association

The International Capital Market Association (ICMA) is a body formed to regulate the practice of issuing new securities into the Euromarket. It does so through a rule book that provides recommendations on the way in which issues should be structured and how the timetable of issuance should be dealt with. In the highly competitive markets of the late 1980s, market share counted for almost everything and profitability came second. The market could not function on this basis long term and ICMA's aim was to establish a stable environment in which bonds may be issued.

8.3.2 The borrowers

Access to the Euromarkets is limited to those institutions and companies with high credit ratings. Many governments fund a proportion of their debt through the Euromarkets along with the supranational bodies such as the World Bank and the European Investment Bank, who are the largest individual borrowers in the market.

In addition to governmental bodies, corporates also tap the market. However, as mentioned above, the ability to enter the Euromarket is restricted to those companies with strong credit ratings and in particular the markets tend towards those focused into banking and other financial services sectors.

8.4 The issuance process

Primary market eurobond issuance is through the process of placing. Prior to the actual placing taking place, there are a number of preliminary discussions and clearances that need to take place.

8.4.1 Preliminary discussions

A large borrower will have a relationship with a number of Eurobond houses. The decision to issue can come either from the borrower who perceives the need for finance or from the issuing house who perceives that there is an opportunity to issue a reasonably priced bond into the market. Once the decision has been taken to issue a new security into the market place, the borrower will embark upon a process of negotiating with a number of Eurobond houses.

The purpose of these negotiations is to establish who will be the lead manager or book runner of the issue and also to lay down the basis terms of the bond that will be issued. These terms will include the coupon, the maturity and any covenants that may need to be granted to make the bond acceptable to the market place. In these discussions, the borrower will be able to see the type of debt that they will be able to issue. The lead managers will be able to satisfy themselves that the issue will be a success.

Once both sides are agreed, the issue will proceed. At this stage, the lead manager is awarded the mandate. It may well be the case that the borrower has a relationship with a number of Eurobond houses and in these situations it is common for them to insist that whilst there is one lead manager, there are a number of other co-lead managers who are other banks with whom the borrower has a relationship.

8.4.2 The requirement for listing

Another key decision to be taken at this stage is whether or not to list the Eurobond on one of the various exchanges. Almost inevitably a Eurobond will be listed, normally on either the London or Luxembourg Exchange. The reason for this is that certain institutions and investors by their trust deeds are prohibited from investing in securities that are not listed on a formal exchange and consequently, if Eurobond issuers did not seek a listing, then they would be restricting a demand for their stocks.

A second reason for listing is that it will provide the stock with a fallback should the Euromarkets fail, since as they are listed on a domestic Exchange they will be able to trade in that domestic market.

As mentioned above, new Eurobonds are issued through a process of placing. However, within this general approach to issuance there are a number of variants.

8.4.3 The traditional syndicate method

In the 1980s, when Eurobond issuance began to rise rapidly, a syndicate system of issuance started to develop. This system encouraged a large number of Eurobond houses to participate in each issue. At the head of the syndicate, there would be the lead manager or book runner and potentially a number of co-leads. Below this senior management group there would be the management group made up of a number of Eurobond houses, chosen normally for their ability to place bonds with underlying customers.

Houses would be invited to join the management group in line with their ability to place and the markets to which they had principal access. The invitation to join the syndicate is in the form of the invitation telex, which contains a number of important details of the issue. As a further tier even below this there might be a selling group. A selling group consisted of a number of small houses and banks who were allocated a very limited tranche of the issue to place. Frequently, they were only included in the selling group as a courtesy gesture to the borrower or to other members of the management group.

The grey market

Until recently, there was frequently a considerable period between the announcement of the issue and the actual launch. This period became known as the grey market and participants in the Euromarkets were able to buy and sell the security on an **if, as and when issued** basis. Once the management and selling groups had been established during this grey market, the issue was launched and the bond allocated between the lead managers and the management group and selling group, in line with allotment telexes.

All Eurobond houses receiving stock as part of this initial allotment received a form of concession on the price, with the largest concession being reserved for those brokers taking the greatest proportion of the issue and a special concession being granted to the lead manager, referred to as the **praecipium**.

The primary market

From the launch date, the stock entered what became known as the primary market. The primary market was the period of selling down of the bond and could last up to four weeks. During this period, syndicates that had particularly large selling groups often ran into difficulties.

Institutional investors perceived the selling group was often made up of banks, which themselves had a limited ability to place the bonds. Consequently, the institutions brought pressure on those banks to pass the bonds to them along with a proportion of the selling concession, thereby partially deflating the primary market for other Eurobond houses who were trying to place the stock.

In the mid to late 1980s, the competition to become the lead manager of an issue became so intense that the margins on a bond would frequently be trimmed down to the point where it was uneconomic to purchase it. This led to a fall in the value of the bond as it was launched. However, most mandates contain a clause that oblige the lead manager to stabilise the issue.

Stabilisation

Stabilisation obliges the manager to buy back stock in order to support the price in the market. The lead manager, however, did not have to bear the whole of this cost since they were normally able to reclaim stabilisation costs from the management group in the form of reduced management fees. It was this process of stabilisation and the reduction of management fees that eventually highlighted the uneconomic structure of most Eurobond issues.

Developments

Since the late 1980s, it has been more conventional for Eurobonds to be issued through small syndicates of maybe half-a-dozen Eurobond houses, each of which have a very strong ability to place the stock with its client base. It has also meant that Euro issues have to be more accurately priced and the overly competitive pricing of the late 1980s has to a great extent disappeared, although there are still occasional issues which would seem to reflect the desire for league table position getting the better of economic sense. This growing realism in the Euromarkets has led to an increase in profitability for the issuing houses.

The smaller, more efficient syndicate system now used brings with it one further advantage for the issuer in that it is now possible to issue a Eurobond within a very tight time scale, potentially moving from decision to issue to closing within a matter of days rather than weeks. In addition to the slimming down of syndicates, there are a number of other new features in the issuance process that have added to profitability.

The Traditional Syndicate

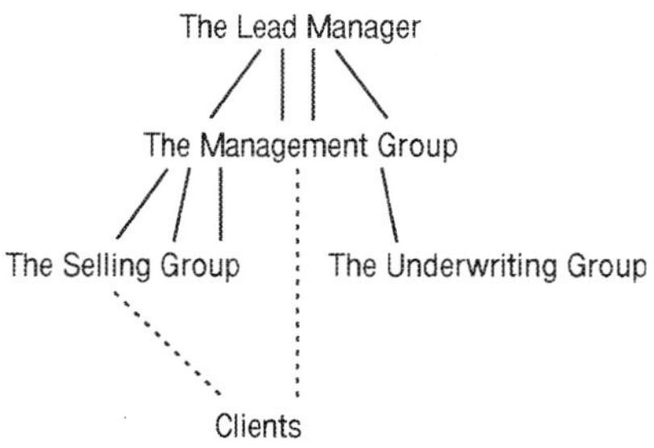

8.4.4 Fixed price reoffers

When IPMA began to introduce rules in order to control stabilisation, the first step was to remove the ability of the lead manager to pass stabilisation costs down to the management group. One way of resolving the problems caused to the lead manager by this was to ensure that the stabilisation need not take place.

Consequently, houses began to use something referred to as the **fixed price reoffer**. The fixed price reoffer states that bonds will not be offered at below the issue price until the syndicate has been broken. The syndicate will be broken when the lead manager believes that the bulk of the issue has been placed.

Obviously, with constraints like this it is important for the other members of the management group to believe that the issue is fairly priced, otherwise they will be left with the stock on their books. This has promoted reasonable and realistic pricing of issues by the lead manager.

8.4.5 Bought deals

Early issues of Eurobonds had been made on an 'open price basis' with the issue terms remaining flexible. The bought deal sets the coupon and issue price at the outset. The obvious risk type of issue is that interest rates will move and thereby leave the issuing house with an 'unsaleable' bond.

With these conditions and the risk taken by the issuing house, it became very important that the issue was placed quickly. Once again, this has led to the formation of smaller, but more powerful, syndicates. In many issues there is no syndicate at all with the bond simply being placed down to clients by the issuing house itself.

8.4.6 New developments

In a move similar to the evolution of bookbuilding in the equity markets, many new issues are aggressively pre-marketed. The issuing house attempts to gauge the markets' appetite for the stock by approaching key clients and attempting to get an indication of interest.

In recent years, this approach has become a part of most issues.

The indications of interest may be firm or simply indicative and give the lead manager some form of guide as to the demand curve for the issue.

More recently still we have seen the development within this structure of the 'pot system'. Under this approach, before allotting securities the lead manager will want to see the order book of the syndicate. Whilst some would argue that this is a logical structure to ensure fair placement of the bonds, others see it as a cynical attempt to gain access to the client base of the syndicate members.

8.5 The secondary market

As mentioned above, the secondary market was initially very limited in many Euro issues. It is still true to say that of the 13,000 or so bonds issued through the Euromarket, no more than a few hundred are actively traded. According to the International Capital Markets Association (ICMA) statistics, over 60% of Eurobonds in issue have fewer than three market makers prepared to trade actively in them.

8.5.1 The International Capital Market Association (ICMA)

The market is governed by ICMA which has been granted designated investment exchange status by FSA. Among its achievements ICMA cites the following.

- The establishment of uniform market practices, which now govern secondary market dealings in the international bond market.
- The introduction of new and standard methods of calculating the yield for international bonds.
- The provision of market information and institutional services to members and the provision of daily electronic and weekly published information.
- The harmonisation of settlement procedures.
- The introduction of annual education seminars.
- The promulgation of recommendations to issuing houses on new issues.
- The maintenance of contracts and information exchanged from central monetary authorities and other regulators.

Certainly over the last few years, ICMA has been able to cultivate an atmosphere of trust in the Euromarkets that did not exist during the 1970s and early 1980s when regulations seemed to be very much a side issue.

8.5.2 The dealing mechanism

The Euromarket is an over-the-counter market place dealing via telephone systems, and using screen information displays through Reuters and Telerate, amongst others. Liquidity in the market tends to be concentrated in the larger issues. Many smaller issues are tied into the swap markets and disappear without trace immediately after issue, only to re-emerge on maturity when they are redeemed.

One method that has been employed to generate a secondary market activity and to enhance the liquidity has been for the issuer to issue a new Eurobond and then follow that up a few months later with a second tranche of the stock into the secondary market. However, regardless of this it tends to be the case that liquidity is focused in those stocks that have just been issued. In order to support this over-the-counter market, the ICMA introduced the TRAX system.

8.5.3 TRAX

The Transaction Exchange System (TRAX) is a real time trade matching and confirmation computer system designed principally for the International Securities Markets. TRAX is a risk management tool designed to eliminate the possibility of costly failed trades by the swift identification of problem trades.

In this system, brokers conducting trades on the secondary market are able to input trade details onto a screen which is then automatically displayed and confirmed by the other party to the trade. Prior to the introduction of TRAX, settlement errors would only be picked up by the two clearing houses and this often resulted in delays of two to three days before problems were resolved. It is an obligation to report trades within 30 minutes.

8.5.4 Coredeal

In the first quarter of 2000, ICMA introduced a screen-based order matching system called Coredeal. This supplements the current role of the reporting dealers with significant volumes of trading.

8.6 Taxation and settlement

8.6.1 Withholding taxes

Since Eurobonds are international bonds and are not issued under the auspices of any domestic economy and therefore are not governed by any domestic withholding tax legislation, all coupons are paid **gross of tax**. This undoubtedly makes Eurobonds tax efficient investments, since the investor receives the gross coupon. The alternative is that the investor receives their coupon net of withholding tax and is then able to reclaim it if he is a non-taxpayer. At present there is some debate within the European Union as to the imposition of withholding taxes. Whilst many nations favour this as a way of combating tax evasion, there are significant concerns with regard to the implications for the UK's position as the key centre for Eurobond trading.

Obviously, in each domestic tax regime the Eurobond interest is taxed in accordance with normal rules.

8.6.2 The clearing houses

Settlement in the Euromarket takes place through two independent clearing houses, Euroclear and Clearstream. Each of these houses was established by a consortium of banks and they both operate the same settlement process with a three-day rolling settlement cycle.

The majority of Eurobonds are immobilised by the two clearing houses and transfers take place through electronic book entry systems. In addition to normal three-day settlement, there is also the possibility of urgent settlement, which takes place on a two-business day basis.

Individual brokers will have accounts with one of the two clearing houses. Trade between brokers operating through different clearing houses is cleared using an electronic 'bridge' for information between Euroclear and Clearstream.

Whilst Euroclear and Clearstream effectively maintain registers of the owners of Eurobonds, these registers are completely outside of the control of governmental authorities.

8.7 Legal form of issue

Most Eurobonds issued are in bearer form. The only real exception to this are bonds that are issued to the US primary market which due to the Tax Equity and Fiscal Responsibility Act (TEFRA) are obliged to be in registered form. Any new issues of bearer bonds are prevented from accessing the American markets (under Regulation 5 of the SEC), until the bond has **seasoned** for a period of 40 days (in Japan the period is 90 days). Innovation in bonds issuance is strong in the Euromarkets and there are a variety of different issues which have taken place.

8.8 Global bonds

With Eurobonds, because of the bearer nature of the instruments, access to certain markets such as the US and Japanese markets is limited, until the **seasoning** period is over.

An alternative is to issue a bond that fulfils all of the local requirements as well as those of the international markets. Global bonds are instruments that fulfil the SEC requirements, and other regime requirements, in addition to the Euromarkets. Consequently, the bonds can be traded around the globe instantaneously.

Global bonds are issued for substantial sums of money and whilst they are undoubtedly more expensive to arrange, they often mean that an issuer will be able to raise all of their required finance in one issue, rather than tapping the market several times.

9 The Differences between the Euromarket and the Domestic Market

	Domestic Market	Euromarket
Size	Small/Medium	Large
Market	Localised	Internationalised
Registered or Bearer	R	B
Withholding Tax	20%	None

The divide between the markets has been blurred over the past few years, particularly in currencies such as sterling. At present, there is little divide between the Eurosterling sector and the domestic market.

Chapter Roundup

You need to be able to

- Describe the characteristics of corporate bonds including
  - coupon types.
  - redemption terms.
  - security.
  - covenants.
- Contrast various methods of credit enhancement, including
  - subsidiary guarantees.
  - monoline insurance.
  - asset backing.
- Describe the characteristics of corporate debt markets.

Test Your Knowledge

Check your knowledge of the Chapter here, without referring back to the text.

Briefly describe the following:

1. The distinction between sinking funds and serial notes.
2. The distinction between a stepped coupon bonds and a step-up clause.
3. Monoline insurance.
4. The distinction between unsecured holding company debt and holding company debt subjet to a subsidiary's guarantee.
5. Asset securitisation.
6. The distinction between a negative pledge and a pari-passu clause.
7. The default rate.
8. Preferred securities issued by financial institutions.
9. PIBS and PSB.
10. Structural financial products.

---

11. Walt Disney is issuing a 100-year dollar denominated bond with a coupon 40 bp above the coupon on the 15-year dollar bond it issued recently. You work for an insurance company and have been asked to explain the reasons why Walt Disney is issuing such a bond and the advantages and disadvantages to investors such as yourselves.

---

12. Your US $ bond fund is considering investing in asset-backed securities such as bonds backed by mortgages, credit card receivables, bank cheques, or pools of non-investment grade corporate debt.

    One example of such an issue is one by the mortgage securitisation arm of XYZ Bank. A recent issue of $700m of residential mortgage-backed bonds was divided into three tranches.

    Class A1 $105m Average life 2.05 years
    Coupon 8 bp over 3-month LIBOR, stepping up to 20 bp over 3-month LIBOR in March 2008
    Call option March 2008
    Issue Price $100.00
    Ratings: Aaa (Moody's), AAA (Standard & Poor's)

    Class A2 $560m, average life 4.97 years
    Coupon 13 bp over 3 month LIBOR, stepping up to 50 bp over 3 month LIBOR in March 2008
    Call option March 2008
    Issue Price $100.00
    Ratings: Aaa (Moody's), AAA (Standard & Poor's)

    Class B $35m, average life six years
    Coupon 27 bp over 3-month LIBOR, stepping up to 75 bp over 3-month LIBOR in March 2008
    Call option March 2008
    Issue Price $100.00
    Ratings: AA– (Standard & Poor's)

    Write a brief report for your manager explaining

    (a) The characteristics and pricing of asset-backed bonds, using the above issue as an example.

    (b) The risks and returns associated with such investments.

Test Your Knowledge: Answers

1. A sinking fund is a process by which a proportion of the bonds in issue are redeemed each year. A serial note is one where a proportion of the capital on each bond is repaid each year. Both have the effect of reducing the total debt capital outstanding though the exact method of achieving this differs. (See 3.5)

2. The coupons on a stepped coupon bond are pre-determined at issue and will rise over the life of the bond in pre-determined steps. A step-up clause will have the effect of increasing the coupon rate in the event that the credit rating falls below a certain level. (See 3.4)

3. Monoline insurance is credit insurance taken out by issuers with poor credit ratings in order to enhance the rating (hence attractiveness and marketability) of an issue. Monoline insurers tend to be AAA rated entities and the effect of monoline insurance is that the issuers debt becomes AAA rated. The cost of the insurance is usually a substantial proportion of the credit sprad. (See 4.4)

4. When a group goes into liquidation the process starts at the bottom (lowest sub-subsidiary) and works up to the top (the holding company). Each subsidiary must be liquidated first and any surplus passed up the group structure with the liquidation of the holding company being the final stage.

   Unsecured holding company debt will, therefore, not be dealt with until the final stage and will only be repaid if there is a surplus at that stage. Holding company debt guaranteed by a subsidiary will be dealt with earlier as part of the winding up process for that subsidiary, being effectively treated as part of the subsidiaries debt. (See 3.8)

5. Asset securitisation is a process by which financial assets (e.g. mortgages, credit card receivables etc.) are transferred into (bought by) a special purpose vehicle (SPV), this purchase being financed by the issue of bonds by the SPV. The coupons and repayment of the bonds are financial by the assets transferred. (See 5)

6. A pari-passu clause ensures that any old lenders are granted the same level of security as that given to any new lender. A negative pledge ensures that any new finance cannot have a better level of security than any existing finance. (See 3.9)

7. The default rate is the rate at which bonds of various credit rating fail to pay coupons or repay redemption proceeds on a timely basis. The default rate is frequently used in the context of credit derivatives in order to quantify the potential risk in the underlying securities. (See 4.5)

8. Basel II allows banks to hold 15% of total Tier 1 capital in the form of a special kind of debt, and this is known as innovative Tier 1 capital or preferred securities. As it is debt, the bank gets tax relief on the interest payments. This debt will be more attractive than issuing additional shares because dividends paid on share capital are not an allowable tax deduction and increasing share capital decreases earnings per share. (See 6.3)

9. Permanent interest bearing shares (PIBS) are a form of debt issued by mutual building societies. PIBS from demutualised building societies are known as perpetual subordinated bonds (PSB). As the name suggests, they are perpetual issues with no date for redemption and carry a fixed (or floating) coupon. (See 7.1)

10. Structured debt represents those bonds that are more sophisticated in their structure than conventional plain vanilla paper. The term embraces asset-backed securities and also bonds with embedded options such as credit linked notes. In essence it is about providing bespoke solutions to the financing needs of companies that often might struggle if they tried to issue plain vanilla paper. (See 5.2)

11. The simple logic behind the Walt Disney Corporation's decision to launch the 100-year issue is to obtain long-term committed and relatively cheap finance. A 40 bp increase in spread to increase the term of finance by 85 years seems attractive from the company's point of view.

This 'cheap' finance will then be used to fund projects whose rate of return exceeds the cost of finance, thereby enhancing the profitability of the firm and the equity shareholders' returns.

By buying this bond the insurance company will be able to lock into a relatively guaranteed cash flow for the next 100 years. Whilst no corporate is ever risk free, companies such as Walt Disney are in secure market positions that should enable them to survive in the long term.

The disadvantage of the bond is that, by virtue of the name recognition that Disney has, the yield spread may have been squeezed to such an extent that the risk/reward trade off on this bond may not be as attractive as the returns available on other less well-known bonds with shorter maturities.

The duration of this bond will be relatively high but probably not that much greater than the duration of the 15 year bond. This, however, may infringe the restriction imposed on the firm's investment powers.

Finally, as with many corporate bonds, this issue is likely to be illiquid. This means that the fund's monies are effectively committed to this investment. As such, the fund may wish to consider shorter dated issues that will at least redeem in the next few years.

12. *Tutor's note: in the exam use a report format when laying out your answer.*

(a) Asset backed securities allow for the conversion of relatively illiquid assets into more liquid securities.

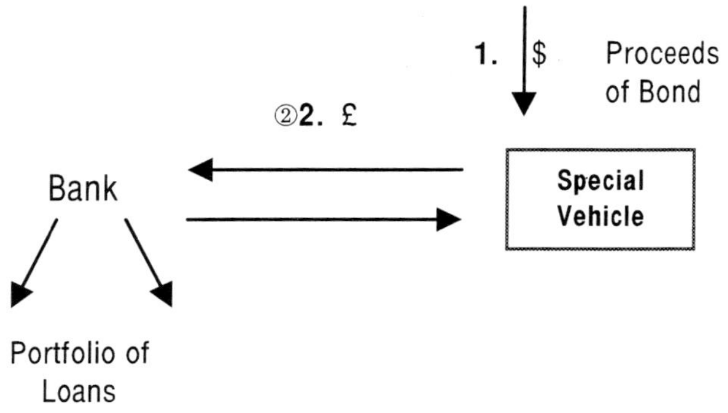

In the above scenario the special vehicle (a shell company) raises funds from a bond issue (1). These funds are then used to purchase a portfolio of financial assets (loans, mortgages or other receivables).

In a simple pass through security any cash generated from the portfolio of assets purchased is then passed through to the bondholders. These types of asset-backed security experience significant volatility with regard to the cash flows received by the bondholders.

In order to minimise these risks to certain bondholders, collateralised mortgage obligations or CMOs were introduced, whereby the bond is split into a variety of tranches. Each tranche is given a different priority within the cash flows.

The two main types are as follows.

- **Sequential Pay Tranches**

  Here the bonds carry a preset coupon (if the portfolio of mortgages, etc. is fixed rate). Any prepayment of capital by the underlying borrowers is initially paid to Category A bonds until they are redeemed. Then Category B bonds are redeemed and so on. The companion class is the last to be paid and therefore bears the greatest risk. Even so, there is volatility for the holders of Category A bonds since they will only be redeemed when repayment takes place.

- **Planned Amortisation Classes**

  In this case there are planned cash flow profiles for different bonds. These profiles are based on conservative assumptions with regard to likely prepayment that should be met. Once again, there will have to be a companion class that carries the risk of uncertainty.

Using the example of the XYZ Bank mortgage-backed bond, we can see different tranches with different expected lives. The different credit ratings reflect the different exposures to default. With the first two tranches being redeemed first the credit risk is borne by the third tranches. In addition, the bonds are floating rate with step-ups in 2004. The initial spreads reflect the cash flow risk.

	Spread	**Step-Up**
A	8 bp	20 bp
B	13 bp	50 bp
C	27 bp	75 bp

An additional risk is presented by the call provisions that exist on these bonds in 2008.

(b) The principal risk associated with MBS securities is that of prepayment.

- **Contraction risk**

  Earlier than expected redemption of the mortgages.

- **Extension risk**

  A slower redemption profile than expected therefore extending the average life.

In addition, subject to the existence of any guarantees, there will be the risk of default. In general, this will be borne by the companion class.

With regard to the XYZ bank issue, as noted above, there are further risks contained in the floating rate nature of the bonds, and in the call options which are exercisable in 2008, when the step-ups are programmed to begin.

The returns should price in these risks, by offering a suitable spread over the equivalent maturity government issue. Whilst these bonds are not normally as risky as conventional corporate debt, due to their asset backing, there are risk factors that must be reflected in the price.

6 Money Markets

INTRODUCTION

Money market instruments represent a source or store for short term cash. Money market instruments are short dated and have very low volatility. They should be regarded as a very safe asset class.

We need to be familiar with the types of fixed interest instrument available in these markets and how the instruments may be used by central banks as a tool for managing their monetary policy.

CHAPTER CONTENTS

CHAPTER LEARNING OBJECTIVES

The syllabus areas covered by this section are

Economics

Students should be familiar with the operations and responsibilities of central banks and national treasuries in the management of the economy and, for those markets for which detailed knowledge is required, possess a knowledge of operations to manage monetary and fiscal policy. A knowledge is also required of the influence of supranational institutions such as the IMF, BIS and EU.

Knowledge of money markets will be limited to the activities of the authorities in the management of interest rate, exchange rate and monetary policy and implications for prices of securities and financing positions.

Government Securities Markets

Students should possess a detailed knowledge of the government securities markets of the UK, US, Japan and Euro and knowledge of the practices and conventions in the Australian and Canadian government securities markets. Beyond a knowledge of their existence and relative size this need not extend to agency, government sponsored enterprise, mortgage or corporate bond markets outside the UK. Students should be familiar with:

- Regulatory Authorities
- Methods and types of Issuance
- Withholding Taxation
- Secondary Market
- Structure
- Dealing Practices
- Price Transparency
- Transaction publication
- Settlement and Custody Practices
- Funding
- Repo/stock borrowing

For the four detailed markets, knowledge should extend to securities which are anomalous for specific reasons e.g. FOTRA or strippability. Students should be aware of the procedures for stripping securities and the implications for rump issues. Students should be aware of the existence of cash – derivative arbitrages and their potential impact upon market price behaviour. Students should be able to calculate the cash/futures price relationship. Students should be familiar with the taxation of UK residents and the taxation of non-residents in the other three detailed markets.

1 The Nature of the Market

The money markets are the focus for trading in short-dated (conventionally with maturities of under one year) interest bearing products and hedging instruments. The market itself is a complex intermeshed structure with a wide variety of instruments.

2 The Instruments

As mentioned above, the normal definition of money market instruments encompasses any instrument with a maturity of under one year. However, in reality, longer dated instruments can come under the aegis of the market. Given the short maturities of the instruments, there is a tendency for them to be discount securities, issued at a discount to par rather than carrying a coupon. However, some securities with a maturity of over one year pay annual coupons.

Whilst it is possible for some of the securities to be in registered form, the conventional approach is for these securities to be in bearer form. The security problems that this raises are normally dealt with through the use of computerised book entry systems.

2.1 Deposits

2.1.1 Introduction

The simplest of all money market instruments is cash. In the deposits market, banks simply take and lay off deposits from each other.

The market is liquid over a wide range of maturities, although primarily less than one year.

Interest is computed on a simple basis, i.e. no compounding for periods less than 12 months. For example, for a £1m deposit for three months (91 days) the interest @ 10% would be

$$£1,000,000 \times 0.10 \times \frac{91}{365} = £24,931.51$$

In the UK, the day count convention is Actual/365, this is also basis adapted by Australia, Canada and New Zealand. Most other markets use the convention of Actual/360. Note this is invariably at variance with the accrued interest convention used in the bond markets where the compound interest approach is applied.

2.1.2 Eurosterling

The historical development of the Euromarkets

In the immediate post-war period, the dollar became established as a quasi-international currency, due to its central position within the Bretton Woods system for foreign exchange rate control. Investors were keen to hold the dollar, and large overseas holdings of dollars started to build up outside the US. This process was accelerated by the start of the 'cold war' when the Eastern European countries repatriated their dollar assets.

The international or 'euro' dollar market gradually evolved from these deposits. London, by virtue of its position as an international banking centre between the two time zones, became the natural home for this market.

Whilst it is possible that there will be a discrepancy between the domestic and the euro rates, due to differences in supply and demand conditions in the markets, normally a process of arbitrage should alleviate relative surpluses and shortages.

With regard to sterling, and most other major currencies, due to the existence of tight exchange controls that prevented currency from leaving the UK, the development of a eurosterling market was limited.

The removal of exchange controls in 1979 has meant that there is no real difference between domestic and international sterling and, consequently, the eurosterling market remains small.

2.1.3 Interbank rates

It is from this, primarily interbank market, that key reference interest rates are produced. To date, the key reference rate has been the **London Interbank Offered Rate (LIBOR)**. Thus far, due to the dominance of London as an international banking centre, rate fixing has not been limited to sterling, extending to most internationally traded currencies. Consequently, many floating-rate deals have been priced off LIBOR rates set in London.

With the advent of the euro, this dominance is under threat. This is particularly true with regard to the establishment of key euro reference rates. The key rival to euro LIBOR is **Euribor**, which is established on the basis of a wider range of quotes from a predominantly Euroland pool of banks. It remains to be seen which rate will be most popular as the basis for trading. However, Euribor starts with several key advantages.

	Euro LIBOR	EURIBOR
Panel	16 major banks active in the euro market in London	Currently 43 banks active in the Euro Zone Money Markets.
Calculation Basis	Discard top and bottom 4 Average remainder	Discard top and bottom 15% Average remainder
Time of Fixing	11:00 London time daily	11:00 CET daily

2.2 Treasury bills

2.2.1 Introduction

A Treasury bill is a promise to repay (**a promissory note**) a set sum of money by the Treasury (via the Bank of England) at a specified date in the future, normally not longer than 91 days.

T-bills are issued by way of a weekly auction and trade at a discount to their face value. Unlike gilts, they are not part of the government' s funding programme per se, but are much more an instrument of monetary policy. The principal use of T-bills is to drain liquidity from the market, thereby making it easier for the authorities to conduct their open market operations pursuant to establishing the interest rate.

The principal measures used to evaluate T-bills are as follows.

Formula to learn

$$\text{Discount rate} = \frac{100 - \text{Discounted value}}{100 \times {}^{\text{Days}}\!/_{365}} \times 100$$

Formula to learn

$$\text{Yield} = \frac{100 - \text{Discounted value}}{\text{Discounted value} \times {}^{\text{Days}}\!/_{365}} \times 100$$

The yield can also be arrived at through the discount rate.

Formula to learn

$$\text{Yield} = \frac{\text{Discount rate}}{1 - \left(\text{Discount rate} \times {}^{\text{Days}}\!/_{365}\right)}$$

Example

91-day Treasury bill issued at 98.

The discount rate

$$\frac{100-98}{100\times {}^{91}\!/_{365}} = 0.0802 \text{ or } 8.02\%$$

The interest rate or yield

$$\frac{100-98}{98\times {}^{91}\!/_{365}} = 0.0818 \text{ or } 8.18\%$$

Alternatively, using the discount rate

$$\frac{0.0802}{1-(0.0802\times {}^{91}\!/_{365})} = 0.0818 \text{ or } 8.18\%$$

It is conventional for bills to trade on the discount rate and this requires the holder to convert to the yield in order to compare with other investments.

2.3 Bills of exchange

2.3.1 Introduction

A bill of exchange is an instrument that is drawn and issued by the seller of goods to the buyer, specifying an amount to be paid either immediately or at some particular date in the future. Once the bill has been accepted by the buyer (by stamping and signing the reverse), i.e. the buyer formally acknowledges the obligation to pay the amount stated, the bearer of the bill is entitled to the proceeds at maturity. The accepted bill may then be discounted, provided the purchaser is willing to take on the credit risk of the bill's acceptor, which is the promise of repayment.

During the 18th century, the practice developed of banks adding their own acceptance to a bill, particularly for foreign trade, which effectively provided the holder with a guarantee of repayment. As this was being done for merchants, the banks in this line of business became known as merchant banks and later formed a group known as the Accepting House Committee, which has evolved into today' s London Investment Banks Association. These guaranteed bills are referred to as 'bank bills' or **'bankers acceptances'**.

If the accepting bank is one of a list of approximately 168 'eligible' banks, maintained by the Bank of England, then it becomes an **eligible bill**.

Whilst it is possible to trade non-eligible bills, the market is limited by the fact that the Bank of England will only trade in eligible bills. This therefore restricts the bills that the discount houses can repo with the bank.

The other prime conditions required by the Bank of England for eligibility are that

- It be drawn in sterling.
- Has a maximum maturity of 187 days.
- Is payable within the UK.
- May not be accepted by a bank that has a direct link with the drawer.

Clausing on a bill

A further condition imposed on a trade bill in the UK is that it must have an underlying commercial substance. The idea behind this is that the bills must not be used as financing instrument other than for working capital. For example, the Bank is prepared for bills to be 'secured' against the receipt of a cash flow under a particular contract (as we saw in our initial description above, this is the way that bills started).

Bills can now be drawn against contracts in general, but not used as a means of creating pure finance for long-term acquisitions. For example, a company may have several contracts that will generate funds in the future. They will be able to draw a bill on their bank (subject to having arranged a facility) with regard to this sum and discount this in order to receive value now rather than later. In the US, the regulation requires that commercial bills be based on specific contracts and this restrictive approach led to the creation of the commercial paper market.

2.3.2 Commercial paper

Many companies began to appreciate that their name was strong enough to enable them to issue discount securities without the need for a bank guarantee. This led to the emergence of the commercial paper market. Commercial paper is simply a promissory note issued at a discount to the face value with maturities normally up to 12 months.

It may be issued via the auspices of a bank guaranteed programme or directly into the market.

2.3.3 Medium term notes

Medium term notes (MTNs) are not strictly a type of security, but rather a facility enabling the issuer to issue a range of stock from one global facility. In the US, the facility can cover maturities of between one-year and 30-year debt. Until recently, the Bank of England imposed a five-year limit on the range of instruments available within a facility – this has now been removed.

The convenience to the issuer is that through one piece of documentation, it is able to issue a variety of paper, thereby saving on issuance costs and enhancing flexibility.

2.4 Certificates of deposit

2.4.1 Introduction

A certificate of deposit (CD) is in effect a securitised bank deposit. Ideally, banks would like to be able to take deposits from customers on the understanding that these deposits would not be repayable within the short term. However, investors are either unwilling to commit their funds for specified time periods (time deposits) or demand too high a premium.

The resolution to this dilemma came in the 1960s with the creation of certificates of a bank deposit that was committed for a period of time. Such certificates carry a fixed coupon rate and have a maturity of up to five years, more normally one year or less. Like any other security, the certificate can be traded enabling the deposit holder to realise the deposit through the sales proceeds and not by withdrawal.

Conventionally, CDs are issued by highly rated banks and therefore carry a limited credit risk. Whilst, unlike the other money market instruments, they do carry a coupon, this is only paid on maturity. The exception to this is that any CD with a maturity of over one year will pay an annual coupon out to the holder.

Once issued, CDs trade on a yield basis. That is to say the amount that is to be paid for the CD means that, given the fixed coupon, the new purchaser will generate the yield at which it is trading.

2.5 Short gilts

With their status as relatively risk-free investments, the money market also trades short-term (normally in market terms with less than five years to go to redemption) gilts. The discount houses are deemed to be market makers in short-term gilts.

In particular, the banks, who are obliged to hold a proportion of their assets in the form of liquid investments, are active in the short gilts market. This is because, whilst offering a competitive return, the gilts are also highly liquid, enabling the banks to swiftly realise their positions if so required.

2.6 The repo market

Exam tip

Questions in this area have become quite common and frequently involve some calculations along the lines of the illustrations shown, see Winter 2008 Question 3, Summer 2007 Question 2, Summer 2006 Question 2, Winter 2004 Question 3, Winter 2002 Question 6.

2.6.1 Introduction

On 1 January 1996, the Bank of England introduced an open repo market in the UK, bringing the UK into line with the other major government bond markets in both America and continental Europe.

In essence, a repo is a relatively straightforward and simple transaction. The term 'repo' stands for 'sale and repurchase agreement' and, in its basic form, is not vastly dissimilar to pawnbroking.

Effectively, the holder of an asset (in this case, a bond) approaches somebody who has excess cash (the pawnbroker or repo house) although, as we will see later on, the repo house itself is simply a reflection, perhaps, of savers elsewhere in the financial system, such as the institutions. The holder of the bond sells their asset to the pawnbroker and receives cash in return. This sale, however, is not an outright sale. What it represents is a conditional sale for, at the same time as the sale and passing of cash takes place, a repurchase is agreed. This repurchase takes place at a second date and at a different price. The price differential reflects an interest cost to the borrower of the funds calculated using the local money market convention. As with pawnbroking, the longer the term of the loan, the higher the mark-up in the final price to reflect greater interest cost.

Equally, following our analogy with pawnbroking, if the repurchase transaction is not fulfilled, i.e. the original bondholder does not repurchase their bond on the pre-set date at the pre-set rate, then the bond becomes the property of the pawnbroker and they can then sell the bond in order to release their cash. In effect, what they have made is a **collateralised loan**. Default on the repayment simply means that the collateral reverts to the lender, allowing them to release their funds.

In basic terms, there are two types of repo transaction. The simplest form of transaction which we will cover is a sell/buyback arrangement. As we will see, there are a number of structural difficulties involved in this type of operation. More conventionally, there are also what we would term classic repos, which are specific instruments designed to overcome some of the shortcomings of sell/buybacks.

Finally, there is a further type of transaction (stocklending), which in many ways replicates one of the aspects of the repo market.

2.6.2 Sell/Buyback

Sell/buyback arrangements are the simplest type of repo transaction and simply involve the creation of two deal tickets – an initial sale ticket, selling the bond to the lender, with a post-dated buy ticket agreeing to buy the bond back at a date in the future. The difference in the two prices represents the repo interest on the loan of cash. Other than these two tickets, there is no formal documentation for sell/buyback arrangements and, in that sense, they are regarded as being simpler and more convenient. Equally, a firm's systems will not have to be amended in order to take account of the transactions, since effectively all you have are two straightforward trades that can be booked in the normal fashion.

Example

A is the owner of £5m nominal of Treasury 7½% stock currently priced at £98.531250 carrying 45 days' interest (based on a 181-day coupon period). A sell/buyback is arranged with B for 31 days at a rate of 6%.

Current value

	(£)
Current clean price £5m @ 98.531250 =	4,926,562.50
Accrued interest $£5m \times \frac{0.075}{2} \times \frac{45}{181} =$	46,616.02
Current dirty price	4,973,178.52

This value of £4,972,795.38 is, therefore, the principal value of the loan. Interest on this will, therefore, amount to

$$£4{,}973{,}178.52 \times 6\% \times \frac{31}{365} = £25{,}342.77$$

Consequently, the amount to be repaid in a month's time is

	(£)
Current dirty price	4,973,178.52
Future interest (next 31 days)	+ 25,342.77
Future dirty price in 31 days	4,998,521.29

This interest must then be reflected in the second deal which then returns the stock to the original owner. In terms of the forward price booked onto the dealing ticket this will give

	(£)
Future clean price in 31 days	4,919,792.01
Accrued interest: $£5m \times \frac{0.075}{2} \times \frac{45+31}{181} =$	78,729.28
Future dirty price in 31 days	4,998,521.29

This final price represents the effective forward clean price taking into account the interest on the 'loan' of cash and the accrued interest.

Disadvantages of sell/buyback transactions

Whilst it may, on the face of it, appear that having no special documentation requirements or systems requirements might make sell/buyback transactions attractive, there are a number of difficulties that go along with this simplicity. Firstly, the lack of formal documentation creates a number of different legal problems. One of these is associated with the payment of coupons.

The essence of all repo transactions is that the ultimate ownership of the bond, subject to the repayment of the principal, remains with the underlying holder. In effect, the person who uses the pawnbroker still has the underlying asset until they default. If a sell/buyback transaction overlaps a coupon payment, there are a number of issues that need to be raised.

Technically, under a sale and buyback agreement, the legal ownership has been passed to the lender and, therefore, they would be the recipient of the coupon. In economic terms, however, the real ownership of the coupon still lies with the borrower and it would be important to ensure that the pricing of the forward trade is also priced in any coupon that should have been, or was, received during the term of the loan.

A second issue that arises from the lack of documentation in these situations is that of security and margining. As we will see, one of the virtues of a formal repo transaction is that there will be a degree of security in the form of margining. Margining can take place even in the context of sale and buyback transactions. The way in which margining would work in this situation is that, rather than lending the whole value of the bond at the outset, the lender may choose to pass over only a proportion of the value, perhaps, for example, 98% of the face value is passed over in loan.

This would then give the lender a greater level of collateral than the loan made and would protect them against adverse price movements in the collateral itself. The underlying price movement in the collateral is only a risk if the borrower fails to pay up on the final date and the collateral becomes the definitive legal possession of the lender.

More formalised repo transactions will allow not only for margining at the outset, referred to as the **initial haircut**, but also throughout the life of the contract.

A final weakness with sale and buyback transactions is that, by their nature, they must be for a fixed term. The deal is struck and the set date for redemption is set. A large proportion of the outstanding repo market in the US is undoubtedly driven by open repos where the agreement exists and can then be terminated at will by either party. Without such notice of termination, the deal simply rolls over on an overnight basis. Therefore, whilst there are a number of significant advantages in simplicity in the documentation behind sale and buyback agreements, there are also significant weaknesses and, as a consequence, it is recommended, certainly by the authorities in each of the major markets, that a more formal and **classic repo** be entered into.

2.6.3 The classic repo

The classic repo is a sale and repurchase agreement and, in that sense, is no different from a sale and buyback. However, rather than being entered into as two separate but linked trades, a repo is one trade drawn up within the context of its own legal framework. The convention in most major markets is to use the PSA/ISMA master legal agreement, as amended in the gilts market by an appendix relevant to the UK gilts industry.

The advantages of this formal legal documentation are many.

- The agreement can lay down the basic events of default and the remedies available to either party in the repo.
- The agreement can allow for a number of enhancements with regard to margining. In particular, it can allow for intra-contract margin calls where, for example, if the value of the collateral backing the repo has fallen, the lender can demand an increase in collateral held to protect themselves against risk. Vice versa, if the value of the collateral has risen, the borrower can take back a proportion of the collateral which has, to date, been locked away.
- The documentation may provide for greater surety and segregation of the assets involved. As we will see later on, there are a variety of different repos, ranging from delivery to hold in custody repos that have different levels of security attached to them.

The basic trade

In essence, the nature of the repo trade is not vastly dissimilar from sale and buyback. There are two legs to the trade, however, there is only one deal. The initial leg passes the bond in receipt for cash in much the same way that the initial bondholder's sale would have realised the cash value of the investment. Within the context of a normal repo, it is at this stage that the first margin is taken out in the form of an initial haircut in that the amount of money lent against collateral will seldom, if ever, be 100% of the value of the bonds.

The haircut taken will depend on a number of factors – the quality of the collateral, the quality of the counterparty and the term of the repo.

General collateral repos

A general collateral repo is a repurchase agreement in which the lender of funds is willing to accept any of a variety of Treasury and other related securities as collateral. The lender is primarily concerned with earning interest on their money and having possession of assets that can be sold quickly in the event of a default by the borrower. Interest rates on overnight general collateral repos on Treasury securities are usually quite close to rates on overnight loans in the federal funds market. This reflects the essential character of a general collateral repo as a device for borrowing and lending money.

Special collateral repos

A special collateral repo is a repurchase agreement in which the lender of funds designates a specific security as the only acceptable collateral. Special collateral repos are generally used to borrow specific securities needed to deliver against short sales.

Other features

As with the sale and buyback, the repo rate is established at the outset. However, the term itself need not necessarily be set at this point. Indeed, as mentioned before, a large proportion of outstanding repo business is on a rolling basis, whereby the term is overnight and the assumption is that the loan will be renewed each day unless either party to the trade wish to leave the market.

Example

Trade date 19 January, value date 20 January. XYZ & Co repos £100m Trs 7.5% stock (with 69 days accrued, 183 days between coupons) for one month (31 days) at 4.75% repo rate.

Clean price	99.2500
Accrued interest $100 \times \frac{0.075}{2} \times \frac{69}{183}$	1.4139
Dirty price	100.6639

20 January

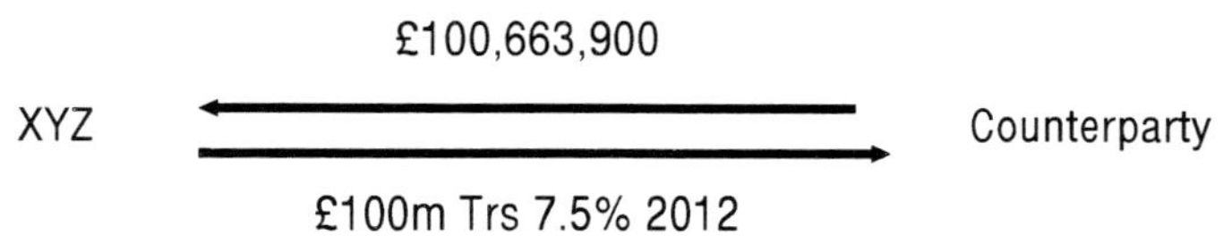

20 February

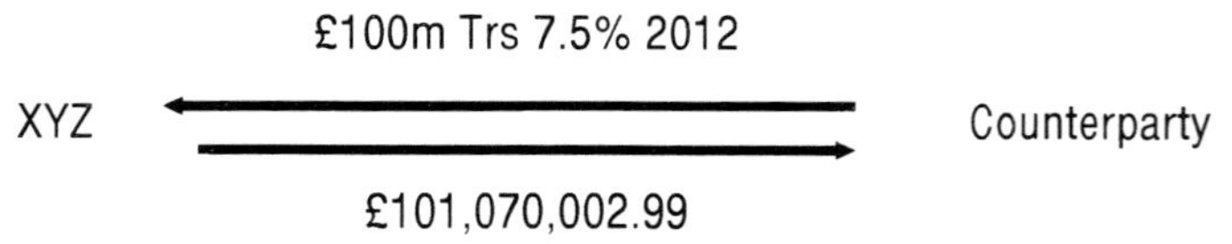

Repo interest at 4.75% for 31 days is

$$£100,663,900 \times 4.75\% \times \frac{31}{365} = £406,102.99$$

Returnable cash = £100,663,900 + £406,102.99 = £101,070,002.99

Whilst rolling repos are, perhaps, the most common form, it is equally possible to have term repos and, if one were to enter into a term repo using the same information as we had for the sale and buyback, the structure of the deal would broadly be very much the same. The initial leg of the transaction would involve the borrower passing the bond to the lender in exchange for a cash payment. This cash payment would represent a proportion of the face value of the bond. Then, at the end of the specified term, the borrower would pass the cash back to the lender, along with the repo interest (again, calculated on a daily basis) and, in return, the borrower would receive the bond back.

We noted above that there was a significant weakness with sale and buyback arrangements when the loan extended over a coupon date, in that the coupon would go to the lender but, in truth, belonged to the underlying holder. One of the advantages of formal repo arrangements is that the repo agreement itself will contain terms requiring that all coupons received during the term of the repo are immediately passed to the underlying owner and not, as is the case with sale and buyback, wrapped up in the final settlement price.

It is in the area of risk that classic repos possess the greatest advantages over sale and buyback arrangements.

The risks of repo and margining

From the point of view of the lender, a repo is a simple loan transaction. They lend their surplus cash in return for interest and are supported as collateral by the holding of the bond during the life of the contract. As with any loan, the principal risk taken by the lender is that of a **counterparty risk** in that they have lent money to an individual or institution and there is always the risk of default in that they will not repay. This counterparty risk is, to some extent, minimised in the repo transaction by the passing of collateral and, in this sense, the lender then obtains an element of **market risk**. This market risk arises from the fact that the underlying assets may deteriorate to such an extent that, should the counterparty fail on the repayment date, then the lender would be left with insufficient collateral compared to the amount of the loan.

This is why repo arrangements allow for ongoing margin calls to be made against the borrower.

Initial margins

As mentioned above, initial margins will be taken out in the form of a haircut on the original loan given against collateral. These haircuts will reflect a number of factors.

- The credit rating of the supply of collateral to, in part, reflect the counterparty risk that exists.
- The term of the repo.
- The maturity of the collateral and its underlying duration and, therefore, sensitivity to interest rates.
- The scarcity of the collateral.
- The legal agreements supporting the repo for, if there is a legal agreement allowing for variation margin, the initial margins do not have to be too punitive.

Variation margin

Variation margin will allow for the collateral to be marked to market throughout the life of the repo. This may be on a daily basis or it may be at specific dates throughout the term of the repo. Many agreements will specify a frequency of marking to market and, indeed, within this, a level of variation requiring that within small tolerances, even where the collateral falls in value, no additional margin is required to be put up, reducing the transaction costs.

The availability of variation margin obviously reduces the level of credit risk that exists on repo transactions. Whilst there is still counterparty risk, the variation margin should ensure that the collateral more than repays the principal of the loan.

The term of repos

As with most money markets, the terms available are varied, ranging from overnight repos to term repos, going out as far as one year and, potentially, further. The vast majority of activity tends to be condensed around the one day to six months time range. Again, as mentioned earlier, the market contains a significant amount of open repo business, whereby there is no specified redemption date set at the outset of the contract. The contract simply rolls until either party decides to terminate the arrangement.

In addition to term, i.e. fixed term repos and open repos, there are also **flex repos**. Flex repos have a fixed term and, indeed, a fixed repo rate. The difference here is that the amount of drawdown is determined by the borrower as and when they see fit. For example, under a flex repo, a borrower may be given a facility to borrow against collateral at 6% for the next six months. This facility may extend to the level of £10m and can be drawn down as and when the borrower wishes to raise the finance.

The nature of custody and collateral risk

Thus far, we have seen that the collateralisation of a repo tends to mean that there is a lower degree of risk attached to the lender in this process. However, much depends upon the nature of the collateral and the way in which it is held.

Delivery repo

By far the safest form of repo is a delivery repo, under which the stock is actually delivered to the account of the lender, thereby ensuring that they have absolute control over the collateral. This will be important in certain repo transactions where the intent of the lender is not simply to lay off excess funds, but actively to borrow the stock in question. In that situation, they will need to have delivery in order to obtain the stock that they require.

Hold-in custody

A riskier form of repo is a hold-in custody repo, whereby the collateral is not delivered by the borrower, but simply held within their own books and records in a separate custody account. In colloquial terms, this is often referred to as a 'trust me' repo.

In many ways this is unsatisfactory, since the lender has no control over the collateral and does, in very simple terms, have to trust the borrower's integrity. This has, in the past, led to a number of situations where repo transactions have been abused. The most obvious fraud here being to use the same collateral for several repo loans, effectively gearing the book up substantially using the funds raised in this way to speculate on the market and, hopefully, to win.

The risks associated with hold-in custody repos are commensurably greater and, therefore, the rewards offered must be higher and the rates will tend to be above the inter-bank rates. As we will see later on, in general terms for most repo transactions, the rates would tend to lie below the inter-bank rate, reflecting the collateralised nature of the loan and its higher degree of safety.

Whilst hold-in custody has a lack of appeal in many respects with regard to safety, in certain situations, such as unsecuritised mortgages and direct loan books, there is no alternative, since the legal transfer cannot be effected and unwound in the same way as securities backed repos. However, the repo lender must take the nature of collateral risk here into account when pricing the spread over the inter-bank rates.

Safe-keeping repo

One step on from the hold-in custody repo, but not quite the full level of the delivery repo, a safe-keeping repo transfers the collateral into the lender's name in a segregated account at the borrower's bank or custodian. The involvement of the third party generates a greater level of satisfaction and safety from the point of view of the lender in the repo transaction but, of course, there are still fears. In particular, fears of collusion between the borrower and their custodian.

Tri-party repo

One way of avoiding these fears would be to establish an independent third party who would receive the collateral and maintain it for the underlying lender. There are a number of cost advantages to be derived from tri-party repos and, from many lenders' point of view, it avoids the unnecessary paperwork of actually receiving delivery whilst effectively achieving the same level of control.

2.6.4 The reverse repo

Thus far, we have consciously been focusing on the repo transaction as a way of borrowing money. Anybody doing the repo is selling a bond in order to gain cash now. They are obliged to pay that cash back in the future with interest in order to release their collateral. This is, undoubtedly, the biggest element of the international repo market, allowing the big securities houses to finance their inventory in bonds, buying the bond and then 'repoing' the bond out in order to get back the cash. This cash can then be reutilised buying more bonds which, in turn, can be 'repoed', and so on and so forth, gearing up the house's position.

Thus far, we have referred to the other side of the repo as the lender of cash. In technical market jargon, the borrower is doing the repo and the lender is doing the reverse repo. In the reverse repo, the lender receives the stock in exchange for cash. They then receive the cash back and pass the stock back.

It is in this sense that the repo market can be perceived in part to be a stock borrowing market for the lender of cash, i.e. the person taking out the reverse repo, is, in effect, borrowing the stock and the nature of the agreement is that they will, effectively, have ownership rights over that stock (depending on the type of delivery given) until the repo is unwound.

Repo as stock borrowing

Stock borrowing is essential where a securities house has taken a short position in a stock. For example, in the gilts market, if a house wishes to go short of a specific issue and they sell in the market, then they will be expected to deliver that bond to their purchaser the next day. Unless they physically buy back in the market place, they will not be able to do this and, if they do, then they will no longer be short. Stock borrowing allows a short position taker to borrow stock from a long-term investor who is not looking to sell immediately, in order to satisfy their settlement requirement the next day. When the firm that takes the short position closes their position out in future by buying stock into the short, they must then pass this stock back to the underlying owner.

Equally, stock borrowing is a vital feature of any market where the penalties for failed settlements are high. For example, a broker may believe that they have agreed to buy bonds which they then sell on. If the initial purchase is not delivered on time, then they will be faced with the situation where they are expected to deliver stock that they do not have. Euroclear and Clearstream offer stock borrowing facilities, but at high rates of interest.

In the context of the repo market, the reverse achieves exactly what a borrower of stock wants, in that the lender of funds receives the stock as collateral, which they can then use. For this to be true, it would, of course, be a requirement that this repo was a delivery repo with the delivery of stock going to the lender of cash.

Equally, due to the nature of the short deal, it would be a requirement that, rather than being general collateral, which would allow the collateral to be replaced throughout the life of the repo, it must be a specific collateral repo with a particular bond effectively being borrowed for a specific term, although these can be open specific repos.

Due to the nature of this trade, the rates involved will often be very different from those available on general collateral repos. Within the general collateral market, the laws of supply and demand basically favour the lender on the assumption that it is the need of the borrower to borrow cash. In the specific repo market, the laws of supply and demand would tend to favour the borrower.

The borrower in the repo transaction is the borrower of cash. The borrower of cash is going to provide a specific bond as collateral. This specific bond, which they will deliver to the lender of cash, is a bond that the lender requires in order to cover their own short positions. Now, the spread of specific collateral rates against general collateral rates will depend upon a number of factors.

- The availability of the stock.
- The size of the position.
- The term of the repo.

Spreads could vary from anything down to 10/20 basis points up to hundreds of basis points. Taking an extreme position, if a house was short and desperate to obtain stock to cover their short position, then the advantage to the borrower of cash and lender of security is that they could borrow money at rates significantly below LIBID.

It must be emphasised, however, that the vast majority of repo transactions will be general collateral financing transactions, rather than specific collateral stock borrowing transactions.

2.6.5 Securities lending

Having just dealt with the particular situation of reverse repos with specific collateral as a form of stocklending, let us now look at the conventional stocklending market.

The conventional stocklending market is a straightforward one. Certain institutional investors tend to be long of particular stocks, which they are holding for the long term. Market traders can borrow these stocks in order to cover their short positions. These short positions may be as a result of failed trades, or they may be specific trading stances taken to benefit or speculate on changing rates in the market.

Until the introduction of the open repo market, there was only a very limited facility for stock borrowing in the UK, being accessible solely by market makers through a specific group of intermediaries, the Stock Exchange Money Brokers.

If a market maker wished to borrow stock, then they would approach a money broker who, in turn, would approach an institution. The institution would be prepared to lend the stock, but only at a fee. Initially, these fees were fixed at approximately 75 basis points. However, once negotiation was allowed, the fees began to fall rapidly to 20-30 basis points.

Once the trade has been agreed, then it is possible for the institution to pass the bonds in question to the money broker who, in turn, would pass them to the market maker. The market maker would then be able to use these bonds to settle their short transactions in the market. In order to protect the institution against credit risk of the market makers' defaulting, rare though this would be, given the support given to market makers by the DMO, the market maker would pass collateral to the institution. In reality, it is more likely that the market maker would pass collateral to the Stock Exchange Money Broker, who would hold this on behalf of the underlying institution.

At the end of the agreement, the bonds would be purchased in the market by the market maker in order to close out their short position. These bonds would then be transferred back to the underlying institution, along with the borrowing fee. Once the stocks have been returned, then the collateral would be released back into the market maker's hands.

In this way, it is not vastly dissimilar from the reverse repo trade that we have just seen. Indeed, carrying on the similarity, all coupons arising under stocklending would have to be paid immediately to the underlying institution. This involves the market makers who are borrowing stocks over coupon dates, manufacturing coupons and passing them back to the institutions.

The institutional investors receive their reward in this system through the fee paid when the stock is returned. In the reverse repo market, the institutions receive their reward, not through a fee specifically paid to them, but through the interest rates which they receive. We saw in the reverse repo market that the interest rates for specific collateral may be considerably below the market rates. This would enable the institution to effectively borrow money secured against the collateral of the specific bond required by the other party to the deal at low rates. They would borrow money at low rates and then reinvest this money at higher rates in the conventional money markets, the return between the borrowing cost and the investment return being their fee for lending the stock.

Stocklending vs Repo

Stocklending

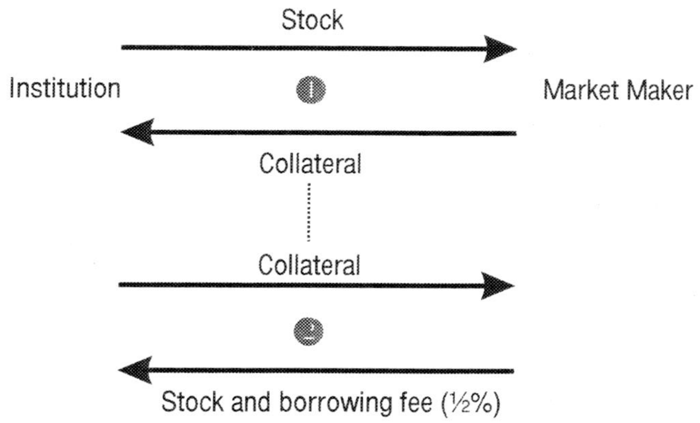

Repo

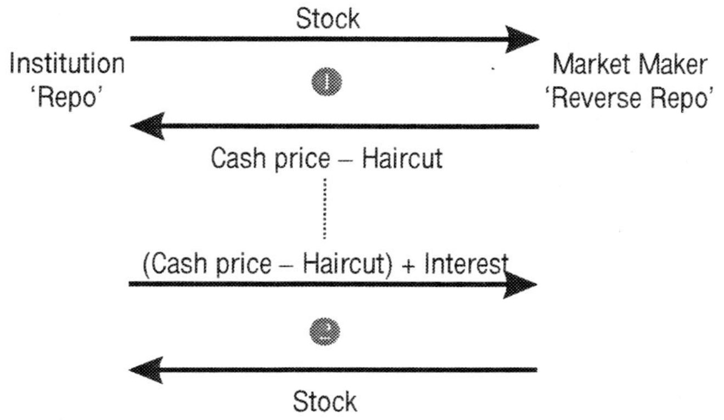

The key difference is that with stock borrowing the collateral backing the loan of securities can be a variety of assets whereas with a repo it must be cash.

The fundamental difference between the reverse repo market and stocklending is that, under stocklending, the institution does not have to do anything; they will simply receive a fee at the end of the process. Whereas, through the repo trade, they will have to take money on and lay it off into the market in order to make their return.

In this sense, it is argued that there will still be a role for stocklending, even after the repo market is opened, simply through some institutional investors neither having the will nor the ability to play the money markets, yet still wishing to enhance returns on their portfolio in a relatively riskless way through stocklending.

2.6.6 Summary of types of repo transaction

As we have now seen, there are two basic types of repo trade. The sale and buyback is a very simplistic trade, which contains with it a number of contractual risks. The classic repo is a legally structured borrowing/lending agreement collateralised by the holding of bonds. One form of this, the specific collateral repo, can, in some ways, be a surrogate for stocklending.

2.6.7 The use of repo

In summary, there are several main uses of the repo market.

To borrow money

The primary use of the repo market for the securities houses will be to enable them to borrow money at relatively attractive rates. The rates will be attractive due to the collateralised nature of the borrowing and will tend, dependent upon the type of delivery, to be sub-LIBOR. This ability to borrow, backed on the collateral of their bond holdings, enables securities houses to finance geared books. If the house has £100m in capital and it chooses to invest all of this into the bond markets, then they could buy a position of £100m.

With the access to the repo markets, the house can then repo the bond out, retaining its underlying economic interest in that bond and use the cash proceeds to buy a second bond position. This second bond position can equally be 'repoed' out and a third bond position can be taken. Assuming that each time the full value is obtained through the repo market, ignoring all initial haircuts, then, at this stage, the firm will have been able to take an economic exposure to £300m worth of bonds, as opposed to its initial position of only £100m.

This ability to borrow money on the collateral of the bond positions and the gearing that opens up for the bond houses is the key driver to the repo market.

The ability to lend money

It takes two sides and two views to make every market. There are clearly people who wish to be able to borrow money on the collateral of their bond portfolios in order to release the cash which is locked inside those investments. For this to be possible, there must also be people who wish to lend money. The lenders are able to obtain fair reward for minimal risk. At present, banks, institutions, securities houses and local government with surplus cash are able to access rewards through the inter-bank market, lending money at LIBID and below.

The inter-bank market, however, is not riskless. There is always the counterparty risk attached to these loans. The repo market provides an attractive and relatively riskless market for depositors and, whilst the returns will normally be below LIBID, the level of risk involved is not as great. Indeed, it will always be possible to enhance returns above LIBID, and even above LIBOR, if the lender is prepared to take additional risk.

This additional risk may take a number of forms.

- Lower grade collateral.
- Custody risk in the form of hold-in custody repos.
- Term risk on longer term repos, where the markets will tend to be thinner and the spreads, therefore, wider.
- Counterparty risks with lower grade borrowers.

The ability to borrow stock

The access through the reverse repo market to stock borrowing allows full and open access to a market which has, to date, been solely the preserve of the market makers. The ability to borrow stock allows all individuals to cover themselves against failed trades, and it will also allow individuals to take short positions in the stocks which they particularly want to protect themselves against.

To date, ordinary market participants have not been able to short specific sectors of the bond market. If, for example, a fund manager was holding a bond portfolio focused around the seven-year maturity band in the yield curve, then their only method of hedging this through the futures market would be to sell the long gilt future. Whilst it would be possible through the use of hedge ratios to take account of the differential volatility between the two instruments involved, it would not be possible to hedge against differential movements in the yield curve.

For example, if, in the above example, the fund manager is trying to hedge the seven-year bond portfolio with the ten-year gilt future, then if the yield curve rises in the medium range and bond prices fall, and the fund manager has hedged himself to the long gilt future, his hedge will be ineffective. The price of their underlying bonds will have fallen because yields in the seven-year range have changed. However, since yields at the long end have not altered, then the value of the future will remain unchanged and, whilst the logic behind a hedge is that the loss in the cash market is offset by gain in the futures market, this will not have taken place.

Repo quotes in the market

The following rates are taken from the US market and reflect the nature of repo rates versus the underlying inter-bank market. Note, repos are priced using money markets conventions to make them consistent with these short-term loans/ borrowing.

	Deposit	Borrow
Inter-bank		
1-month money	6.00	6.12
Repo		
1 month	5.80	5.93

As we can see from this example, the current repo rates lie below the inter-bank rate. As mentioned above, this is no surprise since the repo represents a collateralised and, therefore, safer form of both lending and borrowing. Whilst it is dangerous to generalise, this type of spread of 20bp below would not be uncommon.

The quoted rates represent the rates available for general collateral repo. Specific collateral repo would, undoubtedly, be on wider spreads against the inter-bank, potentially lying considerably below the current rates, reflecting specific pressures on a bond. A piece of market jargon often used is **'trading special on repo'**, reflecting the particular supply and demand pressures on an individual stock.

As mentioned earlier on, this can result in a spread against the inter-bank rates of anything from tens to hundreds of basis points. Also, of course, the spreads will be affected by a number of other factors, such as the mode of delivery. Hold-in custody will, undoubtedly, have to offer slightly higher rates than delivery repos. The nature of the counterparty will, again, be affected and reflected in the repo rate. Depositors will be able to get better rates from slightly riskier borrowers, such is the nature of all borrowing and lending markets and, within this, of course, the volatility and quality of the underlying collateral will again affect the actual spreads given on a particular trade.

2.6.8 The market in repos

In broad terms, there are two key components to the repo market: people who wish to borrow money and people who wish to lend money, with a small sub-set within that of those people who wish to borrow specific stocks. In order to facilitate the smooth working of the market and to make a profit themselves, there are repo houses who are prepared to sit in between the two and run a book. These repo houses effectively act as unofficial and uncommitted market makers to the process.

These principal trading desks will offer two-way market spreads on repos, quoting the work rate for the repo and the reverse repo. As with most market making activities, for the majority of participants and for most of the time, the principal traders will be operating on a matched book basis, taking money in and laying it out.

Certainly, for many of the repo desks one of their key customers will be their own bond book, where they will be seeking to finance their inventory and to cover any short positions.

Equally, it is entirely plausible that a repo trader may wish to take a mismatch position in order to speculate on movements in the market, converting what could be seen as an ancillary function of the bond desk into a potential profit centre. This mismatch book could take the form of a traditional banking role with the desk borrowing short term on overnight rolling, and therefore floating repos and lending longer term at fixed rates, trying to profit from the 'normal' differential between the two terms.

This will create an exposure for the desk, even though the stock taken in has been repoed out on the other side. The exposure here is to the rollover of the finance at the then market rate. For example, if the desk borrows three-month money and lends six month, taking a turn of 30bp, this could be wiped out when the finance rolls over in three months' time. What the desk is doing is taking a position based on the expected outturn of rates.

In addition to the principal books that will be operating in the repo market, there will also be a number of agency brokers. These brokers will act both on a name passing and a matched principal trade basis, bringing together two parties to a trade. In particular, there is a clear role for them in the context of specific repos in particular stocks, where they are effectively acting as stock borrowers and stock lenders.

2.6.9 The legal documentation

Crucial to ensuring the operation of a safe and efficient repo market is the legal documentation that supports the agreement.

The ICMA Global Master Repurchase Agreement

The ICMA GMRA is becoming the industry standard and has been adopted by the DMO with an appendix covering the gilt-edged market's special conventions. The main contents simply clarify the points raised thus far with regard to margining and coupon.

Basic terms

- Legal ownership is transferred by the first leg of the repo. However, the primary economic interest is held by the initial bondholder. Where the repo extends over a coupon date, the coupon received by the then holder of the bond must be passed to the underlying owner.
- The rights of substitution are clearly defined.
- The events of default clause is designed to give redress to the non-defaulting party. This is of particular relevance in the context of an open repo which is left to roll. The events that constitute default are fairly obvious and include failure to repay, failure to maintain margin to the required level, suspension or expulsion from an exchange and insolvency. There is, however, no cross-default clause linking to other debt.
- Representations and warranties from both parties to the deal are included within the agreement. If it is subsequently apparent that any of these representations is untrue or false, then this too will constitute an event of default; the representations given extend to cover items such as the legal capacity to enter into repo deals. This is particularly an issue in the US where many investors are restricted in the activities that they can undertake.
- A large part of the agreement is concerned with the provision and maintenance of the required margin.

The gilt market annex

This annex to the main agreement simply amends the documentation to take account of the peculiarities of the gilt-edged market. In particular, it lays down the settlement conventions to be adhered to.

2.7 Floating rate notes and other debt

As with the short gilts, other forms of 'low risk' debt will also be traded through the money markets, including local authority issues and highly rated corporate issues. In particular FRNs, which are linked to the short-term money market rates, are traded. The market will tend to prefer those issued by banks and building societies, since these will obviously carry very limited credit risk.

3 The Participants in the Market

3.1 Bank of England

As with the gilt-edged market, the Bank of England is a key player in the market. However, here the Bank's role is different, focusing much more on the implementation of policy than the raising of finance. It is through the money markets that the Bank is able to dictate the direction of interest rates and monetary policy.

Its final role in the market is as the 'Lender of the Last Resort', whereby the Bank ensures that the market will not fail to meet its obligations. As the Barings crisis showed, this is not a blank cheque to the industry. The Bank will, however, step in where there is a 'systemic' risk to the market.

3.2 The banks

The principal users of the market are the banks who use the market to trade their own liquidity positions. Banks are faced with a dilemma with regard to liquidity. A bank takes deposits from its customers and then wishes to lend the money on to borrowers. In simple terms, the bank makes its profits from the difference between the deposit and lending rates.

The banks, in order to maximise their potential profit, would like to be able to lend the entire deposit out. However, they are constrained pragmatically by the need to maintain a proportion of liquid assets to satisfy the needs of their customers and, more importantly, by the prudential supervision of the Bank of England. The Bank dictates that each bank shall retain a proportion of its deposits in the form of liquid assets. These liquid assets partly comprise physical cash, but also certain liquid assets.

There are also many foreign and merchant banks which do not have access to a branch network in the UK and therefore need to obtain deposits via the wholesale rather than retail markets – hence, the frequently used term for the money markets, the interbank market.

With the deregulation of the building society market in the mid-1980s, they too have assumed an important role in the market acting predominantly in the same way as the ordinary banks, which is in effect what they now are.

3.3 Companies

In addition to the banks (and financial institutions), larger corporates are also involved in the market, partly obtaining short-term flexible finance, but also using the derivative instruments to hedge their interest rate exposure.

3.4 Institutional investors

All portfolios will maintain a portion of the fund in the form of cash and near-cash instruments. The money markets provide an obvious and safe channel through which these liquid assets can be made to generate a return.

3.5 Intermediaries

In any market such as this, opportunities always exist for traders to intermediate between buyer and seller, exploiting anomalies in the relative prices of the instruments. The most important intermediaries in the market are the deposit brokers.

These firms act as IDBs for the banking market. If a bank receives a large deposit in a particular currency, then they may not wish to take the full exposure onto their book. Or indeed, the bank may not be allowed to take the full exposure under the Bank's prudential supervision rules. They are able to off-load the position through the market via the currency deposit brokers (CDBs).

The initial market for these brokers is anonymous. Terms are asked for a borrower of $xx million. Once a potential lender has provided a rate, then this rate is communicated to the underlying borrower. If the rate is acceptable to the borrower, then the name is passed to the lender. At this stage, the lender can reject the name on the basis that the lending bank's book is already at its limit to the borrower in question. If the name is rejected, the potential borrower will be informed only that the rate was withdrawn without being told of the counterparty. Once the name has been accepted, then the names are passed to both sides of the deal.

With the introduction of the repo market, a number of repo dealers have emerged. Most of these intermediaries started as adjuncts to the large bond desks. Initially, they acted as an interface between the needs of the proprietorial bond desks and the larger institutional client of the firm, effectively borrowing funds on a secured basis from the cash rich institutions. This role then extended to stock borrowing activity through the reverse repo.

Some houses then began to run 'matched books', whereby the repo desk takes positions with the rest of the market whilst balancing its exposure overall. This matching is not, however, perfect. Whilst the desk will take in and lend out the appropriate volume of money, the maturities may differ. In common with normal banking markets, the desks will tend to borrow short and lend long in order to exploit the normal upward slope to the yield curve and the yield pick up it offers.

The Bank considered whether it was necessary to create market makers in this market. In the end, they decided that it was best left to an unstructured environment. Their reasoning was that if the market needed market makers then, effectively, they will evolve from the current system. If, on the other hand, they are not required, then it would cause significant problems to impose them on the market.

At present, some of the repo desks occasionally quote indicative prices on the main screen services, but there is no obligation.

The secured nature of the repo transaction has led to it becoming one the principal ways in which the institutions lend their excess cash to the market. Estimates now suggest that over half of the overnight lending which takes place in the market is through repo.

4 Dealing

The market is an over-the-counter market, with deals being struck over the telephone. Deals concluded before noon are normally for same-day settlement, all other trades settle on the following day.

5 Settlement

CREST, part of Euroclear, operates the computerised book entry settlement system for the London market. Given that most money market issues, in particular Treasury bills and certificates of deposits, are bearer instruments, there are considerable security problems involved with physical transfer of these assets. Consequently, the bulk of issues are immobilised at the Bank of England, and CREST operates a book entry system to enable holders to transfer their holdings to new purchasers.

Whilst a number of firms have accounts with the CREST, it is conventional for non-account holders to settle using a settlement agent who holds an account with CREST. It is, however, still possible for physical settlement to take place either completely outside CREST or by delivery into, or out of, physical certificates.

6 The Operation of UK Monetary Policy Through the Money Markets

6.1 The establishment of the interest rate target

In May 1997, the incoming Labour government announced that it intended to pass operational responsibility for monetary policy to the **Bank of England**. From this point on, the Bank would set rates in order to achieve a level of inflation within the target range set by the Government. This target was initially set at a long run rate of 2½% with a leeway on either side of 1%. The intention behind this band is to ensure that the bias of policy will not be overly deflationary. In December 2003, the inflation target was lowered to 2% (with the same 1% leeway either side of the target). This change was due to the adoption of a new measure of inflation, the Consumer Price Index (CPI).

Without the target range, the temptation for the Bank would be to operate an overly cautious monetary policy and thereby induce a deflationary bias to the economy. In the US, this bias is avoided by the requirement that the Fed control inflation whilst at the same time trying to maintain the highest level of employment possible.

In order to set the appropriate rate of interest, the **Monetary Policy Committee (MPC)** meet on a monthly basis. This committee decide whether to maintain, increase or decrease rates by a simple majority of members. The membership of the committee comprises the Governor of the Bank, the two Deputy Governors, the Bank officials responsible for economic forecasting and the debt markets and four independent economists (at least, one of whom is from industry).

The committee meet on the first Wednesday of the month and then vote the following morning. Whilst the result is announced immediately, the minutes are not released for two weeks. This is in line with the equivalent procedures in the US relating to the conduct of the Federal Open Markets Committee (FOMC), although in the States, the delay is six weeks.

Once announced, the Bank then sets about ensuring that three-month money rates remain at or around this target rate. This is achieved through the Bank of England's daily operations in the money market.

6.2 The Bank of England's daily operations

The money markets are characterised by large value short-term flows.

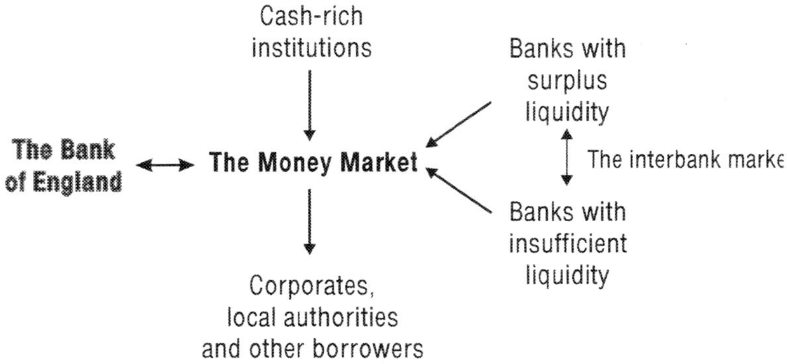

As we have already seen, there are a variety of instruments through which these flows can pass, ranging from bills and CDs to straightforward cash and repo transactions. Taken together, these flows represent the effective supply and demand for short-term funds. As in any market, the interplay between supply and demand creates the price, in this case the interest rate. It is into this mix of demand and supply that the Bank of England operates.

Every morning, the Bank of England establishes its estimate of the daily in and outflows of the system. In doing this, the Bank is using the results of its monitoring of the markets. In particular, the Bank is looking at the flows between the public and the private sector.

At 09:45, the Bank publishes its estimate of the likely shortfall or surplus in funding in the market place.

At this stage, the Bank of England may offer to support the market by providing additional liquidity. Normally, it will only offer to provide assistance at this stage if the shortage is particularly large. On those days in the month when the MPC is meeting, the first round will take place at 12:15, following the announcement of the Committee's decision at 12:00. If the Bank wishes to provide support, then they will invite eligible participants to tender relevant securities for repo. Details of any support provided will be published within 15 minutes.

In the past, the list of eligible participants was relatively limited (basically, the discount houses), however, it has now been expanded to cover any bank, building society or securities firm that can satisfy the Bank that they

- Are subject to appropriate prudential supervision.
- Have the technical capability to respond quickly and efficiently to the Bank's operations.
- Will maintain an active presence in the gilt repo and/or bill markets, thus contributing to the distribution of liquidity around the system.
- Will participate regularly in the Bank's operations (note there is no requirement for anyone to take part in the Bank's weekly tender of T-bills other than this implicit pressure).
- Will provide the Bank with useful information on market conditions and developments.

Failure to comply with these requirements may result in a participant being dropped from the list of eligible counterparties, either on a permanent or temporary basis.

In response to an offer of assistance, the counterparties will be able to tender eligible securities for repo with the Bank. The list of eligible securities comprises gilts, marketable HM Government foreign currency debt and eligible bills (Treasury and eligible local authority and bank bills). In certain circumstances, the Bank will offer assistance through outright purchases of eligible securities.

Any repo will normally be for a maximum maturity of two weeks, although the Bank reserves the right to restore its previous facility (which was started in 1994) of twice-monthly repos with one-month maturities. This will be used if the burdens imposed on the Bank by the daily operations become too intense.

At present, it is envisaged that the finance provided will be of a fixed rate nature, though the Bank reserves the right to operate on a variable rate basis.

The Bank revises its forecasts at 14:30 and again may at this stage open itself up to the counterparties as a source of funding. Details of any assistance provided will be released within 15 minutes.

The process will be conducted again at 15:30, when the Bank will review and revise its forecasts of the liquidity shortage or surplus and again may offer repo and outright purchase facilities. At this stage, the rate applied will be set by the Bank and will conventionally be above (by 100bps) its normal repo rate. This reflects the Bank's expectation that counterparties who wish to obtain liquidity from the Bank should do so in the rounds of operations at 09:45 and 14:30.

At 16:20, the market has closed and the Bank will publish any further revisions to its forecasts. At this point, the settlement banks will have access to a late repo facility up until 16:30. These repos will normally be of overnight maturity. Once again, the Bank reserves the right to charge a rate above the current repo rate.

Thus far, we have assumed that the bank will be operating in order to provide liquidity. Whilst this is likely to be the normal state of affairs with the participant trying to run on the lowest liquidity positions, it may equally be the case that the market has surplus liquidity. In these cases, the bank will act to absorb the excess money by issuing T-bills. The invitation to tender for these bills will be made in the same way as the offers for assistance on the wire service screens.

Whilst the focus has been on changing rates, it should be remembered that for the most part, the Bank will be acting in the market to maintain rates around their current level. In doing so, it will be basing its operations around base rates.

The base rate is the current target of policy with regard to one-week/three-month rates, i.e. the Bank will operate in the markets to keep one-week/three-month LIBOR around this rate. Commercial banks will use base rates as the foundation for most of their loans because it will remain stable over time. Whilst other rates, such as three-month LIBOR, will tend to fluctuate on a daily basis, necessitating a repricing of their loan book on a regular basis.

The bank is less concerned about overnight rates, which can vary considerably reflecting supply and demand in the market. However, with the advent of the open repo market, the volatility of the overnight rate has diminished considerably.

6.3 Conclusions

Overall, the impact of the reforms that have taken place, in addition to reflecting the reality of the market, have had the effect of moving the UK market into line with the way in which the money markets in the other G7 nations operate. In many ways, the facilities provided will exceed the standards of transparency elsewhere.

7 The Operation of Monetary Policy in Overseas Markets

7.1 Monetary policy in overseas regimes

Around the developed world, most governments have now passed the responsibility for monetary policy to independent, or semi-independent, central banks. There are, however, slightly different objectives that have been set and different methodologies for achieving this.

United States of America
The Full Employment and Balanced Growth Act of 1978 (known as the Humphrey Hawkins Act) specifies that 'The Board of Governors of the Federal Reserve System and the Federal Open Market Committee shall maintain long-run growth of the monetary and credit aggregates commensurate with the economy's long-run potential to increase production. So as to promote effectively the goals of maximum employment, stable prices and moderate long-term interest rates.'
The European Central Bank (ECB) and the European System of Central Banks (ESCB)
The ECB established under the Maastricht Treaty is also charged with maintaining price stability. The ECB will achieve its task through the ESCB, which functions as a network of National Central Banks (NCBs). Article 105 of the Treaty states that 'The primary objectives of the ESCB shall be to maintain price stability. Without prejudice to the objective of price stability the ESCB shall support the general economic policies in the Community.'
Japan
Article 1 of the Bank of Japan law states that 'The Bank of Japan shall pursue as its objectives the control of currency and finance and maintenance and the fostering of the credit system pursuant to the national policy in order that general economic activities of the nation might be adequately be enhanced.'

7.2 United States

7.2.1 Introduction

Monetary policy in the US is established by the Federal Reserve Bank (the Fed). There are two key interest rates to watch in the US market.

The Federal (Fed) funds rate

Banks hold deposits with the Fed in order to settle interbank transaction. Where these deposits are too high, the surplus will be lent on an overnight basis to other members of the system. These deposits and loans give rise to the Fed funds rate. This rate effectively sets the tone for money market rates and is manipulated by the Fed.

The Fed has an objective rate for Fed funds that is not published. The market employs special analysts – '**Fed watchers**', many of whom are ex-employees of the Fed – to attempt to uncover this target rate and anticipate changes. The key source of information on the Fed's policy stance has, in the past, been the minutes of the monthly meeting of the Federal Open Markets Committee (FOMC).

This Committee meets to discuss the pressures that exist on the economy and the policy response required. The minutes are released six weeks later.

The watcher will also closely scrutinise the statements made by members of the FOMC in order to identify concerns over the direction of policy, which will then be reflected in changes in the rates. Equally, the daily operations of the trading desk of the New York Fed will be dissected in order to strip out policy changes from the normal technical adjustment that the central bank has to make in the money markets.

In recent years, the Fed has taken to making announcements accompanying actual changes in the rates so as to reduce the uncertainty in the market.

The discount rate

The discount rate is the rate at which the Fed is prepared to lend to banks. This money can only be used for limited adjustment purposes and the rate can be seen as the floor to the Fed funds rates. Changes in the discount rate are strong indicators as to the change in Fed funds rates.

7.2.2 The policy instruments

Repos

Unlike the UK, repos and the repo rate are crucial levers of policy. The Fed uses repos either to alleviate short-term shortages or to signal a change in policy. It is the ability to differentiate between these two objectives that marks out a successful Fed watcher.

Matched sales

If there is a temporary excess of liquidity, then the Fed may relieve this, or signal a move to higher rates, through matched sales or reverse repos.

Outright purchases and sales

The Fed may intervene in the market through outright purchases and sales of government securities in order to directly affect the reserves of the banking system.

Bank reserve requirements

The Fed also sets the required levels of reserves and therefore is directly able to affect the balance sheets of the banks.

7.2.3 Timing

The repo and matched trade business is normally conducted around 11:30, with outright trades being conducted around 13:00.

7.3 The European Central Bank

7.3.1 Introduction

From 1 January 1999, responsibility for monetary policy within Euroland was passed to the European Central Bank (ECB) is arguably the most independent central bank in the world. This independence is guaranteed by Article 7 of the treaty, which states

> '...neither the ECB, nor a National Central Bank (NCB), nor any members of their decision making bodies shall seek or take instructions from community institutions or bodies, any government of a member state or from any other body'.

The structure introduced by the ECB is modelled very much on the structure of the Fed and its immediate predecessor, the Bundesbank. The ECB is funded by contributions from the National Central Banks (the Central Banks of the 16 Euro member states, ie Bundesbank, Bank of France, etc.).

It is headed by a Governor (and five other executives, all of whom are on non-renewable contracts). These six executives and representatives from the National Central Banks meet monthly to discuss the economic conditions prevalent in Euroland.

The European System of Central Banks (ESCB)

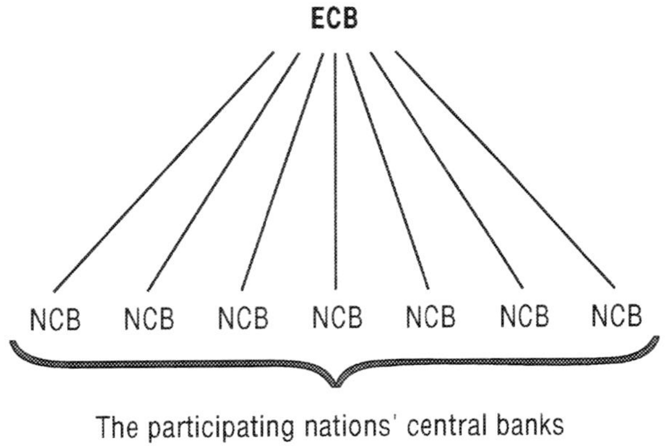

The NCBs act in very much the same way as the federal reserve bank system in the US. Each NCB passes up information about local business conditions to the ECB meetings.

On this information, decisions are then taken on what the direction of policy should be. Unlike the Fed, there is a much greater level of participation from the network of NCBs. Each NCB has a vote as do the six members of the executive. Ultimately, the Governor has the casting vote.

The remit set for the ECB within the Maastricht Treaty is to achieve price stability. The definition of this task was left to the ECB itself. The ECB has decided to use a combination of targets. Many commentators suggested the ECB should target money supply. However, in the absence of any stable link between money supply and inflation, they have elected to target inflation directly with a reference target of price inflation of 2% or less. Supporting this, there are some broader monetary targets reflecting the monetarist leanings of several members of the executive.

Once the council has decided upon the rate of interest in the economy that it believes to be appropriate, it will then instruct the NCBs to operate in the conventional way, through the money markets to achieve the chosen rate. Supporting this will be the ECB and their commitment to enter into repo trades to support this chosen rate.

Again, in line with the practices of the Bundesbank, there will be a channel within which rates can fluctuate. The limit on this channel are the rates at which banks can either borrow from or deposit monies with the ECB.

Euro Short-term Interest Rates Illustrated

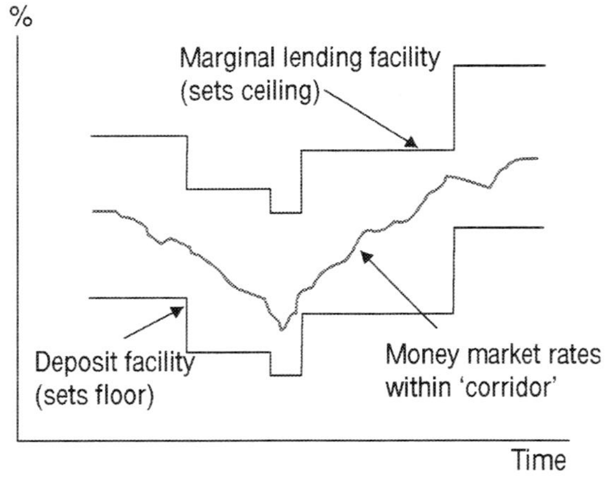

Concerns about the effectiveness of the ECB

There are a number of major concerns with regard to the role of the ECB.

- There is relatively little openness and accountability. Unlike other central banks, there is no formal publication of minutes at present.
- The relatively large number of votes held by the NCBs (16 out of 22) may well lead to some friction, particularly in the case of nations where the policy imposed by the majority is not what they require locally. This will be exacerbated by a relatively low-staff level (500 at the ECB compared with over 50,000 employed by the 12 NCBs).
- Whilst many of the council members have considerable experience, no one really has any experience of the new combined Euroland economy. Consequently, it is entirely possible that key signals will be missed. There is also the fear voiced by some economists that in a bid to gain credibility, the ECB will take an overly aggressive stance and thereby tighten policy too much.
- Whilst, after Bundesbank pressure, the ECB does have the ability to impose minimum reserve conditions, it does not have a role in the regulation of the banking markets. This has traditionally been a convenient route through which the central bank has been able to control monetary conditions.

Overall, there are a number of concerns as to the effectiveness of the ECB. Only time will tell how serious these concerns are and how effectively they can be dealt with.

7.4 Japan

7.4.1 Introduction

Whilst the Fed is fundamentally independent, the relationship between the **Bank of Japan (BoJ)** and the government is closer with the government having representatives on the key committees.

However, in many other ways, the two systems are similar. As in the US, there are two key rates.

Uncollateralised overnight call rate (UC Rate)

This rate is the equivalent of the Fed funds rates in the US and is the key indicator of the policy objective of the BoJ.

The basic discount rate and basic loan rate

This rate provides a limit to money market rates in Japan and again, as in the US, it tends to play a confirmatory or lagging role in the identification of policy trends. The BoJ will intervene in the market so as to reduce or increase the UC rate, the basic discount rate provides an upper limit to the UC rate.

Instruments of policy

Whilst the principal policy weapons will be a combination of outright transactions and repos, the BoJ also has the ability to alter the reserve requirements of the banks. The BoJ reserves requirement is set on a monthly basis, running from the 16th of one month to the 15th of the next.

In addition, the BoJ is also able to exert a degree of moral influence over the market to ensure that they get their own way.

Timing

The BoJ's estimates of liquidity for a day are announced between 17:20 and 18:20 on the previous day. The BoJ will then intervene the next morning in accordance with its policy objectives.

CHAPTER ROUNDUP

You must be able to describe

- The various money market instruments
- The market participants
- The role of the Bank of England
- Treasury Bills

  $$\text{Discount rate} = \frac{100 - \text{Discounted value}}{100 \times {}^{\text{Days}}\!/_{365}} \times 100$$

  $$\text{Yield} = \frac{100 - \text{Discounted value}}{\text{Discounted value} \times {}^{\text{Days}}\!/_{365}} \times 100$$

  $$\text{Yield} = \frac{\text{Discount rate}}{1 - \left(\text{Discount rate} \times {}^{\text{Days}}\!/_{365}\right)}$$

- You must be able to calculate repo costs and the returnable cash under a repo.

TEST YOUR KNOWLEDGE

Check your knowledge of the Chapter here, without referring back to the text.

1. (a) What is the interest on a 8% CD with a principal amount of $100,000 issued for 90 days?
   (b) What difference would it make if the principal was £100,000?
   (c) Assume the dollar CD is sold after 30 days when interest rates have risen to 10%.
      (i) How much will the purchaser be prepared to pay for the CD?
      (ii) What return has the seller earned?

2. £500,000 of 181 day commercial paper is issued at £483,266.10. What is the discount to yield?

3. Describe the role of the MPC.

4. It is currently 7 March 2005. You have $1m available for investment until 2 May 2005. You obseve the following prices for different money market securities maturing on 2 May 2005.

   (a) T-bill Nominal value $1m
   Market price $991,300

   (b) Certificate of Deposit Nominal value $1m
   Coupon 6%, Original Maturity 180 days
   Market Price $1,020,947.60

   Any surplus funds can be invest in a time deposit with a maturity of 2 May 2005 at 5.00% per annum. There is also available to you a $50,000 credit line at 6.50% per annum.

   (i) Compare the dollar outcome of either investing in (a) or (b).

   (ii) Describe three alternative money market instruments available to investors for short maturities and comment on their relative attractiveness in different economic scenarios.

5. A UK Treasury 5% is priced at £102.17 based on its GRY of 4.76%. It pays its semi-annual coupon on 7 June and 7 December each year. Calculate the repurchase price for a 3 month repo from 1 February assuming 3-month LIBOR of 4.5%, given that gilt repos trade at 10 basis points under LIBOR and given that it is not a leap year.

6. You have been asked by your senior manager to explain the impact of two features in the UK gilt market, namely the gilt repo market and gilt strips. In particular, you are asked to explain how fixed income funds under your control can take advantage of these changes.

TEST YOUR KNOWLEDGE: ANSWERS

1. (a) Interest = $\$100{,}000 \times 8\% \times \frac{90}{360}$ = \$2,000.00

   (b) Interest = $£100{,}000 \times 8\% \times \frac{90}{365}$ = £1,972.60

   (c) (i) The purchaser will be prepared to pay

   $$\frac{\$102{,}000}{1+\frac{0.10\times60}{360}} = \$100{,}327.87$$

   (ii) The original cost was

   $$\frac{\$102{,}000}{1+\frac{0.08\times90}{360}} = \$100{,}000.00$$

   hence the seller has earned \$327.87, i.e.

   $$\frac{\$327.87}{\$100{,}000} \times \frac{360}{30} = 0.0393 \text{ or } 3.93\% \text{ p.a.}$$

2. $$£483{,}266.10 = \frac{£500{,}000}{1+\frac{Y\times181}{365}}$$

   gives

   $$1 + \frac{Y\times181}{365} = \frac{500{,}000}{483{,}266.10}$$

   $$365 + Y \times 181 = 377.64$$

   $$Y = \frac{377.64365}{181} = 0.07 \text{ or } 7\%$$

3. See Section 6. The MPC are charged with the task of controlling UK inflation, keeping it at or around 2%. The MPC aim to achieve this through the control of interest rates.

4. (i) **T-bill**

7 March	56 days	2 May
\$991,300	→	1,000,000.00
\$8,700	surplus to invest @ 5% for 56 days	8,767.67
		1,008,767.67
CD		
\$1,020,947.60	→	1,030,000.00
	$1{,}000{,}000 \times 6\% \times \frac{180}{360}$	
20,947.60	Borrowed for 56 day @ 6.5%	(21,159.40)
		1,008,840.60

The CD offers the greater return but is also the marginally higher risk investment carrying as it does the risk of default.

(ii) Alternative money market instruments could include

- Short-dated bonds (government and corporate).
- Floating rate notes.
- Commercial paper.
- Bills (commercial/eligible or bank bills).
- Repos.
- Cash deposits.

The variety of instruments on offer reflects the risk-reward spectrum provided by the market. All will be driven to a great extent by the same set of expectations of short-term rates. Higher returns as in the case of the T-bill vs CD analysis will generally reflect additional risk in the form of credit and/or liquidity.

Short-dated bonds should price in much the same way as T-bills with spreads to reflect credit risk for corporate paper. Trade bills and bank bills contain varying degrees of credit risk dependent upon the backing for the issue.

Similarly with commercial paper the return will depend upon the credit backing for the paper. The market in 'junk' or higher yielding CP that has emerged over the past few years is an example of the higher risk segment of the market.

5. **1 May value**

	(£)
Clean price	102.170000
Accrued interest $100 \times \frac{0.05}{2} \times \frac{56}{182} =$	0.769231
Dirty price	102.939231

Day count		Days	Days in Period	Repo Days	Days 2
December	From last coupon (inclusive)	25	25		25
January	To day before settlement	31	31		31
February			28	28	28
March			31	31	31
April			30	30	30
May			31		
June	To day before next coupon		6		
		56	182	89	145

Repo

Interest at 4.4% (4.5% – 0.1%) for 89 days is

$$102.939231 \times 0.044 \times \frac{89}{365} = 1.104411$$

giving returnable cash of

	(£)
1 February Dirty Price	102.939231
Repo interest	1.104411
1 May Dirty Price	104.043642

1 May value

	(£)
1 May Dirty Price	104.043642
Accrued interest $100 \times \frac{0.05}{2} \times \frac{145}{182}$	1.991758
1 May Clean Price	102.051884

Repurchase price = £102.051884

6. **What is a Repo?**

In essence, a repo is a relatively straightforward and simple transaction. The term 'repo' stands for 'sale and repurchase agreement' and, in its basic form, is not vastly dissimilar to pawnbroking.

Effectively, the holder of an asset (in this case, a bond) approaches somebody who has excess cash (the pawnbroker or repo house) although, as we will see later, the repo house itself is simply a reflection, perhaps, of savers elsewhere in the financial system, such as the institutions. The holder of the bond sells their asset to the pawnbroker and receives cash in return. This sale, however, is not an outright sale. What it represents is a conditional sale – at the same time as the sale and passing of cash takes place, a repurchase is agreed. This repurchase takes place at a second date and at a different price. The price differential reflects an interest cost to the borrower of the funds. As with pawnbroking, the longer the term of the loan, the higher the mark-up in the final price to reflect greater interest cost.

Equally, following our analogy with pawnbroking, if the repurchase transaction is not fulfilled, i.e. the original bondholder does not repurchase their bond on the pre-set date at the pre-set rate, then the bond becomes the property of the pawnbroker and they can then sell the bond in order to release their cash. In effect, what they have made is a **collateralised loan**. Default on the repayment simply means that the collateral reverts to the lender, allowing them to release their funds.

Thus far, we have consciously been focusing on the repo transaction as a way of borrowing money. Anybody undertaking a repo is selling a bond in order to gain cash now. They are obliged to pay that cash back in the future with interest in order to release their collateral. This is, undoubtedly, the biggest element of the international repo market, allowing the big securities houses to finance their inventory in bonds, buying the bond and then 'repoing' the bond out in order to get back the cash. This cash can then be reutilised buying more bonds which, in turn, can be 'repoed', and so on and so forth, gearing up the house's position.

Thus far, we have referred to the other side of the repo as the lender of cash. In technical market jargon, the borrower is undertaking the repo and the lender is undertaking the reverse repo. In the reverse repo, the lender receives the stock in exchange for cash. They then receive the cash and return the stock.

It is in this sense that the repo market can be perceived in part to be a stock borrowing market for the lender of cash, i.e. the person taking out the reverse repo, is, in effect, borrowing the stock, and the nature of the agreement is that they will, effectively, have ownership rights over that stock (depending on the type of delivery given) until the repo is unwound.

The Uses of a Repo

- As an outlet for surplus funds the repo will allow the fund to lend its surplus cash at minimum risk.
- As a method for borrowing cash (if permitted under the terms of the fund management agreement).

- It is also in this sense that the repo can be used to perfect the pricing of bond futures, since the repo rate is what used to be the implied repo in the cash and carry arbitrage. Indeed, repos in many respects replicate the futures market. If we were to take a position in a bond we could then repo the bond in order to obtain cash. This cash could then be reinvested into the bond creating a similar effect to the gearing obtained by futures. This time, however, it would be possible to gear up on specific bonds rather than be constrained by the existence of standardised futures contracts.
- The stock borrowing element of a repo in addition to allowing the fund (if permitted) to go short of stock will more conventionally allow the fund to obtain lending fees on the existing stocks held in the portfolio.

What is a Strip?

The strips system takes an ordinary bond and breaks it down into its component parts. Each flow from a bond is converted into a zero coupon bond.

For example, a five year bond with a semi-annual coupon of 6% would become ten zero coupon bonds, one for each of the individual coupon flows of £3. These are known as the '**Tint**'. These zero coupon bonds range in maturity from six months to ten years. In addition, there is another zero coupon bond formed out of the principal, known as the '**TP**'.

The Uses of the Strips Market

- Given that the strips market is derived from the same market as the underlying bonds then the possibility of arbitrage exists between the two to ensure that prices are consistent.
- The yield derived from the strips market are the spot yields that can be derived from the GRYs. They will not tie up absolutely since there is not perfect liquidity over the range of maturities in the market.
- There will be substantial interest in the long end of the market, since by buying the strip the investor will be able to expose himself to greater interest rate risk than by going through the conventional market. The 26-year bond may have a duration of ten years, however the 'TP' (stripped zero based on the principal) will have a duration equal to the maturity, therefore 26 years. These longer durations are essential for some of the more structured fund management techniques, such as immunisation.
- The development of a full strips market has enabled the investors in the US Treasuries market to create highly structured strategies based on the movement of the yield curve. It will also allow for the creation of more structured products to be created. For example, annuities for set periods can be created by purchasing the appropriate series of strips.

The impact of the repo market has been to increase the liquidity of the gilts market by attracting more participants (initially at the expense of futures market volumes). It is likely that the strips market when it is introduced will have a similar impact. However, there are concerns that it might lead to a more volatile market stemming from the ability to take geared and short positions.

7 International Markets

INTRODUCTION

The objective of this session is to expand the candidate's knowledge to cover the bond markets of other major countries.

Investment is now very frequently conducted on an international basis and we need to be aware of the main instruments available in other major markets.

CHAPTER CONTENTS

CHAPTER LEARNING OBJECTIVES

The syllabus areas covered by this section are

Government Securities Markets

Students should possess a detailed knowledge of the government securities markets of the UK, US, Japan and Euro and knowledge of the practices and conventions in the Australian and Canadian government securities markets. Beyond a knowledge of their existence and relative size this need not extend to agency, government sponsored enterprise, mortgage or corporate bond markets outside the UK. Students should be familiar with:

- Regulatory authorities
- Methods and types of Issuance
- Withholding taxation
- Secondary market
- Structure
- Dealing practices
- Price transparency
- Transaction publication
- Settlement and custody practices
- Funding
- Repo/stock borrowing

For the four detailed markets, knowledge should extend to securities which are anomalous for specific reasons e.g. FOTRA or strippability. Students should be aware of the procedures for stripping securities and the implications for rump issues. Students should be aware of the existence of cash – derivative arbitrages and their potential impact upon market price behaviour. Students should be able to calculate the cash/futures price relationship. Students should be familiar with the taxation of UK residents and the taxation of non–residents in the other three detailed markets.

Exam tip

Questions from this Section are factual discussions either stating characteristics or comparing markets. For example, which markets issue index linked products (Summer 2004, Question 7), how do coupon frequencies vary (Summer 2000, Question 7).

1 The Non-Euroland Markets

1.1 US bond markets

1.1.1 Introduction

Segmentation of the US Bond Markets

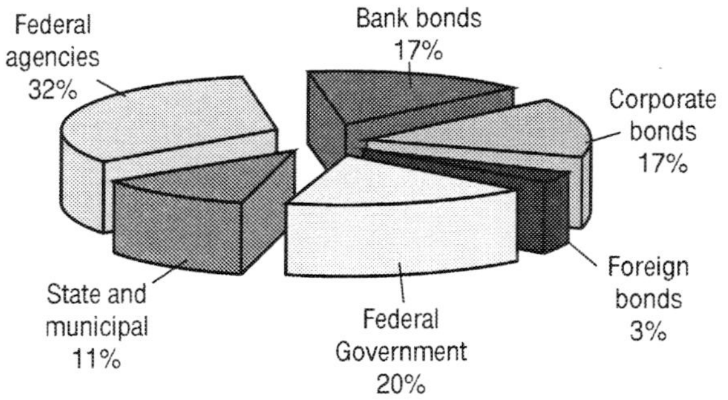

1.1.2 The government bond market

The US government bond market is the largest in the world having expanded rapidly in the 1980s. This size is evident in both the quantity of issuance in the primary market and volumes of activity in the secondary market.

The market is not dissimilar in structure from the UK gilts market. This is due to the UK reforms that have been designed to bring the two markets into line. Indeed, the general direction of all government bond markets has been towards greater 'fungibility' or similarity, with the US being seen as the role model.

The Fed

The key player in the market is the **Federal Reserve** (the 'Fed'). As the US central bank, the Fed, through **open market operations**, manipulates liquidity to control US monetary policy. The Fed is largely independent, the only political involvement comes in the appointment of the board. To this extent, many argue that the Fed is less independent than the Bundesbank. However, in many ways this possibility of political influence is more apparent than actual. For if a President were to try to 'rig' the Fed, then it is likely that the markets would react unfavourably and the benefits of credibility would be eroded very quickly.

The Fed's own publications summarise the objectives of the Board of Governors and the 12 Federal Reserve banks as being the following.

- Conducting the nation's monetary policy by influencing money and credit conditions in the economy in pursuit of full employment and stable prices. However, the clear focus of policy is towards the latter of these two objectives in the belief that price stability is a prerequisite for higher levels of employment.
- Supervising and regulating banking institutions to ensure the safety and soundness of the nation's banking and financial system and to protect the credit rights of consumers.

- Maintaining the stability of the financial system and containing the systemic risk that may arise in financial markets.
- Providing certain financial services to the US government, the public, financial institutions, and foreign official institutions, including playing a major role in operating the nation's payments system.

The Treasury

The Treasury is part of government and responsible for the issuance of debt in order to fund the deficit.

1.1.3 Types of issue

Main Issues

There are three main types of instrument issued.

- **Treasury bills (T-bills)** – These have a maturity of three months to one year and are issued at a discount to face value.
- **Treasury notes (T-notes)** – These are coupon securities and are issued with initial maturities of between two and ten years.
- **Treasury bonds (T-bonds)** – These are again coupon securities and are issued with an initial life of over ten years.

All US bonds are quoted on a clean basis. The coupon paying bonds all pay semi-annual coupons and adopt the Actual/Actual basis for accrued interest.

There is a tendency for the market to focus into the liquid issues referred to as the **'on-the-run bond' or 'hot runs'**. These benchmarks are normally the most recent issues; other issues are referred to as 'trade by appointment'.

Treasury Inflation Protected Securities (TIPS)

In 1997, the US government issued treasury inflation protected securities or index-linked bonds for the first time. In part, this was seen as an unusual decision by the markets, who initially viewed it as a worrying sign with regard to the government's commitment to low inflation. The justification is that, far from undermining the government's commitment to low inflation, it actually reinforces it by ensuring that if inflation does take off, government finance cost will likewise rise in nominal terms.

On TIPS, the principle value is adjusted for changes in the CPI to reflect inflation and the coupon is a fixed rate payable on this adjusted value.

The bonds are semi-annual paying with quotations on a dirty basis.

1.1.4 Primary market

The US Treasury is responsible for the issuance of new securities. Issuance takes place on a regular calendar with weekly issues of three or six-month Treasury bills, monthly issues of one-year bills and two and five-year notes, and quarterly issues in set cycles of longer dated stocks. These quarterly issues are referred to as the quarterly refunding. The quarterly refunding simply allows for the Treasury to clarify the current state of the government's finances and to signal changes for the future. The extent of each auction is announced a week in advance of the auction.

In 2001, the government stopped issuing the 30-year T-bond. Ostensibly this was designed to reflect the reduced funding needs of the state. However, increased demands from pension funds and other long-term investors allied with low long-term yields led to their reintroduction in 2006.

T-bonds are issued through competitive auction. Two and five-year T-notes are issued using a uniform price auction, or tender, where each bidder pays the highest accepted yield (i.e. the lowest accepted price).

The competitive auction

The competitive auction in the US is basically the system that was introduced into the UK in 1987. The principal differences are that, in the US, the primary dealers are obliged to bid for stock and bids are on a yield basis (rather than price in the UK). Non-competitive bids are accepted and they **will** be allocated stock at the average of the successful competitive bids.

The lowest accepted bid is known as the '**stop-out yield**' and the difference between this and the average price is the '**tail**'. The amount by which bids exceeded the issue is referred to as the '**cover**'.

1.1.5 Secondary market

Participants and operation

Central to the operation of the market are the **primary dealers**. These firms are the market makers. They are authorised to conduct trades by the Fed and are obliged to make markets in all issues. As with the UK, there are inter dealer brokers (IDBs) to facilitate the taking and unwinding of large positions. There are no money brokers, but there is a full repo market.

Whilst the stocks are listed on the New York Stock Exchange, the market is effectively an over-the-counter market. The market is perhaps the most truly global market. The market has deep liquidity across the maturity range.

The strips market

The development of a full strips market in the US during the early 1980s has enabled the investors in the US Treasuries market to create highly structured strategies based on the movement of the yield curve, and achieve more precise matching of asset and liability cash flows.

1.1.6 Trading, settlement and taxes

All bonds are traded on a clean price basis except for TIPS.

Settlement takes place predominantly through the Fed's wire (book entry system). Settlement is by convention for the next business day, although same day settlement is possible.

There are no withholding taxes on US government securities, which makes them particularly attractive to overseas investors.

1.1.7 Other bond markets

Federal Agencies

These are quasi-governmental institutions established to fill gaps in the US financial markets. They are backed by the guarantee of the US government via the Fed and are therefore riskless. However, they may well trade at a slight premium to the equivalent US government securities principally due to lower liquidity.

The main Federal Agencies are

- **Federal National Mortgage Association (FNMA) ('Fannie Mae').***
- **Government National Mortgage Association (GNMA) ('Ginnie Mae').**
- **Federal Home Loan Mortgage Corporation (FMLMC) ('Freddy Mac').***
- **Federal Home Loan Bank System (FHLB).**
- **Federal Farm Credit Bank (FFCB).**

* Currently in conservatorship by the Federal Housing Finance Agency (FHFA). Conservatorhip, is a US equivalent of receivership in the UK, where new managers try to rescuer a business in financial difficulties.

Prior to its privatisation in 2004, a further federal agency was the Student Loan Association (Sallie Mae), now the SLM Corporation.

Unlike conventional government bonds, which are predominantly redeemed in bullet form, these issues repay a portion of the capital with each coupon payment. In addition to these quasi-governmental organisations, there are also Municipal bonds or 'Muni's' issued by States and districts. These obviously have a higher credit risk and are less liquid. Yield are consequently greater.

Domestic corporate bond markets

Unlike the UK, the US corporate sector has been able to borrow substantial sums via the issue of debt securities. In part, this has been forced upon them by the highly fragmented nature of the domestic banking market. Equally, however, investors are willing to hold corporate debt as part of their portfolios in a way in which UK investors are not.

Yankee bonds

Ever since 1945, the dollar has been the key international currency, and there has been substantial interest from non-US firms in raising dollar finance.

A Yankee is a dollar-denominated bond issued in the US by an overseas borrower. Given that Eurodollar bonds may not be sold into the US markets until they have **seasoned** (a period of 40 days), there is still a divide between the Euromarket and the domestic market. Apart from the access to a different investor base, the market also allows issuers to raise longer term finance, since the American domestic investors are prepared to accept longer maturities.

These domestic and international bonds trade in the same way as shares.

US private placement market

In the US, corporates are allowed to issue bonds into the private placement market without seeking full SEC registration. This access to the market is available to both domestic and overseas issuers, through the market is dominated by US domestic issuers who have chosen not to enter the public market.

The buy side of the market is restricted to certain institutional investors (primarily insurance companies) who are predominantly 'buy and hold' investors. The market is therefore less liquid than the full domestic market, since issues tend to be held to redemption, thereby limiting the secondary market. This thin secondary market is itself a discouragement to potential investors such as the mutual investment funds.

Reflecting the nature of the market as in effect a one-to-one contract, new issue terms are negotiated between the issuer and the lender. This process can take up to eight weeks to complete. Equally, as a consequence, borrowers tend to have to pay a premium over the public market yields. However, they do not have the cost of seeking a credit rating, nor are they bound by the rules of the SEC.

1.1.8 Bond derivatives

The Chicago Mercantile Exchange (CME) trade futures on the 2 year, 5 year, 10 year and 30 year bonds/notes, and options are available on the 5 year, 10 year and 30 year notes/bonds.

1.2 Canadian bond market

1.2.1 Introduction

Segmentation of the Canadian Bond Market

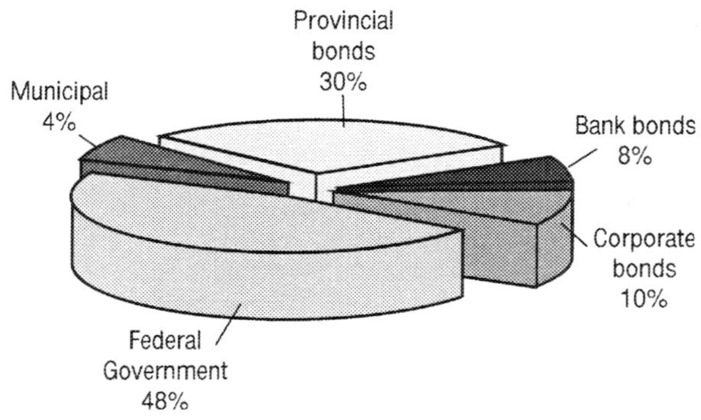

1.2.2 The government bond market

The Canadian government bond market is relatively small compared to other members of the G7. The principal reason for this is that the Canadian system operates on a much more decentralised basis than most other countries. In essence, the provinces act as clearly distinct economic units with their own tax-raising and borrowing powers.

1.2.3 Types of issue

The two major types of issue are

- **Government of Canada Treasury Bills** – short-term discount instruments
- **Government of Canada Marketable Bonds** – coupon paying bonds typically issues with maturities of 2, 5, 10 or 30 years

The bonds are quoted on a clean price basis with accrued interest on the semi-annual coupon calculated Actual/Actual.

In line with many countries who have had a problem with inflation, the Canadian government has issued Real Return (index-linked) bonds. These bonds track the Canadian CPI (Consumer Price Index), pay coupons semi-annually and trade on dirty prices. The inflation time delay is three months, making these bonds an effective hedge against inflation.

1.2.4 Primary market

Bonds are issued by auction, administered by the Bank of Canada on behalf of the Department of Finance.

There is an effective 14 day ex-coupon period. However, all trades are done on a cum coupon basis. Therefore, any seller of bonds during the ex-period must deliver not only the bond, but also a post-dated cheque for the coupon payment.

1.2.5 Secondary market

Given the size of the outstanding market, the secondary market is perhaps surprisingly liquid.

1.2.6 Trading, settlement and withholding taxes

Bonds are settled on a T + 3 basis. A withholding tax of 10% is applicable to most major overseas investors.

1.2.7 Other bond markets

As mentioned above, a large proportion of finance for the Canadian state is provincial debt raised by the quasi-autonomous provinces. Much of this has in the past been raised via the Euromarkets. In particular, the larger borrowers such as Quebec have issued global bonds that qualify as domestic and euro securities.

1.2.8 Derivatives

The Montreal Exchange trades futures on the 2 year and 10 year Government of Canada bonds with notional coupons of 4% and 6% respectively. They also trade options on the 10 year bond.

1.2.9 Economic linkage to the US

The Canadian economy has always been regarded as an adjunct to the US market, and given the size of the US economy and the strong trading links between the two economies, there will always tend to be a relatively high correlation.

1.3 Japanese bond market

1.3.1 Introduction

Segmentation of the Japanese Bond Market

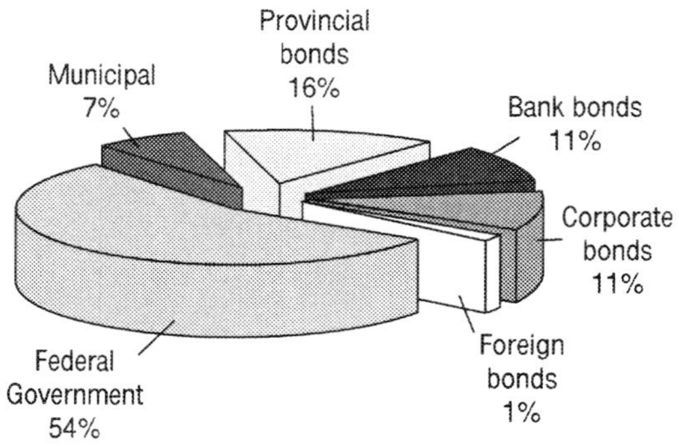

1.3.2 The Japanese government bond market

The Japanese government bond market is the second largest in the world. The market has basically grown from nothing in the early 1960s to its current size. From that point on, the government has consistently borrowed money initially to finance investment in the nation's infrastructure.

However, more recently the poor economic conditions within Japan have led to a need to borrow in order to finance fiscal injections into the economy.

The Japanese bond market is dominated by government bonds. This domination is not in terms of volume, where Japanese Government Bonds (JGBs) account for only half of the market, but in the secondary market where they account for the majority of the secondary market trading.

Initially the market was dominated by domestic investors, however, due both to the size of issuance and the growing importance of the yen, the market has attracted increasing numbers of overseas investors. To aid this internationalisation of the market the government has introduced a number of liberalising measures, though it is still impossible to settle and deliver JGBs outside Japan.

The Japanese market has in the past been regarded as one of the least developed and most 'investor unfriendly' markets amongst the major government bond markets. The Bank of Japan was until recently one of the least independent of all the central banks. However, steps have been taken in order to bring the market into line with the other major markets. These steps have included a greater level of say for the BoJ in the establishment of policy.

It is still the case that many international investors regard the Japanese market as a hostile environment and therefore tend to avoid it. Only 5% of JGBs are owned by non-Japanese citizens.

1.3.3 Types of issue

There are three main types of instrument issued.

- **Treasury bills** – Issued with three and six-month maturities, these are discount securities issued via public auction twice a month. The market is not active and external investors only have limited access.
- **Medium Term Notes** – These are two-year maturity notes that are issued via an auction every two months.
- **Government bonds** – These are conventional debt securities predominantly with a maturity of ten years. The government does issue 'super longs' that have a maturity of 20 years. The Ministry of Finance has also placed a number of 30-year zero-coupon bonds in the past.

All prices are clean and accrued interest on the semi-annual coupon is calculated on the Actual/365 convention. Whilst JGBs do not trade ex-dividend as such, it is not possible to settle in the 14 days prior to coupon payment dates.

In March 2004, Japan issued inflation-linked bonds (ten-year). They are structured similarly to UK ILGs, with a three month inflation lag. They are not available to overseas investors.

The JGBs are referred to as

- **Construction** – these are bonds used to finance development of the infrastructure.
- **Refinancing** – bonds issued to repay maturing debt.
- **Deficit financing** – bonds issued to cover a budget deficit.

In essence, they are all the same semi-annual government bonds. The only difference is that the deficit financing stocks must be approved by the parliament. All new issues now pay their interest on set dates. JGBs can be in either registered or bearer form, and can be converted within two business days.

1.3.4 Primary market

The issue process is more complex than the structure used in most markets with a monthly auction/syndicate issue. In Japan, the syndicate (still dominated by the large investment banks) is allocated 40% of the issue, with 60% sold via public auction. The terms of the issue are set by the Ministry of Finance having taken soundings in the market from the syndicate.

1.3.5 Secondary market

JGBs trade on both the Tokyo Stock Exchange and the Broker Broker (OTC) market settling on a T+3 basis. The market does tend to focus on the 'benchmark' issues, with occasionally 90% of the volume taking place in that stock. However, any issues that are deliverable into the JGB future will possess a fair degree of liquidity.

Whilst a form of repo market ('Gensaki') does exist, it is not as liquid or as important as in many other markets.

1.3.6 Trading, settlement and tax

TSE transactions settle after three days with the OTC taking nine days or more, following a complicated settlement timetable. Settlement is conducted through book entry systems. Withholding tax is levied at 10% where tax treaties exist (most major developed countries), 15% where they do not. Recently, in an attempt to encourage more external participation, withholding taxes for overseas owners have been removed.

1.3.7 Other bond markets

There are a number of important issuers other than the government. In the form of 'quasi-government' there are the agencies and municipal stocks (11%). The banks are large borrowers (19%), using the funds raised in this way to lend to their customers.

As the market in JGBs has become more international, some of this interest has filtered through to the other more domestically orientated markets.

International borrowers are able to access the domestic pool of savings through the issue of Samurai (publicly issued yen bonds) and Shibosai (yen bonds issued via private placement). This is not an important part of the market, with much more being issued in the form of euro-yen (for much the same reasons as the decline of the UK bulldog market).

In addition, there are Daimyo bonds, which are in effect a cross between the Samurai and the euro-yen; domestic bonds with the ability to settle through the normal Eurobond channels. Trading in all of these markets is meagre compared with the volume and liquidity of the JGB market.

1.3.8 Bond derivatives

JGBs Futures are available on the Toyko Stock exchange (TSE) and NYSE Liffe.

1.4 Australian bond markets

1.4.1 Introduction

Segmentation of the Australian Bond Market

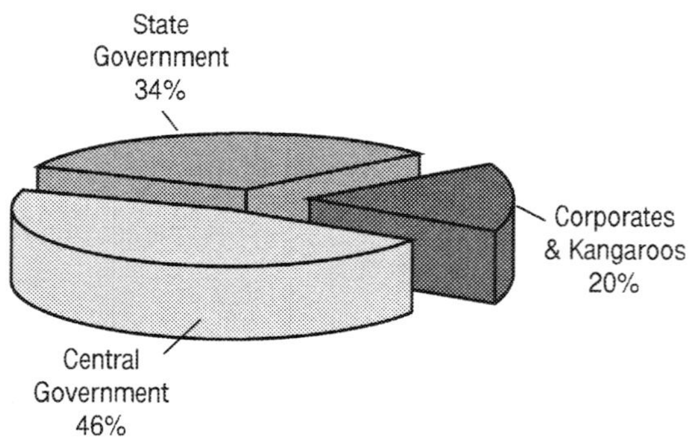

1.4.2 The government bond market

The Australian Office of Financial Management (AOFM) manages Australian Government debt and cash balances via the Reserve Bank of Australia.

1.4.3 Types of issue

The main types of issue are

- **Treasury notes** – short term discount instruments with maturities less than one year.
- **Treasury bonds** – coupon paying securities with maturities up to 15 years

By convention the coupon frequency is semi-annual and accrues on an Actual/Actual basis.

In addition to the conventional bonds, there are also Treasury Indexed Bonds (TIBs). These are capital indexed bonds. In this case, only the capital balance is affected by the actual indexation process. The coupon is simply then calculated on the basis of the set rate as applied to the adjusted capital value. These bonds pay their coupon quarterly. As with most index-linked markets, the liquidity is relatively low.

In addition, there are also Treasury Adjustable Rate Bonds (TABs). These are floating rate instruments and are issued normally with relatively short-dated maturities (three and five-year issues are conventional).

1.4.4 Primary market

The debt is issued by way of a monthly competitive public tender. Whilst relatively large in the past, the sales of these issues has reduced due to the strength of the government's fiscal position.

1.4.5 Secondary market

The secondary market is relatively unstructured with no formal market makers.

As in the UK, the introduction of a full repo market has diminished the level of activity in these contracts, which at one stage was greater than the cash market.

1.4.6 Trading, settlement and holding tax

Settlement is normally on a T + 3 basis. There is still a withholding tax of 10% applicable to overseas residents. This withholding tax is zero for UK and US financial institutions.

1.4.7 Other bond markets

State government bonds

State governments are also significant borrowers in this market. The range of products that they use is very much the same as the Commonwealth Government, including the use of index-linked bonds. The States were the main instigators of the surge in asset-backed bonds in the 1980s as they used bonds to finance projects such as state housing schemes. Each state has its own Central Borrowing Authority or CBA.

In addition to closed auctions (to a restricted panel of bidders), the debt is released by way of taps into the secondary markets and placements.

The secondary market in these securities is relatively limited with only modest activity levels.

Corporate bond markets

The corporate bond market has remained relatively small, however, with the decline in the financing requirements of the government there are signs of a resurgence in corporate bond issuance. In particular, there has been a buoyant market in asset-backed securities.

The Australian equivalent of the Yankee bond market is Kangaroos. These bonds are issued by non-Australian borrowers and are exclusively sold to Australian investors. In addition to Kangaroos, there are Matildas. Matildas are bonds issued by overseas borrowers into the Australian and international markets simultaneously, in essence a global bond issue.

1.4.8 Bond derivatives

The Sydney Futures Exchange offers both futures and options on both the 3 year and 10 year bonds.

1.5 Islamic bond markets

1.5.1 Introduction

Islamic bonds or Sukuk are bond issues that satisfy Islamic principles and have gained Sharia approval. Western style bonds do not satisfy certain Islamic principles, in particular the prohibition of speculation and the payment of interest or any charge simply related to time and much effort has been made in the Islamic world to structure acceptable financial arrangements.

Though Islam frowns on speculation, it does approve of partnerships and risk sharing and Sukuk are based on partnership risk sharing ideas. When investing in such bonds, the Sukuk holder is effectively becoming a part owner of the asset being financed, sharing in profits it generates or losses it incurs. The arrangement is achieved through a special purpose vehicle (SPV) which buys the asset to be financed with the funds raised and acts on behalf of all the Sukuk investors.

In any partnership there are at least two parties involved who may contribute capital, skill and effort, or both. With Sukuk, we have the following parties

- Rab al Mal – provides capital
- Mudarib – provides skill and effort

1.5.2 Types of issue

The main types of issue are

- **Mudaraba Sukuk** – This is the primary type of Sukuk contract where the SPV is the Rab al Mal and company needing finance is the Mudarib. In such an arrangement, all profits are shared as defined in the Sukuk contract, all losses are absorbed by the Rab al Mal. As part of the contract it is normal for the the Mudarib to contract to buy the financed asset at maturity in order to redeem the Sukuk holders. The result of this arrangement can be very similar to that of Western asset-backed bonds depending on how the profit-sharing arrangements are structured.
- **Musharaka Sukuk** – Where all parties contribute both capital and effort. All profits are shared as defined in the Sukuk contract, all losses are absorbed in proportion to capital introduced. This is very dissimilar to Western bonds, Western bond-holders would not expect to contribute anything other than capital.
- **Salam Sukuk** – Has a structure similar to a short term zero-coupon bond which as achieved through a combination of spot and deferred payment sales.
- **Istisn'a Sukuk** – Used in construction contracts where the profits are generated from rents received and the ultimate sale of the property constructed.
- **Ijara Sukuk** – Has a structure similar to a leasing arrangement.

1.5.3 Primary market

Sukuk markets are relatively new and are not yet as developed and standardised as Western markets. They were originated by government entities, particularly that of Malaysia, and government entities still dominate the market, though corporate issues are gaining in importance.

Issuance is achieved in a similar manner to corporate bond issues in the UK, with investment banks underwriting and managing the issues.

1.5.4 Secondary market

Sukuk other than the short-term Salam Sukuk are traded by being listed on stock exchanges, though liquidity levels are currently quite low and many issues are held to maturity.

2 THE EUROLAND BOND MARKETS

With effect from 1 January 1999, the separate bond markets of those nations participating in the first wave of EMU became one single market. This market ranks on as the third biggest market in the world.

Relative Shares of the Euroland Bond Market

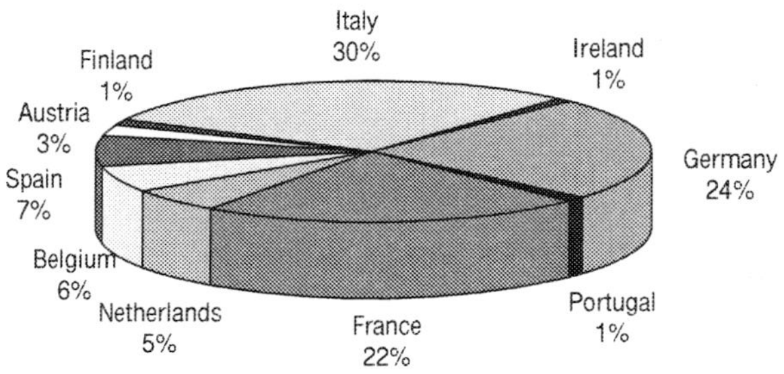

The immediate impact of this was that debt previously denominated in individual currency units was redenominated into euros.

Initially, the markets continued much as they had done before, although all of them share the same currency.

However, reforms rapidly pushed the markets towards greater levels of harmonisation with regard to the structures of the individual markets. All nations moved to the Actual/Actual basis for accrued interest.

2.1 German bond market

2.1.1 Introduction

Segmentation of the German Bond Market

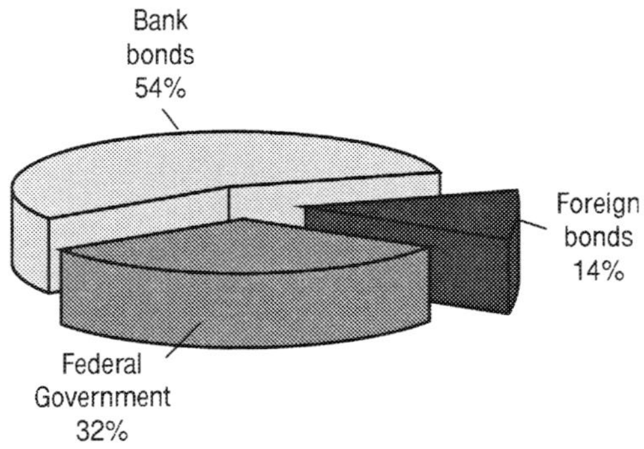

2.1.2 The Government bond market

The German bond market, including government bonds, domestic bonds and Eurobonds, is one of the largest in the world. In contrast to the UK, the Germans have a strong corporate debt market and a much weaker equity market. The bulk of finance for industry is provided through the banks, either as lenders or shareholders, with debt securities other than Eurobonds being less significant. Within the context of debt issuance, it is the banks that issue bonds and then lend on the money to the corporate sector.

The key participant is the Bundesbank, the German central bank. Unlike many of the other central banks, the Bundesbank (Buba) is totally outside political control. The role of Buba is to generate price and currency stability and the politicians have to operate within any constraints that this creates. The Bundesbank is obliged to support the overall direction of Federal Government policy to the extent that this does not conflict with price stability.

2.1.3 Types of issue

There are four main type of instruments issued.

- **BU-Bills** – six-month bills issued at a discount to face value.
- **Bundesschatzanweisungen (Schatze) and Kassenobligationen** – coupon paying bonds with maturities of between two and six years.
- **Bobls (Bundesobligationen)** – These are medium-term issues with lives of up to five years. Initially designed for the domestic market, they have been opened to foreign investment since 1989.
- **Bunds (Bundesanleihen)** – coupon paying bonds with normal maturities of ten years.

2.1.4 Primary market

Primary issuance of bunds is achieved by way of competitive auction.

The primary market in Bobls is still restricted to domestic purchasers and takes the form of a **tap** directly into the secondary market. Once the stock has been listed, then the market is open to all investors.

2.1.5 Secondary market

There are three main domestic routes for trading.

- The domestic stock exchanges (mainly Frankfurt).
- The over-the-counter market.
- The domestic computerised market known as IBIS.

The market is focused on those stocks that are deliverable into the futures contracts of Eurex.

In May 1997, the Bundesbank introduced a domestic strip facility with regard to the Bund market. In addition there is an active domestic repo market.

2.1.6 Trading, settlement and withholding taxes

Settlement date for domestic bond deals is three banking days after the day of dealing. There are no withholding taxes applicable to overseas investors.

2.1.7 Other bond markets

The bulk of the banking sector bond issuance comes in the form of Pfandbriefe. These are effectively bonds collateralised against portfolios of loans. Offenliche Pfandbriefe are backed by loans to the public sector and Hypotheken Pfandbriefe are backed by mortgages. Traditionally, whilst being very secure, they have offered higher yields than bunds by virtue of their illiquidity. This is beginning to change.

The domestic bank bonds are normally issued via placings. A substantial proportion of the market is comprised of Pfandbriefe (mortgage bonds) and Offentliche Pfandbriefe (municipal bonds). The yield spreads on these issues are more a reflection of the liquidity in the market than credit.

2.1.8 Bond derivatitives

Eurex trades futures and options based on the Schatze, Bolb and Bund. These are effectively bond derivatives for the entire Euro zone.

2.2 French bond market

2.2.1 Introduction

Segmentation of the French Bond Market

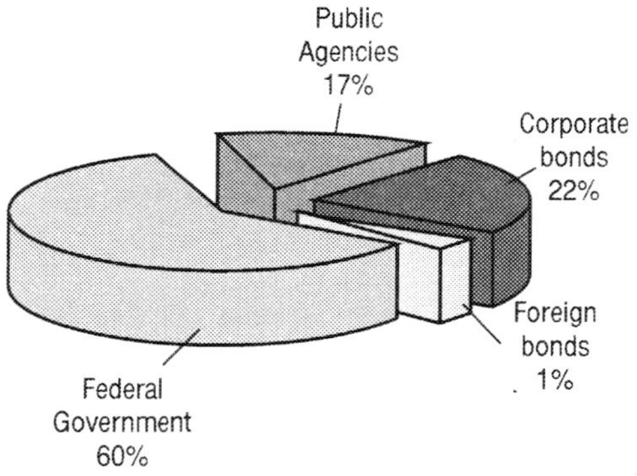

2.2.2 Government bonds

The Banque de France is the central bank in France and the issue of French government bonds is undertaken by the Agence France Tresor, the French debt Agency.

2.2.3 Types of issue

There are three main types of instrument issued

- **Bons du Trésor à Taux Fixe (BTFs)** – These are the French T-bills, issued at a discount to face value and with maturities of 13, 26 and 52 weeks.
- **Bons du Trésor à Taux Fixe et Intéret Annuel (BTANs)** – These are fixed rate coupon paying Treasury notes issued with maturities of between two and five years.
- **Obligations Assimilables du Trésor (OATs)** – These are the conventional coupon paying government bonds with maturities of between seven and 30 years.

The coupon paying bonds all pay annual coupons and adopt the Actual/Actual basis for accrued interest.

Variable rate OATs are also available and these are linked to either long or short-term reference rates. Since the late 1990s the French have been issuing index-linked OATs, once again following the Canadian model, with a three-month delay in the indexation period.

2.2.4 Primary market

Debt is issued by way of monthly auctions to the public. There is, however, a syndicate of banks that the government uses to underwrite issues in particular situations. Issuance takes place in accordance with a preset calendar.

- **BTFs** – Auctioned on weekly basis. The issue is announced on Thursday and the auction takes place on Monday. All bids are on yield basis.
- **BTANs** – Auctions take place on the third working Thursday of the month. The stock to be offered is announced on the Monday preceding the issue. During a six-month period all issues are into the

same two or five-year stock. These stocks are the benchmarks and attract the strongest liquidity. All bids are on a price basis (in basis points).

- **OATs** – Auctions take place on the first Thursday of the month on much the same basis as BTANs. Settlement of the stock purchased in the auction takes place on the 25th of the month.

2.2.5 Secondary markets

The market is focused around market makers who are obliged to make continuous two-way prices in all stock and participate in the auctions. Only the OATs are listed on the Bourse. A substantial amount of trading takes place on the over-the-counter market.

There is an active repo market in French government debt. In addition, the French market has a liquid and efficient strips market.

2.2.6 Trading, settlement and tax

All issues are now in book entry form with no physical delivery. The records are maintained either through RELIT, the domestic system, or Euroclear or Clearstream. Settlement is on a three-day basis.

Settlement is either cash or, for external holders of the bonds, follows the normal Euroclear and Clearstream timetable. Full facilities are available for investors to hold French government debt through Clearstream and Euroclear. BTANs settle on the T + 1 basis for domestic holders.

There are no withholding taxes applicable to overseas investors for French bonds.

2.2.7 Other bonds markets

As noted above, over half the market is made up of debt issues from the public corporations. These stocks are not, for the most part, guaranteed by the government, but the corporations concerned do possess strong credit ratings. They have established their own market structure in order to facilitate trading in their stocks. All issues are by way of a placing through a syndicate of mainly local banks.

Gradual deregulation is easing up the market. The removal of stock queues should have the effect of allowing faster access to the market and therefore enable firms to exploit swap opportunities.

2.3 Italian bond market

2.3.1 Introduction

Segmentation of the Italian Bond Market

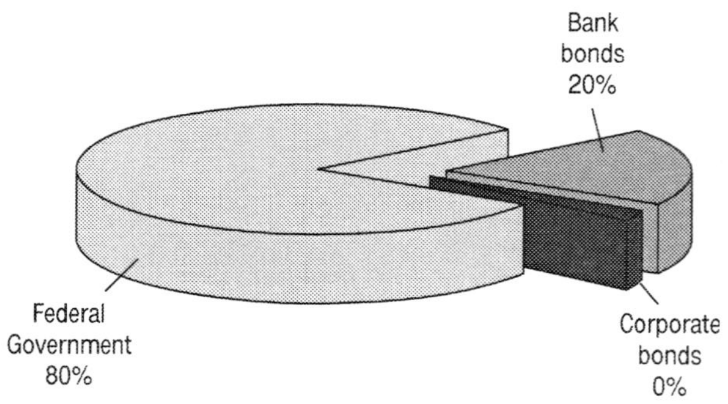

2.3.2 Government bonds

Italian government bonds are issued by the Dipartimento del Tesoro, the Italian debt management agency.

2.3.3 Types of issue

There are three main types of issue

- **Buoni Ordinari del Tesoro (BOT)** – discount instruments with maturities of three, six and twelve months.
- **Buoni del Tesoro Poliennari (BTPs)** – coupon paying bonds issued into the five to seven-year maturity ranges, although some maturities of ten years have now been issued along with limited issuance at the 30-year mark.
- **Certificati di Credito del Tesoro (CCTs)** – a form of floating rate notes. The coupon rate is established by adding a fixed margin to the BTP yield, as determined in the market. The normal maturity of these issues is between five and ten years.

The coupon paying bonds all pay a semi-annual coupon and adopt the Actual/Actual basis for accrued interest.

Whilst the BTPs and CCTs are bullets, the government has also issued Certificati del Tesoro con Opzione (CTOs), which are six-year bonds with an optional redemption after three years. The redemption is at par multiplied by the difference between 100 and the issue price.

In common with the UK, the Italian authorities have also issued index-linked CTRs. In 1995, the authorities commenced the issuance of zero-coupon bonds targeted primarily at the retail sector called Certificati del Tesoro a zero coupon (CTZs).

2.3.4 Primary market

BOTs are auctioned twice monthly, at the middle and end of the month. The auction is run on a competitive basis, unlike the issue of BTPs, which is conducted through a monthly uniform price auction or tender.

2.3.5 Secondary market

Trading takes place through one of three markets. The Stock Exchange is by far the smallest of the three and lists the issues on call. In response to the inadequacy of the stock market, an OTC market was established using Reuters screens to display price information. This too has proved to be unsuccessful and now the market has switched to the Telematico market, where primary dealers focus the liquidity of the market. Maximum liquidity is generated in the new issues immediately post-issue.

2.3.6 Trading, settlement and tax

Settlement takes place on the basis of three business days for domestically settled trades. Settlement takes place in book entry form through specified accounts held at the Bank of Italy. As with most European bond markets, settlement facilities are available through Euroclear and Clearstream on a T + 3 basis.

There are no withholding taxes on Italian government bonds.

2.4 Dutch bond market

2.4.1 Introduction

Segmentation of the Dutch Bond Market

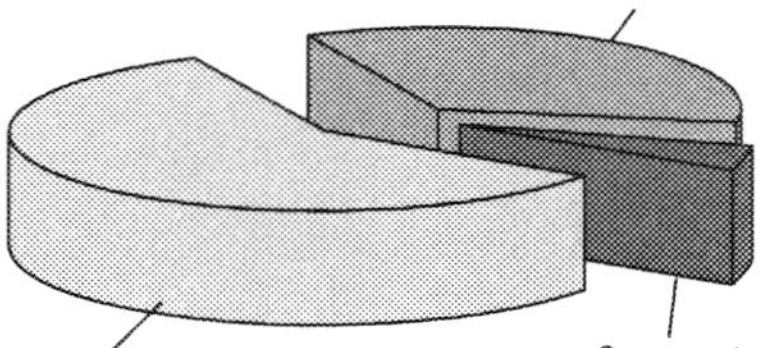

2.4.2 Government bonds

The Dutch domestic market in bonds is dominated by the Dutch government bond issues, which represent over 60% of the total outstanding amount.

2.4.3 Types of issue

There are two primary issues

- **Dutch Treasury Certificates (DIC)** – short dated discounts instruments
- **Dutch State Loans (DSL)** – Longer term coupon paying bonds.

The coupon paying bonds pay an annual coupon and apply the Actual/Actual basis for accrued interest.

2.4.4 Primary markets

All new issues are undertaken by the Dutch State Treasury Agency in the form of bullets. The main insurance method is via an auction though smaller issues may be by direct tap into the secondary market.

2.4.5 Secondary market

The government issues trade freely on both the Amsterdam Exchange (ASX) and the Amsterdam Interprofessional Market (AIM).

2.4.6 Trading, settlement and withholding tax

The settlement convention is three business days with all stock being held in dematerialised form. Interest is paid on an annual basis on either the 1st or 15th of the month. There is no withholding tax for overseas investors.

2.4.7 Other bonds

Local Authorities are also substantial borrowers in the capital markets. In addition, the banks issue a variety of bonds into the debt market. These tend to dominate the non-government bond market by virtue of their high credit rating. Whilst other corporates do issue bonds, they represent only a small proportion of the market.

2.5 Spanish bond market

2.5.1 Introduction

Segmentation of the Spanish Bond Markets

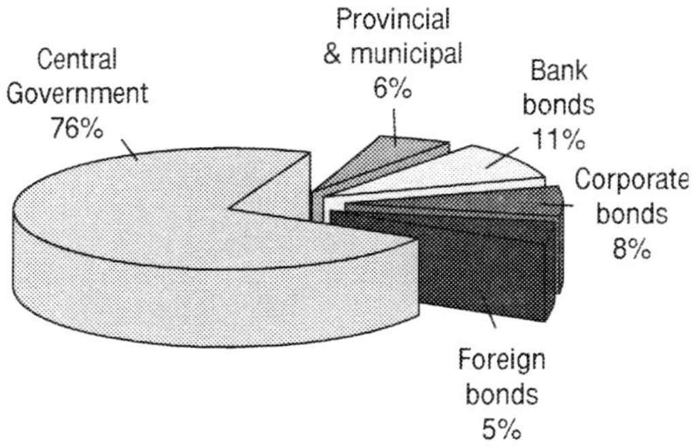

2.5.2 Government bonds

The Tesoro Publico undertakes the issue of Spanish Government bonds. The majority of the issues are Euro denominated, though there are are small non-euro issues, mainly in US dollars and sterling.

2.5.3 Types of instrument

There are three types of instrument.

- **Letras del Tesoro (Treasury bills)** – zero-coupon bonds issued at a discount to their face value with a maximum life of 18 months, to date they have only been issued with maturities of three and 12 months.
- **Bonos del Estado (Bonos)** – These are coupon paying bonds with lives of three to five years.
- **Obligaciones del Estado** – These are coupon paying bonds with a maturity over five years, usually 10 years and 30 years.

All maturities pay annual coupons, are issued as bullets and are redeemable at par. Prices are quoted clean with accrual interest calculated on a Actual/Actual basis.

2.5.4 Primary markets

All bonds are now issued through monthly auctions. These issues take place on a set calendar announced at the start of the year. The coupon for the next three issues is announced prior to each auction. In line with most markets, issuance tends to focus into the reopening of existing bonds in order to deepen liquidity.

2.5.5 Secondary market

The secondary market functions around a market maker 'blind' (anonymous) system. Trading is conducted electronically without knowledge of the identity of the counterpart. There is a second level market that deals with smaller orders on a named basis.

Both Repos and strips are traded on the secondary market.

2.5.6 Trading, settlement and withholding tax

Bonds settle on a T + 3 basis. There are no withholding taxes on Spanish bonds.

3 Summary of Major International Government Bond Markets

	US T-Bond	German Bund	French OAT	Italian BTP	UK Gilt	Japan (JGB)
Coupon Frequency	Semi-annual	Annual	Annual	Semi-annual	Semi-annual	Semi-annual
Settlement	Same/next day	3 business days	3 business days	3 business days	Same/next day	3 business days
Registered or Bearer	R	R	R	R or B	R	R or B
Normal Life	Life of over 10 years	Mostly 10 years	Issued with lives of between 7 and 30 years	Usually 5-7 years, but have been as long as 10 years	Varied	10 years, some super longs with life of 30 years
Quotation	1/32 Converting to 1/100	1/100	1/100	1/100	1/100	1/100
Withholding Tax (for Overseas Investors)	None	None	None	None	None	None
Medium-Term Debt	T-note life of 2 to 10 years	Bobls with lives of up to 5 years and Schatz with lives of 2 to 6 years	BTAN life of 2 to 5 years	CTOs with lives of up to 6 years	–	–
Settlement Agencies	Federal Reserve	Kassenvereine and Euroclear and Clearstream	Relit, Sicovam and Euroclear and Clearstream	Bank of Italy, Euroclear and Clearstream	CGO/CREST, Euroclear, Clearstream and RBNY.	Tokyo Stock Exchange
Accrued Interest Convention	$\frac{\text{Actual}}{\text{Actual}}$	$\frac{\text{Actual}}{\text{Actual}}$	$\frac{\text{Actual}}{\text{Actual}}$	$\frac{\text{Actual}}{\text{Actual}}$	$\frac{\text{Actual}}{\text{Actual}}$	$\frac{\text{Actual}}{365}$

Perhaps the most important point to note is that US T-bonds are priced in 32nds. If a T-bond is quoted at \$102-20 this is \$102 $^{20}/_{32}$ or \$102.625. We are liable to be given prices on this basis and should always quote prices on this basis, however all calculations are most conveniently undertaken in decimals so we will need to convert from 32nds to decimals at the start and may need to convert from decimals to 32nds at the end.

One further little complication here is that we may be given a quote of \$102-20+. This should be interpreted as \$102-20.5, i.e. \$102 $^{20.5}/_{32}$ or \$102.640625.

4 Emerging Bond Markets

4.1 The risk-reward payoff

The bull market of the 1990s reduced yields in the developed markets to such a level that investors began to look outside the traditional markets for higher returns. Higher returns will only come with higher risk, but in a diversified portfolio this level of risk might be acceptable. In this light, the emerging bond markets offer an attractive investment opportunity. Indeed, many saw the market as significantly undervalued offering attractive returns.

The risks involved in emerging markets

Political risk

Unstable governments create a number of risks for potential investors. Included amongst these are default risks on government bonds, nationalisation and the potential expropriation of assets held within the economy. The move towards democratic regimes in Latin America was one of the key prerequisites for the development of international activity. The recent experience of the Russian market, however, highlights the possibility of default.

The imposition of exchange controls is also a potential threat with the risk that the currency will be **closed**, effectively blocking the ability of remitting the capital back to the investor's country.

Exchange risk

Where these currencies are subject to market forces, they are often prone to extreme fluctuations as market sentiment moves. These fluctuations are often so extreme as to remove the profit that the investor has made in local currency.

Corporate risk

As with any investment into a company, the investor must assess the risk of the company concerned. This is often more difficult in emerging markets due to the lack of formal information and the absence of credit rating agencies.

This is often exacerbated by the risk that the information that is available is either false or inaccurate. Once again, this will serve to heighten the risks that are faced by the investor and will obviously discourage many.

Local market risk

There is obviously a risk in using the local market. For example, potential loss through the failure of an undercapitalised local brokerage, or inefficient systems resulting in delayed settlement.

In addition, there are other risks associated with local settlement and custodial arrangements, all of which must be addressed prior to large-scale institutional inward investment.

Market inefficiencies

Arguably a benefit as opposed to a risk, in these markets knowledge and expertise can be fairly thinly spread. Consequently, it may be possible to pick up bargains that in more mature markets either would not or should not appear.

These risks were reflected in the Mexican peso crisis of 1994 and very strongly in the Asian bond market crisis of 1997/8.

4.2 The Brady bonds

A particular sub-niche of the emerging market comprises Brady bonds created in 1989.

The Brady plan

The Brady plan has also acted as a promoter of growth and activity in the emerging bond markets. Brady plans reflect the fact that the debtor nations would never be able to repay their existing debt, built in the 1970s and that it is better to get something out of this than to persist in the belief that the debt has some value. Accordingly, the creditors agree to forgo some of the debt in order to restructure the debt into a more tradeable form.

The basis of any Brady plan was be the adoption and approval by the IMF of domestic policies which would, in the IMF's view, stabilise the country's economy. Once the economic plan has been agreed, the IMF/IBRD would lend the nation enough money, along with its own reserves, to buy specially created US Treasury zero-coupon bonds. These zeros were lodged in New York and represented the collateral for the capital value of the bonds.

Those investors holding debt were then be invited to surrender their debt in return for these collateralised bonds issued by the debtor nation. To reflect the fact that the original loan is unsustainable, the investors surrendering the debt received either bonds representing a proportion of the debt surrendered or the full value of the debt in bonds with a coupon below the market rate.

The creditor now had an asset which it is able to trade and the nation had a debt burden it could service.

If all else failed, then the holders of the bonds knew that the bond they are holding is backed by a US Treasury zero-coupon bond. Indeed, most plans also collateralise the coupon stream for the next 12 to 18 months using other investment grade bonds.

This arrangement between the debtor nations and the holders of the debt reflects economic rationality, a rationality many argue that was not present in the initial loans.

4.3 Conclusions

Emerging markets are undoubtedly more volatile and consequently offer the attraction of higher returns in order to compensate for the greater risks involved. The key risk to monitor is credit risk with the additional factor of significant currency risk when the bonds are denominated in the local currency.

As ever with credit risk, the fundamental truths apply. The risk is determined by the likelihood of default coupled with the severity of loss in the event of default and the likely timing of any default. This will always make the pricing of this debt more problematic than the debt of the developed nations where these factors are to an extent more predictable.

CHAPTER ROUNDUP

You need to be familiar with the

- Government bond markets.
- Types of issue.
- Primary issuance.
- Secondary markets.
- Other bond markets.
- Bond derivatives.

for the major international markets.

TEST YOUR KNOWLEDGE

Check your knowledge of the Chapter here, without referring back to the text.

1. Which major markets issue index linked products?

2. Describe the settlement periods of the major markets.

3. Which major markets charge withholding taxes on UK investors?

4. You are the manager of a US dollar-denominated bond fund run on behalf of a life company and you have noted that the US Government has index-linked bonds in issue. Write a short paper explaining the advantages and disadvantages of including index-linked US Government bonds in your portfolio. State whether or not the fund should invest in these instruments given that the yield on the ten-year benchmark US Treasury bond is 6.69% and the **real** yield on the ten-year index-linked US Treasury bond is 3.59%.

TEST YOUR KNOWLEDGE: ANSWERS

1. UK, US, Canada, Japan, Australia, France, Italy. Index linked issues have not been undertaken by Germany, Holland or Spain.

2. Next business day is adopted by the UK, US.

   T + 3 is adopted by Canada, Japan, Australia and all Euroland markets.

3. Canada, Japan (until recently).

4. *Tutor's note: the question requested a report and marks would have been awarded for report format.*

Treasury Inflation Protected Securities (TIPS)

In May 1996 the US Government decided to issue index-linked bonds for the first time. In part this was seen as an unusual decision by the markets, who initially viewed it as a worrying sign with regard to the government's commitment to low inflation. The justification is, however, that far from undermining the government's commitment to low inflation it reinforces it by ensuring that if inflation does take off, government finance cost will rise correspondingly, in nominal terms.

The first issue took place in 1997 and the format of the issues is in line with the Canadian model. The bonds are quarterly paying with quotations on a dirty basis.

Advantages

- They are real assets.
- They may prove useful in any measure of solvency for a life fund.
- They provide an element of diversification within a fixed income portfolio by creating an exposure to real and not nominal rate movements.

Disadvantages

- The inflation link is to CPI and it might be a more effective hedge for many funds for the link to be to an earnings measure.
- Until the market develops the bonds will tend to be illiquid.

In evaluating the current yields we will use the Fisher relationship.

$(1 + r) = (1 + R)(1 + i)$

Where

r = nominal rates
R = real rates
i = expected inflation

On the current basis the nominal yield of 6.69% and the real yield of 3.59% show that the current market estimate of future inflation is around 3%. This would appear a little less than generous and at this stage I would recommend that we stick with the conventional US Treasuries.

8 Bond Returns or Yields

INTRODUCTION

The objective of this session is to introduce various return measures that may be used in the context of fixed income securities and further aspects that follow on. You need to be familiar with the alternative measures, their uses and their limitations.

In studying this area, we should always bear in mind the relationship between risk and return, that is if we are looking to an investment that offers a higher return then we must expect to face a higher risk. This section concentrates on the return aspect, the risk dimension is considered in the next section.

Questions regularly arise from the ideas in this section.

CHAPTER CONTENTS

CHAPTER LEARNING OBJECTIVES

The syllabus areas covered by this section are

Economics

Students should have broad understanding and knowledge of international and domestic affairs which impact upon financial markets. This would include current levels of yields and exchange rates and for those market for which detailed knowledge is required, a thorough knowledge of current concerns in the marketplace. Taxation might be an example of this latter point. Students should possess a broad understanding of the principal theories of economic and financial behaviour. For example, purchasing power parity, capital asset price and arbitrage price theories.

Analysis

Students should possess a broad understanding of both static and dynamic methods for the analysis and construction of fixed income securities containing both certain and contingent cashflows. Variable rate securities will be included. Students should be aware of the limitations of assumptions and mathematical techniques upon results. Although analysis will be concerned principally with 'risk–free' securities, students should be aware of the further considerations for 'risky' securities and the effect they may have on expected return. Students should possess a thorough comprehension of single–period and multi–period, single currency and multi–currency portfolio management theory.

Yields

- Yield curves and surfaces
- Term structures of interest rates

1 RETURNS MEASURES – THE YIELD

Exam tip

> Calculations may be required for any of the following measures in a compulsory Section A question.

The value of any investment will depend on the return that it generates and the risks inherent in those returns. In bond markets, the single most important measure of return is the bond yield. There are, however, several different yield measures which we may wish to calculate, each having its own uses and limitations. For each of these measures, we need to know

- How it is calculated.
- Its uses.
- Its limitations.

1.1 The flat yield

1.1.1 Calculation

The simplest measure of the return used in the market is the flat (interest or running) yield. This measure looks at the annual cash return (coupon) generated by an investment as a percentage of the cash price. In simple terms, what is the regular annual return that you generate on the money that you invest?

Formula to learn

$$\text{Flat yield} = \frac{\text{Annual coupon}}{\text{Market price}}$$

Example

We hold 10% Loan stock (annual coupon) redeemable at par in four years. The current market price is £97.25. Calculate the flat yield.

Solution

The flat yield for the above would be

$$\text{Flat Yield} = \frac{10.00}{97.25} = 0.10283 \text{ or } 10.283\%$$

1.1.2 Uses

This measure assesses the annual income return only and is most appropriate when either

- We are dealing with irredeemables, which pay no return other than a coupon into perpetuity; or
- Our priority is the short-term cash returns that the investment will generate.

1.1.3 Limitations

This measure, while of some limited use (particularly in the short term), has three important drawbacks for the investment markets.

- In addition to the coupon flows, bonds may have returns in the form of the redemption moneys. Where the bond has been purchased at a price away from par, this will give rise to potential gains and losses, which are excluded from the calculation.
- The calculation completely ignores the timing of any cash flows and the time value of money.
- With some bonds (floating rate notes or FRNs), the return in any one period will vary with interest rates. If the coupon is not constant, then this measure is only of historic value unless the predicted return is used.

These limitations combine to make the flat yield of only marginal use.

1.2 The Japanese gross redemption yield

1.2.1 Calculation

The idea behind the Japanese Gross Redemption Yield (GRY) calculation is to overcome the first of the limitations of the flat yield noted above, specifically that any gains or losses to redemption are ignored. This measure recognises that the total return in any period is a combination of both income and capital components, i.e. the coupon received plus any gain (minus any loss) for the period.

The Japanese method for calculating the GRY is to take the flat yield and then add the average annual capital gain (or deduct the average annual loss) to redemption, stated as a percentage of the current market price. Thus, we can state the Japanese GRY as follows.

Formula to learn

$$\text{Japanese GRY} = \frac{\text{Annual coupon}}{\text{Market price}} + \frac{\text{Average annual capital gain to redemption}}{\text{Market price}}$$

Or

$$\text{Japanese GRY} = \frac{\text{Annual coupon}}{\text{Market price}} + \frac{\frac{\text{Redemption price} - \text{Market price}}{\text{Years to redemption}}}{\text{Market price}}$$

Example

We hold 10% Loan stock (annual coupon) redeemable at par in four years. The current market price is £97.25. Calculate the Japanese GRY.

Solution

The Japanese GRY for the above would be

$$\text{Japanese GRY} = \frac{10.00}{97.25} + \frac{\frac{100.00 - 97.25}{4}}{97.25}$$

$$= \frac{10.00}{97.25} + \frac{0.6875}{97.25}$$

$$= 0.10283 + 0.00707 = 0.10990 \text{ or } 10.99\%$$

1.2.2 Uses

The main use of this method is to provide a quick and easy way of assessing the GRY that takes into account all of the returns, income and capital.

It should be noted that it is not an absolutely accurate measure of return, since it assumes linear capital growth rather than the more realistic compound growth. As a result, it is liable to overstate the effects of any capital gain or loss. Furthermore, this inaccuracy increases the further away a bond is from maturity.

It does, however, serve as a useful tool in determining the true GRY as we illustrate below.

1.2.3 Limitations

Whilst this method does overcome the first limitation of the flat yield, i.e. its failure to account for any capital gains or losses to redemption, it does not overcome the other noted drawbacks, specifically

- The calculation completely ignores the timing of any cash flows and the time value of money.
- With some bonds (FRNs), the return in any one period will vary with interest rates. If the coupon is not constant, then this measure is only of historic value unless the predicted return is used.

The first of these limitations can only be overcome through the use of discounted cash flow techniques as illustrated below. The second is a valid limitation of all yield measures.

1.3 Gross redemption yield

1.3.1 Calculation

The gross redemption yield (GRY) resolves the issue of the redemption values **and** the time value of money by using discounted cash flow techniques.

The gross redemption yield is the internal rate of return (IRR) of

- The dirty price paid to buy the bond.
- The gross coupons received **to redemption**.
- The final redemption proceeds.

Mathematical formulation

This could be expressed mathematically as follows.

When GRY = r, then

Formula to learn

$$\text{Price} = \sum \frac{C_t}{(1+r)^t} + \frac{R}{(1+r)^n}$$

Alternatively, this may be expressed as

Formula to learn

$$\text{Price} = \frac{C_1}{(1+r)} + \frac{C_2}{(1+r)^2} + \frac{C_3}{(1+r)^3} + \cdots + \frac{C_n + R}{(1+r)^n}$$

It should be noted that these formulae **cannot** be algebraically solved (except in very rare circumstances) and that the process of interpolation described below represents the only practical method.

Interpolation approach

The interpolation approach is based on the fact that there is an inverse relationship between yields and bond prices, i.e. as yields rise, bond prices fall, and vice versa.

In order to calculate the GRY, we select two interest rates and calculate the net present value of the bond cash flows at each of these two rates. These calculations establish two reference points in terms of values and rates, which can be used to determine a linear relationship between changes in the bond price and changes in interest rates. We can then interpolate between the two, i.e. use this relationship to establish what rate gives rise to a zero NPV, giving the GRY (IRR).

The true relationship between bond prices and interest rates is **not** linear, hence this calculation is only an approximation.

This process is graphically illustrated below for our 10% four-year Loan stock, where 5% and 15% have been used as reference rates.

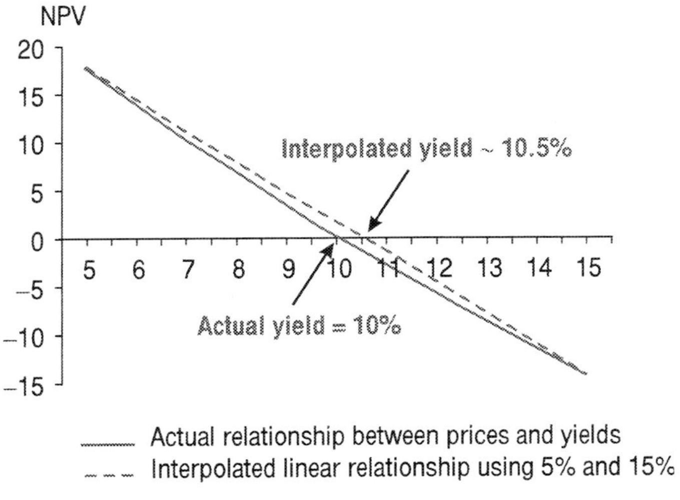

As this diagram illustrates, the process of interpolation is not absolutely accurate since, as we have already noted, the relationship between prices and interest rates is **not** linear. Furthermore, this inaccuracy increases if the two reference points are widely dispersed. It is therefore essential that our two selected rates are close to the actual GRY in order to produce an accurate result.

To get an indication of which rates are suitable, we should use either

- The conclusions established above regarding coupon rates, interest rates and bond prices; or
- The flat yield or Japanese GRY assessments.

Example

We hold 10% Loan stock (annual coupon) redeemable at par in four years. The current market price is £97.25. Calculate the GRY.

Solution

Assessing the rates to try based on current market value

Since the current market value is below par, it must be that the coupon rate is below prevailing interest rates or the yield. As a result, we should select some higher rates for our GRY computation. We could perhaps try 11% as our first reference point, then select something slightly higher or lower for the second, depending on what results were obtained from the first.

Assessing the rates to try based on flat yield and Japanese GRY

The flat yield completely ignores any gain (or loss) to redemption and hence will understate (overstate) the GRY. We established above that the flat yield (coupon return) on this bond is 10.283%.

The Japanese GRY overstates the effect of any gain or loss to redemption as we noted above, hence it will overstate the GRY if there is a gain, and understate it if there is a loss. We established above that the Japanese GRY on this bond is 10.99%.

The flat yield and Japanese GRY therefore represent two rates, one of which is normally higher than the GRY, and one of which is normally lower, though both may well be close to it. As such, they may well represent two good reference rates to try in our interpolation process.

Note that we said **normally** higher/lower, not always. There is one circumstance where this is not the case and this is when a bond is valued at par. In this situation, there will be no gain or loss to redemption and hence, all three measures will produce the same return.

The relationship between these three measures could be summarised as follows.

Bond Value	Relationship
Above par (loss to redemption)	Flat yield > GRY > Japanese GRY
At par	Flat yield = GRY = Japanese GRY
Below par (gain to redemption)	Flat yield < GRY < Japanese GRY

Conclusion

Whichever method we use to establish reference rates, we need to try rates above 10% for this example. The approach would be to select and try one rate, say 11%, and see if this gives a positive or negative NPV. If the NPV is positive, then our second selected rate needs to be even higher to try to establish a negative NPV, on the basis of the inverse relationship between prices and interest rates. Conversely, if the NPV is negative, then the second selected rate needs to be lower.

In this example, a rate of 11% was tried first, giving a negative NPV. A second (lower) rate of 10.5% was then selected, giving a positive figure.

Using the annuity formula

Time	Cash Flow (£)	DF (10.5%)	PV (10.5%) (£)	DF (11%)	PV (11%) (£)
0	(97.25)	1	(97.25)	1	(97.25)
1–4	10.00	$\frac{1}{0.105}\left(1-\frac{1}{1.105^4}\right)$	31.36	$\frac{1}{0.11}\left(1-\frac{1}{1.11^4}\right)$	31.03
4	100.00	$\frac{1}{1.105^4}$	67.07	$\frac{1}{1.11^4}$	65.87
Net present value			1.18		(0.35)

Yield assessment

We have found that the rate of 10.5% is too low and 11% is too high, hence the GRY lies between these two points.

The total range of values covered as a result of this 0.5% (11% – 10.5%) yield difference is a value of £1.53 (£1.18 + £0.35). We need to move so far from 10.5% towards 11% that we eradicate £1.18 of this £1.53. The GRY is, therefore

$$\text{GRY} = 10.5 + \frac{118}{153} \times (11.0 - 10.5) = 10.886\%$$

Note. The actual GRY is 10.8842%, hence this calculation has proved accurate to better than one basis point. If we required any greater accuracy, we could reassess the GRY taking 10.886% as a starting reference rate and continuing through a process of iteration with closer reference rates until we achieve the level of accuracy required.

1.3.2 Uses

This measure overcomes the major deficiencies highlighted in relation to the flat yield and the Japanese GRY. It considers all cash returns and exactly when they occur.

As a result, the GRY represents a realistic measure of the expected overall return from a bond at any point in time.

1.3.3 Limitations

Assumes rates remain constant

As a measure of predicted return, the yield is limited, since it **assumes that interest rates remain constant throughout the period and hence, that any coupon receipts may be reinvested at the same rate as the yield**. If this is the case, then the GRY does represent the return achieved. If rates vary, however, the return achieved will differ from the GRY.

Example

If the above bond priced at £97.25 and on a GRY of 10.8842% is held to maturity, what will be the value of the portfolio at maturity and the return achieved by a fund manager, assuming interest rates

- Remain constant.
- Fall to 9% after two years.

Solution

Calculating the terminal value at the redemption date and hence the annual return achieved for each scenario gives the following.

Constant interest rates

Time	Cash Flow (£)	CF	Terminal Value (£)
1	10.00	1.108842^3	13.6336
2	10.00	1.108842^2	12.2953
3	10.00	1.108842	11.0884
4	110.00	1	110.0000
			147.0173

Return achieved

The annualised return achieved can now be calculated as

$$1+r=\sqrt[4]{\frac{147.0173}{97.2500}}=\sqrt[4]{1.511746}=1.108842$$

Giving

r = 0.108842 or 10.8842%

Hence, we can see that with constant interest rates, the yield at acquisition does represent the return achieved to maturity.

Changing interest rates

The calculation of the terminal value at redemption will now need to reflect the change in interest rates after two years. The terminal value will now be as follows.

Time	Cash Flow (£)	CF	Terminal Value (£)
1	10.00	1.108842×1.09^2	13.1742
2	10.00	1.09^2	11.8810
3	10.00	1.09	10.9000
4	110.00	1	110.0000
			145.9552

Return achieved

The annualised return achieved can now be calculated as

$$1+r=\sqrt[4]{\frac{145.9552}{97.2500}}=\sqrt[4]{1.500825}=1.10683$$

Giving

r = 0.10683 or 10.683%

Hence, we can see that with changing interest rates, the yield at acquisition does **not** represent the return achieved on holding the bond to maturity. In this case, the return is lower as reinvestment rates have fallen.

Assumes held to maturity

If the bond is not held to redemption, but sold at some earlier date, then the return achieved will be a function of the price of the bond (hence, interest rates) at the disposal date.

Example

If the above bond priced at £97.25 and on a GRY of 10.8842% is held for one year and sold on GRY of 10%, what return will have been achieved?

Solution

To calculate the return achieved, we must firstly calculate the selling price of the bond at the end of one year. This, however, is simple here, since we are pricing a 10% bond on a 10% yield its price will be par. As a result, the amount realised at the end of the year is as follows.

Selling Price	(£)
Coupon for the year	10
Sale proceeds	100
	110

Hence, based on an investment of £97.25, the return achieved has been

$$\text{Return} = \frac{110.00 - 97.25}{97.25} = 13.11\%$$

which clearly differs from the GRY of the bond at acquisition.

Conclusion

If interest rates remain constant throughout the period to redemption, then the GRY will represent the return that will be achieved throughout any holding period. If interest rates change, then the return achieved will alter as reinvestment returns and selling prices (if not held to maturity) change.

One further criticism of the yield measure is that it ignores reality in that we discount all future flows at the same rate when, as we shall see from the yield curve, the required rate of return for cash at different future dates varies.

1.4 The net redemption yield

1.4.1 Calculation

The GRY measures the gross return before the effects of taxation. The net redemption yield (NRY) is the return that the investor can expect net of taxation.

The NRY is most appropriate for individual investors to help them assess their after-tax returns. As each individual has a different tax position, the NRY will obviously be different for different individuals. The market convention is to compute the NRY at assumed levels of personal tax such as 40%.

Though less appropriate, the NRY may be calculated for corporate investors. Unfortunately, the tax treatment of individual and corporate investors differs, adding a minor complication.

Individual investors

The tax treatment for individuals is that coupon income is subject to income tax, however the capital gain (or loss) on gilts and sterling non-convertible debt is tax free.

The net redemption yield can, therefore, be calculated as the internal rate of return (IRR) of

- The dirty price paid to buy the bond.
- The **net** coupons received **to redemption** (net of the appropriate rate of tax).
- The final redemption proceeds.

The net redemption yield for individual investors can be formulated as

Formula to learn

$$\text{Price} = \sum \frac{C_t(1-T_p)}{(1+r)^t} + \frac{R}{(1+r)^n}$$

where

r = NRY

T_p = personal tax rate

Alternatively, this may be expressed as

Formula to learn

$$\text{Price} = \frac{C_1(1-T_p)}{(1+r)} + \frac{C_2(1-T_p)}{(1+r)^2} + \frac{C_3(1-T_p)}{(1+r)^3} + \cdots + \frac{C_n(1-T_p)+R}{(1+r)^n}$$

Once again, it should be noted that these formulae **cannot** be algebraically solved (except in very rare circumstances) and that the IRR interpolation approach represents the only practical method.

Note. It is possible to get a quick approximation to the NRY by using an approach similar to that for the Japanese GRY, but using the coupon net of tax for the first part of the calculation, i.e.

Formula to learn

$$\text{NRY} \approx \frac{\text{Annual net coupon}}{\text{Market price}} + \frac{\left(\frac{\text{Redemption price} - \text{Market price}}{\text{Years to redemption}}\right)}{\text{Market price}}$$

Example

We hold 10% Loan stock (annual coupon) redeemable at par in four years. The current market price is £97.25. Calculate the NRY for a 40% taxpayer.

Solution

Assessing the value at two rates

Since the GRY was known to be somewhere between 10% and 11%, then two reasonable rates to use would be 6% and 7%, roughly 60% of the GRY rates, giving

Time	Cash Flow (£)	DF (6%)	PV (6%) (£)	DF (7%)	PV 7% (£)
0	(97.25)	1	(97.25)	1	(97.25)
1–4	10.00	$\frac{1}{0.06}\left(1-\frac{1}{1.06^4}\right)$	20.79	$\frac{1}{0.07}\left(1-\frac{1}{1.07^4}\right)$	20.32
4	100.00	$\frac{1}{1.06^4}$	79.21	$\frac{1}{1.07^4}$	76.29
			2.75		(0.64)

Yield assessment

We have found that the rate of 6% is too low and 7% is too high, hence the NRY lies between these two points.

The total range covered is a value of £3.39 (£2.75 + £0.64), and the NRY is therefore

$$\text{NRY} = 6.0 + \frac{275}{339} \times (7.0 - 6.0) = 6.811\%$$

Note. As for the GRY, this calculation provides a very close, though not absolutely accurate, answer. The actual NRY is 6.8084%, hence this calculation has again proved accurate to better than one basis point.

Approximation method

Had we used the Japanese style approximation, we would have calculated

$$\text{NRY} = \frac{6.00}{97.25} + \frac{\frac{100.00 - 97.25}{4}}{97.25}$$

$$= \frac{6.00}{97.25} + \frac{0.6875}{97.25}$$

$$= 0.06170 + 0.00707 = 0.06877 \text{ or } 6.877\%$$

You will note that this is less accurate, but still reasonably close.

Corporate investors

For corporate investors, the tax treatment of the income and gain elements of the return on a bond are identical, they are both taxed as income.

As a result, ignoring the time delay on the payment of the tax, the net redemption yield for a corporate investor can be calculated as

Formula to learn

$$\text{NRY} = \text{GRY} \times (1 - T_C)$$

where

T_C = corporate tax rate

Example

We hold 10% Loan stock (annual coupon) redeemable at par in four years. The current market price is £97.25. Calculate the NRY, assuming a 40% corporate tax rate.

Solution

We earlier noted the GRY of this stock to be 10.8842%, hence at 40% corporation tax

NRY = 10.8842 × 0.60 = 6.531%

Effect of the tax difference

For individual investors, any gain is tax free, but any loss does not attract tax relief. For corporate investors, gains are taxed and losses are tax allowed.

Individual investors are, therefore, in the superior tax position if bonds are trading below par (e.g. low-coupon bonds), since this gain to maturity goes untaxed. This can be seen from the above example where the NRY is greater for the individual investor (6.811% vs 6.531%), with the bond trading below par at £97.25.

Corporate investors are, however, in the superior tax position where bonds are trading above par (e.g. higher coupon bonds), since these will suffer a loss to maturity that will be tax allowable for them but not for individuals.

1.4.2 Uses

Since it is based on discounted cash flow techniques, as is the GRY, this measure overcomes the major deficiencies highlighted in relation to the flat yield and the Japanese GRY. It considers all cash returns and exactly when they occur and their tax implications for the investor.

The NRY therefore represents a realistic measure of the expected overall return to the investor at any point in time net of taxes.

1.4.3 Limitations

The limitations of the NRY are as for the GRY, specifically it only represents the net return that will be achieved if interest rates to maturity remain constant throughout the holding period.

1.5 Gross equivalent yield or grossed-up NRY

1.5.1 Calculation

As we noted earlier, the tax status for individual investors holding gilts or sterling non-convertible debt is that coupons are taxed, but any capital gain is not. This may be contrasted with an investment in shares where both income and capital are subject to tax.

The Gross Equivalent Yield (GEY) calculates the gross return required from a fully taxed source of income in order to produce the same after-tax return as a particular bond. This calculation only has any relevance for individual investors, since for corporate investors, both income and gains are taxed, i.e. for them a bond is a fully taxed source of income.

The approach to the calculation is to measure the after-tax return that the bond is providing using the NRY calculation, which the fully taxed source of income will need to match, then gross this up for the appropriate tax rate to see what gross return is required from that source. The calculation is

Formula to learn

$$GEY = \frac{NRY}{1 - T_p}$$

where

T_p = the personal tax rate upon which the NRY was calculated

Example

We hold 10% Loan stock (annual coupon) redeemable at par in four years. The current market price is £97.25 based on a GRY of 10.8842% and an NRY of 6.8084% for a 40% taxpayer. Calculate the GEY.

Solution

The flat yield for the above would be

$$GEY = \frac{6.8084}{0.60} = 11.3473\%$$

Clearly, this is a higher return than the GRY, which may have been anticipated, since this bond is valued below par, hence generating a tax-free gain to maturity. Any fully taxed alternative would need to match this gain **after tax** and hence requires a higher return before tax.

Conversely, if the bond is valued above par, then the capital loss it will suffer to maturity would **not** attract tax relief, whereas it would on the fully taxed alternative. As a result, a much higher capital loss could be sustained on the fully taxed alternative whilst still having the same effect net of tax. The result is that the GEY will be lower than the GRY in this situation.

If a bond is valued at par, then the two measures will be identical as there will be no capital gain or loss, hence the tax treatment will be the same.

The relationship between these two measures and the flat yield could be summarised as follows.

Bond Value	Relationship
Above par (loss to redemption)	Flat yield > GRY > GEY
At par	Flat yield = GRY = GEY
Below par (gain to redemption)	Flat yield < GRY < GEY

1.5.2 Uses

The use of this measure is to enable comparison of the returns of alternatives regardless of their tax treatment.

It does **not** represent the pretax return the bond will offer that is given as accurately as can be by the GRY. Instead, it provides a benchmark for appraising alternatives that are fully taxed.

1.5.3 Limitations

Since it is based on the NRY, its limitations are as for that measure, specifically it only represents the gross return required from the alternative if interest rates to maturity remain constant throughout the holding period.

In addition, the calculation only caters for one tax rate, hence we must assume that this will also be constant to over the period.

1.6 Gross redemption yield – further considerations

1.6.1 Introduction

Though we noted and illustrated some limitations of the GRY as an assessment of the return a bond will pay, it still represents the best assessment of the potential pre-tax returns from a bond at any point in time and is the major return measure considered when appraising bonds.

We illustrated above how we could calculate the GRY for a plain vanilla bond paying a fixed annual coupon to maturity and being redeemed at par. You may also have noted from the above GRY examples that the bond had also just paid a coupon, as the first coupon was always one year away.

We now need to consider how to extend these ideas to cover some other types of bonds and dates through the coupon payment period.

Specifically, we need to consider the calculation for

- Bonds paying a semi-annual (or even more frequent) coupons.
- Double dated bonds
- Bonds between coupon payment dates
- Floating rate bonds, where the coupon varies with interest rates.
- Portfolio yield
- Yield to call for callable bonds
- Yield to average bonds
- Index-linked bonds, where the cash returns vary with inflation.
- Risk-adjusted yield and yield degradation

1.6.2 Calculation for semi-annual coupons

In the calculations that we have entered into so far, we have assumed an annual coupon. With a semi-annual coupon, the calculation would be similar, with the exception that the coupon would be half the annual amount and would arise twice as frequently (every six months).

For example, with a 10% four-year semi-annual bond, there would be eight £5 coupons paid every six months up to redemption. How can we incorporate these semi-annual cash flows into our IRR calculation?

As we did earlier, the way to deal with this is to work in semi-annual terms, i.e. take one time period to be six months, and discount the half-yearly cash flows at a semi-annual rate of return.

Example

We hold 10% Loan stock (semi-annual coupon) redeemable at par in four years. The current market price is £97.25. Calculate the GRY.

Solution

We will consider one unit of time to be six months and try to establish a semi-annual (six-monthly) yield.

This bond will pay £5 every six months for the next eight periods (four years), at which date it will be redeemed at par. Based on its current market price (below par), we know that the total return exceeds 5% every six months, hence we try two higher rates – say 5.2% and 5.5%.

The calculation is then as follows.

Time	Cash Flow (£)	DF (5.2%)	PV (5.2%) (£)	DF (5.5%)	PV (5.2%) (£)
0	(97.25)	1	(97.25)	1	(97.25)
1–8	5.00	$\frac{1}{0.52}\left(1-\frac{1}{1.052^8}\right)$	32.06	$\frac{1}{0.055}\left(1-\frac{1}{1.055^8}\right)$	31.67
8	100.00	$\frac{1}{1.052^8}$	66.66	$\frac{1}{1.055^8}$	65.16
			1.47		(0.42)

Hence, the semi-annual GRY (six-month yield) can be calculated as

$$GRY = 5.2 + \frac{147}{147-(42)} \times (5.5-5.2) = 5.433\%$$

To convert this to an annual yield, **the market convention is simply to multiply this semi-annual yield by two**, i.e. the quoted gross redemption yield is twice the semi-annual rate. Here that would give a quoted yield of 10.866% (5.433% × 2).

This does not give a completely accurate assessment of returns, since it ignores the compounding effect of interest rates within any year. It is, however, the market convention, and you must therefore be aware of it. The mathematically correct method of annualising the return is to apply the following formula.

Formula to learn

$$\text{Annualised return} = (1 + r)^2 - 1$$

1.6.3 Calculation for double dated bonds

The assessment of the GRY for double dated bonds follows the same principles as our normal calculation. The only extra point to factor in is what is the redemption date.

The answer here is consistent to that outlined in the pricing section. Specifically we need to determine whether the bond offers a relatively cheap source of finance (in which case the issuer will run it to the latest possible date) or one expensive source (in which case the issuer will redeem as soon as possible, refinancing at a lower rate if necessary).

This determination can be achieved by reference to the price. If a bond is priced below par it is paying a relatively low coupon which represents cheap finance to the issuer. Conversely, if the bond is priced above par it must be paying a relatively high coupon, representing an expensive source to the issuer. So we can summarise as follows.

Bond Price	Redemption Date
Below par	Latest
Above par	Earliest

1.6.4 Calculation for bonds between coupon payment dates

The approach for determining the GRY of bonds between coupon payment dates follows the same logic. That is we need to pick two rates, assess the NPV at those rates and establish the GRY through interpolation of those results. The only issue here is in establishing the NPV where we need to use the idea of pricing between coupon dates introduced in the section on pricing.

Example

Calculate the GRY of the above semi-annual coupon bond if it is now 40 days later, i.e. 40 days into its next coupon period (which is 184 days long), and the bond is now priced at £99.00.

Solution

Time	Cash Flow (£)	DF (5%)	PV (5%) (£)	DF (5.5%)	PV (5.5%) (£)
0	5.00	1	5.00	1	5.00
1–7	5.00	$\frac{0}{0.05}\left(1-\frac{1}{1.05^7}\right)$	28.93	$\frac{1}{0.055}\left(1-\frac{1}{1.055^7}\right)$	28.41
7	100.00	$\frac{1}{1.05^7}$	71.07	$\frac{1}{1.055^7}$	68.74
PV Cum-Interest at Next Coupon Date			105.00		102.15
Discounted back for 144 days			$\times\frac{1}{1.11\frac{3}{4}}$		$\times\frac{1}{1.11\frac{3}{4}}$
PV 40 days through period			101.07		97.96
Price 40 days through the period			99.00		99.00
NPV 40 days through the period			2.07		(1.04)

Hence the semi-annual GRY is now

$$GRY = 5.0 + \frac{2.07}{2.07-(1.04)} \times (5.5-5.0) = 5.33\%$$

And so the quoted yield would now be 10.66% (5.33% × 2).

1.6.5 Evaluation of floating rate bonds

We established earlier the following formula for the evaluation of a floating rate bond.

Formula to learn

$$\text{FRN Price} = \frac{\text{Next coupon} + \text{Par value}}{1 + r \times \text{Days}/365}$$

This relationship can also be used 'in reverse' to calculate the yield to the next coupon payment date.

Example

If an FRN is priced at £102 when we are three months into the annual coupon payment period, what yield is it trading on, assuming interest rates were 10% at the last reset date?

Solution

$$102 = \frac{10+100}{(1+r)^{3/4}}$$

Giving

$$(1+r)^{3/4} = \frac{10+100}{102} = \frac{110}{102} = 1.07843$$

Therefore

$$1 + r = \sqrt[3/4]{1.07843} = 1.10592$$

r = 0.10592 or 10.592%

1.6.6 Portfolio yield and maturity

When considering a portfolio of bonds, it may be appropriate to consider the yield of the portfolio.

The true portfolio yield, would look at the individual components in the portfolio and their associated cash flows. Once the cash flows have been identified, then the yield can be derived in the same way as the yield on an ordinary bond, i.e. by discounting the portfolio cash flows back to the present value. This could clearly be a quite involved calculation if we have, say, semi-annual bonds with long maturities so the question to ask is whether there are any reasonable alternatives.

One alternative that may come to mind is to take a weighted average of the yields of the bonds in the portfolio. If one bond is yielding 5% and another is yielding 7% then in a 50:50 portfolio the yield would surely be 6% wouldn't it? The answer is that if the two bonds concerned had the same maturity then this would give a reasonable approximation. If, however, the bonds had different maturities, say 5 and 10 years respectively, then this calculation ignores the fact that we are getting the higher yield for longer – it effectively assumes that we receive them for the same term.

The best approximation to the portfolio yield that takes account of both the yields on the bonds and their terms is to weight the bond GRYs by nominal values and BPVs, though duration or modified duration may be used in place of BPV if they are more readily available. Duration, modified duration and BPV are all covered later in this Study Text. Using this we have.

$$\text{Portfolio yield (approx 1)} = \frac{\Sigma \text{GRY} \times \text{Nominal} \times \text{BPV}}{\Sigma \text{Nominal} \times \text{BPV}}$$

An alternative approximation is to weight the bond GRYs by both value and modified duration, though again, using duration or BPV in place of modified duration provide reasonable alternatives.

$$\text{Portfolio yield (approx 2)} = \frac{\Sigma \text{GRY} \times \text{Market value} \times \text{Modified duration}}{\Sigma \text{Market value} \times \text{Modified duration}}$$

Note that these are all alternative approximations and you should use whatever is most convenient based on the information given.

Example

The following two bonds are held in a portfolio.

Bond	Coupon	Maturity (Years)	GRY	Portfolio nominal	Duration	Modified Duration	BPV
A	6%	2	3%	30	1.945	1.888	0.01996
B	4%	3	5%	70	2.884	2.747	0.02672

The true portfolio yield is 4.526%. Calculate the approximate portfolio yield. Note that this example is more fully illustrated in the appendix to the risk chapter where we introduce duration, modified duration and BPV.

Solution

Portfolio yield (approx 1) $= \dfrac{\Sigma \text{GRY} \times \text{Nominal} \times \text{BPV}}{\Sigma \text{Nominal} \times \text{BPV}}$

$= \dfrac{3\% \times 30 \times 0.01996 + 5\% \times 70 \times 0.02672}{30 \times 0.01996 + 70 \times 0.02672} = 4.515\%$

Portfolio yield (approx 2) $= \dfrac{\Sigma \text{GRY} \times \text{Market value} \times \text{Modified duration}}{\Sigma \text{Market value} \times \text{Modified duration}}$

$= \dfrac{3\% \times 105.740 \times 1.888 + 5\% \times 97.277 \times 2.747}{105.740 \times 1.888 + 97.277 \times 2.747} = 4.144\%$

The first approximation is clearly very close to the actual yield of 4.526%

1.6.7 Yield to call

So far our calculations have been made on the assumption that the bond is held until maturity. There is an obvious problem with callable (double dated) bonds in that the holder will not know when the bond is going to redeem. The yield to call attempts to evaluate the return on a bond based on the period up to the call date.

The most common solution is to assess whether early redemption seems likely (based on the bond's price relative to par) and use either one of the extremes. If the bond is trading above par then this indicates that the coupon is above the market level. Logically, the issuer will then retire the debt at the earliest opportunity and replace it with lower coupon issues. In this situation, it makes sense for the yield calculation to be based on the earlier of the two dates. If the bond is pricing below par, then the opposite holds true.

Another possible solution to this problem is to calculate the yields on a variety of possible scenarios and then produce a weighted average.

1.6.8 Yield to average life

Where a bond has a set redemption schedule with the principal being repaid over a period of time, the most appropriate measure will be the **yield to average life**. This measure reflects the fact that there is a certainty to the redemption pattern on this bond that does not exist with a callable bond.

Example

Nominal value \$200m redeemed in three instalments.

Year 8	Year 9	Year 10
\$50m	\$50m	\$100m
@ 110	@ 105	@ 100

Calculate the yield to average life

Solution

Time (t)	Redemption (Rv)	Proportion of Issue (Pr)	Average Redemption Value (ARV = Rv × Pr)	Time Weighted ARV (ARV × t)
8	110	0.25	27.50	220.00
9	105	0.25	26.25	236.25
10	100	0.50	50.00	500.00
			103.75	956.25

Average life = $\frac{956.25}{103.75}$ =9.217 years

This may alternatively be reduced to the following formulae

Formula to learn

$$\text{Average redemption value} = Rv_1 \times Pr_1 + Rv_2 \times Pr_2 + \cdots + Rv_n \times Pr_n$$

and

Formula to learn

$$\text{Average life} = \frac{(Rv_1 \times Pr_1 \times N_1) + (Rv_2 \times Pr_2 \times N_2) + \ldots + (Rv_n \times Pr_n \times N_n)}{(Rv_1 \times Pr_1) + (Rv_2 \times Pr_2) + \ldots + (Rv_n \times Pr_n)}$$

where

Rv_1 = the redemption value at the first redemption date
Pr_1 = the proportion of the issue redeemed at the first redemption
N_1 = the number of years to the first redemption date

Using the details from the example

Average redemption value = (110 × 0.25) + (105 × 0.25) + (100 × 0.50) = 103.75

$$\text{Average life} = \frac{(110 \times 0.25 \times 8) + (105 \times 0.25 \times 9) + (100 \times 0.50 \times 10)}{(110 \times 0.25) + (105 \times 0.25) + (100 \times 0.50)} = 9.217 \text{ years}$$

Having established the average life (AVL) and the average redemption value (ARV), the final stage is to calculate the yield to average life (YAL). This will be achieved by using the same approach as for all other GRY calculations but taking the redemption value as the average redemption value, and the redemption date as the average life. Mathematically this could be described as follows

Formula to learn

$$\text{Current price} = \frac{C}{(1+YAL)} + \frac{C}{(1+YAL)^2} + \cdots + \frac{C+ARV}{(1+YAL)^{AVL}}$$

This would be best undertaken as a standard tabular GRY calculation.

1.6.9 Evaluation of index-linked bonds

We established earlier the following relationship for the evaluation of index-linked gilts.

Formula to learn

Real price = PV of the original cash flows at real rates – the price quoted for 3 month ILGs
Nominal price = Real price × (1 + i) – the price quoted for 8 month ILGs

This latter relationship may be expressed as

$$\text{Real price} = \frac{\text{Nominal price}}{(1+i)}$$

And we can use this to calculate the real yield through interpolation. The approach is a normal GRY calculation, the only difference being that we need to incorporate the adjusted price (the left-hand side of the above equation).

With an index-linked gilt (ILG), all the cash returns, both coupon and redemption proceeds, vary with inflation since the issue reference date.

Example

A notional index-linked stock is in issue, carrying a coupon of 3% paid semi-annually. The stock was issued some years ago when the index was 100 (three months prior to the issue date) and will redeem in ten years. The reference RPI (three months prior to the payment date) for the coupon just paid is 140. The bond is currently trading at £133.25.

Calculate the real and nominal GRY when future annual inflation is expected to be 5% p.a.

Solution

The assumed inflation rate of 5% p.a. corresponds to 2½% on a semi-annual basis – dividing by two for consistency with GRY assessments.

Adjusted market value

The real pre-inflation market value is then

$$\text{Real price} = \frac{\text{Nominal price}}{(1+i)} = \frac{133.25}{1.40} = £95.18$$

NPV calculations based on adjusted market value

The Japanese GRY for this bond works out at over 1.75%, hence trying this as a first rate, then selecting a suitable second rate based on the results gives

Time	Cash Flow (£)	DF (1.75%)	PV (1.75%) (£)	DF (1.80%)	PV (1.80%) (£)
0	(95.18)	1	(95.18)	1	(95.18)
1–20	1.50	$\frac{1}{0.0175}\left(1-\frac{1}{1.0175^{20}}\right)$	25.13	$\frac{1}{0.018}\left(1-\frac{1}{1.018^{20}}\right)$	25.01
20	100.00	$\frac{1}{1.0175^{20}}$	70.68	$\frac{1}{1.018^{20}}$	69.99
			0.63		(0.18)

Yield assessment

We have found that the rate of 1.75% is too low and 1.80% is too high, hence the real GRY lies between these two points.

Real GRY

The total range covered is a value of £0.81 (£0.63 + £0.18), and the real semi-annual GRY is therefore

$$\text{GRY} = 1.75 + \frac{63}{81} \times (1.80 - 1.75) = 1.789\%$$

and the real annual GRY would be quoted as twice this, i.e. 3.578%.

Nominal GRY

To establish the nominal GRY, we once again need to utilise the Fisher relationship, i.e.

$(1 + r) = (1 + i)(1 + R)$

Giving the nominal semi-annual yield as

$(1 + r) = 1.01789 \times 1.025 = 1.04334$

Hence

$r = 0.04334$ or 4.334%

And from this, we can establish the nominal quoted GRY as 8.668% (4.334% × 2).

Use of the real yield

Once the real yield has been established, it can be used to compare with the nominal yields on offer from the conventional gilts to arrive at the breakeven yield. We illustrate this diagrammatically below.

Note. We have simplified here to illustrate the idea by using addition of real returns and inflation rather than the Fisher relationship. Strictly speaking, the Fisher relationship should be applied.

Example

Conventional gilts are yielding 10% against a real yield of 4% on an ILG. Which should we invest in?

Solution

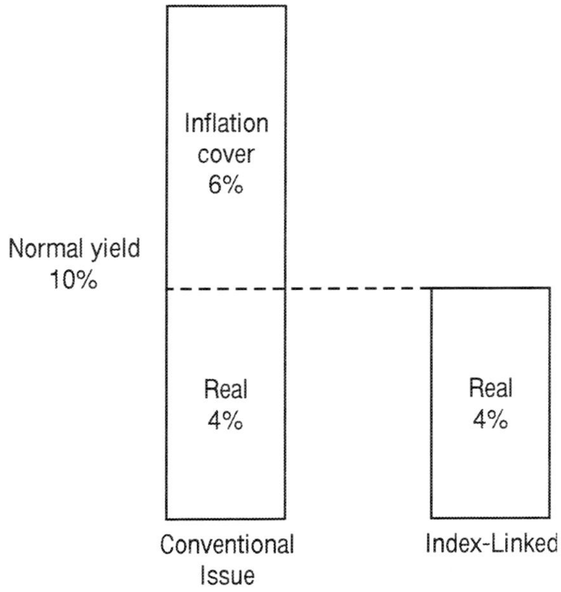

If inflation is greater than the 6% currently built into the nominal yield on the conventional, then it makes sense to invest in the index-linked stock, since this will generate the higher real return.

For example, if the expected rate of inflation is 7%, the real return on the conventional stock will only be 3% (10% – 7%) as compared with 4% on the index-linked, or the nominal return on the ILG will be 11% (4% + 7%) rather than the 10% on the conventional.

Note. For this analysis to be accurate, the comparison stock ought to be common in as many respects as possible. There is no value in comparing the nominal yield of a conventional short-dated high-coupon stock with that of a low-coupon long-dated index-linked stock. The market services that are available will often use a variety of stocks to make their comparisons.

1.6.10 Risk adjusted yield and yield degradation/default loss rates

One of the assumptions of the normal GRY calculations is that the bond (or bonds in the portfolio) will be held to maturity, and implicit within that is that the bond (or portfolio) will pay all of its cash flows. With high grade bonds this assumption may not be unreasonable, however with lower grade investments it may be less appropriate.

The GRY is the IRR of all cash flows that could be received. The risk adjusted yield is the IRR of all the cash flows we expect to receive taking account of any annual expected loss rate from bonds that may go into default along with any estimate of any future recovery of these losses.

The yield degradation is the difference between these two figures (usually expressed in basis points), i.e.

Yield degradation = GRY – Risk adjusted yield

Though it does not precisely take account of time and discounting, it is possible to estimate the risk adjusted yield mathematically. If Y is the current GRY of the portfolio then, assuming all other things remain equal and that there are no losses, the expected value in one year could be determined using terminal value ideas as

Future value = Current value $\times$ (1 + Y)

If, however, the portfolio suffers an annual **default rate** of D, then the future value should be reduced by this amount, giving

$$\begin{aligned}\text{Future value} &= \text{Current value} \times (1 + Y) \times (1 - D)\\ &= \text{Current value} \times (1 + Y - D - YD)\end{aligned}$$

Where Y and D are both small percentages, YD is negligible, leaving

Future value = Current value $\times$ (1 + Y – D)

And so considering the return on the portfolio we have

Risk adjusted yield = (Y – D)

If, however, the portfolio experiences a **recovery rate** of R from any defaulting securities, then the default loss is not the full amount D but is reduced to D(1 – R), giving

Risk adjusted yield = (Y – D(1 – R))

A yield degradation of

Yield degradation/default loss rate = D(1 – R)

1.7 Alternative yield calculators

1.7.1 Performance yield

A performance yield measures the return on a bond over a specific period. It can either be computed on an historic or predictive basis. The historic basis reviews the holding gain over the period of ownership.

Formula to learn

$$\text{Holding period return} = \frac{(\text{Sales proceeds} + \text{Coupons received}) - \text{Purchase price}}{\text{Purchase price}}$$

Alternatively, by predicting interest rates into the future it would be possible to perform the same calculation using the predicted value on sale as the consideration at sale.

1.7.2 Realised yield or horizon yield

The methodology that we have used above gives us a simple holding period return. An alternative is to build in the time value of money.

The calculation of the holding period return or realised or horizon yield can be defined as follows.

Formula to learn

$$\text{Horizon yield} = \sqrt[n]{\frac{\text{Terminal value}}{\text{Price}}} - 1$$

where

n = the number of years to horizon

We used this calculation earlier when discussing the limitations of the GRY is assessing the returns realised if rates changed.

2 Term Structure of Interest Rates and Yield Curve

2.1 Introduction

In all of our evaluation exercises so far, we have applied the same interest rate in discounting the cash flows regardless of when they arise. But is this reasonable?

Example

What will be the market values of two zero-coupon bonds which are identical in all respects, except that one matures in one year and the other in five years, if the interest rate is 10%? How will these values change if interest rates fall to 9%?

Solution

Maturity	10%	9%	Change
1 year	$MV = \frac{100}{1.10} = 90.91$	$MV = \frac{100}{1.09} = 91.74$	£0.83 or 0.913%
5 years	$MV = \frac{100}{1.10^5} = 62.09$	$MV = \frac{100}{1.09^5} = 64.99$	£2.90 or 4.671%

In both absolute and relative terms, the five-year bond shows significantly more price volatility, hence we may conclude that the five-year bond is a more risky investment.

One of the fundamental precepts of investment appraisal is that if an investor faces a higher risk, then he will demand a higher return. On the basis of this, it is unreasonable to be applying the same required return to these two bonds – the required return on a longer dated bond should be at some premium over that of a shorter dated bond to reflect the additional risk, i.e there should be a term structure to these rates.

Thus, there should be some term structure to interest rates and bond yields, which we would normally expect to rise as we consider investment cash flows further and further into the future.

2.2 Spot rates

Exam tip

> Questions involving the calculation of forward rates from spot rates and spot rates from forward rates are quite common, e.g. Winter 2007 Question 5, Summer 2003 Question 4.

2.2.1 Introduction

As we have just seen, cash flows at different dates are subject to different risks and should, therefore, be discounted at different rates. However, if the cash flows from a one-year bond should be discounted at a certain rate, then why should the first-year coupon from a five-year bond (received on the same day) be discounted at a different rate (the yield on the five-year bond)? Both represent cash in one year, hence both represent equal risk to an investor.

What we should have are various rates of interest which are appropriate for cash flows at certain dates, regardless of whether they are from a one-year bond or a five-year bond. These are the spot rates.

The spot rate is the rate of interest that the market demands for money from now to a specific future time, i.e. the rate for one-month money or one-year money or five-year money. If we wished to invest cash today for one year, we could do so at the one-year spot rate.

So far, when pricing bonds, we have applied the same interest rate in discounting the cash flows regardless of when they arise. To establish the market value of a bond, we have applied the relationship

$$\text{Price} = \frac{C_1}{(1+r)} + \frac{C_2}{(1+r)^2} + \frac{C_3}{(1+r)^3} + \cdots + \frac{C_n + R}{(1+r)^n}$$

where r is the GRY of the bond. A more appropriate method of valuing fixed income securities may be to approach the instrument in a slightly different way.

In essence, a coupon bond is a composite investment made up of individual flows. For example, if we have a 10% three-year bond, this can be regarded as a package of four individual flows: £10 after one year, £10 after two years, £10 after three years and the redemption value, £100 after three years. This is represented diagrammatically below.

Coupon Bond
(10% three-year maturity)

A Series of Strips

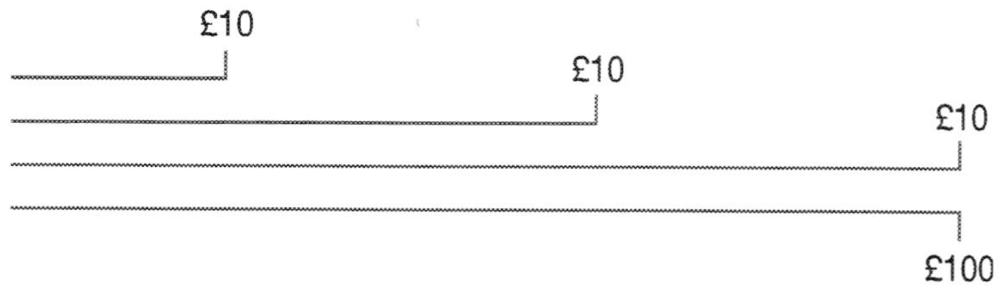

The gross redemption yield attempts to apply one rate of interest to all of those flows to bring them back down to their present value. It would perhaps be more appropriate to regard each flow as an individual zero-coupon bond and value each one at an appropriate rate of interest. The total value of the bond would then be the summation of these individual amounts.

Hence, to correctly evaluate a bond, we should discount each of its cash flows at the rate appropriate for their timing, i.e. the above price relationship should be restated as

Formula to learn

$$\text{Price} = \frac{C_1}{(1+r_1)} + \frac{C_2}{(1+r_2)^2} + \frac{C_3}{(1+r_3)^3} + \cdots + \frac{C_n + R}{(1+r_n)^n}$$

where $r_1, r_2, r_3, \ldots r_n$ are the relevant spot rates, given the timing of the bond cash flows.

Whilst spot rate quotes are currently available in the money markets, these are only available for relatively short periods, hence we have a practical difficulty in applying this idea in the UK at present.

Spot rates for longer maturities are available from the zero-coupon bond or strips market where it is possible to trade government bonds as either the full coupon bond or as a series of zero-coupon strips.

If, however, we are dealing in markets which are not fully developed, and such rates are not directly available, then an alternative is to derive the spot rate from the normal bond prices as we illustrate below.

2.2.2 Link between spot rates and bond yields

Our starting point in this session was to determine yield measures, though this hinged on us being able to firstly establish the bond value. These yield calculations should perhaps be considered the end stage of the process, with bond prices being derived from spot rates, and bond yields being derived from these prices.

Bond evaluation

What we have arrived at is that in order to correctly evaluate a bond, we need to discount its cash flows at appropriate spot rates, i.e.

$$\text{Price} = \frac{C_1}{(1+r_1)} + \frac{C_2}{(1+r_2)^2} + \frac{C_3}{(1+r_3)^3} + \cdots + \frac{C_n + R}{(1+r_n)^n}$$

GRY

The GRY is then the one rate, r, which satisfies the relationship

$$\text{Price} = \frac{C_1}{(1+r)} + \frac{C_2}{(1+r)^2} + \frac{C_3}{(1+r)^3} + \cdots + \frac{C_n + R}{(1+r)^n}$$

Therefore, we can state that

> The Gross Redemption Yield on a bond is a form of weighted average of the spot rates used to discount each flow.

The derivation below, of spot rates from yields, may help to clarify this relationship.

2.2.3 Derivation of spot rates in undeveloped markets

As we noted above, spot rates are potentially available from the money markets and the zero-coupon bond or strips markets. If, however, we are dealing in markets which are not fully developed, then an alternative is to derive the spot rate from the normal bond prices.

Example

Establish the one-year, two-year and three-year spot rates from the following data regarding three annual coupon bonds.

Maturity	Coupon (%)	Price (£)	GRY (%)
1 year	10	99.50	10.55
2 years	11	98.25	12.04
3 years	9	90.56	13.00

Solution

One-year spot rate

This can be established from the details of the one-year bond. For the one-year bond, there is a single flow of £110 (the coupon £10 and the redemption value of £100) in one year's time. The price of this bond has therefore been established by discounting this cash flow at the one-year spot rate, i.e.

$$\text{Price} = \frac{C+R}{1+r_1}$$

Giving

$$99.50 = \frac{110.00}{1+r_1}$$

Rearranging this gives

$$1 + r_1 = \frac{110.00}{99.50} = 1.1055$$

Hence

$r_1 = 0.1055$ or 10.55%

Two-year spot rate

For the two-year spot rate, it is necessary to use the one-year spot rate and turn to the two-year bond. Here, we have two flows: £11 coupon in one year's time and £111 (£11 coupon and £100 redemption) in two years' time. Again, the price of the bond will have been determined using the spot rates, i.e.

$$\text{Price} = \frac{C}{(1+r_1)} + \frac{C+R}{(1+r_2)^2}$$

Giving

$$98.25 = \frac{11.00}{1.1055} + \frac{111.00}{(1+r_2)^2}$$

$$98.25 = 9.95 + \frac{111.00}{(1+r_2)^2}$$

$$88.30 = \frac{111.00}{(1+r_2)^2}$$

Rearranging this gives

$$(1 + r_2)^2 = \frac{111.00}{88.30} = 1.2570$$

Giving

$1 + r_2 = \sqrt{1.2570} = 1.1212$

Hence

$r_2 = 0.1212$ or 12.12%

Three-year bond

In the case of the three-year bond, the coupon in each of the first two years is £9. In the third year, the coupon will be paid with the redemption money, making a total payment of £109. The market value of the bond will therefore have been established as

$$\text{Price} = \frac{C}{(1+r_1)} + \frac{C}{(1+r_2)^2} + \frac{C+R}{(1+r_3)^3}$$

Giving

$$90.56 = \frac{9.00}{1.1055} + \frac{9.00}{1.1212^2} + \frac{109.00}{(1+r_3)^3}$$

$$90.56 = 8.14 + 7.16 + \frac{109.00}{(1+r_3)^3}$$

$$75.26 = \frac{109.00}{(1+r_3)^3}$$

Rearranging this gives

$$(1 + r_3)^3 = \frac{109.00}{75.26} = 1.4483$$

Giving

$$1 + r_3 = \sqrt[3]{1.4483} = 1.1314$$

Hence

$r_3 = 0.1314$ or 13.14%

Conclusion

If we now compare the three yields and spot rates, we find the following.

Time	**Spot Rate (%)**	**GRY (%)**
1 year	10.55	10.55
2 years	12.12	12.04
3 years	13.14	13.00

You will note that the one-year yield and spot rate are identical, since this bond simply pays its one cash flow at that date. For the other two bonds, the yields are slightly below the spot rates, illustrating that it represents a weighted average of those rates.

We can also intuitively justify the numbers that we have derived above. The yield is, as we have seen, a complex weighted average of the spot rates. In the above example, the yield on the three-year bond is 13%. This is a weighted average of 10.55%, 12.12% and 13.14%, heavily biased towards the final three-year spot rate. Simply looking at this in this light, the yield of 13% would appear to make sense.

As mentioned above, it may not be necessary to derive the spot rates using the above formulation. In markets such as the US, where an active Strips or zero-coupon market exists then this market will generate the spot rates.

An alternative methodology for deriving spot rates

So far, we have adopted a method which is referred to as 'boot-strapping' to derive spot rates from the current yield structure. In this process, we have used progressively a one-year, two-year, three-year and four-year bond to derive the appropriate spot rates and then we use these rates in deriving the subsequent yearly rates.

Whilst this method will provide us with a correct estimation of spot rates, there are a number of problems involved with it.

- It requires an even distribution of bonds across the maturity spectrum and indeed, within that a complete range of bonds, i.e. we would need to have a one-year, two-year, three-year and four-year maturity, **and**
- To derive a ten-year spot rate using the boot-strapping methodology, we would have to go through the process of deriving all the intermediate spot rates, since only by having the one-year, two-year, three-year, four-year, etc. spot rates would we be able to get to the ten-year rate.

An alternative method would allow us to directly derive the ten-year spot rate.

The price arbitrage method

Under this method, it will be possible to directly derive a ten-year spot rate from a series of bonds without the need to go for all of the intermediate phases.

In order to derive spot rates, all that is required is that we establish a portfolio of bonds partly in the form of a short position, partly in the form of a long position, which creates for us a zero coupon of the appropriate maturity. To do this we will need two bonds of the same maturity but with different coupons.

For example, it is possible to derive the three-year spot rate using a three-year 10% priced at £107.87 and a three-year 5% bond priced at £94.75.

In this case, what we would do is to short the three-year 10% bond. In essence, this establishes a negative position over the next three years with a £10 coupon flow going out in each of the first two years and the coupon redemption stream in the final year being 110. To offset this, we would then establish a long position of two 5% three-year bonds. This would again generate a series of flows over the three years with two lots of a £5 coupon coming in Years 1 and 2 and two lots of £105 coming in Year 3.

	Cost	Coupon	Redemption
Short one 10% bond	(107.87)	(10)	(100)
Long two 5% bond	189.50	10	200
Net	81.63	–	100

The net result of this portfolio is to establish a zero-coupon bond with a maturity of three years and from this, we can derive a three-year spot rate as follows.

For the 3 year spot rate

$$(1 + r)^3 = \frac{100.00}{81.63} = 1.2250$$

$$1 + r = \sqrt[3]{1.2250} = 1.070$$

$$r = 0.070 \text{ or } 7.0\%$$

The above example used a particularly convenient mix of coupons enabling us easily to establish the position of short one lot of the high-coupon bond and long two lots of the low-coupon bond. However, the approach will work with any combination of coupons.

For example, imagine the two bonds available are a 10% and 7.5% coupon. This time to create the zero position, it will be necessary to go short three lots of the 10% bond and long four lots of the 7.5% bond. Once again, the coupon positions will net to zero leaving a single redemption flow maturing in three years' time.

Example

The following 3 year bonds are in issue

A a 9% bond priced at £93.07
B a 5% bond priced at £83.34

Determine the three year spot rate.

Solution

In order to synthesise a 3 year zero-coupon bond we will need to set up the following portfolio

	Cost	Coupon	Redemption
Short five 9% bonds	(465.35)	(45)	(500)
Long nine 5% bonds	750.16	45	900
Net	284.71	–	400

The portfolio synthesises a three year zero coupon investment with redemption proceeds at £400 and a cost of £284.71.

So for the 3 year spot rate

$$(1 + r)^3 = \frac{400.00}{284.71} = 1.4049$$

hence

$$1 + r = \sqrt[3]{1.4049} = 1.1200$$

giving

$$r = 0.1200 \text{ or } 12\%$$

2.3 Forward rates

Exam tip

Questions are frequently set with respect to the determination of forward rates, e.g. Summer 2008 Question 5, Winter 2006 Question 9, Summer 2005 Question 6.

2.3.1 Introduction

A spot rate is a rate of interest that can be agreed today for a deposit or borrowing from today for a fixed period. A forward rate is a rate of interest that can be agreed today for a deposit or borrowing from one future date to another.

The use of forward rates is to allow people to lock rates today for any future deposit or borrowing in order to avoid the risk of adverse interest rate movements before actually undertaking the deposit or borrowing.

Clearly, no one ever knows future interest rates with certainty, hence the borrower or depositor may find that the normal market rate ultimately proves to be better or worse than the forward rate that he has locked into. However, by locking in today with forward rates as, say, a borrower, we are avoiding the difficulty that we would suffer if interest rates rose, but giving up the opportunity of a benefit if interest rates fall.

The motivation here is to fix a rate, and hence cash flow levels, at something that represents a definitely affordable cost or reasonable income, e.g. locking into a fixed rate mortgage that you know you can afford rather than risking the variable rate. In the fullness of time, the variable rate may turn out to be lower, but that lost opportunity is the price paid to avoid risk of rates moving up dramatically, which they have been known to do.

2.3.2 Derivation of bond forward rates

How then does a bank determine today the rate that it is prepared to offer in, say, one year's time for a one-year borrowing? Does it take a guess as to what interest rates will be at that time and take the risk of being wrong? This idea does seem to pose an intriguing problem as if the borrower is avoiding risk, then the bank must be taking it on.

Banks could adopt this approach, i.e. guessing what interest rates will be next year, though this could hardly be considered prudent and would undoubtedly result in disaster. There must be some other factors at work here.

The answer lies in the idea of arbitrage. That is, if the bank is happy to lend to someone today for two years at the two-year spot rate, then they should be happy to agree today to lend to two people over the same period (one for the first year and one for the second) so long as the total returns are the same. The first year borrower would be charged the one-year spot rate, as this is the rate appropriate for his borrowing term. The second year borrower would be charged the forward rate for a one-year borrowing starting in one year's time.

Similarly, there should be no difference between investing the money for two years and investing it for one year and agreeing now to roll this over in a year's time into another one-year deposit.

Either arrangement could be pictured as

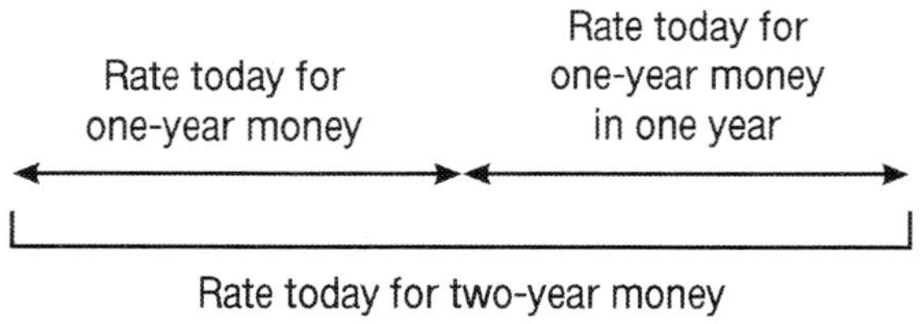

Mathematically, the relationship that we have here is

Formula to learn

$$(1+r_1)\times(1+{}_1f_2)=(1+r_2)^2$$

where

r_1 and r_2 are the one and two-year spot rates respectively.

${}_1f_2$ is the forward rate from Time 1 to Time 2.

The forward rate is **not** necessarily the rate that will eventually be available in the market in a year's time. As we have already noted, this cannot be predicted with certainty.

Example

Calculate the forward rates that would be available, given the results that we established above regarding spot rates, specifically

Time	Spot Rate (%)
1 year	10.55
2 years	12.12
3 years	13.14

Solution

Forward rate – $_1f_2$

Using the above relationship gives

$(1 + r_1) \times (1 + {}_1f_2) = (1 + r_2)^2$

$1.1055 \times (1 + {}_1f_2) = 1.1212^2$

$$1 + {}_1f_2 = \frac{1.1212^2}{1.1055} = 1.1371$$

Hence
$_1f_2 = 0.1371$ or 13.71%

Here, the one-year spot rate is lower than the two-year spot rate and consequently, the forward rate must be higher to compensate.

Forward rate – $_2f_3$

This relationship can easily be extended to cover other periods, for example, agreeing to borrow for two years at the two-year spot rate followed by a third year at the forward rate should cost the same as three years at the spot rate. Hence

$(1 + r_2)^2 \times (1 + {}_2f_3) = (1 + r_3)^3$

$1.1212^2 \times (1 + {}_2f_3) = 1.1314^3$

$$1 + {}_2f_3 = \frac{1.1314^3}{1.1212^2} = 1.1521$$

Hence

$_2f_3 = 0.1521$ or 15.21%

Here, the two-year spot rate is lower than the three-year spot rate and consequently, the forward rate must be higher to compensate.

Forward rate – $_1f_3$

Another way that could be agreed today for a three-year borrowing is one year at the spot rate followed by a two-year forward rate starting in one year's time. This would give

$(1 + r_1) \times (1 + {}_1f_3)^2 = (1 + r_3)^3$

$1.1055 \times (1 + {}_1f_3)^2 = 1.1314^3$

$$(1 + {}_1f_3)^2 = \frac{1.1314^3}{1.1055} = 1.3101$$

Giving

$1 + {}_1f_3 = \sqrt{1.3101} = 1.1446$

Hence

${}_1f_3 = 0.1446$ or 14.46%

Here, the one-year spot rate is lower than the three-year spot rate and consequently, the forward rate must be higher to compensate.

2.3.3 Link between spot rates and forward rates

Forward rates therefore equate to the term structure of spot rates.

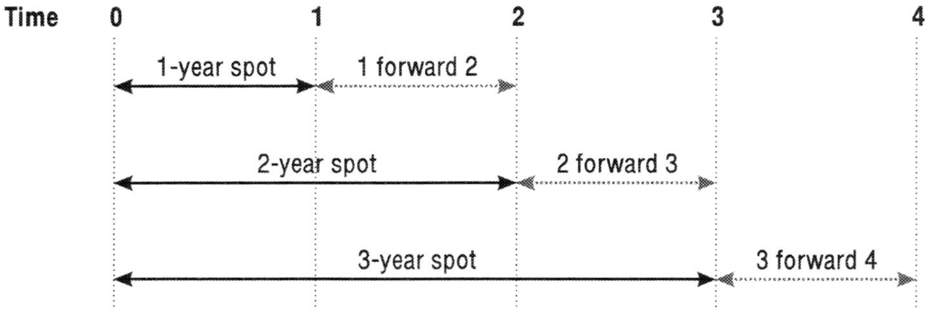

1-year spot	$(1 + r_1)$
2-year spot	$(1 + r_1) \times (1 + {}_1f_2) = (1 + r_2)^2$
3-year spot	$(1 + r_1) \times (1 + {}_1f_2) \times (1 + {}_2f_3) = (1 + r_3)^3$
4-year spot	$(1 + r_1) \times (1 + {}_1f_2) \times (1 + {}_2f_3) \times (1 + {}_3f_4) = (1 + r_4)^4$

The formulae above demonstrate the relationship between spot rates and forward rates. If we are given the spot rates for any period of time, then we can derive the associated forward rates as we have shown. Similarly, if we are given the forward rates, we can use these to determine the associated spot rates.

What we have not determined is how the market works, e.g.

- Are spot rates determined first by the consensus view as to required returns for given periods from now, from which forward rates may be derived?
- Or are forward rates determined first by the consensus view as to future interest rates, from which spot rates may be deduced?

Ignoring the problem of which is derived from which for now, and simply concentrating on the relationship between these rates, we can see that spot rates may be equated to the current one-year spot rate, as expanded by the forward rates going out into the future.

For example, the two-year spot rate equates to the current one-year rate and the one-year rate in one year's time; whereas the three-year spot rate equates to the one-year rate multiplied by the one-year rate in one year and the one-year rate in two years. Therefore, one can state that

> The spot rate equates to the geometric mean forward rate.

We will return to the causality of this relationship later.

2.3.4 Derivation of money market forward rates

Exam tip

> Last examined in Summer 2008 Question 5.

The method of calculating forward money market rates follows the same principles but applies simple interest conventions.

Example

The spot rate for 3 months (91 days) is 6% and for 6 months (183 days) is 7%. Calculate the three month forward rate in three months time for a sterling investor.

Solution

We are looking to assess the forward rate for the last 92 days (183 – 91) of the six month period.

For the first 3 months

$$r_1 = 6\% \times \frac{91}{365} = 1.495890\%$$

For the full 6 months

$$r_1 = 7\% \times \frac{183}{365} = 3.509589\%$$

And applying

$$(1 + r_1)(1 + {}_1f_2) = (1 + r_2)$$

gives

$$1.01495890 \times (1 + {}_1f_2) = 1.03509589$$

and so

$$(1 + {}_1f_2) = \frac{1.03509589}{1.01495890} = 1.0198402$$

giving

${}_1f_2 = 0.0198402$ or 1.98402% for the 92 days

the quoted rate will, therefore, be

$$\text{Forward rate} = 1.98402 \times \frac{365}{92} = 7.87\%$$

2.4 Relationship between yields, spot rates and forward rates

Exam tip

> Most recently examined in Summer 2008 Question 6

We have briefly described above the relationship between yields and spot rates, and the relationship between spot rates and forward rates. We are now going to consider how all three interact mathematically (again ignoring causality for now). This is most easily achieved with an example.

Example

A series of 10% annual coupon paying bonds are in issue with maturities from one to ten years. The following has been established from these bonds.

Year	Forward (%)	Spot (%)	Yield (%)
1	–	7.00	7.00
2	8.0	7.50	7.48
3	9.0	8.00	7.94
4	9.0	8.25	8.16
5	9.5	8.50	8.38
6	10.0	8.75	8.59
7	10.0	8.92	8.74
8	9.5	9.00	8.82
9	9.0	9.00	8.82
10	8.0	8.90	8.77

Plot these rates on a graph to visualise/determine how the rates interact.

Solution

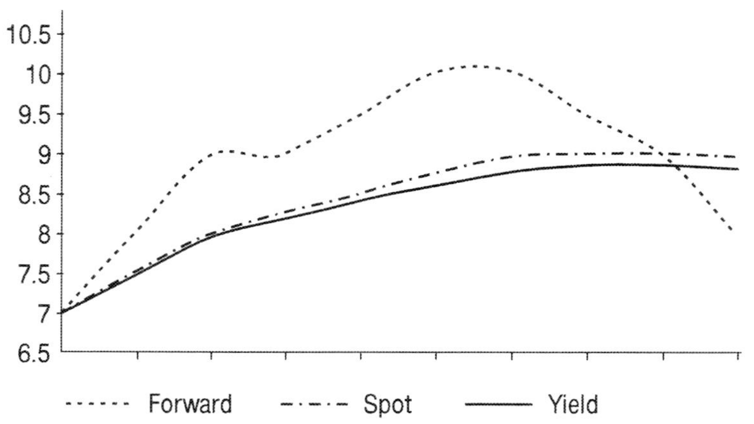

Spot rates equate to the geometric mean of the forward rates and as such, their movements lag behind those of forward rates, effectively smoothing out much of the abruptness demonstrated by them. Similarly, the yield is a weighted average of the spot rates and hence demonstrate less volatility still.

When rates are rising, at first we see that forward rates rise rapidly, with spot rates next, closely followed by yield curves. For the longer dated stocks, our scenario gave falling rates and once again, we see the greatest volatility demonstrated by forward rates, with spot rates and yields lagging somewhat, and yields again showing the least volatility.

In a normal rising term structure environment, we would therefore expect to see the following relationships between yields, spots (the term structure of interest rates or zero-coupon curve) and forwards.

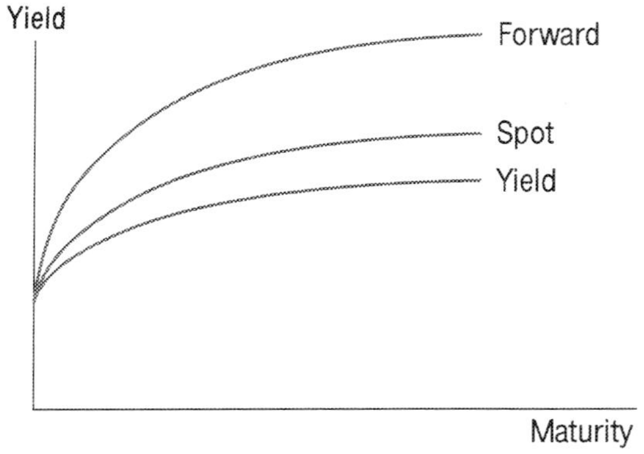

We can see that the increase in forward rates rapidly outpaces that of spot rates and yields.

In the case where short-term rates are high the opposite will be true, with the forward curve pulling the spot rate and yield curve down.

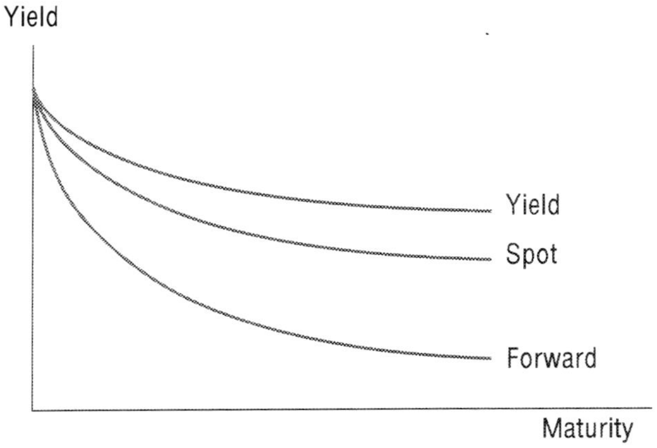

2.5 The yield curve

Exam tip

> Questions involving the discussion of the factors influencing the shape of the yield curve arise in all three sections of the exam. Section A questions require brief definitions (e.g. Winter 1996 Question 4). Section B questions tend to require a yield curve forecast (covered in a later chapter), Section C questions require a broader discussion or explanation of the shape of a given yield curve (Summer 1999 Question 16).

2.5.1 Introduction

The yield curve demonstrates the relationship between bond yields and their maturities and is very closely linked to the term structure of interest rates.

Normal yield curve

The normal shape of the yield curve is illustrated below.

The Normal Yield Curve

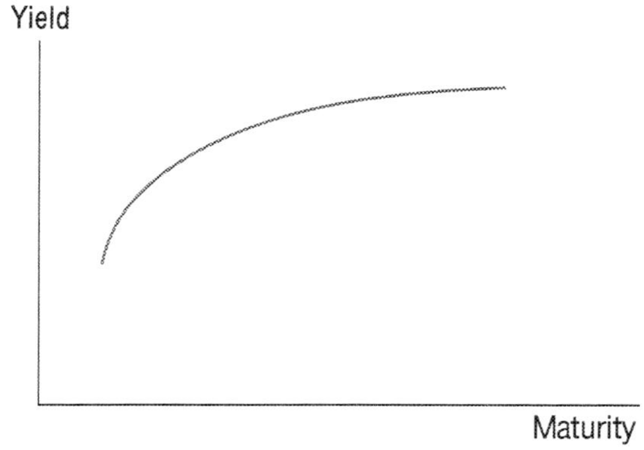

This curve clearly demonstrates the point made earlier, i.e. longer maturity results in higher risk which, in turn, results in higher returns or yields.

Use of this relationship

One use of this relationship is in evaluating bond issues or trades by determining the yield to use for discounting its cash flows. As we are aware, we may establish the market value of a bond by applying the relationship

$$\text{Price} = \frac{C_1}{(1+r)} + \frac{C_2}{(1+r)^2} + \frac{C_3}{(1+r)^3} + \cdots + \frac{C_n + R}{(1+r)^n}$$

where r is the GRY of the bond. If we can determine a suitable yield for a bond to use in this relationship, then we will be able to value it accurately. We will see, however, that this may not be as easy as it seems, and that there are other factors that need to be considered.

Problem with these ideas

Unfortunately, the yield curve does not always follow the shape described above, indeed occasionally it becomes inverted with short-term yields exceeding longer term ones as shown below.

The Inverted Yield Curve

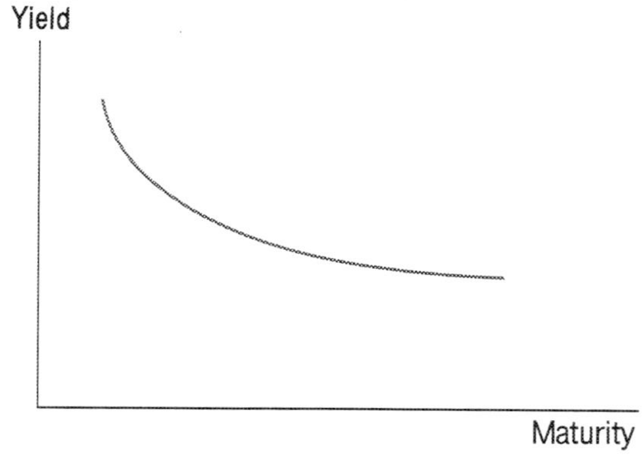

This appears to contradict our fundamental idea that higher risk means higher return, one of the cornerstones of investment theory. Hence, we need to consider what factors determine the shape of this curve. There are clearly some other forces at work here in addition to the simple risk/return relationship that we have considered so far.

2.6 Shape of the yield curve

2.6.1 Introduction

What, then, determines the shape of the yield curve? The risk/return relationship is one factor at work here but, as we noted earlier, there must be other, perhaps more, significant factors, otherwise we would never see an inverted yield curve.

A number of theories have been advanced to explain the shape of the yield curve. These are outlined below.

2.6.2 Liquidity preference

Liquidity preference theory states that if an investor's money is invested in longer term (and therefore riskier) stocks, then they will require a greater return or **risk premia**. Short-term liquid stock carries a lower risk and therefore requires a lower return.

As regards causality, this theory assumes that spot rates are established by the market from which forward rates and yields may be derived.

This risk premium gives rise to the normal upward sloping yield curve.

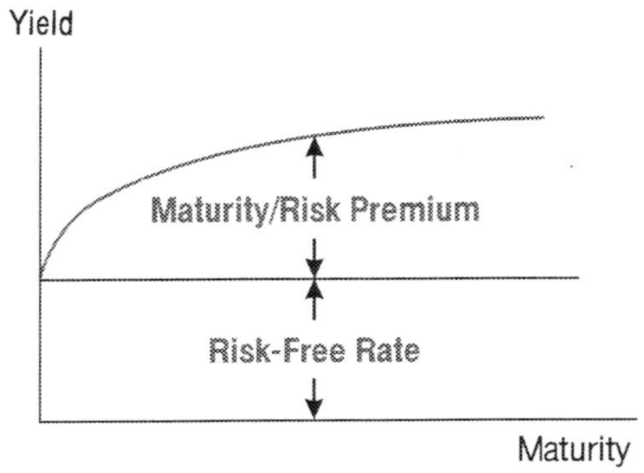

This maturity premium may invert in high-yield environments. This is because as yield levels rise towards historically high levels, then the expectations of investors will shift to the belief that rates will fall and consequently prices will rise. If this is the case, then investors would benefit from holding longer dated and therefore more volatile stock. Consequently, investor pressure would force the longer yields down relative to the less volatile shorter yields.

2.6.3 Expectations theory

Basic theory

Pure expectations theory takes us back to the linkage between spot and forward rates. This theory argues that the yield curve is a reflection of spot rates and that spot rates in turn are a reflection of the market's expectation of forward rates. As we have seen, the yield is the weighted average of spot rates and spot rates equate to the geometric mean of forward rates.

As regards causality, this theory assumes that forward rates are established by the market from which spot rates, and hence yields, are derived.

If we consider the data we used above for relating forward rates, spot rates and yields, we may conclude that the upward slope of the yield curve reflects the market's expectations that interest rates will rise in the short term. The yield then begins to tail off towards the end, reflecting a fall back in interest rates from their peak of 10% down to 8%, giving rise to a mild hump in the yield curve at the longer end.

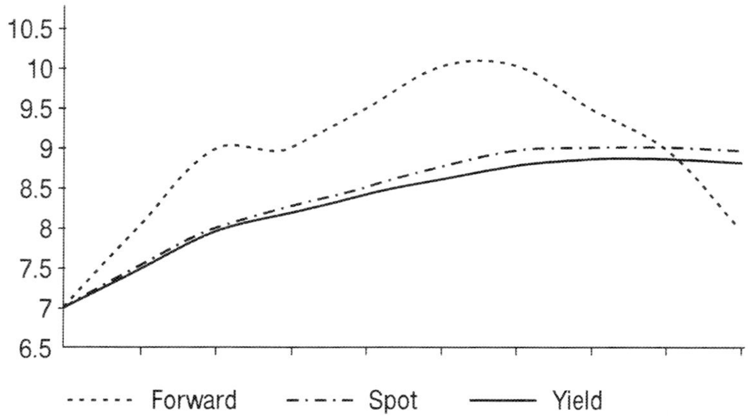

The steepness of the yield curve would therefore also be a reflection of the expected rate of change in forward rates. The faster the expected change, the steeper the yield curve.

In this case, we were dealing with a rising yield curve environment. The opposite would be true of a falling yield curve environment.

Intervention

The only point on the yield curve which can be fixed is immediate short-term rates by the Bank of England through its operations in the money markets. If short-term interest rates are high, the market's expectation will be that rates will fall. This would lead to a downward sloping yield curve referred to as an 'inverted' curve for which the relationship between forward rates, spot rates and yields is shown below.

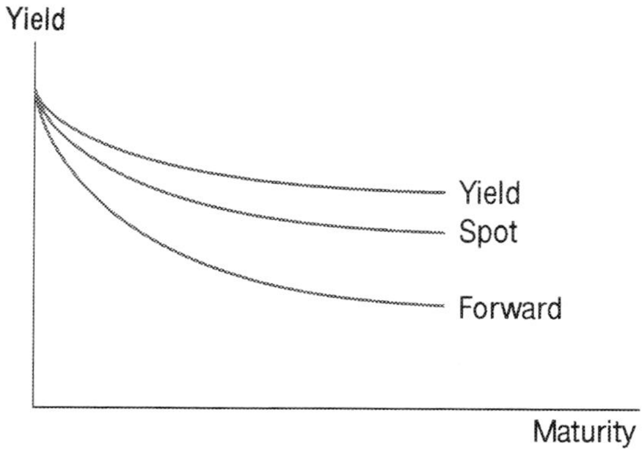

Future inflation

Another element of the market's expectations will be the expectations of inflation. If the market believes that inflation will rise in the future, then the yields on the longer dated stocks will have to rise in order to compensate investors for the fall in the real value of their money. The expectation of inflation is much more of a problem with the long rather than the short end.

2.6.4 Preferred habitat and market segmentation – demand effects

Preferred habitat or market segmentation is not a theory to explain the full shape of the yield curve as such. Rather, it should be viewed as an addenda to the above two theories to help explain certain other features observed in the markets, such as humped yield curves in relation to the liquidity preference theory.

Certain maturity ranges are appropriate to particular types of investors. In the UK, the short end of the market is dominated by the financial sector (maintaining a proportion of their assets in liquid investments) and general insurance companies, whereas the long end is dominated by institutional investors such as pension funds and life assurance companies.

In effect, this gives rise to two markets concentrated at different ends of the yield curve. The impact of this concentrated demand at these two ends is that prices are driven up and hence, yields fall below those that may otherwise have been expected at these points. This may result in a discontinuity or hump in the yield curve.

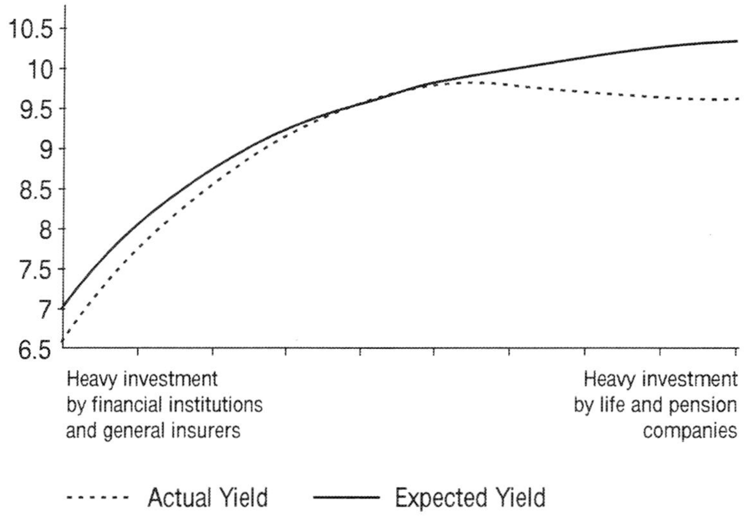

2.6.5 Supply-side factors

The availability or supply of stocks in certain maturity ranges may lead to either an excess or shortage of stock and consequently, an anomalous yield on some stocks. This is more often a problem at the long end of the yield curve where governments may be priced out of the issuance market.

Both during the buy-back period of the late 1980s and the issuance surge of the early 1990s, it is argued the government's funding policy created considerable strains on the shape of the yield curve. In the late 1990's in particular, the government held back from issuing at the longer end of the yield curve, due to the belief that longer rates were too high, and this led to a shortage of stock forcing prices up and yields down. Since 2001, the government has increased its funding requirements and as a result the distortions have been greatly diminished.

2.6.6 A combination approach

As we have seen, there are several explanations for the shape of the yield curve, ranging from the theoretical pure expectations model to the more pragmatic segmentation theory. There is, however, no reason why only one need be chosen to explain the shape of the curve.

Whilst the yield curve will undoubtedly reflect risk/return effects, it will also reflect expectations and other influences. It is certainly possible to argue that the short term is dominated by expectations of future rates, whereas the medium and long term may be more influenced by the expectations of inflation and the liquidity premia, both overlaid by the effects of supply and demand.

2.6.7 Critically appraising the alternative theories

The basic alternative theories explaining the shape of yield curves are that it is driven by

- The liquidity premium and preferred habitat models.
- Market expectation of future interest rates.

The pure expectations theory of the yield curve suggests that the only real driver to yields and spot rates is the market expectation of future interest rates. Therefore, if the market's expectation of future interest rates is flat, the yield curve, the spot curve and the forward curve would be straight lines running out together from the current rate as illustrated below.

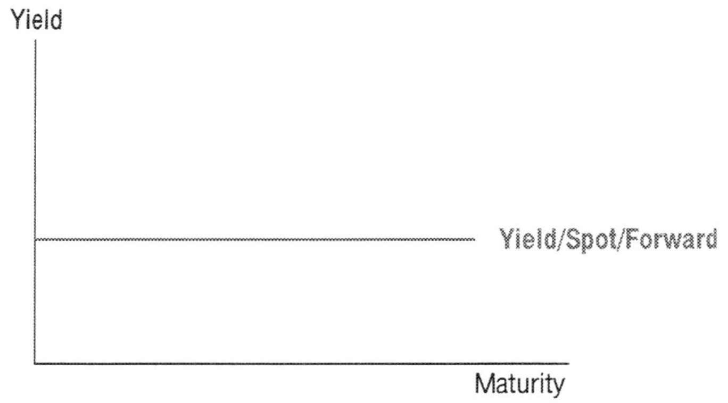

However, if the other theories are correct, it may well be the case that even if the market's expectation of interest rates were that there would be no change, then the yield curve might have an upward slope as a result of the liquidity premia.

Wherever the yield curve is upward sloping, the spot rate will lie above it and the forward rate will lie above that. This would therefore tend to insert an upward bias into forward rates.

It is often the case when analysing the market that the following situation occurs. An upward-sloping yield curve gives rise to an upward-sloping spot rate curve and in turn suggests an expectation of forward rates rising, yet the market's anticipation of forward rates is not as dramatic as the forward curve.

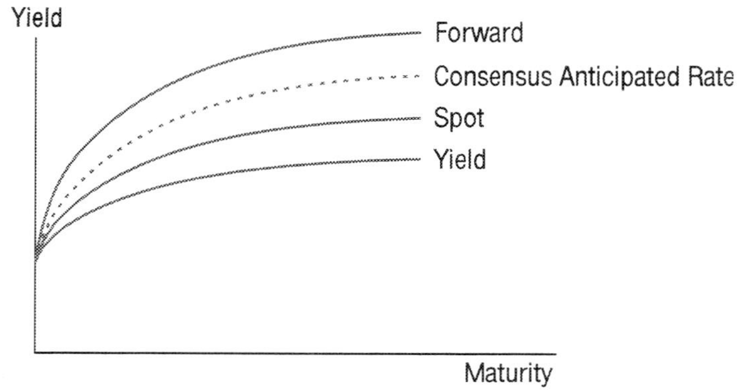

In itself, this would cause only a limited amount of difficulty, however the forward rates that we have derived thus far are used in the calculation of a variety of interest rate derivative products and, in particular, form the basis of pricing for the short sterling contract available on Euronext.liffe and the bespoke forward rate agreements available in the over-the-counter market. It would seem, therefore, somehow anomalous that the market is prepared to offer contracts linked to forward rates when it is not necessarily what they would expect to see.

For example, the one-year forward derived from current market rates might be 7½%, whereas the expectation in the market might be 7¼%. In this case, there is a natural advantage for anybody wishing to lock into deposit rates, and a cost to anybody wishing to lock into borrowing rates.

It is possible to argue that that difference represents the price that borrowers have to pay in the market to secure the rate and is the innate cost in terms of time value on the option that they are buying. It would also reflect, perhaps, a natural bias in the market that it is more likely that borrowers will want to hedge their risk than depositors, particularly in an upward yield environment and consequently, the price they have to pay is slightly above expectation. This is the cost of certainty to them.

To an extent, however, this undermines the pure expectations theory that suggests that everything is driven off the back of forward interest rates and many commentators argue that the key determinant is the spot rate; forward rates are merely an arbitrage from spot rates that we then use to price a variety of interest rate products.

Equally, it is possible to argue that the forward rate **is** the market rate and that any consensus simply represents the views of the City economists, which the traders simply do not believe.

The truth is probably that the combination approach is the valid one. With certain individuals in the market believing one theory and others believing the alternative, it is likely that their actions, and hence the market, are driven by both.

2.7 Construction of the yield curve for bond pricing

The yield curve demonstrates the relationship between bond yields and their maturities. As we noted earlier, one use of this relationship is in evaluating bond issues or trades by determining the yield to use for evaluation purposes in the relationship

$$\text{Price} = \frac{C_1}{(1+r)} + \frac{C_2}{(1+r)^2} + \frac{C_3}{(1+r)^3} + \cdots + \frac{C_n + R}{(1+r)^n}$$

where r is the GRY of the bond. If we can determine a suitable yield for a bond from the yield curve, then we will be able to fairly value it using this relationship.

Unfortunately, it is not possible in most markets to simply plot the yields of the available stocks and then fit a curve to the data. This simplistic approach would ignore some of the key factors that affect the yield and mislead the user of the yield curve.

One of the most important distorting factors is the coupon available. In the UK gilts market for example, there are a large number of issues of the same basic maturity, each with a different coupon. The coupon distorts the yield due to the taxation treatment applied to capital gains in the UK.

Example

There are three stocks with a maturity of approximately four years. The coupons available on these bonds are 3%, 6% and 9% respectively. If the market is expecting a return of 6% on bonds of this maturity, then the 6% bond will be priced at par.

Due to its low coupon, the 3% bond will be priced at a discount to par. Since it will be redeemed at par in four years' time, realising a gain (and that gain will be tax free to a private investor), this will make it attractive to tax-paying individuals. The increase in the demand for this stock will force the price up and the yield down.

Conversely, a capital loss will arise on the 9% bond, making it less attractive (since all the coupon is taxed). Hence, demand will fall and yields rise.

2.7.1 Conclusion

Whilst it might be expected that all stocks of a similar maturity and credit risk ought to have the same yield, this will not be the case. **Higher coupon stocks will have higher yields, and lower coupon stocks lower yields**.

Consequently, the yield information used to plot the yield curve would look as follows.

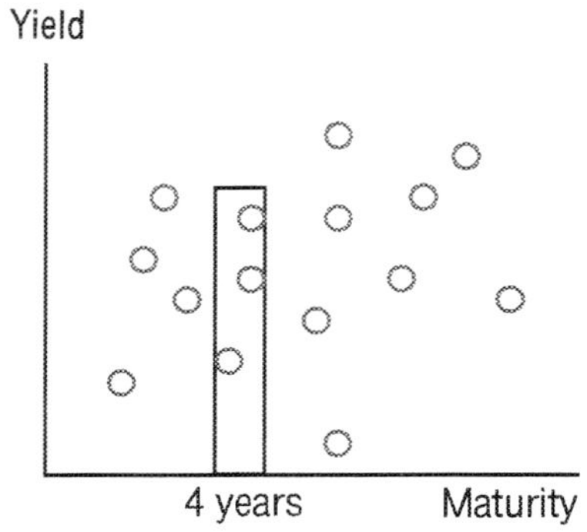

At the four-year range, there are three different yields reflecting the different coupons. Which do we use to evaluate a bond or set the coupon level for a new issue?

There are a number of solutions to this problem, using

- Spot rates if they are available (seen above).
- Restricted coupon yields.
- Par yields.

2.8 Restricted coupon yield curves

To overcome the problem of coupons and other factors distorting the yield curve, it is possible to construct a restricted coupon yield curve. Here, the yields of a limited number of bonds with coupons in a limited range, say 9% to 11%, are plotted and a curve is then fitted to these data.

The obvious limitation with this approach is that it is not a full picture of the market and may easily be distorted by other variables and maturity gaps in the coupon range.

2.9 Par yields

Exam tip

> This tends to be examined as a compulsory Section A calculation, e.g. Winter 2005 Question 8.

The par yield is the coupon that would have to be offered on a bond in order for it to be priced at par using the appropriate spot rates. The relationship that we need to solve is

$$100 = \frac{C}{(1+r_1)} + \frac{C}{(1+r_2)^2} + \frac{C}{(1+r_3)^3} + \cdots + \frac{C+100}{(1+r_n)^n}$$

Where C is the par yield and r_1, r_2, ...r_n the spot rates for each period.

Example

Using the spot rates derived earlier in our example (see Section 2.2.3) and based on a three-year bond, the par yield is calculated as follows.

Solution

$$100 = \frac{C}{1.1055} + \frac{C}{1.1212^2} + \frac{C+100}{1.1314^3}$$

$$100 = 0.9046C + 0.7955C + 0.6905C + 69.05$$

$$100 - 69.05 = 2.3906C$$

$$30.95 = 2.3906C$$

$$C = \frac{30.95}{2.3906} = £12.95 \text{ or } 12.95\%$$

The par yield curve is used in a number of ways, but is particularly useful in the pricing of new issues, since new bond issues are generally priced close to par. The Debt Management Office also uses the par yield to price loans between government departments.

The use of the par yield to price new gilt issues is becoming less of a feature of the gilts market, as the Debt Management Office is seemingly preferring to opt for coupon standardisation. Issuing bonds in the range $6^1/_2\%$ to 8%.

2.10 Yield surfaces

Exam tip

> The effect of tax on bond yields has been examined most recently in Winter 2006 Question 8.

A yield surface is a three-dimensional representation of the yield curve. The normal two-dimensional curve plots yield against the maturity. With a yield surface, the third dimension is the coupon.

The reason for this is the impact of tax for the individual investor. As we noted under the NRY earlier, for an individual investor the coupon is taxed whereas any gains/losses are not taxed/allowed.

High coupon bonds trading above par will, therefore, suffer a high tax on the high income but get no allowance for the capital loss to maturity. Low coupon bonds, on the other hand, will be trading below par, they will suffer low tax on the low coupon and the gain to maturity will be tax free.

As a result, low coupon bonds are highly attractive to higher rate taxpayers, driving their prices up and their yields down. Higher coupon bonds are relatively unattractive driving prices down and yields up.

If we could establish the yield surface, then this would provide an appropriate yield for a bond, given its maturity and coupon.

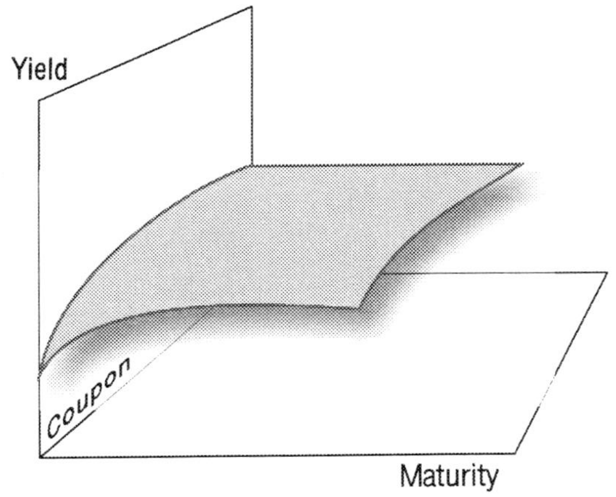

2.11 Yield curve comparison techniques

2.11.1 Yield curve differentials

By comparing one yield curve with another it is possible to draw conclusions about the relationship between the two economies.

For example, using the following yield curve information for the German and French markets as at December 1998. In this case, the two yield curves had almost completely converged as a prelude to EMU. Any residual differences reflected the distortion caused by liquidity and investor preference.

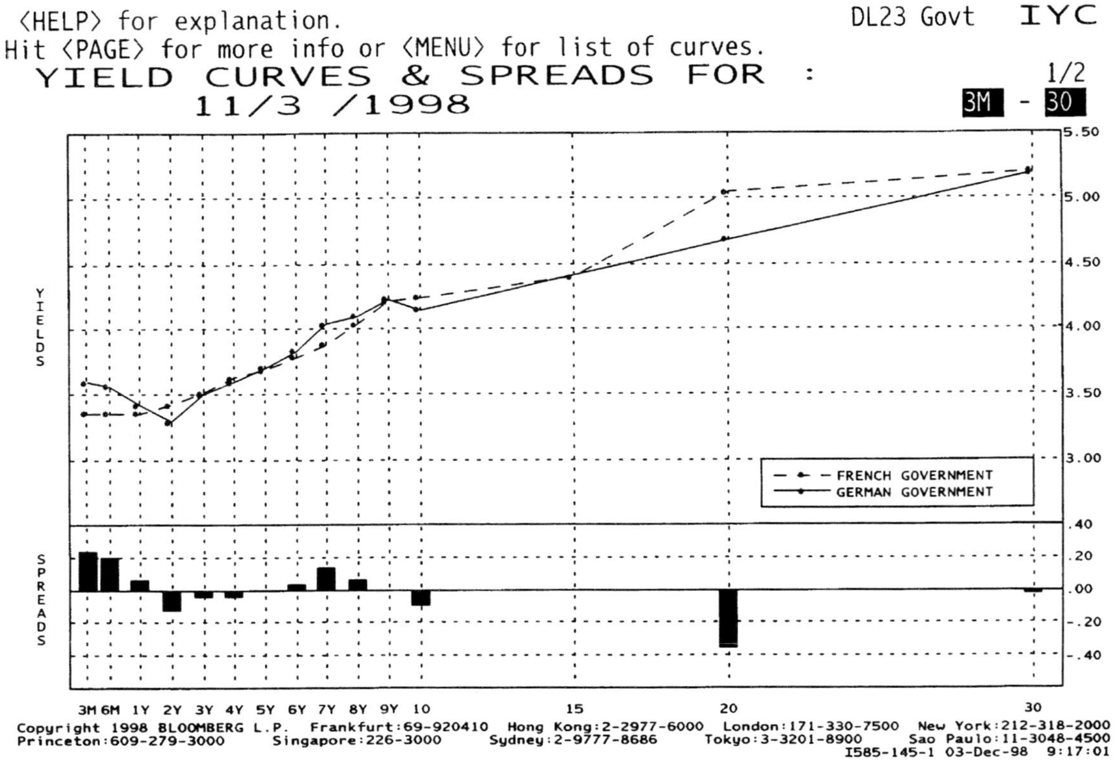

Economies that are closely linked together are characterised by particularly small yield spreads.

The greater the difference between the two yield curves, the greater the degree of **desynchronisation** between the two economies.

Chapter Roundup

- **Yields**
  - $$\text{Flat yield} = \frac{\text{Annual coupon rate}}{\text{Market price}}$$
  - $$\text{Japanese GRY} = \frac{\text{Annual coupon rate}}{\text{Market price}} + \frac{\frac{\text{Redemption price} - \text{Market price}}{\text{Years to redemption}}}{\text{Market price}}$$
  - GRY = IRR calculation

  You must be able to calculate each both at and between coupon payment dates for all types of bond (fixed coupon index-linked etc.) and discuss their uses and limitations.

- **Term structure of interest rates**

  You must be able to

  - Calculate spot rates and forward rates from bond prices.
  - Calculate spot and forward rates for money markets.
  - Discuss the factors influencing the shape of the yield curve.

TEST YOUR KNOWLEDGE

Check your knowledge of the Chapter here, without referring back to the text.

1. A 6% long government bond pays interest half-yearly. Two months after payment of interest the dirty price is £62.50. What is the interest yield?

2. Conversion 10¼% stock was quoted at £104.91 on Tuesday 23 February. Interest payment dates are 22 May and 22 November. What was the interest yield on 23 February?

3. You buy £10,000 nominal of 3½% War Loan on Tuesday 2 September cum div and pay £3,915.10 excluding transaction costs. Interest payment dates are 1 June and 1 December. Calculate the interest yield on 2 September.

4. Calculate the redemption yield of a bond bought for £91.99 with four full years to maturity and paying a 7% annual coupon.

5. A £100 bond is priced at £101.73 with an 11% coupon payable at the end of each of the next three years, and is then redeemable at par. What is its yield to maturity?

6. An 8% Treasury is redeemable in four years, it has a market value of £102.00.

   (a) Assuming annual interest payments calculate

   (i) The net present value of the gilt at 7% assuming a nil rate taxpayer.
   (ii) The gross redemption yield of the gilt.
   (iii) The net redemption yield of the gilt assuming a 40% taxpayer.
   (iv) The gross equivalent yield.

   (b) Recalculate the quoted gross redemption yield assuming semi-annual interest payments.

7. A bond pays an annual coupon of 10% once each year; the current year's coupon payment has just been made. The bond is currently quoted at 90 and it will be redeemed at par in eight years' time.

   Requirements

   (a) Calculate the redemption yield and flat yield of the bond.

   (b) Compute the holding period return for the bond if it is sold after four years for 98.

   (c) Calculate the realised return on the bond if intermediate coupon receipts can be reinvested at 8% per annum and that the bond is sold for 98 after four years, just after receipt of the coupon payment.

   (d) Outline the limitations of redemption yields when used in investment analysis.

8. The characteristics of two bonds are as follows.

Bond I: Coupon rate 10%, paid annually; redeemable at par (100%). Bond redeemable in one year, when final coupon will also be paid (the current coupon has just been paid). Market price 100.

Bond II: Coupon rate 12%, paid annually: redeemable at par (100%). Bond redeemable in two years' time. Two remaining coupon payments to be made, the last on the redemption date. Market price 106.93.

Requirements

(a) Compute

(i) The redemption yields of both bonds.
(ii) The one and two periods spot rates.
(iii) The implied forward rate from period one to two.

(b) Distinguish between the 'yield curve' and 'term structure' and outline the potential problems in determining each.

9. A 2% Index Linked is redeemable in three years. It was issued some time ago and you have just bought it at a price of £118.60. RPI details for the period prior to the issue and purchase are as follows.

	Issue	Purchase
0 months before	113	138
1 months before	112	137
2 months before	111	136
3 months before	110	135

If expected inflation is 4% p.a. (a flat rate), calculate the real and nominal gross redemption yield on your purchase of the gilt assuming it pays a semi-annual coupon.

10. (a) Illustrate the shapes that the yield curve can take and explain how these shapes may arise.

(b) One-year bonds are currently selling to yield 8% and two-year bonds are selling to yield 9%. What is the market's current expectation of one-year interest rates one year from now? Explain the factors that you would consider if you wished to invest for two years and had only the above two alternatives from which to choose.

(c) Explain how yield curves will differ between

(i) Bonds issued for equal maturities by companies with materially different ratings.
(ii) Bonds issued for equal maturities by an AAA rated company and the UK Government.

11. Musings plc has recently divested itself of a UK subsidiary and has realised

£50 million as a result. The Board of Musings has belatedly begun to consider possible long-term uses for these funds and expects to take up to 12 months to formulate a strategy for their use. In the meantime, as Corporate Treasurer, you have been instructed by the Board to invest the surplus funds. In conveying these instructions Musings' Finance Director commented that investment prospects were good since he expects interest rates to rise. After analysis of market rates you have observed an inverse yield curve for maturity periods of up to one year.

Requirements

(a) Explain the term 'inverse yield curve' and how such a curve can arise.
(b) Comment on its significance for the investment policy.

12. (a) One-year government bonds currently yield 5 7/8% per annum with two-year and three-year yields at 6 1/8% and 6% respectively.

    What risk-free rates are currently implied for one-year maturities in (i) one year and (ii) two years' time?

    (b) The sterling money market currently charges 6% per annum for time deposits with 91-day maturities (LIBOR). Dealers generally feel that this will ease to 5% per annum in three months' time.

    What would you expect six-month (182 day) LIBOR to be today?

13. **Yield Curve Analysis**

    (a) Explain what is meant by the yield curve. In what different ways could the yield curve be constructed and using what measures of yield? What are the limitations of the different methods used?

14. Calculate all the spot and forward interest rates from the following information.

Gilt	Coupon (%)	Maturity (Yrs)	Price (£)
A	8	1	101
B	10	2	105
C	12	3	110

15. The term structure is as follows.

	Year One	Year Two	Year Three	Year Four	Year Five
Spot rate	5% p.a.	6% p.a.	8% p.a.	9% p.a.	9% p.a.

Bond A has a coupon rate of 10% per annum and is redeemable at par at the end of five years; Bond B also has a coupon rate of 10% and is redeemable at par at the end of three years. The coupon is paid once per annum and has just been paid.

Requirements

(a) Calculate the current prices of both bonds.

(b) Calculate the expected return on each bond over the coming year, assuming the term structure to be unchanged at the year end.

(c) Discuss the bond strategies suggested by your answer in (ii).

16. Given the following information, calculate all the spot and forward interest rates, i.e. the term structure of interest rates.

Gilt	Maturity (yrs)	Price (£)
Treasury 8½%	1	100
Exchequer 9¼%	2	102
Treasury 10%	3	104

17. From prevailing bonds' prices current spot interest rates have been calculated.

Maturity	Spot Rate
1-year to June 2006	7.50%
2-year to June 2007	7.20%
3-year to June 2008	7.00%
4-year to June 2009	6.80%
5-year to June 2010	6.50%
6-year to June 2011	6.25%

(a) What shape is this yield curve? What conclusions do you draw from this?

(b) Calculate, using the spot rates, the clean market prices of the following bonds

(i) 5% Treasury June 2008 (3-year maturity)
(ii) 15% Treasury June 2009 (4-year maturity)
(iii) 5% Treasury June 2010 (5-year maturity) assuming annual coupon payments for simplicity.

(c) Which of the three bonds in (ii) would you expect to have the highest gross redemption yield and why?

(d) If all yields to maturity were to fall by 1%, which of the three bonds in (ii) would experience the greatest percentage price change?

18. (a) Given the following prices for annual coupon bonds, what is the implied three-year spot rate?

Maturity	Price	Coupon
1-year	100.00	8%
2-year	98.60	7.5%
3-year	97.20	7.25%

(b) Explain the importance of spot rates for the fixed income fund manager.

TEST YOUR KNOWLEDGE: ANSWERS

1. Interest yield = $\frac{\text{Coupon}}{\text{Clean price}} = \frac{6.00}{62.50-(3\times 2/6)}$ = 9.76%

2. The interest yield = $\frac{10.25}{104.91}$ = 0.0977 or 9.77%

3. The interest yield on 2 September was $\frac{3.50}{38.252}$ = 0.0915 or 9.15%

4. The flat yield (annual income return) on this bond is 7.61% (7.00/91.99). Clearly since it is priced so far below par there is a definite annual gain to be added to this income to get the total return or GRY. Hence for interpolation we will try 8% and 10%.

Time	Cash Flow (£)	DF (8%)	PV (8%) (£)	DF (10%)	PV (10%) (£)
0	(91.99)	1	(91.99)	1	(91.99)
1	7.00	$\frac{1}{1.08}$	6.48	$\frac{1}{1.10}$	6.36
2	7.00	$\frac{1}{1.08^2}$	6.00	$\frac{1}{1.10^2}$	5.79
3	7.00	$\frac{1}{1.08^3}$	5.56	$\frac{1}{1.10^3}$	5.26
4	107.00	$\frac{1}{1.08^4}$	78.65	$\frac{1}{1.10^4}$	73.08
			4.70		(1.50)

$$\text{GRY(IRR)} = 8\% + \frac{4.70}{4.70-(1.50)} \times (10\% - 8\%) = 9.52\%$$

5. The flat yield (annual income return) on this bond is 10.81% (11.00/101.73). Since the price is a little above par there will also be a small annual loss in capital value to be deducted from this income to get the total return or GRY. Hence for interpolation we will try 10% and 11%.

Time	Cash Flow (£)	DF (10%)	PV (10%) (£)	DF (11%)	PV (11%) (£)
0	(101.73)	1	(101.73)	1	(101.73)
1	11.00	$\frac{1}{1.10}$	10.00	$\frac{1}{1.11}$	9.91
2	11.00	$\frac{1}{1.10^2}$	9.09	$\frac{1}{1.11^2}$	8.93
3	111.00	$\frac{1}{1.10^3}$	83.40	$\frac{1}{1.11^3}$	81.73
			0.76		(1.73)

$$\text{GRY(IRR)} = 10\% + \frac{0.76}{0.76-(1.73)} \times (11\% - 10\%) = 10.3\%$$

6. (a) (i) **Net Present Value**

Time	Cash Flow (£)	DF (7%)	PV (£)
0	(102)	1	(102.00)
1–4	8	$\frac{1}{0.07}\left(1-\frac{1}{1.07^4}\right) = 3.387$	27.10
4	100	$\frac{1}{1.07^4}$	76.29
			1.39

(ii) **GRY**

Time	Cash Flow (£)	DF (8%)	PV (£)
0	(102)	1	(102.00)
1–4	8	$\frac{1}{0.08}\left(1-\frac{1}{1.08^4}\right) = 3.312$	26.50
4	100	$\frac{1}{1.08^4}$	73.50
			(2.00)

$$GRY = 7 + \frac{1.39}{1.39 - (2.00)} \times (8 - 7) = 7.41\%$$

(iii) **NRY**

Time	Cash Flow (£)	DF (4%)	PV (4%) (£)	DF (5%)	PV (5%) (£)
0	(102.00)	1.0000	(102.00)	1.0000	(102.00)
1–4	4.80 (W)	3.6300	17.42	3.5460	17.02
4	100.00	0.8548	85.48	0.8227	82.27
			£0.90		£(2.71)

$$NRY = 4 + \frac{0.90}{0.90 - (2.71)} \times (5 - 4) = 4.25\%$$

Workings

Post-tax income = 8 × (1 – 0.40) = £4.80

(iv) **Gross Equivalent Yield**

Gross equivalent yield = 4.25/0.60 = 7.08%

This is alternatively called the grossed up net redemption yield.

(b) **Semi-Annual Coupon**

Time (Half Years)	Cash Flow (£)	DF (4%)	PV (4)% (£)	DF (5%)	PV (5%) (£)
0	(102)	1.0000	(102.00)	1.0000	(102.00)
1–8	4	6.7327	26.93	7.0197	28.08
8	100	0.7307	73.07	0.7894	78.94
			£(2.00)		£5.02

$$\text{Semi-annual yield} = 3 + \frac{5.02}{5.02-(2.00)} \times (4-3) = 3.715\%$$

GRY = Twice semi-annual yield

= 2 × 3.715 = 7.43%

7. (a) Using the bond valuation model

The flat yield = Coupon/price 10/90 = 11.1%

To find the true GRY the following formula will be required.

$$\text{Price} = \text{Coupon} \times \frac{1}{r}\left(1-\frac{1}{(1+r)^n}\right) + \frac{\text{Redemption}}{(1+r)^n}$$

Substituting in values of 11% and 13%

11%	13%
£4.85	– £4.40
£9.25	

The total range covered is a value of £9.25 and the point of balance is

$$11\% + \left[(13\%-11\%)\times\frac{£4.85}{£9.25}\right] = 12.05\%$$

(b) The holding period return, if the bond is sold for 98 after four years, is found by solving

$$\frac{(\text{Sales proceeds} - \text{Purchase price}) + \text{Coupons received}}{\text{Purchase price}} \times 100$$

$$\frac{(98-90)+40}{90} \times 100 \times ¼ = 13.33\%$$

An alternative is to regard the exercise as a four-year bond with maturity proceeds of £98 and annual coupons of £10 and solve for the yield.

(c) The compound value of coupons reinvested at 8% to a period four years, hence

	$10 \times (1.08)^3 =$	12.59
	$10 \times (1.08)^2 =$	11.66
	$10 \times (1.08) =$	10.80
		10.00
		45.05
Proceeds of sale of bond		98.00
		143.05

The holding period return r, is then given by

$90\,(1 + r)^4 = 143.05 \quad r \approx 12\%$.

(d) The main limitations of redemption yields are as follows.

- The reinvestment rate assumptions.
- The averaging impacts.
- The assumptions that the bond will be held to maturity.

8. (a) (i) The redemption yield of Bond I will be 10% (its coupon rate) since it is selling at par, while the redemption yield for Bond II is found by solving

$$106.93 = \frac{12}{1+r} + \frac{112}{(1+r)^2}$$

which yields r = 8.1%

Note. An approximation would be to use the Japanese method to calculate the GRY.

(ii) The one period spot rate will be the yield on a one-year pure discount bond, i.e. 10%.

The two period spot rate is computed by solving

$$106.93 = \frac{12}{1.10} + \frac{112}{(1+SR)}$$

Which yields an annualised, two period spot rate of 8%

(iii) The implied forward rate = $\frac{1.08^2}{1.10} - 1 = 6\%$

(b) The yield curve is the plot of redemption yields against maturity, while the terms structure entails plotting spot rates against time. Amongst the problems associated with determining the yield curve are coupon effects and other heterogeneities (such as tax status, call features) across bonds. As there are insufficient pure discount bonds to determine the full term structure, it is generally estimated using regression-based techniques.

9. **Semi-Annual Coupon**

Relevant RPIs are those eight months prior to any cash flow, i.e.

- Issue date RPI = 110
- Last coupon RPI = 135

Nominal price = Real price × (1 + i)

$$118.60 = \text{Real price} \times \frac{135}{110}$$

$$\text{Real price} = \frac{118.60}{\frac{135}{110}} = 96.64$$

where

I = Cumulative inflation in the last coupon calculated by reference to the relevant RPI.

Real Yield

Time (Half Years)	Cash Flow (£)	DF (1%)	PV (1%) (£)	DF (2%)	PV (2%) (£)
0	(96.64)	1.000	(96.64)	1.000	(96.64)
1–6	1.00	5.796	5.80	5.601	5.60
6	100.00	0.942	94.20	0.888	88.80
			£3.36		£(2.24)

$$\text{Real Semi-Annual GRY} = 1 + \frac{3.36}{3.36-(2.24)} \times (2-1) = 1.60\%$$

Nominal Yield

Nominal Semi-Annual GRY = (1.016 × 1.02) – 1 = 0.03632 or 3.632%%
Nominal Annual GRY = 2 × 3.632 = 7.26%

10. **Yield Curves**

(a) *Factors affecting the shapes of the yield curve*

Expectations – if investors expect interest rates to rise, then the yield curve will be upward sloping. If rates are expected to fall then the yield curve will be downward sloping.

Liquidity preference – other things being equal, investors prefer to have ready access to their money. This means that they would tend to prefer to make short-term rather than long-term investments and therefore need to receive a higher rate to make longer term investments attractive. This would suggest that the yield curve should be upward sloping.

Risk – the longer investments are tied up, the more risk there is that returns will be more variable than expected. Longer term investments therefore require an additional risk premium over short-term investments, suggesting that the yield curve should be upward sloping.

Inflation – the cumulative effect of inflation plus the risk of inflation increasing in the future means that longer term investments need to give a higher return, causing the yield curve to rise.

Market segmentation – there may be high supply compared to demand or vice versa at a particular range of maturities or level of coupon, giving rise to distortions in the yield curve.

The main shapes that may arise as a result of these influences are as follows.

Positive, normal or rising yield curve

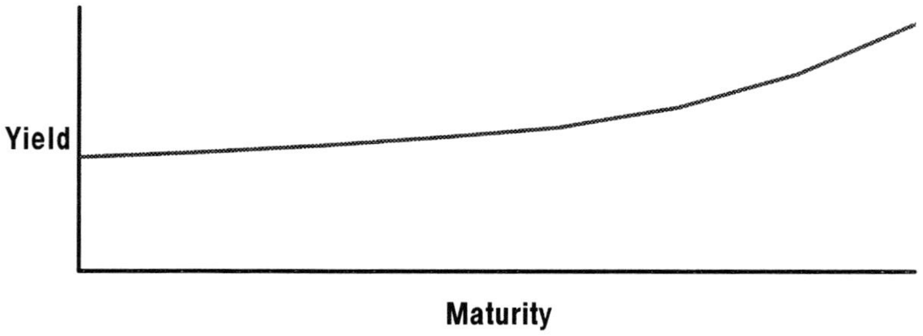

Negative or inverse yield curve

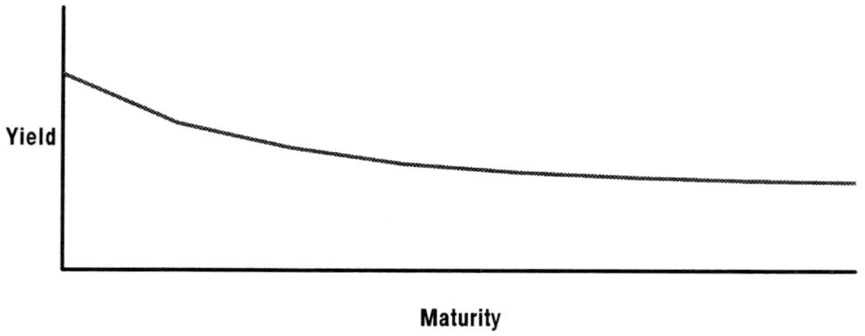

(b) Assuming that the two year bond does not pay interest until maturity, the market expectation for one year interest rates in one year from now is given by the value of f in the equation

$1.08 \times (1 + f) = 1.09^2$

$f = 10\%$

The assumption that the bonds only pay interest on maturity can be demonstrated by considering the cash flows relating to the two bonds.

	Bond 1 (£)	Bond 2 (£)
Market value	(100.00)	(100.00)
Redemption in one year	108.00	–
Redemption in two years	–	118.81
Yield	8%	9%

For the two situations to be identical, the investor in bond 1 should be able to reinvest the £108 so as to earn £118.81 a year later. This occurs at interest rates of 10%.

The same would not be the case if the yield on bond 2 were made up of an annual coupon, for example.

	Bond 1 (£)	Bond 2 (£)
Market value	(100.00)	(100.00)
Redemption in one year	108.00	9.00
Redemption in two years	–	109.00
Yield	8%	9%

In this case, the approach would be to first calculate the spot rate for flows in two years' time, as follows.

$$100 = \frac{9}{1.08} + \frac{9}{(1+r_2)^2}$$

$r_2 = 9.05\%$

The one-year rate in one year's time is then given by

$1.08 \times (1 + f) = 1.0905^2$

$f = 10.1\%$

Other factors to consider

Assuming that the funds are available for two years, the two possibilities are that they are invested in the two year bond or that they are invested for one year and subsequently reinvested. Theoretically, both methods give the same expected result, given the calculations above.

Investment for two years gives a certain return of 9%, assuming that any interest proceeds in one year's time can be reinvested at this rate. Investment for one year gives an uncertain return, since rates in one year's time may have changed from those predicted. This may give a higher or lower overall return, depending on the direction in which rates have moved. This uncertainty could be removed by using hedging instruments such as FRAs, but since the FRA price would be based on yield curve information anyway, the final return would probably be very similar to that of the two year bond.

The company's own view on interest rates, compared with that of the market, may indicate which of the above it feels to be the better alternative in terms of yield.

Tying up the funds for two years reduces the flexibility of the company's position. If the funds are required earlier than anticipated, then investing in a two year bond will mean that the bond may have to be sold in the market place for an uncertain sum. If the bond cannot be sold or the company is unwilling to adopt this route, the company will have to borrow additional money. This will inflate the balance sheet, use up credit facilities and involve losing money on the spread between borrowing and depositing.

Investing the funds for only one year will enable the reinvestment to be done with better knowledge as to when the funds will actually be needed. This will avoid many of the above problems.

(c) (i) *Companies with materially different ratings*

The main distinction between the two companies is one of risk. The company with the lower rating will have a far higher perceived default risk than the highly rated company.

This means that overall the required yields on bonds issued by the lower rated company will be higher at any maturity. However, the difference in yields between the two companies will widen at longer maturities. The reason for this is that investors will perceive that locking up funds with the riskier company for a longer period of time enhances the chance that insolvency will occur, due to economic and other unpredictable factors. One of the basic ideas behind the yield curve is that longer maturities demand higher yields due to higher risk involved in tying up funds for so long.

To summarise, the yield curve for the lower rated company will generally have higher yields in the first place. Assuming a normal yield curve, the slope of the curve for the lower rated company will be steeper.

(ii) *AAA rated company and UK government debt*

Government debt is traditionally viewed as being as close to risk free as can be achieved. As such, gilts command the lowest yields. AAA companies are also perceived to be very low risk and can command low yields. This means that the yields required on gilts will be very low and only slightly lower than those required on AAA debt. This will particularly be the case for very short-term debt, where the perceived risk of the AAA company's debt is extremely low.

At more distant maturities, UK gilts will still be perceived to be relatively low risk. However, there is a greater risk attached to the debt of an AAA company for several reasons. Increased time spans always increase risk and it may be the case that the rating of the company will have deteriorated significantly in, say, five years' time. The company's prospects and cash flows may significantly worsen even though it is at present seen to be in a very attractive market place. There have been many examples of large companies that have fallen in this way due to either incompetent management or extreme adverse economic conditions. Alternatively, there is the risk that the company will gear up significantly through a junk issue, for example, which will affect the quality of its existing debt adversely and result in higher yields being demanded.

This means that, at the longer end of the yield curve, the gap between Government and AAA company securities will widen.

11. **Inverse Yield Curve**

(a) The inverse yield curve can be shown diagrammatically as follows.

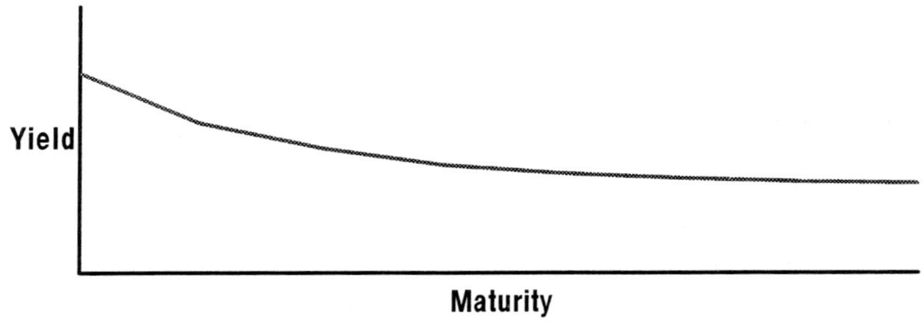

It relates to the situation when yields on long-term bonds are lower than those on short-term bonds. It arises when investors are expecting interest rates to fall in the future from a current high rate. Although factors such as risk aversion and preference for liquidity mean that investors usually demand higher returns from longer term instruments, the expectation of falling interest rates is sufficient to compensate for this and to drag the slope of the curve down.

(b) The existence of the inverse yield curve over the coming year indicates that yields on short-term instruments of, say, one month are higher than those on longer term instruments of one year. Investing in a one-year bond will give a lower yield than investing in, say, a six-month bond.

This does not necessarily imply that the company should invest in the short-term bond to achieve the higher yield available. Since the money is to be invested for a year in total, investment in a short-term instrument will necessitate reinvestment, which may be at a lower yield. The efficient market hypothesis would argue that the expected yield at which the funds could be reinvested will result in the return for the whole year being equivalent to the yield on the one-year bond. For example, if six-month bonds were yielding 15% now and one-year bonds were yielding 10%, the efficient market hypothesis would argue that the expected yield at which the six-month funds could be reinvested in six months' time would be given by the value of r in the following equation.

$1.075 \times (1 + f) = 1.1$
$f = 0.023$ or 2.3%

On an annual basis, this would give a yield for six-month bonds in six months' time of 4.6%.

Notwithstanding the above prediction, the finance director believes that interest rates are going to rise. If this actually occurs, it will clearly be best to invest for as short a time as possible and then lock into the higher yields when interest rates increase. The problem is that the finance director may be incorrect in his belief that interest rates will increase. The yield curve indicates general market expectations and there is no reason to believe that the finance director is a superior forecaster or has superior knowledge than the market in general. This means that investing on the basis of his beliefs may not be in the company's best interests.

The objective of maximising yield is not the only factor to be considered in deciding on the appropriate maturity in which to invest. The funds may be required in advance of the 12-month period. Locking up the money in a one-year bond may therefore be disadvantageous. Either the bond will need to be sold, possibly at a capital loss, or the company will have to borrow money, using up credit lines, inflating the balance sheet and suffering the difference between the borrowing and depositing rates.

Overall, it may be appropriate for the company to invest the funds in a range of maturities to give it flexibility, while maximising the expected yield on the surplus funds in the meantime.

12. **Government Bonds**

(a) There is insufficient information given in the question to calculate the expected future rates precisely. Assuming that the bonds are UK Government bonds and pay interest semi-annually, information on the coupon levels and yields for bonds maturing at six monthly intervals is required. This would enable spot rates to be calculated and expected forward rates to be derived.

With the information given in the question, it is necessary to make assumptions. The easiest assumption is the bonds are zero coupon bonds, meaning yield information given is equivalent to spot rate information.

An alternative assumption would be to assume that the bonds pay interest annually and are all priced at par – this would enable spot rates to be estimated for each of the three years. Given the time available in the exam and the fact that this would involve more work, the first assumption is probably best, although both approaches are probably inaccurate.

(i) One-year rate in one year's time

$1.05875 \times (1 + f) = 1.06125^2$

$$f = \frac{1.06125^2}{1.05875} - 1 = 0.06376 \text{ or } 6.376\%$$

(ii) One-year rate in two years' time

$1.06125^2 \times (1 + r) = 1.06^3$

$$r = \frac{1.06^3}{1.06125^2} - 1 = 0.0575 \text{ or } 5.75\%$$

(b) **Six-month rate**

$$\left(1 + 0.06 \times \frac{91}{365}\right) \times \left(1 + 0.05 \times \frac{91}{365}\right) = 1 + r$$

$r = 0.02761$ or 2.761%

$$\text{Annualised} = 2.761\% \times \frac{365}{182} = 5.54\%$$

13. **Yield Curve Analysis**

(a) This section requires a reasonably detailed theoretical knowledge of the yield curve, how it is constructed and the limitations of analysis using particular types of yield curve. Students should be aware of the basic description of the yield curve, what information it provides and how it can be used. Detailed knowledge of the different methods of preparing the yield curve is less important, although the disadvantages of using gross redemption yields and the importance of allowing for the problem of comparing high and low coupon bonds should be appreciated. An answer should cover the following main areas.

Basic description of the yield curve

- Diagram comparing bond yields and maturities.
- Constructed by obtaining data for various maturity dates and drawing line of best fit on the graph, either visually or by using more sophisticated techniques.
- Ideally, maturities should be close together to give a more accurate picture.
- Can be constructed for any period of time, from a few months to a number of years.
- Can be used to determine market expectations of interest rates and to analyse whether a particular bond is appropriately valued or not.
- In order to have valid comparisons, need to compare similar bonds in terms of credit risk, etc.

Use of gross redemption yield as the measure of yield

- Very common technique.
- Essentially the internal rate of return of all the bond's cash flows.
- Easy to calculate.
- Although quick and easy, it is difficult to obtain meaningful information when comparing the GRYs of different bonds if the bonds have different maturities or different levels of coupon. The reason for this is that the IRR as a measure is not really designed to be of use for comparison purposes. It is merely the discount rate that makes the future cash flows of a bond equivalent in present value terms to its existing market value.
- The GRY approach assumes that the same discount rate should be used to discount all the flows of the bond regardless of when they occur. This ignores the fact that investors may actually use a different discount rate for flows that occur at different times.
- The IRR of the bond is in fact just an amalgamation/average of all the different interest rates that have been used by the investors. It implies that two five year bonds, one with a high coupon and one with a zero coupon could be valued using the same gross redemption yield.
- The GRY approach by itself does not recognise that different bonds have different volatility in price. Low coupon bonds' prices are more volatile than those of high coupon bonds. To an extent, this can be compensated for by using techniques such as duration and modified duration.
- The GRY approach ignores the fact that different types of bond, e.g. high and low coupon bonds, have different yields due to tax factors, for example.

Alternatives to the simple GRY approach

- Constructing a three-dimensional yield surface enables the yield to be compared not just to maturity but to a second factor, which would typically be coupon. The three axes of the graph would therefore be yield, maturity and coupon. This removes the distortion caused by comparing high and low coupon bonds on the traditional graph with two axes. It is, however, more difficult to construct and harder to visualise than the simpler model.
- Use of the spot rate curve or the zero coupon curve. This assumes that investors do not view a bond as a series of flows and apply one discount rate (the IRR/GRY) to all the flows. Rather they treat each flow of the bond as a separate bond with only one flow on its maturity, i.e. a zero coupon bond and calculate the market value of each flow separately, using a discount rate that reflects the date on which the flow occurs (the spot rate for that date). These spot rates are shown on the yield curve. This yield curve avoids the problem of comparing GRYs for what could be very different bonds and the problem of high and low coupons.
- For example, a bond paying interest of £10 in one year's time and interest of £10 plus capital redemption of £100 in two years' time would be treated as one zero coupon bond paying £10 in one year's time and another zero coupon bond paying £110 in two years' time. Each bond would be valued separately, the first using the spot rate applicable to one year flows and the second using a different spot rate applicable to flows in two years' time. The total bond value would be the aggregate of the two separate market values.
- Use of the par yield curve. Assumes all bonds are trading at par, which means that the GRY is the same as the income yield of a bond and removes any distortion due to different coupon levels. Used by the Bank of England.

14. **One year spot rate from A**

$$101 = \frac{8+100}{1+r_1}$$

$$1 + r_1 = \frac{108}{101} = 1.0693$$

$$r1 = 1.0693 - 1 = 0.0693 \text{ or } 6.93\%$$

Two year spot rate from B

$$105 = \frac{10}{1.0693} + \frac{10+100}{(1+r_2)^2}$$

$$105 = 9.352 + \frac{110}{(1+r_2)^2}$$

$$95.648 = \frac{110}{(1+r_2)^2}$$

$$(1 + r_2)^2 = \frac{110}{95.648} = 1.150$$

$$1 + r_2 = \sqrt{1.150} = 1.0724$$

$$r_2 = 1.0724 - 1 = 0.0724 \text{ or } 7.24\%$$

Three year spot rate from C

$$110 = \frac{12}{1.0693} + \frac{12}{1.0724^2} + \frac{12+100}{(1+r_3)^3}$$

$$110 = 11.222 + 10.434 + \frac{112}{(1+r_3)^3}$$

$$88.344 = \frac{112}{(1+r_3)^3}$$

$$(1 + r_3)^3 = \frac{112}{88.344} = 1.268$$

$$1 + r_3 = \sqrt[3]{1.268} = 1.0823$$

$$r_3 = 1.0823 - 1 = 0.0823 \text{ or } 8.23\%$$

1 forward 2

$$1.0693 \times (1 + {}_1f_2) = 1.0724^2$$

$$1 + {}_1f_2 = \frac{1.0724^2}{1.0693} = 1.0755$$

$${}_1f_2 = 1.0755 - 1 = 0.0755 \text{ or } 7.55\%$$

2 forward 3

$$1.0724^2 \times (1 + {}_2f_3) = 1.0823^3$$

$$1 + {}_2f_3 = \frac{1.0823^3}{1.0724^2} = 1.1024$$

$${}_2f_3 = 1.1024 - 1 = 0.1024 \text{ or } 10.24\%$$

1 forward 3

$1.0693 \times (1 + {}_1f_3)^2 = 1.0823^3$

$(1 + {}_1f_3)^2 = \dfrac{1.0823^3}{1.0693} = 1.1856$

$1 + {}_1f_2 = \sqrt{1.1856} = 1.0889$

${}_1f_3 = 1.0889 - 1 = 0.0889$ or 8.89%

15. (a) **Bond Values**

		Bond A		Bond B	
Time	**DF**	**Cash Flow**	**PV**	**Cash Flow**	**PV**
1	$\frac{1}{1.05}$	10	9.53	10	9.53
2	$\frac{1}{1.06^2}$	10	8.90	10	8.90
3	$\frac{1}{1.08^3}$	10	7.94	110	87.32
4	$\frac{1}{1.09^4}$	10	7.08		
5	$\frac{1}{1.09^5}$	110	71.49		
			104.94		105.75

(b) **Return in One Year**

Values in One Year

		Bond A		Bond B	
Time	**DF**	**Cash Flow**	**PV**	**Cash Flow**	**PV**
1	$\frac{1}{1.05}$	10	9.53	10	9.53
2	$\frac{1}{1.06^2}$	10	8.90	110	97.90
3	$\frac{1}{1.08^3}$	10	7.94		
4	$\frac{1}{1.09^4}$	110	71.49		
			104.30		107.43

Returns over the Year

$$\text{Holding Period Return} = \frac{(Ve + D) - Vs}{Vs}$$

$$\text{Bond A} = \frac{(104.30 + 10.00) - 104.94}{104.94}$$

$$= 0.0892 \text{ or } 8.92\%$$

$$\text{Bond B} = \frac{(107.43 + 10.00) - 105.75}{105.75}$$

$$= 0.1104 \text{ or } 11.04\%$$

(c) **Strategies**

Holding bonds generates returns in two ways.

- Coupons received.
- Capital gain realised if interest rates fall.

Where we have a stable and upward sloping term structure of interest rates, bonds will be moving to lower discount rates as they move towards maturity and hence will be generating a capital gain. The scale of this gain is a function of the timing of the cash flows and where the curve slopes.

For Bond B, the major cash flow (the redemption proceeds) moves from a discount rate of 8% to 6% generating a significant gain. For Bond A, this gain is not apparent as the major cash flow is discounted at 9% in both years.

In practice, it is unlikely that term structures will be constant over a year and hence risk (duration and the likely changes in term structures) as well as return would need to be considered.

16. **One year spot rate**

$$r_1 = \frac{108.5 - 100}{100} = 0.085 \text{ or } 8.5\%$$

Two year spot rate

$$102 = \frac{9.25}{1.085} + \frac{9.25 + 100}{(1+r_2)^2}$$

$$102 = 8.5253 + \frac{109.25}{(1+r_2)^2}$$

$$93.4747 = \frac{109.25}{(1+r_2)^2}$$

$$(1 + r_2)^2 = \frac{109.25}{93.4747} = 1.1688$$

$$1 + r_2 = \sqrt{1.1688}$$

$$r_2 = \sqrt{1.1688} - 1 = 0.0811 \text{ or } 8.11\%$$

Three year spot rate

$$104 = \frac{10}{1.085} + \frac{10}{1.0811^2} + \frac{10 + 100}{(1+r_3)^3}$$

$$104 = 9.217 + 8.556 + \frac{110}{(1+r_3)^3}$$

$$86.227 = \frac{110}{(1+r_3)^3}$$

$$(1 + r_3)^3 = \frac{110}{86.227} = 1.2757$$

$$1 + r_3 = \sqrt[3]{1.2757} = 1.0845$$

$$r_3 = 1.0845 - 1 = 0.0845 \text{ or } 8.45\%$$

1 forward 2

$$1.085 \times (1 + {}_1f_2) = 1.0811^2$$

$$(1 + {}_1f_2) = \frac{1.0811^2}{1.085} = 1.0772$$

$${}_1f_2 = 1.0772 - 1 = 0.0772 \text{ or } 7.72\%$$

2 forward 3

$$1.0811^2 \times (1 + {}_2f_3) = 1.0845^3$$

$$(1 + {}_2f_3) = \frac{1.0845^3}{1.0811^2} = 1.0913$$

$${}_2f_3 = 1.0913 - 1 = 0.0913 \text{ or } 9.13\%$$

1 forward 3

$$1.085 \times (1 + {}_1f_3)^2 = 1.0845^3$$

$$(1 + {}_1f_3)^2 = \frac{1.0845}{1.085} = 1.1756$$

$$1 + {}_1f_3 = \sqrt{1.1756} = 1.0843$$

$${}_1f_3 = 1.0843 - 1 = 0.0843 \text{ or } 8.43\%$$

17. (a) The shape of the yield curve is inverted indicating that the short yields are currently high and expected to fall over the next few years. However, the slope is not particularly marked and therefore is not predicting a rapid fall.

(b) (i) Current price $= \frac{5}{1.075} + \frac{5}{1.072^2} + \frac{105}{1.07^3} = 94.71$

(ii) Current price $= \frac{15}{1.075} + \frac{15}{1.072^2} + \frac{15}{1.07^3} + \frac{115}{1.068^4} = 127.63$

(iii) Current price $= \frac{5}{1.075} + \frac{5}{1.072^2} + \frac{5}{1.07^3} + \frac{5}{1.068^4} + \frac{105}{1.065^5} = 93.55$

(c) All of the bonds will be influenced by the pull to redemption that would tend to indicate that Bond B (with the highest coupon) would be trading on the highest yield. However, with an inverted yield curve, the short-dated stock should trade at a higher yield than the others.

In the UK, the impact of coupon is a strong influence on the yield. Lower coupon stocks trade below par generating a tax-free gain. Consequently, these stocks attract greatest interest from the public. The effect of this is to force the price of low coupon stocks up thereby reducing the yield. Higher coupon stocks of the same maturity will consequently trade at a higher yield.

(d) Bond C has a longer maturity and a lower coupon and will therefore have the highest duration and, consequently, greatest sensitivity to the fall in interest rates of 1%.

18. (a) **1 Year spot**

$$100 = \frac{108}{(1+r)} \quad \text{Therefore } r = 8\%$$

2 Year spot

$$98.60 = \frac{7.50}{(1+r_1)} + \frac{107.50}{(1+r_2)^2}$$

$$98.60 = \frac{7.50}{1.08} + \frac{107.50}{(1+r_2)^2}$$

$$98.60 = 6.94 + \frac{107.50}{(1+r_2)^2}$$

$$91.66 = \frac{107.50}{(1+r_2)^2}$$

$$(1+r_2)^2 = \frac{107.50}{91.66} = 1.1728$$

$$(1+r_2) = \sqrt{1.1728} = 1.0829$$

$$r_2 = 1.0829 - 1 = 0.0829 \text{ or } 8.29\%$$

3 Year spot

$$97.20 = \frac{7.25}{(1+r_1)} + \frac{7.25}{(1+r_2)^2} + \frac{107.25}{(1+r_3)^3}$$

$$97.20 = \frac{7.25}{1.08} + \frac{7.25}{1.0829} + \frac{107.25}{(1+r_3)^3}$$

$$97.20 = 6.71 + 6.18 + \frac{107.25}{(1+r_3)^3}$$

$$84.31 = \frac{107.25}{(1+r_3)^3}$$

$$(1+r_3)^3 = \frac{107.25}{84.31} = 1.2721$$

$$(1+r_3) = \sqrt[3]{1.2721} = 1.0835$$

$$r_3 = 1.0835 - 1 = 0.0835 \text{ or } 8.35\%$$

(b) Spots are used to evaluate bonds by inserting into the ordinary bond formula and solving for the present value. Technically, this is deemed to be a more appropriate form of valuation.

Once the spot rates have been derived, it is possible to project the forward rates, the expected interest rate in a future period. Forward rates are used to evaluate many derivative products.

9 Bond Risk and Risk Analysis

INTRODUCTION

Whenever we are considering any investments there are two very important aspects to consider, the return the investment will offer and the risk we face with that investment.

This section reviews the risks inherent in investing in bonds, how the risks may be measured or assessed and how these measurements may be used.

A full appreciation of risk is essential for successful investing and the ideas in this section are regularly examined.

CHAPTER CONTENTS

Chapter Learning Objectives

The syllabus areas covered by this section are

Analysis

Students should possess a broad understanding of both static and dynamic methods for the analysis and construction of fixed income securities containing both certain and contingent cashflows. Variable rate securities will be included. Students should be aware of the limitations of assumptions and mathematical techniques upon results. Although analysis will be concerned principally with 'risk–free' securities, students should be aware of the further considerations for 'risky' securities and the effect they may have on expected return. Students should possess a thorough comprehension of single–period and multi–period, single currency and multi–currency portfolio management theory.

Credit Analysis

- Sovereign and corporate
- Ratings
- Default experience

Students will not be required to perform higher mathematical calculations, to derive any theoretical proofs, or to know any formulae other than for the topics marked (*) above to satisfy the requirements of the paper. Should other formulae be necessary they will be given. An awareness of the limitations of the mathematical techniques is necessary. Students may expect applications of analytic techniques in practical examples.

1 The Risks of Holding a Bond

1.1 Introduction

An investor in a fixed income security is exposed to a number of different risks, and any complete assessment of a bond must include consideration of these factors. These bond risks include the following.

1.1.1 Interest rate risk

This is probably the most important risk because of the powerful relationship between interest rates and bond prices. Duration and modified duration (volatility) are the means of measuring this risk. Convexity is the measure that is used to explain the variation away from the predicted return.

1.1.2 Credit and default risk

Credit and default risk is the risk of the issuer defaulting on its obligations to pay coupons and repay the principal. The ratings by commercial rating companies can be used to help assess this risk.

1.1.3 Inflation risk

Inflation risk is linked to interest rate risk, as interest rates rise to compensate bondholders for inflation.

1.1.4 Liquidity and marketability risk

This has to do with the ease with which an issue can be sold in the market. Smaller issues especially are subject to this risk. In certain markets, the volume of trading tends to concentrate into the 'benchmark' stocks, thereby rendering most other issues illiquid. Other bonds become subject to 'seasoning' as the initial liquidity dries up and the bonds are purchased by investors who wish to hold them to maturity.

1.1.5 Issue specific risk

There may be factors specific to the issue, which tend to either increase or decrease the risk, e.g. issuer options such as the right to call for early redemption or possibly, holder options.

1.1.6 Fiscal risk

Fiscal risk represents risk that withholding taxes will be increased. For foreign bonds, there would also be the risk of the imposition of capital controls locking your money into the market.

1.1.7 Currency risk

For any investor purchasing overseas or international bonds, there is obviously also the risk of currency movements.

1.1.8 Leveraged buyout risk

Risks arising if the issuer is subject to a takeover, especially if it is highly leveraged.

2 Interest Rate Risk

Exam tip

Questions involving the calculation, properties and uses of the various measures in this section arise quite frequently. It is notable that these calculations have become much more in depth in more recent sittings, e.g. Summer 2008 Question 1, Winter 2006 Question 3, Summer 2006 Question 1, Winter 2005 Question 4, Summer 2003 Question 1.

2.1 Introduction

The most predictable of these risks is the interest rate risk. Within bond markets, this is sometimes referred to, somewhat confusingly, as the **volatility**. The sensitivity of any bond to movements in the interest rate will be determined by a number of factors.

2.1.1 Sensitivity to maturity

Longer-dated bonds will be more sensitive to changes in the interest rate than shorter dated stocks as illustrated by these prices for three 12% bonds of differing maturity subject to differing GRYs.

Coupon %	Maturity (Years)	Price for a GRY of		
		8%	10%	12%
12	4	£113.24	£106.34	£100.00
12	7	£120 83	£109.74	£100.00
12	26	£143.23	£118.32	£100.00

In this example, it is the price of the 26-year bond which exhibits the greatest range as the yield alters (moving from £143.23 to par). The logic behind this is that the longer dated bond is more exposed to the movements of the yield, since it has longer to go to maturity.

2.1.2 Sensitivity to coupon

With regard to the level of coupon, it is the lower coupon stocks that demonstrate the greatest level of sensitivity to the yield.

Coupon %	Maturity (Years)	Price for a GRY of		
		9%	10%	11%
5	15	£67.75	£61.97	£56.85
10	15	£108.06	£100.00	£92.81
15	15	£148.30	£138.03	£128.76

In this example, the price of the 5% bond moves from £61.97 when the GRY is 10% to £67.75 if GRY drops to 9% (a fall of 9%) to £56.85 if GRY rises to 11% (a fall of 8.2%). The other bonds, whilst exhibiting the same overall relationship, are not as responsive to the alteration in the GRY. The 10% bond rises by 8% and falls by 7.1%.

It should be noted that the relationship between the coupon and maturity and the price are not symmetrical (equal for both a rise or a fall in GRY). This is a relationship that we will return to later and is known as **convexity**.

The logic behind this relationship is that the lower coupon bonds have more of their value tied up in the terminal value. The ultimate low-coupon bond is, after all, the zero-coupon bond where the entire value is in the final payment.

2.1.3 The impact of the yield

If yields are particularly high, then the flows in the future are worth relatively little and the sensitivity is diminished. Conversely, if the yield is low, then the present value of flows in the future is enhanced and the bond is more sensitive to the changing GRY.

2.1.4 Summary

Long dated > Short dated

Low coupon > High coupon

Low yields > High yields

Whilst these simple maxims are good indicators of the likely sensitivity to fluctuations in the rate of interest, they do not allow for two bonds to be compared.

For example, which of the following is likely to be the most sensitive to a rise in interest rates – a high-coupon long-dated stock or a low-coupon short-dated stock? It was for this reason that in the 1930s, a composite measure of interest rate risk was devised – the **duration**.

2.2 Macaulay duration

2.2.1 Introduction

As we have just seen, cash flows at different points in time have different sensitivities to rate movements (different risks). A bond may be thought of as an amalgamation of differently timed cash flows each with their own sensitivity. Hence, the sensitivity of a bond to changes in rates must be a weighted average of the sensitivities of the individual cash flows. This is a bond's duration.

2.2.2 Definition

Duration is the weighted average length of time to the receipt of a bond's benefits (coupon and redemption value), the weightings being the present value of the benefits involved.

This concept can be shown diagrammatically

Duration

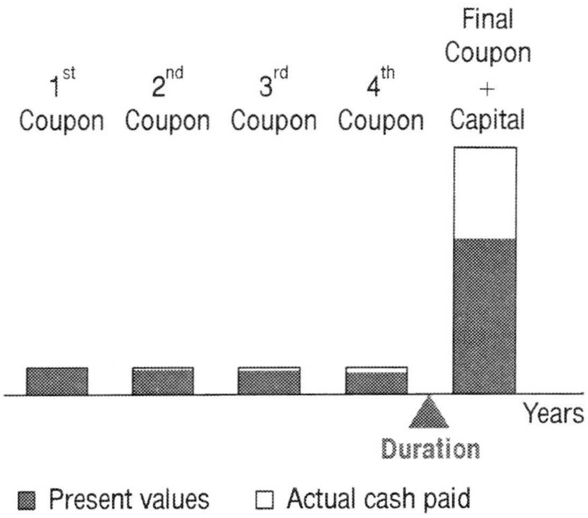

where the fulcrum or point of balance represents the duration of the bond.

2.2.3 Calculation

Mathematically, duration can be expressed using the following formula.

Formula to learn

$$\text{Macaulay duration (D)} = \frac{\sum(t \times PV_t)}{\text{Price}}$$

Or

Formula to learn

$$\text{Macaulay duration (D)} = \frac{\text{Sum of the time-weighted present-value}}{\text{Price}}$$

where

PV_t = present value of cash flow in period t (discounted using the redemption yield)

This may look difficult, but can be easily calculated in a table that simply adds one column to the one used for evaluation.

Example

What would be the duration of a three-year 9% annual coupon bond trading with a GRY of 8%?

Solution

Time	Cash Flow (£)	Discount Factor	Present Value (£)	Weighted (t × PVt)
1	9.00	$\frac{1}{1.08}$	8.33	8.33
2	9.00	$\frac{1}{1.08^2}$	7.72	15.44
3	109.00	$\frac{1}{1.08^3}$	86.53	259.59
			102.58	283.36

Using the above, the duration is

$$\text{Duration} = \frac{283.36}{102.58} = 2.7623 \text{ years}$$

2.2.4 Use

The uses of duration are

- As a measure of relative risk for a bond in a similar fashion to the standard deviation or the beta for a share. The higher the duration of the bond, the higher its risk or interest rate sensitivity.
- To calculate modified duration (discussed below).
- In the determination of the portfolio holdings necessary to establish a bond fund management strategy called immunisation. This is not covered in this section, but dealt with in the fund management section later.
- To approximate the portfolio yield (see the Appendix to this section)

2.2.5 Properties of duration

The basic features of sensitivity to interest rate risk are all mirrored in the duration calculation.

- **Longer dated bonds** will have longer durations.

  Note. The duration of an irredeemable = $1 + \frac{1}{\text{Yield}}$.
- **Lower coupon bonds** will have longer durations. The ultimate low-coupon bond is a zero-coupon bond where the duration will be the maturity.
- **Lower yields** will give higher durations. In this case, the present value of flows in the future will fall if the yield increases, moving the point of balance towards the present day, therefore shortening the duration.

The duration of a bond will shorten as the lifespan of the bond decays. However, the rate of their decay will not be the same. In our example above, a three-year bond has a duration of 2.7623 years. In one year's time, the bond will have a remaining life of two years, and a duration based on the same GRY of 1.9182 years. The lifespan has decayed by a full year, but the duration by only 0.8441 of a year.

The following graph shows the relationship between duration and maturity for a number of bonds at a GRY of 10%.

Exam tip

> Covered in Winter 2007 Question 1.

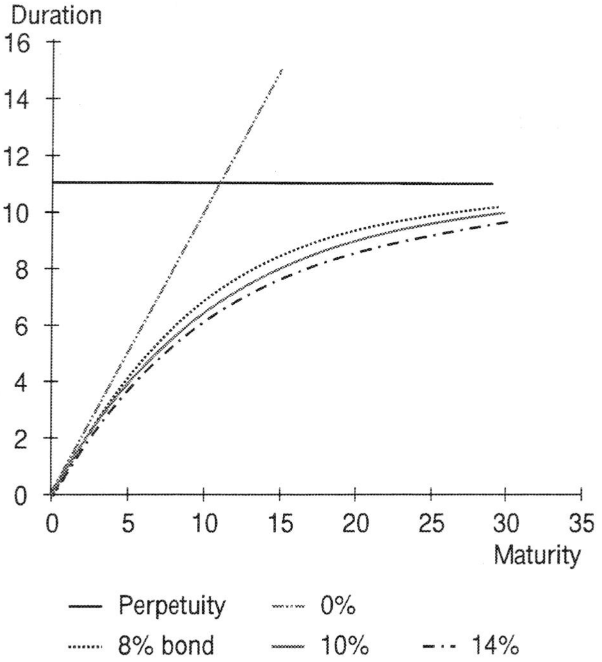

The duration of a zero-coupon bond equates with its maturity since there is only one flow to weight.

For coupon bonds there is a finite limit on duration set by the valuation of a perpetuity. With an irredeemable bond or a very long-dated bond, it is effectively a perpetuity. A perpetuity is a perpetual income stream going into the future.

One note of caution – for very low coupon bonds their duration will initially track the zero-coupon relationship. However, eventually they will be drawn back to the perpetuity. This will mean though that it is possible for their duration to rise above the perpetuity level.

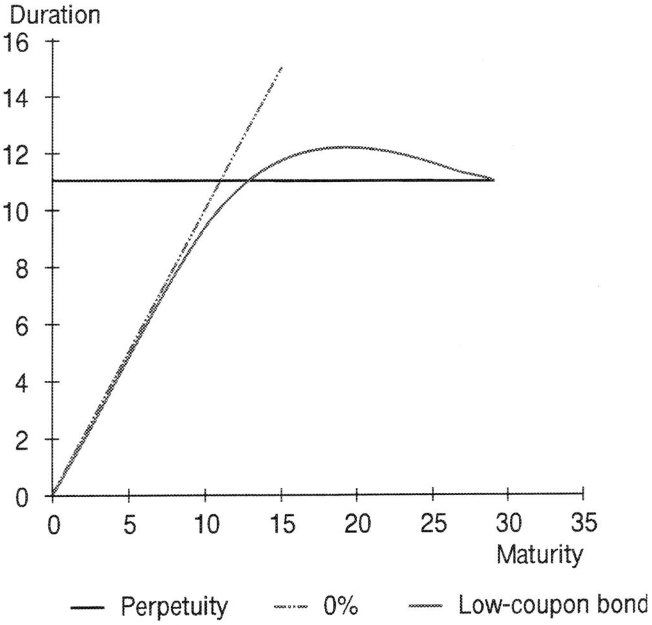

2.3 Modified duration/Volatility

2.3.1 Introduction

At the same time as the Macaulay duration was being promoted as a means of expressing the sensitivity of a bond to movements in the interest rate, Hicks was developing a formula to explain the impact of yield changes on price. Not surprisingly, the two measures are linked.

Hick's basic proposition was that the change in yield multiplied by this sensitivity measure would give the resultant percentage change in the bond's price, i.e. the volatility gives the percentage change in price per unit change in yield.

2.3.2 Definition

Modified duration is the percentage change in the price of a bond arising from a 1% change in yields.

2.3.3 Calculation

The modified duration formula may be derived through the use of calculus, specifically differentiation of the price equation with respect to yields. Fortunately, there is an easier definition, specifically

Formula to learn

$$\text{Modified Duration/Volatility} = -\frac{\text{Macaulay duration}}{1+\text{GRY}}$$

Some texts do not include the minus sign in the calculation of modified duration but insert it on use. We have included it here to emphasise the inverse relationship between prices and yields, i.e. as yields rise, prices fall.

2.3.4 Use

The use of modified duration is to provide a first estimate of the change in the price of a bond that will result from a given change in yields. It can also be used to calculate an approximate portfolio yield (see appendix)

Example

Using the example from above

$$\text{Modified duration} = -\frac{2.7623}{1.08} = -2.5577$$

This is negative, hence we can state that the price will **fall** by 2.5577% or £2.62 (102.58 × 2.5577%) for every one percentage point **increase** in the yield – we must bear in mind the inverse relationship.

Based on this, calculate the change in price and the new resulting price, if yields

- Fall 0.5%.
- Rise 1.0%.

Solution

Yields fall 0.5%

Alternative 1 – First principles

Bearing in mind the inverse relationship, if yields **fall** 0.5%, then prices will **rise** by £1.31 (£2.62 × 0.5) to £103.89 (£102.58 + £1.31).

Alternative 2 – Mathematical relationship

This relationship may be expressed mathematically as

Formula to learn

Proportionate change in price = MD × ΔY

where

MD = modified duration
ΔY = percentage change in the gross redemption yield (expressed as a decimal)

Applying this relationship gives

Proportionate change in price = MD × ΔY = –2.5577 × (–0.005) = 0.01279 or 1.279%

This is a positive figure, hence prices will rise by 1.279% or £1.31 (£102.58 × 1.279%) as calculated above in Alternative 1 above.

The first principles approach is certainly easier and more intuitive when we are only considering modified duration. The second mathematical relationship approach comes in to its own, however, when we try to incorporate the effects of convexity below.

Yields rise 1.0%

Alternative 1 – First principles

Bearing in mind the inverse relationship, if yields **rise** 1.0%, then prices will **fall** by £2.62 (£2.62 × 1.0) to £99.96 (£102.58 – £2.62).

Alternative 2 – Mathematical relationship

Proportionate change in price = MD × ΔY = –2.5577 × (+0.010) = –0.025577 or –2.5577%

This is a negative figure, hence prices will fall by 2.5577% or £2.62 (£102.58 × 2.5577%) as calculated above in Alternative 1 above.

Comments

If a full DCF pricing exercise is carried out, we would find that the prices would become £103.90 if yields fell 0.5% to 7.5%, and £100 if yields rose 1.0% to 9.0%. The modified duration calculation produces a quite accurate result for small changes in yields, however it becomes increasingly inaccurate for larger shifts.

2.3.5 Properties of modified duration

As the modified duration is derived from the Macaulay duration, it shares the same properties.

- **Longer dated bonds will have higher modified durations**

  Note. The modified duration of an irredeemable $= -\frac{1}{\text{Yield}}$.

- **Lower coupon bonds will have higher modified durations.**
- **Lower yields will give higher modified durations.**

The higher the modified duration value, the greater the sensitivity of that bond to a change in the yield.

The Relationship Between Duration and Modified Duration for a Coupon Bond

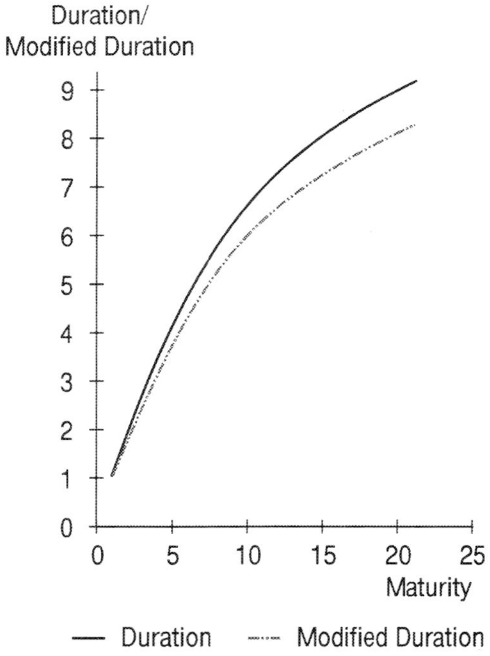

2.4 Convexity

2.4.1 Introduction

Modified duration predicts a linear relationship between yields and prices. If the modified duration is 2, then if yields rise by 1%, the price will fall by 2%. If the rise in yields had been 3%, then the fall in price would have been 6%.

The Price/Yield Relationship Given by the Modified Duration

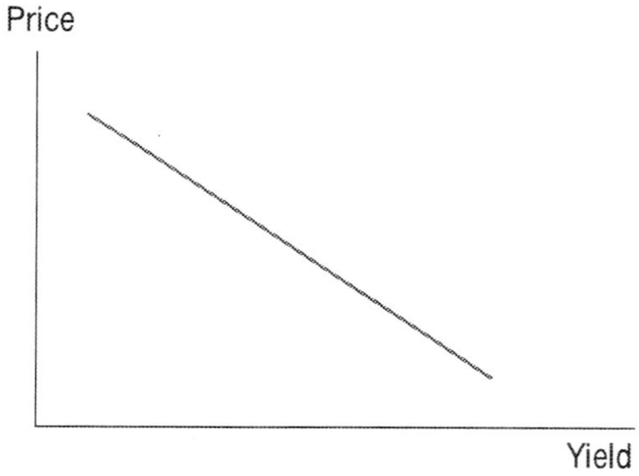

The slope of the line is the modified duration.

However, as the yield changes, so will the duration and consequently, the modified duration. It is this that gives rise to the concept of convexity.

The Impact of Changing Yields on the Modified Duration

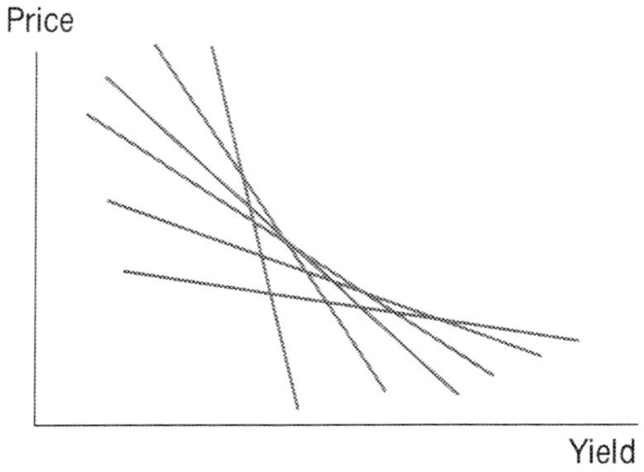

As the yield falls, the duration will increase and therefore, so will the modified duration. As modified duration increases, the line will steepen.

The actual relationship between the yield and price is given by the convex function that these individual linear relationships describe. We are after all aware that the relationship between bond prices and interest rates is not linear. The actual relationship between prices and yields is curved, with increases in yields resulting in prices falling, but at a reducing rate, as illustrated by the example at the start of this session.

The actual convex relationship and the linear one predicted by the modified duration formula are illustrated below.

Convexity

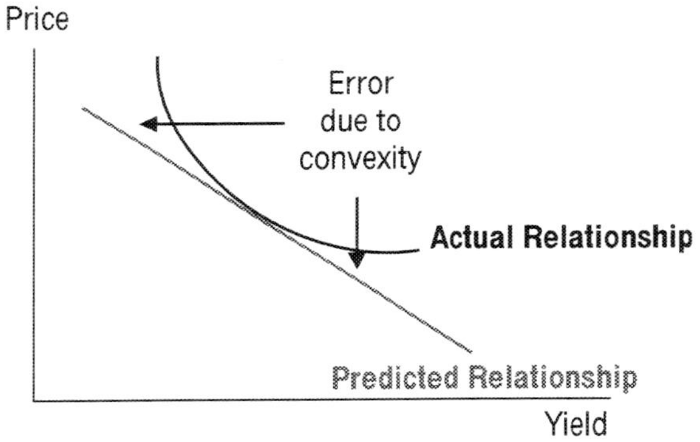

The impact of convexity will be that the modified duration will tend to **overstate the fall in a bond's price and understate the rise**. However, for relatively small movements in the yield, the modified duration will be a good estimate; the problem of convexity only becomes an issue with more substantial fluctuations in the yield.

2.4.2 Definition

Convexity is the change in the modified duration with respect to yields.

2.4.3 Calculation

The convexity formula may be derived once again through calculus, being a function of the second derivative of the price equation with respect to yields.

Formula to learn

$$\text{Convexity} = \frac{\sum t(t+1)PV_t}{\text{Price}(1+GRY)^2}$$

Note. Some texts include a ½ in this formula, others include the ½ when it is used within further calculations. How and when this ½ is included is of no relevance to its use as long as all calculations are done consistently.

Once again, this does not look like a very pleasant formula. However, it may easily be dealt with by extending our tabular duration calculation.

Example

Based on the previous duration calculation, calculate convexity (C).

Solution

Time	Cash Flow (£)	Discount Factor	PVt (£)	t × PVt (£)	t(t + 1)PVt (£)
1	9.00	$\frac{1}{1.08}$	8.33	8.33	16.66
2	9.00	$\frac{1}{1.08^2}$	7.72	15.44	46.32
3	109.00	$\frac{1}{1.08^3}$	86.53	259.59	1,038.36
			102.58	283.36	1,101.34

Hence

$$\text{Convexity} = \frac{\sum t(t+1)PV_t}{\text{Price}(1+\text{GRY})^2}$$

$$\text{Convexity} = \frac{1{,}101.34}{102.58 \times 1.08^2} = 9.2048$$

2.4.4 Use

The use of convexity is to

- Give a more accurate assessment of the change in the price of a bond that will result from a given change in yields.
- Indicate the risk of a bond fund immunisation strategy by comparing the convexity of the alternatives. Note, the relative convexity is unaffected by the consistent inclusion or exclusion of the ½ in the calculations. Once again, this is not covered in this section, but dealt with in the fund management section later.

Example

Using our ongoing example, calculate the change in the price of the bond, and the new resulting price, if yields

- Fall 0.5%.
- Rise 1.0%.

Solution

Yields fall 0.5%

Alternative 1 – Using an average modified duration

As we noted above, modified duration changes as yields change, hence using it to forecast price movements will lead to inaccuracies. To overcome this, we could use the convexity information to calculate the average modified duration over the given range of yields and use this to more accurately assess the change in prices as follows.

Modified duration at 8% GRY		–2.5577
Change due to convexity if yields fall 0.5% (–0.005)	9.2048 × (–0.005)	–0.0460
Modified duration at 7.5% GRY		–2.6037
Average modified duration	(–2.5577 – 2.6037) ÷ 2	–2.5807

Giving

Proportionate change in price = Average MD × ΔY = –2.5807 × (–0.005) = 0.01290 or 1.290%

Hence, prices will rise by £1.32 (£102.58 × 1.290%) to £103.90 (£102.58 + £1.32).

Alternative 2 – Mathematical relationship

Note, we could calculate the above average modified duration from the originally calculated modified duration (MD) as

$$\begin{aligned}\text{Average MD} &= \text{MD} + \tfrac{1}{2}\text{C} \times \Delta\text{Y} \\ &= -2.5577 + \tfrac{1}{2} \times 9.2048 \times (-0.005) \\ &= -2.5807\end{aligned}$$

Substituting this into the above price change formula would give

$$\begin{aligned}\text{Proportionate change in price} &= \text{Average MD} \times \Delta\text{Y} \\ &= (\text{MD} + \tfrac{1}{2}\text{C} \times \Delta\text{Y}) \times \Delta\text{Y} \\ &= \text{MD} \times \Delta\text{Y} + \tfrac{1}{2}\text{C} \times \Delta\text{Y}^2\end{aligned}$$

That is, this whole average modified duration approach may be combined into a single formula to speed the calculation and expressed mathematically as

Formula to learn

$$\text{Proportionate change in price} = \text{MD} \times \Delta\text{Y} + \tfrac{1}{2}\text{C} \times \Delta\text{Y}^2$$

where

MD = modified duration at the original GRY
C = convexity at the original GRY
ΔY = percentage change in the gross redemption yield (expressed as a decimal)

Applying this relationship gives

$$\begin{aligned}\text{Proportionate change in price} &= \text{MD} \times \Delta\text{Y} + \tfrac{1}{2}\text{C} \times \Delta\text{Y}^2 \\ &= -2.5577 \times (-0.005) + \tfrac{1}{2} \times 9.2048 \times (-0.005)^2 \\ &= 0.01290 \text{ or } 1.290\%\end{aligned}$$

This is a positive figure, hence prices will rise by 1.290% or £1.32 (£102.58 × 1.290%) as calculated above in Alternative 1.

Yields rise 1.0%

Applying the formula gives

Proportionate change in price $= MD \times \Delta Y + \frac{1}{2}C \times \Delta Y^2$

$= -2.5577 \times (+0.010) + \frac{1}{2} \times 9.2048 \times (+0.010)^2$

$= -0.02512$ or -2.512%

This is negative, hence prices will fall by £2.58 (£102.58 × 2.512%) to £100.00, which we know to be correct.

2.4.5 Properties of convexity

Not all bonds have the same degree of convexity. The general rule is that bonds with a higher duration will exhibit the greatest degree of convexity.

The Maturity Effect

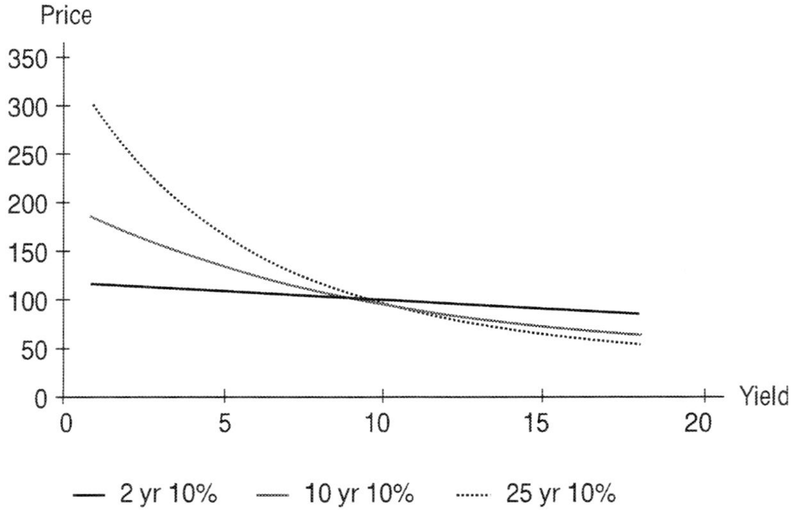

For bonds with the same duration, it will be the higher coupon bonds that will be the most convex. The reason for this is that the lower coupon bonds, for example 0% bonds, will have durations that will change little with the alteration in yield. In the most extreme form, the 0% bond will have a duration equal to its maturity and this will not alter as yields move.

The Coupon Effect

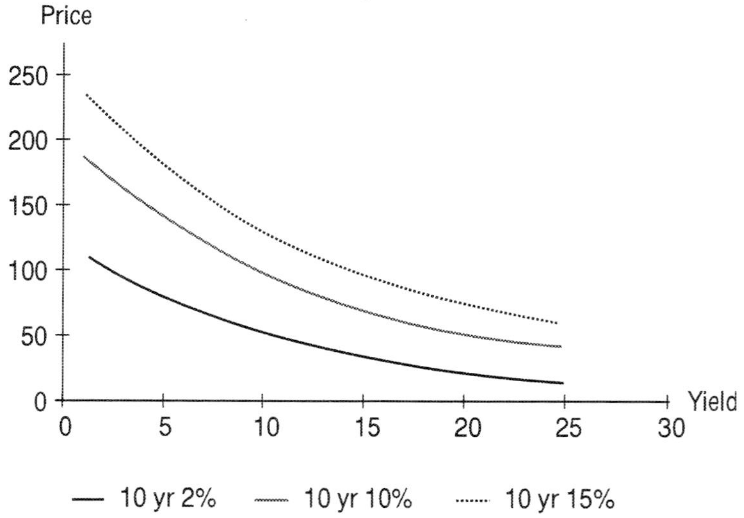

Investors may be prepared to pay for convexity. In a volatile market, the convex bonds at any particular maturity interval will outperform the bonds with lesser convexity.

It will also be possible to construct portfolios with enhanced convexity. This will be achieved through the use of barbell structures.

Example

Based on the following 10% bonds, construct a portfolio at bonds A and C that reflects the duration of bond B and determine the convexity of this portfolio.

Bond	Maturity (Years)	Duration (Years)	Convexity
A	5	4.170	0.097
B	15	8.317	0.434
C	30	10,370	0.787

Solution

Using the date from above, we can see that the 10% bond with a life of 15 years has a duration of 8.317 years and a convexity of 0.434. By buying a combination of the short and long-dated issues, it will be possible to replicate that duration exposure (weighted average of portfolio).

($p_a \times$ Duration of 5-yr bond) + [(1 – p_a) $\times$ Duration of 30-yr bond)] = 8.317

where

Pa = the proportion of the 5-year bond purchased

$(p_a \times 4.17) + [(1 - p_a) \times 10.37)] = 8.317$

$4.17\ p_a + 10.37 - 10.37\ p_a = 8.317$

$2.053 = 6.20\ p_a$

$p_a = 0.331$

Proof

$(0.331 \times 4.17) + [(1 - 0.331) \times 10.37] = 8.317$

This will preserve the sensitivity of the portfolio in duration terms but in terms of convexity

$(0.331 \times 0.097) + [(1 - 0.331) \times 0.787] = 0.559$

As opposed to the actual convexity of the 15-year bond which was 0.434.

Once again, this example demonstrates the linkage between dispersion and convexity. The portfolio of two bonds that simulates the 15-year bond has the same duration but a greater dispersion of cash flow and therefore a greater convexity.

2.5 Semi-annual coupons

The process for calculating duration, modified duration and convexity does not alter when we are dealing with semi-annual coupons, though we must do all the calculations on a semi-annual basis. That is, we take time 1 to be after the first half year, time 2 after the second half year etc, calculate the duration, modified duration and convexity on a half yearly basis, then apply the impact of changes in the semi-annual yield to give the results.

Example

A 5 year semi-annual 9% bond is currently achieving a quoted yield (twice the semi-annual yield) of 9%. Calculate the duration, modified duration and convexity for this bond and estimate the price change that will arise if the yield changes to

- 8%.
- 10%.

Solution

This bond will be paying a coupon of £4.50 each half year and achieving a semi-annual yield of 4.5%, hence it will be trading at par. The proof of this and the calculation of duration, modified duration and convexity is as follows.

Time ($^1/_2$ years)	Cash flow (£)	PV (£)	tPV (£)	t(1 + t)PV (£)
1	4.5	4.3062	4.3062	8.6124
2	4.5	4.1208	8.2416	24.7247
3	4.5	3.9433	11.8300	47.3200
4	4.5	3.7735	15.0941	75.4705
5	4.5	3.6110	18.0551	108.3309
6	4.5	3.4555	20.7332	145.1323
7	4.5	3.3067	23.1471	185.1768
8	4.5	3.1643	25.3147	227.8320
9	4.5	3.0281	27.2526	272.5263
10	104.5	67.2905	672.9044	7,401.9487
	Price	100.0000	826.8790	8,497.0746

Semi-annual

Duration $\frac{826.8790}{100} = 8.2688 = 4.1344$ years

Modified duration $-\frac{8.2688}{1.045} = -7.9127 = 3.95635$ annualised ($\div 2$)

Convexity $\frac{8{,}497.0746}{100 \times 1.045^2} = 77.8103 = 19.4526$ annualised ($\div 2^2$)

Quoted yield changes to 8%

If the quoted yield falls by 1% p.a. this corresponds to a semi-annual fall of 0.5%, i.e. $\Delta Y = -0.005$. Applying the formula, we would expect the price to rise by

$$\begin{aligned}\text{Proportionate price change} &= MD \times \Delta Y + \tfrac{1}{2}C \times \Delta Y^2 \\ &= -7.9127 \times (-0.005) + \tfrac{1}{2} \times 77.8103 \times (-0.005)^2 \\ &= 0.039564 + 0.000973 = +0.040537 \text{ or } +4.05\%\end{aligned}$$

If you recalculate the bonds value on the basis of a yield of 8% you will find the value is £104.06, a rise of 4.06%.

Quoted yield changes to 10%

If the quoted yield rises by 1% p.a. this corresponds to a semi-annual increase of 0.5%, i.e. $\Delta Y = +0.005$. Applying the formula, we would expect the price to fall by

Proportionate price change $= MD \times \Delta Y + \frac{1}{2}C \times \Delta Y^2$
$= -7.9127 \times (+0.005) + \frac{1}{2} \times 77.8103 \times (+0.005)^2$
$= -0.039564 + 0.000973 = -0.038591$ or -3.86%

If you recalculate the bonds value on the basis of a yield of 10% you will find the value is £96.14, a fall of 3.86%.

2.6 Callable bonds

2.6.1 The nature of callable bonds

Callable bonds enable the issuer to repurchase the bond at a set price prior to its stated maturity. For example, a bond with a 105 call could be bought back by the issuer at a price of £105.

A call option should not be confused with a redemption clause. It is often the case that a bond may be redeemed under predetermined circumstances, so long as the redemption is not being refinanced by a new bond issue. For example, a company may have excess cash balances (possibly due to the sale of assets) available to retire the bond.

2.6.2 The impact of a call provision on the price-yield relationship

The price of a callable bond will change at a different rate to the price of an equivalent straight bond as interest rates change.

You will recall that the relationship between the price and yield of a straight bond is as follows.

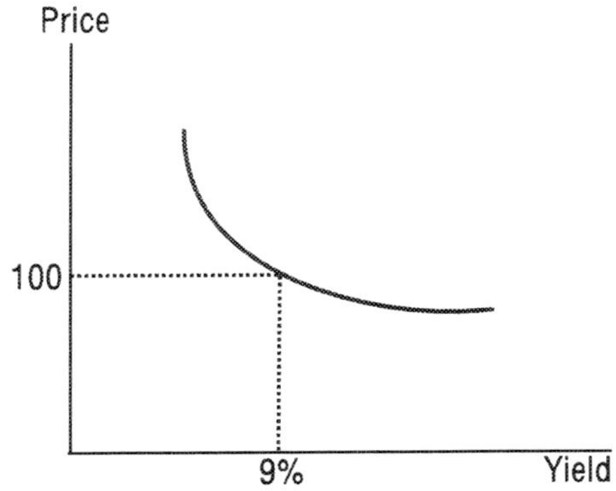

In other words, as interest rates fall, the price of the bond continues to rise.

For a callable bond (assuming that it is callable immediately), the price will not rise as much – for a given fall in interest rates – as a straight bond. For example, take a bond that can be called at 105. As interest rates fall, bond prices rise. The price of a straight bond will continue to rise as interest rates fall and may go above 105. However, the price of the callable bond can never rise above the call price of 105, since the company can buy it back at that price.

Consequently, as interest rates fall, the rate at which the price of the callable bond increases will be slower than the rate at which the straight bond price increases. Once the callable bond price is close to 105, it will hardly change at all, even if interest rates continue to fall.

Price/Yield Curve
for a Straight versus a Callable Bond

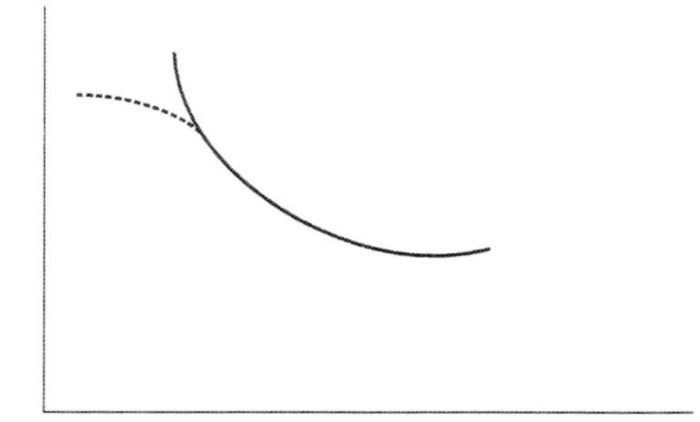

The curve to the right gives the price/yield relationship for both bonds. However, at lower interest rates, the relationships diverge, with the straight bond's price continuing to rise while the price of the callable bond first increases at a declining rate, then stays static.

The fact that price changes decline as interest rates fall is sometimes referred to as **price compression**.

2.6.3 Duration for a callable bond

For callable bonds, duration and related measures can be calculated based on the final maturity or on the first call date. The latter assumes that the bond will be called at the first call date. The duration to first call will be lower than the duration to final maturity, since it assumes a shorter effective maturity.

2.6.4 Convexity for a callable bond

The fact that the price of a callable bond hardly changes when interest rates fall to low levels means that the change in price will be **less** than that predicted by modified duration to first call. This is unusual, since it was noted above that modified duration always understated a rise in price and overstated a fall in price. As a result, convexity had to be added to the price change due to modified duration.

For a callable bond at low interest rates, the change due to convexity will be **deducted** from the change due to modified duration rather than added. This is known as **negative convexity**.

2.6.5 Breaking a callable bond into its component parts

A callable bond could be viewed as a straight bond with an embedded option. The company has sold a straight bond to investors but at the same time has bought a call option from the investors, enabling the company to buy back the straight bond at the agreed call price.

As a result, the proceeds on the issue of a callable bond are less than that for an equivalent straight bond. The company effectively receives the proceeds from the straight bond, but then uses part of those proceeds to buy a call option from the bond investors. The net proceeds received are therefore lower.

The bond investor's position is as follows.

Long callable bond = Long straight bond and short call option

The value of this is given by

Formula to learn

Callable bond value = Straight bond value – Issuers call option value

If the value of the call option increases, then the value of the callable bond will decrease. For example, an increase in the price of the straight bond (caused by a decrease in interest rates) will also result in an increase in the intrinsic value of the call option. Although the straight bond will increase in value, the call option also increases in value, meaning that the callable bond value hardly changes at all.

If interest rates are very high, then the call option will be deeply out-of-the-money, meaning that its value will change by very little for a change in interest rates. Therefore, the price behaviour of the callable bond mimics the behaviour of the straight bond.

An increase in expected volatility of interest rates will increase the value of the option, since it makes the bond price more volatile. This will reduce the value of the callable bond.

2.6.6 Call-Adjusted yield

Call-adjusted yield is calculated by stripping out the value of the option from the callable bond.

We know from above that the relationship between the price of a straight bond and a callable bond is as follows.

Callable bond value = Straight bond value – Call option value

The value of the callable bond is available in the market. The value of the call option can be estimated using option pricing models. Hence, the value of the straight bond within the callable bond can be inferred.

This analysis is a simple example of a more complex technique, Options Adjusted Spread (OAS). As in this case, all the OAS attempts is to remove the impact of any option embedded with the bond. This time, rather than simply create a value, the OAS tends to look at the spread over a government bond.

The yield of this straight bond can then be calculated – this is then referred to as the call-adjusted yield. It can be compared to yields on comparable straight bonds. If it has a lower yield, then it is overvalued (rich). If it has a higher yield, then it is undervalued (cheap).

2.6.7 Call-adjusted modified duration

It is possible to calculate a call-adjusted modified duration for a callable bond. This reflects the fact that the bond price will hardly move when interest rates are low and falling, but will move almost like a straight bond if interest rates are high and rising.

The call-adjusted modified duration depends on three factors.

- The duration of the straight bond implicit in the callable bond.
- The ratio of the price of the non-callable bond to the callable bond. The callable bond is always worth less than the straight bond or the same amount. It cannot be worth more since the option in the call bond will not have a negative value. If interest rates are very high, the option value will be low, meaning that the price of each bond would be very close. If interest rates are low, the value of the option will be high, meaning that the prices of each bond will diverge.
- The sensitivity of the price of the option to the change in the price of the underlying straight bond (i.e. the option's delta). As the bond price moves, the price of the option will move. This will affect the overall value of the callable bond, reducing its price as the option's value increases.

Where interest rates are very low, the price of the callable bond will hardly move as interest rates change. Its call-adjusted modified duration will be virtually zero. If interest rates are very high, then the price of the callable bond and the price of an equivalent straight bond will almost move in line. Its call-adjusted modified duration will be almost equal to that of the straight bond.

It is possible to calculate call-adjusted convexity using similar principles. This is determined by the above three factors plus the convexity of the straight bond and the convexity of the call option.

Puttable bond

Puttable bonds enable the holder to redeem the bond at a set price prior to its stated maturity. For example, a bond with a 95 put could be sold back by the issuer at a price of £95. The price of a puttable bond will, therefore, change at a different rate to the price of an equivalent option free bond as interest rates change.

Again, as we noted above, for an option free bond, as interest rates rise, the price of the bond continues to fall. For a puttable bond (assuming that it is puttable immediately), for a given rise in interest rates the price will not fall as much as a straight bond. For example, take a bond that is puttable at 95. As interest rates rise, bond prices fall. The price of a straight bond will continue to fall as interest rates rise and may go below 95. However, the price of the puttable bond can never fall below the put price of 95, since the investor can sell it back at that price.

The convexity of a puttable bond therefore remains positive, becoming more positive as it approaches the put price.

2.7 Simpler measures of sensitivity

Exam tip

Most recently examined in Winter 2009 Question 2, Winter 2008 Question 2.

2.7.1 Price value of a basis point (PVBP)/Basis point value (BPV), Dollar value of one basis point (DV01)

Sometimes referred to as the **price value of a basis point (PVBP)** or **the dollar value of a basis point, dollar value of an 01 or Dollar duration**. This is the change in price if the yield changes by one basis point. The more sensitive stocks will have a high PVBP. **Note.** The term dollar duration is usually applied to a 1% (100bp) change in yield.

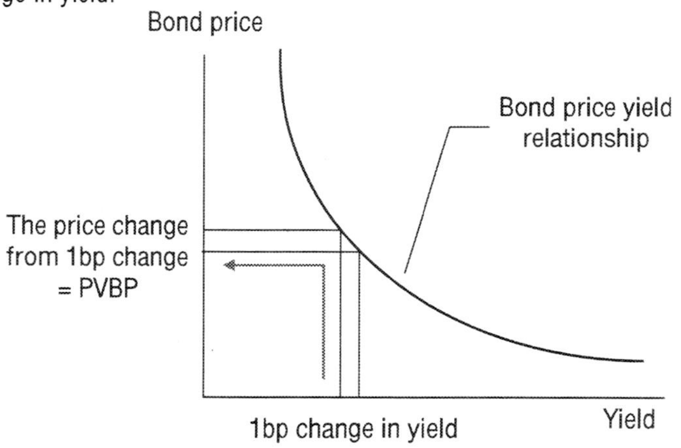

As we can see from the above diagram, this measure is in essence the same as the modified duration, since for a given yield change (a basis point) we can predict the change in price.

Calculation

Modified duration gives the percentage change in price for a 1% change in yield. One basis point is a 0.01% change in yields. As a result the change in the price for a one basis point change in yield will be

Exam tip

$$PVBP = Price \times MD \times 0.0001$$

This calculation ignores convexity which, over a one basis point yield will probably be negligible.

Example

Determine the PVBP for the 3 year 9% bond we have been using in this section priced at £102.58 and with a modified duration of –2.5577.

Solution

PVBP = £102.58 × –2.5577 × 0.01%
= £102.58 × –2.5577 × 0.0001 = –£0.0262

Alternative calculation

As an alternative, we could reassess the bond price at a GRY of either 7.99% or 8.01% (one basis point difference) and measure the price movement to four decimal places.

	(£)
Price at 8.00%	102.5771
Price at 7.99	102.6033
PVBP	(0.0262)

Use of PVBP in estimating price change

Example

If the yield on the above bond rises 6 bp what will be

- The change in price.
- The new price.

Solution

Change in price = 6 × (–£0.0262) = –£0.1572 or – £0.16

New price = £102.58 – £0.16 = £102.42

The properties of PVBP are the same as modified duration as demonstrated by the following graph.

PVBP Against Maturity

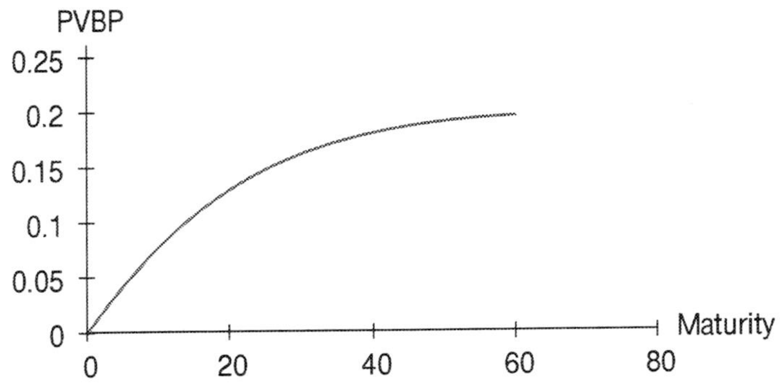

Equally, it shares the same limitations. PVBP is a linear estimate of a convex relationship and as such is only accurate for small variations of yield.

2.7.2 Yield difference of a tick

The yield difference of a tick is a measure of sensitivity is expressed in terms of the required movement in yield in order to shift the price by one tick, for example, it prices arequoted in 32nd.

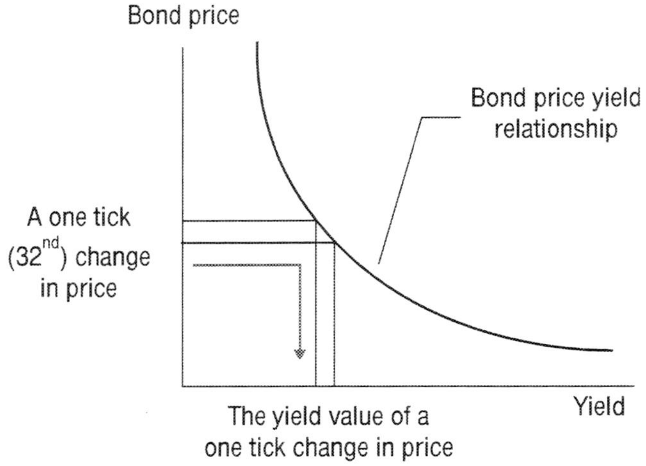

As the previous diagram demonstrates, this measure is in effect the inverse view of the PVBP (and therefore modified duration), this time looking at the required movement in yields in order to generate a specified change in price.

Once again, this is a simple linear approximation to a convex relationship and as such is inaccurate for large movements.

Calculation of yield value of $\frac{1}{32}$

From modified duration we have

Proportionate change in price = MD $\times \Delta Y$

and so, taking account of the current price we will have

Change in price = Price $\times$ MD $\times \Delta Y$

To assess the yield movement for a give change in price we need to rearrange this formula to solve for ΔY as follows

$$\Delta Y = \frac{\text{Change in price}}{\text{Price} \times \text{MD}}$$

And so if the price change is one tick we will have the yield difference of one tick as

Exam tip

$$\text{Yield value of a tick} = \frac{\text{Tick value}}{\text{Price} \times \text{MD}}$$

Example

Calculate the yield difference on our 3 year 9% bond priced at £102.58 with a modified duration of –2.5577, when

- Tick size = £0.01
- Tick size = $^1/_{32}$

Solution

Tick size = £0.01

$$\Delta Y = \frac{0.01}{102.58 \times (-2.5577)} = -0.000038111 \text{ or } -0.003811\%$$

Tick size = $\frac{1}{32}$

$$\Delta Y = \frac{0.03125}{102.58 \times (-2.5577)} = -0.0001191 \text{ or } -0.01191\%$$

Use of yield value in estimating price change

Example

If the price rises £0.16 on the above bond what is the change in yield?

Solution

Yield value at one tick (£0.01) = 0.003811%

Yield value at 16 ticks (£0.16) = 0.061%

This is approximately the same as before.

The smaller the value, the greater the level of sensitivity. Again, the more sensitive bonds will be those with a longer maturity/lower coupon. This is, however, a blunter method of calculating the sensitivity.

3 Other Risk Factors

3.1 Introduction

At the beginning of this section on risk, we established a number of factors that contribute to bond risks, specifically

- Interest rate risk.
- Credit and default risk.
- Inflation risk.
- Liquidity risk.
- Issue specific factors.
- Fiscal risk.
- Currency risk.
- Leveraged buyout risk.

With government gilts, interest and inflation risk represent the greatest dangers to the investor; there is no possibility of default or liquidity problems. Government gilts can therefore be considered a benchmark against which required yields for other bonds could be assessed.

The normal form of evaluation of non-government bonds is to judge them by virtue of such a benchmark government bond establishing the required yield difference between the two stocks and then investigating discrepancies which may be generated by the market.

The Required Yield	**(%)**
Yield on the equivalent benchmark gilt	X
Yield premium for additional credit risk	X
Yield premium on rights given to the issuer (calls)	X
Yield give up on option given to the holder (conversion and put premium rights)	(X)
Yield mark up for liquidity risk	X
Yield change for tax advantage/(disadvantage)	X
	X

The key reasons for a variance in the yield between a corporate issue and a government bond will be

- Credit rating.
- Name recognition.
- Liquidity.

In addition, the perceived security of the market place is important. In particular, government bond markets will attract money in volatile market places due to the **flight to quality**. The variety of other features that may be added to the bond may create uncertainty and therefore detract from the bond's value rather than add to it.

3.2 Leveraged buyout risk

A leveraged buyout is not dissimilar to a young family buying a house with a mortgage. Typically, a young family will not have much of its own capital or personal equity and so will take out a large mortgage to achieve a purchase. In such situations it is not unusual to have a 90% or 95% mortgage with the remainder of the purchase price being financed by the couple's personal equity, indeed 100% mortgages have been available for suitable borrowers.

With a mortgage, the debt is secured on the assets (the house) acquired and the family must generate sufficient income to service the mortgage payments. The risk to the mortgage lender is that the family may not be able to service the mortgage and default, though since the mortgage is secured on the asset the lender does have some security.

A highly leveraged buyout is the purchase of the voting shares (the takeover or privatisation) of a target company where a very large part of the finance, commonly 90% to 95%, is financed through debt. This debt is usually fixed rate, though, given the risks involved, it may be at a fairly high rate and have a low junk bond rating. Financing the purchase in this way allows the transaction to proceed without the buyer needing to have, or commit, much of their own capital. Through this highly leveraged approach, even the largest public companies are not immune from becoming targets.

As with a mortgage, the leveraged buyout debt will be secured on the assets being acquired (and possibly also assets of the acquiring company), and the acquired business must generate sufficient cash to service this debt.

The commercial rationale for a buyout is that the acquirer believes that the performance (profitability and cash generation) of the target business can be significantly improved by operational and management changes along with the sale of non-performing and non-core assets. The purchaser will usually be looking to achieve this over a period if three to five years after which the business will be sold or re-floated providing them an exit route. The purchaser may, therefore, consider highly leveraged finance because

- **Minimal own capital** – There is a minimal requirement to commit the purchasers own capital.
- **Discipline of debt** – Large interest and debt repayment requirements instil great discipline in management towards achieving their targets of improving performance and operating efficiency. This can force management to focus on certain initiatives such as divesting non-core businesses, downsizing, cost cutting or investing in technological upgrades that might otherwise be postponed or rejected outright. In this way, the use of debt serves not just as a financing technique, but also as a tool to force changes in managerial behaviour.
- **Benefit of gearing** – Where profitability and cash generation do improve, gearing has the effect of amplifying the benefit to the shareholders. For example, if a business generates 100 profit but must pay 95 of debt interest it has 5 left for shareholders. If it can achieve a 5% profit improvement to 105 then after deducting the 95 interest this leaves 10 for shareholders, a 100% gain to equity. Indeed most leveraged buyout firms look to achieve a return in excess of 20%.
- **Tax advantages of debt** – Payments of debt usually attract tax relief, reducing one of the most significant costs of the business.

A special case of such acquisition is a management buyout (MBO), which occurs when a company's managers buy out the shares of the company.

The problems associated with highly leveraged transactions, and consequent risks to bond investors, are

- **Default** – With such high leverage there is a significant risk of default if unforeseen events, such as recession, litigation, or changes in the regulatory environment, result in the businesses cash generation falling short of anticipated levels, leading to difficulties in meeting scheduled interest payments. As noted above, the associated debt finance usually has junk bond status and if the business suffers poor performance the assets may be insufficient to repay the debt. Where this arises, as it historically has, any benefit that the purchaser has made through salaries, dividends etc. has effectively been at the expense of the debtholders.

  At the very least, the increase in the fixed costs of the acquired business arising from the higher interest payments will reduce the business's ability to weather downturns in the business cycle, again creating risk for debt holders.

  This risk may be reduced in highly leveraged situations by requiring the purchasers to provide personal guarantees or offer security based on personal assets. Though such security may fall far short of what may be required to repay the debt, it does ensure that the actions of the purchaser are in line with the interests of the bond holders.
- **Short-termism** – With a three to five year exit target, the managers of the business are liable to concentrate on short-term policies, potentially at the expense of the long-term development of the business. Since the debt is liable to remain on the company's balance sheet as part of the financing of the business beyond this time, such a concentration is not in the best interest of the bondholders. Once again, the alignement of management and bondholder interests may help minimise this risk.
- **Distraction** – In troubled situations, management teams of highly levered firms may become distracted by dealing with lenders concerned about the company's ability to service debt, rather than concentrating on dealing with the underlying business problem. Such a distraction is of benefit to no one.

3.3 Measures of total risk

Thus far we have considered specific measures of sensitivity derived from bond valuation models. There are some other measures of risk/dispersion that we can use. These come from the study of statistics.

Tutor's note. No calculation of these values will be expected in your exam and consequently no formulae have been given.

3.3.1 Standard deviation

In statistics, we examine the properties of sample data. Some measures, such as the mean (average), look at location/central tendency. Other measures focus on the degree of dispersion within data. The most important measure of dispersion is the standard deviation, usually designated as σ in any calculations. From these basic measures we can then create more complex models of expected movement and attach degrees of certainty to these outcomes. In this sense, we are taking past data and deriving expectations of likely future values.

In the context of bonds, it would be possible to look back at price data or information with regard to returns. We could calculate the average return and then the standard deviation. The standard deviation would indicate the range of returns in the past. For example, the average return might be 5.6%, with a standard deviation of 1.2%.

Without delving into the detail of this area, there are some conventional distributions of data within statistics. One of these is the Normal distribution. Large sample sizes will tend to a Normal distribution. One of the key features of the Normal distribution is that approximately 100% of the expected values will lie within 3 standard deviations of the average. In this case, we could therefore be virtually certain that the returns would lie within the normal expected range, 5.6% ± (3 × 1.2%), i.e. 2% to 9.2%.

If we were to accept a lower level of certainty, we would get a narrower range of expected returns. For example, within a Normal distribution 95% of the expected values would lie 1.96 standard deviations either side of the mean. In this case, in the range 5.6% ± (1.96 × 1.2%), i.e. 3.25% to 7.95%. This gives us a narrower range of expected values, but a greater risk that values will fall outside of this range.

3.3.2 Variance

The standard deviation is simply the square root of the variance. Within statistics the variance has properties that make it easier to manipulate.

3.3.3 Semi-variance

This only looks at the distribution of data beneath the mean. The variance and standard deviation both consider data above and below the mean and attach equal importance to these numbers. The semi-variance is arguably more relevant to cautious investors who perceive the risk of loss as more important.

3.3.4 Portfolio risk and portfolio theory

If we know the standard deviation of each of the bonds in our portfolio how do we determine the overall portfolio position.

We noted in the yields section that the portfolio return may be calculated as the weighted average of the individual bond yields. For two securities this could be expressed as

Formula to learn

$$r_{a+b} = p_a r_a + p_b r_b$$

where

r = return on the bonds
p = proportion of the portfolio invested in each bond

Unfortunately the assessment of portfolio risk is a little more complicated. It needs to take account of the proportions invested in each bond, the risks of each bond and also the diversification effects. The relationship here is

$$\sigma_{a+b} = p_a^2\sigma_a^2 + p_b^2\sigma_b^2 + 2p_ap_b\sigma_a\sigma_b Cor_{ab}$$

where

σ = risk of bonds
p = proportion of the portfolio invested in each bond
Cor = correlation coefficient of the bonds returns which factors in any diversification benefit

3.4 The Capital Asset Pricing Model

3.4.1 Introduction

Let us consider a highly diversified investor who has spread his funds across the full stock market, with some also invested in risk-free investments. What returns will he achieve and what risk will he face?

If

r_m = returns expected from investing in the **market portfolio** (a portfolio representative of the whole stock market, e.g. a tracker fund)

r_f = returns from risk-free investments

β = proportion of his funds invested in the market portfolio

then, considering the returns he can expect to receive and the risks he will face, we have the following.

3.4.2 Return

The proportion of his money invested in the market portfolio β will return r_m, and the remainder invested risk free $(1 - \beta)$ will generate r_f. Hence, his full portfolio will generate the sum of these amounts, i.e.

$$r = \beta r_m + (1 - \beta)r_f$$

which can be algebraically rearranged, giving

$$r = \beta r_m + r_f - \beta r_f$$

$$r = r_f + \beta(r_m - r_f)$$

3.4.3 Risk

The risk that he will face (only systematic risk since he is diversified) will only be in relation to the proportion of funds he has invested in the market portfolio, since his other investment is risk free. This level of systematic risk he faces will therefore be

$$\sigma_s = \beta\sigma_m$$

where

σ_s = the systematic risk in the portfolio

σ_m = the risk (systematic) in the market portfolio

NB: So far, we have talked about β as the proportion of funds invested in the market portfolio. It can also be more usefully viewed as the proportion of **market portfolio risk** that we are willing to face, since a simple rearrangement of the above equation gives

Formula to learn

$$\beta = \frac{\sigma_s}{\sigma_m}$$

It is this latter way of viewing β, as the proportion of the market portfolio risk, that is going to give us the relationship we need between risk and return.

3.4.4 The model

Considering the above equations, for any given level of risk in relation to the market portfolio $\left(\beta = \frac{\sigma_s}{\sigma_m}\right)$, the return an investor can achieve by a broad investment in the stock market and risk-free investments is given by

$$r = r_f + \beta(r_m - r_f)$$

As a result, he would only consider an alternative investment opportunity with the same level of systematic risk if it offered a higher return. Hence, this relationship gives the minimum acceptable return for an investment based on its level of systematic risk.

Plotting this relationship on a graph gives the Securities Market Line (SML) as follows, which clearly shows the relationship between relative levels of risk (β) and corresponding expected returns.

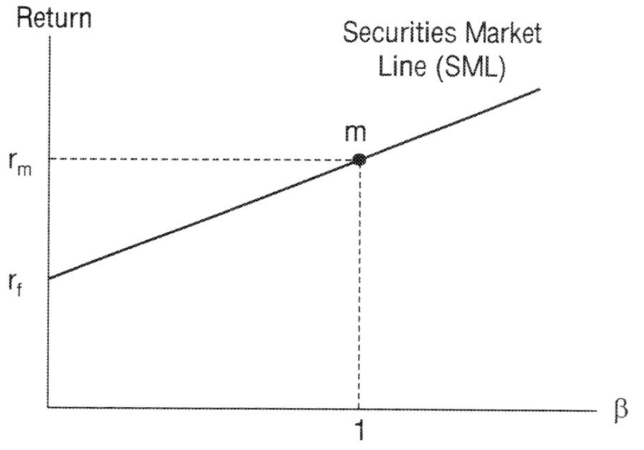

3.4.5 Conclusion

Thus, for an investment whose risk relative to the market portfolio is given by β, the expected return is given by the Capital Asset Pricing Model (CAPM) formula

Formula to learn

$$r = r_f + \beta(r_m - r_f)$$

where

r_m = the return expected from the market portfolio
r_f = the return offered by a risk-free security
β = the risk of the investment opportunity relative to that of the market portfolio (systematic risk only)

That is, the investor can expect to achieve the risk-free return (r_f) plus a proportion of the **market risk premium** ($r_m - r_f$) based on the levels of relative risk (β) he is willing to face.

Any difference between the actual return achieved and this expected return is referred to as alpha (α)

Example

For example, suppose that the risk-free rate of return is 6%, and the market is expected to return 14%, what return would a diversified investor require from an investment with a β of

- 0
- 0.5
- 1
- 1.5

Solution

Using

$$r = r_f + \beta(r_m - r_f)$$

gives

β = **0**	r = 6% + 0 × (14% – 6%) = 6%
β = **0.5**	r = 6% + 0.5 × (14% – 6%) = 10%
β = **1**	r = 6% + 1 × (14% – 6%) = 14%
β = **1.5**	r = 6% + 1.5 × (14% – 6%) = 18%

3.4.6 Investment appraisal under CAPM

Investment appraisal under CAPM amounts to plotting investments' expected returns and betas on the SML graph as follows.

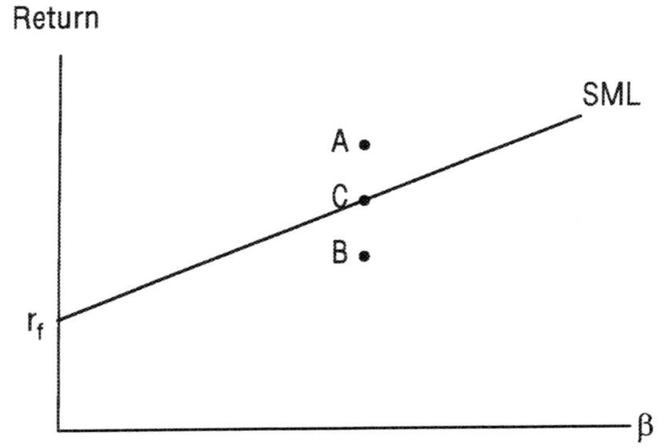

Investment A, lying above the SML, would be accepted by an investor as it is offering a return higher than that required for its level of risk, i.e. it is **undervalued**.

Investment B, lying beneath the SML, would be rejected as its current return is too low, i.e. it is **overvalued**.

Investment C, lying on the SML, is currently correctly priced in the market. An investor should be indifferent to the choice between buying it or not.

3.4.7 Forming portfolios using CAPM

We can use the CAPM to assist in the formation of portfolios where we have determined the degree of risk that the client is willing to face.

An individual seeking a high return would need to take on more risk. Thus, we would need to construct a portfolio with a high β. A portfolio with a β greater than 1 could be expected to give returns greater than those of the market, but at a correspondingly enhanced level of risk.

A young pension fund may be prepared to undertake a similar investment strategy with the view that there will be long-term benefits.

A mature pension fund, on the other hand, is liable to be seeking a safer portfolio and would, therefore, prefer a portfolio with a β less than 1. Clearly, as the proportion of risk-free investments is increased in our portfolio (and the proportion of equities reduced), the portfolio β reduces towards 0.

4 CREDIT ANALYSIS

Exam tip

> Credit analysis quite frequently arises in optional 15 mark Section C questions, e.g. Summer 2002 Question 14, Summer 2001 Question 9.

4.1 Introduction

The objective of credit analysis is to assess the ability of a borrower to service and repay its loan obligations.

In evaluating credit risk there are three key issues to be borne in mind.

- How probable is it that a default will take place?
- How severe will the loss be if there is a default?
- When will any default take place (near term/far term)?

It is the answers to these three questions that allow you to fully appraise the credit risk that you face.

4.2 Evaluating sovereign credits

In analysing sovereign credits we are usually reviewing the best credits in the market. This is particularly true where governments are raising debt in their own currency, since, in the short term, they will be able to print additional money supply in order to meet their obligations.

However, where governments begin to borrow in other currencies and when the economic fundamentals are not as strong, then the credit begins to weaken.

4.2.1 Company versus country analysis

As with all credit analysis, the objective of country credit analysis is to assess the ability and willingness of the company to service its debt obligations on a timely basis. Differences between company and country analysis can be summarised as follows.

- Countries cannot be forced to make debt payments, meaning that willingness to pay is an important feature. Politicians may suspend payments for various reasons.
- Data on countries will come from different sources from company data. Company data includes, amongst others, annual reports, whereas country data includes newspapers, research documents, rating agencies, etc.

- It is difficult and costly to do due diligence on a country compared to a company, since it involves visiting the country and meeting with a wide range of people.
- Subjective factors are more important when analysing countries, such as interpreting political and economic developments.

4.2.2 Risk factors

Political risk

The following political risk factors will affect a country's willingness to service its debt obligations.

- **The system of government and decision making** – a strong system of control (e.g. China) can improve creditworthiness, whereas a weak splintered political system (e.g. Italy) reduces creditworthiness.
- **Ideological beliefs** – the ideologies of parties in power and in opposition can be important. Ideology may mean that the party in power is likely to suspend debt payments or that a strong party in opposition can prevent desirable policies being put through.
- **Political longevity and succession** – a system that allows long-term policies to be enacted and ensures a smooth transition of power will improve creditworthiness.
- **Degree of integration with the outside world** – isolated countries (politically or financially) will be less creditworthy, e.g. North Korea.
- **Domestic stability and regional security** – internal dissension (e.g. Israel) or threats of external aggression (e.g. Kuwait) can reduce creditworthiness.
- **Labour relations and other demographic factors** – the existence of strong, but hostile, labour unions or a poor population may force governments to seek internal popularity at the expense of foreign lenders, thereby reducing creditworthiness.

4.2.3 Economic risk

Indicators of economic risk are as follows.

- Countries with high levels of **natural resources** have more flexibility than countries that rely on external natural resources. A major example here is oil.
- A **well-diversified economy** with a **large private sector** improves economic efficiency within the country.
- Strongly **growing and developing economies**, producing exportable goods and services will be better risks.
- **Fiscal and monetary performance** should be satisfactory, aimed at maintaining low inflation and keeping a balanced budget.
- **High inflation and high unemployment** will destabilise a country, reducing confidence and investment.
- A **convertible currency** and a country **without exchange controls** will promote confidence, attract investment and prevent the flight of capital.
- A country with an **open system of trade**, little protectionism, diversified exports and international competitiveness will generate more foreign currency to repay foreign debt.
- High **imports of consumer goods** indicate outflows of foreign currency, restricting the ability to service foreign debt. **Imports of intermediate or capital goods** indicate a growing economy producing final goods, possibly with higher exports.

- Sources of **foreign exchange earnings**, such as invisible exports, and transfers received from overseas workers will increase the supply of foreign currency.
- **Excessive reliance on weak trading partners** can put pressure on a country's trading performance. For example, countries that relied excessively on the former Soviet Union as an export market suffered on its separation.
- The higher the level of **foreign exchange reserves**, the better the ability of the company to service overseas obligations in times of a liquidity crisis. Foreign exchange reserves should cover at least three months of imports, indicating a satisfactory level of liquidity. A liquidity problem may cause a rescheduling of foreign debt.
- The size of the **current account deficit** indicates the net financing required by the country. It can be compared to the GDP of the country, with anything above 3% meriting close attention.
- The **nature of foreign investment** should be considered. Direct investment is more stable than portfolio investment in financial assets, since it reduces exposure of such flows to changes in interest rates and business confidence.
- The level of **external debt to current account earnings** should be examined. A common guide is that this should not exceed 2× for investment grade countries. Some analysts also examine the ratio of debt to GDP. However, this ratio is potentially misleading, since a country could have a large GDP but a fairly small amount of exports. If this is the case, it may not be able to generate foreign exchange. Another ratio often used is the level of external debt net of foreign assets to current account earnings. However, the weakness of this ratio is that the debt and assets may not match in terms of maturities and holders, making netting-off less appropriate.
- Analysing the **breakdown of debt** by lender, borrower, instruments, maturity and currency helps assess exposure to short-term problems. For example, excessive reliance on short-term debt can lead to a withdrawal of facilities if confidence declines. This can create a liquidity crisis.
- The ratio of **debt servicing costs to current account earnings** gives an indication of the country's ability to meet all the servicing costs of debt, both interest and principal. This should be 25% or less for investment grade countries.

4.2.4 Analysing sovereign credits in the wake of EMU

Historically, developed governments raising finance in their own currency have been awarded AAA ratings. This reflects the key advantages that they possess

- Access to the tax system to raise revenue; and
- The ability to 'print money' at least in the short term.

The start of EMU has radically changed this for those nations entering the system. In effect, it will be as if the government is issuing debt in a foreign currency where, of course, credit risk is a feature.

The degree of credit spread built into the market depends in part on the credibility that the market attributes to the 'no bail out' clause in the Maastricht Treaty.

Article 104 b

The community shall not be liable for nor shall it assume the commitments of any participant nation.

If this clause is upheld, then each nation will have to stand alone. This has, to an extent, been shown in the past EMU credit ratings, which reflect the 'old' foreign currency debt ratings.

	Pre-EMU		Post-EMU
	Domestic	Foreign	
Austria	AAA	AAA	AAA
Belgium	AAA	AA+	AA+
Finland	AAA	AA–(+)	AAA
France	AAA	AAA	AAA
Germany	AAA	AAA	AAA
Ireland	AAA	AA	AAA
Italy	AAA	AA+(–)	A+
Luxembourg	AAA	AAA	AAA
Netherlands	AAA	AAA	AAA
Portugal	AAA	AA–	AA
Spain	AAA	AA	AA+

Source: Standard & Poor's

The ratings for non-domestic currency debt, and now euro debt, reflect the market's perceptions of the economic health of the nations concerned and factor in support issues such as the level of reserves held by the government/central bank.

A key difference between the pre and post-EMU bond markets is the degree of in-built liquidity within the 'domestic' government bond market. Whilst nations maintained their individual currencies, there was a natural tendency for domestic residents to hold a proportion of their wealth in local currency debt. With the advent of the euro, and the consequent absence of currency risk, these investors are able to hold their assets in whichever Euroland government's debt they choose.

4.2.5 Summary of key ratios in analysis of sovereign debt

Ratio	Purpose
External debt ÷ Current account earnings (debt ratio)	Looks at the size of the debt relative to ability of country to generate foreign currency earnings – 200% or less is desirable for investment grade countries.
Debt servicing ÷ Current account earnings (debt service ratio)	Looks at the total servicing costs of debt relative to ability of country to generate foreign currency earnings – 25% or less is desirable for investment grade countries.
Current account balance ÷ GDP	Looks at the net financing requirement compared to the size of the country's economy – less than 3% is desirable.
Foreign exchange reserves ÷ One month's imports (import cover)	Measures ability of the country to deal with liquidity crisis – three months' cover is desirable.
Budget balance ÷ GDP	Looks at the government's financial discipline.

4.3 Credit analysis for corporate bonds

In the credit analysis of corporate bonds credits there are many more factors to take into consideration. Firstly, we will consider the general considerations before moving on to more detailed issues.

4.3.1 Industry considerations

Economic cyclicality

The responsiveness of an industry to cyclical factors should be considered. Industries may closely track GDP growth (e.g. retailers). Alternatively, they may be defensive stocks with relatively slow growth (e.g. utilities).

A company's growth should be compared to the growth trend of its own industry and any differences should be analysed and explained.

The particular factors driving growth in an industry should be identified. Some industries are more responsive to demographic factors than general economic trends, such as nursing homes, the growth of which is linked to the ageing of the population. Banks, in contrast, have earnings linked to interest rate changes.

Growth prospects

This is related to economic cyclicality.

Growth prospects have a number of financial implications for companies. A high-growth company will need to find funds for expanding its capacity. The source of these funds should be considered (debt or external equity).

Although in the short term, growth will mean that a company is demanding cash, a fast growing company has more scope for credit improvement than a company in a declining industry.

Research and development

In order to achieve or maintain growth, a company may need to spend significant amounts of cash on research and development. This in itself represents a drain of cash. A company that fails to invest in research and development will find its profits and cash position improved as a result. However, in the long run it could find its performance deteriorating.

A qualitative problem with research expenditure is whether it is being spent in the right areas. If a company fails to identify the direction in which technology is heading, it may find that its expenditure is largely wasted.

Competition

More competition increases credit risk.

Increasing competition will reduce prices and increase costs. In an international market, competitive forces will be framed by exchange rate movements.

Competition within an industry will largely be determined by the market structure, being monopoly (regulated or unregulated), oligopoly or free competition.

Overcapacity will increase the level of competition.

Sources of supply

Companies with guaranteed stable, low-cost sources of supply will be favourably placed compared to companies without such sources. For example, paper companies need a readily available cheap source of wood pulp, i.e. forest lands.

Companies that suffer increasing costs from their suppliers need to be able to pass those costs on to their own customers, otherwise their margins will be restricted and their credit quality is reduced.

Regulation

Regulation itself is not a credit problem. However, the credit analyst will need to look at regulation and see whether it is resulting in excessive costs for the industry, highly restricted prices and restrictions on the company making good business decisions.

Labour

A heavily unionised industry that is highly militant is going to increase credit risks. The historical occurrence of strikes, the likelihood of future strikes, the relative power of the unions and related factors should be considered.

In non-union industries, the supply and demand situation for labour should be considered. It may be that labour can extract high wages from the companies in the industry and hence, reduce profitability.

More labour-intensive industries will give greater cause for concern than less labour-intensive industries.

Accounting

Any special accounting practices in an industry need to be taken into account by a credit analyst when considering a company.

Care should be taken when using accounts, since the data will be historic and the directors have significant scope for presenting results in a flattering manner.

4.3.2 Financial analysis

Obviously one key source of information in determining the viability of a company will be the financial statements. However, the financial statements may require some adjustment before they are of real use.

Adjustments to book values in the accounts

Purpose of the adjustments

- To make the accounts more relevant for analytical purposes. Book values are fairly meaningless in this context, since they do not represent the current market values of any assets and liabilities.
- To promote a comprehensive examination of the company's financial position.

Adjustments to assets

Assets should be adjusted to an approximation of their current market value, since they act as support and protection for creditors.

Adjustments to liabilities

Liabilities should be adjusted to their current market values. Where debt has a high or low coupon, for example, the market value will be different from the book value.

Off-balance sheet items should be added into liabilities. These could include unconsolidated subsidiaries whose activities are integral to the firm.

Cash flow analysis

In all businesses "cash is king" and it is cash flow that is crucial in ensuring that a business is capable of surviving. Consequently, analysis has moved in recent years to a much greater focus on the cash flow position of the business.

Purpose of the analysis

- To establish the company's ability to generate cash sufficient to cover its operating requirements.
- To assess the role of different sources of financing.
- To understand the impact of accounting policies on cash flow classification.

Cash flow from operations

When analysing cash flow from operations, the following points should be considered.

- The trend of cash flow through time should be examined.
- The ability of the company to convert net income into cash flow. A company may have net income but, if its working capital levels are increasing rapidly, a large proportion of income may not become cash flow.
- Although a company may have positive cash flow before capital expenditure due to the adding back of the depreciation charge, it should be remembered that depreciation represents to some extent a charge for replacement levels of capital expenditure.
- Some items included in operating cash flow are not truly operational. These include dividends and interest income and interest paid. It is usually appropriate to strip these out and analyse them separately.
- The impact of accounting policies on operating cash flow should be allowed for.

Free cash flow

There is no one definition of free cash flow. Broadly speaking, it is the cash available to a company after it has made all its mandatory payments in the year. Items that are mandatory or non-discretionary might be considered to include the following.

- Interest paid.
- Taxation.
- Replacement capital expenditure.
- Preferred dividends.

Payments that are more discretionary include the following.

- Equity dividends.
- Expansion capital expenditure.
- Repayment of debt and equity balances.

Some debt repayments may be scheduled and hence, they would be mandatory as opposed to discretionary.

A company should be able to cover its mandatory payments, leaving some surplus cash for making any discretionary payments thought appropriate. If these cash flows are insufficient, then any deficit will need to be met by debt or external equity being raised. In the short run, this may be satisfactory if there are genuine reasons why short-term cash flow is insufficient to cover mandatory payments. However, in the long run, such a failure indicates potential bankruptcy.

EBITDA

Most business income and expenses are a consequence of transactions that result in cash flows, however depreciation and amortisation are two often quite significant expenses charged against profits that do not relate to current year cash flows. Depreciation and amortisation are notional charges against profit to recognise the use of a fixed asset. The term depreciation refers to tangible assets such as property, equipment etc, whereas the term amortisation is used in the context of intangibles such as trade marks, publishing rights and goodwill. For fixed assets, the cash flow arises when it is acquired, however the use of the asset is recognised in the income statement as depreciation or amortisation as it is used over the future years.

EBITDA stands for earnings before interest, tax, depreciation and amortisation and can be considered to be an approximation to the pre-tax cash flows of a business arising as a consequence of how it is trading and may be used as an indication of the level of interest payment, hence debt, that the business can sustain.

Ratio analysis

Key ratios are as follows.

Interest cover

Formula to learn

$$\text{Interest cover} = \frac{\text{Income before interest and taxes}}{\text{Debt interest charges}}$$

The higher the interest cover, the safer the company. For unsecured debtholders, interest cover should be calculated based on total interest paid since they rank last for any payments. For secured debtholders, it is more appropriate to calculate the ratio based on interest charged in relation to just secured debt since these payments have priority over payments to unsecured debtholders.

An alternative ratio to interest cover is fixed charge cover.

Formula to learn

$$\text{Fixed charge cover} = \frac{\text{Income before interest lease payments and taxes}}{\text{Debt interest} + \text{Lease payments} + \text{Grossed-up preferred dividend}}$$

The benefit of fixed charge coverage is that it allows for other sources of financial risk in addition to the published debt balances.

Standard & Poor's levels of interest coverage for ratings were as follows in the 2000s.

	Interest Coverage (×)
AAA	23.8
AA	13.6
A	6.9
BBB	4.2
BB	2.3
CCC	0.4

Gearing in the balance sheet

A common ratio measuring balance sheet gearing or leverage is debt to total capitalisation or capital employed.

Formula to learn

$$\text{Debt to total capital} = \frac{\text{Total long-term debt}}{\text{Total long-term capital}}$$

The lower the percentage, the safer the company. Where a company has a high level of gearing, the analyst must ensure that it has an adequate margin of safety, being the amount by which its operating income exceeds its fixed obligations. This relates to the concept of free cash flow considered above.

When looking at gearing, the existence of off-balance sheet exposure, such as guarantees of other companies' debt or high levels of operating leases, should be taken into account.

Standard & Poor's levels of debt to total capital for ratings were as follows in the 2000s.

	Debt to Total Capital (%)
AAA	6.2
AA	34.8
A	39.8
BBB	45.6
BB	57.2
CCC	101.2

In addition to calculating a debt to total capital figure based on balance sheet figures, the analyst should look at the market value of the equity. Where a company has negative stockholders' equity on its balance sheet (e.g. due to a stock repurchase financed by a major leveraged recapitalisation), the balance sheet ratio may overstate the debt to total capital. However, if the stock market capitalisation is still sufficiently high, it could indicate a company that has little difficulty in servicing its debt obligations.

Evaluating the debt included in the ratio

Whether the debt is fixed or floating should be considered. A company paying floating rates may find that an increase in interest rates increases its costs, but also causes demand for its products to fall, reducing profits and interest coverage substantially.

Generally, a company with a low proportion of floating rate debt is preferable from a credit viewpoint.

The maturity structure of the debt is important. If debt is due for refinancing in the near future, it may be that the cost of interest after refinancing could increase considerably.

The bank lines available to the company should be analysed, identifying how much has been drawn down and how much is still available. Any security given to the banks should be identified. A company that has drawn down all of its bank lines and is in slightly distressed circumstances may find it hard to renew the bank finance.

Cash flow

A relevant cash flow ratio is cash flow to debt.

Formula to learn

$$\text{Cash flow to debt} = \frac{\text{Net income} + \text{Depreciation} + \text{Amortization} + \text{Deferred taxes}}{\text{Total debt}}$$

Alternatively, cash flow could be defined as cash from operations in the cash flow statement.

When looking at cash from operations, the quality of the cash flow should be considered. For example, if a company is receiving dividends from subsidiaries, the ongoing sustainable level of dividends should be identified.

Standard & Poor's levels of funds from operations to total debt for ratings were as follows in the 2000s.

	Funds from Operations to Total Debt (%)
AAA	167.8
AA	77.5
A	43.2
BBB	34.6
BB	20.0
CCC	2.9

Net assets

A relevant ratio here is net assets to total debt.

Formula to learn

$$\text{Net assets to debt} = \frac{\text{Net assets}}{\text{Total debt}}$$

The liquidation value of the assets should be taken into account when doing this calculation, not the value of assets in the balance sheet.

Since looking at the liquidation value of assets is relevant in a bankruptcy situation, the analyst must consider the impact of bankruptcy on the company.

The impact of intangibles in the balance sheet on ratio calculations

When a company has significant intangible assets on its balance sheet, the analyst should look at the market value of the intangibles compared to the balance sheet value. If the balance sheet value is excessively high, the intangibles should be written down.

In a distress situation, writing down intangibles to zero may be the most appropriate approach.

Unfunded pension liabilities

A large unfunded pension liability will make the company's credit position less attractive. A large unfunded liability might constrain the company's ability to make sensible commercial operating decisions.

The assumptions used by a company in calculating its pension plan status should be reviewed to ensure that they are not excessively optimistic.

Age and condition of plant and equipment

A company with a high average age for its plant is probably operating inefficiently and will need to replace much of the plant in the near future to remain competitive. Large future capital expenditure is therefore a possibility, making the company's cash flow position less secure.

In addition, having a very old plant is probably resulting in an excessively low depreciation figure, leading to overstated earnings.

Working capital

Relevant ratios here include the current ratio and the acid test (quick) ratio.

Formula to learn

$$\text{Current ratio} = \frac{\text{Current assets}}{\text{Current liabilities}}$$

Formula to learn

$$\text{Acid test ratio} = \frac{\text{Current assets} - \text{Inventories}}{\text{Current liabilities}}$$

The stronger the company's liquidity, the more able it is to resist an economic downturn.

In addition to the above ratios, it is important to understand the links between working capital and cash flow generation. A company could generate a high current ratio and acid test ratio by building up inventories and receivables. However, this does not mean that it has good liquidity.

Analysing the components of return on equity

The analysis of return on equity can take several forms. One well-known approach is the Dupont system, which breaks down return on equity into the following areas.

Formula to learn

$$\text{Return on equity} = \text{Net profit margin} \times \text{Total assets turnover} \times \text{Financial leverage}$$

Formula to learn

$$\text{Return on equity} = \frac{\text{Net income}}{\text{Equity}} = \frac{\text{Net income}}{\text{Revenue}} \times \frac{\text{Revenue}}{\text{Total assets}} \times \frac{\text{Total assets}}{\text{Equity}}$$

The analyst should look at the changes in each ratio over at least five years and over one business cycle. The company's ratios and how they have changed should be compared to the industry average, with any differences being investigated and satisfactory explanations being found.

4.3.3 Illustration plc

We will illustrate the above ratios with the following example.

Balance sheet as at 31 December

	(£'000)	(£'000)
Non-current assets		
Intangible		3,926
Tangible		18,731
Investments		842
		23,499
Current assets		
Inventory	19,420	
Receivables	27,882	
Investments	3,926	
Cash	6,425	
		57,653
Total assets		**81,152**
Share capital		
£1.00 NV Ordinary shares		17,925
Preference shares		837
Reserves		
Share premium account reserve		2,455
Revaluation reserve		2,681
Retained earnings reserve		9,143
Shareholders' funds		33,041
Creditors due after one year		
5% secured loans*	2,073	
7% unsecured loans	2,372	
		4,445
Creditors due within one year		
Bank overdraft	17,079	
Trade payables	18,702	
Tax	1,625	
Others	6,260	
		43,666
Total liabilities		**81,152**

* In issue throughout the year.

Income statement account

	(£'000)
Revenue	135,761
Cost of sales*	(83,604)
Gross profit	52,157
Distribution costs	(22,961)
Administration costs	(22,712)
Operating profit	6,484
Interest received	365
Interest paid	(3,176)
Profit before tax	3,673
Tax	
Corporation tax	(1,372)
Profit after tax	**2,301**
Dividends	
Ordinary	1,120
Preference	84
	1,204
Earnings per share	12.37p
Dividend per share	6.25p

* Cost of sales includes:	
– Depreciation	15,462
– Amortisation	1,287
– Lease payments	628

EBITDA

	(£'000)
Operating profit	6,484
Depreciation	15,462
Amortisation	1,287
EBITDA	23,233

Interest cover

	(£'000)
Operating profit	6,484
Interest received	365
Income before interest and tax	6,849
Interest paid in total	3,176
Interest paid on secured loans (2,073 × 5%)	104

$$\text{Interest cover (total)} = \frac{\text{Income before interest and taxes}}{\text{Debt interest charge}} = \frac{23,233}{3,176} = 7.32\text{x}$$

$$\text{Interest cover on secured loans} = \frac{\text{Income before interest and taxes}}{\text{Secured debt interest charge}} = \frac{23,233}{104} = 223.4\text{x}$$

Fixed charge cover

	(£'000)
Operating profit	6,484
Interest received	365
Lease payments	628
Income before interest, lease payments and tax	7,477

	(£'000)
Debt interest	3,176
Lease payments	628
Grossed up preferred dividend (84 ÷ 0.9)	96
Debt interest + Lease payments + Grossed-up pref div	3,960

$$\text{Fixed charge cover} = \frac{\text{Income before interest lease payments and taxes}}{\text{Debt interest + Lease payments + Grossed-up preference dividend}}$$

$$= \frac{7,477}{3,900} = 1.92\text{x}$$

Gearing

	(£'000)
Long-term debt	4,445
Shareholders' funds	33,041
Long-term capital employed	37,486

$$\text{Debt to total capital} = \frac{\text{Total long-term debt}}{\text{Total long-term capital}} = \frac{4,445}{37,486} = 0.119 \text{ or } 11.9\%$$

Cash flow to debt

	(£'000)
Net income (profit after tax)	2,301
Depreciation	15,462
Amortisation	1,287
Deferred tax charge	–
Estimated cash flow after tax	19,050

	(£'000)
Long-term debt	4,445
Short-term debt (loans and overdrafts)	17,079
Total debt	21,524

$$\text{Cash flow to debt} = \frac{19,050}{21,524} = 0.89$$

Net assets to debt

$$\text{Net assets to debt} = \frac{\text{Net assets}}{\text{Total debt}} = \frac{33,041}{21,524} = 1.54$$

Current ratio

$$\text{Current ratio} = \frac{\text{Current assets}}{\text{Current liabilities}} = \frac{57,653}{43,666}$$

Acid test ratio

$$\text{Acid test ratio} = \frac{\text{Current assets} - \text{Inventories}}{\text{Current liabilities}} = \frac{57{,}653 - 19{,}420}{43{,}666}$$

Return on equity

	(£'000)
Total shareholders' funds	33,041
Preference shares	(837)
Equity shareholders' funds	32,204

$$\text{Return on equity} = \frac{\text{Net income}}{\text{Equity}} = \frac{2{,}301}{32{,}204} = 0.071 \text{ or } 7.1\%$$

4.3.4 Covenants indentures and charges

Covenants are terms and conditions attached to a bond issue. They can be features of both the domestic or Euromarkets. The level of covenants that are attached to an issue will depend very much on the creditworthiness of the borrower concerned. If the borrower is in need of funds, then the lenders will be able to enforce particularly onerous covenants.

One of the key issues in appraising credit risk is the likely severity of any loss. Crucial in limiting the loss suffered will be the protection afforded by covenants. Following on from the first question of credit analysis, i.e. "How likely is it that there will be a default?", these covenants will be most important in the context of riskier debt.

Bonds with a greater coverage from either covenants or charges will be referred to as senior debt and will trade accordingly. The benefits of senior status are more important in the context of lower quality debt where the risk of default is greater and consequently, the protection afforded by the charges more valuable.

4.3.5 Credit analysis in the context of portfolios

When reviewing the credit risk implicit in a portfolio of bonds, the key issue is the amount of diversification. If the portfolio is invested solely into the bonds of one company, then the fund is exposed to the specific risk of that security. On the other hand, where the fund is divided between two bonds in different sectors, a proportion of the risk is diversified away. As more and more securities are included in the portfolio, the specific risk of the portfolio is diversified away. It is in this area that models such as the Capital Asset Pricing Model (CAPM) may be useful within bond funds.

In this context many funds may feel able to take on a higher degree of risk with a proportion of the portfolio and invest into higher yielding (or riskier) debt.

A variety of more complex models (e.g. creditmetrics) have developed over the past few years to help with evaluating the credit risk of a portfolio. However, as with all econometric models, the results are limited by the quality of input data. The more complex models combine traditional credit appraisal with value at risk (VAR) approaches to create probability distributions of potential losses.

4.4 Evaluating high yield bonds

Exam tip

> Last examined in Winter 2007 Question 12.

4.4.1 Analysis of high yield bonds

High yield bonds and junk bonds

A distinction could be drawn between high yield bonds and junk bonds. Both have high yields and trade primarily on the basis of their creditworthiness. However, junk bond yields reflect the poor quality of the issuer. High yield bonds, in contrast, may reflect other factors such as the small size of the issuer or a lack of credit history. In fact, such a firm may have good underlying credit quality.

Since many high yield bonds have a short history, the analysis of junk bonds involves projections and a weighting towards credit analysis techniques bordering on those used to appraise equity.

Reasons why high yield bonds have often been ignored by analysts include the following.

- Many investors are confined to investing in investment grade securities.
- In the past, there was lack of liquidity and stability in the market.
- It has been difficult to obtain a diversified portfolio of high yield bonds.
- Small firms found it hard to issue high yield debt due to the lack of large buyers.

However, there are good reasons for investing in such bonds.

- **Enhanced yield** – The yields that they offer are much better than those available on investment grade debt and, if careful analysis is undertaken, this is only slightly reduced by default risk.
- **Capital appreciation** – Investing in bonds where credit quality is improving will not only yield high coupons, but also capital appreciation, as the bond price rises.

The approach to high yield analysis

The general approach is the same as with any bond. However, since the companies will often be smaller or less well known, more time will be required to complete the analysis. In addition, each bond will have a high degree of specific risk due to the fact that these bonds trade on the basis of creditworthiness of the individual company. As a result, a portfolio of bonds will need to be built up to reduce specific risk. This means that the analysis will need to cover companies in a number of sectors.

Key areas of analysis are as follows.

- Level of competition in the industry.
- Cash flow generation.
- Net assets.
- Management quality.
- Level of leverage.

Competition

It is often the case that firms that issue high yield debt are small in relation to their industry. This poses significant risks, since pricing policy in the industry will usually be driven by the larger players.

A small firm that has to follow prices set by larger companies must have a cost structure that does not offer a significant disadvantage to those larger companies, otherwise it will go bankrupt in a sustained price war.

A small firm must therefore either be cost efficient, or it must have a strategy built on product differentiation. If it follows the price differentiation approach, the analyst must ensure that it can maintain its edge in the chosen niche.

Cash flow

For a normal debt analysis, ratios such as cash to total debt are used. However, for a high yield analysis, it is more relevant to look at cash to total cash requirements. The company must be able to generate enough cash to cover interest payments and any operational requirements such as research and development expenditure.

It is likely that a small firm will not have the ability to borrow significant amounts of new debt to see it through a period of restructuring. Hence, it must have sufficient cash flow to see its way through a period of weak economic activity.

The analysis of cash flow should not just focus on immediate cash flow and the ability to cover immediate interest payments. It is often the case that part of the interest on a high yield bond is paid in kind (see below for more details), by the issue of additional bonds. The analyst must ensure that there is the ability to service this new debt in cash when it becomes due.

In addition to cash flow from operations, the impact of cash from asset sales should be considered. It may be that sales of assets are an integral part of a program to pay down debt in a highly leveraged situation. The analyst should analyse the likely sales price, the estimated time it will take to sell the assets and the impact if the sale proceeds or time to sale are delayed. There is a risk that the company may not have the financial flexibility to deal with unexpected delays in sale or lower sale prices. Potentially, the company could breach indenture provisions.

Net assets

The asset backing for the debt must be estimated, looking at the estimated liquidation value of assets on the balance sheet. Real estate holdings could be of particular importance in this area.

The quality of the assets should be considered. Factors to consider here include the following.

- It may be that the assets are already the subject of a lien elsewhere.
- The assets may not have been well maintained, significantly reducing their value.
- The assets may be used to secure new senior debt to which the high yield bonds are subordinated.
- Some assets may be spun off to the equity investors in the company, depriving bondholders of protection.
- The location of the assets could be important. It may be hard to obtain control of assets located overseas, depending on the local foreign exchange and bankruptcy laws.

Management

A strong high quality management is essential. Factors to consider include the following.

- Strong financial controls.
- Strong marketing.
- Incentives to succeed.
- No excessive reliance on one person, particularly if soon to retire.

Gearing/Leverage

The impact of the high degree of leverage implicit for high yield bonds should be considered. It may adversely affect the financial flexibility of the firm. When looking at balance sheet leverage, ratios based on both book values and market values should be used. As a company's market value increases, this indicates that the market is prepared to accept a higher degree of borrowing. Alternatively, it means that the company can refinance some existing debt at lower rates of interest, improving cash flow coverage and profitability.

4.4.2 Special types of high yield bonds

Exchangeable variable rate notes

EVRNs have the following features.

- Subordinated.
- Medium term.
- Quarterly interest.
- On issue, there is often a teaser period where the interest rate is set quite low. Subsequently, it will be reset by reference to indices such as prime rate or Treasury bill rates.
- The issuer may have the option to convert the securities into fixed rate notes with predetermined features as regards coupon, maturity and call provisions. Typically, such a conversion feature must be exercised after five years.

Usable bonds

These are bonds that have a warrant attached that gives the right to acquire shares in the company. When the warrant is exercised, the investor has the right to use the bond to pay for the common stock instead of paying cash. For these purposes, the bond will be valued at par.

As a result of this ability to use the bonds to pay the strike price of the warrants, these are sometimes called synthetic convertibles.

The value of these bonds is often highly correlated with the value of the company's equity and the amount of usable bonds outstanding that are available to pay for exercise of the warrants.

Springing issues

These securities change their characteristics if a triggering event occurs. For example, subordinated debt might become senior debt if the company repays its existing senior debt. Alternatively, warrants might become immediately exercisable if the company is taken over.

When analysing springing securities, a key feature is the likelihood of the triggering event occurring, since this will fundamentally affect their nature.

Pay in kind securities (PIKS)

With PIKS, the issuer has the option to pay interest in cash or by issuing additional securities in lieu of cash for a specified period of time. When additional securities are issued, the interest due is effectively being rolled up into the principal sum outstanding.

The benefit of PIKS for the issuer is that they give financial flexibility.

When analysing PIKS, the analyst should use discounted cash flow techniques. This is because the value of any payments in kind is equal to the value of the securities being issued.

4.4.3 Performance of high yield securities

Default risk

The key risk with a high yield security is default risk.

Studies in the US have indicated that the default rate typically changes from 4% to 10%. The rate is highly correlated to the economic cycle. In addition it is important to look at the default rates by industry.

In order to minimise the risk of loss through default, a portfolio will need to be diversified.

Where a default occurs in the portfolio, continuing analysis is required. It may be the case that the defaulting company will be able to resume payments in the future. Alternatively, the issuer might issue common stock to the debt investors in return for cancellation of the debt, which could become worth far more.

4.4.4 Suitability of high yield debt as an investment

What represents an ideal investment is not as simple as looking at the nominal returns, rather the assets utilised by any investor need to be suited to their investment objectives and constraints.

To understand the type of investor for whom a particular investment may be suitable, we need to examine the characteristics of that investment and match them to clients with corresponding needs.

The defining characteristic of higher yielding debt is a bond that is rated below investment grade when it is issued, i.e. a junk bond. Such bonds subject investors to a higher exposure to credit and default risk but in return offer a high yield.

High yield bonds not only respond to changes in interest rates but are also very sensitive to changes in credit spreads. Furthermore in a recession, when interest rates are being reduced, bond prices may be expected to rise. Whilst this may be the case for investment grade bonds, increased credit spreads and the increased potential of default for junk bonds tends to lead to their prices falling.

The other side of this coin, however, is that when interest rates are rising in the recovery phase of an economic cycle and investment grade bond prices are falling, the prices of junk bonds tends to rise on narrowing credit spreads and reduced default risk.

One final characteristic to mention is that many high yield issues are made by smaller companies. As a result they tend to be relatively low volume issues and, as a consequence, liquidity tends to be low. Such bonds will, therefore, typically be bought and held to maturity.

Emerging market debt is a term used to refer primarily to the sovereign debt of less developed countries, often debt that is beyond their apparent ability to repay. The term may also encompass corporate debt, though typically in emerging markets this is provided by banks.

Historically, emerging market debt has been issued in, for that country, foreign currencies, most usually dollars or more recently Euros. Most recently, however, emerging countries have been issuing bonds in their domestic currencies in order to finance domestic obligations such as domestic pensions funding.

Emerging market debt, in common with high yielding debt, tends to have a credit rating below investment grade and therefore has similar characteristics of high yield, high risk and low liquidity. Potentially the main difference between the two classes being the additional currency exposure contained within an emerging market investment. Other differences, however, include

- The remedies for sovereign debt defaults are not the same as the remedies for domestic higher yielding debt defaults. If the sovereign government chooses to default there is little if any recourse available to the investor.
- Political and economic difficulties in emerging countries have historically been known to lead to them over-borrowing and assuming excessive risk.

High yielding bonds and emerging market debt are, therefore, both characterised by high returns, high volatility and low liquidity, along with a currency exposure on emerging market debt.

As a result of these characteristics, such investments are most suitable as a minor more speculative component of a large long-term portfolio with more certain liabilities/outflows – portfolios where the risk can be absorbed through the funds risk tolerance and diversification and the low liquidity can be sustained through high liquidity elsewhere. They may, perhaps, be used as a partial, alternative to equities given their risk/return characteristics so long as liquidity is less of an issue.

As a consequence of their risk characteristics many funds, such as pension funds and general insurance funds, may be prohibited from investing in them, though they would be a perfectly appropriate asset class for a pension fund to hold assuming the fund manager had sufficient expertise or used the services of a specialist manager. They may also be suitable for life assurance funds (e.g. financing annuities) since both pension funds and life funds tend to be large long-term investment funds with a large diversified spread of assets that can cater for low liquidity over a limited range of their assets.

4.5 Investing in distressed companies

4.5.1 Bankruptcy

Investing in the securities of bankrupt companies

It is often the case that investors avoid buying securities in bankrupt companies, for understandable reasons. However, this approach is misconceived, for the following reasons.

- Bankruptcy may be the start of a reorganisation that gives the company a fresh start. The analyst must identify the company with prospects and avoid the company that is never going to recover.
- Securities in bankrupt companies can often be bought at very cheap prices. They then subsequently recover, giving a profit to the purchaser.

Investors either own securities in bankrupt companies by default or they buy the securities after the company has become bankrupt.

4.5.2 Companies becoming bankrupt

It is not usually a surprise when a company becomes bankrupt, as the process usually takes a number of years of deteriorating performance. The major situation when this is not the case is when a company suffers a sudden loss. This will often be flagged in the notes to the accounts concerning contingent liabilities.

4.5.3 Analysis of companies in reorganisation

Investing in Vulture Funds or Individual Securities

A vulture fund is where a group of investors pool their resources to obtain a large stake in a bankrupt company's bonds. This can give them significant influence in the bankruptcy process. This approach is risky, since a reorganisation may cause such securities to lose value, depending on the allocation of equity in the business.

An alternative approach is to buy securities in a specific company, which is more suited to individual investors. The benefit of this is that it does not necessarily involve a large investment in one company and allows investors to diversify. Although reducing exposure to one company, it has the scope to be very profitable.

When investing in a company, the investor may invest for one of two reasons.

- A belief that the company itself will improve, giving an improvement in value for all securities.
- Although the company itself may not prosper, the return on the particular security is quantifiable because of the asset backing.

Identifying appropriate companies

There are a vast number of companies that file for bankruptcy each year. In order to identify appropriate companies for investment, the following process should be followed.

- Obtain details of companies that have gone bankrupt from the financial pages of a newspaper.
- Avoid very small companies or securities that are not publicly traded. In these circumstances, it will be difficult to obtain the necessary financial information or to buy the securities.

Avoid companies that have failed through operational difficulties, since this may involve a long and difficult turnaround. Companies that have gone bankrupt through a poor financial structure but have a good operational base are more likely to be good candidates for investment.

APPENDIX

Portfolio yield

A method of approximating the **portfolio yield** without scheduling the portfolio cash flows and determining the IRR is to weight the individual bond yields appropriately as we discussed in the yields chapter earlier in this Study Text.

As we noted then, the best approximation to the portfolio yield that takes account of both the yields on the bonds and their terms is to weight the bond GRYs by nominal values and BPVs, though duration or modified duration may be used in place of BPV if they are more readily available.

$$\text{Portfolio yield (approx 1)} = \frac{\Sigma \text{GRY} \times \text{Nominal} \times \text{BPV}}{\Sigma \text{Nominal} \times \text{BPV}}$$

An alternative approximation is to weight the bond GRYs by both value and modified duration, though again, using duration or BPV in place of modified duration provide reasonable alternatives.

$$\text{Portfolio yield (approx 2)} = \frac{\Sigma \text{GRY} \times \text{Market value} \times \text{Modified duration}}{\Sigma \text{Market value} \times \text{Modified duration}}$$

Note that these are all alternative approximations and you should use whatever is most convenient based on the information given.

The purpose of this appendix is to illustrate these alternatives now that we have introduced duration, modified duration and BPV.

Example

The following two bonds are held in a portfolio

Bond	Coupon	Maturity (Years)	GRY	Portfolio nominal
A	6%	2	3%	30
B	4%	3	5%	70

Calculate the true portfolio yield and the approximate portfolio yield

Solution

Bond A

Time	Cash flow	DF (3%)	PV (3%)	tPV
1	6	$\frac{1}{1.03}$	5.825	5.825
2	106	$\frac{1}{1.03^2}$	99.915	199.830
			105.740	205.655

$$\text{Duration} = \frac{205.6556}{105.740} = 1.945$$

$$\text{MD} = \frac{1.945}{1.03} = 1.888$$

BPV = 105.740 × 1.888 × 0.0001 = 0.01996

Bond B

Time	Cash flow	DF (5%)	PV (5%)	tPV
1	4	$\frac{1}{1.05}$	3.810	3.810
2	4	$\frac{1}{1.05^2}$	3.628	7.256
3	104	$\frac{1}{1.05^3}$	89.839	269.517
			97.277	280.583

$$\text{Duration} = \frac{280.583}{97.277} = 2.884$$

$$\text{MD} = \frac{2.884}{1.05} = 2.747$$

BPV = 97.267 × 2.747 × 0.0001 = 0.02672

Portfolio

Based on the portfolio nominal holdings we can calculate the portfolio value as

Portfolio value = 0.30 × 105.740 + 0.70 × 97.277 = 99.816

And the portfolio cash flows as

Time	Bond A		Bond B		Portfolio
	100%	30%	100%	70%	
1	6	1.80	4	2.80	4.60
2	106	31.80	4	2.80	34.60
3			104	72.80	72.80

The GRY of these portfolio cash flows can be calculated as 4.526%, giving

Time	Cash flow	DF (4.526%)	PV (4.526%)	tPV
1	4.60	$\frac{1}{1.04526}$	4.401	4.401
2	34.60	$\frac{1}{1.04526^2}$	31.668	63.331
3	72.80	$\frac{1}{1.04526^3}$	63.747	191.241
			99.816	258.973

$$\text{Duration} = \frac{258.973}{99.816} = 2.595$$

$$\text{MD} = \frac{2.595}{1.04526} = 2.483$$

BPV = 99.816 × 2.483 × 0.0001 = 0.02478

Alternatives

Weighting the portfolio GRY by nominal value and BPV gives

Portfolio yield (approx 1) $= \frac{\Sigma \text{GRY} \times \text{Nominal} \times \text{BPV}}{\Sigma \text{Nominal} \times \text{BPV}}$

$$= \frac{3\% \times 30 \times 0.01996 + 5\% \times 70 \times 0.02672}{30 \times 0.01996 + 70 \times 0.02672} = 4.515\%$$

Weighting the portfolio GRY by market value and duration gives

Portfolio yield (approx 2) $= \frac{\Sigma \text{GRY} \times \text{Market value} \times \text{Modified duration}}{\Sigma \text{Market value} \times \text{Modified duration}}$

$$= \frac{3\% \times 105.740 \times 1.888 + 5\% \times 97.277 \times 2.747}{105.740 \times 1.888 + 97.277 \times 2.747} = 4.144\%$$

Summarising

If we consider all of the possibilities we would find the following

True portfolio GRY	4.526%
Weighting by nominal and BPV	4.515%
Weighting by nominal and duration	4.552%
Weighting by nominal and modified duration	4.545%
Weighting by market value and BPV	4.104%
Weighting by market value and duration	4.154%
Weighting by market value and modified duration	4.145%

Clearly the closest approximation uses the nominal value and BPV.

CHAPTER ROUNDUP

- **Risk**

  You must be able to calculate and use

  – Macaulay duration (D) = $\frac{\sum(t \times PV_t)}{Price}$

  – Modified Duration/Volatility = $-\frac{\text{Macaulay duration}}{1+GRY}$

  – Convexity = $\frac{\sum t(t+1)PV_t}{Price(1+GRY)^2}$

  – PVBP = Price × MD × 0.0001

  – Yield value of a tick = $\frac{\text{Tick value}}{Price \times MD}$

  You must be able to describe

  – The impact of bond call features on convexity.
  – Bond credit ratings.
  – The factors involved in credit analysis.

TEST YOUR KNOWLEDGE

Check your knowledge of the Chapter here, without referring back to the text.

1. If a eurosterling bond has three years to redemption, pays a 9% annual coupon, with interest rates at 10%, and is priced at £97.51, what is the duration, modified duration and PVBP of the eurosterling bond?

2. If the coupon rate on a bond increases, what will be the impact on its duration, modified duration and PVBP?

3. Treasury 10% is redeemable in exactly three years and pays interest annually. Calculate the duration, modified duration and PVBP if the price is £101.935.

4. A bond has three years to redemption at par and pays an 8% coupon payable at the end of each of the three years. Interest rates are 9.5% and it is currently priced at £96.24. What is the duration, modified duration and PVBP of this bond?

5. A bond is priced at £113.75 and has a modified duration of 3.45. If yields rise by ½%, what will the new price of the bond be?

6. Exchequer 14% is repayable in exactly 1½ years. It has a quoted gross redemption yield of 10% and a price of £105.446.

   Calculate the duration, volatility and convexity of the gilt.

7. The following information relates to two gilts.

Treasury 10%	1 year to maturity	Price	£101.85
Treasury 9%	2 years to maturity	Price	£100.925

   (a) What are the one and two-year spot rates, and the forward rate for lending in one year's time?

   (b) What is the duration of the above Treasury 9% gilt, calculated using the redemption yield rate, and how useful is such a measure? Assume interest is paid yearly.

   (c) What are the principal problems of using redemption yields when comparing two gilts with the **same** maturity date?

8. The term structure of interest rates, as expressed in annualised spot rates, has been determined as follows.

	One Year	Two Years	Three Years	Four Years	Five Years and Beyond
Spot rate	12%	10%	10%	11%	9%

   Two bonds, with the following characteristics are now under consideration.

   Bond I: Annual coupon rate 10%; redeemable at par (100%) in five years' time; coupon has just been paid.

   Bond II: Coupon rate zero; redeemable at par (100%) in four years' time.

Requirements

(a) Compute the price of both bonds, assuming the coupons on Bond I are paid annually.

(b) Compute the implied forward rates from years one to two and years two to three.

(c) Assuming the prices that you computed in Part (a), calculate the redemption yields for both bonds on an annual and semi-annual compounding basis, and comment upon your results.

(d) Compute the durations of both bonds and indicate which bond you would select if interest rates are expected to fluctuate in the future.

(e) Discuss briefly the factors that are likely to generate a term structure of the type featured in this question.

(f) Briefly outline the advantages and disadvantages of index-linked gilts over more traditional gilts, relating your answer to the term structure described in this question.

9. A Treasury 8½% Bond 2004 is currently quoted at 85 and can be assumed to have exactly ten years to maturity. Interest is paid half-yearly with the first payment due in six months' time. The duration of the gilt has been calculated as 6.62 years.

Requirements

(a) Calculate the yield to redemption of the gilt.

(b) Explain how the duration of the gilt is calculated.

(c) Briefly compare the use of changes in redemption yield and duration as measures of volatility in evaluating fixed interest securities.

(d) Explain the impact on duration under each of the following conditions.

(i) The coupon rate is lower than 8½%.

(ii) The yield to redemption is lower than that calculated in (a) above.

(iii) The maturity is shorter than ten years.

10. Data on two bonds is summarised below.

	Coupon Rate	Maturity Date	Current Price	Redemption Price
Bond A	0%	1 year	91	100
Bond B	10%	5 years	100	100

Requirements

(a) Compute the duration of each of the bonds.

(b) Describe how duration will change if

(i) The coupon rate on B increases.
(ii) The redemption yields on both bonds increase.
(iii) The maturities of both bonds increase.

(No further computations are necessary to answer (b) (i), (ii) and (iii).)

(c) Indicate which of Bonds A or B would be preferable if interest rates are anticipated to decline over the forthcoming year.

11. Write brief notes on the following.

- Duration.
- Convexity.
- Risk-free yield curve.
- Basis risk.
- Repos.

12. Bonds I and II both have five years to maturity, when the bonds will be redeemed at par. They both pay a coupon once per annum and have just paid their latest coupon. Bond I has a coupon of 5%, while Bond II pays a coupon of 10%. The term structure is flat and both bonds have yields to maturity of 8% per annum.

Requirements

(a) Compute the durations and convexities of both bonds and comment upon your results.

(b) Calculate the percentage change in the price of each bond when interest rates increase by 3% along the whole yield curve.

(c) Discuss the implications of your answers in Parts (i) and (ii) for investing in bonds.

(d) Outline what other factors you would take into account if the two bonds are

Eurobonds denominated in yen and you are a UK investor.

13. A default free bond with a coupon rate of 10%, which is payable annually, will be redeemed at par at the end of five years. The coupon on the bond has just been paid. The current one-year spot rate is 10% and the various one-year forward rates are as follows.

From End of Year	% p.a.
1	11
2	12
3	13
4	14

Requirements

(a) Compute the current price of the bond.

(b) Derive the term structure of interest rates.

(c) If the bond is callable at a 5% premium at the end of Year 3, calculate the yield to call and yield to maturity of the bond and comment upon your results.

(d) Briefly outline the usefulness of convexity to an investor and indicate when it can become negative.

14. You hold, on 15 October 2005, $5m nominal of a non-callable World Bank 6½% Eurobond with maturity date 15 October 2010. The yield on the bond is currently 8.42% and its price is $92.42 with a duration of 4.40.

You wish to switch into an 8.25% Treasury bond with a maturity date of 15 October 2023, priced at $100.38, with a yield of 8.21%, and duration of 9.69 without altering your interest rate exposure.

(a) Determine the appropriate nominal amount of the Treasury bond that you should buy.
(b) By how much will your new investment fall in value if yields rise 25 bp?
(c) What would be the rationale behind such a switch and what are its potential returns and risks?

15. A debt portfolio consists of two Eurobonds issued by the Russian Ministry of Finance (rated B3 by Moody's and CC by Standard & Poor's). These bonds are dollar-denominated and pay coupons annually. From your market knowledge, you would price a new issue for the Russian Ministry of Finance at 4.20% over US Treasury bonds when yields are expressed in annual equivalents.

Bond	Nominal	Coupon	Maturity	Yield %	Price	Duration
A	$1m	15%	3.33 years	10.7	$121.38	2.661
B	$1m	3%	3.25 years	10.7	$81.97	3.049

(a) Estimate the duration of the portfolio.

(b) The quoted yield on a three-year US Treasury note is 6.40%. At what price would you expect a 10% coupon three-year Brazilian dollar-denominated Eurobond to be issued to yield 4.50% over Treasuries in annual yield equivalent terms?

(c) You are considering selling short the Brazilian bond in an amount which will match the duration of the Russian bond portfolio position. How much of the Brazilian bond should you sell short?

(d) What risks are inherent in this duration-neutral position?

16. A small debt portfolio consists of $1m nominal of each of two bonds issued by XYZ plc in the dollar Eurobond market: XYZ 10% 31/01/2009 and XYZ 8% 31/12/2008. It is currently 30 September 2005. You know that XYZ paper is typically priced at 1.20% over the equivalent US Treasury bond yield (annual basis). At present, equivalent maturity Treasuries are yielding a quoted 6.5% on a semi-annual basis.

(a) Calculate the market value of the portfolio, taking into account accrued interest.

(b) Estimate the duration of the portfolio.

(c) If the yield on equivalent US Treasuries rose from 6.50% to 7.50%, what would be the proportionate change in the XYZ portfolio?

17. You work for the finance director of a company that is considering its first Eurobond issue and therefore requires a credit rating. Write a paper to the Finance Director explaining the main factors that the two rating agencies, Standard & Poor's and Moody's, will take into account in order to determine your company's credit rating.

18. You manage a Eurobond portfolio and have 2% of the portfolio invested in a Standard & Poor's single A credit-rated US corporate bond. The US company concerned has just been put on Credit Watch by Standard & Poor's.

Write a report to your Senior Manager explaining what a single A credit rating is and the likely implications of the credit watch move.

19. You have just joined a UK fund management firm that is considering launching a US bond fund. You have been asked to explain some concepts unfamiliar to the senior managers. One of these is that of a callable bond. Write a brief report defining a callable bond, explaining its primary characteristics in terms of duration and convexity, with the aid of a diagram and make recommendations as to when these bonds might be appropriate investments for the fund.

TEST YOUR KNOWLEDGE: ANSWERS

1.

Time	Cash Flow (£)	DF (10%)	PV (£)	tPV (£)
1	9.00	$\frac{1}{1.10}$	8.18	8.18
2	9.00	$\frac{1}{1.10^2}$	7.44	14.88
3	109.00	$\frac{1}{1.10^3}$	81.89	245.67
			97.51	268.73

$$\text{Duration} = \frac{268.73}{97.51} = 2.76 \text{ years}$$

$$\text{Modified duration} = -\frac{\text{Macaulay duration}}{1+\text{GRY}} = -\frac{2.76}{1.10} = -2.509$$

PVBP = Price × MD × 0.0001 = £97.51 × (–2.509) × 0.0001 = –£0.0245

2. Low-coupon bonds are more sensitive to interest rates than higher coupon bonds and therefore have higher durations. If the coupon increases the duration decreases.

3. The flat yield (annual income return) on this bond is 9.8% (10.00/101.935). Since the price is a little above par there will be a small annual loss in capital value to be deducted from this income to get the total return or GRY. Hence for interpolation we will try 9% and 10%.

Time	Cash Flow (£)	DF (9%)	PV (9%) (£)	DF (10%)	PV (10%) (£)
0	(101.935)	1.0000	(101.935)	1.0000	(101.935)
1	10.000	0.9174	9.174	0.9091	9.091
2	10.000	0.8417	8.417	0.8264	8.264
3	110.000	0.7722	84.940	0.7513	82.645
			0.596		(1.935)

$$\text{GRY} = 9\% + \frac{0.596}{0.596-(1.935)} \times (10\% - 9\%) = 9.235\%$$

Duration Calculation

Time	Cash Flow (£)	DF (9.235%)	PV (£)	tPV (£)
1	10	$\frac{1}{1.09235}$	9.155	9.155
2	10	$\frac{1}{1.09235^2}$	8.381	16.762
3	110	$\frac{1}{1.09235^3}$	84.393	253.179
				279.096

$$\text{Duration} = \frac{279.096}{101.935} = 2.74 \text{ years}$$

$$\text{Modified duration} = -\frac{2.74}{1.09235} = -2.508$$

PVBP = £101.935 × (–2.508) × 0.0001 = –£0.0256

4.

Time	Cash Flow (£)	DF (9.5%)	PV (£)	tPV (£)
1	8.00	$\frac{1}{1.095}$	7.31	7.31
2	8.00	$\frac{1}{1.095^2}$	6.67	13.34
3	108.00	$\frac{1}{1.095^3}$	82.26	246.78
			96.24	267.43

$$\text{Duration} = \frac{£267.43}{£96.24} = 2.78 \text{ years}$$

$$\text{Modified duration} = -\frac{2.78}{1.095} = -2.539$$

PVBP = £96.24 × (–2.539) × 0.0001 = –£0.0244

5. Proportionate change in price = MD × ΔY = –3.45 × 0.005 = –0.01725 or –1.725%

This is a negative figure, hence prices will fall by 1.725% or £1.96 (£113.75 × 1.725%) to £111.79 (£113.75 – £1.96).

6. Since the quoted gross redemption yield is 10%, the discount rate to apply to the semi-annual flows is 5% (the quoted rate being twice the semi-annual rate). Hence

Time	t(1 + t)	Cash Flow (£)	DF (5%)	PV (£)	tPV (£)	t(1 + t)PV (£)
1	2	7	$\frac{1}{1.05}$	6.6667	6.6667	13.3334
2	3	7	$\frac{1}{1.05^2}$	6.3492	12.6984	38.0952
3	4	107	$\frac{1}{1.05^3}$	92.4306	277.2918	1,109.1672
				105.4465	296.6569	1,160.5958

$$\text{Duration} = \frac{296.6569}{105.4465} = 2.8133 \text{ half-years or } 1.4067 \text{ years}$$

$$\text{Modified duration (volatility)} = -\frac{2.8133}{1.05} = -2.6793 \text{ in semi-annual terms}$$

$$\text{Convexity} = \frac{1{,}160.5958}{105.4465 \times 1.05^2} = 9.9832 \text{ in semi-annual terms}$$

7. (a) **Spot rates** – one-year (since no six-month bond is given the assumption will have to be made that these bonds pay annual coupons).

$$(1 + r) = \frac{C + R}{\text{Current price}}$$

Inserting the values that we have for the one-year bond gives

$$(1 + r) = \frac{£110}{£101.85} = 1.08 \text{ or } 8\%$$

This then is the yield on one-year money.

For the two-year spot rate it is necessary to turn to the two-year bond. Here we have two flows; £9 coupon in one year's time and £109, coupon and redemption, in two years' time.

$$\text{Current price} = \frac{\text{Coupon}}{(1+r_1)} + \frac{\text{Coupon and redemption}}{(1+r_2)^2}$$

Substituting the values for the two-year bond and using the one-year spot rate to discount the flow in one year's time, we can solve for the two-year spot rate.

$$£100.925 = \frac{£9}{(1.08)} + \frac{£109}{(1+r_2)^2}$$

$$£100.925 = £8.33 + \frac{£109}{(1+r_2)^2}$$

$$£100.925 - £8.33 = \frac{£109}{(1+r_2)^2}$$

$$(1 + r_2)^2 = \frac{£109}{92.595}$$

$$(1 + r_2)^2 = 1.177$$

$$(1 + r_2) = \sqrt{1.177} \text{ (or } 1.177^{½}\text{)}$$

$$(1 + r_2) = 1.085$$

$$r_2 = 0.085 \text{ or } 8.5\%$$

Forward rates

$$(1 + r_1) \times (1 + {}_1f_2) = (1 + r_2)^2$$

Rearranging the formula gives

$$(1 + {}_1f_2) = \frac{(1+r_2)^2}{(1+r_1)}$$

Inserting the values

$$(1 + {}_1f_2) = \frac{(1+0.085)^2}{(1+0.08)} = 1.09$$

$${}_1f_2 = 0.09 \text{ or } 9\%$$

(b) **Duration – using the approximate yield of 8.45% (can work out using the interpolation method)**

Time Period	Flow (£)	PV @ 8.45% (£)	PV × Time (£)
1	9	8.30	8.30
2	109	92.68	185.36
		100.98	193 66

$$\frac{193.66}{100.98} = 1.91 \text{ years}$$

(c) The yield can be distorted by a number of factors.

- Liquidity. Not all gilts are equally liquid.
- Coupon (gains tax implications); and different durations.

8. (a) The value of Bond I will be

$$\frac{10}{1.12} + \frac{10}{1.10^2} + \frac{10}{1.10^3} + \frac{10}{1.11^4} + \frac{110}{1.09^5} = 102.77$$

The value of the pure discount bond, II, will be

$$\frac{100}{1.11^4} = 65.87$$

(b) The implied forward rate from period one to two will be

$$\frac{1.1^2}{1.12} = 1.08 \text{ (i.e. 8\%)}$$

and from period two to three will be $\frac{1.1^3}{1.1^2} = 1.10$

(c) The redemption yield for bond I, r, can be found from the relationship

$$\text{Price} = \text{coupon} \times \frac{1}{r}\ [1 - \frac{1}{(1+r)^n}] + \frac{\text{Redemption}}{(1+r)^n}$$

$$102.77 = 10 \times \frac{1}{r}\ [1 - \frac{1}{(1+r)^n}] + \frac{100}{(1+r)^n}$$

By interpolation, the value of r is found to be 9.29%.

Since the semi-annual rate equals $(1+r)^{1/2} - 1$, the redemption yield with semi-annual compounding is 4.54%.

The redemption yield for the pure discount bond will equal the spot rate, i.e. 11%. The semi-annual rate will be 5.36%. In both cases, the semi-annual rates are less than half the annual rates. The duration of bond I, in terms of redemption yields, is

$$\sum_{t=1}^{5} \frac{t \times C(t)}{(1+r)^t}$$

(where *C(t)* is the coupon/principal paid in period *t*) which equals 4.18 years.

(d) The duration of Bond II will equal its term to maturity, i.e. four years, since it is a pure discount bond.

Bond II, i.e. the bond with the lowest duration, would be selected if risk minimisation is the objective being pursued. If an active rate anticipation strategy is being followed, the bond selection will depend upon the direction of the interest rate shift, i.e. if an increase, the shorter duration will be chosen, while for a decrease the longer duration bond will be selected.

(e) The factors likely to generate the term structure include

- Monetary policy.
- Inflationary expectations.
- Risk premia.
- Market segmentation, i.e. banks etc. operating at the short end, pension funds, etc. at the long end.

(f) Indexed-linked gilts provide returns denominated in real terms, i.e. inflation protection. Their usefulness depends upon inflationary expectations. In this case the inverted structure of yields indicates tight monetary policy presumably in order to control inflation. If inflation starts to come down then monetary policy will be eased. There may be arbitrage possibilities available between the index-linked and the conventional stocks based on this potential fall in inflation.

9. (a) **Yield to redemption**

Time ($^1/_2$ years)	Cash Flow (£)	DF (5%)	PV (5%) (£)	DF (6%)	PV (6%) (£)
0	(85)	1	(85.00)	1	(85.00)
1–20	4¼	12.4622	52.96	11.4699	48.75
20	100	0.3769	37.69	0.3118	31.18
			5.65		–5.07

R_1 = 5%
N_1 = 5.65
R_2 = 6%
N_2 = –5.07

Using the following formula

$$GRY = R_1 + R_1 \frac{N_1}{N_1 - N_2}(R_2 - R_1)$$

Redemption yield equals

$$GRY = 5 + \frac{5.65}{5.65 - (5.07)}(6\text{–}5) = \mathbf{5.527}$$

Annual ERY = 11.05% (5.257% × 2)

(b) **Duration (D)** of the gilt is calculated as the weighted average length of time before each receipt from the gilt, the weights being the present value of each receipt at the gross redemption yield.

As a formula

$$D = \frac{\Sigma tPV}{Price}$$

where

D = duration in years
t = period to each interest receipt or redemption date
PV = the present value of each coupon flow

(c) Duration is a better measure of volatility for coupon bonds as it measures the weighted average time until cash flow and is thus a more representative measure of the bond's overall cash flow sensitivity to interest rate changes. Duration takes into account coupon, yield to maturity and time to maturity.

(d) (i) Duration will increase. As the coupon decreases, a higher weight is given to the redemption payment.

(ii) Duration will increase. As rates decline, all cash flows increase in value but the longest ones increase at the greatest rate.

(iii) Duration will decrease. There is a reduction in total coupon payments and a shortening of time until the redemption payment.

10. (a) The duration of **Bond A** is the same as the maturity date, i.e. one year.

Bond B – as the redemption price is 100, the GRY is the same as the coupon, i.e. 10%. Assuming annual coupon payments (this is what the Examiner assumed but it is not obvious from the question).

Time	Cash Flow	10% Factor	PV	tPV
1	10	0.9091	9.09	9.09
2	10	0.8264	8.27	16.54
3	10	0.7513	7.51	22.54
4	10	0.6830	6.83	27.32
5	110	0.6209	68.30	341.50
			100.00	416.99

Duration = (416.99/100) = **4.17 years**

Assuming semi-annual coupon payments and a semi-annual GRY of 5% we have

Time ($^1/_2$ years)	Cash Flow	5% Factor	PV	tPV
1	5	0.9524	4.762	4.762
2	5	0.9070	4.535	9.070
3	5	0.8638	4.319	12.975
4	5	0.8227	4.114	16.456
5	5	0.7835	3.918	19.590
6	5	0.7462	3.731	22.386
7	5	0.7107	3.554	24.878
8	5	0.6768	3.384	27.072
9	5	0.6446	3.223	29.007
10	105	0.6139	64.460	644.600
			100.000	810.778

Duration = (810.778/100) = 8.108 half years or 4.05 years

(b) Duration will

(i) Decrease.
(ii) Decrease for B, stay the same for A.
(iii) Increase.

(c) If interest rates are expected to fall, B would be preferred since its longer duration will magnify the price increase.

7. **Duration**

- An indicator of volatility.
- Generally, low coupon bonds and bonds with more distant maturities exhibit higher volatility. As interest rates change, the market price of such a bond moves by a greater amount than a bond with a closer maturity and a higher coupon.
- Duration reflects both maturity and the level of coupon. The more distant the maturity and the lower the coupon relative to the capital value on redemption, the longer the duration of the bond, i.e. the longer the duration the more volatile the bond.
- Duration is the weighted average length of time to the receipt of the bond's benefits (being coupon and redemption), the weightings being the present value of the benefits concerned. For a zero coupon bond, the duration will be the maturity of the bond, since there is only one date when benefits are received. For any other bond, the duration will be less than its maturity.
- In addition to measuring the volatility of one bond relative to another, duration is of use in portfolio immunisation and in hedging of interest rate risk. In order to achieve effective matching of assets and liabilities, both the asset and liability portfolio should have the same duration. In addition, if a security is held for its duration, then the gross redemption yield of the security on the date of purchase will be realised, whereas if it is sold at any other date and not held to maturity this is not the case.

Convexity

- Relates to estimates of by how much a bond's price will change given a particular change in interest rates.
- The relevant estimate is made by using the theory of modified duration.
- The estimate is inaccurate since it assumes that the proportionate change in price of the bond given a change in yield is constant. In fact, the higher the original price, the higher the proportionate change.
- The inaccuracy is referred to as convexity.
- Given very small changes in yield, the inaccuracy of the estimate is very small, but it becomes more important as greater changes are considered.
- Convexity tends to overestimate falls in price if interest rates increase and underestimate increases in price if interest rates fall. As such it can be seen to be good news to the investor since the expected loss will always be more than the actual loss and the expected gain will be less than the actual gain after a change in interest rates.
- The graph below demonstrates convexity.

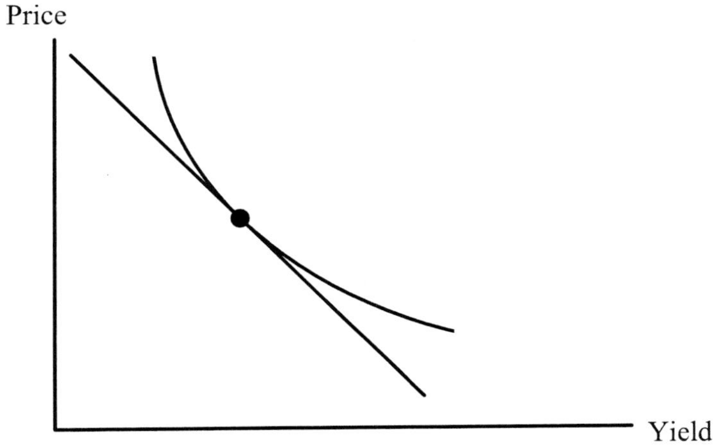

The straight line indicates the predicted price for a particular change in interest rates using the theory of modified duration. The curved line indicates the actual change in price.

Risk-Free Yield Curve

- The yield curve is a diagram or graph plotting the yields available on bonds of different maturities.
- Generally, the shape of the yield curve is expected to be sloping upwards, i.e. higher yields are required for more distant maturities. This is supposed to be due to a number of factors, such as investor expectations that rates will rise, expectations of inflation in the future, higher risk in longer term investments requiring higher yields as compensation and the preference of investors to have liquid short-term investments in order to be able to access their money quickly.
- In order to get a yield curve that is comparing like with like and to identify how maturity is affecting yield as accurately as possible, it is desirable to have investments that are similar in every possible way except for maturity. Risk-free instruments would match this criterion fairly closely.
- The closest approximations to risk-free investments are index-linked gilts, where credit risk and inflation risk are virtually eliminated.
- Inspecting the yield curve for index-linked gilts will enable us to more closely identify the fundamental factors causing changes in yield, particularly if this curve is then compared to a yield curve for non-index-linked gilts.

Basis Risk

- Type of interest rate risk.
- It gives rise to variability in expected returns due to changes in interest rates affecting different instruments in different ways.
- It arises due to the different markets reflecting slight variations in the nature of individual instruments, their liquidity and credit risk.
- An example would be the difference between the cash market and the interest rate futures market.
- The implication is that an instrument purchased to hedge against a particular position may not be an exact hedge due to basis risk.

Repos

- Sale and repurchase agreement.
- Bond holder sells bond to raise cash and simultaneously agrees to repurchase in the future at a specified price.
- Difference between sale and repurchase price reflects interest over the period.
- Effectively a loan secured on the bond. Due to the security can obtain very fine rates.

12. (a) **Duration and Convexity**

Bond I

Time	Cash Flow (£)	DF (8%)	PV (£)	tPV (£)	t(t + 1)PV (£)
1	5.00	$\frac{1}{1.08}$	4.63	4.63	9.26
2	5.00	$\frac{1}{1.08^2}$	4.29	8.58	25.74
3	5.00	$\frac{1}{1.08^3}$	3.97	11.91	47.64
4	5.00	$\frac{1}{1.08^4}$	3.68	14.72	73.60
5	105.00	$\frac{1}{1.08^5}$	71.46	357.30	2,143.80
			88.03	397.14	2,300.04

$$\text{Duration} = \frac{397.14}{88.03} = 4.511 \text{ years}$$

$$\text{Convexity} = \frac{2{,}300.04}{88.03 \times 1.108^2} = 22.4$$

Bond II

Time	Cash Flow (£)	DF (8%)	PV (£)	tPV (£)	t(t + 1)PV (£)
1	10.00	$\frac{1}{1.08}$	9.26	9.26	18.52
2	10.00	$\frac{1}{1.08^2}$	8.57	17.14	51.42
3	10.00	$\frac{1}{1.08^3}$	7.94	23.82	95.28
4	10.00	$\frac{1}{1.08^4}$	7.35	29.40	147.00
5	110.00	$\frac{1}{1.08^5}$	74.86	374.30	2,245.80
			107.98	453.92	2,558.02

$$\text{Duration} = \frac{453.92}{107.98} = 4.204 \text{ years}$$

$$\text{Convexity} = \frac{2{,}558.02}{107.98 \times 1.108^2} = 20.31$$

Although both bonds have the same time to maturity, Bond II has the lower duration and convexity due to its higher coupon rate resulting in the bond 'repaying' capital somewhat more rapidly.

(b) **Price Change**

The proportionate change in a bond's price will be given by

$$\text{Adjusted percentage price change} = \text{MD} \times \Delta Y + \tfrac{1}{2} \times C \times \Delta Y^2$$

where

MD = modified duration
ΔY = change in the gross redemption yield stated as a decimal
C = convexity

Bond I

$$MD = \frac{-4.511}{1.08} = -4.177$$

Adjusted percentage price change $-4.177 \times 0.03 + ½ \times 22.4 \times 0.03^2 = -0.11523$ or -11.523%

Bond II

$$MD = \frac{-4.204}{1.08} = -3.893$$

Adjusted percentage price change $-3.893 \times 0.03 + ½ \times 20.31 \times 0.03^2 = -0.10765$ or -10.765%

(c) **Implications**

Three factors affect the duration, modified duration and convexity of a bond, specifically

- **Maturity** – longer maturity $\Rightarrow$ higher values of each.
- **Coupon** – lower coupon $\Rightarrow$ higher values.
- **Yields** – lower yields $\Rightarrow$ higher values.

Parts (a) and (b) above illustrate the second of these points.

When interest rates are expected to rise (fall) investors should shorten (lengthen) the duration of their bond investments as they will wish to minimise (maximise) their interest rate sensitivity.

(d) **Other Factors if Yen Eurobonds**

If the bonds are yen Eurobonds, the major other dimension to consider is the yen/pound exchange rate and the relative shifts in, say, yen Eurobond and sterling Eurobond yield curves.

Exchange rate fluctuations will introduce an extra risk dimension for the UK investor. Yen Eurobonds will fluctuate in yen terms in response to fluctuations in the yen yield curve.

13. (a) **Bond Pricing**

Time	**Cash (£)**	**DF**	**PV (£)**
1	10	$\frac{1}{1.10}$	9.09
2	10	$\frac{1}{1.10 \times 1.11}$	8.19
3	10	$\frac{1}{1.10 \times 1.11 \times 1.12}$	7.31
4	10	$\frac{1}{1.10 \times 1.11 \times 1.12 \times 1.13}$	6.47
5	110	$\frac{1}{1.10 \times 1.11 \times 1.12 \times 1.13 \times 1.14}$	62.44
			93.50

(b) **Term Structure of Interest Rates**

One year	$1 + r_1$	$= 1.10$	$= 1.1000$	$r_1 = 0.1000$ or 10.00%
Two year	$1 + r_2$	$= \sqrt{1.10 \times 1.11}$	$= 1.1050$	$r_2 = 0.1050$ or 10.50%
Three year	$1 + r_3$	$= \sqrt[3]{1.10 \times 1.11 \times 1.12}$	$= 1.1100$	$r_3 = 0.1100$ or 11.00%
Four year	$1 + r_4$	$= \sqrt[4]{1.10 \times 1.11 \times 1.12 \times 1.13}$	$= 1.1149$	$r_4 = 0.1149$ or 11.49%
Five year	$1 + r_5$	$= \sqrt[5]{1.10 \times 1.11 \times 1.12 \times 1.13 \times 1.14}$	$= 1.1199$	$r_5 = 0.1199$ or 11.99%

(c) **Yields**

Yield to Call

Time	Cash Flow (£)	DF (14%)	PV (14%) (£)	DF(15%)	PV (15%) (£)
0	(93.50)	1	(93.50)	1	(93.50)
1–3	10.00	$\frac{1}{0.14}\left(1-\frac{1}{1.14^3}\right)$	23.22	$\frac{1}{0.15}\left(1-\frac{1}{1.15^3}\right)$	22.83
3	105.00	$\frac{1}{1.14^3}$	70.87	$\frac{1}{1.15^3}$	69.04
			0.59		(1.63)

$$\text{Yield} = 14\% + \frac{59}{59-(163)} \times 1\% = 14.27\%$$

Yield to Maturity

Time	Cash Flow (£)	DF (11%)	PV (11%) (£)	DF (12%)	PV (12%) (£)
0	(93.50)	1	(93.50)	1	(93.50)
1 – 5	10.00	$\frac{1}{0.11}\left(1-\frac{1}{1.11^3}\right)$	36.96	$\frac{1}{0.12}\left(1-\frac{1}{1.12^3}\right)$	36.05
5	105.00	$\frac{1}{1.11^3}$	59.35	$\frac{1}{1.12^3}$	56.74
			2.81		(0.71)

$$\text{Yield} = 11\% + \frac{281}{281-(71)} \times 1\% = 11.80\%$$

Given the current yields, it is unlikely that the bond will be called. If interest rates fall (and market values rise) the issuing company may choose to redeem the bond and refinance at a new lower cost.

(d) **Convexity**

Convexity, in conjunction with modified duration, is useful for providing an accurate assessment of the change in the price of a bond that will result from a given change in interest rates. Any assessment undertaken with modified duration alone will tend to understate the new value, and convexity evaluates this understatement.

Convexity is normally positive, i.e. it needs to be added to the modified duration prediction to assess the actual price change. If, however, the bond has a call feature as above then convexity will turn negative as interest rates fall and prices rise towards the call price that sets an upper value to the bond. Modified duration would predict that prices would rise above this value, hence convexity would be negative.

14. (a) This question requires the use of a hedge ratio.

$$\frac{\Delta Pe}{\Delta Pt}$$

In the context of Modified Duration

$$\frac{\frac{-1}{1+Ye} \times De}{\frac{-1}{1+Yt} \times Dt}$$

where D = Macaulay Duration

Substituting the details from the question

$$\frac{\frac{-1}{1.0842} \times 4.4}{\frac{-1}{1.0821} \times 9.69} = 0.4531968$$

Therefore, the fund will need to purchase (in terms of nominal value)

$$\frac{\$5m \times \$92.4 \times 0.4531968}{100.38} = \$2.086m$$

(b) The second part of the question then goes on to deal with the impact of a 25 bp movement in the yield.

Using the following formula (ignoring convexity)

$$\Delta P = MD \times \Delta Y \times P$$

Substituting in the values for the T-bond

$$\left[\frac{-9.69}{1.0821}\right] \times 0.0025 \times (\$2{,}086{,}294 \times 1.0038) = \$46{,}883$$

(c) The basic rationale for the switch is a policy switch moving the portfolio to the longer end of the yield curve in the anticipation of a non-parallel shift in the yield curve.

Non-parallel shifts in the yield curve will, however, alter the relative durations of the bonds and alter the overall sensitivity of the portfolio.

The cash freed by the switch must be invested in cash products otherwise the overall duration of the portfolio will have been altered.

15. (a) $$\frac{(121.38 \times 2.661) + (81.97 \times 3.049)}{121.38 + 81.97} = 2.817$$

(b) US Treasury – Semi-annual basis

Eurobond – Annual basis

$$\frac{6.40}{2} = 3.20 \Rightarrow (1 + r)^2 - 1 = (1.032)^2 - 1 = 6.50$$

Plus mark-up

$$6.50 + 4.50 = 11.00$$

$$\text{Price} = \frac{10}{1.11} + \frac{10}{(1.11)^2} + \frac{110}{(1.11)^3} = 97.56$$

(c) Duration of Brazilian bond

$$\frac{1\times PV_1 + 2\times PV_2 + 3\times PV_3}{\text{Price}}$$

$$\frac{(1\times 9.01) + (2\times 8.12)+(3\times 80.43)}{97.56} = 2.732$$

Russian bond portfolio = 121.38 + 81.97 = 203.35

Using a modified duration hedge ratio

$$203.35 \times \frac{2.817/1.107}{2.732/1.11} = 210.245$$

In terms of nominal value

$$\frac{210.245}{97.56} = 215.5$$

or $2,155,000

(d) Basis risk

- The risk of an uneven yield change.
- Convexity.
- The risk of different credit risk changes.

Also

Practical issues of being able to buy the appropriate amount of the Brazilian bond.

16. (a) $\$1 \text{ million} \times \frac{112.812}{100} + \$1 \text{ million} \times \frac{106.482}{100}$

1,128,120 + 1,064,820 = 2,192,940

(b) 10% Bond $\frac{320.298}{112.812} = 2.839$

8% Bond $\frac{301.192}{106.482} = 2.829$

Portfolio $= [\frac{1128}{2193} \times 2.839] + [\frac{1065}{2193} \times 2.829] = 2.834$

(c) $2193 \times \frac{2.834}{1.07806} \times \frac{1.0}{100} = -57,652$

Workings

Conversion of the yield into true annualised form

6.50% = 3.25% per $^1/_2$ year

$(1 + r)^2 - 1$	= 6.606	
	1.200	mark-up (per question)
	7.806	

10% 2002

	Jan 1999	Jan 2000	Jan 2001	Jan 2002
4m	10	10	10	110
	$^1/_3$	$1^1/_3$	$2^1/_3$	$3^1/_3$

$$\frac{10}{(1.07806)^{1/3}}+\frac{10}{(1.07806)^{1^1/_3}}+\frac{10}{(1.07806)^{2^1/_3}}+\frac{110}{(1.07806)^{3^1/_3}}$$

112.812 =	9.753	9.046	8.391	85.622
	× $^1/_3$	× $1^1/_3$	× $2^1/_3$	× $3^1/_3$
320.298 =	3.251	12.062	19.580	285.405

(Note that another approach would have been to evaluate the bond at the next coupon date and then discount the resultant value back, but since we were required to compute duration, this would have been inadequate.)

8% 2002

	Jan 1999	Jan 2000	Jan 2001	Jan 2002
4m	10	10	10	110
	$^1/_4$	$1^1/_4$	$2^1/_4$	$3^1/_4$

106.482 =	7.851	7.283	6.755	84.593
	× $^1/_4$	× $1^1/_4$	× $2^1/_4$	× $3^1/_4$
301.192 =	1.963	9.103	15.199	274.927

17. The main factors that will be taken into account for a corporate borrower are as follows.

- **Industry environment**

  Key to the analysis of the business must be the overall prospects for the industry.

- **Competitive position**

  How does the company fit within the industry?

- **Accounting data**

  This begins with a full review of the accounting policies adopted by the firm. Much of the ratio analysis applied by the rating agencies is driven by the cash flow statement.

- **Management's financial policy**

  The management's philosophy is explored in order to assess the resilience of the firm to changes in the future.

- **Profitability**

  The earnings power of the company is one of the most important gauges of a company's ability to meet its obligations.

- **Financial leverage and asset protection**

  Obviously one of the key determinants of the company's credit rating is the current level of gearing.

- **Cash flow adequacy**

  Comparison of the company's historical and projected cash requirement with its ability to generate funds internally.

- **Financial flexibility**

  How capable is the company of dealing with potential shocks?

- **State ownership and local ownership blocks**

  The impact of state ownership and local ownership blocks can be substantial in some economies.

- **Access to local sources of finance**

  Local market strength may allow the company access to finance in times of stress.

18. Stock is currently A, which is still an investment grade stock, albeit with a degree of repayment risk.

The credit watch is likely to signal a downgrading of the credit status of the stock. However, this may not happen and the current rating may be affirmed, or increased.

Even if the bond were downgraded to BBB it would still retain its investment grade status. Only if the review downgrades the rating to BB would the bond be classified as speculative.

The impact of the review will be to increase yields and therefore reduce the value of the bond. The shift from A to BBB is likely to result in a rise in yields of between 25-40 bp.

The credit watch itself will involve a closer monitoring of the company and its prospects.

Impact on the Fund

- If the bond was bought with the intention of holding to maturity then as such there is only the opportunity cost of the fall in the secondary market value.

However, there is the increased risk of default in the future.

- If the fund now covenants limiting its exposure to speculative grade securities then these limits may be breached.
- Overall, the risk of the portfolio has been increased with no enhancement of return.

Actions

The market price will already reflect the possible outcome of the credit watch. The full implication of a downgrade may not be factored into the price. However, any sale to limit losses will obviously preclude gains to be made from a potential affirmation of the rating.

19. *Tutor's note: this is a report, therefore construct in report format, i.e. To, From,etc.*

A callable bond is a bond that can be redeemed prior to the set final redemption date. In this instance, the option of early redemption lies with the issuer, hence the term callable bond. If the right had been given to the holder it would be referred to as a putable bond. An example of a callable bond would be one of the UK Government Gilts; Treasury 13½% 2004-08. In this case, the government has the right to redeem the bond from 2004 but must have redeemed it by the final redemption date in 2008. With most callable bonds the call right is not as explicit as in this example and the bond will be stated as though it were just a simple bullet bond with one redemption date. Within the terms of the bond there will then be the possibility of early redemption.

Duration

Duration is problematic due to the variability of the maturity and coupon flow. The most likely basis for working out duration is to take the assumption that one or other of the extreme points makes a logical choice. This will be determined by the coupon rate offered on the bond and your expectation of yield into the market and may indeed be determined by the current price. What is the market on consensus building on this basis? The only problem with using this method for working out duration is that if market circumstances and expectations change abruptly, then the duration of a portfolio could change significantly, as a bond which had been categorised as redeeming in five years shifts to a ten year redemption point, consequently moving duration.

Convexity

Convexity is normally based upon the duration measure you have chosen previously. The only issue is that with a callable bond there will be negative convexity as the price rises towards the call price.

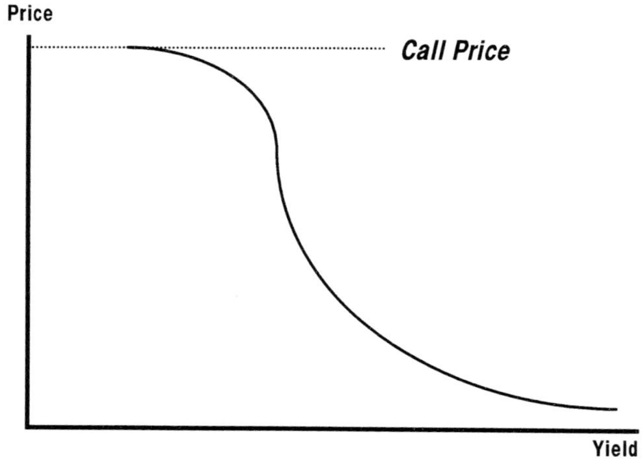

Yield

The logic is that the yield price relationship will no longer hold as the price rises towards the redemption point, since the bond will be redeemed at the redemption value and not at any higher price.

Overall, callable bonds do represent a problem for any fund, in that they have the capacity to change from being a medium-dated bond to a long-dated bond, depending on market circumstance. Therefore, of course, the fund has no control over these bonds, the right to call lying firmly with the issuer.

10 Derivatives

INTRODUCTION

Futures and options provide investors with tools that allow them to speculate on the change in the price of some asset. They also provide tools that facilitate efficient management and risk control within a fund.

We therefore need to be familiar with the basic characteristics of futures and options, with the characteristics of some specific contracts that may be useful to the fixed income investor and with how these instruments may be used by either fund managers or speculators.

Questions regularly arise from the ideas in this chapter

CHAPTER CONTENTS

Chapter Learning Objectives

The syllabus areas covered by this section are

Form and Structure of Securities

Students should be familiar with the form and structure of fixed income securities.

- Call features
- Embedded options

Analysis

Students should possess a broad understanding of both static and dynamic methods for the analysis and construction of fixed income securities containing both certain and contingent cashflows. Variable rate securities will be included. Students should be aware of the limitations of assumptions and mathematical techniques upon results. Although analysis will be concerned principally with 'risk–free' securities, students should be aware of the further considerations for 'risky' securities and the effect they may have on expected return. Students should possess a thorough comprehension of single–period and multi–period, single currency and multi–currency portfolio management theory.

Swap analysis

- Interest rate and currency

Security and portfolio management techniques

Risk Assessment

- Basis and hedging

Students will not be required to perform higher mathematical calculations, to derive any theoretical proofs, or to know any formulae other than for the topics marked (*) above to satisfy the requirements of the paper. Should other formulae be necessary they will be given. An awareness of the limitations of the mathematical techniques is necessary. Students may expect applications of analytic techniques in practical examples.

1 Introduction

Exam tip

> Questions from this chapter tend to either be basic definitions in Section A (e.g. Winter 2008 Questions 5 and 6, Summer 2008 Question 2, Winter 2006 Question 7, Summer 2006 Question 3, Winter 2005 Question 3), or more detailed discussions of their fund management uses in optional 15 mark Section C questions (e.g. Winter 2006 Question 12, Summer 2002 Question 17).

In the minds of the general public, and indeed those of many people involved in the financial services industry, futures and options are considered to be very complicated. They also seem to have little to do with the real world. Television coverage showing pictures of young traders in brightly coloured jackets shouting at each other in an apparent frenzy makes it difficult to imagine that what they are engaged in may be of enormous value to the smooth functioning of the economy.

At the heart of futures and options is the concept of deferred delivery. Both instruments allow you, albeit in slightly different ways, to agree **today** the price at which you will buy or sell an asset at sometime in the future. This approach differs from normal everyday transactions. When we go to a supermarket, we pay our money and take immediate delivery of our goods. Why would someone wish to agree today a price for delivery at sometime in the future? The answer is **certainty**.

Imagine a farmer growing a crop of wheat. To grow such a crop costs money: money for seed, labour, fertiliser and so on. All this expenditure takes place with no certainty that when the crop is eventually harvested, the price at which the wheat is sold will cover these costs. This is obviously a risky thing to do and many farmers will be unwilling to take on this burden. How can this uncertainty be avoided?

By using futures or options, the farmer will be able to agree **today** a price at which the crop will ultimately be sold in maybe four or six months' time. This enables the farmer to achieve a minimum sale price for his crop. He is no longer subject to fluctuations in wheat prices. He knows what price his wheat will bring and can thus plan his business accordingly.

From their origins in the agricultural world, futures and options have become available on a wide range of other assets, from metals and crude oil to bonds and equities. To understand futures and options properly requires some application. There is the relevant terminology to master, and definitions to be understood but, at heart, they are really quite simple. They are products which allow you to fix today the price at which assets may be bought or sold at a future date.

2 Futures

2.1 Definition of a future

> A future is an agreement to buy or sell a standard quantity of a specified asset on a fixed future date at a price agreed today.

There are two parties to a futures contract, a buyer and a seller whose obligations are as follows.

- The buyer of a future enters into an **obligation** to buy on a specified date.
- The seller of a future is under an **obligation** to sell on a future date.

These obligations relate to a **standard quantity** of a **specified** asset on a **fixed future date** at a **price agreed today**.

2.1.1 Standard quantity

Exchange-traded futures are traded in standardised parcels known as **contracts**.

For example, a futures contract on lead might be for 25 tonnes of the metal, or a currency future might be for €125,000. The purpose of this standardisation is so that buyers and sellers are clear about the quantity that will be delivered. If you sold one lead future, you would know that you were obligated to sell 25 tonnes of lead.

Futures are only traded in whole numbers of contracts. So, if you wished to buy 50 tonnes of lead, you would buy two lead futures.

2.1.2 Specified asset

Imagine that you entered into a futures contract on a car. Let us say you buy one car futures contract that gives you the obligation to buy a car at a fixed price of £15,000, with delivery taking place in December.

It is obvious that something very important is missing from the contract, namely any detail about what type of car you are to buy. Most of us would be happy to pay £15,000 for a Porsche, but rather less happy if all our £15,000 bought was a Citroen 2CV.

All futures contracts are governed by their contract specifications, and these legal documents set out in great detail the size of each contract, when delivery is to take place, and what exactly is to be delivered. It is not enough to know that a lead futures contract is for 25 tonnes of the metal. Users will also want to know the level of purity and shape of the metal in which they are dealing.

2.1.3 Fixed futures date

The delivery of futures contracts takes place on a specified date(s) known as **delivery day(s)**. This is when buyers exchange money for goods with sellers. Futures have finite lifespans so that once the **last trading day** is past, it is impossible to trade the futures for that date.

At any one time, a range of delivery months may be traded, and as one delivery day passes a new date is introduced.

2.1.4 Price agreed today

The final phrase in the definition is the most important of all. The reason why so many people, from farmers to fund managers, like using futures is (as was explained in the introduction to this chapter) that they introduce certainty.

Imagine a farmer growing a crop of wheat. In the absence of a futures market, he has no idea whether he will make a profit or a loss when he plants the seeds in the ground. By the time he harvests his crop, the price of wheat may be so low that he will not be able to cover his costs. However, with a futures contract, he can fix a price for his wheat many months before harvest. If, six months before the harvest, he sells a wheat future, he enters into an obligation to sell wheat at that price on the stipulated delivery day. In other words, he knows what price his goods will fetch.

You might think that this is all well and good, but what happens if there is a drought or a frost which makes it impossible for the farmer to deliver his wheat?

Futures are tradeable, so although the contract obligates the buyer to buy and the seller to sell, these obligations can be **offset** by undertaking an equal and opposite trade in the market.

For example, let us suppose a farmer has sold 1 September wheat future at £120 per tonne. If, subsequently, the farmer decides he does not wish to sell his wheat, but would prefer to use the grain to feed his cattle, he simply buys 1 September future at the then prevailing price. His original sold position is now offset by a bought position, leaving him with no outstanding delivery obligations.

This offsetting is common in future markets; very few contracts run through to delivery.

2.1.5 Margining

When futures positions are opened, an initial deposit of collateral is required by the clearing house to ensure that potential future losses can be met – this is known as **initial margin**. The profit or loss associated with a futures position is the number of ticks movement multiplied by the tick size. Daily profits and losses associated with a position have to be paid to or are received from the clearing house, via a system known as daily settlement. The daily payments are referred to as **variation margin**.

The variation margining system ensures that margin deposits are adjusted for market movements, so that adequate collateral is in place at all times. As futures are margined, large trading positions can be taken with relatively small amounts of capital, since only the initial and variation margin payments have to be met, rather than the full value of the underlying bonds. This has the effect of **gearing** potential profits and losses, making futures markets attractive to speculators.

2.1.6 Clearing house

Role of the clearing house

A **clearing house** is a highly capitalised central counterparty for all exchange traded transactions.

Whenever a deal is undertaken between two traders in a system involving a clearing house the deal is effectively split and, through a process called novation, the clearing house becomes the counterparty to each side of the trade, guaranteeing that trade. Its high capitalisation endows the clearing house with a very strong status as a counterparty – its credit standing being much higher than that of almost any trading counterparty.

For derivative products, that credit standing is further enhanced through the operation of a standard margining system under which gains and losses may be realised on a daily basis, limiting the clearing houses risk exposure.

Clearing houses also offer an important market oversight role that is not present in the current system. Fulfilling such a function is essential in a major market

The advantages of a clearing house are, therefore:

- The existence of a highly capitalised central counterparty.
- The existence of a standard margin system
- The existence of an oversight system to ensure market stability
- Standardisation of products and contracts, removing some of the differences that arise in bilateral agreements.
- Potentially, a wider range of investments
- More liquid markets – with more people trading, market liquidity should improve markedly.
- Cheaper trading arising through economies of scale, though this depends on the efficiency of the settlement agencies.
- Cost savings to investors who will only need to understand the one standard product and only need the one settlement platform, reducing back office costs.

Clearing house risks

The prerequisites to operating as a clearing house are

- Very high capitalisation levels validating the role of central counterparty
- Highly efficient systems, processes and procedures in order to accurately fulfil the clearing function on a timely basis.

- The adoption of an appropriate margin system in order to minimise the clearing house exposure.

The risks major faced by a clearing house would result form anything that may adversely effect these primary requirements and would include

- The failure of a counterparty – potentially leaving the clearing house with an uncovered position and a shortfall in margin. In such a situation the clearing house would enter the market as principal, entering a trade to balance the position inherited. In addition, any initial margin payment would, in probability, cover the margin requirements for that day so the effects should be minimised.
- The failure of a major market participant – and the possible consequent disruption to markets.
- The loss of capital that could result from a counterparty failure in extreme circumstances or with extreme positions – a position risk limit would be advisable.
- Systems failures – the losses that could result from errors and failures in the clearing system and the likely consequent legal challenges.

Minimising clearing house risks

It therefore follows that clearing house risk can be minimised by

- The adoption of a suitable margin system utilising
  - Initial margin – based on the worst probable single period price movement to cover against a failure whilst the clearing house establishes an offsetting position
  - Variation margin – being the periodic cash settlement of any gains and, more importantly, losses.

  Both of these would most probably be daily, though the facility to call intra-day margins should exist.
- The adoption of a netting system for clients so that their overall exposure can be continuously monitored, along with the adoption of position risk limits to try to ensure that clients are not becoming over-exposed. The clearing house should also have the facility to close out any over-exposed positions.
- Client agreements containing standard procedures for dealing with
  - Systems failures
  - Dispute resolution
  - Refinancing/raising capital in the event of a major default that turns out to be not fully covered

2.2 Futures v Forward contracts

The definition of a forward contract is very similar to that of a future in that it is an agreement to buy or sell a specific quantity of a specified asset on a fixed future date at a price agreed today. The differences between futures and forward contracts can best be summarised in the following table.

Attribute	Futures	Forward Contracts
Traded	Exchange traded	OTC
Quality and Quantity	Standardised by the exchange for all products	Specified in the contract
Delivery Dates	Standard fixed dates	Specified in the contract
Liquidity/Ability to Close Out	Generally good liquidity/easy to close out	May be limited
Counterparty Risk	None due to the workings of the clearing and settlement system	Default risk exists
Costs/Margin	Relatively low initial costs (margin)	Costs specifically agreed, may be high
Regulation	Significant regulation and investor protection	Less regulated

2.3 Price and fair value

2.3.1 Cash/futures relationship

If we were to compare the cash market price of lead with the futures price for delivery in three months, we might observe the following prices.

Cash price of lead $350 per tonne

Three-month future $360 per tonne

Why should the futures price be higher than the cash price? Intuitively, we might think that the futures price is higher because it indicates that the price of lead is due to rise. This explanation of futures pricing is only part of the story. Futures prices are in fact the product of the interplay between a number of factors, including supply and demand in the cash markets, interest rates, sentiment, and practical issues such as dividend yields and transportation costs.

2.3.2 Basis

Basis is the term used to describe the numerical difference between a cash price and a futures price. Basis is normally quoted as the cash price minus the futures price.

Formula to learn

Basis = Cash price – Futures price

Example

Cash price of wheat = £120 per tonne

Price of July future = £125

The basis is therefore

120 – 125 = –5

In this case, the basis is 'negative'; in some markets, this would be described as '£5 under futures'.

If the calculation gave rise to a positive number, the basis would be described as positive or as 'over futures'.

Although cash and futures prices generally move broadly in line with one another, the basis is not constant. During some periods, cash prices move faster than futures. At other times, futures outpace the cash market.

This movement in basis is brought about by a variety of factors. Most important is the relationship between supply and demand. Under normal conditions, futures prices of physical commodities are higher than cash prices. The reasons for this are discussed later, but where futures prices are higher than cash prices, the market is said to be in **contango**.

However, this normal or contango situation in which futures prices are higher than cash prices can be radically altered if there is some short-term lack of supply. If, for example, there is very little zinc available for delivery, the price demanded for what little is available can be very high indeed.

Markets in which futures prices are lower than cash prices are said to be in **backwardation**. The terms contango and backwardation are not used in all markets. Sometimes, when futures are higher than cash prices, the market is said to be at a **premium**; when futures are lower than cash, it is said to be at a **discount**.

The availability of supply, and hence the basis, is also subject to seasonal influences. For example, the wheat market will tend to be oversupplied at harvest time and undersupplied at other times. This will reflect itself in futures prices, where you may see certain months in contango and others in backwardation.

2.3.3 Basis risk

Changes in basis represent a threat and an opportunity to futures users. To illustrate this, let us consider a farmer who has undertaken a short hedge (holds the stock, sells the future) to protect himself against a price fall on 10 February.

	Cash Price		Futures Price		Basis
10 February	140	–	150	=	–10
10 July	120	–	135	=	–15
	(20) Loss		15 Profit		

As can be seen, the hedge has not been entirely effective: a £20 fall in the price of cash wheat has only been partially offset by a £15 gain in the futures market. This difference emerges because the cash price has moved further than the futures price. In other words, there has been a change in basis.

When the basis becomes more negative or less positive, as above, it is said to **weaken**.

When the basis becomes more positive or less negative, it is said to **strengthen**.

Basis changes do occur and thus, they represent potential profits or losses to investors. Notwithstanding the fact that the relationship between cash and futures may vary, the risk this represents is very much smaller than the risk of remaining unhedged. In short, basis risk is smaller than outright risk.

2.3.4 Fair value

For markets where there is an adequate supply of the assets subject to delivery, it is possible to calculate a 'fair' or theoretical price of a future.

The fair value of a future is the price at which investors are indifferent as to whether they buy the underlying asset or the future.

Imagine a jeweller who knows that he will need to buy 5oz of gold to make wedding rings in three months' time. He has two ways in which he can guarantee the price of gold: he can either buy the physical metal now or, alternatively, buy the gold future that will deliver in three months' time.

If he buys physical gold, he will pay for it immediately. The money to finance this purchase will come either from borrowing it or withdrawing it from his bank account. However, if he finances the purchase, there will be an interest rate penalty in the form of paying off his loan, or a loss of interest on his credit balances. In addition, the gold will need to be insured and safely stored between the point of purchase and sale.

If instead he buys the future, he will only pay for the gold in three months' time. In addition, he will also save on storage and insurance costs. Altogether, it would seem that using the future is preferable to buying the gold. However, in futures markets, as in life, money is not given away. The futures price, if it is fairly priced, will incorporate the costs of finance, storage and insurance.

The reasons these costs are included are best explained if we look at the future from the seller's rather than the buyer's perspective. If you were a prudent futures seller, you would not simply sell the future at some arbitrary price. You would calculate how much it would cost you to get the gold to delivery at no risk. This would require that the moment you sold the gold future, you would prepare to meet the delivery obligation by buying cash gold and hold and insure it through to delivery day. As the seller will incur these costs, known collectively as the **cost of carry**, he will add these to the cash price of gold to find the minimum acceptable selling price of the future.

2.3.5 Calculating fair values

Example

Cash gold is $355 per oz, interest rates 5% per annum and insurance and storage charges a further 0.5% per annum.

Calculate the cost of carry by working out how much the cost of finance and other charges will be for a three-month (90-day) period (note that when dealing in US dollars, it is conventional to use a 360-day year.) Then calculate the fair price of the future.

Solution

$$\text{Cash} \times (\text{Interest rate} + \text{Storage/insurance}) \times \frac{\text{Days}}{360}$$

$$\$355 \times 5.5\% \times \frac{90}{360} = \textbf{\$4.88 Cost of carry}$$

To find the fair value, add the cost of carry to the cash price.

$4.88 + $355 = $359.88

The fair value of the three-month future is $359.88.

In the example above, we have calculated the fair value of a gold future. We could equally easily calculate the fair value of other futures, as long as the market has adequate supply. For futures on bonds, equities and currencies the mathematics becomes more complicated, but the same principles apply.

In the gold example above, we calculated the fair value by adding the cash price to the cost of carry.

Formula to learn

Cash price + Cost of carry = Fair value

For a bond index future, such as the UK gilt future, the same calculation is undertaken. However, as the cash asset here is bonds, the carrying charges are different.

If you own a bond, you will receive coupons. Bonds, unlike gold, pay income, therefore, the cost of carry equals the finance cost less the coupons received.

Example

Let us try and price the UK gilt future, given the following information.

Cash Price:	£105
Interest rate:	6% per annum
Coupon yield:	4% per annum
Days until expiry:	91 (182 days in coupon period)

Solution

			(£)
Cash price			105.00
Cost of carry			
■	Interest	$105 \times 6\% \times \frac{91}{365}$	1.57
■	Coupon	$105 \times 2\% \times \frac{91}{182}$	(1.05)
Future price			105.52

When there is restricted availability of the underlying asset and the market is in backwardation, it is impossible to calculate fair values.

2.3.6 Arbitrage

Arbitrage is an activity in which traders (arbitrageurs) seek to make riskless profits from exploiting mispricings between markets.

We have established that for most futures it is possible to calculate a fair value. If the future is not trading at its fair value, this will mean that it is, in theoretical terms, either cheap or expensive. When this occurs, arbitrageurs will sell what is expensive and buy what is cheap, whilst at the same time undertaking an offsetting trade in the cash market. For example, if the future is expensive relative to fair value, the arbitrageur will

- Sell futures and buy underlying asset – a cash & carry arbitrage.

If the future is cheap, he will

- Buy futures and sell underlying asset – a reverse cash & carry arbitrage.

The activity of the arbitrageur in buying 'cheap' assets and selling 'expensive' ones will tend to bring the future back to its correct level. This is because sellers will appear if the future is expensive and drive the price down and vice versa.

Whilst most ordinary investors do not have the low costs necessary to make arbitrage economically viable, the fact that many professionals undertake this activity is highly important, as it maintains the linkage between cash and futures markets.

Although professional traders might theoretically be expected to undertake arbitrage as soon as the future trades at variance to its fair value, even professionals have some costs. Thus, in reality, the future must move some way above or below fair value before arbitrageurs will appear. Exchange fees, taxes and bid/offer spreads all mean that there is an area, known as the arbitrage **channel**, either side of fair value within which arbitrage will not take place. As costs vary between participants, so also does the width of the channel.

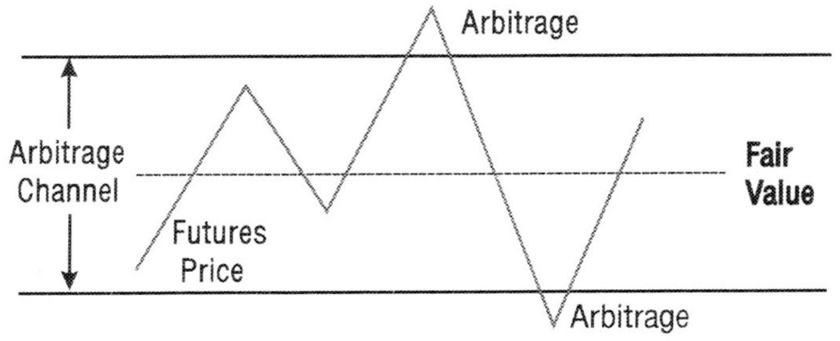

2.3.7 Convergence

Once a future reaches its last trading day, the cost of carry will be nil. At the moment of delivery, the futures market and the cash market will have the same price, as both quotes will be for the immediate delivery of the underlying asset. This coming together of the future and cash is known as **convergence**, and it is the only time in a future's life when it necessarily has the same price as the cash market.

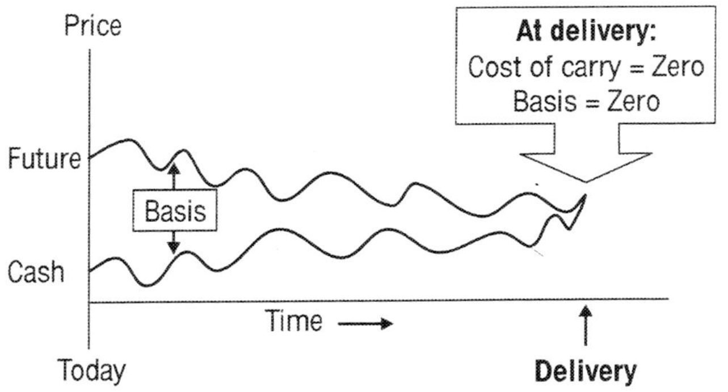

2.4 Using futures

All sorts of people use futures. Some, like the wheat farmer, may use them to reduce risk, others to seek high returns – and for this, be willing to take high risks. Futures markets are in fact wholesale markets in risk. They are markets in which risks are transferred from the cautious to those with more adventurous (or reckless) spirits. The users of futures fall into one of three categories: the **hedger**, the **speculator** and the **arbitrageur**, whose motivations are as follows.

- **Hedger**: someone seeking to reduce risk.
- **Speculator**: a risk taker seeking large profits.
- **Arbitrageur**: seeks riskless profits from exploiting market inefficiencies, it is the activity of arbitrageurs that ensure the above pricing relationship applies.

In the remainder of this section we will look at the use of futures by speculators and hedgers.

2.4.1 The speculator – buying a future

Introduction

A transaction in which a future is purchased to open a position is known as a **long futures position**. Thus, the purchase of the oil future would be described as **going long of the future** or simply **long**.

The purpose of undertaking such a transaction is to open the investor to the risks and rewards of ownership of the underlying asset by an alternative route.

Example

On 1 May, a speculator thinks that the situation in the Middle East is becoming more dangerous and that war is imminent. If war takes place, he would expect oil supplies to become restricted and the price of oil to rise.

The current cash price of oil is $19.00 per barrel, and the futures price is $20.50. The speculator does not have the facilities to store the oil at present.

How can he use the futures market to buy in anticipation of this price rise, and what will his position be if the price rise does occur on 21 May (cash price becoming $35, futures price being $30)?

Solution

Action 1 May: Buy 1 July Oil Future at $20.50

Since he does not have the facilities to store the oil, he cannot use the cash market, hence the speculator could buy 1 July oil future at $20.50 per barrel. Thus, he is now obliged to buy one contract (here 1,000 barrels) to be delivered on 1 July.

Action 21 May: Sell 1 July Oil Future at $30

Following the price rise, our speculator can now sell this contract at $30.00 per barrel, realising a profit of $9.50 per barrel or $9,500.

The reason the speculator has made a profit is that the futures market has risen in response to a rise in the cash market price of oil. Generally, futures prices can be expected to move at substantially the same rate and the same extent as cash market prices. This is a far from trivial observation. The cash market and the futures market in this example have both risen: the cash market from $19 to $35 – an increase of $16 per barrel; and the futures market from $20.50 to $30.00 – a rise of $9.50.

The reasons why the price movement should normally be substantially the same in both markets, and why they may differ, are explained in the next chapter.

Summary of position

Risk	Almost unlimited – The maximum loss would occur if the future fell to zero. For our oil speculator, this would be if the July future fell from $20.50 to 0.
Reward	Unlimited – As the futures price could rise to infinity, the profit is potentially unlimited.

2.4.2 Speculation – selling a future

Introduction

A transaction in which a future is sold to open a position is known as a **short futures position**. Thus, the sale of the oil future would be described as **going short of the future** or simply **short**.

The purpose of undertaking such a transaction is to open the investor to the opposite risks and rewards of ownership of the underlying asset.

Example

On 1 July, a speculator feels that the oil market is becoming oversupplied and that oil prices will fall. On that date, the September futures contract is trading at $22.00 per barrel.

How can the speculator use the futures market to profit from this situation and what will be his profit if the price fall does occur on 14 July, when the futures price has fallen to $20.00 per barrel?

Solution

If a speculator thinks that an asset price will fall, he will seek to make a profit by selling the future at the currently high price and subsequently buying it back at a low price. This is not an activity commonly undertaken in the cash markets and therefore needs a little explanation.

There are two ways of making profits.

- Buy at a low price and sell at a high price. For example, we may buy a house at £80,000 and sell it at £100,000 making a £20,000 profit.
- In futures markets, it is equally easy to sell something at a high price and buy it back at a low price. If you thought the property market was going to fall, you could sell a house at £100,000 and buy it back at £80,000 again realising a £20,000 profit.

In the actual property market, it is not easy to go **short** of a house, but in the futures market, in which deliveries are at some future date, it is straightforward.

Action 1 July: Sell 1 September Oil Future at $22

The speculator is committing himself to delivering an asset he does not own on 1 September.

Action 14 July: Buy 1 September Oil Future at $20.00

By 14 July, the future price has fallen and the speculator **buys back** his short futures position, thus extinguishing any delivery obligations. The profit can be calculated again as $2.00 per barrel or $2,000 in total.

Summary of position

Risk	Unlimited.
Reward	Limited, but large. The future can only fall to zero.

2.4.3 Hedging – protecting against a fall

Speculators use futures to take on risks in the hope of large profits. Hedgers use futures to reduce the risk of existing cash market positions. They are motivated by a need for certainty and security.

Let us think about the position of an oil producer. The producer's profitability will be determined largely by the price of crude oil. When times are good, and the demand for oil is high, he will make good profits. However, if oil prices fall, he may find that the market price for oil is so low that the price does not cover the costs of extracting the oil from the ground. It is in helping people such as this that futures have their most important application.

The following graph shows the oil producer's exposure to the price of oil.

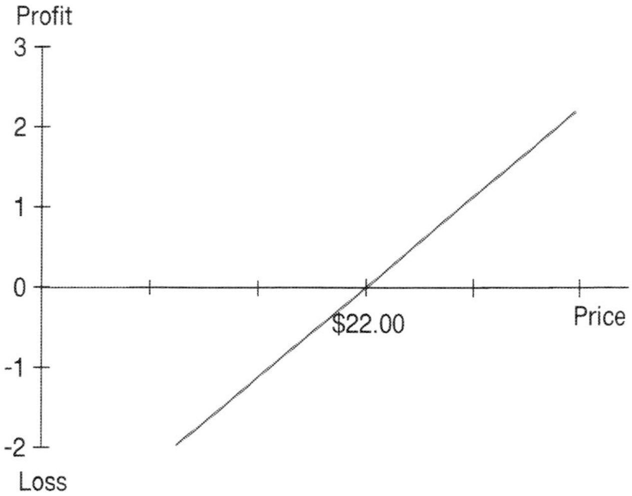

This shows that if prices go up, so do profits; if the price falls below a certain level, losses will emerge. This position is described as a **long position**.

How can the risk from a fall in price be reduced?

This can be done by selling futures and thereby entering into a contract that will obligate the futures seller to deliver oil at some time in the future at a price agreed today.

Through this mechanism, the oil producer can establish a sale price for his, say, July production of oil some time in advance, without having to wait until July when the price may be much lower. When futures are sold to hedge a long cash market position, it is known as a **short hedge**.

The theory of futures hedging is based on the future's position, producing profits or losses to offset the losses or profits in the cash market.

Example

An oil producer will have 100,000 barrels of crude oil available for delivery in July. He is nervous about the price of oil and expects it to fall sharply. On 1 May, the cash market price of oil is $22 a barrel, and the July future is trading at $23.

How can he use the futures market to hedge his position and minimise the risk of owning the asset (note, one contract is 1,000 barrels), and what will his position be if by 15 June the price has fallen to $18 in the cash market and $19 in the futures market?

Solution

Action 1 May: Sell 100 July Oil Futures at $23

(100 because each contract represents 1,000 barrels, and the producer is hedging 100,000 barrels.)

The oil producer is now long in the physical market (that is, he has 100,000 barrels for July delivery). He is also short 100,000 barrels in the futures market.

Action 15 June: Buy 100 July Oil Futures at $19

The profit from the futures trade should, if we have constructed the hedge properly, compensate the producer for the fall in oil prices. Let us see if this is true by first calculating the futures profit and then calculating the oil market loss.

Futures profit

Profit per barrel = \$4.00 per barrel (\$23.00 – \$19.00)
Total profit = \$400,000 (\$4.00 × 100,000 barrels)

Cash market loss

Loss per barrel = \$4.00 per barrel (\$18.00 – \$22.00)
Total loss = \$400,000 (\$4.00 × 100,000 barrels)

As can be seen, the profit and loss net each other out, demonstrating that the fall in oil prices did not hurt the producer.

It can be shown on a graph as follows.

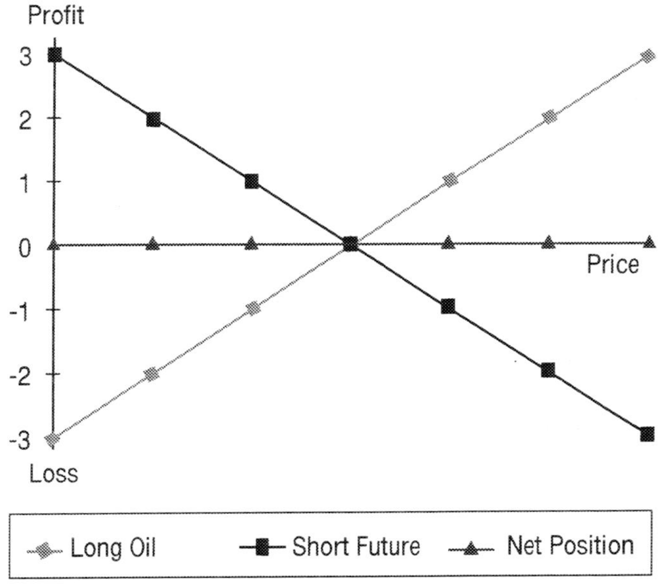

Whether the price of oil goes up or down, the producer need not worry as he has, by selling futures, **locked in** a sale price for his oil.

The numbers in this example are slightly unrealistic, as there is a perfect offset between cash and futures markets. In the real world, futures do not always move precisely in line with the cash market. This point will be examined in more detail later on.

In the example above, we have seen how futures can be used to protect the oil producer against a price fall with a short hedge.

Short hedge: Protects against price fall

2.4.4 Hedging – protecting against a rise

The scenario that we are considering here is that an investor wishes to acquire an asset at some time in the future when cash is available, but is concerned that the current price may rise making the asset unaffordable. He therefore wishes to protect against this price rise.

Example

A chemical company, whose principal raw material is crude oil, is becoming nervous about a rise in oil prices.

The current cash price of crude oil is \$18.00, and the November future trades at \$18.50 per barrel.

How can the company use the futures market to hedge against any price rise and what will their position be if the cash price rises to \$24.00 and the futures price to \$24.50 on 10 October?

Solution

To protect itself against the possibility of a rise, the company could agree today the price it will pay for oil to be delivered in November. To guarantee the purchase price, all the company need do is buy or go long in the futures contract.

Action 20 September: Buy 10 November Oil Futures at $18.50

(To hedge its requirement for 10,000 barrels)

Action 10 October: Sell 10 November Oil Futures at $24.50

Has the hedge worked?

Cash market loss

To find out, let us see how the price rise would have affected the cost of purchasing the physical oil.

	£
Cash price on 10 October	24.00
Cash price on 20 September	18.00
Cost increase per barrel	6.00

For the quantity required by the chemical manufacturer (10,000 barrels), this movement would have increased its costs by $60,000 ($6 × 10,000).

This increased cost should, in whole or in part, be offset by the futures profit.

Futures profit

	£
Futures price on 10 October	24.50
Futures price on 20 September	18.50
Futures profit per barrel	6.00

Hence, the total profit on the futures contract is $60,000, which covers the price increase.

Thus, whilst the physical oil will now cost more to acquire, the extra cost of purchase will in fact be covered by the futures profit.

	£
Cash price of 10,000 barrels of oil at 10 October	240,000
Less futures profit	(60,000)
Net cost	180,000

This equates to $18 per barrel, the cash price on 20 September.

This is an example of a long hedge, which protects against a rise.

Long hedge: Protects against a rise

2.4.5 Summary

In short hedges, you sell futures to protect an existing holding.

In long hedges, you buy futures to protect an anticipated holding.

2.4.6 Cross-hedging

Unfortunately, it may be the case that there is no futures contract based on the underlying cash instrument to be hedged, and a contract based on a similar underlying must be used. This is known as cross-hedging.

In such a situation, the hedged asset and the futures contract may not move together precisely. As a result, the investor will end up with some residual risk. This risk will depend on such factors as

- Risk levels of the two instruments.
- Coupon levels.
- Maturity dates.
- Time span covered by the hedged underlying instrument and the instrument delivered under the future.

2.5 Some specific contracts and their uses

2.5.1 Introduction

In order to understand the use of futures to a fund manager we need to be familiar with contracts he may wish to use, how he may use them and why. We consider three contracts, in particular

- Three-month sterling future.
- UK gilt future.

One bit of terminology we will introduce here is the **tick**. There are two aspects to this.

- The **tick size** is the smallest permitted quote movement on one contract.
- The **tick value** is the change in the value of one contract if there is a one-tick change in the quote.

These two factors enable us to calculate our futures dealing profit or loss by using

Formula to learn

Profit = Quote change in ticks × Tick value × Number of contracts

When we look at the Three-Month Sterling Futures contract in particular, it will be most convenient to calculate the profit this way.

2.5.2 Three-month sterling future

Purpose and characteristics

The purpose of the three-month sterling contract is to provide a means to gain or hedge interest rate exposure for a period of three months from a given future date.

The general characteristics of the contract are as follows.

Unit of trade

The unit of trade = £500,000, i.e. the contract measures the effects on the total interest costs of interest rate changes on a notional borrowing of £500,000 for three months.

Note. The £500,000 does not change hands, just the interest effect.

Delivery

This contract is **cash settled**, that is the two parties simply settle up by the payment from one to the other of the difference in value between the interest bill for three months at the rate agreed when the contract was traded and the actual rate that arises.

Quotation

Formula to learn

> Quotation = 100 – Rate of interest

where the rate of interest is the **forward rate** for the three months from the delivery date. Hence, if three-month forward rates from the delivery date are 8%, the contract will be quoted at 92 (100 – 8). Note, this is a forward money market rate, ie forward rate calculated based on the simple rate convention applied in that market.

Tick

The tick size, the smallest permitted quote movement, is 0.01, i.e. one basis point, which corresponds to a tick value of £12.50 (£500,000 × 0.01% × $^3/_{12}$).

Uses

As we indicated above, we may use this contract to gain exposure to, or hedge exposure against, interest rate movements.

Example

If a speculator believes interest rates will, say, rise, then he will know that this contract will fall in value. He could then open his position by selling now at a high price and buying to close his position later, realising a profit if his view turns out to be correct.

Three-month forward rates from June are currently quoted as 8.26%. The speculator sells 107 contracts now (January) and closes out his position in May when the three-month forward rates from June have moved to 9.14%. What gain does he make?

Solution

	Forward Rate	Quote
Sell in January	8.26%	91.74
Buy in May	9.14%	90.86
		0.88 = 88 ticks

Hence, the total profit on the 107 contracts will be

Profit = Ticks × Tick value × Number of contracts
= 88 × £12.50 × 107 = £117,700

Example

An investor wants to borrow £5m for three months from June, but is worried that interest rates will rise from their current levels. The forward rate for three months from June is currently quoted as 7.23%.

What action should the borrower take now?

If the rate has risen to 8.8% by June, what position will he be in?

Solution

Action now

If the borrower is correct that interest rates are rising, then he will suffer a higher interest burden than at present. He therefore needs a futures position that will yield profits when interest rates rise to offset this loss. Hence, as for our speculator above, he should sell futures contracts, and in particular sell ten contracts, since each one will hedge £500,000 of the loan.

Final position

Cash position

	(£)
Interest actually paid on loan £5m × 8.80% × $^3/_{12}$	110,000
Interest due at original rate £5m × 7.23% × $^3/_{12}$	90,375
Extra interest suffered	19,625

Futures position

	Forward Rate	Quote	
Sell in January	7.23%	92.77	
Buy in June	8.80%	91.20	
		1.57	= 157 ticks

Hence, the total profit on the 10 contracts will be

Profit = Ticks × Tick value × Number of contracts
= 157 × £12.50 × 10 = £19,625

and will exactly offset the extra interest suffered.

2.5.3 UK gilt future

Purpose and characteristics

The purpose of UK Gilt futures contract is to provide a means to gain or hedge exposure to UK gilts. It can be considered as similar to the FTSE Index futures in that it can be used in the management of bond funds to hedge or gain exposure. It effectively represents a bond index contract.

The general characteristics of the contract are as follows.

Unit of trade/Lot size/Contract size

The unit of trade = £100,000 nominal of a notional 6% gilt, i.e. gilts with a nominal value of £100,000.

Delivery

This contract is **physically settled**, that is the seller of the future must deliver gilts and the buyer must pay the pre-agreed price. Clearly, however, there is a problem here with the contract being based on a notional gilt. To overcome this difficulty the exchange specify a range of eligible deliverable gilts for each delivery date that the seller may choose to satisfy delivery, and the seller decides which gilts he delivers. The decision is always to deliver whichever is cheapest at the delivery date, referred to as the cheapest to deliver (CTD).

These eligible deliverable gilts all have differing maturities and coupons, hence differing prices and differing interest rate sensitivities. To try to cater for these price and sensitivity differentials, the exchange calculates a **price factor** or **conversion factor** or **delivery factor** for each deliverable gilt before trading starts in the contract, i.e. a scaling factor that will be applied to the futures price in order to determine the price actually paid for the delivered gilt. The relationship between the price of the CTD and that of the future being

Formula to learn

CTD gilt price = Futures price × Price factor

The seller of the future also has the choice as to which date to make delivery. The contract is due for delivery on any day in the delivery month. The seller will therefore decide whether he would prefer to receive the accrued interest from holding the gilt for the month, or hold cash on deposit earning interest.

If interest rates are low compared to the coupon rate, then he will hold the gilt as long as possible, making delivery on the last day. If, however, interest rates are high compared to coupon rates, then he will deliver on the earliest date and hold cash.

Quotation

The quotation is similar to gilts quotes, i.e. price per £100 of nominal value.

Tick

The tick size, the smallest permitted quote movement, is £0.01 per £100 nominal value, which corresponds to a tick value of £10 (£100,000 × 0.01 × $^1/_{100}$).

Uses

As we indicated above, we may use this contract to gain exposure to, or hedge exposure against, movements in bond markets.

Example

We are managing a £20m bond portfolio and we believe that the market is about to fall. The gilt future currently stand at 105.

The alternatives that we have are as follows.

- Sell the portfolio and move into cash – this will avoid the market fall, but will clearly incur massive dealing costs.
- Set up a short hedge using the futures contract.

Short hedge

The future is quoted at 105, hence each contract will hedge £105,000 (£105 × $\frac{100,000}{100}$) of our exposure.

To hedge the full portfolio, we will therefore need 190.48 contracts (£20m ÷ £105,000). However, we can only deal in whole contracts, therefore we will sell 190 contracts (the closest whole number).

Let us now consider what our position is if the portfolio (and the futures contract) fall 10% points.

Cash position

	(£)
Old portfolio value	20,000,000
New portfolio value = £20m × 90%	18,000,000
Loss	2,000,000

Futures position

	Points
Sold at	105.00
Bought to close position at (105 × 90%)	94.50
Gain	10.50 = 1,050 ticks

Hence, the total profit on our 190 contracts will be

Profit = Ticks × Tick value × Number of contracts
= 1,050 × £10.00 × 190 = £1,995,000

As we can see, our futures profit almost exactly cancels the loss on the portfolio and hence represents a good hedging strategy.

2.5.4 Hedge ratio

Exam tip

Last examined in Summer 2008 Question 2, Winter 2007 Question 2.

One assumption we have made here is that our portfolio has the same volatility as the future. If this is not the case, then we may need to sell more or less contracts to achieve the hedge. The important determinant is the relative volatility.

If our portfolio is 10% more volatile than the future we will incur a 10% bigger loss on the asset. To hedge this we will need a 10% larger gain on the futures contract which can only be achieved by having 10% more, or 1.1 times as many, futures contracts. this 1.1 is our hedge ratio here and to hedge with futures, we should use

$$\text{Number of contracts} = \frac{\text{Portfolio value}}{\text{Futures value}} \times h$$

where h is the hedge ratio, which reflects the relative volatilities of the portfolio and the hedging instrument. For the Gilt future

$$h = \frac{\text{Modified duration of portfolio}}{\text{Modified duration of future}}$$

Number of contracts to hedge a portfolio – Method 1

Pulling these ideas together, the number of contracts to hedge a portfolio can be calculated as

$$\text{Number of contracts} = \frac{\text{Portfolio value}}{\text{Futures value}} \times \frac{\text{Portfolio MD}}{\text{Futures MD}}$$

Where MD = modified duration

One question that is left, however, is what is the modified duration of the gilt futures contract, ie. what will be the percentage change in the price of that contract for a 1% change in yields? The answer here is that it is the same as the modified duration of the CTD. Remember that we have.

CTD gilt price = Futures price × Price factor

Since the price factor is fixed, a 10% change in the price of the CTD will result in a 10% change in the price of the future, i.e. they have equivalent volatilities or equivalent modified durations. As a result, we may alternatively write this expression as

$$\text{Number of contracts} = \frac{\text{Portfolio value}}{\text{Futures value}} \times \frac{\text{Portfolio MD}}{\text{CTD MD}}$$

Basis point value

Modified duration expresses the sensitivity of a bond's price to a change in yield. Thus, if a bond has a modified duration of 8.62, this would imply that for a 1bp change in price the bond would change in price by 0.0862%. To convert this sensitivity into a price change, we would simply multiply by the current market price. For example, for a bond with a modified duration of 8.62 and a market price of £100, the fluctuation in price for a 1bp movement would be £0.862.

The present value of a basis point (PVBP) measures the absolute change in the price of a bond for a 1 basis point (0.01%) change in yield.

To find the PVBP one undertakes the following calculation.

Formula to learn

$$\text{PVBP} = \text{Modified duration} \times \text{Dirty price of bond} \times 0.0001$$

For example, for a bond with a modified duration of 3.5 years and a dirty market price of 98

$$\text{PVBP} = 3.5 \times 98 \times 0.0001 = 0.0343$$

Sometimes, the PVBP is shown as the impact on £100,000 nom rather than £100 nom as above.

Number of contracts to hedge a portfolio – method 2

Depending on the information provided, the earlier calculation may or may not be the most convenient way of assessing the required number of contracts to hedge a portfolio. The following shows an algebraic rearrangement that brings us to an alternative formulation. It is useful for those who are interested, however all that is needed for the exam is the final result.

The formulation above is

$$\text{Number of contracts} = \frac{\text{Portfolio value}}{\text{Futures value}} \times \frac{\text{Portfolio MD}}{\text{CTD MD}}$$

Now

$$\text{CTD gilt price} = \text{Futures price} \times \text{PF}$$

where PF = Price factor of the CTD, hence

$$\text{CTD value} = \text{Futures value} \times \text{PF}$$

or

$$\text{Futures value} = \frac{\text{CTD value}}{\text{PF}}$$

giving

$$= \frac{\text{PF}}{\text{CTD value}}$$

Substituting this in the original formulation gives

$$\text{Number of contracts} = \frac{\text{Portfolio value} \times \text{PF}}{\text{CTD value}} \times \frac{\text{Portfolio MD}}{\text{CTD MD}}$$

or

$$\text{Number of contracts} = \frac{\text{Portfolio value}}{\text{CTD value}} \times \text{PF} \times \frac{\text{Portfolio MD}}{\text{CTD MD}}$$

Now this could be broken down further as

$$\text{Number of contracts} = \frac{\text{Portfolio nominal} \times \text{Portfolio price}}{\text{CTD nominal} \times \text{CTD price}} \times \text{PF} \times \frac{\text{Portfolio MD}}{\text{CTD MD}}$$

Which could be expanded to

$$\text{Number of contracts} = \frac{\text{Portfolio nominal}}{\text{CTD nominal}} \times \frac{\text{Portfolio price}}{\text{CTD price}} \times \text{PF} \times \frac{\text{Portfolio MD}}{\text{CTD MD}}$$

Which could then be rearranged as

$$\text{Number of contracts} = \frac{\text{Portfolio nominal}}{\text{CTD nominal}} \times \text{PF} \times \frac{\text{Portfolio price}}{\text{CTD price}} \times \frac{\text{Portfolio MD}}{\text{CTD MD}}$$

or

$$\text{Number of contracts} = \frac{\text{Portfolio nominal}}{\text{CTD nominal}} \times \text{PF} \times \frac{\text{Portfolio price} \times \text{Portfolio MD}}{\text{CTD price} \times \text{CTD MD}}$$

Now we defined earlier

$$\text{PVBP} = \text{MD} \times \text{Bond price} \times 0.0001$$

And so substituting this into the top and bottom lines of the last part of this formula gives

$$\text{Number of contracts} = \frac{\text{Portfolio nominal}}{\text{CTD nominal}} \times \text{PF} \times \frac{\text{PVBP of portfolio}}{\text{PVBP of CTD}}$$

Please note once again, you do not need to learn the above algebraic rearrangement, but you do need to be comfortable with the conclusion summarised below.

Number of contracts to hedge a portfolio – summary

We therefore have two equally valid alternatives for calculating the number of contracts to hedge a portfolio

$$\text{Number of contracts} = \frac{\text{Portfolio value}}{\text{Futures value}} \times \frac{\text{Portfolio MD}}{\text{Futures CTD MD}}$$

or

Formula to learn

$$\text{Number of contracts} = \frac{\text{Portfolio nominal}}{\text{CTD nominal}} \times \text{PF} \times \frac{\text{PVBP of portfolio}}{\text{PVBP of CTD}}$$

Which of these to apply depends on the information given in any question.

Example

The cheapest-to-deliver gilt trades at a dirty price of £108.125, with a modified duration of 7.12 and has a price factor of 1.17124.

A bond to be hedged trades at a dirty price of £102.3125 and has a modified duration of 5.37. You are long 2,000,000 nom of this bond. How many futures should be sold to hedge this position?

Solution

Alternative 1

Applying the original formula

$$\text{Number of contracts} = \frac{\text{Portfolio value}}{\text{Futures value}} \times \frac{\text{Portfolio MD}}{\text{CTD MD}}$$

We are given

Portfolio nominal = 2,000,000
Portfolio (bond) price = £102.3125
Portfolio (bond) MD = –5.37
CTD price = £108.125
CTD MD = 7.12
PF = 1.17124

So

$$\text{Portfolio value} = 2{,}000{,}000 \times £102.3125 = £2{,}046{,}250.00$$

and

$$\text{Futures price} = \frac{£108.125}{1.17124} = £92.31669$$

As a result

$$\text{Futures value} = £92.31669 \times \frac{100{,}000}{100} = £92{,}316.69$$

And applying the original formula

$$\text{Number of contracts} = \frac{\text{Portfolio value}}{\text{Futures value}} \times \frac{\text{Portfolio MD}}{\text{CTD MD}}$$

Gives

$$\text{Number of contracts} = \frac{£2{,}046{,}250.00}{£92{,}316.69} \times \frac{-5.37}{-7.12} = 16.7 \text{ (or 17) contracts}$$

Alternative 2

Applying the second version

$$\text{Number of contracts} = \frac{\text{Portfolio nominal}}{\text{CTD nominal}} \times \text{PF} \times \frac{\text{PVBP of portfolio}}{\text{PVBP of CTD}}$$

We are given

Portfolio nominal = 2,000,000
Portfolio (bond) price = £102.3125
Portfolio (bond) MD = –5.37
CTD price = £108.125
CTD MD = 7.12
PF = 1.17124

So

Bond PVBP = $-5.37 \times £102.3125 \times 0.0001 = -0.0549418$

CTD PVBP = $-7.12 \times £108.125 \times 0.0001 = -0.076985$

And applying the second formula

$$\text{Number of contracts} = \frac{\text{Portfolio nominal}}{\text{CTD nominal}} \times \text{PF} \times \frac{\text{PVBP of portfolio}}{\text{PVBP of CTD}}$$

Gives

$$\text{Number of contracts} = \frac{2{,}000{,}000}{100{,}000} \times 1.17124 \times \frac{0.0549418}{0.076985} = 16.7 \text{ (or 17) contracts}$$

Other methods of measuring relative volatility can be used, such as using regression analysis. This approach models the historic price behaviour between the target bond and the CTD and calculates a correlation coefficient. Such an approach can be particularly useful for non-sovereign bonds where credit risks are high.

Despite the apparent sophistication of these methods, there are a number of potential shortcomings.

First, the CTD can change. CTD changes occur where either yields or the slope of the yield curve changes. Another connected problem is that as yields change over the lifespan of the hedge, so too will the relative sensitivities of the bonds. Not all bonds will be equally sensitive – a property known as convexity.

The final problem is that the hedge ratios rely on there being parallel changes in the yield curve to be effective. If there is a change in the slope, the hedge will not be efficient; this problem can be particularly acute when the CTD and the target bond have significantly different maturities.

3 Traded Options

3.1 Definition

An option is a contract that confers upon the buyer the right, but not the obligation, to buy or sell an asset at a given price on or before a given date.

Again, all the comments related to standard quantities, specified assets, fixed future dates and price agreed today (that we noted above for futures) still apply.

3.2 Using options

3.2.1 Speculation – buying an option

Conventionally, a speculator anticipating a rise in the price of cocoa would straightforwardly buy cocoa for immediate delivery and then store the goods, hoping to sell them for a profit once the price rose. If we imagine that the price of cocoa is £600 per tonne and that the speculator buys just one tonne, the expenditure would be £600.

Another way of representing the hope of a rise in cocoa prices would be to buy a cocoa option – specifically, an option that would give the right, but not the obligation, to buy cocoa at a price of £600 per tonne for a period of three months. The purchase of this option would cost, say, £5 a tonne.

Remember that an option is a contract for a future delivery, so it would not be necessary to pay £600 in the first instance; the only money to be invested at this point is the £5. If an option on one tonne of cocoa was bought, it would only cost £5 immediately.

One advantage is immediately apparent. Options are cheaper than purchasing the underlying asset.

Example

If three months later, as expected, the price of cocoa has risen from £600 per tonne to £700 per tonne, what will be the position of

- The speculator who bought physical cocoa?
- The speculator who bought the cocoa option?

Solution

Physical cocoa

	(£)
Sale price	700
Purchase price	(600)
Profit	100

On an investment of £600, the investor has made a profit of £100 in just three months.

Cocoa option

Now, let us look at the profit for the options buyer. Three months ago, he entered into a contract that gave him the right, but not the obligation, to buy cocoa at £600. When purchased, that right cost just £5 per tonne.

With cocoa now trading at £700, the right to buy at £600 must be worth at least £100 – the difference between the current price and the stated price in the contract.

This right to buy at £600 was purchased for £5. With the market price at £700 at the end of the option's life, the option will now be worth £100, hence

	(£)
Sale price	100
Purchase price	(5)
Profit	95

On an investment of £5, a £95 profit has been achieved. In percentage terms, this profit is spectacularly greater than on the conventional purchase and sale of physical cocoa.

One important thing to note is that options are tradeable instruments. It is not necessary for the underlying asset to be bought or sold. What more commonly occurs is that **options** are bought and sold. Thus, an option bought at £5 could be sold to the market at £100 realising a £95 profit with the investor never having an intention of buying the underlying asset.

At this stage, it is necessary to introduce some of the vocabulary used in the options market.

3.3 Terminology

In the definition of an option given earlier, an option was described as being the right, but not the obligation, to **buy or sell**. The right to buy and the right to sell are given different names.

- The right to buy is known as a **call option**.
- The right to sell is known as a **put option**.

The rights to buy (call) or sell (put) are held by the person buying the option who is known as the **holder**.

The person selling an option is known as a **writer**, who is obliged to make (call) or take (put) delivery of the asset if it is exercised. With respect to exercise, this may be

- **European Style** – which means the option can only be exercised at its termination or **expiry date**.
- **American Style** – which means the option can only be exercised at any time on or before its expiry date.

The following diagram shows the relationship between holders and writers.

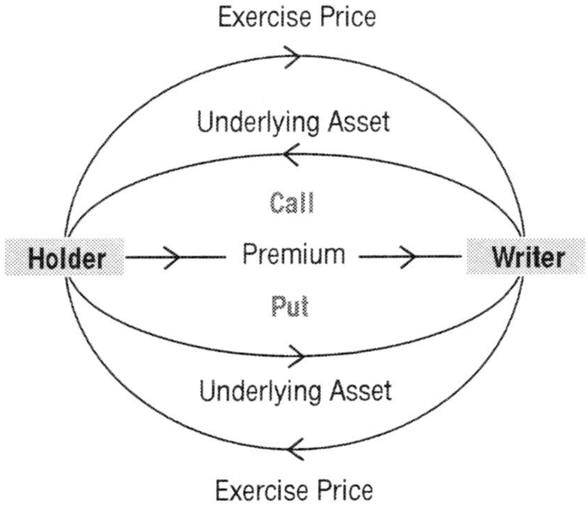

The first thing to understand is the flow of option **premium**. Premium is the cost of an option. In our cocoa example, the premium was £5 and this is paid by the holder and received by the writer.

In return for receiving premium, the writer agrees to fulfil the terms of the contract, which of course are different for calls and puts.

3.3.1 Call options

Call writers agree to deliver the asset underlying the contract if **called** upon to do so. When options holders wish to take up their rights under the contract, they are said to **exercise** the contract. For a call, this means that the writer must deliver the underlying asset for which he will receive the fixed amount of cash stipulated in the original contract.

Thus, for a cocoa call option that gives the holder the right, but not the obligation, to buy at £600, which would mean that the writer would be required to deliver cocoa to the holder at £600. The option's holder will only want to buy at £600 when it would be advantageous for him to do so, i.e. only when the real or market price is somewhat higher than £600. If the market price were less than £600, there would be no sense in paying more than the market price for the goods.

Call options writers run very considerable risks. In return for receiving the option's premium, they are committed to delivering the underlying asset at a fixed price. As the price of the asset could, in theory, rise infinitely, they could be forced to buy the underlying asset at a high price and to deliver it to the option's holder at a much lower value. The price at which an option's contract gives the right to buy (call) or sell (put) is known as the **exercise price** or **strike price**.

3.3.2 Put options

The dangers for put options writers are also substantial. The writer of a put is obligated to pay the exercise price for assets that are delivered to him. Put options are only exercised when it is advantageous for the holders to do so. This will be when they can use the option to sell their assets at a higher price than would be otherwise available in the market.

3.3.3 Summary

To summarise, options writers, in return for receiving premium, run very large risks. This is similar to the role undertaken by insurance companies. For a relatively modest premium, they are willing to insure your house against fire, but if your house burns down, they will be faced with a claim for many thousands of pounds. The reasons why insurers and options writers enter into such contracts are that houses don't often burn down, and markets don't often rise or fall substantially.

If writers price options properly, they hope to make money in most instances. Options writing is not for the faint-hearted, nor for those without substantial resources. That said, many conservative users do write options as part of strategies involving the holding of the underlying asset. Such uses, which are **covered**, are much less risky and are discussed later.

When investors buy or hold options, the risk is limited to the option's premium. If the market moves against them, they can simply decide not to exercise their options and sacrifice the premium. Remember, options holders have the right, **but not the obligation**, to buy (call) or sell (put). If it does not make sense to buy or sell at the exercise price, the holder can decide to **abandon** the option.

3.4 The uses of options

3.4.1 Buying a call

Introduction

Buying a call is motivated by a view that an asset's price will rise.

Risk – The investor's risks are limited to the premium he pays for the options. So, if the 80 call could be bought for a premium of 5, this 5 is all he risks. The premium of the call option will only be a fraction of the cost of the underlying asset, so the option can be considered less risky than buying the asset itself.

Whilst this is true, remember that the whole premium is at risk, and it is easy to lose 100% of your investment, albeit a relatively small amount of money.

Reward – The rewards from buying a call are unlimited. As the contract gives the holder the right to buy at a fixed price, this right will become increasingly valuable as the asset price rises above the exercise price.

Imagine an investor who buys one XYZ call option that gives him the right, but not the obligation, to buy the XYZ asset at a fixed price of 80 between now and the option's expiry date in January. The cost of this option is 5.

If the asset price rises to 120, the right to buy at 80 (i.e. the premium of the 80 call) must be worth at least 40. The net profit for the call would be 35 (40 – 5). Of course, if the price of XYZ falls below 80 at the option's expiry date, the 80 call will be worthless and 100% of the initial 5 invested will be lost. This loss occurs because no sensible person would want the right to buy at 80 if they could buy the asset more cheaply elsewhere.

Graphically

By using graphs we can show how much an option will be worth at expiry.

On the vertical axis of the graph is profit/loss and on the horizontal axis is the asset price.

Holder of 1 XYZ January 80 Call – Premium 5

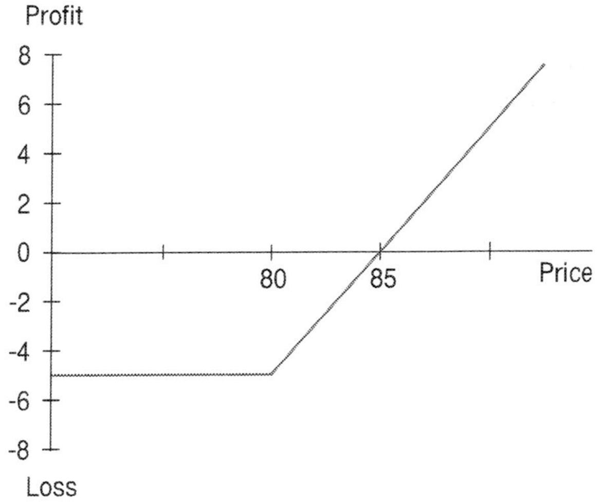

The graph shows that losses of 5 are made anywhere below 80, whilst profits emerge above 85. The breakeven point is represented by 85. This is the point at which the original investment is recouped, and it is calculated by simply adding the premium to the exercise price, e.g. 80 + 5 = 85. The buying of a call to open a position is known as a 'long call'.

Use for speculation

A speculator may adopt this position if he is strongly bullish, i.e. he believes that prices will rise significantly. Through the option the speculator can gain exposure to the asset at a fraction of its cost.

Use for hedging

A hedger could use this trade to hedge a future cash receipt against future price rises in a similar manner to a long hedge with futures. The difference between these two positions is that with futures the value of the position rises if prices rise and falls if prices fall, whereas with options the value rises as prices rise but there is a limited price fall potential. The premium on the option is effectively paying for this limit on the price all potential.

3.4.2 Selling a call

Introduction

Risk – Selling a call, or writing a call, of a call without at the same time being in possession of the underlying asset is extremely risky. The risk is unlimited because the writer has a duty to deliver the asset at a fixed price regardless of the prevailing asset price. As the share price could, in theory, rise to infinity, the call writer assumes an unlimited risk. This strategy is sometimes called **naked** call writing and as it suggests, can leave you feeling very exposed.

Reward – You might ask why someone would assume such an unlimited risk. The answer, of course, is the hope of a profit. The maximum profit the writer can make is the premium he receives. Let us look again at an 80 call with a premium of 5. The seller of this call will receive the 5 premium, and as long as the asset price at expiry is less than 80, no one will rationally want to exercise the right to buy. The graph for selling a call is set out below. You will see that it is the equal and opposite of buying a call.

Graphically

Writer of 1 XYZ January 80 Call – Premium 5

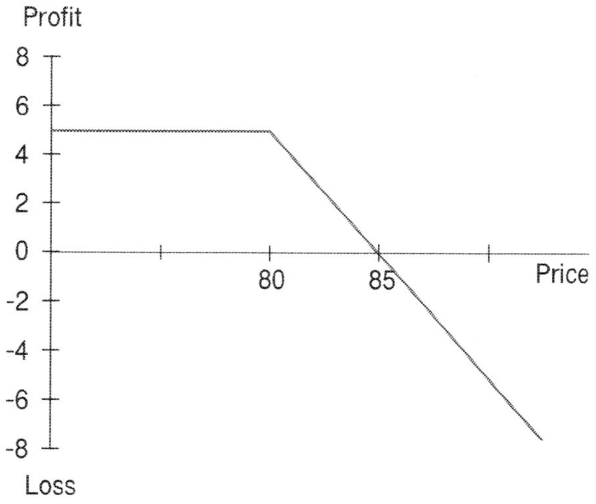

Use for speculation

As the graph demonstrates, the call writer believes that the asset price is likely either to stay the same or fall. If this happens, the writer simply pockets the premium received and will not have to deliver the asset. The selling of a call to open a position is known as a 'short call'.

Use for hedging

A fund manager may choose to write call options on assets he holds in his portfolio, referred to as writing a covered call.

The manager would consider this strategy in a static market. If the manager holds assets where he believes that prices are unlikely to move, hence the fund is not performing, he can write call options and boost fund performance by the premium received. If prices remain static or even fall, then the fund will have benefited from that premium receipt. If prices rise, the fund is still better off until the strike price is reached. The manager therefore needs to write out-of-the-money options, i.e. options that are not currently worth exercising and which he believes will never be worth exercising.

Another potential use would be if the manager has a target selling price. Writing a call results if selling at that target price if it is reached while also boosting performance by the premium received.

3.4.3 Buying a put

Introduction

Risk – As when buying a call, the risk of buying a put is limited to the premium paid. The motivation behind buying a put will be to profit from a fall in the asset's price. The holder of a put obtains the right, but not the obligation, to sell at a fixed price. The value of this right will become increasingly valuable as the asset price falls.

Reward – The greatest profit that will arise from buying a put will be achieved if the asset price falls to zero.

Graphically

Holder of 1 XYZ July 80 Put – Premium 8

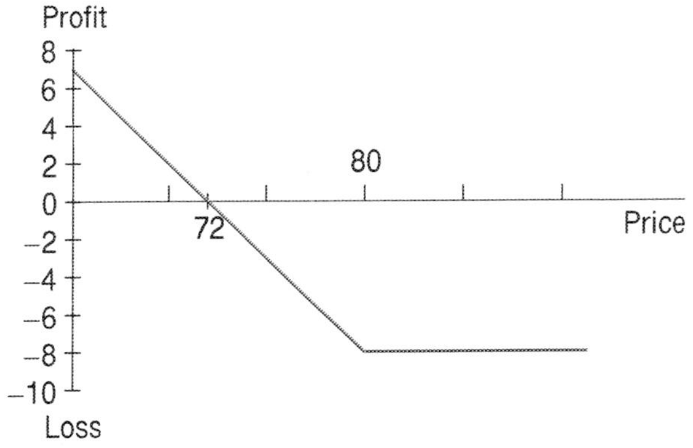

The breakeven point, and maximum profit, is calculated by deducting the premium from the exercise price, e.g. 80 – 8 = 72. Like the purchase of a call, the premium needs to be recovered before profits are made. The buying of a put to open a position is known as a 'long put'.

Use for speculation

A speculator may adopt this position if he is strongly bearish, i.e. he believes that prices will fall significantly. Again, through the option the speculator can gain exposure to the asset at a fraction of its cost.

Use for hedging

A hedger could use this trade to hedge a fund against price falls in a similar manner to a short hedge with futures.

The difference between these two positions is that with futures the value of the value of the overall position is hedged against a price fall and against a price rise. The net value remains almost constant irrespective of market movements.

When buying a put, the value of the total position is hedged against a price fall but the fund can benefit from a price rise. The premium effectively pays insurance on the floor value of the fund. Ths may be referred to as a protective put position.

3.4.4 Selling a put

Introduction

Risk – Selling a put is dangerous, as the writer enters into an obligation to purchase an asset at a fixed price. If the market price of that asset falls, the put writer will end up paying a large amount of money for what could be a valueless asset. The worst case will arise when the asset price falls to zero. If this happens, the loss will be the exercise price less the premium received.

Reward – The put option writer hopes that the put will not be exercised. This will occur if the asset has a price above the exercise price at expiry. The maximum reward is the premium received. The selling of a put to open a position is known as a 'short put'.

Graphically

Writer of 1 XYZ July 80 Put – Premium 8

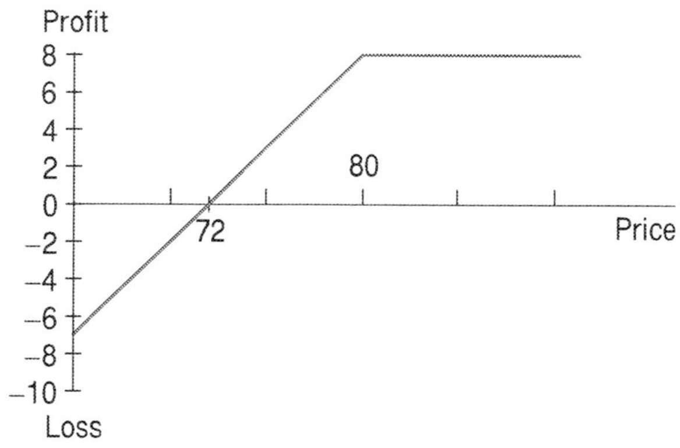

Use for speculation

A speculator would consider this position if he is neutral to mildly bullish about the asset, i.e. he believes that prices are either static or going to rise slightly. If he is correct then he will benefit from the premium receipt.

Use for hedging

A fund manager may choose to write put options on short positions in his portfolio.

The manager would consider this strategy in a static market. If the manager is short assets where he believes that prices are unlikely to move, hence not performing, he can write put options and boost fund performance by the premium received.

If prices remain static or even rise, then the fund will have benefited from that premium receipt. If prices fall, the fund is still better off until the strike price is reached. The manager therefore needs to write out-of-the-money options, i.e. options that are not currently worth exercising and which he believes will never be worth exercising.

3.4.5 Summarising

The four basic strategies outlined above form the building blocks of all the more complicated option techniques. You should ensure that you are clear about three things.

- What is the motivation behind each trade?
- What are the risks associated with them?
- What are the rewards?

3.4.6 Options trading strategies

Motivation

Before embarking on a discussion of the attributes of some options trades, let us first think about the reasons why they are undertaken and we need to consider

- Speculators
- Hedgers

Speculators

The first and most obvious reason for speculating in the markets is that investors have a view on their future direction, be it up or down. These are **directional** trades and may be either **bullish** (the investor feels the market is likely to go up) or **bearish** (the investor feels the market is likely to go down). Investors may also feel the market is likely to go up or down very markedly, or only slightly. The four basic option trades accommodate these views.

People also trade because they feel the market is likely to be highly volatile or remain broadly static. These investors do not know in which direction the market may move, but have opinions as to its likely variability. These types of trades are known as **volatility** trades, and options are unique in allowing investors to trade in this way.

Directional trades

Strategy A	Long Call
Motivation	**Directional, very bullish**
Construction	Opening purchase of a call. Choice of call depends on degree of bullishness; buy out-of-the-money options if very bullish, in-the-money options if less so.
Key Formulae	**Maximum risk:** Premium paid **Maximum reward:** Unlimited **Breakeven at expiry:** Exercise price + Premium
Comments	Position suffers from time decay (see valuation of options).

Example

Buy 100 Call @ 7

Graph

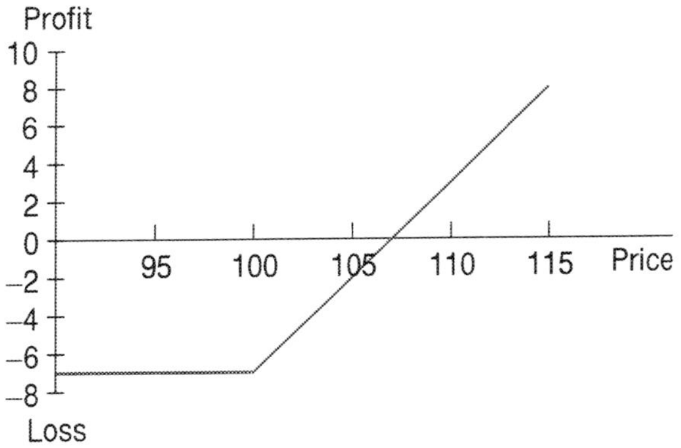

Table

Stock Price	90	95	100	105	110	115
Intrinsic Value	0	0	0	5	10	15
Profit/Loss	–7	–7	–7	–2	3	8

Strategy B	Short Call
Motivation	**Directional, bearish**
Construction	Opening sale of a call. Choice of call depends on degree of bearishness. Sell in-the-money call if very bearish, out-of-the-money if less so.
Key Formulae	**Maximum risk:** Unlimited **Maximum reward:** Premium received **Breakeven at expiry:** Exercise price + Premium
Comments	Position helped by time decay (see valuation of options).

Example

Graph

Sell 100 Call @ 7

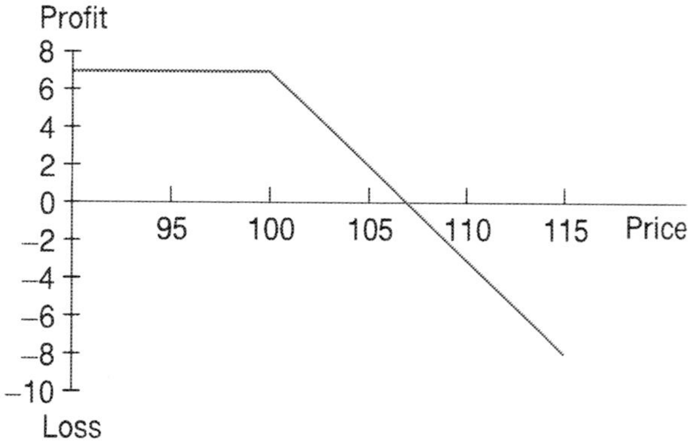

Table

Stock Price	90	95	100	105	110	115
Intrinsic Value	0	0	0	5	10	15
Profit/Loss	7	7	7	2	–3	–8

Strategy C	Long Put
Motivation	**Directional, very bearish**
Construction	Opening purchase of a put. Choice of put depends on degree of bearishness. Buy out-of-the-money put if very bearish, in-the-money if less so.
Key Formulae	**Maximum risk:** Premium paid **Maximum reward:** Exercise price – Premium **Breakeven at expiry:** Exercise price – Premium
Comments	Position suffers from time decay (see valuation of options).

Example

Graph

Buy 100 Put @ 6

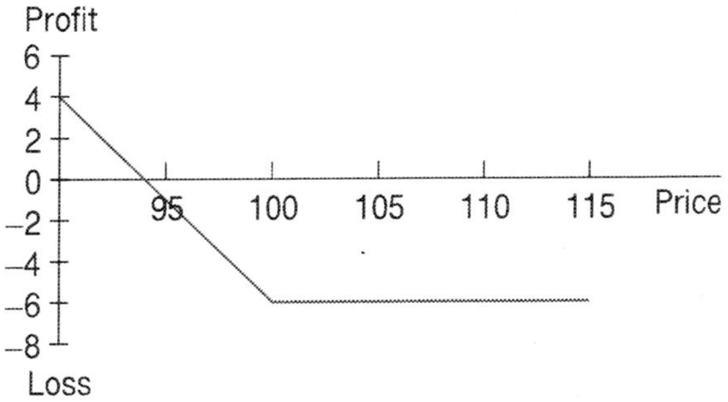

Table

Stock Price	90	95	100	105	110	115
Intrinsic Value	10	5	0	0	0	0
Profit/Loss	4	–1	–6	–6	–6	–6

Strategy D	Short Put
Motivation	**Directional, bullish**
Construction	Opening sale of a put. Choice of put depends on degree of bullishness. Sell in-the-money put if very bullish, out-of-the-money if less so.
Key Formulae	**Maximum risk:** Exercise price – Premium **Maximum reward:** Premium received **Breakeven at expiry:** Exercise price – Premium
Comments	Position helped by time decay (see valuation of options).

Example

Graph

Sell 100 Put @ 6

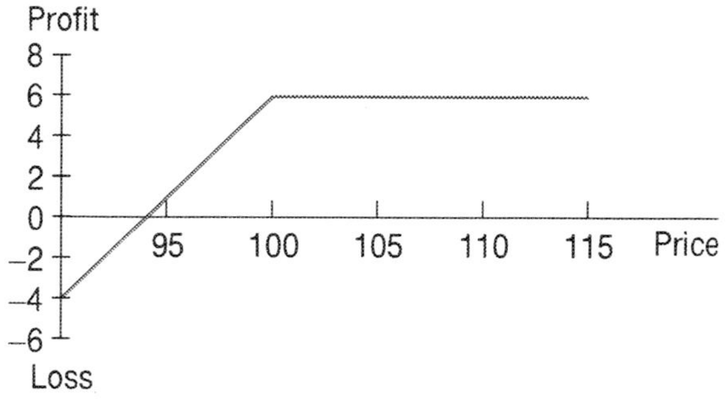

Table

Stock Price	90	95	100	105	110	115
Intrinsic Value	10	5	0	0	0	0
Profit/Loss	–4	1	6	6	6	6

Volatility trade

Strategy E	Long Straddle
Motivation	**Volatility – undertaken to exploit increasing variability**
Construction	Purchase of call and put with same exercise price and expiry.
Key Formulae	**Maximum risk:** Premiums paid **Maximum reward:** Unlimited **Breakeven at expiry:** Upside: Exercise price + Both premiums Downside: Exercise price – Both premiums
Comments	Prone to severe time decay if position held near to expiry (see valuation of options).

Example

Buy 100 Call @ 7, Buy 100 Put @ 6

Graph

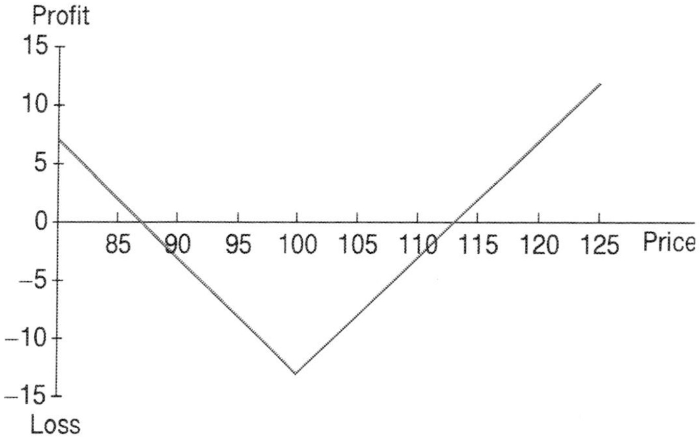

Table

Stock Price	80	85	90	95	100	105	110	115	120	125
100 Call Intrinsic Value	0	0	0	0	0	5	10	15	20	25
100 Call Profit/Loss	–7	–7	–7	–7	–7	–2	3	8	13	18
100 Put Intrinsic Value	20	15	10	5	0	0	0	0	0	0
100 Put Profit/Loss	14	9	4	–1	–6	–6	–6	–6	–6	–6
Profit/Loss	7	2	–3	–8	–13	–8	–3	2	7	12

Hedging

A second group of users may be those who hold assets and are looking to protect or boost the returns in some way. Hedgers may wish to protect themselves against the fall in the asset price. Alternatively they may be looking to boost their performance in a static market.

Protect against a price fall

If we hold an asset and are concerned that prices may fall we can protect this position by buying a put option.

If prices do fall then we can exercise the put and sell the asset at a guaranteed value. If, however, prices rise then we will still benefit as we will retain the asset and abandon the put.

Strategy G	Protective Put
Motivation	**Directional, bullish, but with limited downside risk**
Construction	Long position in stock/future and purchase of put.
Key Formulae	**Maximum risk:** Initial value of stock/future – Exercise price + Put premium **Maximum reward:** Unlimited **Breakeven at expiry:** Initial value of stock/future + Put premium
Comments	Classic options hedge of long position in underlying; protects downside but allows profit if market advances. More flexible and thus more expensive than short hedge with futures.

Example

Graph

Buy Stock @ 99, Buy 100 Put @ 6

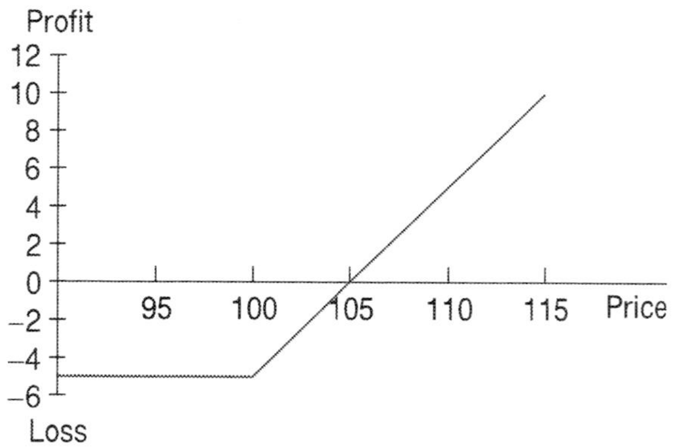

Table

Stock Price	90	95	100	105	110	115
Stock Profit/Loss	–9	–4	1	6	11	16
100 Put Intrinsic Value	10	5	0	0	0	0
100 Put Profit/Loss	4	–1	–6	–6	–6	–6
Profit/Loss	–5	–5	–5	0	5	10

Boost income in a static market

If we hold an asset with a the current price of 99 and we believe the price is unlikely to move, we could, say, write 105 calls and receive the premium.

If we are correct and the price does not move then we will retain the asset and have the premium received as a boost to our income.

Alternatively, if the price does rise the option may be exercised against us but we are covered against this event as we already have the asset available to deliver.

Strategy H	Covered Call		
Motivation	**Directional, bullish-neutral, subject to strike**		
Construction	Long position in stock/future, and sale of call. If call sold is out-of-the-money, the trade is bullish; if at-the-money call is sold, trade is neutral.		
Key Formulae	**Maximum risk:**	Initial value of stock/future – Call premium	
	Maximum reward:	Exercise price – Initial value stock/future + Call premium	
	Breakeven at expiry:	Initial value of stock/future – Call premium	
Comments	Very familiar investment strategy that can enhance returns in static markets, whilst also providing limited protection against falls. (Protection = Call premium)		

Example

Buy Stock @ 99, Sell 105 Call @ 4

Graph

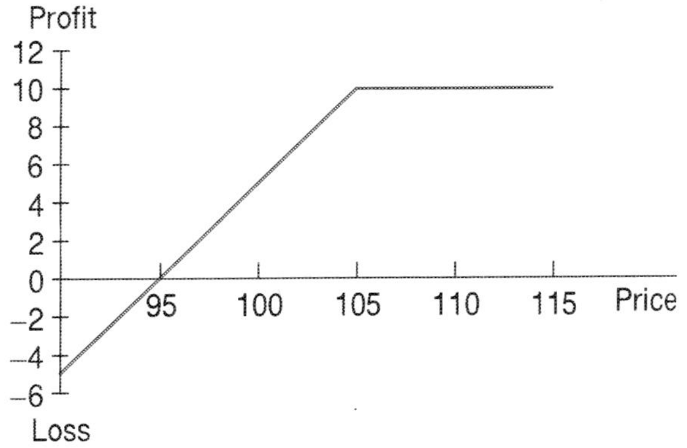

Table

Stock Price	90	95	100	105	110	115
Stock Profit/Loss	–9	–4	1	6	11	16
105 Call Intrinsic Value	0	0	0	0	5	10
105 Call Profit/Loss	4	4	4	4	–1	–6
Profit/Loss	–5	0	5	10	10	10

We can see that this strategy gives a gain of 10 at any price above 105. With the original asset alone we would need the price to rise to 109 to achieve this gain. If markets are non-volatile this strategy can be very beneficial for a portfolio.

3.5 Some specific contracts and their uses

3.5.1 Options on bonds

The options discussed so far have been options which, upon exercise, result in the purchase or sale of a tangible underlying security such as a share.

More common than these types of options are options on futures. This apparently complex term merely describes options, the exercise of which results in a long or short futures position.

Thus, the exercise of a **long call** results in the holder establishing a **long futures** position in the same delivery month.

The exercise of a **long put** results in the holder establishing a **short futures** position in the same delivery month.

To complement trading in its futures contracts, NYSE Liffe offers options on its more liquid futures contracts, including some government bond contracts.

The option on the long gilt future is used as an example. The December 112 call provides the right to purchase the December futures contract at £112. Each option is based on one futures contract with the tick size being the same as the futures contract at 0.01 (£10). Unlike most other options, the option premium is not payable when the position is opened. The option premium is marked to market and profits and losses settled daily, as with futures.

3.5.2 Interest rate options

Interest rate options are available as OTC products. There are three basic structures: the cap, the floor and the collar. In common with other OTC structures they offer considerably more flexibility than their exchange-traded cousins, especially options on short-term interest rate futures.

The Cap

The cap gives the buyer the right, but not the obligation, to fix the cost of borrowing.

Caps are most commonly used by variable rate borrowers to fix the maximum they will pay.

For example, a corporate treasurer buys a 6% cap on a notional amount of £10m.

At the rollover date, the cap strike rate is compared with an agreed benchmark, usually three-month LIBOR. If the strike is below the benchmark the option is exercised and the cash difference is delivered.

If the benchmark were 7% and the period three months, the settlement amount would be

$1\% \times £10m \times {}^{3}/_{12} = £25,000$

If, however, the strike is above the marked rate, the option is simply abandoned.

Although the cap may appear to the buyer to be one option, it is in fact a series of European style calls on the agreed benchmark with, normally, quarterly settlements.

The table below shows the structure of a two-year cap.

March	3 months
June	6 months
Sept	9 months
Dec	12 months
March	15 months
June	18 months
Sept	21 months
Dec	24 months

Caps (and floors) are available in all the major currencies. The normal dealing size is \$5-\$50m and maturities are usually between one and five years. The premiums are quoted on basis points.

Caps offer an OTC alternative to a strip of put options on short-term interest rate futures.

The floor

The OTC equivalent to a call option on a short-term interest rate future. The floor enables the buyer (usually a depositor) to obtain protection against falling interest rates. As with the cap, it is a cash-settled European style option in which, usually, quarterly settlements are made against a benchmark index. Settlement is usually made against the offer rate (e.g. LIBOR), although LIBID is the rate more likely to be achieved.

Liquidity and availability are somewhat more restricted than in the cap market.

The collar

The collar is the combination of both a cap and a floor in the same product at different strikes and is comparable to options 'cylinders' and 'fences'.

Two varieties are available.

Borrower's collar

A cap is purchased to protect against rises. This purchase price is offset in whole or in part by the sale of a floor. The sale of the floor limits the borrower's ability to take advantage of falls in interest rates.

Interest rate collar

Buy 10% cap

Sell 5% floor

The Collar

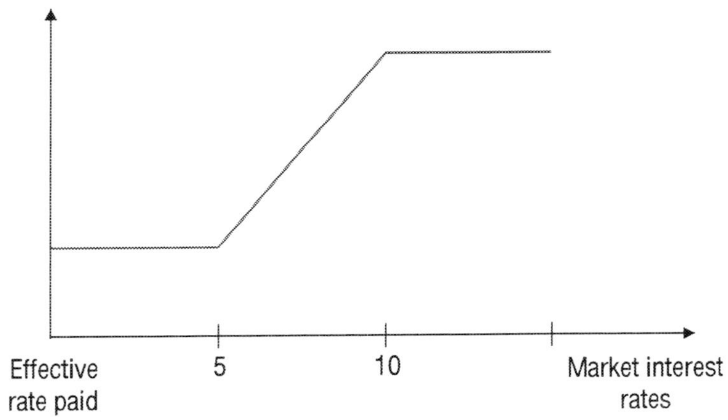

As can be seen, a synthetic bull spread is created.

Investor's collar

This is constructed in a reverse style, e.g. the cap is sold and the floor is purchased.

Interest rate guarantees

These are simply options on FRAs (like options on futures) or one-period caps/floors.

They work in exactly the same way as caps and floors, but simply relate to one period.

Captions and floptions

Captions and floptions are options on either caps (captions) or floors (floptions or floortions).

Although these sound complicated, they do have important applications for hedgers who face a contingent interest rate risk, but are uncertain as to whether or not an interest rate exposure may occur.

The pricing of such options on options (sometimes called compound options) is more complex. A model was devised by Geske to price these products and is a variation on the Black Scholes model. In the Geske model, the value of the underlying asset is substituted by the strike of the underlying cap/floor.

Swaptions

These are options on, normally, coupon swaps (see later). They come in two varieties.

Receiver swaptions – the buyer has the right, but not the obligation, to receive fixed and pay floating.

Payer swaptions – the buyer has the right, but not the obligation, to pay fixed and receive floating.

Swaptions are usually European style and are comparable to interest rate caps. There are, of course, some differences.

The swaption allows the holder the right to pay (or receive) a specific fixed rate and receive (or pay) a floating rate for an agreed term. The swaption can only be exercised into the underlying interest rate swap **once**.

A cap agreement gives the right to fix a series of individual interest payments. Thus, the cap tends to be more expensive because the holder has multiple exercise dates, can benefit if rates fall during the life of the agreement and can limit his loss potential if interest rates have risen at any point.

Rate spread options

These products offer a basis play between two benchmark rates.

For example, an investor may think the spread between US dollar LIBOR and Euribor is expected to widen. To receive the anticipated increase, the investor would buy the call spread and upon exercise, receive the increased differential multiplied by the notional amount and the number of days.

Better performance bond options

Better performance options pay the greater of two assets' returns over the period to exercise, if both are positive. These may have important applications for money managers who are uncertain as to which of two assets to invest in.

Average rate (Asian) options

When exercised, average rate or Asian style options pay out the difference between the strike rate and the average interest rate for the period of the option. Alternatively, the structure may set the strike as the average over the whole period. Cash compensation is delivered if the strike is below the actual interest rates achieved at the rollover dates within the term of the option.

Average rate options expose the issuer to less risk than the cap/floor (where in-the-money differences are exchanged between the fixed cap rate and the benchmark at each rollover). Consequently, premiums are lower. Generally, average rate options are priced at about 65% of either cap or floor premiums.

3.6 Summary of exchange traded bond products

We illustrated the use of bond and interest rate futures and options above by reference to products traded in the UK on NYSE Liffe. There are various products available internationally, all of which have very similar uses and characteristics and the following gives a brief summary of the various futures contracts and indicates where options are available on those contracts.

3.6.1 Bond futures and options

Exchange Product	Size	Tick	Tick value	Option available	Notional coupon	Underlying maturities
NYSE Liffe						
Long gilt	£100,000	0.01	£10	Y	6%	8y 9m to 13 years
Medium gilt	£100,000	0.01	£10	N	6%	4 to 6 years
Short gilt	£100,000	0.01	£10	N	6%	1y 6m to 3y 3m
JGB	¥100,000,000	0.01	¥10,000	N	6%	7 to 11 years
Eurex						
Euro-Bund	€100,000	0.01	€10	Y	6%	8.5 to 10.5 years
CME						
30 yr T-Bond	$100,000	1/32	$31.25	Y	6%	>15 years
10 yr T-Bond	$100,000	1/64	$15.625	Y	6%	6y 6m to 10years
5 yr T-Note	$100,000	1/128	$7.8125	Y	6%	4y 2m to 5y 3m
3 yr T- Note	$200,000	1/128	$15.625	Y	6%	2y 9m to 3years
2 yr T- Note	$200,000	1/128	$15.625	Y	6%	1y 9m to 2years

Note, this is not intended as a comprehensive list, simply an illustration of the main derivatives and their key characteristics.

Perhaps the most important point to note is that US T-bonds are priced in 32nds. If a T-bond is quoted at \$102-20 this is \$102 $^{20}/_{32}$ or \$102.625. We are liable to be given prices on this basis and should always quote prices on this basis, however all calculations are most conveniently undertaken in decimals so we will need to convert from 32nds to decimals at the start and may need to convert from decimals to 32nds at the end.

One further little complication here is that we may be given a quote of \$102-20+. This should be interpreted as \$102-20.5, i.e. \$102 $^{20.5}/_{32}$ or \$102.640625.

3.6.2 Short term interest rate (STIR) futures and options

Exchange Product	Size	Tick	Tick value	Option available
NYSE Liffe				
3m sterling	£500,000	0.010	£12.50	Y
Eurex				
3m Euribor	€1,000,000	0.005	€12.50	Y
CME				
3m Eurodollar	$1,000,000	0.010	$25.00	Y

3.7 Options pricing

3.7.1 Futures/options compared

Options pricing has similarities with futures pricing. The cost of finance and the passage of time are important considerations. However, remember that the products have different attributes; delivery of futures is an obligation, but delivery of options is only a possibility. It is in the evaluation of whether or not an option is likely to be exercised that some of the complexities emerge.

Options are priced according to probability and it is in working out how to price probability that some complicated mathematics are used as we will see later.

3.7.2 Intrinsic value and time value

Why are some options more expensive than others? Below are the printed prices for call options on a particular asset. The underlying price is 98.

Exercise Price	Expiry Date		
	January Premium	April Premium	July Premium
70	29	31	32
80	20	22	23
90	12	14.5	16
100	5	10	13
110	4	6.5	8
120	2	4	5

Two influences on options prices are readily apparent

- Exercise price.
- Time.

Compare the value of the January 70 call and the January 90 call from the table. The 70 call is priced at 29 whilst the 90 call is priced at 12. Why?

Remember that we are looking at call options, i.e. the right to buy. The value of the 70 call is greater than the 90 call because the right to buy at a low price (70) must be more attractive than the right to buy at a high price (90).

Why is the 70 call priced at 29?

We can readily explain at least part of the premium. If we bear in mind that the underlying stock is trading at 98, the right to buy at 70 must be worth at least 28. If the 70 call was worth less than 28, it would be possible to buy the call, exercise it to acquire stock and immediately sell the stock at the market price of 98 and thereby realise a risk-free profit. Markets do not give away money. The 70 call with an underlying stock at 98 must be worth at least 28. This value of 28 is known as the option's **intrinsic value**.

The option is not just valued at 28, its price is 29, so where does the difference of 1 come from?

This part of the premium is known as **time value**. The amount of time value in an option is a function of probability, of the chance of further movements in the underlying asset.

The premium of the 70 call is made up of two things, namely intrinsic value and time value.

Formula to learn

Intrinsic value + Time value = Premium

28 + 1 = 29

Not all options have intrinsic value. If you look at the table, you will see the premium of the January 120 call is 2. The 120 call has no intrinsic value because it gives the right to buy at a level above the current price of 98. It is therefore of no immediate value. However, because things may change between now and expiry, the option has 2 of time value.

At expiry, no time is left, so an option is worth its intrinsic value or nothing. The table below gives the expiry values of call options with the underlying at 98.

Exercise Price of Call	Value
70	28
80	18
90	8
100	0
110	0
120	0

Options which have intrinsic value, hence are worth exercising, are described as being **in-the-money**. The intrinsic value of an in-the-money option is the difference between the share price and the exercise price.

Options which are not worth exercising only have time value and are described as being **out-of-the-money**.

Practitioners sometimes describe options as being **at-the-money**. This term has nothing to do with intrinsic value, it merely describes the option exercise price that is nearest to the current underlying price. Thus, the 100 call from the table, as the exercise price nearest the underlying (98), would be the 'at-the-money' option.

3.7.3 Time decay

From the table of prices, we can see that the January 70 call is priced at 29, the April 70 at 31 and the July 70 at 32. You will notice from these, and from the other options, that the more life remaining in an option, the more expensive it is.

This is very similar to the insurance market. If you asked an insurance company to give you two quotes, one for six months' cover on your car and one for 12 months, the quote for a year would be much more expensive. This is because the insurance company would be taking the risk over a longer period. Similarly, options writers will want larger rewards for taking larger risks.

Another point to note about time value is that it is not evenly distributed across all the different exercise prices for a particular expiry.

For the March calls with an underlying price at 98, time values are distributed as follows.

Exercise Price	Premium	Intrinsic Value	Time Value
70	29	28	1
80	20	18	2
90	12	8	4
100	5	0	5
110	4	0	4
120	2	0	2

You see that time value is greatest for the 100 exercise price, i.e. the at-the-money option. This is always the case with options and is again related to the probability of whether an option will be exercised.

The 70 call has a time value of only 1 because it is almost inevitable that the option will be exercised; the 120 call also has a time value of 2 because it is likely to expire unexercised. All the uncertainty, and thus all the time value, is concentrated in the 100 call. This is because there is an approximately 50/50 chance of the option being exercised or not. This uncertainty represents risk, and where there is risk, time value will always be higher.

The final point to note about time value relates to the pace of time decay as expiry draws near. We have already observed that time value erodes as expiry draws near, but it is important to understand that such erosion does not take place evenly. As expiry approaches, the pace of decay increases dramatically.

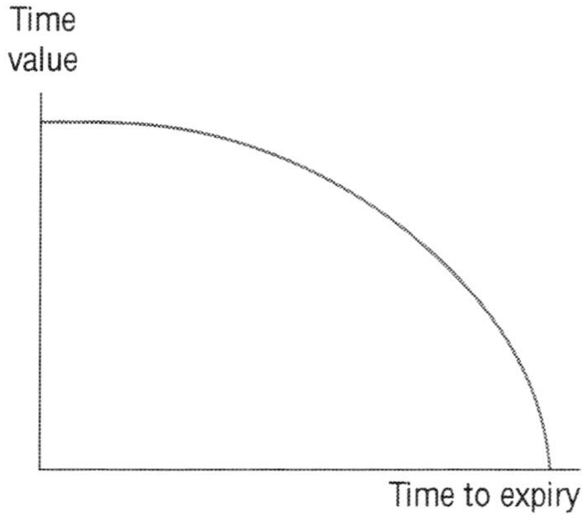

The erosion of time value has important consequences for investors.

For options holders, the passage of time is painful in that, all other things remaining equal, every day that passes means their options lose value, i.e. **holders are hurt by time decay**.

Conversely, options writers welcome the passage of time as again, all other things remaining equal, the options they originally sold are worth less as each day passes, i.e. **writers are helped by time decay**.

Advisers should be conscious of time decay when talking to investors, particularly if contemplating buying options with a short time until expiry.

3.7.4 Volatility

Aside from time and underlying security price, the most important other factor is option **volatility**.

Volatility is a measure of how much an underlying price varies. If an underlying asset varies a great deal, the risk for the options writer becomes larger and the premiums they demand rise accordingly. If, however, an option is sold on an unvolatile asset, the premiums will be lower. At times of crisis or change, such as wars or elections, people become uncertain about the future. This uncertainty brings with it higher options premiums.

This is analogous to the insurance market. If you were an insurer and you were asked to quote a premium for an 18-year old and a 40-year old driving the same model of car, the premium you would demand of the 18-year old would invariably be much higher than that for the 40-year old. This would be reasonable as the likelihood of the 18-year old crashing his car and making a claim is statistically much greater than that of the older driver doing so. Where risks are perceived to be higher, so too are the premiums.

The challenge for all options traders is to know how risky or volatile an asset may be in the future so that they can make appropriate option prices. Regrettably, we cannot know what will happen in the future, so options traders analyse how variable an asset has been in the recent past and use this to estimate how variable it may be in the future. This type of volatility is known as **historic volatility**.

The impact of changes in volatility is quite straightforward.

- If volatility rises, call and put premiums increase.
- If volatility falls, call and put premiums decrease.

3.7.5 Other influences

There are two other influences on options premiums, namely interest rates and, for stock options only, dividends.

For options on physicals

Interest Rate Rise: Call Premiums Rise
Put Premiums Fall

This is a cost of carry feature similar to that for futures. The writer of call options will be borrowing to hold shares as a hedge against the options he has written and any rise in interest rates is detrimental to him, increasing his cost of carry hence increasing the premium he must charge.

The writer of puts, on the other hand, will be depositing cash from the short shares position he has set up as a hedge. Any increase in rates will be beneficial to him, reducing his cost of carry and correspondingly reducing the premium he will demand.

For options on futures (When the premium is paid immediately)

Interest Rate Rise: Call and Put Premiums Fall

For options on futures, since the future has no up-front cost there is no need for the writer to borrow to buy the asset in order to hedge his position, so the cost of carry feature of physicals does not apply. When the premium is paid immediately in full however, the writer gains the benefit of that premium and the higher the interest rate the greater the benefit to the writer, hence the lower the premium needs to be.

For options on futures (When the premium is margined)

Interest Rate Rise: No Influence

For options on futures where the premium is margined, neither the cost of carry feature of physicals nor the benefit received from receiving the up-front premium are relevant. The rates therefore have no noticeable effect.

Asset yields

The asset yields on investments also influence option prices through their influence on the cost of carry as we saw with futures. The yield has the opposite effect to interest rates and though the coupon may be fixed for most bonds it does vary for some and for bond portfolios.

The writer of call options, who is borrowing to hold bonds as a hedge against the options he has written, will benefit from coupons received on those bonds, reducing his cost of carry. The writer of puts, on the other hand, will have a short bonds position as a hedge. Any increase in coupon yield will be detrimental to this position, increasing his cost of carry.

3.7.6 Summary of factors

Pulling the above points together, we have six factors affecting the price of an option which can be put in three broad groupings as follows.

- Asset price
- Exercise price

} Intrinsic value factors

- Volatility
- Time to Expiry

} Risk factors

- Interest rates
- Asset yields

} Cost of carry factors

A change in any one of these factors will lead to a change in the value of the option, and impacts will be as follows.

Increase in	Impact On	
	Call Option	Put Option
Share price	Up	Down
Exercise price	Down	Up
Volatility	Up	Up
Time to Expiry	Up	Up
Interest rates	Up	Down
Dividend yields	Down	Up

3.8 Option price sensitivities – The Greeks

3.8.1 Introduction

As we have just seen, the price of an option is driven by a number of factors, so a question that arises is how prices move as these factors change.

3.8.2 Delta (δ)

Definition

Delta is the rate of change of an option's premium with respect to the underlying security.

If we plot the values of a call option against the value of the underlying asset, we get the following.

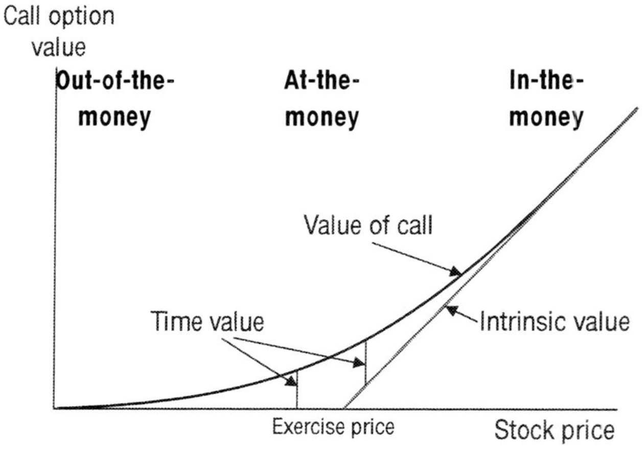

Options that are out-of-the-money show very little sensitivity to share price movements, an option price may only rise by 1p for a 10p asset price rise. Options that are in-the-money are much more sensitive, showing almost a one for one price relationship. This relationship between the option price and the underlying asset price is given by the option delta.

Delta can be viewed in the following three ways.

- Delta is the rate of change of an option's premium with respect to the underlying security. For example, an option with a delta of 0.25 can theoretically be expected to move at one quarter of the amount of the underlying. If the underlying goes up or down by 4, the option could be expected to go up or down by 1, all other factors remaining constant.
- It follows from this that delta is also the riskless hedge ratio, ie number of shares that would be required to hedge a particular option position. For example, if the delta of a call (put) is 0.25, the holder of a call (put) is theoretically long (short) a quarter of a bond, and needs to sell (buy) 0.25 bonds to achieve the hedge. In this example, the call holder's position at this instant is equivalent to a long position in a quarter of a bond, i.e. the holder will make or lose money at a quarter of the rate of a share.
- Delta can also be viewed as representative of the probability that an option will expire in-the-money. Thus, a delta of 0.25 or 25% means that there is only a small chance of being in-the-money; a delta of 0.9 or 90% gives an obviously higher chance.

Use of delta

Delta (δ) may be used to provide a first estimate of the change in the price of an option that will result from a given change in the price of the underlying asset.

Example

A bond is priced at 90, and a corresponding 100 call has a premium of 6 and a delta of 0.4. Calculate the change in premium, and the new resulting premium, if the bond price

- Falls 3
- Rises 5

Solution

Bond Falls 3

This relationship may be expressed mathematically as

Formula to learn

Change in premium = $\delta \times \Delta S$

where

δ = option delta
ΔS = change in the bond price

Applying this relationship gives

Change in premium = $\delta \times \Delta S = 0.4 \times (-3) = -1.2$

Giving a new premium of 4.8 (6.0 – 1.2)

Bond rises 5p

Change in premium = $\delta \times \Delta S = 0.4 \times 5 = +2.0$

Giving a new premium of 8.0 (6.0 + 2.0)

Comments

Note that these are just first estimates since the delta changes as the share price changes. This is dealt with under gamma below.

Delta hedging – Delta neutral positions

Whilst the delta of a futures/underlying position remains constant, option deltas are dynamic. This presents problems to hedgers who often like to have a delta position of zero (sometimes called a delta neutral position), which gives them no exposure to movements in the underlying asset price.

Example

A bond has a price of 96 and our holding could be hedged by shorting 200 futures. Call options written on that bond have a premium of 2.26 and a delta of 0.4.

- Construct a delta neutral position.
- Determine how this position will change as the underlying share price moves.

Solution

Delta neutral position

When we are looking to hedge we need to set up a position such that the gain on the derivative offsets the loss on the asset being hedged. We know that bond options settle into the bond futures and we saw earlier how to calculate the number of futures contracts to hedge a position, so the number of bond options must be related. The additional problem with options is their delta. Futures have no delta (it is effectively 1), options on the other hand have a delta that is always less than one.

To lead into this, imagine that an option is a contract over just one asset and has a delta of 0.4. This means that if the asset price moves by 1 the option price will only move by 0.4. If we wished to hedge the asset price movement then it would not be sufficient to use one option for each asset since a 0.4 gain will not offset a loss of 1. To hedge the asset exposure we need to use 2.5 options contracts (giving a gain of $0.4 \times 2.5 = 1$) per asset.

The relationship may be extended to

Formula to learn

$$\text{Number of options to hedge a position} = \text{Number of futures to hedge the position} \times \frac{1}{\text{Option delta}}$$

So for our scenario we would have

$$\text{Number of options} = 200 \times \frac{1}{0.4} = 500$$

Movements in the underlying

Such neutrality is only real for as long as the delta of the option remains the same. This means that the position is only technically delta neutral for infinitesimally small changes in bond price. Should the option move further in or out-of-the-money, the neutrality will be lost, necessitating a readjustment of the position when the delta changes significantly.

The problem with not adjusting a delta neutral position is that the value of the portfolio will decline as the bond price moves in either direction. This is because as the stock price rises, the delta of the call option will increase and the loss on the short call position will accelerate. We therefore lose out on the relative price movements.

As the value of the bond falls, the delta of the option reduces. This means that its price falls at a slower rate compared to the bond. Thus, the gains we make on the short call are less than the losses we suffer on the long bond position.

This could be represented on a graph as follows.

Value of a Portfolio Delta Neutral at a Stock Price of 36

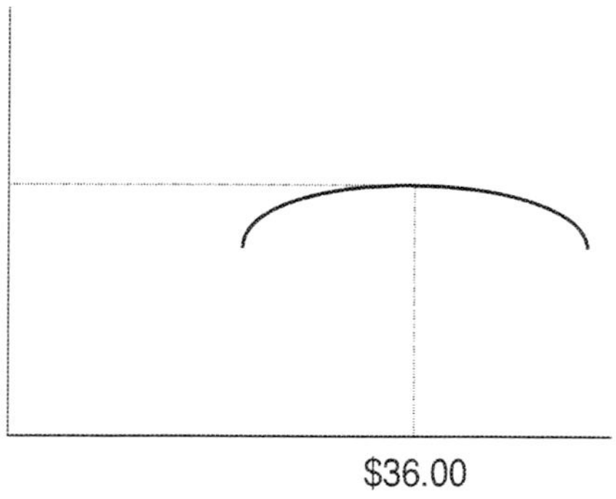

3.8.3 Gamma (γ)

Definition

Gamma is the rate of change of delta with respect to the underlying security.

As noted earlier, the delta of the underlying asset or futures contract is **always** 1. If you are long a future, you have a positive delta; if short, a negative delta of 1.

Whilst the delta of a futures/underlying asset position is static, option deltas are dynamic. An option's sensitivity to price changes does **not** stay constant, rather it changes as the underlying asset price moves and time to expiry shortens. Deep in-the-money options normally have deltas near 1; at-the-money options have deltas of approximately 0.5; deep out-of-the-money options have deltas near to zero. As options move in-to and out-of-the-money, their deltas change and the gamma reflects the rate of this change.

These dynamics presents problems to hedgers who often like to have a delta position of zero (sometimes called a delta neutral position), which gives them no exposure to movements in the underlying as long as the deltas of the options remain the same. Should any of the options move further in or out-of-the-money, the neutrality will be lost, necessitating a readjustment of the position. Traders can achieve a delta neutral position, but if this is done by using options with high gammas, the comfort of the hedge can be illusory.

Options that are at-the-money and close to expiry have the highest gammas, thus particular care needs to be taken if such options are used in a hedge. Out-of-the-money options have low or zero gammas, as the options will have deltas of zero. Similarly, in-the-money options which will already have deltas of 1 will have zero gammas, as these options are bound, subject to an extraordinary move, to expire in-the-money.

Referring back to the earlier delta diagram

- Delta is **the slope** of the value line ranging from 0 (when deeply out-of-the-money) though 0.5 (when at-the-money) to 1 (when deeply in-the-money).
- Gamma is **the curve** of the value line, indicating how the slope, i.e. delta changes. The curve is greatest for at-the-money and gradually reduces (as the line becomes increasingly straight) as the option is more in or out-of-the-money.

Use of gamma

Gamma can be used to give a more accurate assessment of the change in the premium of an option that will result from a given change in the share price.

Example

Extending our earlier example, a share is priced at 90, and a corresponding 100 call has a premium of 6, a delta of 0.4, and a gamma of 0.007. Calculate the change in premium, and the new resulting premium, if the share price

- Falls 3p.
- Rises 5p.

Solution

Share falls 3p

Alternative 1 – Using an average delta

As we noted above, delta changes as the share price changes, hence using it to forecast price movements will lead to inaccuracies. To overcome this, we could use the gamma to calculate the average delta over the given range of share prices and use this to more accurately assess the change in premiums as follows.

Delta at share price of 90p		0.4000
Change due to gamma if shares fall 3p	0.007 × (–3)	– 0.0210
Delta at share price of 87p		0.3790
Average delta	(0.4000 + 0.3790) ÷ 2	0.3895

Hence

Change in premium = Average $\delta \times \Delta s = 0.3895 \times (-3) = -1.1685$

Giving a new premium of 4.8315 (6.0000p – 1.1685p)

Alternative 2 – Mathematical Relationship

Note, we could calculate the above average delta from the original delta (δ) and gamma (γ) as

$$\begin{aligned}\text{Average } \delta &= \delta + \tfrac{1}{2}\gamma \times \Delta S\\ &= 0.4000 + \tfrac{1}{2} \times 0.0070 \times (-3)\\ &= 0.3895\end{aligned}$$

and substituting this equation in the above premium change formula gives

$$\begin{aligned}\text{Change in premium} &= \text{Average } \delta \times \Delta S\\ &= (\delta + \tfrac{1}{2}\gamma \times \Delta S) \times \Delta S\\ &= \delta \times \Delta S + \tfrac{1}{2}\gamma \times \Delta S^2\end{aligned}$$

That is, this whole average delta approach may be combined into a single formula to speed the calculation and expressed mathematically as

Formula to learn

$$\text{Change in premium} = \delta \times \Delta S + \tfrac{1}{2}\gamma \times \Delta S^2$$

where

δ = option delta at the original share price
γ = options gamma at the original share price
ΔS = change in the share price

Applying this relationship gives

$$\begin{aligned}\text{Change in premium} &= \delta \times \Delta S + \tfrac{1}{2}\gamma \times \Delta S^2\\ &= 0.400 \times (-3) + \tfrac{1}{2} \times 0.007 \times (-3)^2\\ &= -1.1685\end{aligned}$$

This is a negative figure, hence the premium will fall by 1.1685p to 4.8315p (6.000 – 1.1685p) as calculated above in Alternative 1.

Share rises 5p

Applying the formula gives

$$\begin{aligned}\text{Change in premium} &= \delta \times \Delta S + \tfrac{1}{2}\gamma \times \Delta S^2 \\ &= 0.400 \times 5 + \tfrac{1}{2} \times 0.007 \times 5^2 \\ &= 2.0875\text{p}\end{aligned}$$

This is positive, hence the premium will rise by 2.0875p to 8.0875p.

Gamma hedging

As was discussed above regarding delta hedging, it is also appropriate to hedge a position's gamma. As the gamma is the sensitivity of the delta to the underlying, it is also a reflection of how frequently a portfolio would have to be rehedged to maintain its delta. One thing to note with gamma hedging is that unlike delta hedging, it cannot be done by adjusting the amount of underlying in the portfolio. This is because the gamma of the underlying asset is zero. Therefore, gamma hedging will necessitate adjusting the gamma via options, which will make it more expensive. Typically therefore, it will be done less frequently.

3.8.4 Theta (θ)

The theta of an option reflects the rate of change of the option price with respect to time.

As we are aware, the price or premium of an option is a combination of intrinsic and time value. If all other factors remain constant, by how much will the time value, hence the premium, move over a period of, say, one day?

Theta is an absolute measure, hence if an option has a premium of 1.50 and a theta of 0.05, the next day, all other things remaining equal, the option will have a value of 1.45.

The relationship here (all other factors being equal) is

Formula to learn

$$\text{Change in premium} = \theta \times \Delta T$$

where

θ = option theta at the original date
ΔT = number of days that have elapsed

For buyers of options, theta is negative, buyers suffer from time decay. For sellers of options, theta is positive, sellers benefit from time decay.

The buyer of an option may be concerned by this, as the value of his investment (the price of his option) falls as time moves towards expiry. He will therefore require a return from other factors, such as the movement in the underlying asset price, that will more than offset the loss due to time decay over any specified period. The theta provides a means for assessing this time decay.

As we indicated earlier, the rate of time decay is non-constant, i.e. the theta of an option also varies with time. As options move towards expiry, the rate of time decay increases, hence theta attracts a larger value.

3.8.5 Vega (or Kappa) (κ)

The vega (or kappa) of an option reflects the rate of change of the option price with respect to volatility.

As an asset becomes more/less volatile, option premiums rise/fall. Vega assesses this rate of change.

The relationship here (all other factors being equal) is

Formula to learn

Change in premium = $\kappa \times \Delta\sigma$

where

κ = option vega (kappa) at the original volatility
$\Delta\sigma$ = change in the volatility

The higher the vega, the greater the impact on an option premium for a given change in volatility. This may be of use to speculators in assessing volatility trades such as straddles and strangles.

At-the-money options have the greatest sensitivity to volatility, i.e. have the greatest vega. Options that are deeply in-the-money or out-of-the-money have little sensitivity to volatility and hence, very low vegas.

Although an at-the-money option has the highest vega, this vega is relatively insensitive to changes in volatility itself. However, the vega of options which are deeply in or out-of-the-money are more sensitive to changes in volatility.

3.8.6 Rho (ρ)

The rho of an option measures the rate of change of an option price with respect to interest rates.

We are aware that interest rates influence option premiums, though the impact on calls and puts differs. Rho measures the sensitivity to this change and can be used to assess risk in an option in times of interest rate volatility.

The relationship here (all other factors being equal) is

Formula to learn

Change in premium = $\rho \times \Delta r$

where

ρ = option rho at the original rate of interest
Δr = change in the interest rate

3.8.7 Combined

Combining all of the above individual factors gives

Formula to learn

Change in premium = $\delta \times \Delta S + \frac{1}{2}\gamma \times \Delta S^2 + \theta \times \Delta T + \kappa \times \Delta\sigma + \rho \times \Delta r$

3.8.8 Lambda (λ)

The lambda of an option, like the delta of an option, indicates the sensitivity of the option price to changes in the price of the underlying asset. The difference is that the delta measures the absolute change in the option price per unit change in the asset price, whereas the lambda gives the percentage change in the option price for a 1% change in the asset price. That is where the delta is an absolute measure, the lambda is a relative measure.

The lambda therefore reflects the relative returns that can be made. If an option has a lambda of 2, then a 1% movement in the asset price will result in a 2% movement in the option price, all other factors being equal. As such, lambda reflects the gearing that can be achieved through investing in the option.

In common with the delta, however, the lambda is not constant, but changes as the underlying asset price changes. As a result, it is only valid for small movements and would not perfectly assess the relative position due to a larger price movement.

3.9 Protecting and hedging with options

3.9.1 Protecting

As we noted when we considered options strategies earlier, the aim of protecting a bond/bond portfolio with options is to

- Place a minimum value on an existing portfolio – protective put.
- Place a maximum price on a future purchase – long call.

The number of contracts for either purpose is the same number as we calculated earlier for hedging with the bond futures contract, the options being on the futures contract, ie.

$$\text{Number of contracts} = \frac{\text{Portfolio value}}{\text{Futures value}} \times \frac{\text{Portfolio MD}}{\text{Futures CTD MD}}$$

On exercise

- A long call settles into a long futures position.
- A long put settles into a short futures position.

3.9.2 Hedging

When hedging with options rather than with futures we have one more factor to contend with, the option delta. Futures effectively have a delta of one, and the formulae established above are based on this. When using options that have deltas less than one we will need to scale up the number of contracts accordingly in order to get the correct offsetting effect as we discussed under detla hedging above

$$\text{Number of option contracts} = \text{Number of futures contracts} \times \frac{1}{\text{Option delta}}$$

The issue that arises with options (that is not an issue with futures) is that the option delta changes as the bond price changes. Therefore if an investor wishes to maintain a delta neutral position he will need to constantly monitor and adjust the position. In doing this he will need to consider the cost and benefit of the continuous rebalancing. On balance, it may well be best to hedge with in-the-money options where the changes in delta will be low and the options are reasonably sensitive to price movements in the underlying bond.

4 Interest Rate Swaps

Exam tip

> Most recently examined in Summer 2008 Question 4.

4.1 Definition

An interest rate swap is a contract which commits two counterparties to exchange, over an agreed period, two streams of interest payments, each calculated using a different interest rate index, but applied to a common notional principal amount.

4.1.1 Key points

Only interest is exchanged in the swap; there is no exchange of principal. Interest rate swaps do not, therefore, impact on the balance sheet, only on the profit and loss account. They are therefore classed as 'off balance sheet instruments'.

Movements in the interest cash flow streams take place at intervals during the swap's life and are normally netted. For example, in a swap in which one side is paying a fixed rate and the other a floating rate, such as six-month LIBOR, only the cash difference is exchanged. This reduces credit risks between the counterparties.

4.1.2 A basic interest rate swap

The cash flows in a basic interest rate swap could be pictured as follows.

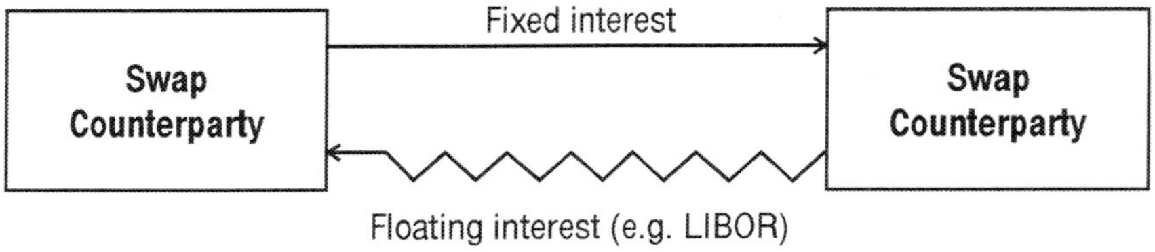

4.2 Terminology

4.2.1 Coupon swap

Definition

A coupon swap involves the exchange of a fixed interest rate (e.g. the coupon payment on a bond) for the floating rate as measured by an index such as LIBOR. These are sometimes called fixed against floating or generic swaps.

Counterparties to a coupon swap

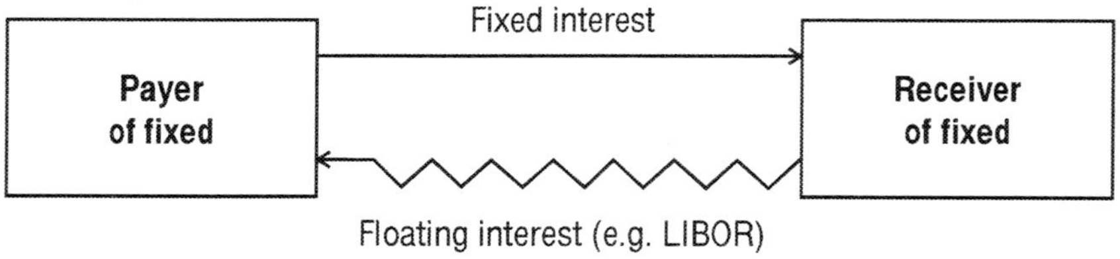

Counterparties – Alternative terms

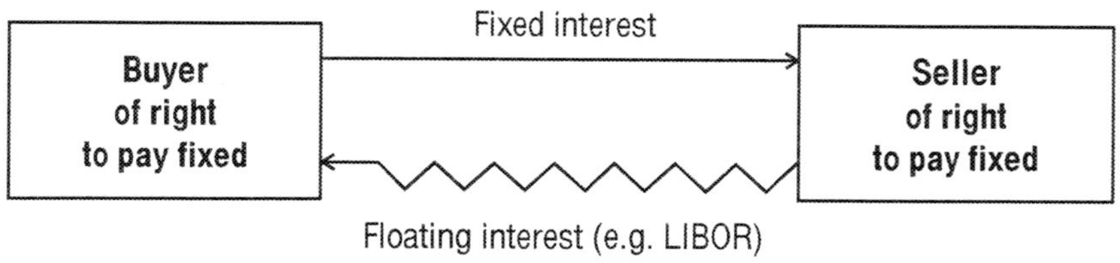

4.2.2 Basis swap

Definition

It is possible to swap two interest streams which are both calculated using floating interest rates, e.g. 3 month LIBOR vs 6-month LIBOR.

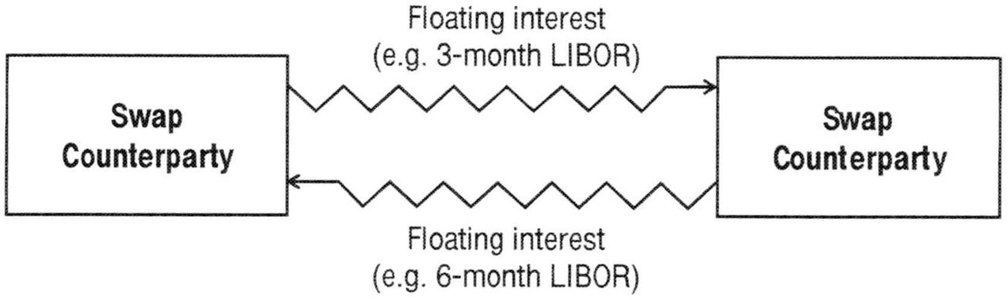

Counterparties to a basis swap

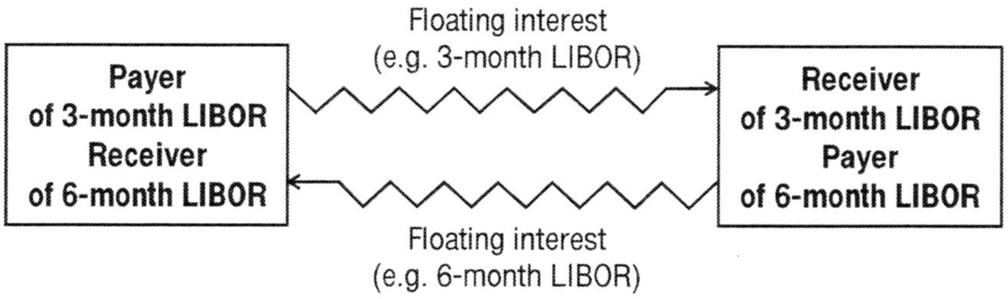

4.2.3 Term swap

A swap with a lifespan of more than two years.

4.2.4 Money market swap

A swap with up to two years of life when originally negotiated.

4.2.5 Asset swap

When the interest streams being exchanged through an interest rate swap are funded with interest received on specific assets, the swap is called an asset swap. Asset swaps may also be coupon or basis swaps and are covered in more detail later in this chapter.

4.3 Dealing

4.3.1 Inception

The market in interest rate swaps is an over-the-counter (OTC) market. Trading is conducted over the telephone, and price information is disseminated through quote vendor systems, such as Reuters and Telerate.

In interest rate swaps, the floating rate in a coupon swap (the most common type of swap) is assumed to be 6-month LIBOR. Negotiation therefore concentrates on the fixed rate, sometimes called the swap rate.

There are two methods of quoting the fixed rate: the all-in price, or as a swap spread on a benchmark rate.

All-in prices

A quote for a one-year swap may be given as 8.00%-7.85%. This is a two-way price in which the dealer would pay a fixed rate of 7.85% and would look to receive 8.00% fixed. The dealing spread of 15 basis points represents the dealer's profit.

Swap spreads

In more liquid interest rate swaps markets, such as the US, the use of all-in terms for quoting the fixed rates in coupon swaps has been replaced by the convention of quoting in two parts: a swap spread and a benchmark interest rate.

The benchmark interest rate is usually the yield on the 'on the run' (most actively traded) bond, with a remaining life similar to the swap. When the swap is agreed, the spread and the benchmark are fixed.

Example

	Swap Spread	Bond Yield
Two Years	21/25	5.70–5.75

The spread is quoted bid/offer in basis, hence this quote corresponds to an all-in price of 5.91-6.00.

As such, the swap spread is the difference between the fixed swap rate for a specific term and the yield on a gilt of equivalent maturity. Since swaps have a AA credit rating and gilts are rated AAA, what does this swap spread give us?

Historically, government bonds have always been used as a benchmark for the evaluation of other securities, with a premium added to account for credit/default risk. To act as a good benchmark, however, the following attributes are required.

- Size
- Liquidity
- Length of maturity
- Consistency
- Transparency

Evaluative uses

Historically, the second of these (liquidity) has, on occasion, been brought into question due to the distortions of:

- Government deficits/surplus leading to an increase/reduction in new issues and an excess/shortage of supply especially at longer maturities.
- Short-term rates being increased to control inflation resulting in an inverted yield curve contrary to the conventional risk-return trade-off.

The swaps market does not suffer from these distortions, hence swap rates arguably represent a more realistic benchmark rate for evaluation purposes. By adjusting the gilt yield curve by the swap spreads we can, arguably, construct a better benchmark.

Trading uses

Swap spreads and movements in swap spreads give an indication of credit risk/credit conditions and how conditions are changing (spreads widening or narrowing).As a result, this alternative undistorted benchmark gives an indication of the position in the economic cycle which may be of great use to fund managers.

In addition, fund managers can trade on these spreads to take advantage of such movements.

4.3.2 Termination and assignment

Termination and assignment are two methods by which counterparties can exit their swap positions. A third route, the reversal, in which an equal and opposite position is taken, is also available.

Termination is simply the mutual cancellation of the swap. Assignment is the process through which existing swaps are sold to new counterparties.

When a swap is terminated or assigned, it is valued and a cash compensation paid to the party that is in-the-money.

The termination value will be the NPV of the cash flows (see valuation below). Assignment values are calculated in the same way, although the pricing can be complicated by credit issues.

4.4 Uses of interest rate swaps

As with futures and options, there are three basic motivations: speculation, hedging and arbitrage.

4.4.1 Speculation

Interest rate swaps can be used to take risky positions independent of any underlying instruments. In a coupon swap

- **The payer of fixed interest** is exposed to the risk of an interest rate fall but will benefit if rates rise, since he is in the same commercial position as an issuer of a fixed coupon bond or fixed rate mortgage borrower.
- **The receiver of fixed interest** is exposed to the risk of an interest rate rise but will benefit if rates fall, since he is in the same commercial position as an investor in a fixed coupon bond.

4.4.2 Hedging

Swap hedges work in a very similar way to futures hedges, in that swaps are used to establish an equal and opposite position.

For example, assume a bank has invested its assets in fixed rate bonds, but has liabilities (depositors) to whom it has to pay floating rates. The bank is exposed to rising rates which will increase its payments without the benefit of increased returns on its bonds.

This position could be hedged using swaps, and the cash flows for the hedged arrangement are illustrated below.

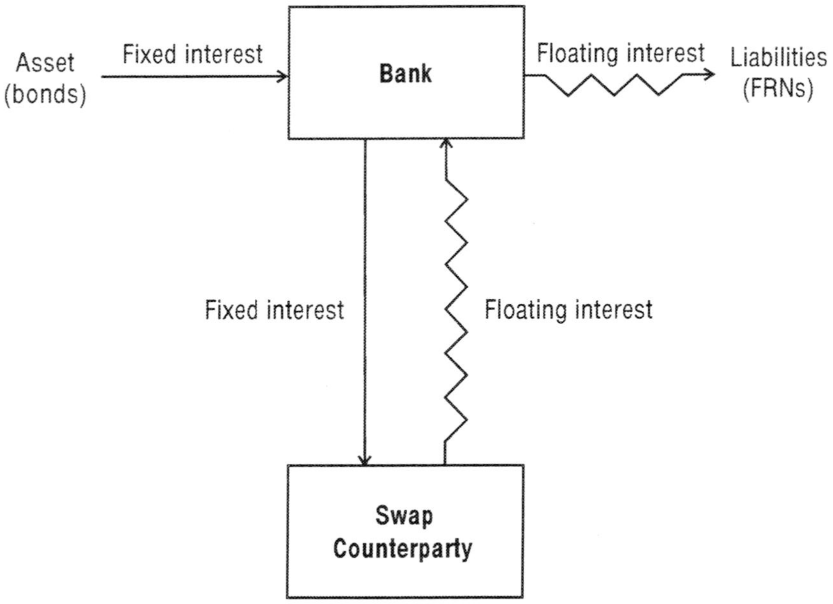

In this hedge, the bank

Receives	Fixed interest from the bonds. Floating interest from the swap counterparty.
Pays	Floating interest to depositors. Fixed interest to the swap counterparty.

In this way, the mismatch between the asset and liability cash flows is overcome.

Example

An institution raises money by issuing a five-year bond at a yield of 8.75%, but would prefer floating rate funding. Five-year swaps are quoted at all-in rates of 8.95-9.075. How could the institution change its interest rate exposure to floating rates and what would be the all-in cost of its borrowing after swapping?

Solution

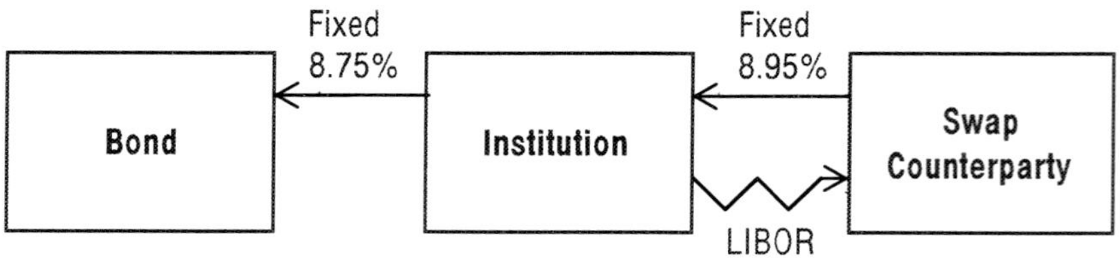

Summary of cash flows

Cost of bond:	–8.75%
Fixed receipts via swap:	+8.95%
Floating payments via swap:	LIBOR
Net cost of borrowing:	**LIBOR – 20 basis points**

4.4.3 Arbitrage

Another important use of interest rate swaps is arbitrage. Indeed, it was the driver behind the early development of the market. The arbitrage occurs because the fixed rate bond market and the floating rate banking markets have differing perceptions of an institution's credit risk.

The result of collaboration between two institutions that are viewed differently by the markets can result in an interesting example of financial alchemy. The following example illustrates this point.

Example

Let us take two companies who have a borrowing need for $100m for six years.

Company A	AAA rating	Requires floating funds
Company B	BBB rating	Requires fixed funds

Available rates

	Bond Market	Bank Market
Company A	8.20%	LIBOR + 35bp
Company B	10.10%	LIBOR + 125bp
Advantage of A over B	1.90%	0.90%

Whilst A can raise cheaper finance in both markets, Company B has a comparative advantage in the floating market. This is because it only pays 0.9% more in the bank market as opposed to 1.9% in the bond market.

This difference is known as the market arbitrage and is the result of differing perceptions by lenders in the two markets.

This arbitrage is 1% (1.9 – 0.9) and can be exploited by companies A and B working in collaboration.

Swap structure

Each company raises money in its market of comparative advantage (A fixed, B floating) and they, say, share the arbitrage equally (50bp each). The arrangement could be viewed as

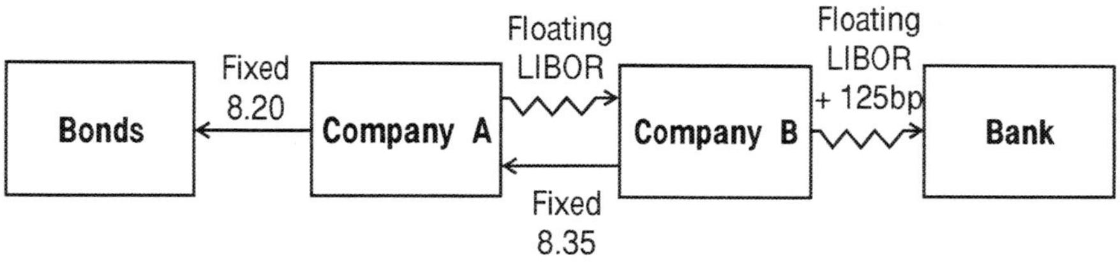

Company A		Company B	
Pays	Fixed 8.20% Floating LIBOR	**Pays**	Fixed 8.35% Floating LIBOR + 125bp
Receives	Fixed 8.35%	**Receives**	Floating LIBOR
Net	LIBOR – 15bp	**Net**	Fixed 9.60%

Each company ends up 50bp better off. Company A at LIBOR – 15bp (rather than LIBOR + 35bp), and Company B with fixed funds at 9.60% (rather than 10.10%).

The above example illustrates an important feature of the swap market: swaps enable borrowers to raise funds in the market to which they have best access, but to make interest and principal payments in a preferred form or currency. This separation of the funding decision and the choice of servicing debt enables borrowers to exploit their comparative advantages.

A more likely arrangement would involve an intermediary, perhaps a bank, who would also take a share of this arbitrage benefit. Perhaps, the arrangement would be as follows.

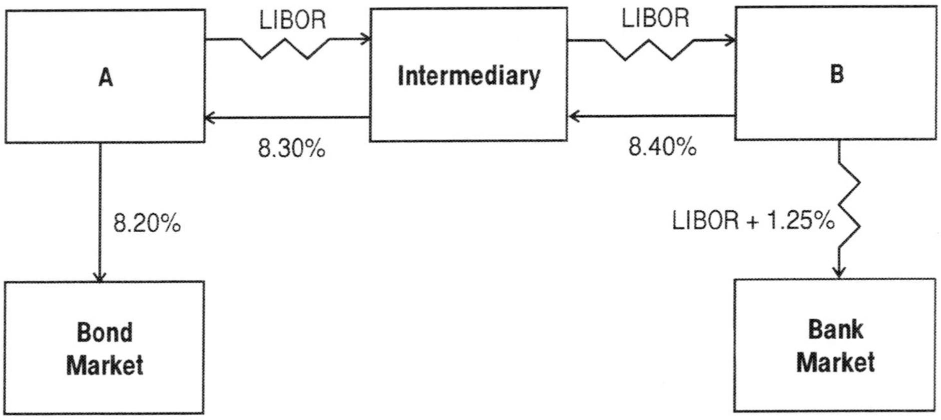

Net Positions		
LIBOR – 10bp	10bp	9.65%
Best if Arranged Individually		
LIBOR + 35bp	0bp	10.10%
Benefit		
45bp	10bp	45bp

4.5 Swap valuation

4.5.1 Introduction

In all swaps, there must be an equality between the value of the two legs at the inception date. The value of the swap at its start date is zero, with the net present value of one leg equalling the net present value of the other. If this were not the case, one party would be unable to rationalise entering into the swap, as they would immediately suffer a loss.

At any later date, the present value of the two legs may vary as spot rates change and the swap may have a value being the difference between the present values of the two legs.

The value of the swap to either counterparty at any time will be given by

Formula to learn

Swap value = Difference between PV of cash flows swapped

Swap value = PV of cash flows acquired – PV of cash flows sold

4.5.2 Approach

The neatest approach to valuing an interest rate swap is to use bond pricing ideas along with the ideas of arbitrage. Arbitrage ensures that if there are two different ways of achieving the same end result, then they must have the same value, and when it comes to swap cash flows, it is quite easy to replicate them with fairly simple instruments.

The cash flows that the payer of fixed interest (receiver of floating) would experience are identical to those that would be experienced if he borrowed with a fixed rate bond and invested the proceeds raised in a floating rate note (FRN). That is, throughout the term of the swap, he would pay fixed and receive floating. At the termination date, the capital flows cancel, with the capital received on the maturity of the FRN repaying the fixed borrowing.

As such, the value of a swap to the swap buyer could be established as the difference between the value of a FRN and a fixed rate bond as follows.

Value of swap

Value to Payer of Fixed	(£)
Value of FRN asset	X
Value of fixed coupon bond liability	(Y)
Value of swap	Z

And we can use the bond valuation ideas.

FRN Price

Formula to learn

$$\text{FRN Price} = \frac{\text{Next coupon} + \text{Par value}}{1 + rt}$$

where t is the time to the next coupon in years and r is the annualised spot rate to the next coupon payment date.

Fixed coupon bond price

Formula to learn

$$\text{Fixed coupon bond price} = \frac{C_1}{(1+r_1)} + \frac{C_2}{(1+r_2)^2} + \frac{C_3}{(1+r_3)^3} + \cdots + \frac{C_n + R}{(1+r_n)^n}$$

where r_1, r_2, r_3, ...r_n are the relevant spot rates given the timing of the interest cash flows.

4.5.3 Value at inception

The pricing of interest rate swaps is concerned with the determination of the rate for the fixed interest leg, as traditionally, the floating rate leg is simply an agreed benchmark such as 6-month LIBOR.

If we remember that in the generic interest rate swap, no money passes between the payer and receiver at the initiation of the swap, this must mean that the net present value of the fixed leg equals the net present value of the floating leg at inception. Using this gives

Value to Payer of Fixed	(£)
Value of FRN asset	X
Value of fixed coupon bond liability	(Y)
Value of swap	0

When issued, an FRN is always valued at par and therefore the problem is identifying the coupon to price the bond at par, the par yield.

Example

What is the required swap rate for a five-year swap with annual payments on a notional principal of £100? Twelve-month LIBOR is 10% and the following spot rates are observed.

Year	(%)
1	10
2	11
3	12
4	13
5	14

Solution

Value of FRN

This calculation is not strictly required, but included here for illustration.

$$\text{FRN Price} = \frac{\text{Next coupon} + \text{Par value}}{1+rt} = \frac{110}{1.10} = 100$$

Value of swap and fixed rate bond

Value to Payer of Fixed	(£)
Value of FRN asset	100
Value of fixed coupon bond liability	(100)
Value of swap	0

Coupon on fixed rate bond

We now need to find the fixed rate necessary to result in a par value on the 'bond' a calculation known as the **par yield**

$$\text{Fixed coupon bond price} = \frac{C}{1.10^1} + \frac{C}{1.11^2} + \frac{C}{1.12^3} + \frac{C}{1.13^4} + \frac{C+R}{1.14^5}$$

$$= \frac{C}{1.10^1} + \frac{C}{1.11^2} + \frac{C}{1.12^3} + \frac{C}{1.13^4} + \frac{C}{1.14^5} + \frac{100}{1.14^5}$$

Gives

$100.00 = 0.9091C + 0.8116C + 0.7118C + 0.6133C + 0.5194C + 51.94$

$100.00 = 3.5651C + 51.94$

$48.06 = 3.5651C$

Hence, the fixed interest cash value is

$$C = \frac{48.06}{3.5651} = 13.48$$

Which, on a £100 nominal value, corresponds to a coupon rate of 13.48%.

This approach, where the values of inception are equal, is also called a par swap.

4.5.4 Later valuation

As we have noted, the value of a generic interest rate swap at its start date will be zero. At any later date, the present value of the two legs may vary as spot rates change and the swap may have a value being the difference between the present values of the two legs, which can again be established using the above idea.

We can see that as interest rates rise and the market value of bonds fall, the buyer's position (payer of fixed) will be showing a gain and the seller a loss. This is what we would expect. When interest rates rise, fixed rate payers gain and floating rate payers lose.

Example

The above swap is to be valued one year later, when the spot rates have fallen to

Year	(%)
1	9
2	10
3	11
4	12

Solution

Approach 1

Value of original swap using prevailing spot rates

Value of FRN

$$\text{FRN Price} = \frac{\text{Next coupon} + \text{Par value}}{1 + rt} = \frac{109}{1.09} = 100$$

Value of Bond

Time	Cash Flow	DF	PV
1	13.48	$\frac{1}{1.09^1}$	12.37
2	13.48	$\frac{1}{1.10^2}$	11.14
3	13.48	$\frac{1}{1.11^3}$	9.86
4	113.48	$\frac{1}{1.12^4}$	72.12
			105.49

Value of Swap and Fixed Rate Bond

Value to Payer of Fixed	(£)
Value of FRN asset	100.00
Value of fixed coupon bond liability	(105.49)
Value of swap	(5.49)

Hence

Swap value to buyer (payer of fixed) = –5.49
Swap value to seller (payer of floating) = +5.49

i.e. locking in to a fixed rate (the buyer) loses money when we experience generally declining interest rates, whereas paying variable rates (the seller) results in a gain.

Approach 2

Step 1 New swap rate par yield calculation

$$100.00 = \frac{C}{1.09^1} + \frac{C}{1.10^2} + \frac{C}{1.11^3} + \frac{C}{1.12^4} + \frac{100}{1.12^4}$$

$$100.00 = 0.9174C + 0.8264C + 0.7312C + 0.6355C + 63.55$$

$$36.45 = 0.9174C + 0.8264C + 0.7312C + 0.6355C$$

$$36.45 = 3.1105C$$

Hence, the fixed interest cash value is

$$C = \frac{36.45}{3.1105} = 11.72$$

Which, on a £100 nominal value, corresponds to a coupon rate or swap rate of 11.72%.

Value of FRN

$$\text{FRN Price} = \frac{109}{1.09} = 100$$

Value of bond

Time	Cash Flow	DF (11.72%)	PV
1	13.48	$\frac{1}{1.1172^1}$	12.07
2	13.48	$\frac{1}{1.1172^2}$	10.80
3	13.48	$\frac{1}{1.1172^3}$	9.67
4	113.48	$\frac{1}{1.1172^4}$	72.84
			105.38

You will note that this value is the same as to Approach 1, though if we had not rounded rates and PV's there would be a slight difference as we are using one average rate of 11.72% as representative for all four years, which could never be 100% accurate. It does, however, represent a quick method when spot rates are not immediately available but swap rates are.

Value of swap and fixed rate bond

Value to Payer of Fixed	(£)
Value of FRN asset	100.00
Value of fixed coupon bond liability	(105.38)
Value of swap	(5.38)

Hence

Swap value to buyer (payer of fixed) = –5.38
Swap value to seller (payer of floating) = +5.38

4.5.5 Sensitivity of swap to rate changes

We have just established that the value of a swap to the buyer can be determined by assessing the net value of an FRN asset and a bond liability. If we wish to determine the sensitivity of the swap to changes in rates we need to consider the sensitivities of a portfolio of these bonds by an assessment of their duration, modified duration or BPV (DV01).

We considered assessing the duration, modified duration or BPV (DV01) of both individual bonds and bond portfolios earlier in this Study Text so do not repeat ourselves here.

4.6 Forward rate agreements

Exam tip

Most recently examined in Summer 2009 Question 6.

4.6.1 The use of forward rate agreements

Interest rate swaps are usually appropriate for longer term interest rate exposures and are often used for maturities of between two and five years, possibly going out even further. Forward rate agreements (FRAs) are usually appropriate for shorter term hedging strategies. They enable a company to fix its interest rate for a particular future period, i.e. they allow a company to lock in to a relevant forward rate of interest for a specified future term.

An FRA is a contract between counterparties for a fixed interest rate on a notional principal sum with a specified value date (start date) and maturity (end date). Note that, as with an interest rate swap, there is no exchange of principal. Rather, this is an agreed notional sum on which the contract is based, and compensation is paid or received if the interest rate at the value date differs from the contracted FRA rate.

Example

A company has borrowings of £100m, with interest payable quarterly at a rate of LIBOR + 1%. It is concerned that in three months' time, interest rates will rise, increasing its interest cost for the period from three months' time to six months' time. Accordingly, it buys a 3 v 6 FRA with a notional principal of £100m at an interest rate of 7%. This effectively locks it into a LIBOR rate of 7%, giving an overall cost for this future period of 8% (LIBOR + 1%).

At the value date in three months' time, LIBOR is 9%. Hence, the company's actual borrowing cost has risen to 10% (LIBOR + 1%). Under the FRA, however, it receives a compensating payment at a rate of 2%, being the difference between the prevailing LIBOR (9%) and the contracted FRA rate (7%) at the value date. Its net cost is therefore 8% for the three months (quoted on an annual basis).

Note that the actual receipt under the FRA will usually take place at the beginning of the period to which it relates (the value date), whereas interest is usually paid in arrears (maturity). As a result, the payment under the FRA is the discounted value of the difference, the discount rate being the appropriate market rate of interest.

Looking at this numerically gives

	(£'000)
Actual interest cost payable at **maturity** – £100m × 2.5% (10% × $^3/_{12}$)	2,500
Difference under the FRA at **maturity** – £100m × 0.5% [(9% – 7%) × $^3/_{12}$]	(500)
Net cost at maturity	2,000

The net cost clearly being 2% for the period, or 8% p.a.

The actual compensation payment received at the **value date** would be the present value of this £500,000 discounted at the prevailing LIBOR rate of 9% p.a. (2.25% for the three-month period), i.e. 500,000 × $^1/_{1.0225}$ = £488,998.

5 Short-Term Currency Swaps

5.1 Definition

A short-term currency swap is a contract that commits two parties to exchange pre-agreed foreign currency amounts now and re-exchange them back at a given future date (the maturity date). The flows are capital only; there is no direct interest payment involved.

5.2 Terminology

5.2.1 Primary and secondary currencies

Primary currency

One currency is defined as the primary currency, and most deals are structured such that the nominal value of the primary currency exchanged on the two dates is equal.

Secondary currency

The other currency is the secondary currency, and the nominal value of this exchanged on the two dates is a function of the spot rate and the swap market forward rate.

5.2.2 Buyer and seller

Terms

The terms buyer and seller are a little awkward in relation to currency dealing, since each party is giving (selling) one currency and receiving (buying) the other.

The terms buyer and seller relate to these swap arrangements from the point of view of the primary currency cash flows at inception. The **buyer** is the person who, at inception, purchases the primary currency (selling the secondary currency); the seller is the individual who, at inception, sells the primary currency (buying the secondary currency).

Cash flows

Buyer		Seller
At inception	←— Buy $1.5m (primary currency) ——	At inception
	—— Sell £1m (secondary currency) —→	
At maturity	—— Sell $1.5m (primary currency) —→	At maturity
	←— Buy £0.95m (secondary currency) ——	

5.2.3 Synthetic Agreement for Forward Exchange (SAFE)

A SAFE is a variation on the short-term currency swap, in which there is no actual exchange of principal at inception or at maturity, the arrangement being a contract for differences based on notional cash sums.

When the two parties agree to execute a SAFE, they agree the exchange rates at which the notional deals will be executed at inception and maturity. At maturity, one party pays to the other the difference in the value of the secondary currency between the rate originally contracted and the rate actually prevailing.

5.3 Dealing

The market in short-term currency swaps, as for interest rate swaps, is an OTC market. Trading is conducted over the telephone and price information is disseminated through quote vendor systems, such as Reuters and Telerate.

The quotes are as a swap spread on the current spot rate.

5.4 Using short-term currency swaps

5.4.1 Hedging

Short-term currency swaps provide an alternative to forward exchange rate agreements (see the next chapter) through simultaneously entering swap and spot deals. The arrangement may result in a better forward exchange rate being achieved as a result of differences between interest rates in swap and money markets.

The swap deal is chosen to achieve the correct cash flows at the maturity date, as could be achieved through the use of a forward exchange contract. The spot deal is undertaken to cancel the initiation leg of the swap so that the net position is that the only cash flow occurs at maturity. This is most easily seen with an example.

Example

A sum of $3m is to be received in three months from a US customer. The current spot rate is $1.733:£1, and three-month swap market interest rates are 10% in the UK and 4% in the US. How can a swap arrangement be structured to translate this amount into sterling, and what will the sterling receipt be in three months?

Solution

The swap arrangement needs to be selling US dollars in three months, hence buying US dollars now. If the US dollar is the primary currency, we need to be the buyer of the swap.

Based on the information provided, the relevant exchange rates and corresponding secondary currency (sterling) values are

Now: spot rate = 1.7330 $\Rightarrow$ £1,731,102

3 months: forward rate = $1.7330 \times \dfrac{1.01}{1.025} = 1.7076 \Rightarrow$ £1,756,812

The whole deal can therefore be structured as

Spot Market	Swap Market – Now	Swap Market – 3 months
Sell \$3,000,000	Buy \$3,000,000	Sell \$3,000,000
Buy £1,731,102	Sell £1,731,102	Buy £1,756,812

Spot Market and Swap Market Now: These cancel out, resulting in a net zero cash flow at inception

Swap Market 3 months: Leaving the second leg as the only actual commercial cash flow

5.4.2 Speculation

Since short-term currency swaps reflect forward exchange rates and respond to interest rate differentials, a speculator may use them to speculate on future

- Forward exchange rate spreads.
- The changes in interest rate differentials.

If, for example, a speculator believed that US rates were going to rise relative to UK rates in the near future, then the forward exchange rate on the US dollar would move to a lower premium, resulting in less pounds sterling being received per US dollar for forward exchange deals at that future date.

Entering a swap as in the above hedging example would, therefore, result in a gain to the speculator.

A buyer gains and a seller loses when the primary currency interest rate increases in relative terms.

Example

A speculator enters the above swap transaction, buying \$3m in the belief that US interest rates will increase in the near future relative to UK rates. Next day, US rates move up to 5% to support the dollar, keeping the spot rate at 1.733, but UK rates are unaltered. What will be the speculator's gain or loss?

Solution

With US rates at 5%, the three-month forward exchange rate, and sterling value corresponding to \$3m, will be

Forward rate = $1.7330 \times \dfrac{1.0125}{1.025} = 1.7119 \Rightarrow$ £1,752,439

The speculator can now close out his swap position with a forward exchange contract buying \$3m in three months for £1,752,439, hence realising a sterling profit of £4,373 (£1,756,812 – £1,752,439) at maturity.

6 Long-Term Currency Swaps

Exam tip

Most recently examined in Summer 2008 Question 4.

6.1 Introduction

The long-term currency swap was the original swap product; in its contemporary form, it dates back to 1976, but it did not really take off until 1981, when a deal was done between IBM and the World Bank.

In terms of size, currency swap volume is now dwarfed by the single currency interest rate swap market.

6.2 Definition

A long-term currency swap is a contract that commits two counterparties to exchange, over an agreed period, two streams of interest payments in different currencies and, at the end of the period, to exchange the corresponding principal amounts at an exchange rate agreed at the start of the contract (there may or may not be an exchange of principal amounts at the start of the contract).

6.2.1 Key elements

Thus, broken down into its constituent parts, we might see

- A UK corporate contracted to pay a US bank the interest payments on $15m at a rate agreed when the swap is negotiated.
- A US bank contracted to pay the UK corporate the interest payments on £10m at a rate agreed when the swap is negotiated.
- At the end of the, say, three-year term of the swap, the principal amounts involved would be exchanged, with the UK corporate paying the US bank $15m and receiving £10m.

You will immediately notice two important differences between currency swaps and interest rate swaps.

- The cash flows involved take place in two currencies.
- There is an exchange of principal amounts.

As a result of these differences, the currency swap can help reduce, or increase, exposure to both currencies and interest rates.

6.3 Terminology

As with interest rate swaps, there are many different structures that have developed from the simple currency swap outlined above. Some of the more important ones are listed below.

6.3.1 The currency swap

As with so much of the jargon of the financial industry, different practitioners often use the same term to mean different things but, strictly speaking, a currency swap is a swap involving the exchange of two fixed interest streams in different currencies with an exchange of principal at maturity.

This could be represented on a diagram as follows.

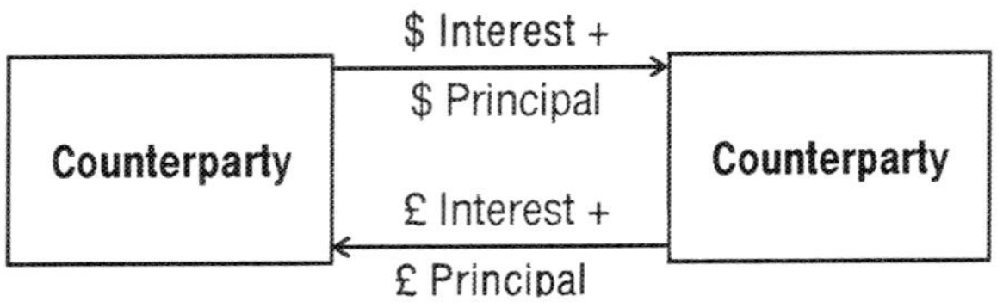

Some currency swaps may involve exchange of principals both at the beginning and end of the term. These are undertaken when the swap is associated with new borrowings by either or both of the counterparties. This form of currency swap – sometimes called a cash swap – was, in fact, the first manifestation of the product, and was introduced to overcome some of the difficulties of back-to-back or parallel loans.

6.3.2 Cross-currency swaps

Cross-currency swaps involve an exchange of interest streams in different currencies, of which at least one is at a floating rate of interest.

These swaps could therefore include

- **Cross-currency coupon swaps**, in which a fixed rate is exchanged for a floating rate; or
- **Cross-currency basis swaps**, in which two floating rates in different currencies are exchanged.

6.3.3 Asset swaps

Currency swaps in which the interest streams are backed by cash flows from assets.

6.3.4 Diff swaps

A diff(erential) or quanto swap is a special type of cross-currency basis swap, which does not involve any exchange of principal whatsoever. Both streams of interest payments through a diff are calculated with reference to the same notional principal amount of the same currency. For example, a $/€ diff swap would typically involve an exchange of six-month LIBOR € for a six-month US LIBOR. Both interest rate streams would be paid in euro.

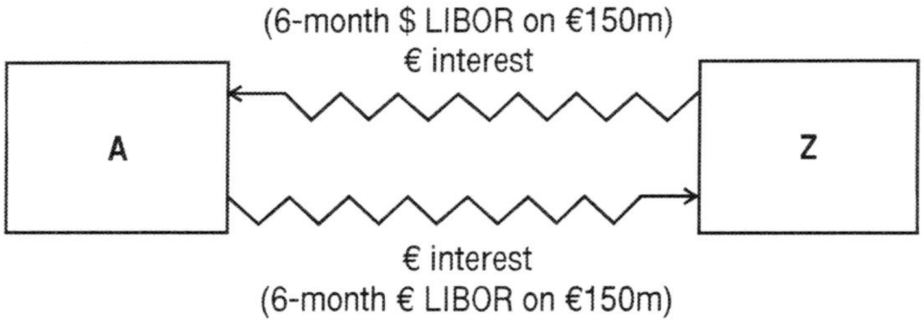

6.3.5 Circus swaps

A circus swap is a swap made up of a cross-currency coupon swap (fixed against floating) and a single-currency coupon swap. The purpose is to synthesise either a pure fixed against fixed currency swap or a cross-currency basis swap.

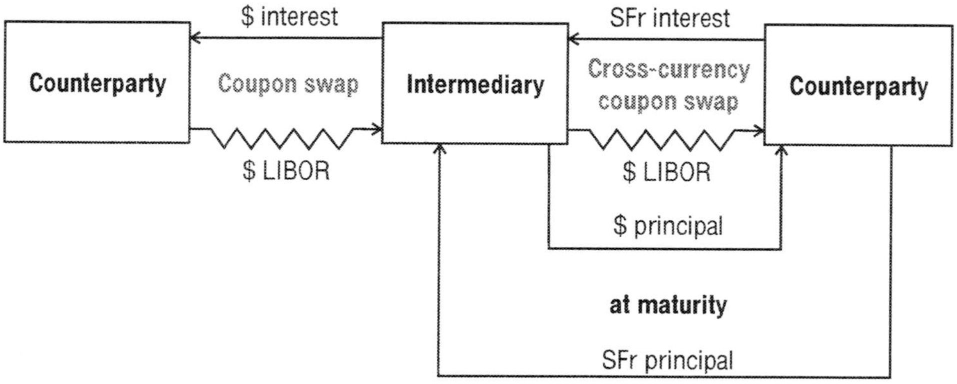

6.4 Dealing

It is conventional with interest rate coupon swaps to use six-month LIBOR as the standard index for the floating rate, thus leaving the fixed rate to be agreed. With currency swaps where a currency is also involved, the standard is to use six-month US dollar LIBOR.

Cross-currency basis swaps also use six-month US dollar LIBOR as a reference with the other floating rate (say, six-month UK LIBOR) being quoted as a margin over or under LIBOR in the non-dollar currency.

For example, a £/$ cross-currency basis swap might be quoted at +10, meaning the swap is between US dollar LIBOR on one hand and sterling LIBOR plus 10 basis points on the other.

Conventionally, currency swaps are quoted in terms of all-in prices, i.e. as absolute interest rates as two-way prices, e.g.

	7.15%		7.25%
Receive	7.15% fixed	Pay	7.25% fixed

6.5 Uses of currency swaps

6.5.1 Speculating

Although currency swaps create exposures to both fluctuations in interest rates and exchange rates, they are not used as trading vehicles in the same way as futures. This is because of the credit risks involved in exchanging principals. Currency swaps are therefore used exclusively for hedging and arbitrage.

6.5.2 Hedging

Imagine a British pharmaceutical company which has issued a dollar bond to finance development. The company expects the dollar to appreciate and sterling interest rates to fall.

If this happens, the foreign currency liability (the bond) will increase in sterling terms, and the cost of servicing the bond begins to look increasingly unattractive. Which swap structure could be used to achieve the required end of accessing lower UK rates and fixing the sterling value of the liability?

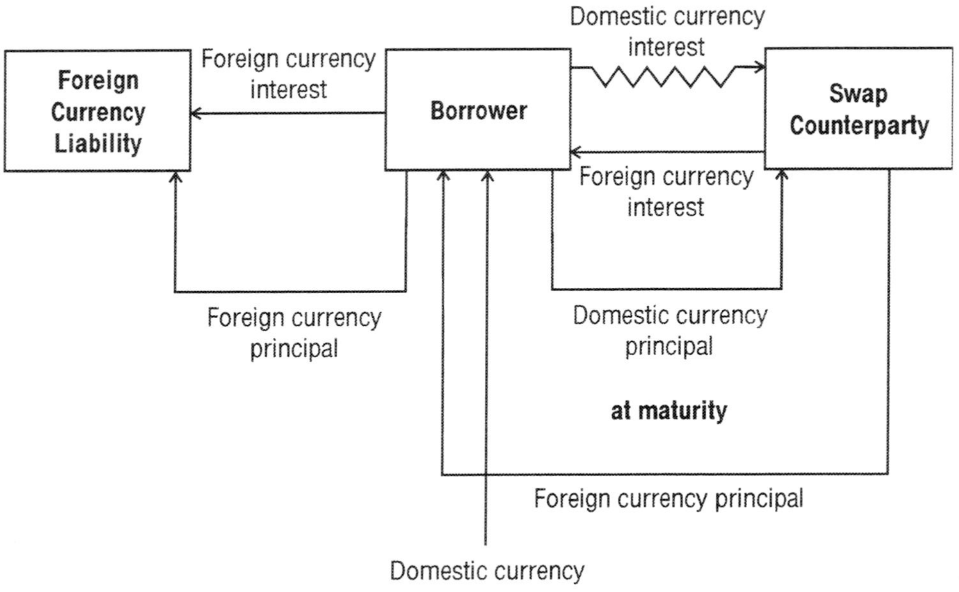

In the previous example, it was assumed that the British company could access the US bond market. In reality, the UK company might have a comparative advantage in its domestic corporate bond market and therefore raise funds there and swap the sterling into dollars at the start of the swap.

These are just two simple examples of swap hedges – there are, of course, many other potential uses.

6.5.3 Arbitrage

Currency swaps can be used in a similar way to interest rate swaps to arbitrage comparative advantage in different markets. It is also possible to arbitrage absolute advantage. For example, a Swiss company may be able to borrow dollars more cheaply than Swiss francs (perhaps, because the domestic Swiss market is already saturated with its paper), and a US company may be able to borrow Swiss francs more cheaply than dollars for the same reasons.

The appeal of new issue arbitrage using currency swaps is that borrowers can separate their funding decisions from risk management decisions about currency and interest rate risk.

6.6 Valuation

Once again, in order to initially conclude the swap deal, the present value of the swapped future cash flows must be identical, hence the value of the swap is zero. The swap will attract a value if these present values change as a result of interest and foreign exchange rate movements.

The valuation of a long-term currency swap (as for all swaps), requires us to evaluate the present values of the two legs and determine the difference. Once again, however, the cash flows involved are identical to those for two bonds, this time in two different currencies. The bonds may be either fixed or floating rate. However, the approach to both of these was discussed above under interest rate swaps and the problem, once again, amounts to that of bond valuation.

If, for example, we have entered into a swap under which we pay sterling and receive dollars, then the cash flows are identical to those of borrowing in sterling and investing in dollars. Hence, the value of the swap to us could be calculated as

Value to Payer of Sterling	(£)
Value of dollar bond asset	X
Value of sterling bond liability	(Y)
Value of swap	Z

The approach is to evaluate each bond separately in its own currency based on the relevant currency cash flows and spot rates. These present values can then be translated into the same currency using the prevailing spot exchange rate and hence, the swap value, being the difference between these two values, can be determined in that currency.

Example

Two years ago, a UK company and a US company entered into a six-year currency swap under which the UK company agreed to pay 6% on a notional borrowing of $8.5m in exchange for the US company paying 9% on a notional borrowing of £5m, with an exchange of these capital amounts at maturity.

The current term structure of interest rates is flat in both countries – at 5% in the US and 10% in the UK. The exchange rate is $1.50:£1. What is the value of the swap to the UK corporate?

Solution

Sterling bond value

Time	Cash Flow (£)	DF 10%	PV (£)
1	450,000	$\frac{1}{1.10^1}$	409,091
2	450,000	$\frac{1}{1.10^2}$	371,901
3	450,000	$\frac{1}{1.10^3}$	338,092
4	5,450,000	$\frac{1}{1.10^4}$	3,722,423
			4,841,507

Dollar bond value

Time	Cash Flow ($)	DF 5%	PV ($)
1	510,000	$\frac{1}{1.05^1}$	485,714
2	510,000	$\frac{1}{1.05^2}$	462,585
3	510,000	$\frac{1}{1.05^3}$	440,557
4	9,010,000	$\frac{1}{1.05^4}$	7,412,549
			8,801,405

Swap value

Value to Payer of Dollars	(£)
Value of dollar bond liability ($8,801,405 ÷ 1.50)	(5,867,603)
Value of sterling bond asset	4,841,507
Value of swap	(1,026,096)

7 Asset Swaps

7.1 Single currency asset swap

Exam tip

> An asset swap is an interest rate swap plus a bond. Full analysis needs you to schedule the cash flows individually and then deal with them. Don't let the terminology frighten you, take it step-by-step

An asset swap is a package that consists of the fixed cash flows of a bond and an agreement to swap these fixed cash flows for a series of floating payments. The reference rate for the floating payments is normally LIBOR.

Consider the following example that demonstrates the motivation and use of an asset swap. A company is borrowing at LIBOR and wishes to invest in a floating rate note. However, because the FRN market is small compared to the fixed coupon bond market the company is going to achieve its aim by investing in a fixed coupon bond and then swapping the fixed coupon for a floating rate of interest.

The fixed coupon bond can be a fairly illiquid Eurobond (for example) that pays a coupon above the current swap rate. In exchange for paying this coupon to its swap counterparty, the company will receive a floating rate that is at premium over LIBOR. These flows can be shown below.

1. Company is borrowing at LIBOR.

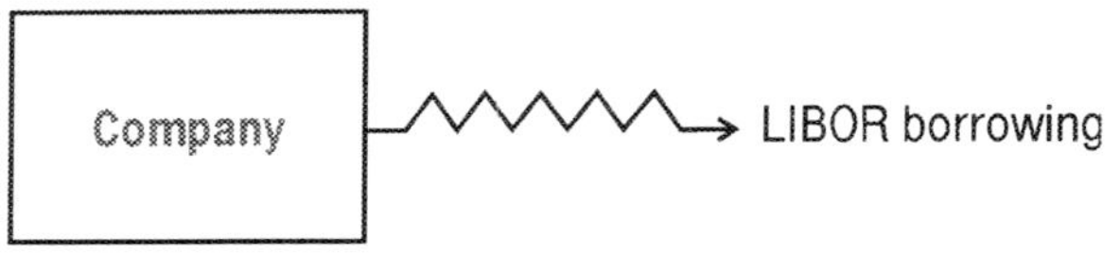

2. Company Invests in a Fixed Coupon Bond, e.g. a Eurobond Paying 8% Coupon.

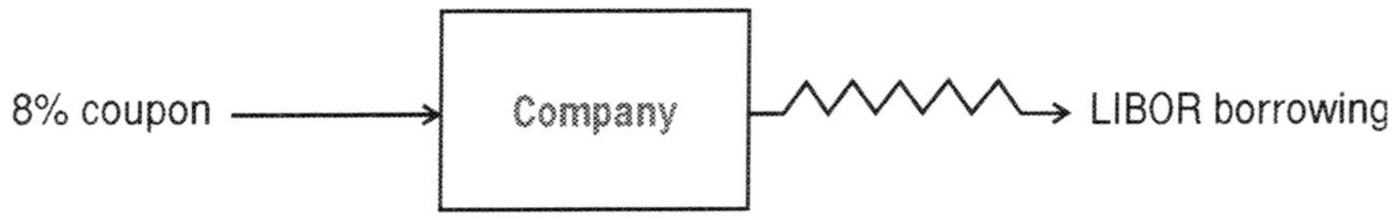

3. Company Swaps Fixed Coupon for Floating.

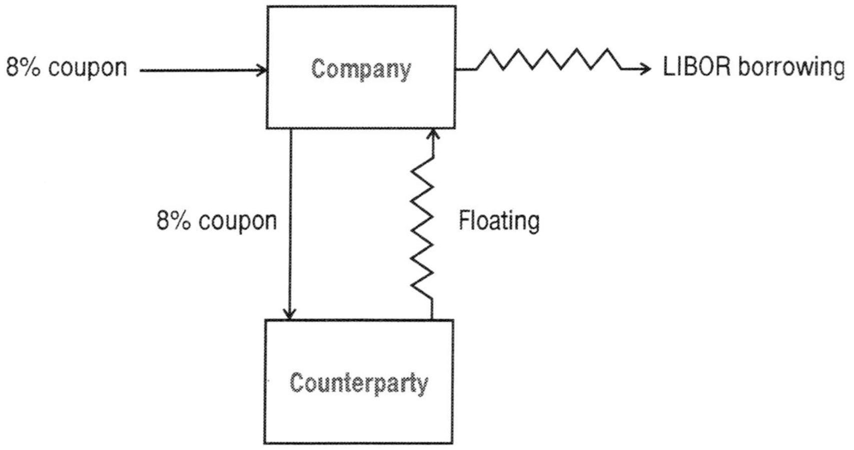

4. If the coupon is above the par swap rate and the swap is going to be priced at par, then the floating rate will be a spread over LIBOR relating to the difference between the coupon and the par swap rate. If, for example, the par swap rate was $7\frac{1}{2}\%$, the asset swap would look as follows.

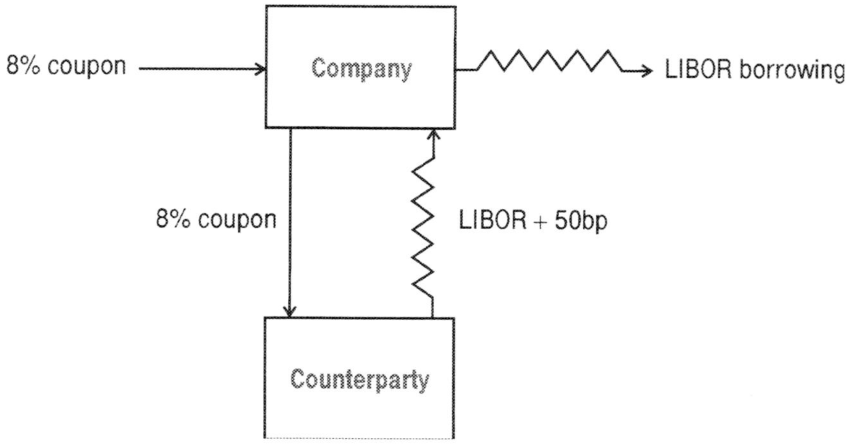

It can be seen from the above that the company can achieve sub-LIBOR funding (L – 50bp) and thereby enhance its returns.

The above calculations are somewhat simplified, as they have assumed that the underlying fixed coupon bond was trading at par. If this is not the case, the floating rate will have to be adjusted to reflect the difference between the par value of the bond and the market value of the bond.

The reasoning behind this is that asset swaps are typically sold as a package. In the above example, the company would buy the bond, typically at par, from the counterparty and then swap the cash flows from the bond for floating. If the market value of the bond is greater than par, the counterparty must be compensated for the fact that they are receiving less than the market value. The way this compensation works is for the counterparty to pay a lower floating rate, over the life of the swap, to the company. This reduction to LIBOR will have the same PV as the difference between the par value and the market value of the bond.

In the above example, let us say that the market price of the 8% coupon bond was £105, but the company and counterparty entered into a three-year par value asset swap.

We must calculate what adjustment to LIBOR over the next three years has a present value of £5. To do this, we need the spot rates.

Year	**(%)**
1	6.0
2	6.5
3	7.0

$$£5 = \frac{C}{1.06} + \frac{C}{1.065^2} + \frac{C}{1.07^3}$$

C = £1.89

The difference of £5 in the price today is the same in present value terms as £1.89 per £100 for each of the next three years.

The resulting floating rate would be

LIBOR + 50bp – 189bp = LIBOR – 139bp

An alternative to a spread over/under LIBOR could be a one-off payment at the start of the swap equal to the PV of the difference.

It is usual to trade asset swaps by quoting the asset swap spread. This is the spread referred to above that is necessary to price the swap at par. Obviously, this spread will be different for different underlying fixed coupon bonds.

The above example had the fixed rate in the swap equal to the coupon on the bond. If the fixed rate in the swap was the current swap rate, then the company could make a profit equal to the difference between the coupon and the swap rate. This is shown below.

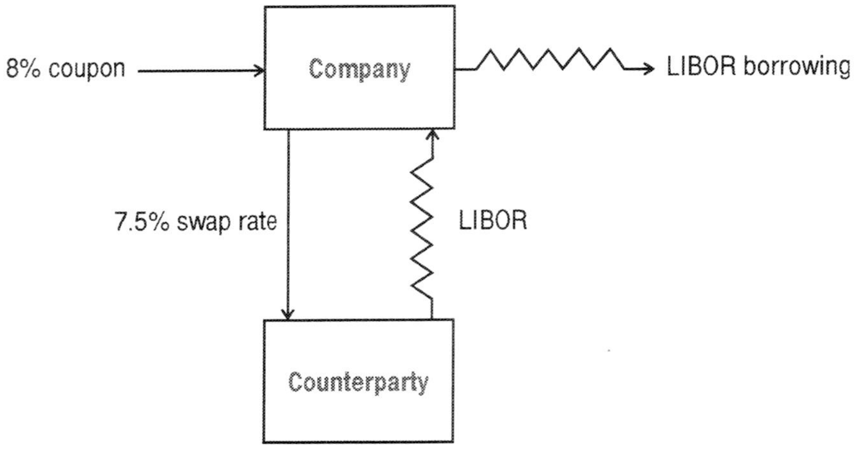

Assuming the underlying bond is trading at par, the company is making an arbitrage gain of 50bp.

7.2 Cross-Currency Asset Swap

The basic asset swap has all its cash flows in one currency. It is possible to combine an asset swap with a cross-currency basis swap to gain an exposure to a second currency.

1. Company enters into a £ asset swap.

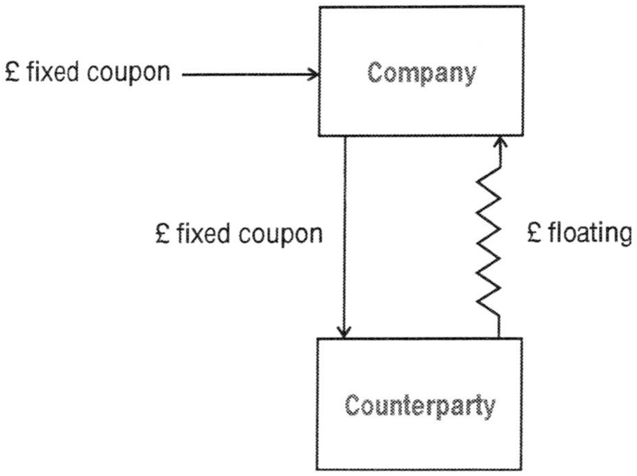

2. Company also enters into a currency basis swap exchanging floating £ for floating $.

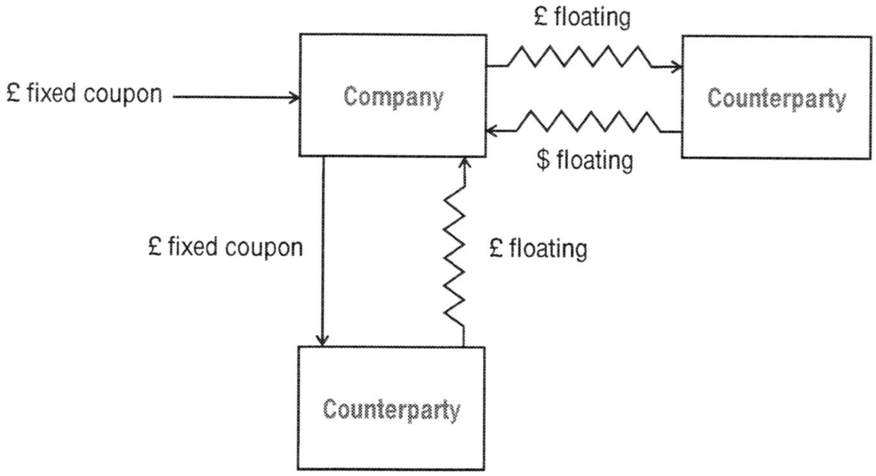

Net result is that fixed £ coupon has been swapped into floating $ interest.

8 Credit Derivatives

8.1 Features of credit derivatives

Credit derivatives are financial instruments that transfer credit risk from one counterparty to the other. Particular features are as follows.

- Specifically tailored and negotiated.
- May be options, forwards or swaps.
- Referenced to the credit characteristics of a particular asset or issuer or to a particular credit index.
- Usually cash settled.

Credit derivatives should be distinguished from other debt derivatives such as T-bond futures, etc. Whereas other debt derivatives typically offer protection against market risk (changes in interest rates), credit derivatives offer protection against the specific entities credit risk (changes in spreads and credit rating changes).

8.2 Uses of credit derivatives

Credit derivatives can be used to reduce credit exposure or to enhance credit exposure. They represent a more efficient way of controlling credit exposure than buying and selling the underlying assets because of the transaction costs and tax problems of the latter route.

8.3 The importance of credit risk

8.3.1 Types of credit risk

Introduction

There are three separate components of credit risk, as follows.

- Default risk.
- Spread risk.
- Downgrade risk.

8.3.2 Default risk

The default risk is the risk that the issuer will default on his obligations. and is assessed by rating agencies. The percentage of issuers expected to default in a particular population of issuers is referred to as the **issuer default rate**.

An alternative measure for defaults is the **dollar default rate**, which measures the percentage of par value that has defaulted. This is less commonly used by rating agencies since the credit decision is made irrespective of issuer size.

When bonds default, investors do not necessarily lose all of their money. They may recover some of their investment. The amount expected to be recovered is referred to as the **recovery rate**.

Assume that you invest \$1,000 in a bond portfolio with a default rate of 5% and a recovery rate of 40%. You expect 5% of bonds to default and on these bonds, to lose 60% of the money invested. Your expected losses are therefore $1,000 \times 0.05 \times 0.6$ = \$30 or 3%. This is **default loss rate** and is much lower than the default rate.

Analysis of the default loss rate is particularly important when investing in a wide portfolio of bonds. If the loss rate is sufficiently low, it is possible for there to be defaults in the portfolio but for the portfolio still to outperform a portfolio of Treasury securities, due to its higher yield.

8.3.3 Spread risk

The yield on bonds is made up of two major components, being the yield on Treasury bonds of the same maturity plus a spread. Part of this spread reflects the risk of default and is referred to as the credit spread. If investors are concerned that the risk of default is increasing, the credit spread will increase to allow for this. The increase in the required yield will reduce the price of the bond.

Generally, credit spreads widen in times of recession.

8.3.4 Downgrade risk

The credit risk of bonds is assessed by the various rating agencies, such as Moody's and Standard & Poor's. They will issue bonds with a credit rating. Should they decide to downgrade this rating, the credit spread will increase, causing the bond price to fall. Alternatively, an upgrade will cause the credit spread to reduce.

It is possible to prepare a rating transition matrix, which gives the historical percentage of bonds in a particular rating category that have been upgraded or downgraded over a given timescale. This can assist in assessing the downgrade risk.

8.3.5 Reasons for selling credit protection

Reasons why people might sell credit protection and assume credit risk are as follows.

- In recent history (up to the 2008 credit crunch), there have been more credit rating upgrades than downgrades. This was partly because the stock market bull run has encouraged new equity issues by riskier companies, which have often been used to reduce debt levels.
- A strong economy has resulted in good operating performance from companies, improving their credit risk.
- A number of high yield issuers in the small to mid-cap sectors have been acquired by relatively large and mature companies. This has reduced credit risk.
- As a result of the strong economy, banks have been providing term loans to riskier companies at better rates than those available in the high-yield bond market. These companies have therefore been redeeming high-yield bonds and refinancing with bank loans. The premium on redemption has enhanced returns on high-yield portfolios.

8.4 Credit Options

8.4.1 Credit options on an underlying asset

Introduction

Credit options on underlying assets are of two major types.

- Binary options with a predetermined payout.
- Binary options with a payout based on credit rating.

Binary options with a predetermined payout

This is where there is a fixed payout on the default of a specified asset. If the asset is in default on the expiration of the option, a fixed payout is made. If there is no default by expiry, the option lapses worthless.

Alternatively, the payout may be based on a specified ratings downgrade or on the net worth of the bond issuer falling to a specified level, rather than on default.

A European option is where exercise can only take place on expiration, while an American option is where the option can be exercised up to expiration. The American option will be worth more, since the investor receives the payoff more quickly when default occurs before expiration. The present value of the payment to the investor is therefore greater.

Binary options based on credit rating

The payoff of a binary option may be based on the credit rating of the issuer, rather than being a fixed amount. In addition, the option may be embedded in the bond by the issuer.

There are various ways in which these options may be structured.

8.4.2 Credit options on a spread

Payoff on a credit spread call option

The payoff on a credit spread option is based on the difference between the strike spread for the option and the actual spread of the specified instrument. The actual amount payable is calculated as follows.

Formula to learn

Payoff = (Actual spread – Strike spread) × Notional principle × Risk factor

The risk factor is based on the interest rate sensitivity of the specified instrument. It gives the dollar value of a 1bp change in spread and is calculated by reference to duration and convexity.

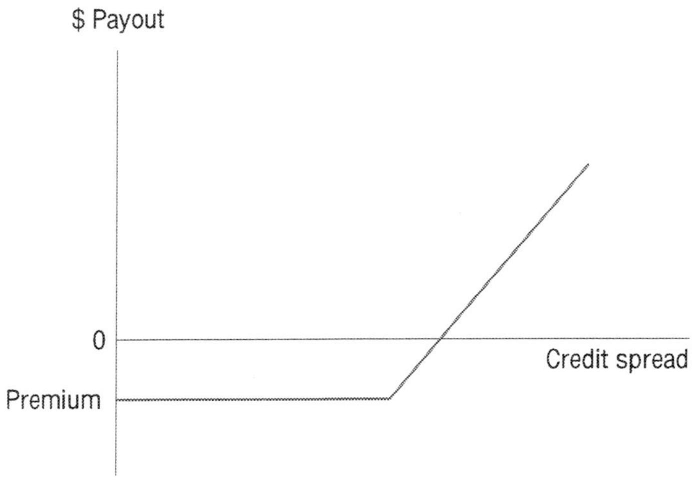

Unlike the put options noted above in relation to credit options on underlying assets, the payoff for credit spread options is independent of the level of interest rates. This is because the calculation of the payoff does not incorporate the risk-free rate. It is only based on the spread.

8.4.3 Uses of credit spread options

Relative value options

Credit spread options are relative value options, since they are based on movements in spreads. The option only gives a profit if the spread changes, rather than if the total yield changes.

If the general level of interest rates increased, but the spread stayed constant, the option would not give any profit.

If the general level of interest rates stayed the same, but the spread increased beyond the strike spread, the option would make profits. As a result, it is an underperformance option.

Gaining exposure to overvalued bonds

One possible use of a credit spread option would be to take advantage of a perceived overvaluation of a bond, i.e. its spread is too low. Instead of selling the bond, the investor could buy a call option on the spread. When the bond's spread widens, the option will give profits.

Using credit spread options to enhance income

A fund manager planning to buy an issue could sell a put option on the issue at a spread of, say 400bp, agreeing to physically settle the option by buying the bond at that spread.

When the option is exercised, the manager will take delivery of the bond that he was intending to buy anyway. In addition, the manager will have received the premium income from the option. This effectively reduces the purchase price.

The manager would write such an option when he believed that the spread will not move wider than 400bp.

Analysis of credit spreads

Credit spreads could be analysed from a macroeconomic or a microeconomic viewpoint.

- **Macroeconomic viewpoint.** A worsening economy will lead to wider spreads, due to the flight to quality (and vice versa in a booming economy).
- **Microeconomic viewpoint.** The spread of a particular issuer might change due to its operating performance.

8.5 Credit forwards

8.5.1 The nature of credit forward contracts

Credit forwards represent an obligation rather than an option. They can be useful, for example, when a high yield portfolio has performed well with narrowing spreads, and investor wishes to lock in gains to date.

When an investor purchases a credit forward contract (which would be tailored to relate to the underlying portfolio), the investor will receive compensation if spreads increase. This will compensate for any fall in the value of the underlying portfolio.

If spreads decrease, the value of the portfolio would increase. However, the investor would be obliged to make a payment under the forward contract.

The payment or receipt under the forward contract is calculated as follows.

Formula to learn

Payment = (Spread at maturity – Contract spread) × Notional principal × Risk factor

As with credit spread options, the risk factor is based on the duration and convexity of the underlying and represents the interest rate sensitivity to a 1bp change in spread.

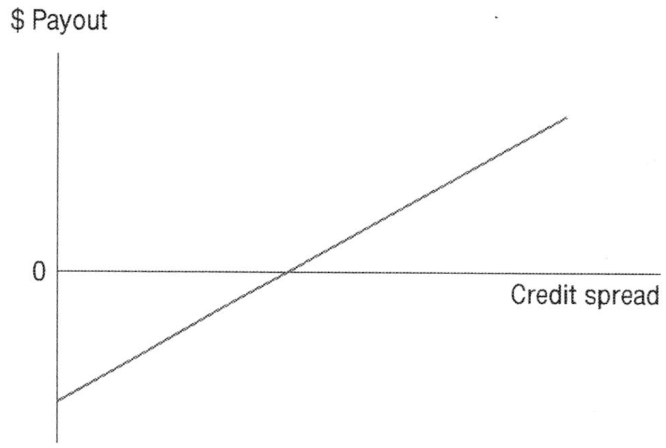

8.6 Credit swaps

8.6.1 Credit default swaps

Credit default swaps (CDSs) are something of a misnomer. In reality, they are not swaps, but more accurately reflect insurance contracts on which the insurance premium is referred to as the **credit default swap spread.**

As we can see, at present there are a wide variety of credit derivative products available. Credit default swaps are, however, the most widely available and tradeable products in the market.

A credit default swap may be based upon the credit status of a single reference asset. The buyer of the swap pays a periodic premium to the protection seller, with the credit swap only paying out on the occurrence of a credit event in relation to that reference asset.

A credit event would, under ISDA definitions, include

- Bankruptcy
- Obligation acceleration (where a payment becomes due early)
- Obligation default (a failure to pay)
- Restructuring – though this may be difficult to define precisely

A credit default swap as described may be referred to as a single name credit swap as it is referenced to a single asset.

An alternative to this single name swap is a portfolio credit default swap where the seller is exposed to the risk of one or more constituents of a portfolio of assets.

A variation on this idea of a portfolio default swap is the basket default swap where the seller is exposed to, say, the first default in the basket (first-to-default swap). Protection is provided for the whole basket but on the occurrence of the specified credit event (eg first default for a first-to-default swap) the basket swap settles and closes (the insurance expires) and the buyer is exposed to the credit risk of the remaining assets in the basket. In this way, the swap seller is only exposed to the potential loss on one defaulting asset, though that exposure is on all of the assets in the basket.

In a diversified basket of bonds the risk of there being several defaults is low and hence the basket default swap may provide adequate protection at a reduced cost to a full portfolio credit default swap.

Basket swaps are commonly first-to-default basket swaps, however they may be a second-to-default basket swap or an nth-to-default basket swaps.

CDS as insurance

Credit default swaps can be constructed so as to give credit insurance. The investor who is holding a bond with credit risk can make a payment the **credit default swap spread** to the credit swap dealer. In exchange, should the specified asset or portfolio of assets default, the dealer will make a payment to the investor.

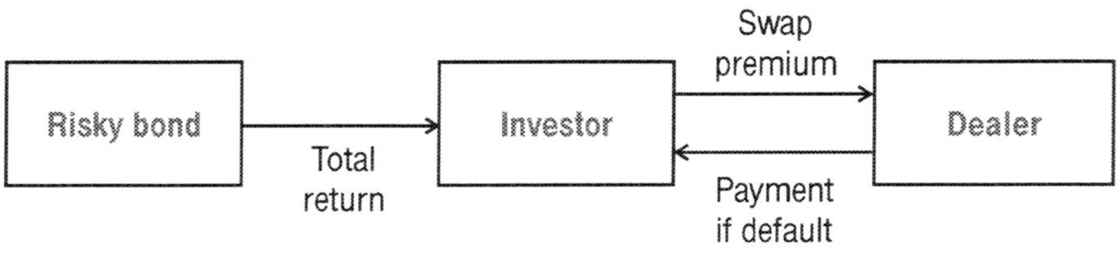

Example

An investor holds a risky bond that is yielding 7.8% and the credit default swap spread on that bond is 2.3%. If the investor buys the swap (takes out the insurance) covering his full exposure, what is the net effect of this arrangement and the net return received?

Solution

The net effect of the arrangement is to convert the bond into a risk-free investment. If the bond does not default the investor will receive a net return of

	%
Bond yield	7.8
Credit default swap spread	(2.3)
Net return	5.5%

If the bond does default, the investor receives 5.5% up to the default date and will then be able to exchange the bond for par and reinvest those funds at whatever rate is then available.

CDS spread

The periodic payment made by the investor may be made quarterly, semi-annually or yearly.

The pricing of these swaps is relatively straightforward when one bond is being insured. It is based on the following factors.

- The probability of default.
- The expected recovery value given a default.

The value of the credit default swap spread (the premium payment) will be equal to the present value of the expected net cost of the dealer due to default, ie

CDS spread (in £'s) = PV expected loss based on default probabilities and recovery rates

or

CDS spread (%) = PV loss as a percentage of the par value × Default probability over swap period

The credit default swap spread will, therefore, vary as economic conditions vary. In strong economic times the probability of default will be low and the expected recovery rate may be high leading to a low spread. Conversely in poor economic times the spread will be high.

Movements in the spread are, therefore, an indication of the market consensus on the current economic conditions and it is possible for speculators to use this as the basis for a trading strategy. To determine the profits from such a trade (buying and selling CDSs) we need to know the change in the value of our position as the spread moves. With a bond, we can assess the change in value per basis point change in yields through the BPV (or DV01). Similarly, with CDSs we can assess the change in the value of the position with the CDS spread DV01, this gives the change in the value of the position per 1bp change in the credit default spread.

CDS spread time value

As we have already noted, the CDS spread in effectively an insurance premium that is influenced by time. As we noted

CDS spread (%) = PV loss as a percentage of the par value × Default probability over swap period

As we move through the swap period the default probability will fall reducing the value of the CDS. For example, if a CDS is entered with an original term of twelve months then the CDS spread will reflect the probability of a loss over those twelve months. By the last day of this term when there is only one day left in the term the relevant amount is the probability of default on this last day which is clearly vastly lower than the probability of default over an entire year.

CDS spreads effectively have a time value component like options, indeed there are similarities between CDSs and par valued put options on the same asset.

Implied default probability

Based on the above, the CDS spread can be assessed as

CDS spread = PV expected loss based on default probabilities and recovery rates

or

CDS spread = PV loss as a percentage of the par value × Default probability over swap period

And this can be used to price the spread.

Alternatively it can be used in reverse. Given the market CDS spread and an assessment of recovery rates we can use this formulation to determine the market assessment of default probabilities, the implied default probability.

Example

The CDS spread is 2.5% on an asset where the present value of any loss (net of any recovery) expressed as a percentage of the par value is 60%. Calculate the default probability.

Solution

CDS spread = PV loss (net of any recovery) as a percentage of the par value × Default probability

CDSs for a portfolio

When the swap is on a bond portfolio, the pricing is slightly more involved and will need to reflect the following.

- The credit quality of each of the individual bonds.
- The default correlation between the bonds in the portfolio. This is difficult to measure and makes pricing difficult.

When a credit default swap relates to one period, it is very similar to a credit put. The investor makes a premium payment and receives compensation if the bond defaults.

When the credit default swap relates to a number of periods, there are some differences between a put option and the swap, as follows.

- The premium is paid periodically rather than all being paid upfront, in the case of the swap.
- The investor can receive a number of payments from the dealer if the credit quality of the bond deteriorates over time, in the case of the swap.

Hedging with CDSs

A bondholder can use CDSs in one of two ways

- Hedging for default
- Hedging for credit spread

Hedging for default

If we wish to hedge against the potential default of a bond we will purchase CDSs covering 100% of the nominal exposure we have. If we are holding £50m of a risky corporate bond we would purchase £50m of CDS coverage. This was the basic idea we used when introducing CDSs above. In the event of default we would get 100% recovery of the underlying par value.

The relationship to apply here is simply

Required CDS principal = Bond principal to hedge

Hedging for credit spread

Alternatively we may be less concerned by default but wish to hedge ourselves against any variations in the credit spread of a bond or portfolio and this requires a slightly different approach. What we are looking for here is that if our portfolio falls by, say, £1m if credit spreads widen by 1bp then our hedge will gain £1m to offset this loss.

Now, as we noted earlier, CDSs are, in many respects, related to options and the relationship between the bond credit spread and the CDS spread is very similar to the relationship between an asset and an option on the asset. CDSs effectively have a delta that we would need to factor in to achieve this hedge.

The relevant factors that needs to be considered here are

- The bond credit spread BPV or credit spread DV01
- CDS spread BPV or credit spread DV01 on the same principal

If, say the credit spread DV01 for our bond position was £10,000 then we may find that the CDS spread DV01 over the same principal sum is £5,000 (an effective delta of 0.5). To hedge the bond portfolio credit spread we would need to double the CDS coverage to give the appropriate offset.

The relationship to apply here is

$$\text{Required CDS principal} = \text{Bond principal to hedge} \times \frac{\text{Bond credit spread DV01}}{\text{CDS credit spread DV01 on same principal}}$$

Example

We hold £20m nominal of a bond with a credit spread DV01 of £32,000.

A credit default swap over the same principle sum would have a CDS spread DV01 of £9,600.

What CDS principal do we require to

- Hedge against default
- Hedge against credit spread

Solution

Hedge against default

Required CDS principal = Bond principal to hedge = £20m

Hedge against default

$$\text{Required CDS principal} = \text{Bond principal to hedge} \times \frac{\text{Bond credit spread DV01}}{\text{CDS credit spread DV01 on same principal}}$$

$$= £20\text{m} \times \frac{32{,}000}{9{,}600} = £66.67\text{m}$$

Exchanging risky credit flows with guaranteed flows

This form of credit swap can be pictured as follows.

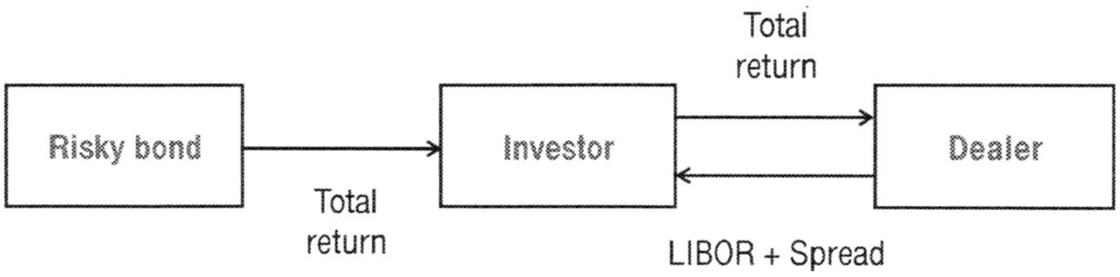

The dealer will be making a payment based on the Notional principal × LIBOR + Spread.

Where the total return from the bond is negative, e.g. due to a fall in value for the bond, the dealer will have to make an extra payment to the investor, in addition to the LIBOR-based payment.

Where the total return from the bond is positive, the investor will have to pass this return on to the dealer.

Any decline in value of the bond will need to be significant and confirmed by an independent source. For example, there may be a requirement for a credit rating downgrade. In addition, there may be an allowance for a recovery rate on the bond.

This type of swap is economically the same as a short bond position. The investor is selling the bond and investing the proceeds in a floating rate note.

Large banks can use credit default swaps in various ways.

- They can provide credit protection. This is a natural add-on to their credit protection business in areas such as letters of credit.
- They can use default swaps to hedge their own credit exposure. This can be a way of extending credit to a customer without keeping exposure to that customer.
- They can shift their credit exposure between industries and regions by taking different sides on different swaps.

Exchanging credit risks

Institutions can use default swaps to exchange credit risks, as follows.

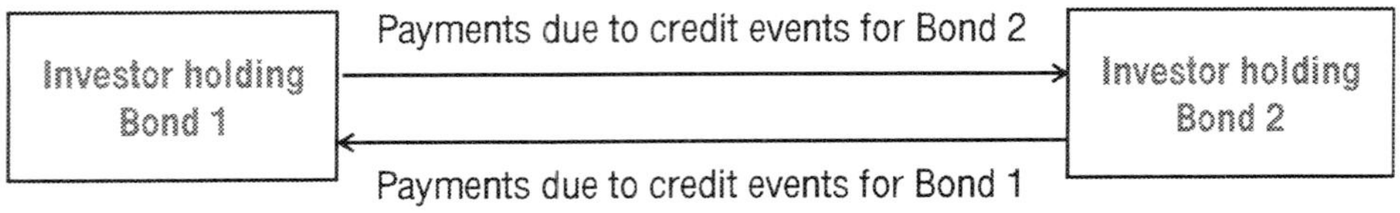

In these and other default swaps, the method used to determine any payment can vary. For example, the swap could state the exact amount of any payment or may base it on the difference between the strike price and the value of the bond after the credit event has occurred.

8.6.2 Credit spread swap

A credit spread swap allows firms to trade smaller shifts in a borrower's credit rating short of outright default. One party makes payments based on the yield to maturity of a specific issuer's debt and the other makes payments based on comparable sovereigns' bond yield plus a spread reflecting the difference in credit rating.

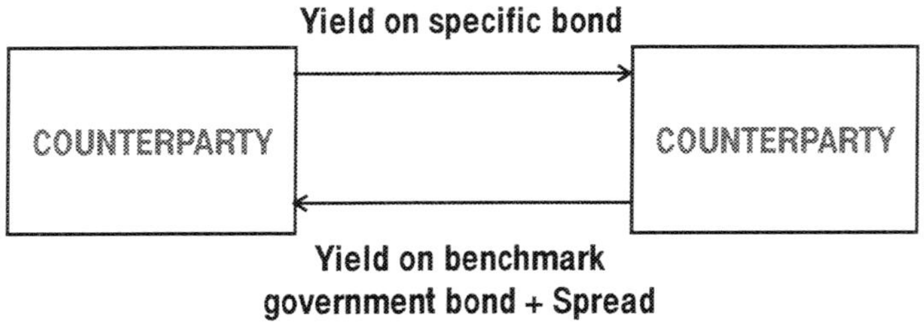

If the above two flows are equal at inception of the swap, any change in credit rating of the specified bond relative to the benchmark will result in a payment being made from one party to the other.

This, like the total return swap, allows an investor to lock in a specific spread above a benchmark yield. Naturally, one of the prime causes of the spread is the difference in credit rating between the corporate bond and the government bond.

Variations on the above could see a swap between yields on a specific bond above a benchmark and the yield between two other bonds, or swap the spread on one security above a benchmark with a spread on another security above a benchmark.

8.6.3 Total return credit swaps

These are, in effect, a type of asset swap.

The purpose of total return swaps

Total return credit swaps are designed to enhance credit exposure. The purchaser of the swap obtains the full credit exposure of the specified asset.

The purchaser of the swap may make a payment based on LIBOR + Spread to the counterparty of the swap. In exchange, the purchaser receives all cash flows from the specified bond, including any appreciation of the bond. If the bond depreciates in value, the purchaser of the swap will have to make a payment to the counterparty.

The purchaser of the swap has not purchased the underlying assets, just the exposure to their credit risk.

The payer of the total return, i.e. the counterparty of the swap purchaser, may own the assets prior to entering into the swap. Alternatively, he may buy the assets after entering into the swap.

An example of a total return swap structure is as follows. In this case, the dealer has borrowed money at LIBOR to buy the asset and then agreed to pay the total return on the asset to the investor. In exchange, the investor is paying LIBOR + Spread. The dealer's net return is therefore the Spread over LIBOR.

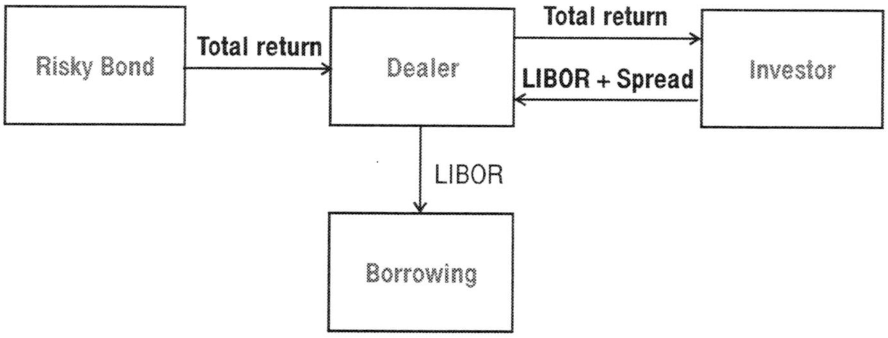

With this type of swap, there is no credit event and no contingent payment. There is an exchange of payment at the end of each period, unless default occurs, in which case the next payment is brought forward to the time of default and the contract is terminated.

The payer of the total returns has hedged the economic risk of the asset, whilst the receiver has the exposure of the asset without having the operational complications of buying it. It is possible to introduce variations on a plain vanilla structure by incorporating puts and calls to establish caps or floors on the returns of the underlying assets. The finance leg can similarly incorporate caps and floors to control financing costs. These types of swaps will always be cash settled and will be marked-to-market periodically.

If during the term of the swap the reference asset defaults, the buyer of the swap, who owns the asset, will receive from the swap seller an amount in cash equal to the difference between the last mark-to-market price and the market value after the default.

8.6.4 Benefits of total return swaps

The benefits of purchasing a total return swap compared to buying the underlying asset are as follows.

- There is no need to finance the purchase of the underlying asset. Instead, the swap purchaser pays a fee to the dealer.
- The total return payer can earn a fee while removing the credit risk from an asset on his balance sheet.
- The total return receiver can obtain an economic exposure that would take several cash market transactions to implement. It can give exposure to a diversified portfolio of risky assets. As a result, the approach is efficient.
- The total return receiver can benefit from the skills of the total return payer. The bank that is selling on the credit risks will have originally selected appropriate risks for inclusion in the portfolio.
- It gives leverage.

Chapter Roundup

The key issues in this section are

- Definition of futures and options
- Characteristics and uses of
  - Three month sterling future
  - UK Gulf future
- Speculative use of futures
  - Profit = Quote change in ticks × Tick value × Number of contracts
- Hedging use of futures, what risks are hedged and what remain
  - $\text{Number of contracts} = \frac{\text{Portfolio value}}{\text{Futures value}} \times \frac{\text{Portfolio MD}}{\text{Futures/CTD MD}}$
  - $\text{Number of contracts} = \frac{\text{Portfolio nominal}}{\text{CTD nominal}} \times \text{PF} \times \frac{\text{PVBP of portfolio}}{\text{PVBP of CTD}}$
- Speculative use of options and basic option strategies
- You need to be able to describe
  - The cash flows involved in the various swap arrangements, contrasting the different types.
  - The uses of the various types of swap arrangement from either a speculative or hedging viewpoint.
  - Describe the use of swap spreads.

Test Your Knowledge

Check your knowledge of the Chapter here, without referring back to the text.

1. You own a portfolio of gilts and are concerned that interest rates may rise in the near future. What strategy could you employ to fully protect your portfolio value and what strategy would offer partial protection?

2. Why may a fund manager write call options on shares he holds in his portfolio?

3. Identify the profits and losses from the following transactions.

   (a) You write a call option at an exercise price of £5.00 for a premium of £0.50 per share. The price goes to £5.30 at the time of maturity.

   (b) You buy a put option at an exercise price of £1.20 for 10p per share and the share price goes to £0.90.

   (c) You write a put option at an exercise price of £1.20 for 10p per share and the share price goes to £1.70.

   (d) You write the put in part (c) above and buy the share at its current market price of £1.30. Subsequently, the share price rises to £1.70.

4. What is the motivation for a long straddle and what are the attributes of the position?

5. You are managing a bond portfolio with a 12m nominal value. The PVBP for the bond is –£0.053. The price factor for the CTD is 1.18 and its PVBP is –£0.072. Calculate the number of gilt futures needed to hedge the portfolio.

Tutor's note: The questions in this section are more complex than those normally encountered in this exam. *They are included merely to give worked examples of the mathematical techniques involved in this area.*

6. You wish to hedge £4,500,000 nominal of Conversion 9½ 2015 by selling gilt futures contracts against your position. The Conversion 9½ 2015 is currently priced at £103.5975 (including accrued interest) with a gross redemption yield of 9.01% and a duration of 7.57. The cheapest to deliver gilt is the Treasury 13½ 2018 priced (to include interest) at £130.125 with a gross redemption yield of 9.21% and a duration of 6.64. The conversion factor for this gilt for the nearby futures delivery date is 1.3068092.

   (a) Estimate the nominal value of the cheapest to deliver gilt that has the same interest risk as your portfolio.

   (b) Estimate the number of futures contracts that you should sell to hedge your portfolio.

   (c) Discuss the reasons why you might wish to undertake such a hedge and the risks associated with it.

7. (a) Explain the meaning of the terms

   (i) Conversion factor
   (ii) Implied repo rate

   with respect to the T-bond futures contract.

(b) The current date is 6 June 1996. Determine the implied repo rate on a 360-day basis for the September T-bond futures contract priced at 82.25 with the following bond.

7.25% coupon, maturity 15 May, 2016, price 76.75, conversion factor 0.91958.

Note that the T-bond futures contract has a nominal value of $100,000 and that you can assume that delivery would take place at the end of the contract month.

8. You are given the following information.

Tenor (Yr)	Zero Rates	Zero Discount Factors	Forward Rates
1	7.0000%	0.934579	7.0000%
2	7.2590%	0.869224	7.5188%
3	7.5260%	0.804386	
4	7.8010%	0.740478	8.6306%
5	8.0860%	0.677877	9.2349%

NB: Assume both floating and fixed rates are one-year rates, 30/360 conventions.

Calculate the missing forward rate.

(b) A client asks for a five-year swap quote to receive fixed, pay floating, at LIBOR flat. Calculate the 'fair' fixed rate.

(c) You have been approached by a counterparty who entered into a seven-year swap paying 8.60% against receiving LIBOR flat two years ago. What payment would you require in order to cancel the swap?

(d) A client has requested a four-year receiver swap, i.e. receive fixed, pay floating, starting in one year's time. If the current five-year swap rate is used on the fixed side, what margin below/above LIBOR will be charged?

9. You are given the following information on the appropriate market interest rates and discount factors for discounting one, two and three year cash flows.

Period	1 Year	2 Years	3 Years
Interest Rate	6.75%	7.25%	8.00%
Discount Factor	0.9346	0.8653	0.7938

You discover that you can buy an AA credit risk corporate bond paying annual interest of 8.5% at a price of 100.75.

(a) Determine the fair level for the interest rate on a three-year interest rate swap, where annual fixed interest is paid, and six-month LIBOR is received. (This is equivalent to determining the par yield on a three-year bond, using the rates given in the table.)

(b) Show via a box diagram how you could make an investment in the AA corporate bond into a synthetic investment in a floating rate note, using the interest rate swap. Mark the interest flows that would take place.

(c) Explain the advantages of investing in a floating rate note via a fixed rate bond plus interest rate swap, compared with direct investment in a floating rate note.

10. You are responsible for a fund that invests in Hungarian government bonds. These have risen in price recently and are beginning to seem 'overbought'. Also, it seems that other fund managers are more or less fully invested up to their asset allocation limits for these types of bonds. You are also worried that inflation data to be released in the next week will be higher than expected and cause yields to rise.

You believe that there will only be a relatively short-term drop in prices so do not want to sell the underlying bonds. Unfortunately, there is no exchange-traded futures market. However, your bank is willing to quote prices (see the table below) on over-the-counter 3-month European options based on HUF500 million of the 10-year bond.

	CALL OPTIONS			PUT OPTIONS		
	Strike Price	Premium (Points)	Vol (%)+	Strike Price	Premium (Points)	Vol (%)
3.0 points ITM*	101.70	3.49	8.25	107.70	4.36	8.25
2.0 points ITM	102.70	2.80	8.12	106.70	3.68	8.12
1.0 point ITM	103.70	2.20	8.00	105.70	2.97	8.00
At-the-money (current price)	104.70	1.67	8.00	104.70	2.32	8.00
1.0 point OTM**	105.70	1.42	8.00	103.70	1.96	8.00
2.0 points OTM	106.70	1.18	8.25	102.70	1.62	8.25
3.0 points OTM	107.70	1.06	8.30	101.70	1.38	8.30

* ITM = In-the-money
** OTM = Out-of-the-money
\+ Vol = Volatility

(a) Outline a possible method to limit losses on your portfolio due to price falls. Provide a payoff diagram for a bond plus option position at option expiry (for bond prices between 98.70 and 110.70). Give reasons for your choice of option type and strike price.

(b) How has the lack of a futures market affected the likely profit or loss on your position compared with the option strategy you recommended?

(c) Suggest follow-up action if prices fall sharply in the next month.

TEST YOUR KNOWLEDGE: ANSWERS

1. To fully protect the portfolio, use a short hedge with futures i.e. set-up a short position in the UK Gilt future.

   To offer partial protection establish a protective put position, i.e. retain the Gilts and buy a UK gilt put option.

2. The position described is writing a covered call and could be because

   - The fund manager believes markets are static and he is looking to boost his fund performance by the premium received.
   - The fund manager has a target selling price for the share and is looking to achieve this and receive the benefit of the premium on the call options written.

3. (a)

Proceeds:	Option premium		0.50
	Exercise price		5.00
			5.50
Cost:	Purchase price		5.30
Profit			£0.20

(b)

Proceeds:	Exercise price		1.20
Cost:	Option premium	0.10	
	Purchase price	0.90	
			1.00
Profit			£0.20

(c)

Proceeds:	Option premium **Profit**	£0.10

Share price rises so option not exercised and expires worthless.

(d)

Proceeds:	Option premium (options not exercised)	0.10
Profit on shares owned 1.70 – 1.30		0.40
Profit		£0.50

4. A straddle is a volatility trade and a speculator would take the long position if he believed that volatility would increase.

   The attributes of the position are that it has a limited loss of the full combined premium paid which arises at the common strike price. On the up-side, there is no limit to the profits achievable.

5. $$\text{Number of contracts} = \frac{12{,}000{,}000}{100{,}000} \times 1.18 \times \frac{-0.053}{-0.072} = 104.233$$

   i.e. 104 Contracts (nearest whole number).

6. (a) £4,500,000 × 103.59375 = £4,661,718.75

$$£4{,}661{,}718.75 \times \frac{7.57/1.0901}{6.64/1.0921} = £5{,}324{,}390.94$$

$$\frac{£5{,}324{,}390.94}{1.30125} = £4{,}091{,}750.96$$

BPP LEARNING MEDIA

(b) $\frac{\text{Nominal amount}}{\text{Contract size}} \times \text{Price factor} \times \text{Hedge ratio}$

Note, the hedge ratio must reflect both relative modified durations and the initial market value.

$$\frac{£4{,}500{,}000}{£100{,}000} \times 1.3068092 \times \frac{6.94}{6.08} \times \frac{103.59375}{130.125} = 53.4 \text{ or } 53 \text{ contracts}$$

(c) This hedge protects the investor against downside risk whilst allowing the possibility of releasing the hedge, by buying an equivalent number of futures contracts to offset the hedge, if the prospects for the market improve.

The principal risk associated with this hedge is that it is only truly effective for parallel shifts of the yield curve.

Equally, there is also the basis risk that the cheapest to deliver stock will change and therefore the efficiency of the hedge will be undermined.

The final risk is that associated with the cash flows, the payment of margin, arising from the futures contract.

7. (a) (i) **Conversion Factor**

Most government bonds futures contracts rely upon a notional bond, rather than a specified individual bond in the market. The conversion factor is created in order to enable the existing bonds within the market to be delivered against settlement of the notional bond in the future. The conversion factor effectively converts the bonds available for delivery into the notional value.

(ii) **The Implied Repo Rate**

The pricing of government bond futures is based upon the cash and carry arbitrage process. Under the cash and carry arbitrage there should be no profit in buying the bonds today and selling the future, since the price of the future should reflect the full cost of buying the bond today and carrying it to the future settlement date.

The costs of carrying the bond are basically the purchase price of the bond, plus the finance cost of carrying that bond to the settlement date of the future, less any yield earned on the bond. This will give us the future value of the bond in question, we use the conversion factor to convert that into today's futures price. If there was any profit in that process, then a cash and carry arbitrage should be undertaken. The implied repo rate is the implied finance cost inside today's futures and cash market price.

Since we can know the bond's cash price, the futures price and what the yield will be on the bond, the only missing element is the finance cost.

(b) **Cash and Carry Arbitrage**

Buy Bond	**Sell Future**
Clean price	*Clean price*
\$100,000 @ 76.75	\$100,000 @ 82.25 × 0.91958
\$76,750	\$75,635.45

Buy Bond

Accrued interest

$$\frac{\$100000 \times 0.0725}{2} \times \frac{22}{184} \text{ (w1)}$$

$433.42

Invoice value

$77,183.42

Sell Future

Accrued interest

$$\frac{\$100000 \times 0.0725}{2} \times \frac{138}{184} \text{ (w1)}$$

$2718.75

Invoice value

$78,354.20

The difference between the two values must therefore be the implied repo rate.

$$\frac{£78354.20 - £77183.42}{£77183.42} \times \frac{360}{116[w2]} = 4.7\%$$

w1

M	J	J	A	S	O	N		
16	30	31	31	30	31	15	=	184 Days in ½ yr
16	6						=	22 Accrued days to 6 June
16	30	31	31	30			=	138 Accrued days to 30 Sept

w2

138 – 22 = 116 Days earned

8. (a) $$\left[\left[\frac{(1.075260)^3}{(1.072590)^2}\right] - 1\right] \times \frac{360}{360} = 8.0618\%$$

(Note that the zero rates are, by convention, assumed to compound annually.)

(b) 100 = 0.934579F + 0.869224F + 0.804386F...

....+ 0.740478F + 0.677877F + 67.7877

100 – 67.7877 = 4.026544F

7.9999% = F

The fixed rate is 7.9999%.

(c) Assume fixed rate in (b) is 8.00%.

The payment will relate to the present value of the 0.60% difference in the five years of the swap's life.

Hence if we assume a notional of $100 the PV is

Time	Notional	Interest Differential	Discount Factor	PV Amount $
1	100	0.60%	0.934579	0.5607474
2	100	0.60%	0.869224	0.5215344
3	100	0.60%	0.804386	0.4826316
4	100	0.60%	0.740478	0.4442868
5	100	0.60%	0.677877	0.4067262

PV = 2.4159264% of notional.

(d)

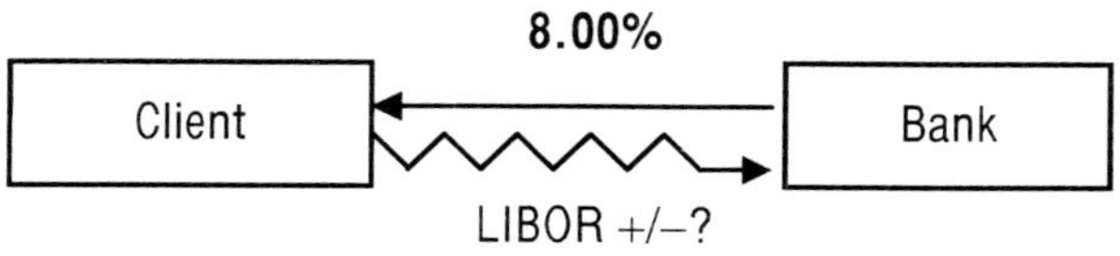

The answer will be the difference between the five year swap rate and the four year deferred start swap rate. As the deferred start swap will have no cash flows in the first year their PVs must be zero.

Consequently, the fixed rate will be

$100 \times 0.934579^{*} = 0.869224F + 0.804386F + 0.740478F + 0.677877F + 67.7877$

$25.6702 = 3.091965F$

$8.3022285 = F$

Therefore, the LIBOR needs to be adjusted by 30.22 bp

LIBOR – 30.22 bp

* The valuation technique employed is that which considers the swap as two bonds (long coupon, short FRN). The 100 therefore represents a fictitious flow that cancels out with the 100 on the other side of the equation. As this 100 is deferred by one year it is discounted using the one year discount factor.

9. (a)

$$100 - (100 \times 0.7938) = 0.9346C + 0.8653C + 0.7938C$$

$$20.62 = 2.5937C$$

$$\frac{20.62}{2.5937} = C$$

$$7.95\% = C$$

(b)

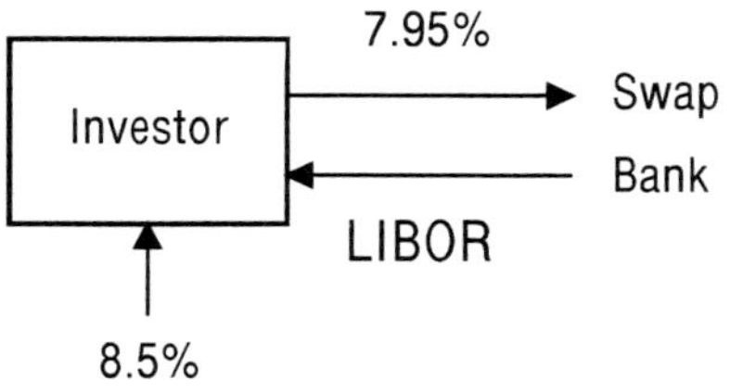

(Note that 7.95% would be subject to some form of spread from the swap bank.)

(c) It would only be advantageous if the return generated by the swap were greater than the relevant FRN. In this analysis it would be important to consider the impact of dealing costs.

10. (a)

- Market has risen.
- Limited buying support.
- Negative inflation data.

All of these factors would suggest a significant fall in prices is a possibility.

Consequently, to protect the portfolio's value the most logical policy would be to

- Buy a put option (OTM would give greater gearing.)

Alternatively

- Writing calls will generate income to offset any fall in portfolio value but this is exposed to the risk of an upside shock forcing prices up.
- By buying a put and writing a call we can create a synthetic future. This will protect against downside movement for a lower establishment cost but also restricts upside potential.

Suggested strategy: buy the 102.70 put. This option is out-of-the-money and therefore relatively cheap. But if the movement is substantial, as may seem likely, it will give us a highly geared return.

Buy 102.70 put

Bond is at 104.70

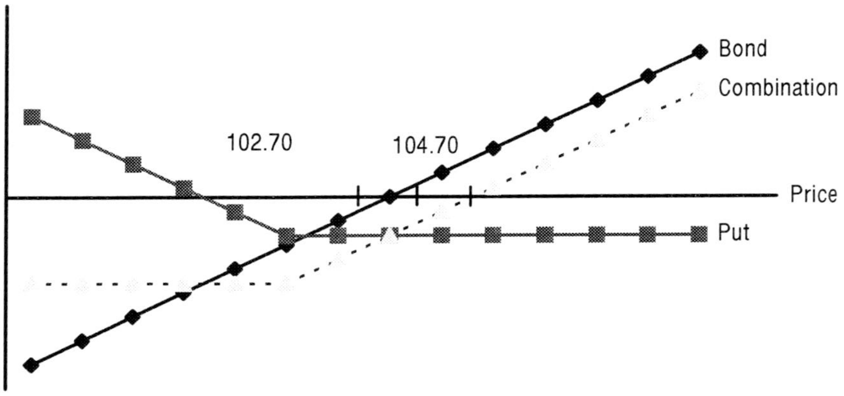

	(Intrinsic–Premium)		
	Bond	Put	Net
97.70	–7	(+5 – 1.62)	–3.62
98.70	–6	(+4 – 1.62)	–3.62
99.70	–5	(+3 – 1.62	–3.62
100.70	–4	(+2 – 1.62)	–3.62
101.70	–3	(+1 – 1.62)	–3.62
102.70	–2	(0 – 1.62)	–3.62
103.70	–1	(0 – 1.62)	–2.62
104.70	0	(0 – 1.62)	–1.62
105.70	+1	(0 – 1.62)	–0.62
106.70	+2	(0 – 1.62)	0.38
107.70	+3	(0 – 1.62)	1.38
108.70	+4	(0 – 1.62)	2.38
109.70	+5	(0 – 1.62)	3.38
110.70	+6	(0 – 1.62)	4.38

(b) A futures market would tend to be a more liquid market place and would therefore allow for the hedge to be unwound in the event of the market view changing.

A futures hedge (which could be created synthetically) would, as mentioned above, protect on the downside but also limit upside potential.

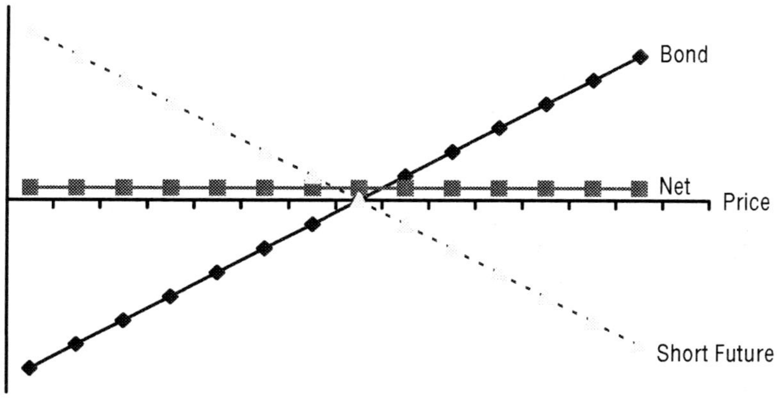

As mentioned above it may be unwound if the market view changes.

(c) Given the European-style nature of the option early exercise to crystallise profits on the option is not a possibility. Equally, trading the option on to a third party is not available either. However, direct negotiations with the bank who wrote the option would be possible.

At this stage, given that our initial view has been vindicated, it might be the right time to consider sealing up our exposure to the market. However, the fund may not be allowed to take more aggressive derivative strategies.

11 Convertibles and Warrants

INTRODUCTION

Convertibles and warrants exhibit the combined characteristics of both bonds and options and so cannot be properly studied until these former areas have been fully digested.

Convertibles and warrants represent a slightly more specialist asset class to many of the others that we have covered so far, and their use in a fixed income context is a little more limited.

Questions quite frequently arise from the ideas in this chapter

CHAPTER CONTENTS

Page

Chapter Learning Objectives

The syllabus areas covered by this section are

Form and Structure of Securities

Students should be familiar with the form and structure of fixed income securities.

- Convertible
- Embedded options

1 Convertibles

1.1 Introduction

Exam tip

> This area gets examined as brief definitions or discussions in Section A questions, e.g. Winter 2009 Question 3, Winter 2007 Question 3, Summer 2006 Question 4, Summer 2003 Question 5. It has also been examined as an optional 15 mark Section C question, e.g. Summer 2008 Question 10, Winter 2003 Question 13.

1.1.1 Definition

A convertible is a fixed income security that offers the holder the right to acquire shares in the issuing company on a specific date or over a specific period, perhaps subject to satisfying certain conditions.

The decision as to whether to convert is solely down to the holder and will only be undertaken if it is to the holder's advantage; there is no obligation on the part of the holder to convert.

In addition to the holder's right to convert, the issuer may also have the right to call (i.e. redeem) the issue if certain conditions are met. This characteristic of having multiple embedded options can make the evaluation of convertibles difficult.

1.1.2 Characteristics

Typically, a convertible will pay a low coupon, though this is compensated by the option to convert into shares at the conversion date. Convertibles are often subordinated, meaning that all 'senior' creditors must be settled in full before any payment can be made to holders in the event of insolvency.

Convertibles are often employed as a form of deferred share. Issuers expect them to be converted into shares at the conversion date.

As a result, convertibles have some of the characteristics of bonds, responding to changes in interest rates, and some of the characteristics of shares, responding to share price movements.

The conversion right can be expressed in a number of ways. By convention, the right is normally to convert the debt into the Ordinary shares of the company in a given **conversion ratio**. For example, £100 nominal is converted into 25 shares (a conversion ratio of 25). The conversion right may exist for a period of time during the bond's life (the conversion window) or may only be available on maturity.

Additional terms may include the following.

- Different conversion ratios at different maturities of the bond.
- The holder of the bond may also be obliged to contribute additional capital on the conversion. For example, £100 nominal of the debt converts into 20 shares and the bondholder is obliged to contribute an additional £2.50 per share. Therefore, each share has an effective cost (assuming the bond is trading at par) of £100/20 = £5 + £2.50 = £7.50.
- Put rights enabling the holder of the bond to force an early redemption of the bond, normally at a premium to the par value.
- Call rights enabling the issuer to call the bond under certain conditions.

When establishing the terms of the convertible, the issuer will normally avoid unduly complicated terms, since this will confuse and thereby dissuade potential purchasers of the bond.

1.1.3 Advantages and disadvantages to the issuer

Advantages

Compared to either a bond or share issue, convertibles offer the following advantages to the issuer.

- No immediate dilution of the current shareholders.
- Lower cost than normal bonds due to a lower coupon.
- Less dilution of earnings per share than either a normal share or bond issue as a consequence.
- Suitable for when assets are not available to secure straight finance.
- Suitable for finance projects with long pay-back periods.

Disadvantage

The disadvantage to the issuer is that if the company fails to perform, it is obliged to make the coupon payments, and ultimately redeem the bond for cash if the holder chooses not to convert. Therefore, the firm cannot be sure that they are issuing deferred share capital when they issue a convertible.

1.1.4 Advantages and disadvantages to the investor

Advantages

The advantages to the investor of a convertible issue are as follows.

- The holder has the security of fixed income, offering downside protection if the shares fall in value, whilst at the same time offering the opportunity to benefit if the shares perform well.
- Convertibles rank above shares in the order of priority on liquidation.
- Convertibles tend to offer higher yields than the underlying shares.
- Convertible bonds tend to have good marketability compared to non-convertible issues.

Disadvantages

The disadvantages to the investor of a convertible issue are as follows.

- Though offering higher yields than the underlying shares, convertibles tend to offer lower yields than equivalent straight bonds.
- The attractiveness of a convertible may be reduced by issuer call options.
- If anticipated share growth is not achieved, the holder will have sacrificed yield for no benefit.

1.2 Valuation of convertibles

Exam tip

> To date, theses ideas have mainly been examined as discussions of the approaches, e.g. Summer 2005 Question 2, Winter 2003 Question 2, however, more recent questions have involved an element of calculation, e.g. Winter 2005 Question 4.

1.2.1 Introduction

When considering holding a convertible or shares in a company issuing one, an investor will need to ensure that it is fairly priced. If it is too expensive, then investors will not buy the convertible stock and the issue will flop. If the price is very cheap, then the company will be obtaining finance on disadvantageous terms, and value for existing shareholders will fall.

Valuation of convertibles is very difficult to do in practice due to the various embedded options that may exist, but various models have been developed. Three common methods are the dividend valuation model, the crossover method and the option pricing method.

1.2.2 Dividend valuation model

Convertible debt generally carries a fixed rate of interest and gives the holder the option to convert it into equity at a certain future date, under terms specified by the company. The impact of this is that the ultimate redemption proceeds may be either

- A cash alternative; or
- Shares.

To apply the dividend valuation model, we need to establish which of these will be preferable at the conversion date and include that as the redemption proceeds in the evaluation.

We can get the market value of the shares at the redemption date by establishing the current market value and growth and extrapolating forward.

Example

A company intends to issue 8% convertible bonds with a nominal value of £100. The conversion terms in five years (at the investors' option) are

- £110 cash.
- 40 shares for every £100 nominal value of stock held (a conversion ratio of 40).

We are also given or have calculated that the current share price is £2.30 and its growth rate is 4% p.a. The investors' required rate of return is 10% p.a. Establish the price at which the bonds will be issued, i.e. the market value of the convertible.

Solution

Conversion option

We need to firstly establish the relevant cash flows, hence we need to determine whether we will be converting or not. Applying four years growth to the current share price gives.

We could calculate the share price in the future using our terminal value ideas as

Formula to learn

$$E_n = E_0(1+g)^n$$

$E_5 = £2.30 \times 1.04^5$
$E_5 = £2.80$

where E_n is the market value of equity at Time n, giving

Hence, in five years, the value of 40 shares will be £112 (£2.80 × 40). Our investor is therefore faced with the option of accepting either

- £110 cash; or
- Shares with a value of £112.

On the assumption that he is rational, he will prefer the shares. We can now follow through the rest of the calculations, using £112 as the redemption proceeds as follows.

Market value of convertible

Time	Cash Flow (£)	Discount Factor	Present Value (£)
1–5	8.00	$\frac{1}{0.10}\left(1-\frac{1}{1.10^5}\right) = 3.791$	30.33
5	112.00	$\frac{1}{1.10^5}$	69.54
Market value			99.87

1.2.3 The crossover method/income-based approach

The crossover method is another application of the dividend valuation model ideas. It is appropriate when there is no pre-determined conversion date, rather the holders have a choice of dates on which conversion can occur and a likely date of conversion needs to be established.

The crossover method assumes that conversion takes place when the income that would be received in the form of dividends from the shares obtained on conversion exceeds the interest receipts from the debt. For this reason, it is also known as the income-based approach.

Example

A company has an existing share price of 140p. Dividends are currently 20p and are growing at a rate of 5%. Investors require a rate of return of 20%. There is some 10% convertible debt in issue, which has conversion terms of 40 shares per £100 of nominal value. What is an appropriate market value for the convertibles?

Solution

The immediate conversion value

The first stage is to value the convertibles on the basis that they are converted into shares immediately. This would give an 'immediate conversion value' of £56.00 (40 shares × 140p). This value represents the present value of all the future dividend payments from one year's time to infinity on the 40 shares.

The income pickup

The convertibles will however be worth more than the immediate conversion value because they will be receiving interest payments of £10 per £100 of nominal value for a number of years. The dividends on 40 shares are only worth £8 a year at present.

The advantage of receiving interest payments rather than dividends can be tabulated as follows.

Year	Interest on Debt (£)	Dividends (5% Growth) (£)	Income Pickup (£)	Present Value of Pickup Discounted at 20% (£)
1	10.00	8.40	1.60	1.33
2	10.00	8.82	1.18	0.82
3	10.00	9.26	0.74	0.43
4	10.00	9.72	0.28	0.14
5	10.00	10.21	–	–
				2.72

After five years, the dividends exceed the interest receipts and therefore, it is assumed that conversion takes place and the investor receives dividends from then on. The value of receiving interest as opposed to dividends for the next four years is £2.72 and hence, the total value of the convertible is £58.72 (£56.00 + £2.72).

It is also common to see this income advantage expressed in percentage terms. Under this approach, a comparison is made between the flat yield on the bond and the current dividend yield on the share.

Formula to learn

Flat yield – Dividend yield = Income advantage

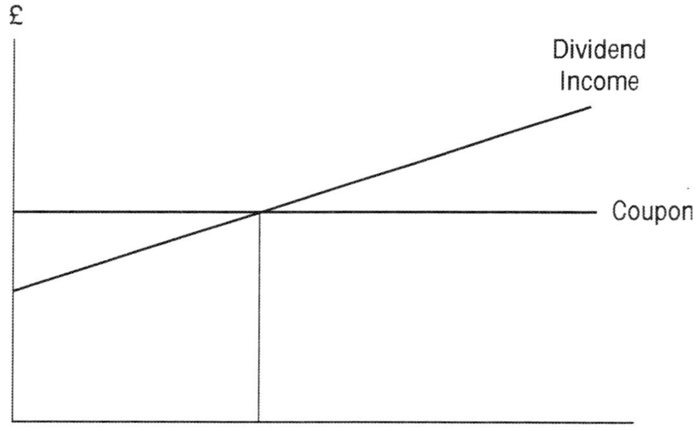

Obviously this exercise date is conditioned by the strategy that the investor is following and the volatility of the underlying share price. If the share price is anomalously high, then it may well be worth considering the exercise of the conversion right immediately in order to take the conversion profit.

Even using more complex, but perhaps more appropriate, options valuation models, the income crossover method has some relevance. Despite their lower coupons, it is still likely to be the case that bond yields on convertible bonds will be higher than dividend yields on shares. Consequently, it would make sense to exercise the conversion right as late as is possible.

It is in this context that many call provisions are utilised. The effect being to force early exercise of the conversion right despite the existence of an income advantage.

1.2.4 Option/warrant pricing method

Convertibles contain an option to acquire equity

The crossover method of valuation is fairly simplistic and easy to calculate. However, it may not give a sensible answer in valuing a convertible because it only focuses on the income differential between the debt and equity alternatives. It fails to take into account the true nature of the convertible, which is that of a bond plus an option (or more probably a warrant – see later) to acquire equity.

As such, a more appropriate method of valuing a convertible would be to use option pricing ideas and warrant pricing ideas discussed later in this section. The option/warrant pricing method recognises that a bond with a conversion right attached is basically a combination of two separate instruments: a low-coupon bond and an option or warrant into the underlying equity.

The conversion right can be expressed in a number of ways. By convention, the right is normally to convert (in a given **conversion ratio**) the debt into the Ordinary shares of the company. For example, £100 nominal is converted into 25 shares. The conversion right may exist for a period of time during the bond's life (the conversion window) or may only be available on maturity.

Additional terms may include

- Different conversion ratios at different maturities of the bond.
- The holder of the bond may also be obliged to contribute additional capital on the conversion, for example, £100 nominal of the debt converts into 20 shares and the bondholder is obliged to contribute an additional £2.50 per share. Therefore, each share has an effective cost (assuming the bond is trading at par) of £100/20 = £5 + £2.50 = £7.50.
- Put rights enabling the holder of the bond to force an early redemption of the bond, normally at a premium to the par value.

When establishing the terms of the convertible, the issuer will normally avoid unduly complicated terms since this will confuse and thereby dissuade potential purchasers of the bond.

Factors affecting option and warrant values

The value of the option will be determined by a number of factors as we have already seen, specifically

- The exercise price of the option.
- The actual price of the underlying share.
- Expected volatility in the price of the underlying share.
- The time to expiry of the option.
- Interest rates.
- Whether a dividend is due to be paid on the share or not in the option period.

1.2.5 Call provisions

Most convertibles contain call provisions allowing the issuer to press for early redemption/conversion. Under these provisions, the issuer can press for redemption. At this point, the holder will have the right to exercise their conversion right or accept the cash repayment.

Some convertibles have a degree of call protection. This call protection may come in either soft form or hard form. Hard form protection prohibits the use of any call provision within a set number of years after issuance. A soft protection prohibits the use of the call provision until such time as the share price has exceeded a pre-set limit.

The existence of these call provisions will have an impact on the underlying value of the option. Once the call threshold has passed, then exercise of the call right must seem likely and consequently, any time value remaining will be lost.

Value of a convertible at its expiry date

A simple example of this technique would be to consider a convertible on its date of expiry. It can either be converted into shares with a value of £120 or redeemed for cash of £100. Clearly, the total value of the convertible is £120. This is made up of its value as straight debt (£100) plus the value of the option to convert into equity, which must be worth an additional £20.

Since the option is at its expiry date, there is no time value, and the whole of the £20 is intrinsic value. Remember that intrinsic value is the difference between the market price of the shares (£120) and the exercise price of the option. In the case of a convertible, the exercise price of the option is the lost proceeds from holding the instrument as straight debt – in other words, £100.

Introducing time value

The absolute **floor value** of the convertible prior to conversion will be the higher of

- The value of the plain vanilla bond (ignoring the conversion right); and
- The value of the bond in terms of the number of shares that could be obtained at their current market price.

Example

A 4% convertible contains the right to convert £100 nominal value into 35 shares or receive cash redemption at par. At present, the shares are trading in the market at £1.25 and 4% redeemable bonds of the same maturity are trading at £88. What is the floor value of this convertible?

Solution

The value of the 4% bond redeeming at the same date (ignoring the conversion right) is £88. The bond could be converted into 35 shares, each with a value of £1.25, that is 35 × £1.25 = £43.75. At this point, the conversion right is of no value, and it is best to regard the bond as a 'straight', i.e. the conversion option has no intrinsic value.

Example

Assume that debt has one year to maturity and will be redeemed for £110 cash. Alternatively, the investor can convert into shares at any time over the next year. The current value of the shares is £120. The debt holder's required rate of return is 10%.

Solution

The value of the instrument now as straight debt is the present value of the proceeds as debt of £100 $\left(\frac{110}{1.1}\right)$. The value in terms of the shares that could be created is £120. The floor value of the convertible will therefore be £120, being the value of the straight debt of £100 plus the intrinsic value of the option of £20.

Whilst this establishes an absolute floor value, the market value of the convertible will obviously be affected by the potential increase in the price of the underlying share. It is likely that the total value of the convertible will be higher than this, due to time value of the option.

Conclusion

If the value of the shares was significantly less than the cash redemption option, then the value of the convertible is likely to be its value as straight debt. The option is significantly out-of-the-money and is almost worthless.

If, however, the value of the shares exceeds the cash redemption price, then the conversion option will have some intrinsic value.

In both cases, however, the conversion option will have some time value, and we could use our options pricing theory to evaluate the option.

Ongoing valuation of a convertible

As mentioned before, a convertible is basically a combination of two instruments and the valuation reflects this.

Example

If we have a convertible on which the underlying bond has a market value of £110 and which gives the right to convert each bond into 25 shares that have a current price of £4.00, then the conversion right only has an **intrinsic value** beyond the point where the share price exceeds £4.40, i.e.

$$\text{Conversion price} = \frac{£110}{25 \text{ shares}} = £4.40 \text{ per share}$$

Once the share price exceeds this point, the conversion right begins to attract a value. The market value will be greater than this simple intrinsic value, since it will reflect the **time value** of the conversion right.

Diagrammatically

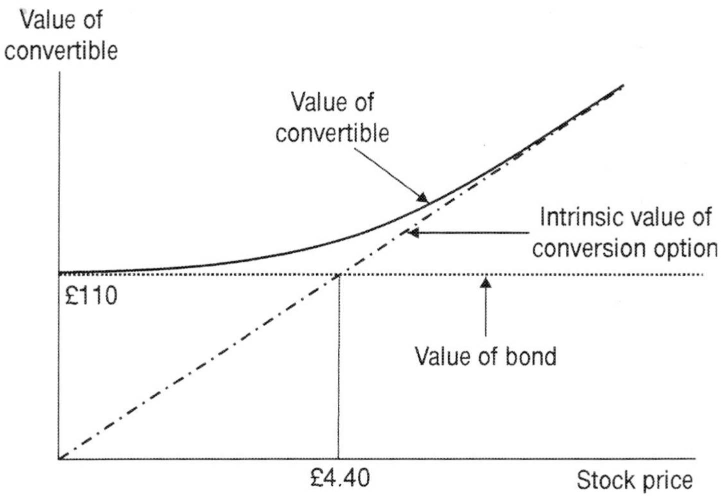

One important point to remember in the valuation of a convertible is that unlike an option where the strike price is fixed, here the conversion ratio is fixed, but the bond price itself will vary.

For example, if the bond increases in value to £120, the breakeven share price becomes

$$\frac{£120}{25 \text{ shares}} = £4.80 \text{ per share}$$

Price of convertible

Using this method, if the convertible results in the issue of new shares by the company (which is most commonly the case) then we havew

Formula to learn

Convertible price = Equivalent bond price + Warrant price

Or, using the warrant pricing formula derived later in this section

Formula to learn

$$\text{Convertible price} = \text{Equivalent bond price} + \frac{A}{1+q} \times \text{Number of shares}$$

where

A = value of an equivalent option derived from a suitable option pricing model.

q = percentage increase in the number of shares in issue once the warrant is exercised (expressed as a decimal).

1.3 Conversion statistics

Exam tip

These relationships are examined either as brief definitions or as calculations e.g. Winter 2005 Question 4, Winter 2003 Question 2.

There are a number of useful statistics that may be employed in the analysis of convertibles, including

- Conversion ratio.
- Conversion value.
- Conversion price.
- Conversion premium.

1.3.1 Conversion ratio

As we noted above

Formula to learn

Conversion ratio = Number of shares received per bond held

In the example above

Conversion ratio = 25

1.3.2 Conversion value

The conversion value represents the value of the convertible if it is converted into shares today, i.e.

Formula to learn

Conversion value = Conversion ratio × Share price

In the example above

Conversion value = 25 × £4.00 = £100

1.3.3 Conversion price

The conversion price represents the price per share at which the convertible has an intrinsic value, i.e. the share price that will result in the shares having the same value as the convertible.

Formula to learn

$$\text{Conversion price} = \frac{\text{Value of convertible}}{\text{Conversion ratio}}$$

In the example above

$$\text{Conversion price} = \frac{£110}{25 \text{ shares}} = £4.40 \text{ per share}$$

1.3.4 Conversion premium

This reflects the excess of the conversion price over the current share price. It should not be confused with an option's premium which represents the value of an option.

Formula to learn

$$\text{Conversion premium} \frac{\text{Conversion price} - \text{Share price}}{\text{Share price}} \times 100\%$$

In the example above

$$\text{Conversion premium} = \frac{£4.40 - £4.00}{£4.00} \times 100\% = 10.0\%$$

In this situation, the underlying share price is going to have to rise by 10.0% before the conversion right has any intrinsic value.

1.4 Exchangeable bonds

Similar to convertibles, exchangeable bonds offer the holder of the bonds either cash or shares. However, in this case, rather than shares in the bond issues they are shares in another company. This is often a way for a company with a significant stake in another company to obtain cheap finance. For example, the *Daily Mail* issued a bond that was exchangeable into Reuters shares.

1.5 Convertible arbitrage

Arbitrage strategies aim to hedge out almost all market risk by taking offsetting positions, often in different but related securities. As such they should be fairly low risk.

Convertible arbitrage is a strategy involving the relationship between the current share price and the price of convertible bonds in issue by a company. The strategy is easy to understand and undertake effectively when the convertible is in the money. In this situation, a large part of the value of the convertible will be the value of the underlying shares into which it can (or soon will be able to) be converted. Because of its option characteristics the value of a convertible should trade at a premium to the value of the underlying shares, but if this premium is too large or too small or even negative than an arbitrage opportunity exists. With a negative premium, for example, the convertible is relatively cheap compared to the shares. We could therefore short the shares and buy the convertibles holding the position until the normal relationship is re-established whilst also picking up the bond yield.

Clearly the strategy involves an element of risk and the major factor influencing this risk is the correlation between the share and the convertible. When it is well in the money this correlation is liable to be quite strong and the risks will be lower. If, however, the convertible is not in the money then the correlation is liable to be weaker and the possibility of the offsetting effect arising is reduced with a corresponding increase in risk.

2 WARRANTS

2.1 Introduction

2.1.1 Definition

A warrant gives the right to the holder to buy shares from the company that issued the warrant at a specified price on or before a specified date.

It can be seen that a warrant is essentially the same as a call option, giving the right to buy a share. The major difference is that warrants are issued by and exercisable on the company, which will issue new shares on exercise. Traded and traditional options are issued by investors and relate to shares already in issue; their exercise does not result in new shares being issued.

Warrants have all the characteristics of call options, such as volatility, risk and valuation factors.

2.1.2 Advantages and disadvantages to the issuer

Advantages

The advantages to a company of issuing warrants include the following.

- Raising immediate cash without the need to finance dividend payments to new shares.
- Increasing the attraction of a debt issue. Many warrants are attached to a debt issue, giving debt investors the added attraction of an 'equity kicker'. This will translate into lower required yields on the debt, meaning that the initial financial burden on the company is lower. After the debt is issued, the warrants are usually detached from the debt and traded separately in the market place.
- Capitalising on an overvalued share price. If the company believes that its share price will fall, then any warrants issued are unlikely to be exercised. This means that the company will receive the money on issue of the warrants but anticipates that it will not have to issue any new shares.

Disadvantages

The disadvantages to the company are that if and when the warrant is exercised

- New shares will be issued by the company, potentially at a significant discount to the then share price.
- The required dividend payments in total may increase dramatically if the share price is not to be adversely affected.

2.1.3 Advantages and disadvantages to the investors

Advantages

An investor will find warrants attractive for various reasons. Warrants offer the following.

- A geared investment in a company's shares, being a cheaper alternative to buying the share itself, much in the same way as for a call option.
- A way of securing an income yield while keeping open the possibility of high equity performance, through buying debt plus warrants from the company. This is similar to the principle of buying a convertible debt issue.

Disadvantages

Disadvantages to the investor are as follows.

- As a geared investment, percentage losses can be extreme if the share underperforms.
- The risk of a takeover. If a company is taken over, it is often the case that the exercise date of the warrants will be accelerated to the takeover date. This will destroy any time value in the warrant, meaning that an investor could suffer a serious loss. If the warrant is out-of-the-money, having just been issued for example, then it may become worthless.

Additional factors when considering an investment in warrants include

- The marketability of the warrant.
- The period to expiry, exercise price and current share price (i.e. basic valuation factors).
- The likelihood that the company's share price will perform adequately.

Note. A warrant holder will not be affected by bonus issues or rights issues because the terms of the warrant will adjust in the same way as the terms of options contracts, outlined above.

Chapter Roundup

You must be able to

- Describe the advantages and disadvantages of convertibles or warrant to both the issuer and the investor.
- Calculate the value or discuss the valuation of a convertible using
  - DCF method
  - Crossover method
  - Optimum pricing method
    - $\text{Convertible price} = \text{Equivalent bond price} + \frac{A}{1+q} \times \text{Number of shares}$

      where A is the value of an equivalent call option
- Calculate the conversion price
  - $\text{Conversion price} = \frac{\text{Value of convertible}}{\text{Conversion ratio}}$
- Calculate the conversion premium
  - $\text{Conversion premium} = \frac{\text{Conversion price} - \text{Share price}}{\text{Share price}} \times 100$

TEST YOUR KNOWLEDGE

Check your knowledge of the Chapter here, without referring back to the text.

1. A company's 9% convertible stands at £115, its ordinary shares at 168p and £100 stock is convertible into 52 shares. What is the premium on the convertible and the conversion price?

2. A company's 10% convertible unsecured loan stock is convertible into 25p ordinary shares at the rate of 35 shares for every £100 stock. The market price of the ordinary shares is 270p and the market price of the convertible is £105. What is the conversion premium or discount?

3. Outline the advantages and disadvantages of convertibles.

4. Outline the pricing approaches for convertibles.

5. You are considering investing in a company's new issue of a 15-year maturity convertible unsecured loan stock, which has a put option attached. The put option allows the investor to put the stock back to the issue after three years at a price that implies a predetermined yield to the investor.

   (a) List the major factors that would influence your analysis of the put option.

   (b) How would the put option (as well as the conversion option) affect your assessment of the credit risk of the convertible as compared with a traditional unsecured loan stock?

6. Your fund holds shares in a UK mining company with international mining interests in a range of commodities. The company announces a £100 million rights issue of £100 of 20 year 4% coupon convertible unsecured loan stock for every 60 shares held. The shares are currently priced at £5.00 per share with a 2.0% gross dividend yield and on a price earnings ratio of 16. The convertible bond includes the right to convert into the shares from three years time to thirteen years time at the rate of 16 shares over £100 nominal of the stock.

   (a) How would you decide whether to take up the rights in the convertible unsecured loan stock?

   (b) Assuming that you do take up your rights, how would you decide when to convert the bond into shares?

   (c) What are the attractions to a company and to an investor of issuing a convertible unsecured loan stock via a rights issue?

7. (a) You have been asked by your senior manager to explain the difference between investing in a bond plus warrants and investing in a convertible bond. In your answer, you should outline the following.

   - The advantages and disadvantages of each from the point of view of the fund manager seeking enhanced returns over conventional fixed income securities.
   - The basic principles and pitfalls in the valuation of warrants and convertibles.

   (b) You have the following information on Northern Foods 6.75% Eurconvertible

Coupon	6.75% semi-annual
Conversion Price	£3.26
Convertible Price	99.25%
Nominal Value	£1,000

   with the current Northern Foods share price at £2.46

   (i) Determine the conversion ratio of the convertible.
   (ii) Determine the conversion parity of the convertible.
   (iii) Determine the conversion premium of the convertible.

Test Your Knowledge: Answers

1. Value of shares = £1.68 × 52 = £87.36

   Premium on convertible = $\frac{£115.00}{£87.36} - 1$ = 0.316 or 31.6%

   The conversion price is $\frac{£115}{52}$ = £2.21

2. Value of shares = 35 × £2.70 = £94.50

   Premium = $\frac{£105.00}{£94.50} - 1$ = 0.01111 or 11.11%

3. See 1.1.3

4. See 1.2

5. (a) The following factors would need to be considered when appraising the value of the put option.

   - The exercise price of the convertible, conversion terms, conversion windows, and the current premium over the share price.
   - Stability of the company's cash flows and the outlook for the share price over the 15 year period.
   - The credit risk of the company.
   - The absolute level of the premium on redemption (and implied yield) and the term structure of interest rates.
   - The mismatch between the put expiry and the conversion right is an important factor to take into consideration. In three years the put will expire and at that time, dependent on the style of the conversion (American or European), a decision will have to be taken as to the value of an extremely long dated option into the equity.
   - We need to compare the yield on the three-year bond using the put premium and the 15-year convertible. If the yield is not significantly greater for the convertible then it would not compensate for the risk.

   (b) In assessing the impact on credit risk the following factors will have to be borne in mind.

   - The put option expires in three years presenting the possibility of early forced redemption at rates above par. The convertible itself matures in 15 years, and presumably has been structured in order to ensure that the conversion of the bond is likely and therefore, repayment of the loan is unlikely.

     Consequently, the company faces the prospect of premium repayment in three years. Is the company prepared for this eventuality?
   - There is the risk that the issue could be perceived as desperation finance with the borrowing being structured to achieve the lowest possible coupon to avoid near-term cash outflows.

6. (a) Decision to take up the convertible will obviously depend upon the valuation applied.

Valuation of the convertible = Bond + Call option

Valuation of Bond

This will be based on the valuation of a 4% straight bond maturing 2008.

This assumes that the dividend yield remains below the bond yield.

Valuation of the Option

This will be driven by the current premium and historic volatility of the contract.

$$\frac{£100}{16} = £6.25 \text{ implied option}$$

$$\frac{£6.25 - £5.00}{£5.00} = 25\% \text{ premium over current market price.}$$

(b) Conversion timing will depend upon

- The option's intrinsic value.
- The relative income flows. Even if the option has an intrinsic value in three years time it would still make sense to delay conversion if the income yield on the bond exceeded that of the equity.

(c) Company

- Less expensive than a public debt issue.
- The issue will give a greater certainty of income flow.

Investor Flexibility

Initially the investor can

- Take up or not.
- Sell right nil paid.

Subsequently, the investor can

- On expiry get back their investment.
- Increase their equity stake.

7. (a) Both convertibles and both with warrants attached offer pretty much the same combination of an equity option linked to a low coupon fixed income instrument.

The equity linkage generates the ability to outperform other fixed income securities. However, as mentioned above, the price that is paid for this comes in the form of a lower coupon and consequently reduced income flow. As a support to the fund the bond element does, however, provide a floor value to the fund.

Warrants have a significant advantage over convertibles in that there is a degree of separability with regard to the option element and the underlying bond. With convertibles the equity element is embedded inside the bond product.

However, with warrants it is possible that there may be different maturity dates on the two instruments. This may result in cash flow implications if the warrant expires before the maturity of the bond.

There are three potential valuation methods.

- Crossover method.
- Discounted cash flow.
- Bond and options models.

The first two methods are to an extent incomplete and somewhat subjective. In particular, they fail to acknowledge any time value implicit in the option element of the product.

The final method, whilst better, is still far from perfect. Its particular problem lies in the valuation of longer dated options.

(b) (i) $\frac{£1,000}{3.26} = 306.748$

(ii) $306.748 \times £2.46 = £754.60$ or £75.46

(iii) £99.25 or £992.50

$\frac{£992.50}{306.748} = £3.2355$

$£3.2355 - £2.46 = 0.7755$

$\frac{0.7755}{2.46} \times 100 = 31.53\%$

12 Foreign Currency and Overseas Investment

INTRODUCTION

Though many investors and investments will be made exclusively in the UK, there are many where an element of overseas investment is involved. Indeed it is very difficult these days to avoid the impacts overseas investment since so many UK companies have overseas operations.

The key things to understand from this section are

- The rewards and risks of overseas investment
- The impact of exchange rate movements and the assessment of forward rates
- The approaches available to investors for the hedging of foreign exchange risk
- The assessment of the returns and risks to a UK investor from investing overseas

Questions do not frequently arise from the ideas in this chapter

CHAPTER CONTENTS

Chapter Learning Objectives

The syllabus areas covered by this section are

Economics

Students should have a broad understanding and knowledge of international and domestic affairs which impact upon financial markets. This would include current levels of yields and exchange rates and, for those markets for which detailed knowledge is required, a thorough knowledge of current concerns in the marketplace. Taxation might be an example of this latter point. Students should possess a broad understanding of the principal theories of economic and financial behaviour. For example, purchasing power parity, capital asset price and arbitrage price theories.

Analysis

Students should possess a broad understanding of both static and dynamic methods for the analysis and construction of fixed income securities containing both certain and contingent cashflows. Variable rate securities will be included. Students should be aware of the of the limitations of assumptions and mathematical techniques upon results. Although analysis will be concerned principally with 'risk-free' securities, students should be aware of the further considerations for 'risky' securities and the effect they may have on expected return, Student should possess a thorough comprehension of single-period and multi-period, single currency and multi-currency portfolio management theory.

Risk assessment

Basis and hedging

1 The Benefits of Overseas Investment

1.1 Introduction

As companies have expanded overseas, world equity markets have developed and foreign exchange controls have been lifted by many countries. Consequently, the importance of understanding, analysing and managing foreign currency exposure has increased.

Investors now have the opportunity to fully diversify their portfolios through overseas investment from around the world. In addition, investors may use a foreign currency as an asset of itself if they believe that it is appreciating relative to their base currency.

Foreign exchange, and the potential for exchange rate fluctuations, adds an extra dimension to the risk/return profile of an overseas investment.

The theoretical benefits of global investing are derived from modern portfolio theory. This argues that all investors invest in an efficient portfolio. An efficient portfolio is one that is not dominated by any other portfolio in terms of risk and return. If we ignore the possibility of a risk-free asset, all efficient portfolios lie on the efficient frontier.

The domestic efficient frontier, obtained when an investor invests only in his own domestic market, is dominated by an efficient frontier that includes global asset portfolios. Overseas diversification benefits include the following.

Markets	▪ Diversification away from reliance on a single economy. ▪ Diversification of portfolio to take in overseas markets.
Industrial Sectors	▪ Investment in sectors not available in the UK, such as mining.
Currencies	▪ Less exposure to one currency. ▪ Exposure to currency risk where the investor feels that this is of benefit.
Correlations	▪ International assets are not perfectly positively correlated to domestic assets.

In addition, overseas diversification offers the potential for extremely **high returns in emerging markets**. The availability of investment trusts investing overseas provides a practical means of achieving a relatively diversified overseas investment at a low level of investment.

2 The Risks of Overseas Investment

Although overseas investment has many advantages, there are also a number of risks of overseas investment, i.e. problems arise through such exposure.

Inherent Risk	▪ High risk in emerging markets due to the unsophisticated domestic investor base and overheating economies. ▪ Political risk in certain volatile countries. ▪ Legal rights of the investor is likely to differ from those in the UK. ▪ Ability of foreign investors to participate/invest.
Liquidity Risk/ Hedging	▪ Ability to realise investment, especially in adverse market conditions. ▪ Lack of developed derivatives for hedging purposes leads to less efficient portfolio management.
Currency Risk/ Hedging	▪ Exposure to adverse currency movements. ▪ Exchange control regulations in certain countries. ▪ Unavailability of suitable currency hedging products.
Lack of Regulation	▪ Lack of market regulation in emerging markets. ▪ Inadequate financial regulation/reporting standards.
Information/ Communications	▪ Inadequate/problematic, e.g. may require foreign language expertise. ▪ Costly to gather. ▪ Unreliability.
Taxation	▪ Potential double taxation problems. ▪ Additional local taxes.

We examine the more significant of these below.

2.1 Foreign exchange risk – The effect of exchange rate movements

The risks an investor may face with respect to foreign currency fluctuations (foreign exchange risk) may be categorised under one of three headings.

- Transaction risk.
- Translation risk.
- Operating or economic risk.

2.1.1 Transaction risk

Definition

Transaction risk is the risk that the sterling value of any foreign currency receipts or payments may vary as a result of exchange rate fluctuations, resulting in a change in the anticipated investment cash flows.

Example

A company holds $5m in US$ bonds to be redeemed in three months' time. The current (spot) exchange rate is $1.60:£1. How much will be received in three months' time if the exchange rate at that date is

- $1.60:£1?
- $1.50:£1?
- $1.70:£1?

Solution

$1.60:£1

At this rate, the sterling amount receivable would be $\frac{\$5,000,000}{1.60}$ = £3,125,000

$1.50:£1

At this rate, the sterling amount receivable would be $\frac{\$5,000,000}{1.50}$ = £3,333,333

$1.70:£1

At this rate, the sterling amount receivable would be $\frac{\$5,000,000}{1.70}$ = £2,941,176

Conclusion

We can see that as a result of a relatively minor fluctuation in exchange rates, the sterling amount receivable has moved dramatically. Clearly, this variability may well effect the decision as to whether the investment should be undertaken.

2.1.2 Translation risk

Definition

Translation risk is the risk that the sterling value of any foreign denominated assets or liabilities, or foreign denominated income or expenses, will vary from one year to the next as a result of changes in exchange rates, which will impact on the investment performance.

Note. This type of risk has no direct cash flow implications. Rather, what we have is variability of reported assets and profits in sterling, which may be caused purely by exchange rate fluctuations, with the assets and profits in local currency terms being fairly stable. As a result, apparent performance may be distorted.

Example

A UK investor holds £100m of US bonds. Interest rates in the US are static, hence bond prices in dollars are stable.

What will be the sterling value of this investment if the exchange rate is

- $2:£1?
- $1:£1?

Solution

	$2:£1		$1:£1	
	$m	£m	$m	£m
Investments	100	50	100	100

What we appear to have is a return of 100%, with the portfolio rising from £50m to £100m. In truth, the true performance of the asset has been zero, it being worth $100m at both the start and end of the year. This apparent spectacular performance in sterling terms completely results from the foreign currency movement across the year. This factor is clearly outside of the control of the investor, and may go the other way just as rapidly.

2.1.3 Operating or economic risk

Definition

Operating or economic risk will not be suffered directly by the investor, though the risks of some of his investments may incorporate this as a function.

Operating or economic risk arises as a result of a company's competitive position. It is the risk that the sterling value of a company's cash flow may vary as a result of foreign exchange fluctuations, regardless of whether

- There is no overseas trade/transactions/assets and liabilities.
- All overseas trade/transactions are fully hedged.

Example 1

A UK tour operator specialises in providing guided tours to overseas visitors. Since operations are conducted in the UK, he bills all of his customers in sterling. His revenue will, therefore, depend on two things.

- The sterling charge per tour sold.
- The number of tours sold.

If sterling were to strengthen, then the tours would appear significantly more expensive to the foreign visitors and hence, the number of tours sold (and consequently, revenue) would fall.

In this example, there is no exporting or importing involved, but the revenues and profits of the company will be impacted upon by exchange rate fluctuations.

Example 2

Jaguar Cars export to the US, where they compete primarily against Mercedes and BMW. As a result, the relative demand for their products depend on their relative cost in dollars which, in turn, depends on the strength of the dollar against sterling and euro, respectively.

Jaguar's US performance is therefore influenced by any relative movement between sterling and euro, even though none of these transactions are being denominated in euro.

2.2 Additional transaction costs

2.2.1 Foreign currency transactions

Dealing in overseas markets will probably have to be done in overseas currencies, incurring dealing costs.

2.2.2 Information gathering

The investor will have less knowledge about overseas markets than his domestic UK market. In itself, this represents a risk that inappropriate investment decisions will be made. In order to avoid this problem, substantial costs will need to be incurred to understand and analyse the overseas companies and markets in which the investor is interested.

2.3 Taxation

2.3.1 Local taxes

Additional tax costs can be incurred when receiving dividends from overseas companies. Initially, the company may suffer high rates of corporate taxation on its profits, reducing its level of post-tax income significantly. Secondly, when dividends are paid over, withholding taxes may be deducted, further reducing the final return to investors.

2.3.2 Double taxation treaties

The cost of overseas taxation will be mitigated by double taxation treaties. These mean that, where overseas tax has already been suffered on income, then additional UK tax may not be payable. Even where the UK does not have a double taxation agreement with another country, it may be the case that the UK tax authorities will give unilateral tax relief to avoid excessive taxation.

2.4 Political risk

Unexpected changes overseas can lead to major catastrophes. Nationalisation of industries without compensation, changes in government, reversals of policy and changes in tax rates will all significantly affect the returns available to investors.

3 Exchange Rate Regimes

3.1 Introduction

In the latter part of the nineteenth century and sporadically in the early twentieth century, the exchange rate regime adopted was that major currencies were effectively fixed against each other by virtue of the Gold Standard. Under the Gold Standard each currency was pegged against gold (into which banknotes were convertible). Therefore, each currency was de facto fixed against the others. This was the first attempt to restrict the volatility of the forex market. This system broke down in the 1920s/1930s.

From 1946 to 1972, the global economy again operated within an environment of **fixed exchange rates**, with sterling and the other currencies pegged to the dollar. This was not an absolute link and sterling was devalued twice, in 1950 and 1967. However, for long periods of time currencies were relatively stable.

In 1972, the sterling rate was allowed to float and supply and demand set the rate. This was a **dirty float** where the Bank of England intervened in order to establish a government set floor, or ceiling, to the exchange rate. Since this point, no truly global exchange rate system has been put in place. However, more localised schemes have been attempted. In Europe, there have been several attempts to stabilise currencies culminating in the EMU. The most effective predecessor was ERM. Under the ERM, currencies were pegged against each other and if the currency moved outside predetermined ranges then intervention was required.

Since the UK's exit from the ERM in 1992, sterling has again floated against the other currencies.

3.2 The impact of the exchange rate regime on economic policy

3.2.1 Fixed exchange rates

Use of monetary policy may well be undermined by the establishment of fixed exchange rates, which effectively act as a constraint on interest rates. Consequently, the objectives of monetary policy may not be achievable within the rate target. Effectively, the government has a choice to attempt to control the exchange rate or the money supply and hence inflation, **but not both**.

With regard to fiscal policy, one of the prime constraints on policy, the risk of **crowding out**, is no longer a problem in the open economy. Since on the assumption that there is full capital mobility, funds will flow in from overseas in order to ensure that the interest rate remains in line with overseas interest rates. There is no restriction on the flow of capital in terms of the fear of exchange rate risk, since rates are fixed.

3.2.2 Floating exchange rates

Within floating exchange rates, the exchange rate is no longer a constraint on monetary policy and, as a result, providing that the government is prepared to abide by the consequences in terms of the exchange rate, there is no longer a policy problem.

In terms of fiscal policy, the problem of crowding out returns since overseas investors will be concerned with the risk of exchange depreciation. As the government attempts fiscal expansion, this crowds out domestic consumption and puts an upward pressure on interest rates. In addition, the increase in interest rates will lead to an appreciation of the exchange rate, thereby reducing the demand for the economy's exports and increasing the level of imports.

3.3 Introduction to EMU

3.3.1 Introduction

On 1 January 1999, the 11 nations participating in the first wave of European Monetary Union (EMU) took the most radical step ever seen in economic policy. In an unprecedented move, they embarked upon the final stage of economic linkage. Under this agreement, first put forward in the 1970s but formally laid down at Maastricht in 1991, the 11 participating nations irrevocably linked their currencies together and formally removed national currencies in 2002.

This system allowed the European Union to fulfil its true economic potential. When compared to the US, the European Union is equal in so many respects, but failed the major economic comparisons. To many commentators, this underachievement was simply a reflection of the inefficiencies caused by individual national currencies. The argument often put forward was that it would be unlikely that the US would have developed as it has if it were not for the single unifying currency.

	Euroland	US	Japan
Population	306m	286m	127m
GDP	$6,121bn	$10,020bn	4,176bn
GDP per capita	$20,000	$35,200	$32,800

Source: National Accounts of OECD countries, Main aggregates, Volume 1

Note. The GDP and GDP per capita are at current prices and exchange rates for 2001.

Traditionally, the European economies have been cyclically linked to the US economy. Arguably, EMU will allows the European economies to assert their real strength. No longer will the US and the dollar be the only global economic superpower. Euroland and the euro has become an engine of the world economy.

3.3.2 The arguments for monetary union

The benefit to trade

The creation of a single currency removed a substantial barrier to the flow of goods between member states of the European Union and reduced hidden transaction cost for intra-European trade. It must be remembered that for the UK intra-European trade is now the most important geographic market. At present, approximately 60% of UK visible trade is with the EU.

In this sense, the Euro perfected the single market regime. Many would argue that a single currency is not a necessary prerequisite for the single market and would point to the various free trade areas that exist in the world without the same currency.

However, in the absence of a single currency, many governments may elect to use devaluation as a weapon of policy. The big question is perhaps whether devaluation is actually a valid tool of economic management or the soft option that governments simply choose to take. The need to devalue is often a product of underlying fundamental problems in the economy, particularly with regard to competitiveness and productivity in the labour market. Arguably, the UK has exploited this flexibility through devaluation and by so doing, for a long time ignored the fundamental flaws that lay within the UK's industrial structure.

If devaluation was used in this way, then it may well have signalled the end of the single market. Without the stability of the single currency, nations would always have had ability to alter their exchange rate and in the end, if this process became too frequent, the whole single market would have broken down amidst a welter of trade barriers. It is this argument that many commentators used to argue that the single market could not survive in the absence of monetary union.

Equally, this may have important implications for those nations who choose not to join the EMU. Given that nations on the outside of the EMU will be able to devalue in order to secure advantage, it is possible that the benefits of the single market, indeed membership of the EU itself, may, in time, be withdrawn from non-participants.

Monetary and price stability

The creation of a single currency monitored and controlled by an independent central bank, the European Central Bank (ECB), charged with creating a stable monetary environment was designed to ensure low inflation.

The role of the European Central Bank

The implicit assumption throughout EMU is that the European Central Bank will be successful in the control of inflation. This will be dependent upon the ability of the Central Bank to select the appropriate targets and receive the appropriate information from a much wider economic base than any individual European central bank had to deal with. However, questions remain regarding the homogeneity of the European economy.

Any lack of homogeneity may hold within it a number of serious flaws for the system. In particular, the main policy weapon used to control inflation is interest rates. The use of interest rates has a markedly different impact on various regional blocks within EMU. In both France and Germany, the vast majority of domestic loans are fixed rate and, as a consequence, households are relatively insulated against interest rate movements.

The opposite is true in the historically higher inflation economies, such as Italy and Spain. As in the UK, the vast majority of domestic credit, particularly in the form of mortgages, is linked very heavily to interest rates with some 80% of existing mortgages being under variable rate plans. Any change in interest rates, which primarily affects the financial sector in both Germany and France, also has a fairly immediate impact upon the consumer sector in Spain and Italy.

However, somewhat perversely, whilst the immediate impact will be greatest amongst the more peripheral members of EMU, ultimately the effect will be greatest on the core members such as Germany and France. The reasons for this lie in the mechanisms through which any rate change is passed down. In Italy, with the vast majority of debt being floating rate in nature, the banks pass the bulk of any increase on. However, in Germany, the inability of the banks to pass on the rate increases, due in part to fixed rate loans, causes strains within bank balance sheets.

In time, the single financial market and the harmonisation and cross-border nature of the banking industry will lead to a greater increase in fixed rate mortgages in both Spain and Italy, thereby creating a consistent and common base.

3.3.3 The implications of EMU for the bond markets

On the positive side, EMU created a large and relatively liquid bond market, which should reduce finance costs. However, even with a wide initial membership the size of the market will not rival the US T-bond market.

Government bond markets immediately pre and post EMU

Pre-EMU

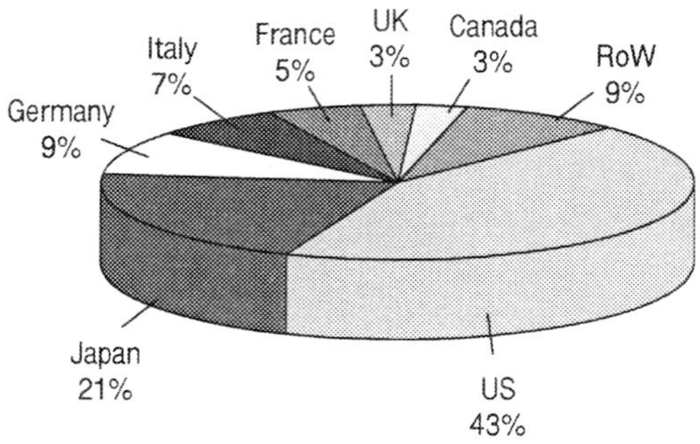

Post-EMU

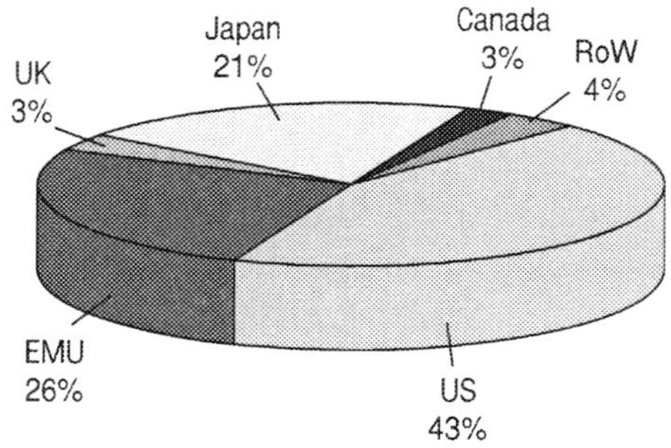

Whilst all the debt of the participant nations became part of one large market, there are effectively sub-markets within this. These sub-markets are driven by the different pools of liquidity and by differing levels of credit perception.

4 Foreign Exchange Rates

In order to be able to analyse foreign currency risk in more detail, it is important to be able to perform basic foreign exchange rate calculations.

4.1 Spot rates

The spot market is the market for immediate currency trades. Delivery will take place two business days after the deal is made. The market has no formal market place and trading takes place via telephones with prices being quoted on screen services.

4.1.1 How spot rates are quoted

The spot market quotes bid/offer prices (spot rates) in the form of a spread, normally based against the US$. The main exceptions to this is £:$ (known as cable) and €:$, where the $ is quoted against the £/€.

Whichever currencies are involved, exchange rates are quoted as the number of units of one currency per single unit of another. For convenience, we will refer to these as the **secondary** and **primary** currencies, respectively. You may also hear them referred to as variable and fixed, or quoted and base – you should view these terms as interchangeable.

As we have just noted, most currencies are quoted against the US$, and any quote where the $ is the secondary or variable currency would be referred to as a **direct** quote (e.g. $s per £1). An **indirect quote** is where the exchange rate is stated with the US$ as the primary currency (e.g. £s per $1).

4.1.2 £/$ Spot rate

1.4275–1.4385

The $ buyer's rate	The $ seller's rate
£1 will get $1.4275	$1.4385 will get £1

Here, the dollar is the secondary currency and sterling is the primary currency.

To assist in remembering which rate to use, remember that the bank always gives you the worst side. For example, if you want to buy dollars with £1, the bank will give you the least dollars it can, i.e. $1.4275 rather than $1.4385 in return. Alternatively, if you have dollars and want to buy £1, then the bank will charge you the most it can, i.e. $1.4385 rather than $1.4275.

4.2 Forward rates

The forward market is a market in currencies for delivery at an agreed date in the future. The exchange rate at which delivery takes place is agreed now.

4.2.1 How forward rates are quoted

Forward rates are quoted as premiums (pm) or discounts (dis) to the spot rate. It is possible for rates to be quoted at par where the spot and forward are the same.

Example

Spot	1.4275-1.4385
One-month forward	0.37-0.35c pm
Three-month forward	1.40-1.38c pm

Calculate the three-month forward rate.

Solution

It is important to note that the premiums and discounts are quoted in cents, whereas the spot rate is quoted in dollars.

A premium implies that the secondary currency is becoming more expensive relative to the primary one, i.e. in the above example, the dollar is strengthening against sterling and as a result, £1 will buy fewer dollars. Hence, to obtain the forward rate, the premium is **subtracted** from the spot rate. Similarly, the discount is added.

This same rule applies regardless of the nature of the quote, **direct or indirect**, since the premium or discount applies to the secondary currency, whichever is the primary one. The rule is that **premiums are subtracted** and **discounts are added**.

Based on the above figures, the three-month forward rate is as follows.

Spot rate	1.4275–1.4385
Less: premium	0.0140–0.0138
	1.4135–1.4247

4.2.2 How forward rates are calculated by the bank

One important factor to be aware of about this market is that it does not necessarily reflect an expectation of what the spot rate will be in three, six or nine months' time. It is simply a mathematical result of the difference in interest rates in the two countries.

Example

In the above example, three-month sterling interest rates were 10%, meaning the interest rate for the three-month period is 2.5% (10 × 3/12); three-month dollar rates were 6%, meaning the interest rate for the three-month period is 1.5% (6 × 3/12).

Now Spot Rate				Three Months' Time Forward Rate
£1,000	→	@ 3-month £ rates at 2.5%	→	£1,025
↓				↓
@ 1.4275				**Therefore @ 1.4136**
↓				↑
$1,427.50	→	@ 3-month $ rates at 1.5%	→	$1,448.91

The forward rate is simply calculated on the basis that the money is invested at the current rate of interest in the two countries. At the end of the period, the relationship between the value of the two deposits gives the forward rate.

$$\frac{1{,}448.91}{1{,}025} = 1.4136$$

If this relationship were not the case, then it would be possible to make an arbitrage profit by borrowing in one currency, converting it at today's spot rate into the other currency and placing this on deposit for, say, three months. At the same time, a forward contract could be taken out to reverse the original spot transaction, locking in a profit.

4.2.3 Interest rate parity formula

Exam tip

This relationship does get examined numerically or as a brief description/definition, see Summer 2005 Question 5.

The link between exchange rates and interest rates can be worked through using first principles as above. Alternatively, the link can be summarised by the **interest rate parity** formula, which says that

Formula to learn

$$\text{Forward rate} = \frac{1+r_s}{1+r_p} \times \text{Spot rate}$$

where

r_s = interest rate for the secondary currency for the relevant period
r_p = interest rate for the primary currency for the relevant period

In the above example

$$\text{Forward rate} = \frac{1.015}{1.025} \times 1.4275 = 1.4136$$

It is worth noting the specific way in which r_s and r_p are calculated. They should be based on the number of days in the period. For example, if dollar interest rates for a three-month (91-day) period are 8%, the relevant value for r_s is (8% × 91/360) 2.02%. If sterling interest rates for a three-month (91-day) period are 10%, then the relevant value for r_p is (10% × 91/365) 2.49%.

The use of a 360-day year for dollar interest rates and a 365-day year for sterling is market convention. When banks work out the yield they wish to pay or receive, they take this into account in their quote.

5 Exchange Rate Forecasting

5.1 Introduction

In order to be able to make informed decisions on currency exposure and overseas investment, it is important to be able to appreciate the factors affecting exchange rates and the likely future direction of exchange rate movements.

Analysis of exchange rates focuses on key economic factors which affect currencies. It considers the performance and interaction of a number of key economic variables, such as growth, inflation and exchange rates. This may be done by constructing a model of the world economy with certain defined relationships and interactions between key variables. Assumptions are made about the key variables and forecasts of exchange rates are produced.

The problem with this approach, known as econometric modelling, is that it is fairly rigid and formal. It is difficult to alter relationships between variables to reflect changing circumstances and the impact of national and international crises.

A more flexible approach is to adopt subjective values, where the forecaster identifies key variables for a period of time and then makes assumptions about these and their relationship to each other over the period.

5.1.1 Shorter term factors affecting exchange rates

Interest rates

In the short term, exchange rates will be influenced by supply and demand for a currency. If, for example, two economies have had stable exchange rates and one decides to increase interest rates, then this change will attract 'hot money' from around the world seeking higher returns, the effect being that the currency will suddenly rise. This exchange rate will however be artificially high – the currencies were previously stable. We would, therefore, expect that the currency would weaken to its original rate over time. As a result, a good estimator of the short-term future exchange rate would be the interest rate parity relationship introduced above, which incorporates the effect of this depreciation over time, i.e.

Formula to learn

$$\text{Future exchange rate} = \frac{1+r_s}{1+r_p} \times \text{Spot rate}$$

where

r_s = interest rate for the secondary currency for the relevant period
r_p = interest rate for the primary currency for the relevant period

Balance of payments

If the UK has a balance of payments surplus, then it is exporting goods with a higher value than it is importing. In order to pay for these goods, overseas customers will need to purchase sterling. Demand for sterling will increase, meaning that the currency will strengthen. Alternatively, if the UK has a balance of payments deficit, then UK companies will need to sell sterling to buy overseas currencies to fund their purchases. This will cause sterling to weaken.

Economic growth

Economic growth will stimulate demand for a currency both through capital flows into the country, due to attractive investment opportunities, and current account flows, due to increased supply and demand for the country's traded goods and services. Alternatively, a credit boom which causes demand for overseas goods and services will cause the currency to weaken.

Fiscal and monetary policies

Taxation and public spending policies have a direct impact on economic growth. Government borrowing plans will impact on interest rates, as will monetary policy, which aims to reduce or increase money supply through changes in interest rates.

Natural resources

The discovery or existence of valuable natural resources, such as oil, can cause a currency to strengthen dramatically.

Currency block membership

Some currencies are pegged to the US dollar, such as certain Middle Eastern currencies. Such formal or informal relationships should be noted, since they will have a key impact on the exchange rate.

Political events

Central bank intervention can affect exchange rates, although experience has shown that it is sometimes the speculators who win the day rather than the central authorities. On top of this, events such as elections, public opinion polls, government ministers' statements and press releases can all affect the exchange rate.

5.1.2 Longer term factors – Inflation and purchasing power parity

Introduction

In the shorter term, the exchange rate is determined by supply and demand factors and, to a greater or lesser extent, market sentiment. Longer term exchange rates are determined by purchasing power parity, which is a relationship between economies and the levels of inflation they suffer. Purchasing power parity (PPP) is best explained by way of a small example.

If a basket of goods costs £100 in London and the same basket of goods costs €160 in Frankfurt, this suggests the exchange rate between the two countries will be £1 = €1.60. However, if the two economies suffer differing rates of inflation, then over time, the exchange rate will alter.

If, after a number of years, the basket of goods now costs £125 in London, due to the impact of inflation on UK prices, and yet it remains at €160 in Frankfurt, this would suggest that the exchange rate between the two currencies is now £1 = €1.28, a decline in the value of sterling.

Short-term supply and demand features may well mask this overall trend, but purchasing power parity gives an underlying theme to the foreign exchange markets. If one economy consistently has an inflation rate in excess of its competitors, then its currency will deteriorate against its trading partners.

The International Fisher Effect

We have seen above that longer term exchange rates are theoretically determined by purchasing power parity and the inflation differential between two currencies. We have also seen above that short-term future exchange rates are determined by reference to interest rate differentials. These two concepts are brought together by the Fisher effect, which links together interest rates, inflation and the foreign exchange markets.

Fisher states that the nominal rate of return (r), i.e. the interest rate charged or monetary return, is equal to the real rate of return (R) adjusted to compensate for the effect of inflation (i) as follows.

Formula to learn

$$(1 + r) = (1 + R)(1 + i)$$

If we now go back to the relationship that we established earlier for short-term exchange rates, we had

$$\text{Future exchange rate} = \frac{1+r_S}{1+r_P} \times \text{Spot rate}$$

Now, the Fisher relationship must apply in all economies, hence

$$\frac{1+r_S}{1+r_P} = \frac{(1+R_S)(1+i_S)}{(1+R_P)(1+i_P)}$$

The assumption of PPP is that the real rate of return, R, should equate between countries in the long term. If this were not the case and one country always offered a superior return, then investors would only invest in that country, resulting in prices rising and returns falling until an equilibrium was reached.

As a result, in the long term, we will have

$$(1 + R_S) = (1 + R_P)$$

These two terms then cancel out in the previous equation as follows.

$$\frac{1+r_S}{1+r_P} = \frac{\cancel{(1+R_S)}(1+i_S)}{\cancel{(1+R_P)}(1+i_P)} = \frac{1+i_S}{1+i_P}$$

This is the International Fisher Effect, that interest rate differentials in the long term equate to inflation rate differentials over the same period.

Making this substitution in our future exchange rate formula above gives us that in the long-term, the difference in exchange rates is generated by the differential in inflation rates, i.e.

Formula to learn

$$\text{Future exchange rage} = \frac{1+i_S}{1+i_P} \times \text{Spot rate}$$

where $(1 + i_S)$, $(1 + i_P)$ reflect the compound effect of inflation over the relevant period.

That is, exchange rate differentials in the long term are driven by inflation rate differentials between the two economies concerned.

6 Hedging of Foreign Currency Risk

Exam tip

This area is examined as a discussion, see Winter 2008 Question 7, Winter 2005 Question 7.

The risk referred to above that movements in exchange rates will cause variability in returns, either in the form of cash flows or asset values, can be reduced or eliminated by use of various foreign currency hedging techniques.

6.1 Forward contracts

6.1.1 Trading

When an importer is buying goods from overseas in foreign currency, he has the risk that when the time comes to pay for the goods, the exchange rate will have moved against him. This risk can be removed by taking out a forward contract for the date he intends to pay for the goods at the date he purchases them. The forward contract fixes the rate today for delivery of the currency at a future date. The relevant rate is the forward rate.

6.1.2 Investment

The same principle can be used by an investor. In our transaction risk example earlier, the returns from the US$ bond were variable, depending on movements in exchange rates.

If we can estimate the expected US$ return in advance, however, then we can take out a forward contract for that amount when we originally purchase the investment, or at some later date.

Example

We hold $5m nominal of US$ corporate bonds when the exchange rate is $1.60:£1, meaning that the sterling value of the bonds is £3.125m. We expect that we will receive a coupon of 8% ($0.4m) and can sell the bonds for $5.06m in a year's time, i.e. we expect a total return of $5.46m in one year. In addition, the forward rate at the beginning of the year for delivery dates one year, hence is 1.56:1. What return can we achieve avoiding currency risk?

Solution

If we take out a forward contract to sell $5.46m for sterling at a rate of $1.56:£1 in one year's time, we will receive £3.50m. This gives a return of

$$R_{£} = \frac{3.500 - 3.125}{3.125} = 12\%$$

6.1.3 Problems with forward contracts

The advantage of the forward contract is that it locks into a certain rate of exchange in the future. There are however a number of problems.

- Since the forward rate is locked into at the outset, the investor cannot take advantage of any favourable exchange rate movements. In our case, for example, if spot rates had been 1.50:1 at the end of the year, then we would in hindsight have done better by not taking out a forward contract at 1.56:1 and instead selling the dollars on the spot market at the rate of 1.50:1.
- The forward contract is for a fixed amount. If the amount of dollars that we receive is different to the amount of the forward contract we have taken out, then the difference will represent an outstanding exposure.
- For example, assume that the worst happens and a US$ corporate bond issuer becomes insolvent and pays no capital or interest. As a result of the forward contract we have entered into, we are now obliged at the end of the year to sell $5.46m for sterling at a rate of 1.56:1. This means that we will have to buy $5.46m on the spot market to complete the transaction and will either make a profit or loss on the transaction, depending on the spot rate.
- It is necessary to estimate the expected proceeds from the investment, which is not easy for risky investments such as equities.
- A series of dividend flows would each require a separate forward contract, increasing costs and administration.
- As the maturity of the investment becomes more distant, it becomes more difficult to obtain competitively priced forward contracts. The reason for this is that the forward market is most active in the three to six-month period. Very long maturities are harder for the banks to cover and hence are more expensive and illiquid.

6.2 Borrowing and depositing

An alternative means of hedging an expected receipt in another currency would be through borrowing and depositing. That is to borrow now in that other currency, convert the money received now into sterling at today's spot rate and place this sterling on deposit, then to use the expected receipt in the other currency to repay the borrowing on maturity.

Example

In our case above, we are expecting to receive $5.46m in one year's time. We can borrow US dollars at an annual rate of 7% and sterling deposits are paying 9.75%. How can we hedge our position?

Solution

We borrow sufficient dollars so that the capital plus interest at 7% comes to $5.46m in one year's time. This will entail borrowing (5.46m/1.07) $5.103m.

This can be converted into sterling immediately using today's spot rate of 1.6:1, giving £3.189m immediately, thus removing exchange rate risk. In one year's time, the borrowing of $5.103m is repaid together with 7% interest of $0.357m, the repayment being funded by the receipt of $5.460m from coupon from and sale of the US$ bonds.

The £3.189m sterling now held can be placed on deposit for the year, growing to £3.500m. This is the same total receipt in one year as it would be, had we taken out a forward contract instead (above). This will always be the case. If there are two ways of achieving the same end result, then they must have the same value as, if they do not, any difference will be arbitraged away.

The key problem with borrowing is that, as with the forward contract, it creates an exposure to foreign currency which will still be there if the expected receipts from the investment do not flow through. In our case, even if we receive no cash from the US$ investment, we are still obliged to repay the dollar borrowing in one year's time and will have to purchase dollars to do so.

6.3 Options

The currency option avoids many of the problems noted above for borrowing and use of forward contracts. The currency option gives the buyer of the option the right, but not the obligation, to buy or sell foreign currency at a specified rate and a specified date or range of dates in the future. The right to buy currency is a call option, the right to sell currency is a put option. The cost of buying the option is the premium.

The key benefit of the option is that it enables the company to benefit from favourable exchange rate movements but protects it from adverse movements. The option need only be exercised if it favours the buyer to do so. This means that an investor could buy an option for the higher range of expected receipts from an investment.

For example, if we were expecting receipts of up to $130, we could buy options to sell the full $130. If the amount received is less than $130, then we only exercise an appropriate amount, and have a choice as to what to do with the remainder. If the dollar has weakened, we can buy dollars at the low price and then sell them, as this option entitles us to, at the higher price. If the dollar has strengthened, then we just let the option expire worthless. Hence, the excess amount covered by the options is not an exposure, as it will never result in a loss.

The problem with an option is that a premium needs to be paid. The larger the amount to which the option relates, the higher the premium. Likewise, the greater the chance that the option can be exercised profitably, the higher the premium.

7 Overseas Investment

7.1 Overseas investment returns

Exam tip

Examined in Summer 2007 Question 2.

7.1.1 Introduction

Any foreign currency fluctuation is liable to impact on the returns on overseas investment. If a currency appreciates by 5% against sterling, then an investment in simply the bank notes of that currency (a 0% return in that currency) would produce a 5% sterling return. If an investment is made in securities that offer a return in the local currency, then the sterling return needs to be amplified by the effects of the exchange gain. This relationship is a compounding one, i.e.

Formula to learn

$$(1 + r_{£}) = (1 + r_{\$})(1 + r_{FX})$$

where

$r_{£}$ = sterling return achieved
$r_{\$}$ = overseas investment return in local currency
r_{FX} = return due to exchange rate fluctuations

This can be demonstrated with a simple example that approaches the problem in two alternative ways.

- First principles.
- The above compounding formula.

Example

A UK investor invests in US bonds that produce a return in dollars of 10% over the period. The exchange rate at the start of the period is \$1.56:£1 and at the end is \$1.50:£1. Calculate the return achieved by the UK investor.

Solution

First principles

Consider what would have happened to an investment of £100 made at the start as follows.

Start Value			$ Return	End Value			£ Return
£		$		$		£	%
100.00	⟶ @1.56	156.00	⟶ +10%	171.60	⟶ @1.50	114.40	14.4

Compounding formula

Clearly, the dollar has appreciated against sterling, moving from 1.56 to 1.50 across the period. The resultant currency return = $\frac{1.56}{1.50}$ = 1.04, i.e. the dollar has appreciated by 4% against sterling. The sterling return can now be calculated using

$$\begin{aligned}(1 + r_£) &= (1 + r_\$)(1 + r_{FX}) \\ &= 1.10 \times 1.04 = 1.144\end{aligned}$$

Hence, $r_£ = 0.144$ or 14.4%

7.1.2 Currency returns

It may appear strange that the currency return has been calculated above as

Formula to learn

$$(1 + r_{FX}) = \frac{\text{Opening exchange rate}}{\text{Closing exchange rate}}$$

when we would normally calculate a gain using

Formula to learn

$$(1 + r) = \frac{\text{End value}}{\text{Start value}}$$

This is due to the way that the rates are quoted above, i.e. as the number of dollars per pound. As a result

- The value of \$1 at the start of the year was $\frac{£1}{1.56}$ = 64.103p.
- The value of \$1 at the year end was $\frac{£1}{1.50}$ = 66.667p.

Hence, the gain was

$$(1 + r) = \frac{\text{End value of \$1}}{\text{Start value of \$1}} = \frac{66.667}{64.103} = 1.04$$

Algebraically, this is

$$(1 + r) = \frac{\text{End value}}{\text{Start value}} = \frac{£1}{1.50} \div \frac{£1}{1.56} = \frac{£1}{1.50} \times \frac{1.56}{£1} = \frac{1.56}{1.50} \text{ as we used above.}$$

If, however, the exchange rates had been quoted against the dollar, i.e. as £0.64103:$1 at the start and £0.66667:$1 at the end, then the currency gain would need to have been calculated as

$$(1 + r_{FX}) = \frac{\text{Opening exchange rate}}{\text{Closing exchange rate}} = \frac{66.667}{64.103} = 1.04$$

What we can see is that the currency gain is calculated by dividing one of the opening exchange rate and the closing exchange rate by the other, but which depends on the way that the exchange rates are quoted.

The best approach may be to determine whether there has been a currency gain or loss and divide the opening and closing rates appropriately.

7.2 Overseas investment risks

As foreign exchange fluctuations augment the returns achieved by a sterling investor, they also augment the risks of overseas investment.

The method we apply here to calculate the total risk (including the foreign exchange effect) represents an approximation, since it assumes an additive rather than a compounding relationship. However, it is reasonably accurate unless risks from either the security or the currency are very large.

The method is based upon the portfolio theory risk combination model introduced in the Bond risk and Risk analysis section.

Formula to learn

$$\sigma_{a+b}^2 = p_a^2\sigma_a^2 + p_b^2\sigma_b^2 + 2p_a p_b \sigma_a \sigma_b \text{Cor}_{ab}$$

taking a as the overseas security and b as the exchange rate, say.

Now normally, when we use this formula, we are splitting our funds between two investments and only part is exposed to one risk and the rest to the other. Here, all of our funds are exposed to both types of risks, hence in this situation

- $p_a = 1$ since all of our money is exposed to the investments risk.
- $p_b = 1$ since all of our money is also exposed to the currency risk.

Hence, the formula becomes

Formula to learn

$$\sigma_£^2 = \sigma_\$^2 + \sigma_{FX}^2 + 2\sigma_\$\sigma_{FX}\text{Cor}_{\$FX}$$

where

$\sigma_£$ = risk to the sterling investor
$\sigma_\$$ = risk of the overseas investment in local currency terms
σ_{FX} = foreign exchange risk
$\text{Cor}_{\$FX}$ = correlation between investment and currency returns

Example

A UK investor invests in US bonds whose risk in dollars is 5%. The exchange rate risk for the same period is assessed at 5%. Calculate the risk to the UK investor if the correlation between currency and security returns are

- 0.4
- –1

Solution

Cor = 0.4

$$\sigma_{£}^{2} = \sigma_{\$}^{2} + \sigma_{FX}^{2} + 2\sigma_{\$}\sigma_{FX}Cor_{\$FX}$$

$$\sigma_{£}^{2} = 5^2 + 5^2 + 2 \times 5 \times 5 \times 0.4 = 70$$

$$\sigma_{£} = 8.3666\%$$

Cor = –1

$$\sigma £^{2} = \sigma \$^{2} + \sigma FX^{2} + 2\sigma \$ \sigma FX Cor\$FX$$

$$\sigma £^{2} = 5^2 + 5^2 + 2 \times 5 \times 5 \times (-1) = 0$$

$$\sigma £ = 0\%$$

As ever, if the returns are perfectly negatively correlated, they may produce a perfect hedge as demonstrated here.

7.3 Impact of foreign exchange on overseas investments

7.3.1 Introduction

The International Fisher Effect referred to above suggests that, in the long run, countries with high nominal rates of interest, and correspondingly high bond yields, will see their currencies depreciate. This means that exchange rate variations and returns from securities may be negatively correlated. This is especially the case for fixed interest securities where yields, interest rates and inflation levels are clearly linked.

Example

The current exchange rate is \$1.50:£1. Interest rates and bond yields in the UK and the US are 8% and 6%, respectively. Estimate the exchange rate in one year and calculate the expected return to a sterling investor from investing in either the UK bond or the US bond.

Solution

Future exchange rate

$$\text{Future exchange rate} = \text{Spot rate} \times \frac{1+r_s}{1+r_p}$$

$$\text{Future exchange rate} = 1.50 \times \frac{1.06}{1.08} = 1.47222$$

Expected returns

UK investor

$r_£ = 8\%$

US investor

$$1 + r_£ = (1 + r_\$)(1 + r_{FX})$$

$$= 1.06 \times \frac{1.50}{1.47222} = 1.08$$

Giving

$r_£ = 0.08$ or 8%

Hence, in deciding whether to invest in overseas bonds or UK bonds, the investor needs to take a view on exchange rate movements. If he believes that the foreign currency will end the year stronger than is implied by interest rate (and bond yield) differentials, then the overseas bond would be expected to produce the superior sterling return. If, however, he expects the currency to be weaker than implied, then the UK bond would be preferable.

By not hedging against foreign exchange risk, an investor can theoretically reduce variability in his real sterling rate of return, since a high nominal rate of interest for an overseas country implies a high inflation rate and a depreciating currency. Alternatively, by hedging against the foreign exchange risk, an investor can fix a certain nominal return in sterling terms.

7.3.2 Active or passive approaches to the currency issue

The investor may adopt an active or passive approach to currency management. Active management may be attractive due to the potentially large gains to be had from correctly forecasting exchange rate movements. However, investors may believe that such an approach is inappropriate for two reasons.

- They do not have the currency expertise themselves. In this case, they may use a currency overlay manager to manage the currency exposure created by their own bond allocation.
- They do not believe it is possible to consistently forecast exchange rate movements reliably. In this case, they may adopt a fully hedged or unhedged portfolio.

Integration of the bond allocation and currency allocation decisions

Many commentators argue that both of the above approaches are sub-optimal and instead propose an integrated approach, where the bond allocation and currency allocation decision are taken together. The reason for this is that the same fundamental economic factors will drive bond prices and exchange rates as we illustrated in the last example.

Hedged and unhedged approaches

Research suggests that a partially hedged approach offers superior risk-adjusted returns to both fully hedged and unhedged approaches for US investors. On this basis, some recommend a 50% hedged benchmark for use by a passive manager or as a starting point for an active manager.

Generally, the hedge ratio for the benchmark should reflect the investment objectives of the investor. For example, an investor concerned primarily with diversification and risk reduction might use a fully hedged benchmark. This is because historically hedged benchmarks have shown greater risk reduction benefits. Although they have higher correlation with the domestic US bond market than unhedged international bonds, they have had a lower standard deviation of returns.

Conversely, an investor concerned primarily with total return and with higher risk tolerance may see opportunities in selecting an unhedged benchmark and giving the manager more ability to adopt active currency management.

7.4 Methods of investing

7.4.1 Direct investment

This has a number of disadvantages and few of the advantages of overseas investment, unless the individual has significant resources, time and knowledge of the local markets in question.

7.4.2 Purchasing shares on the London Stock Exchange

This is cheaper and easier, and the type of overseas company listed in the UK is likely to be reliable and to give out trustworthy and periodic information. It may be difficult to achieve a wide spread of investments however, unless the individual has significant personal resources.

In addition to purchasing shares in overseas companies in London, it is also possible to purchase shares in UK companies that have significant overseas exposure. For example, a company with a number of Japanese motor dealerships could be seen as a play on the Japanese market.

7.4.3 Indirect investment

Investment via unit trusts and investment trusts is probably the easiest and best route for the individual wishing to gain overseas exposure. They give all the above benefits and compensate for most of the problems, such as lack of expertise.

Chapter Roundup

Benefits of overseas investment

Markets	■ Diversification away from reliance on a single economy. ■ Diversification of portfolio to take in overseas markets.
Industrial Sectors	■ Investment in sectors not available in the UK, such as mining.
Currencies	■ Less exposure to one currency. ■ Exposure to currency risk where the investor feels that this is of benefit.
Correlations	■ International assets are not perfectly positively correlated to domestic assets.

Risks of overseas investment

Inherent Risk	■ High risk in emerging markets due to the unsophisticated domestic investor base and overheating economies. ■ Political risk in certain volatile countries. ■ Legal rights of the investor is likely to differ from those in the UK. ■ Ability of foreign investors to participate/invest.
Liquidity Risk/ Hedging	■ Ability to realise investment, especially in adverse market conditions. ■ Lack of developed derivatives for hedging purposes leads to less efficient portfolio management.
Currency Risk/ Hedging	■ Exposure to adverse currency movements. ■ Exchange control regulations in certain countries. ■ Unavailability of suitable currency hedging products.
Lack of Regulation	■ Lack of market regulation in emerging markets. ■ Inadequate financial regulation/reporting standards.
Information/ Communications	■ Inadequate/problematic, e.g. may require foreign language expertise. ■ Costly to gather. ■ Unreliability.
Taxation	■ Potential double taxation problems. ■ Additional local taxes.

Foreign exchange risk

You must be able to describe transaction, translation and economic risk.

Foreign exchange rates

You must be able to

- Calculate forward rates from spot rates.
- Apply the interest rate parity formula
  - Forward rate = $\frac{1+r_s}{1+r_p} \times \text{Spot rate}$
- Forecast longer term
  - Future exchange rate = $\frac{1+i_s}{1+i_p} \times \text{Spot rate}$

  and outline the International Fisher Effect that brings us to this point.

Investments

You must be able to

- Calculate overseas investment returns

  $(1 + r_£) = (1 + r_\$)(1 + r_{FX})$
- Calculate overseas investment risks

  $\sigma_£^2 = \sigma_\$^2 + \sigma_{FX}^2 + 2\sigma_\$\sigma_{FX}\text{Cor}_{\$FX}$
- Discuss the effect of natural hedging.

TEST YOUR KNOWLEDGE

Check your knowledge of the Chapter here, without referring back to the text.

1. The exchange rate with the Euro is 1.50 (i.e. £1 = €1.50). Inflation in the UK is 7% and in the Eurozone is 10%. The required real interest rate in both countries is 3%.

   (a) Use the Fisher relation to estimate the nominal interest rates that will prevail in the UK and Eurozone.

   (b) Use the interest rate parity theory to estimate the one year forward Euro forward rate.

   (c) Use the purchasing power parity theory to determine the expected spot Euro/sterling exchange rate in one year's time.

   (d) Compare your estimate of the current forward rate with the expected spot rate in (b). What does this imply about the need to hedge using the forward markets?

2. From the information given below, calculate the percentage change in each market for

   (a) UK resident investors.
   (b) US resident investors.

Local Index		Start of Year	End of Year
Japan – Nikkei Stock Average		18,000	22,000
US – Dow Jones		2,000	2,200
Rates of exchange			
Japanese Yen	(= £1:)	360	400
US Dollars	(= £1:)	1.60	2.00

3. A European investment denominated in Euros has an expected return and risk (in local currency returns) of 6% and 8% respectively. If the Euro is expected to appreciate by 1% with a standard deviation of 5% and the correlation of the investment and currency returns is 0.2, assess the returns and risks to a sterling investor.

TEST YOUR KNOWLEDGE: ANSWERS

1. (a) **Fisher Relationship**

$(1 + r) = (1 + R)(1 + i)$

r = Nominal interest rate
R = Real interest rate
i = Expected inflation rate

UK

$1 + r = (1 + 0.03)\ (1 + 0.07) = 1.1021$

$r = 0.1021$ or 10.2%

Eurozone

$1 + r = (1 + 0.03)\ (1 + 0.10) = 1.133$

$r = 0.133$ or 13.3%

(b) **Interest Rate Parity Theory**

$$\text{Forward rate} = \text{Spot rate} \times \frac{1+r_{EU}}{1+r_{UK}}$$

The one year forward Euro rate is

$$\text{Forward rate} = 1.50 \times \frac{1.133}{1.1021} = 1.542$$

(c) **Purchasing Power Parity Theory**

$$\text{Expected future rate} = \text{Spot rate} \times \frac{1+i_{EU}}{1+i_{UK}}$$

Expected Euro/sterling exchange rate in one year's time

$$\text{Expected future rate} = 1.50 \times \frac{1.10}{1.07} = 1.542$$

(d) The estimates are the same, therefore, the one year forward rate is the best estimate of the expected future spot rate.

2. (a) **Percentage Change for UK Resident Investors**

Japan

Convert index to sterling

Start 18,000/360 = 50.00

End 22,000/400 = 55.00

$$\text{Percentage change equals } \left(\frac{55.00}{50.00} - 1\right) \times 100\% = 10\%$$

US

Convert index to sterling

Start 2,000/1.60 = 1,250

End 2,200/2.00 = 1,100

Percentage change equals $\left(\frac{1{,}100}{1{,}250}-1\right)\times 100\% = -12\%$

(b) **Percentage Change for US Resident Investors**

Japan

Convert Yen/£1 to Yen/US$

Start 360/1.60 = Yen 225 per US$

End 400/2.00 = Yen 200 per US$

Convert index to US$

Start 18,000/225 = 80

End 22,000/200 = 110

Percentage change equals $\left(\frac{110}{80}-1\right)\times 100\% = 37.5\%$

US

Note the index is (obviously) already in US$, therefore

Percentage change equals $\left(\frac{2{,}200}{2{,}000}-1\right)\times 100\% = 10\%$

3. **Return**

$(1+r_£) = (1 + r_\$)(1+ r_{FX}) = 1.06 \times 1.01 = 1.0706$

$r_£ = 0.0706$ or 7.06%

Risk

$\sigma_£^2 = \sigma_\$^2 + \sigma_{FX}^2 + 2\sigma_\$\sigma_{FX}\text{Cor}_{\$FX} = 6^2 + 5^2 + 2\times 6\times 5\times 0.2 = 73$

$\sigma_£ = 8.54\%$

13 The Macroeconomic Environment

INTRODUCTION

In order to fully understand the operations of a company or the performance of an investment it is necessary to understand the economy in which it operates. The purpose of this section is to gain an understanding of the economic ideas and economic management tools that have been used by governments across the years to control various aspects of the economy such as inflation and unemployment.

Questions do not often arise from the ideas in this chapter

CHAPTER CONTENTS

Chapter Learning Objectives

Economics

Students should possess an understanding of the relevance of economic statistics, such as those listed below and for detailed knowledge markets, be capable of criticising the use of such data, for example, on seasonal, cyclical or revision considerations. For detailed knowledge markets, students should be aware of current levels and recent trends in, for example:

- Monetary and credit aggregates
- Balance of payments
- Indicators of economic growth
- Inflation/price indices

Students should be aware of the relevance of domestic and international capital flows for capital market prices. For detailed knowledge markets, students should be aware of current market conditions and recent trends.

While historic analogy may be useful to illustrate or explain some of these subjects, no knowledge of affairs more than two years prior to the examination will be required.

Students should be able to demonstrate that they are capable of conducting further research into market behaviour. For example, they should be aware of information and data sources.

Exam tip

The ideas in this section are examined as brief definitions and discussions, e.g. Winter 2008 Question 1, Winter 2004 Question 8.

1 Introduction

> "The ideas of economists and political philosophers, both when they are right and when they are wrong, are more powerful than is commonly understood. Indeed, the world is ruled by little else. Practical men, who believe themselves to be quite exempt from any intellectual influences, are usually the slaves of some defunct economists. Madmen in authority, who hear voices in the air, are distilling their frenzy from some academic scribbler of a few years back."
>
> J.M.Keynes

Economics is the study of the allocation of scarce resources amongst competing claims. Many of the issues covered in economics are almost philosophic in their development and as such, there is seldom an absolute answer. Put simply, the objective of economic policy is generally perceived to be the maximisation of the output of the economy, in this way increasing the overall economic welfare of the participants.

Many economists would argue that the only acceptable policy to achieve this is to leave the allocation of resources to **free market forces**. This should ensure that the resources of the economy are fully utilised in the most appropriate combination, reflecting the true preferences of consumers.

The opposite extreme to the free-market argument is the **command economy** where resource allocation and production decisions are taken by a central authority, immune from market forces.

In reality, there are very few economies that conform to either of these two extremes. Most economies are referred to as **mixed**, combining free markets with varying degrees of intervention. In operation, some are biased more towards one extreme than the other.

The study of economics is divided into two elements. **Microeconomics** is the study of the reaction of individuals and firms to economic stimuli. **Macroeconomics** is the study of the economy as a whole and concerns itself with the 'big picture' issues, such as unemployment and growth.

In this session, we will initially explore the theoretical foundations behind the main schools of macroeconomics. Having looked at the theory, we will then move on to consider the way in which economic policy has evolved.

Before we begin to look at the opposing schools of theoretical economics, we will need to build a simple model of how an economy works.

2 THE THEORY OF CIRCULAR FLOW

At the heart of macroeconomics lies a simple theory of circular flow that explains the way in which the economy works. This theory is accepted by each of the different schools of economists. This basic model will then be used to explain the workings of the opposing theories.

At its basic level, an economy can be broken down into two groups, namely the households who own the productive assets of the economy (land, labour and capital), and the firms who employ these resources. The role of the firms is to act as a vehicle through which the various inputs can be pooled. Without these collective vehicles, economic agents would be forced to act individually and the effectiveness of the economy would be undermined. Ultimately, the firms are owned by the households and so all value produced within the firm belongs to the households and is returned to them via the factor incomes. Initially, in a simple economy, the households provide their inputs to the firms in return for the goods produced by the firm.

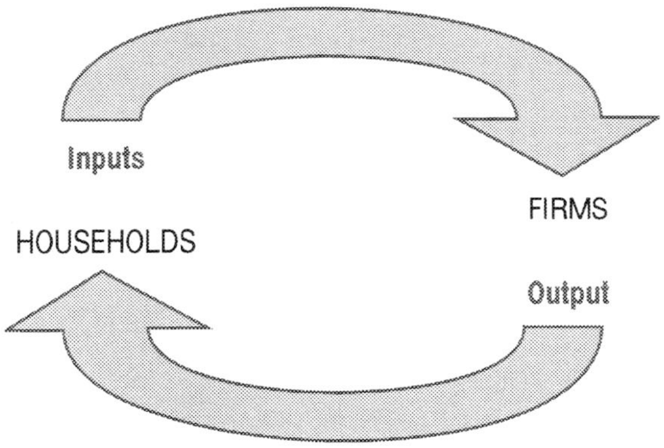

These goods are then exchanged via a process of barter to give consumers the mixture of goods they require. Barter is not a particularly efficient system, since it requires a **mutual coincidence of wants**. As economic society developed, a medium of exchange was required to simplify the process. Money, in all its varied forms, acts as this medium of exchange.

Now, households provide their labour (and other factor inputs such as land and capital) in exchange for a money income. In turn, the households spend this with the firms in purchasing their goods.

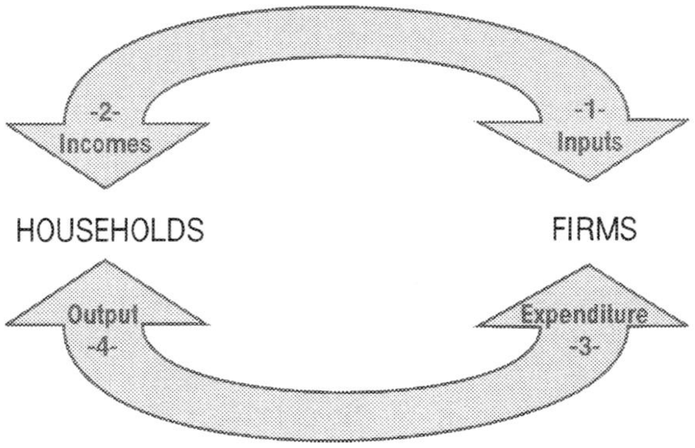

For the system to be at a state of balance (equilibrium), the flows must be equal.

Formula to learn

Outcome = Expenditure = Income

A simple example will serve to explain why these flows must be in balance. The economy produces £1,000 worth of goods; £1,000 worth of factor inputs are supplied in order to produce £1,000 worth of goods, and £1,000 worth of income are paid. These incomes will take the form of wages to labour, rents to land and profit to capital. Ultimately, as mentioned above, given the fact that the households own all of the factors of production, the incomes must reflect the value of the output. If the households spend this £1,000, then the output will be consumed and the economy will have cleared (i.e. all the goods produced have been consumed and the market is ready to start again).

Now, if one household decides that rather than spending their entire income, they will save £100, then £100 leaks from the system. Expenditure will now be £900 and goods worth £900 will be given back to the households. This leaves the households with net savings of £100 and firms with surplus goods also valued at £100. On the assumption that the firms do not wish to hold this increased level of stock, they will respond in the next period by reducing their requirement for factor inputs. From the perspective of the firm, a reasonable estimate of likely sales in the next period would be £900, the sales level that they have just encountered in this period.

In the next period, the firm might demand £800 worth of inputs to produce £800 worth of goods. This, combined with the £100 of stock, will then be enough to meet their estimated demand. The income will go back to the households who will receive £800. The firm's belief must be that the £100 worth of saving during the previous period will now be used up, demanding £900 worth of goods and, thus completely exhausting this period's production and also absorbing the stock that has built up in the previous period.

If, however, the households persisted in saving money, then demand in this period will be even lower, at the level of, let us say, £750. Once again, the household's full income is not being spent, and once again the firms are left with surplus goods on their books. This process of reduction in output will continue until the firms are left with the stock levels they require.

From this example, it can be seen that savings in this simple system result in a decrease in the overall level of output. This phenomenon of savings leading to a decrease in output is referred to as the **paradox of thrift**.

Savings would not be a problem in this system if they were somehow funnelled back into the circular flow. For example, using the numbers above, if the savings of £100 in the first period were placed with a bank, who were then to lend the money to another consumer who wished to spend more than his/her income, the system would retain its balance at an output level of £1,000.

Here, the leakage of £100 in the form of savings is matched by the injection of a further £100 of expenditure by the second consumer. In economics, we would refer to this second consumer's expenditure as **investment**. The system will also be in balance when savings equal investment, i.e. when **leakages equal injections**.

Whilst this seems an overly simplistic model, it lies at the heart of most econometric models of the economy. Obviously, it needs to be expanded further to create a more realistic model.

A second leakage that we can build into this model is taxation. The government removes income from consumers before they can spend it. If the government were simply to sit on this money and do nothing with it, this too would contract the economy, representing an absolute leakage. However, in reality, governments use the money they raise through taxation to finance their expenditure and consequently, the money finds its way back into the system. Once again, so long as leakages and injections are in balance, the economy will remain stable.

The final leakage or injection from our system would be international trade. The purchase of overseas goods by individuals within our economy is a leakage, as demand, which could otherwise have been spent on our own goods, leaks into another economy. Conversely, demand from other economies met by our own production – exports – are injections into our economy. As we will see later when we look at the exchange rate, economists believe that in a perfectly free world, the exchange rate itself will ensure that these two flows are in balance, once again ensuring that leakages equal injections.

This then is our simple model of how an economy works. We have developed it in stages; each stage represents part of the historical development of our own economy moving from a simple barter economy to a complex economy with savings, investments, government taxation and international trade. However, to understand the basics of theoretical economics, we need only consider this fairly simple model.

3 Classical Economics

3.1 The theory of demand and supply

In the world of classical economics, there are two forces that dominate. These are supply and demand – the 'market forces'.

Demand represents the quantity that individuals will buy at a given price. In this context, we are talking about **effective demand**, that is to say a want that the consumer has the resources to satisfy.

The Demand Curve

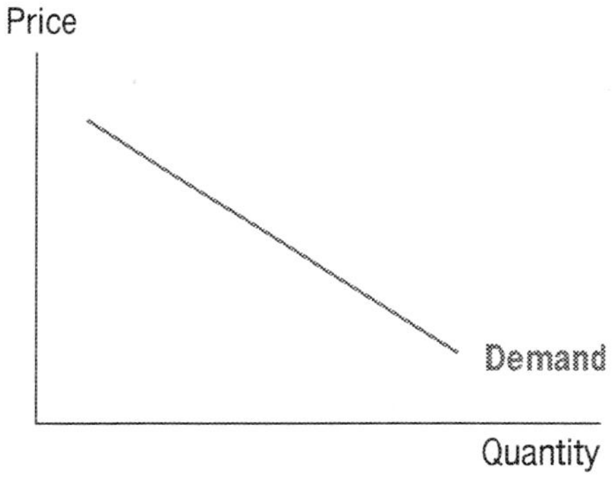

Demand is logically a downward sloping function, since as the price of a good falls, we will demand more of it.

The opposing force to demand is supply. Supply represents the amount of a good that producers are prepared to supply to the market at a given price.

The Supply Curve

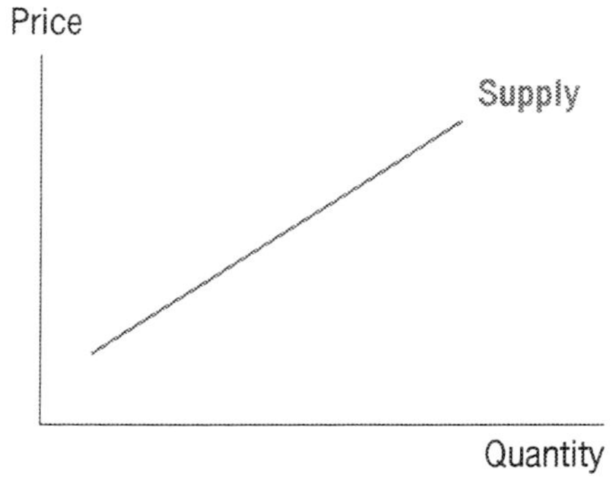

Supply is an upward sloping function. Again, the logic behind this is that as the price rises, producers will be prepared to supply more of that particular good. It is the combination of these two forces – supply and demand – that generates the point of equilibrium.

The Market Equilibrium

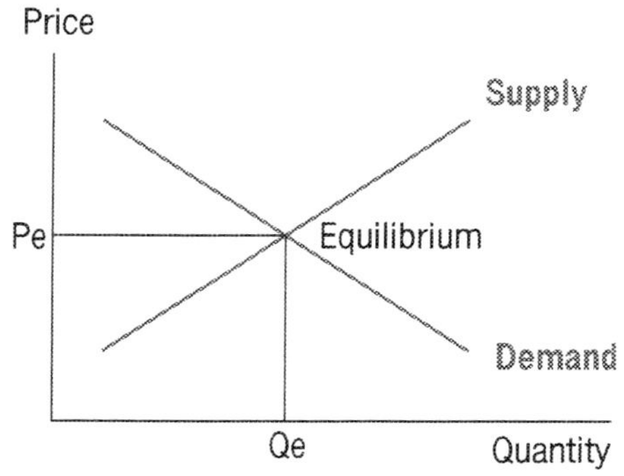

There is one price and one level of output at which supply and demand are in balance. This is the point of equilibrium. At this point and at this price, the amount that consumers are prepared to demand and the amount that the producers supply are in balance (i.e. the market clears).

Classical economists believe that all markets will automatically gravitate to this point of equilibrium. If the price were set too low, then demand would be greater than supply. Those consumers who particularly wanted the goods in question would force the price up, therefore reducing the level of demand and increasing the level of supply. This pressure would continue until the equilibrium point was reached.

Conversely, if prices were set too high, then supply would be greater than demand. Whenever there is oversupply of any good, the price of that good falls. The price will continue to fall until it reaches the equilibrium point where supply and demand are in balance.

Classical economists believe there is nothing that can contradict this power of the market forces that Adam Smith, the first economist, described as **'the invisible hand'**.

3.2 Classical unemployment and self-balancing economy

For the classical economists, unemployment is simply a supply and demand phenomenon taken, in this case, from the labour markets. Unemployment represents the position where the supply of a good – labour – is greater than the demand for that good. This excess of supply over demand represents the unemployed. In very simple terms, the only reason that workers are unemployed is that the price they are charging for wages is too high. If the price were allowed to fall, then more workers would be demanded, and unemployment would be cured.

Indeed, this perceived wisdom, that the only cause of unemployment was too high a wage rate, was maintained right through the inter-war years, and the UK government's only response to the massive unemployment faced at that time was to insist that wages fell further.

Classical Unemployment

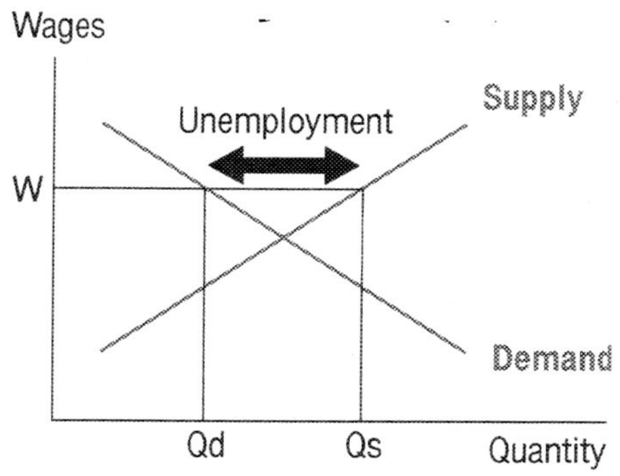

3.3 Say's Law and the long run equilibrium

Classical economists believe that there is no difference between an individual market and the economy acting as a whole. In their view, individual markets will always 'clear' –that is, they will always find their equilibrium where supply equals demand. If individual markets always clear, the economy as a whole must always move to a point of balance.

One of the key elements of classical economics is Say's Law. Say's Law states that supply will create its own demand. In effect, this is saying that where there is an excess of supply, the price will fall, thereby creating demand. The end result of this is that the economy will always move to a point of equilibrium and that point of equilibrium (or balance) will always be the full employment level of activity in the economy. If this were not the case, then those resources that were unemployed would reduce their price so as to ensure that they found employment.

Classical economists therefore believe that in the long run, the economy will always be operating at its full employment level of activity. This is a simple result of market forces and there is nothing that a government can do to alter this process.

Throughout the nineteenth century, economics became known as the 'dismal science', because there was simply nothing the economists could do to make the world a better place. In effect, everything revolves around market forces. Supply must always equal demand and the economy must always be at a point of equilibrium. Short-term phenomena may throw the economy off this point of balance, but these market forces – the invisible hand – will always move us back towards it.

4 The Keynesian Revolution

In the 1920s and 1930s, the UK economy underwent a period of sustained depression. Unemployment did not fall below 10% from 1920 to 1941. The conventional wisdom of the time was wrapped up with classical economics, which suggested that the only cure for unemployment was for wages to fall. The government of the 1920s and 1930s did everything it could to ensure that wages did come down, yet unemployment did not seem to change.

This phenomenon of unemployment not responding to falls in wages was not merely an aspect of the UK's economic history, but was reflected in all of the major industrial economies. It was against this background that John Maynard Keynes developed a different way of looking at the operations of the economic system that has become known as Keynesian economics.

Keynes could see that unused resources in the economy existed. There were empty factories and unemployed labourers, yet the market did not seem to be operating to bring supply and demand into balance. It was at this point that Keynes made a division in economics between micro and macroeconomics. It was Keynes' belief that individual markets may clear, but the whole economy may (for a number of reasons) stick to a particular level of output.

Against this background, Keynes developed the idea that the level of demand for goods and services was the prime motivator of the economy. In his view, it was the absence of this motive power that left the economy stagnating, and more power would need to be injected into the economy to ensure that activity would begin to rise.

Keynes believed that the level of demand in the economy determined the level of output, employment and income. If demand were insufficient, the economy would be underperforming. If demand were excessive, the economy would overheat. However, it would only be purely by chance that the economy might find itself at a point where full employment was achieved without excessive strain.

Having identified demand as the key motivator of the economy, Keynes then moved on to consider the components of demand and how they might be manipulated.

4.1 The nature of demand

From our simple model of the circular flow that we considered earlier, we can see that demand arises in a number of ways. Firstly, there is the demand that consumers have for goods and services. Then there is the demand for investment goods and for government expenditure. Finally, there is the net demand generated by international trade. Keynes considered each of these types of demand in turn, looking at the ways in which they were composed and the influences on them.

4.2 Consumption

The simple assumption of the classical model had been that income is received by households which they then spend. Keynes perceived that it was slightly different, in that the level of expenditure that you incurred was related to, but not coincident with, the level of income you received. In Keynes' eyes, consumption can be described by the following function.

Formula to learn

$$C = a + bY$$

What Keynes is saying in this simple function is that the consumers' demand for goods is made up of two elements. The first element (**a**) is their base consumption – the level of goods they must consume to stay alive. Additional consumption (**b**) is related to their income (**Y**). The logic behind this is that as income increases, consumers will demand more in the way of goods and services. The factor **b** in this equation is referred to as the Marginal Propensity to Consume – the proportion of any increase in income that results in increased expenditure.

If demand is the key motivator of the economy, and demand is determined by the income of the individual, then the classical cure for unemployment of reducing wages and therefore reducing income is, in Keynes' view, always unlikely to work. Rather than enhancing demand, it effectively decreases it.

4.3 Investment

In economics, the term investment means the purchase of goods, not with the aim of immediate consumption. Investment can therefore cover a number of things, including the purchase of plant and machinery and the build up of stocks, both of which are goods that are purchased without being consumed in this period.

BPP LEARNING MEDIA

The level of investment demand is determined in part by the interest rate. If interest rates are low, then it will be profitable to finance an increasing number of projects. Consequently, an increasing number of projects will be undertaken. Therefore, in order to stimulate investment demand, the government needs to ensure that interest rates are low.

However, there is another force at work with regard to investment demand, and this is the level of confidence in the economy. If producers are optimistic, then a variety of investment projects will seem more viable. This highlights one of the weaknesses of monetary policy in controlling investment demand. As we have seen, investment is a function of interest rates and consequently, if rates are forced down, then investment will normally increase. Unfortunately, if the outlook for the economy is depressed then, regardless of the interest rate, investment will be low. This condition has recently been demonstrated by the ineffectiveness of monetary policy in Japan where, despite very low interest rates, investment has remained subdued due to the poor economic outlook.

4.4 Government

The third important source of demand in the economy is the government. The government raises revenue by way of taxation and then spends this money. An alternative to simply raising money through taxation would be either to borrow it or, more simply, to print it. Using any of these routes, the government could expand its expenditure and, therefore, increase the overall level of demand in the economy.

4.5 International trade

The final source of demand in the economy comes from international trade flows. Demand is injected into the system through exports of goods and leaks from the system because of our own imports of overseas produce. As we will see later, the theories of the exchange rate predict that in the long term, imports and exports will be in balance. However, it may be possible for the government, in the short term, to create an imbalance, therefore forcing a higher level of demand into the economy.

In summary, Keynes' belief is that for the economy to be in balance at full employment, the level of demand must be right. He further believed that the economy would not automatically achieve the right level of demand and supply. In short, the economy may stick at a suboptimal position. The solution, as far as Keynes was concerned, was simple – to manipulate demand to ensure that the demand met the right level for the economy's resources.

4.6 How to manipulate this demand?

There are two basic approaches that can be used to manipulate the economy. The choices are monetary and/or fiscal policy.

4.6.1 Monetary policy

Monetary policy means different things to different economists. Put simply, the demand for money arises from the underlying economy. In particular, as the level of transactions rise, the need for money will increase. Based on this demand for money, the authorities have two possible approaches that they can adopt. The government (or more commonly now, the independent monetary authority) can either seek to control the supply of money, in which case the price of money (the interest rate) will fluctuate. Alternatively, the authorities set the interest rate and allow the supply of money to fluctuate. In this sense, it is no different from an ordinary market for any good or service. If the supplier of a good sets a fixed supply of that good and the demand fluctuates, then the price will vary. By varying the supply in line with the level of demand, the supplier will be able to keep the price stable.

In the context of Keynesian economics, the vision is clearly that money supply will be flexed in order to set the interest rate at an appropriate level. However, monetary policy is generally seen as less relevant to Keynesian economists. There are a number of reasons for this. Keynesians believe it is very difficult to control monetary policy correctly and that the effects may be varied and difficult to monitor.

The only area where monetary policy could be used within the Keynesian framework to manipulate demand would be to have an influence on investment expenditure directly, and consumer expenditure in a more indirect fashion.

With regard to the manipulation of investment expenditure, as we have already seen, Keynesians believe that investment is only partly linked to the level of interest rates and, therefore, any impact of a reduction in interest rates may be minimal or non-existent.

The other factor impacting upon investment is the level of confidence or optimism in the economy. If economic agents are not confident about the future, then the interest rate will have a limited impact on the level of investment.

Consequently, monetary policy has a very low profile within Keynesian economics. The emphasis is much more towards fiscal policy.

4.6.2 Fiscal policy

Fiscal policy deals with government expenditure and taxation. Keynesian economics has long been almost exclusively tied to these two policy instruments.

In the event of unemployment, fiscal policy suggests that the government should reduce taxation and increase its own expenditure in order to boost demand in the economy. The effect of this is two-fold.

Firstly, government expenditure increases and, following the multiplier effect discussed below, this will increase the incomes of a large number of participants within the economy. Secondly, by reducing the rate of tax, individuals will have a greater disposable income and therefore will consume more. The end result of this is that overall demand will increase substantially.

Fiscal policy can also be used where the government is dealing with an economy that is overheated. In an economy where demand is greater than the available resources, the result will be **inflation**. Put simply, **'too much money chasing too few goods'**. In this environment, the government should adopt exactly the opposite policy – spending less and taxing more. This will have the effect of reducing demand to a sustainable level.

One important feature that Keynes noted was that it is not essential for the government to inject exactly the right amount of demand into the economy to push demand up to the full employment level. By simply injecting a smaller amount of demand into the economy, it can kick start – **'pump prime'** – the economy, and enable it to reach full employment. This injection of the smaller amount of demand than is required overall relies upon a concept referred to as **the multiplier**.

4.6.3 The multiplier effect

The multiplier effect describes the way in which an increase in the level of demand is transmitted through the economy.

The government might decide to embark upon a new road-building project that will cost £10m. The government pays £10m to the contractors to build the road. The contractors then spend this sum partly on the wages of their employees, and partly on raw materials and profits.

All of these represent income to other groups in the economy. As we saw from Keynes' view of consumption, consumption is based upon your level of income and so, as the workers who were previously unemployed receive wages for building the road, they in turn will spend a proportion of this money. As the workers spend the money, it becomes the income of another participant in the economy and so on.

The beneficiaries of this increased spending by the newly employed workers have also had their income increased and, in turn, they will spend a proportion of this money. The multiplier effect continues to work through the economy until the flows become immaterial.

It can be seen from the multiplier effect that the injection of government demand is simply the catalyst that sets off a chain reaction of individuals' demand. By injecting £10m of additional demand into the economy, the government may be able to achieve a much greater impact on the overall level of demand.

It should, however, be remembered that the multiplier effect works in both ways. So that if the government were to remove £10m worth of demand, the economy would contract substantially.

This doctrine of Keynesian interventionist economics was very attractive to governments and became the mainstay of economic policy in the post-war period. Governments felt they had moved away from the 'dismal science' to a world where economics provided them with the tools they needed to fine-tune and manage the economy.

The problem with Keynesian fine-tuning is that the economy responds in variable degrees to the same impetus and it is impossible to achieve an absolute steady state. Most economies found they were operating around full employment, sometimes with minor unemployment, sometimes with minor inflation, for a number of years.

In the UK, this became known as 'stop-go' economics. The reason for this was partly political (tying booms in with elections). However, to an extent, the cycle would be inevitable due to the lags in receiving information, reacting to the information and finally waiting for the economy to respond to the policy once implemented.

As we have just seen, one of the principal problems faced in implementing Keynesian (and other) economic policy is the lack of accurate and timely information on which to base decisions. The whole process is further complicated by the fact that once a policy has been adopted, the government can never be absolutely sure when it will begin to take effect.

4.7 The impact on the market

Keynesian economics had as its guiding objective the cure for unemployment. It was accepted during the 1950s and 1960s that this may involve a minor level of inflation, but that this was a price well worth paying for full employment.

Throughout the period this led to a gradual increase in the background level of inflation that obviously had an impact on bond yields, particularly at the long end of the yield curve and equity returns.

The use of fiscal policy has a very direct impact on bond markets. In particular, the level of the government deficit tends to vary in line with the economic cycle quite substantially as governments spend heavily in recessions and operate a budget surplus in boom periods. However, provided that the cycles and the economy are not too wide, this impact will not be dramatic.

The Keynesian economics consensus dominated government economic policy in all of the G7 nations, right through the 1950s, 1960s and early 1970s. However, the relationship between unemployment and inflation broke down in the early 1970s, when governments around the world were faced with a phenomenon that Keynesian economics could neither explain nor remedy – the existence of both unemployment and inflation at the same time. This combination of unemployment and inflation is referred to as **stagflation**. At this stage, it was felt that Keynesian economics had failed and a change was called for.

5 THE MONETARIST RESTATEMENT

Monetarism is fundamentally a restatement of classical economic doctrine. It is based firmly on the belief that free markets are the only real solution to economic problems. However, within this, it is not as dogmatic as classical economics, believing that markets will not automatically work, and it offers a number of more pragmatic steps to achieve long-run equilibrium.

5.1 Inflation

In particular, monetarism focuses on the impact of inflation as a distorting influence in the market place. Inflation must be eradicated before any other economic problems can be solved.

5.1.1 The problem of inflation

The problem with inflation is that if it is either too high or too low it may produce fears of a recession, leading to reduced economic activity and higher unemployment. Within financial markets this may be viewed as giving rise to higher risks and lower returns, a very negative combination that can result in heavy selling, possibly leading to a stock market crash.

Impact of too high a level of inflation

- Reduced spending power for individuals, especially those on fixed incomes.
- Erosion of confidence that future returns on investments will cover the costs of capital.
- Higher export prices, possibly offset by a lower exchange rate.
- Increased price instability and noise surrounding price movements.
- Higher nominal interest rates increasing perceived cost of financing.
- Relatively lower real interest rates reducing incentives to lend.

Impact of too low a level of inflation

- May also lead to reduced demand as consumers delay expenditure, reducing potential returns in the short term.
- Real cost of borrowing may be too high, leading to a lower investment.

Monetarism is not a new doctrine and is based upon the **Fisher equation of money**, which was developed in the early twentieth century. Monetarism was new, in that it built this equation into a coherent structure of an explanation of the way in which the economy operates.

5.1.2 The Fisher equation of money

In 1911, Irving Fisher produced the Fisher equation of money. This represented the logical extension of classical economics. This was then developed in the 1950s by Milton Friedman into monetarism.

Formula to learn

$$MV \equiv PY$$

where

M = money supply
V = velocity of circulation
P = the average rate of prices
Y = the real output of the economy

Using the Fisher equation and a number of assumptions, monetarists developed a model that explains why inflation exists. The key assumption that the monetarists make is that the velocity of money is a constant.

Whilst they would admit that this is unrealistic in the long term, they believe that short-term velocity can remain reasonably stable.

The second assumption is that Y – the level of real output of the economy – is governed by long-term growth factors that limit the rate of expansion to a normal rate. Using these two assumptions, we can develop a monetarist assertion about the way in which the economy operates.

> "Inflation is always and everywhere a monetary phenomenon arising from too fast a rate of growth in the money supply over the level of output of the economy."
>
> Milton Friedman

If money supply grows at a faster rate than the economy needs, with velocity held constant, then the only factor that can respond in the Fisher equation of money will be prices. Again, putting it simply, it comes down to too much money chasing too few goods. If there is too much money, it will devalue. Inflation is the way in which money devalues. Once again, in the words of Friedman

> "Inflation is not a capitalist phenomenon, inflation is a printing press phenomenon."

5.1.3 The impact on interest rates

In the first case, any increase in money supply stimulates economic activity beyond its full employment level. This leads to an increase in the demand for money (transactionary demand) and, therefore, can lead to an increase in the interest rate. Whilst this effect may not be certain, the increase in inflationary expectations occasioned by the increase in money supply will definitely lead to an increase in nominal interest rates.

In the longer run, the control of money supply under monetarist policy will bring inflation and interest rates down. So long as the authorities expand the money supply in line with the needs of the economy, there will be price stability and interest rates should not be volatile.

Arguably, monetarist policy should, after some initial instability, bring the overall level and volatility of interest rates down to lower levels. This stability should then remain into the future. When compared to the more sanguine approach that the Keynesians take to inflation, a monetarist policy agenda targets a primary cause of market instability.

5.2 The cure for inflation

If inflation is caused by excessive growth in the money supply, the cure for inflation is simple – control the money supply. In controlling money supply, inflation will automatically be brought under control. Indeed, in its purest form, monetarism exists solely to control money supply, with everything else being left to market forces to bring the economy back to balance.

5.2.1 Definition of the money supply

Before we seek to control money supply, we must understand what it is. Over the past 20 years the government has developed a number of measures of money supply in its attempt to try and control the rate of growth. These measures move in complexity from the simplest measure of money supply (M0) through to the most complex (M5).

Over the years, the government has targeted different measures of money supply. At present, there are only **two measures that are published**. These are **M0 and M4**. However, the first element of M4 is equivalent to a third measure, **M2**.

These definitions increase in complexity from M0, which is the narrowest measure of money, through to M4, which is the widest.

M0

As mentioned above, M0 is the narrowest measure of money available in the UK economy and is sometimes referred to as the **monetary base**. In essence, it is the core of money in the UK – notes and coins. The formal definition comprises the following elements.

Formula to learn

M0 = Notes and coins + Banks' operational deposits at the Bank of England

Another name for M0 is **high-powered money**. The argument is that all the wider measures of money supply derive from M0, therefore in controlling M0, M2 and M4 are also controlled. In practice, this relationship has proved to be less than reliable.

M2

M2 is a measure of transaction balances. It is a wider measure of money supply and brings in a range of other products that can be used to settle debts.

M4

M4 is the widest measure of money supply currently available in the UK. The formal definition of M4 includes all bank accounts held within the system.

Over the last few years, the government has shown a greater interest in the control of M4 than in any of the other monetary aggregates.

5.2.2 Control of the money supply

Once we have defined money supply, we must then attempt to control it to bring the rate of growth of money supply in line with the rate of growth of the real economy. There are a number of ways in which this control of the money supply can be achieved.

Fiscal responsibility

The government must not spend more than it obtains in taxation revenues and it certainly must not resort to the printing presses as a way of financing a budget deficit. Overall, the monetarists believe the government is an all-pervasive and generally malevolent influence on the economy in that large state intervention obstructs the process of free markets.

In capital markets, they believe that large state borrowing to finance expenditure programmes crowds out private sector borrowing and makes the economy less efficient. However, they appreciate the need for certain levels of government expenditure.

Open-market operations

Having reduced the money supply, possibly by running a fiscal surplus – taxing more than they spend – the government may then be able to control the money supply by using open-market operations. Open-market operations are where the central bank either buys or sells government securities in the market place to either add or absorb money. This in itself can be seen as a form of fine-tuning of the money supply.

Direct credit controls

Money in our society is no longer simply notes and coins. Realistically, it comprises all available forms of credit. Therefore, it may make sense to control credit in order to control the money supply. Formal credit controls could be introduced to limit the rate of growth of certain aspects of the money supply.
These controls directly target the banking system through the regulation of loans. Once again, however, this does not fit ideologically with the monetarist approach to the free market and is seldom advocated as a means of monetary control.

This is, however, a technique of monetary control employed by the European Central Bank (ECB).

Conclusion

Whichever method is adopted, the overall objective of the government must be to slow down the rate of growth in money supply so that it balances the **real** rate of growth in the economy.

5.3 Unemployment

The monetarists accept that because of the squeeze in government finances initially required to remove surplus money from the economy, unemployment will result from their policies. However, their assertion is that unemployment would exist anyway and the choice is either between unemployment as a side effect of inflation or unemployment as part of the cure for inflation.

Fundamentally, their views on unemployment are not dissimilar from the classical view that in part, unemployment is a voluntary phenomenon created by workers pricing themselves out of jobs by demanding too high a wage rate. Added to this, monetarists do believe there is a core of unemployment – referred to as the **natural rate** of unemployment – which represents, perhaps, longer structural changes taking place in the economy.

The reason for the persistence of unemployment in the long term is because of the inability of the markets to clear. Inflation is regarded as being one of the key reasons for this inability, in that it establishes a form of static interference that prevents market mechanisms from understanding the messages that are being given to them. The monetarists believe that once inflation is cured, market forces will be able to work more effectively and unemployment will be resolved by the power of the invisible hand.

Often allied with this, monetarists have asserted that there should be **supply-side** economic policies. Supply-side economic policies are designed to free the market and ensure that it is able to respond quickly to market forces. Supply-side economic policies include the removal of union powers, privatisation, reduction of unemployment benefit, retraining schemes, relocation grants and a general increase in the provision of information available to the unemployed.

Monetarists argue that the combination of a low inflation environment and supply-side policies will make sure that market forces work efficiently and effectively to remove unemployment, and that the economy moves to full employment equilibrium.

5.3.1 The impact on the market

In terms of the government bond markets, monetarism should ensure that governments borrow less than they would under equivalent Keynesian policies. The markets themselves will, however, be slightly more volatile due to money supply control.

However, the sole objective of the policy is to control inflation and this will improve the stability of the yields at the long end of the yield curve, as the market will not have to worry about an inflation premium to compensate for risk.

6 The Evolution of Policy

6.1 Summary of the differences between Keynesianism and Monetarism

The two basic theoretical prescriptions then are widely at odds. Keynesianism is an interventionist approach, theorising that the government can intervene to clear markets that fail to work on their own account.

Monetarism (and its earlier incarnation – classical economics) is a free-market, non-interventionist economic policy, relying on market forces, where the only role for government is to ensure that market forces are free to operate in a stable, non-inflationary environment.

In reality, neither appears to work absolutely and after the initial euphoria of the Keynesian revolution in the 1950s and 1960s and the monetarist experiment of the early 1980s, politicians have now moved to a more pragmatic eclectic economic approach, where a variety of policies are used at different times to suit the needs of the economy.

6.2 The eclectic era

From the early 1980s onwards, the government adopted a more pragmatic and less dogmatic stance with regard to economic policy. Ideologically, the approach adopted still owes much to monetarism, in that it focuses on controlling inflation as the central goal of policy. Equally, it uses monetary policy as the key economic lever, with little or no use of fiscal policy to control the economy. However, it uses monetary policy in a Keynesian way in that the level of the interest rate is used to either contract or accelerate economic activity, with less concern being given to the money supply.

If the economy is going too quickly, as evidenced by inflationary pressures, rates rise in order to slow the economy down. Alternatively, if the economy has slowed too far, then the opposite policy of lowering interest rates is used in order to expand economic activity.

Initially, there was no discipline over policy with no clear targets being set. This caused the market some concern, since there was no guarantee that the government would respond to economic pressures in an appropriate or timely manner. These fears seemed justified in the mid-1980s, when inflationary pressures built up with no obvious sign of action from the government. At this point, the markets reacted.

The foreign exchange markets had been liberalised in 1979. Prior to this point, there had been severe restrictions imposed upon the convertibility of sterling into other currencies. As a consequence of the lifting of the controls, capital was able to flow freely into and out of the UK.

In response to a lack of action in 1984, the market sold out of sterling assets, converting into safer, more reliable currencies. The effect of this was to force sterling down sharply. Whilst in general terms a mild decline in a currency might be regarded as an economic stimulus (making exports cheaper at the same time as it discourages imports), a rapid decline in the exchange rate can be very damaging to the economy. Imports that are en route and must be paid for are now much more expensive. Ultimately, there is a risk that the whole country may go bankrupt.

Consequently, the government had to take action to support the currency. Historically, governments have been able to intervene in the forex markets through direct buying and selling of the currency. With the growth of the forex market, this is no longer as effective. Consequently, the most effective intervention technique is via the manipulation of domestic interest rates. If rates are forced up, then this will make the currency more attractive and, therefore, increase demand. In this case, rates were forced up to 14% in order to protect the currency.

In essence, this is what ought to have been done earlier, in that rates should have been pushed up in order to slow the economy down. The market's concern was with regard to inflation, prompting the sell-off of sterling assets. If the authorities had acted earlier by increasing rates, they would not have had to increase rates as aggressively as they ended up doing. The key issue is the whole idea of credibility.

6.2.1 Forex targeting as an approach to credibility

In an attempt to gain credibility, the government adopted the policy of forex targeting. Under this policy, sterling is tied to the currency of a stable inflation nation and this acts as a discipline on policy. To understand this policy, we need to consider the economic underpinnings of the exchange rate.

The exchange rate

Short term – Supply and demand

In the short term, the key factor determining the level of the exchange rate is the supply and demand for currency in the international forex markets.

In a simple world, where the only flows were trade flows, the supply of a currency is created by the imports of that economy. For example, the supply of sterling would be the **supply** of sterling into the forex markets to acquire foreign currency to pay for the **imported goods**, and the **demand** for currency would be the **exports** of that economy since, as a country exports, the countries to which it is exporting will require the appropriate currency to pay for the goods they are purchasing. This leads to a demand for that currency.

The Short-Term Determination of the Exchange Rate

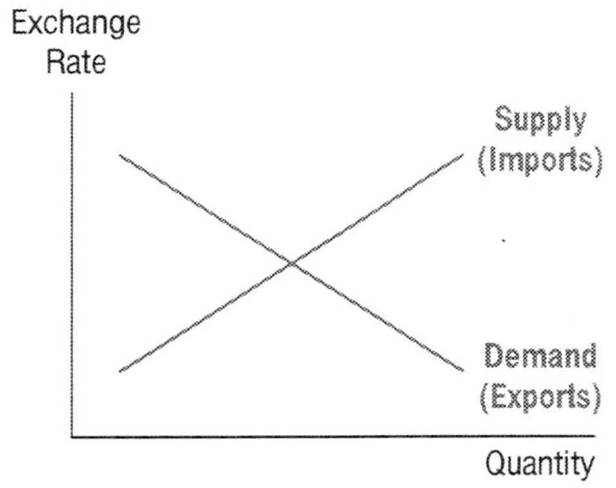

These supply and demand factors should bring the market to an equilibrium rate, and this rate should ensure that the trade flows are in balance.

For example, if an economy is suffering from a deficit on its trading account, i.e. where its imports are greater than its exports, then supply will be greater than demand for that currency. If supply is greater than demand, the price will fall and consequently, the exchange rate will fall. As the exchange rate falls, imports become more costly and exports become cheaper. This will then encourage exporters to produce, and discourage consumers from buying imported goods. As imports fall and exports rise, the balance of trade is brought back into line.

This process of equilibrium is complicated by virtue of the fact that it is not solely trade flows that determine supply and demand for a currency. Over the past 20 years, the world economy has seen the emergence of pools of **'hot money'**, which flow between the international capital centres in order to achieve the highest rates of interest. These flows of investment money can lead to anomalous situations developing with the exchange rate.

For example, in the early 1990s the UK had a substantial trade deficit, which should therefore have forced sterling to fall. However, sterling was supported by high domestic interest rates that encouraged investment flows inwards into the UK, thereby supporting the level of sterling.

Long term – Purchasing power parity

In the short term then, the exchange rate is determined by supply and demand factors and to a greater or lesser extent, market sentiment. Longer term exchange rates are determined by purchasing power parity (PPP), which is a relationship between economies and the levels of inflation they suffer. Purchasing power parity is best explained by way of a small example.

If a basket of goods costs £100 in London and the same basket of goods costs $200 in New York, this predicts that the exchange rate between the two countries will be £1 = $2. However, if the two economies suffer differing rates of inflation then, over time, the exchange rate will alter.

If, after a number of years, the basket of goods now costs £150 in London due to the impact of inflation on UK prices and yet, it only rises to $210 in New York, this would suggest that the exchange rate between the two currencies is now £1 = $1.40 – a decline in the value of sterling.

Short-term supply and demand features may well mask this overall trend, but purchasing power parity gives an underlying theme to the foreign exchange markets. If one economy consistently has an inflation rate in excess of its competitors, then its currency will deteriorate against its trading partners. This pattern is relatively clear in sterling's historic relationships with our major trading partners.

Inflation targets

In the early 1990s the authorities decided to adopt the policy of direct inflation targeting itself. Thus far, policy had revolved around intermediate targets – money supply and the exchange rate. For the first time, the policy would directly target inflation itself. Target ranges were established, initially aiming to keep inflation in the 1% to 4% band.

The chief/sole weapon of policy was still the interest rate – increasing rates to slow the economy down if inflation began to approach the upper end of the target range.

Whilst this development of inflation targets was a welcome clarification of policy, it still had one rather fundamental drawback. The decisions with regard to interest rates were still taken by the Chancellor. This introduced a political element into the policy debate.

Ideally, interest rate policy should be proactive, in that it should try to react ahead of the problem. In normal situations, this is not a problem. However, in the build up to an election, politicians are unlikely to want to increase interest rates regardless of clear signs of overheating. This was the situation the economy found itself in during 1996/7.

Up until this point, the new structure had worked well. Early signs (leading indicators) of overheating had been spotted and action taken. This resulted in a soft landing in 1994/5. A soft landing occurs where policy is directed at slowing the economy down. By acting early, the action does not need to be too extreme and therefore, the economy's reaction is more manageable. The economy slows, but does not fall in value.

An independent central bank

Immediately after the election, the incoming Chancellor (Gordon Brown) took steps to ensure that there would be no repetition of this situation. An independent central bank was required to remove the political dimension and responsibility for monetary policy was passed to the Bank of England. The Monetary Policy Committee (MPC) was formed. The MPC has nine members and comprises five Bank employees and four external economists.

The advantage of this approach is that regardless of the political expediency of the moment, the hard decisions will have to be taken.

The MPC was originally charged with maintaining inflation as measured using the RPI (Retail Price Index) at 2½%. Obviously, it would be impossible to operate with such a rigid target and, consequently, the MPC is allowed a divergence of 1% either side. If actual inflation falls outside of this target range, the Governor of the Bank must justify this to the Chancellor. In 2003, the Chancellor changed the inflation target to 2% as measured using of the CPI (Consumer Price Index) in order to be consistent with other EU members.

Since the transfer of power to the MPC in 1997, inflation has been maintained within the target ranges. If anything, there has been a tendency for caution to prevail in the policy setting process and for long periods of time, inflation has been beneath the target level.

Recession

Historically, policy shifts have been left until too late. Consequently, more extreme actions were required. With more extreme policy actions, the reaction of the underlying economy will be greater. If interest rates go up further and for longer, it is more likely that there will be a hard landing. In a hard landing the economy slides into recession. A recession is defined as two quarters of negative growth in succession.

In 1996, the economy was beginning to overheat mildly. However, with an election in the near future, the Chancellor was unlikely to increase rates. Thus, the risks to the economy were increased.

A recession is usually characterised by

- Falling levels of production.
- Rising unemployment.
- Falling consumer spending.

In a recession, interest rates must be cut in order to stimulate the economy.

Quantitative easing

Exam tip

Most recently examined in Summer 2009 Question 10

Normally, a Central Bank seeks to control the economy through the management of interest rates. If an economy is booming and inflationary pressures are coming to the fore then the Bank will raise rates. Alternatively, if an economy experiencing recessionary conditions, the Bank may seek to stimulate the economy by lowering interest rates. If, however, interest rates are already very low (at or around zero) so there is no further scope for a rate reduction, the Bank may seek to stimulate the economy through quantitative easing.

Quantitative easing is a process by which the Bank attempts to inject cash into the economy with the aim of, through the effects of the bank multiplier, increasing the overall money supply. This is achieved by the Bank purchasing financial assets, mainly short-term government and corporate bonds, from financial institutions (such as banks) using money it has created. Quantitative easing is sometimes described as 'printing money', although the central bank actually creates it electronically 'out of nothing' by increasing the credit in its own bank account.

The intention is that this new money in the hands of the banks can now be lent to customers to be invested, thereby stimulating the economy. There are risks associated with such an approach however, hence it needs to be carefully managed. These risks are discussed below.

Aims of quantitative easing

The issues faced by the Bank of England when it announced its quantitative easing programme in 2008 were

- The economy was weak but interest rates had already been reduced to 0.5%, leaving little scope for further economic stimulus through rate reductions.
- Though interest rates were low, inter-bank rates were quite high as, following the failure of Northern Rock, the banks had little confidence in each other. As a consequence, money market activity had dried up considerably creating further strains on banks and giving rise to the fear of a run on the banks.

The aim of the Bank of England was to positively influence these issues through its quantitative easing programme. Through buying financial assets from banks and replacing them with cash, the banks could have more confidence in each other as well as having the resources to lend to customers. It was hoped that this improvement in confidence would free up the money markets and bring down inter-bank rates allowing normal banking operations to resume. In addition, it was hoped that the new funds would be made available to customers, thereby stimulating the economy.

One final aim of quantitative easing is to create mild inflation. Inflation very low interest rates should encourage consumers to spend now rather than save, thereby again providing a boost to the economy.

Dangers of quantitative easing

As noted above, there are risks associated with a quantitative easing approach, hence it needs to be carefully managed. These risks include the following

- If inter-bank confidence is too low then the amount of money needed to achieve the Bank's objectives may prove to be beyond its scope.
- In difficult economic circumstances the banks may still be reluctant to lend to customers despite the increase in their deposits. They may prefer to pay down debt and improve their balance sheets rather than lend to customers. Consequently, the hoped for economic stimulus may not materialise.
- Alternatively, the policy may be too effective, the economy may be over stimulated leading in a worst case scenario to bubble in the economy with excessive inflation.
- It is very difficult to know what the correct level of quantitative easing is. We are clearly in uncharted economic waters here and it would be very easy to pitch in at the wrong level.
- Finally, sooner or later the Bank will need to reverse the process, selling the financial assets it has acquired for cash. This will reduce the money supply within the banking system which may, if the economy has not recovered, drive it back into recession.

7 Current Issues in Macroeconomics

7.1 The death of inflation

Currently, one of the key questions to be answered in economics is whether inflation has finally been beaten by policy. At first, this may seem to be a rather ambitious statement to make, however, it depends on the view of inflation taken. Whilst we are conditioned to seeing, and expecting, inflation on a regular basis, it can be argued that inflation is simply an aberration of the last quarter of a century and that the norm for the world economy has been a situation where there was low or zero inflation.

The fact that we are able to sustain reasonable levels of economic growth alongside this low inflation has encouraged many to argue that we are in a new era of economics –the 'New Paradigm'.

It is argued that the Keynesian economic policies of the 1950s and 1960s, which attempted to suppress unemployment below its natural or sustainable level, led to the creation of a background level of inflation. Once created, this background level of inflation was then converted into a much more substantial level of inflation by the commodity price shocks of the 1970s.

The big question, therefore, must be what has changed in order to remove inflation from the agenda.

7.1.1 Monetary policy

As we have seen, monetary policy is now more disciplined than before, with a large proportion of the discipline being driven by the financial markets. In addition, the creation of an independent central bank with responsibility for price stability has added even more credibility.

The policy restraint exerted by the financial markets extends also to fiscal policy where, again, government freedom is heavily restricted.

7.1.2 Expectations

Perhaps more crucial than the immediate policy constraint imposed by the markets is the change in the expectations of the key economic players.

It is argued that the opinion formers in the economy have become more rational in their expectation of, and reactions to, changes in economic policy.

7.1.3 Competitive environment

Another crucial element of reformed expectations is the nature of the new, more competitive labour market. The process of structural reform to the UK, and indeed OECD labour markets, has created a market place that is much harsher than before. Workers are now more conscious of their inability to force through wage rises and a large proportion of the work force are rewarded – if not wholly, then in part – by performance-related pay deals.

This has in part reduced downward wage stickiness and enhanced mobility (particularly with regard to skills). However, labour mobility will always be limited in a geographic sense, given the dominance of home ownership and the diminished supply of rented accommodation.

Arguably, if labour is not able to preserve its effective spending power through wage rises, then it must defend it by ensuring that very few, if any, price rises are accepted. The inability of retailers to pass on inflationary price pressures requires them to adopt different strategies to commodity price changes. This effectively severs the link between commodity and retail prices, thereby removing what has been a large erratic element in our inflation history. If the labour market is a more realistic place, then workers will respond in a more rational and predictable fashion to government economic policy, thereby strengthening the argument that low inflation breeds low inflation.

This competitive environment also operates on an international scale, with competitive trade forces exerting downward pressure on UK prices.

7.1.4 Technology

Technological advances are also important in the anti-inflationary atmosphere, particularly with regard to primary raw materials where technological advances are leading to much lower international commodity prices. Equally, technological advances such as the internet allow for much greater visibility of prices and consequently, increased levels of competition.

7.1.5 Conclusion

The key conclusion to draw is that the monetary policy framework can seldom have enjoyed such a supportive environment and this does point to an era of relatively low inflationary pressures.

A note of caution is introduced by many economists who would argue that the old inflationary spirals still exist and that it would only require a number of successful and large wage claims or a series of commodity price shocks to start the spiral moving again.

7.2 Disinflation into deflation

The current forces that are at work in the creation of the new low inflation paradigm may contribute towards the creation of deflation in the global economy. To date, these forces have succeeded in creating disinflation (falling levels of inflation) and many policy makers believe that they can contain levels within inflation targets, which aim at mild sustainable levels of inflation. However, others argue that these forces are so strong that in the end, they will dominate.

7.2.1 The disinflationary forces at work in the global economy

Competition and supply-side reforms

The process of reform that has taken place in the G7 economies has led to a more competitive environment. In this environment, the pressure on prices is downward. This is exacerbated by the internet and information revolution that further erode the power of the producer.

Many argue that these forces have only just begun to have an effect and that once started, this process will continue to exert downward pressure on prices.

The focus of policy

If the central bank continues to fight the battles of the past, there is the risk that overly cautious policy makers will create a policy environment that is too tight and fails to acknowledge the changes in culture that have taken place.

The retreat of the government from the economy

As governments focus on fiscal responsibility and prudence, they may accelerate the slide into deflation and perversely limit the recovery.

The inflationary surge of the past 50 years ties in with the significant expansion of the role of the state. As the government has spent money, it has artificially increased the level of demand in the economy and hence led to inflation. Currently, the fashion in politics is to favour a small/responsible government. Many economists argue that this will then, via the forces of 'crowding in', free up resources for the private sector to expand. However, the evidence to support the expansion of the private sector in response to the reduction in the role of the state is not clear.

Equally, as was seen in Japan, unless the government takes decisive action in response to deflation, the situation can deteriorate and policy becomes difficult to implement.

There is the risk that an overzealous adherence to a balanced budget will also remove some of the automatic stabilisation effects of welfare spending during an economic downturn (and the decelerating influence of taxation during upturns).

Demographics and savings ratios

With an ageing population, in the developed world in particular, it is felt that the mix of consumption and savings will change. The fear is that consumers will switch to a more aggressive savings mentality in order to provide for retirements that they will expect to last longer. The consequence of this will be a decline in the level of demand in the economy.

Conclusions

With all of these forces, it is felt by many that only the first signs of these issues are being seen at present. This has led to the current mild levels of inflation that are being experienced in the global economy. However, this 'new paradigm' might only be a transitional staging post on the way to a sustained era of deflation.

If policy makers are slow to respond to the changing world, then they run the risk of applying the wrong policies. In some ways, this would be a re-run of the 1930s where, in response to the deflationary contraction in the global economy, policy makers focused on economic discipline.

7.3 Deflation

As global disinflation continues, the prospect of deflation or falling prices becomes more likely. This is definitely the case in Japan where, due to a variety of structural problems, the economy has been depressed for over ten years. This has led to very low inflation and now deflation. It is argued by many economists that deflation may already be taking place within several other major economies. The reason that this is not observable lies in the inadequacies within our current inflation measures. At present, inflation is measured by comparing baskets of goods that are repriced monthly. It is argued that these measures fail to take into account improvements in the quality of goods, thereby overstating inflation. Equally, they are not reflective of the goods that people buy. In particular, they fail to incorporate high-tech goods that fall in price over the first few years of their development.

One survey in the US suggested that the impact of these inadequacies was to overstate inflation by around 1½%. This would in effect put the US currently very close to outright deflation.

7.3.1 The impact of deflation

Many economists would argue that deflation is really no better or worse than inflation, simply representing falling rather than rising prices. However, it is perhaps more of a concern that we are approaching a deflationary era from the standpoint of persistent inflation. This will have affected people's expectations and, therefore, may cause problems as they readjust.

7.3.2 The current problem

As mentioned above, the problem at present is not deflation as such, but rather the fact that deflation is occurring after significant and long-term periods of inflation. Inflation, or rising prices, has effectively permeated our expectations and we are accustomed to seeing prices, wages and profits all increasing. Deflation would force these into reverse. Prices would fall logically and therefore, wages should also fall. Equally, profits should fall to reflect the changes in the nominal price level. However, the fear is that if wages and prices start to fall and asset prices then follow, consumers may become too depressed and overly concerned by deflation.

In a deflationary environment, it makes sense for consumers to defer spending, since there is an implied return on deferring consumption even in the absence of interest rates. This deferral of spending may in turn then lead to a further contraction of demand in the economy and so on and so forth, creating a vicious circle of contraction. This is a reflection of the paradox of thrift.

The principal fear of most economists lies in the impact this may have upon the banking markets. Declining profitability and contracting demand may force many companies into default. As the non-performing loans element within the bank's balance sheet increases, depositors may become concerned. Since there will implicitly be a reward to holding cash in the absence of any interest rate (since prices are falling) many investors may choose to take their money out of the banking system. If sufficient numbers choose to do this, the whole process of fractional reserve banking and the money multiplier will start to unravel and the banks may face, at that stage, a liquidity shortage and the possibility of systemic banking collapse.

This is something of a nightmare scenario, although not altogether implausible, given our current circumstances. On a more modest scale, there are other problems associated with deflation. Most notably, government's reliance upon monetary policy will have to change. Over the past 20 years, the dominant theme of economic policy has been the control of economic activity through the use of the interest rate. In a deflationary era, that may become harder to achieve. For example, if the economy starts to slow down, the natural response of policy makers would be to reduce interest rates in order to stimulate growth.

Ultimately, however, they have to appreciate that there is a finite limit beyond which they cannot go. Interest rates cannot be negative, or at least not for any significant period. It might be possible to sustain a minor negative charge as a handling charge, but then only when people have faith in the banking industry.

Once rates have fallen to zero, the government has effectively played every card it has and has nowhere else to go. Equally, deflation in the background will create effective real rates of return that the government will have no control over at all. For example, if interest rates were zero and deflation was 10%, then there would still be an effective real rate of return on holding cash of 10%.

It should be appreciated that this is deflation in the sense of a monetary deflation. There are other deflations that have taken place in the world economy which have been less negative in their nature. For example, in the final quarter of the 19th century, the global economy suffered from technological deflation, where developments in technology and, in particular, transportation allowed prices to fall across a significant range of goods. Rather than having a depressing impact on the global economy, it stimulated the global economy.

Pragmatic mild inflation

The concerns that governments/central banks have with regard to deflation and its potentially depressing influence are reflected in the inflation targets set. For example, the ECB has established a target of 2% or less inflation, as opposed to zero inflation.

The argument used to justify this moderately inflationary environment is that inflation can be tolerated in very mild doses. It may even be supportive of growth, since it creates a slightly positive backdrop to the economy.

It must, however, be emphasised that this is inflation at a modest level. Once inflation goes beyond a certain level, the distortion it creates can be just as debilitating as deflation.

7.4 Government deficits

Over the last 30 years, government deficits have changed dramatically. In the past, whilst governments tended to spend more than they raised in revenue, this excess was not extreme and was often counterbalanced by periods of surplus. Progressively, since the 1970s, government deficits have increased with relatively few periods of repayment. This has been driven by a higher social spend within most economies, accounted for by greater pensions costs and welfare spending.

This has, however, not always been the case. For example, in Japan, much of the expansion in deficit was driven initially by the needs of the economy and the infrastructure investment made by the Japanese government.

The presence of inflation in the past has effectively eroded the impact of increasing deficits. With the economy effectively growing at nominal rates, boosted by inflation, the debt burden does not appear great. With the reduction in inflation and the gradual spiralling of deficits, the real position has been brought home over the last few years. As a result, most governments have started to address the issue of reducing and controlling their deficits. Initially, we must consider the problems created by large government deficits.

Domestically, the crucial difference caused by the growth in government deficits has effectively been a 'crowding-out' of the private sector from the savings market. The primary symptom of this will be an increase in borrowing costs, caused by the presence of the government in the borrowing markets. Many commentators would argue that a large proportion of the increase in real interest rates, which has taken place over the last 20 years, has been driven by the growing demands of government on a shrinking pool of international savings.

Internationally, the effects can be even more important. If the government is borrowing a substantial amount of money, such that it is draining the domestic savings pool, then it may need to call in external capital. This was clearly the case in the American economy during the 1980s, where the substantial deficits accrued by the government attracted large amounts of funds, particularly from Japan. As funds are attracted in, normally by higher interest rates, there is pressure on the currency to appreciate, causing a greater demand for the currency than current supply. An appreciation of a currency will tend to make that country's exports less attractive and imports more attractive. This will effectively lead to a reduction in the overall economic output of the economy and a trade deficit. This was clearly seen in the US throughout the 1980s, where a rapidly increasing trade deficit ran alongside a substantial government deficit.

In addition, significant external debt may render the economy more of a hostage to fortune. If the international markets take a negative view of economic policy, it is more likely that they will sell their holdings, potentially instigating a currency crisis.

Consequently, government deficits need to be tackled. Primarily, this should come through a review of government expenditure and a reduction in the welfare spend. Countries such as the UK and the US have already undertaken much of this process. There has been a gradual transferring of the burden of state spending away from the government and onto the individual through the introduction of personal pensions and private health care, with the state effectively acting as the fall-back for those people who are unable to provide for themselves in any other way.

Many economists would argue that once the situation has been created, it is difficult to resolve, for if a government has a substantial deficit and wishes to reduce it, then by reducing spending or increasing taxation, they will induce a contractionary phase in the economy. This makes it unlikely that any politically motivated government is going to bite the bullet and take such action. Counter to this argument, one might suggest that once governments begin to reduce their intervention in the economy and their expenditure, they will allow much more freedom for the private sector, reducing real interest rates, encouraging investment and encouraging growth. This, effectively, is 'crowding-in' the economy and, as governments gradually retreat, the private sector can expand into the gap left behind, therefore avoiding the need for a full scale contraction.

As a response to the problems caused by these significant deficits, many governments are turning towards some commitment to fiscal discipline. To an extent, these measures will always be open to some doubt, given the inability to separate fiscal policy from the political process. With monetary policy, it is relatively simple to transfer power to the central bank, but with fiscal policy, there is no real possibility of delegation. Consequently, most of these schemes may be seen as flawed but, at least, they create a public statement of intent to control the deficit. In the UK, the Chancellor has committed the government to a policy, under which it is intended that the revenue budget is balanced over the economic cycle, with borrowing only being used to fund infrastructure projects. (This is referred to as *"Gordon's Golden Rule"*.)

Other regimes are slightly more formalised such as the Stability and Growth Pact in the Euro bloc and New Zealand's Fiscal Responsibility Act.

8 Measures of Growth and Economic Activity

There are a variety of important indicators published in the UK and other markets to indicate the level of economic activity and the success, or otherwise, of economic policy.

8.1 Gross domestic and gross national product

The key measures of the level of output of the economy are the **gross domestic product (GDP)** and **gross national product (GNP)**.

The gross domestic product is the total value of output produced in the economy regardless of whom that belongs to. Therefore, it would include the value of cars produced at a Japanese car plant in the UK, but not include the value of produce made in America by UK companies. Gross national product is the value of output of the participants in the economy and therefore includes net property income from abroad.

The gross in the title of each measure refers to the sum before making allowance for the depreciation in the capital stock of the economy. Every year, a certain increase in output has to take place in order to repair the damage to capital stock in actually producing that volume of activity. The net measures of product are net of allowances for capital depreciation.

Both the GDP and GNP figures are used as measures of growth in the economy. The rate of growth indicates the position of the economy within the economic cycle and, therefore, in part predicts what action the government will take – whether expansionary or contractionary – depending on the governmental stance.

National Income Accounting

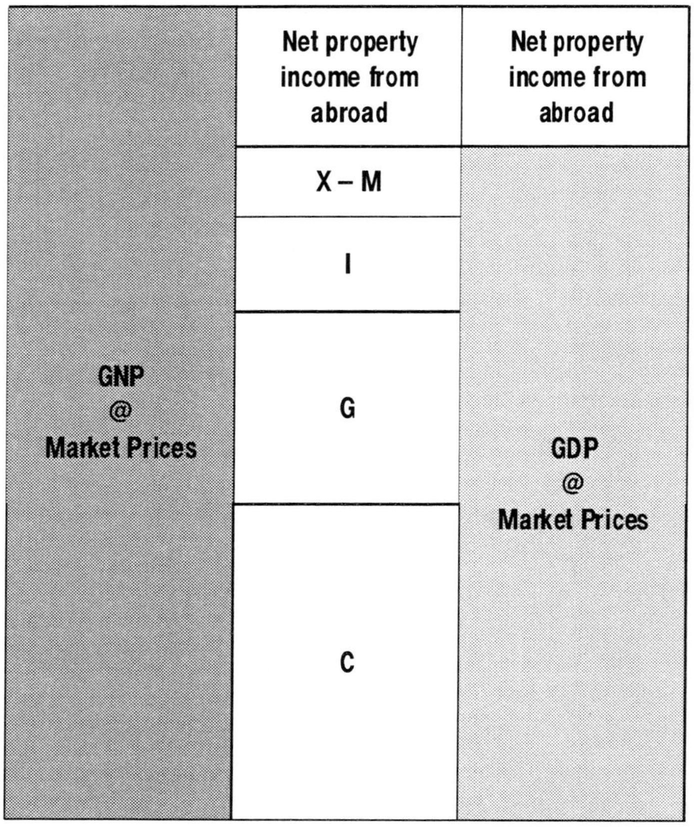

Source: Begg Fisher Dornbusch

In an attempt to strip out the impact of inflation from the figures, a variety of methods are used. One common approach is to create a measure of inflation in the economy, referred to as the GDP price deflator, and use this to scale back the money values to real values. In essence, this exactly mirrors the indexation process on index-linked securities, but in reverse.

The GDP figure is perhaps the most important barometer of economic wellbeing. It is released quarterly and is then revised to remove some of the distortions that creep into the estimation process. One of the most important issues is the relationship of the actual data to trend.

8.2 Output gaps

Linked to the GDP is the output gap. This endeavours to measure the extent to which the economy is operating either above or below its capacity constraint. The capacity constraint represents the ceiling of activity based on the economy's current resources. This ceiling will rise over time at a rate determined by the increased availability of new resources within the economy as adjusted by any increases in productivity. The UK has demonstrated growth at an average annual trend rate of growth of 2¼% over the last 50 years. However, many commentators are now of the opinion that the market reforms of the past few years have increased the ability of the economy to deliver growth. Consequently, many would now estimate sustainable growth at 2½%.

Where the economy is operating below capacity, inflationary pressures will tend to be relatively low. If the output gap closes and the economy starts to operate at or above the ceiling level, then this will put strains on the factor markets (labour, etc.), and this will lead to inflation.

UK Output Gap

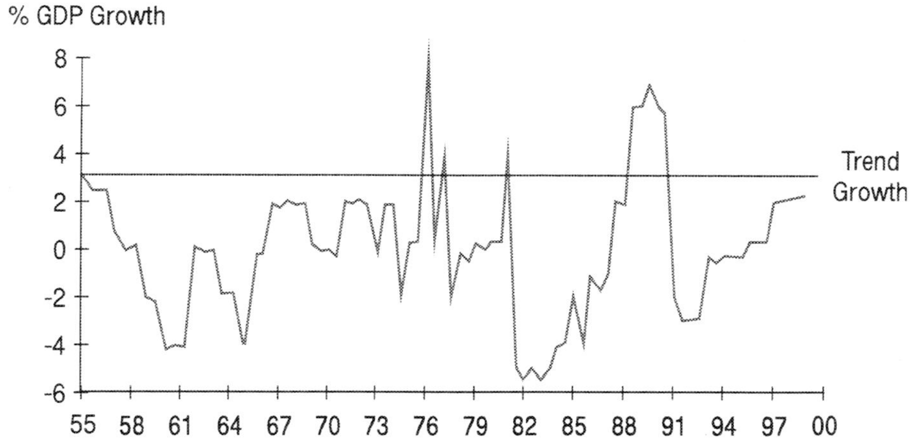

8.3 Asset prices

Asset prices, such as house prices and stock market values, are important leading indicators of economic activity. In the UK, house prices have historically been the most important in the mind of the consumer. As house prices rise, consumers feel more confident and increase their spending. This is often referred to as the **wealth effect**. As we have seen, rising spending is a potentially inflationary force in as much as it outstrips the ability of the economy to deliver. Stock market values can, to a lesser extent, deliver the same effect.

These forces also work in the opposite direction. If asset values fall, the negative wealth effect can be equally powerful in a downward direction. Rapid asset price falls can trigger off a significant contraction of demand. More often, the asset price decline is in response to a tightening of monetary policy. Therefore, the wealth effect simply exacerbates the existing contractionary conditions in the economy. This can lead to a more extreme response than the policy makers had intended.

8.4 Confidence indicators

There are regular surveys conducted of business and consumer confidence. These surveys measure the responses of the sample group to a series of standard questions. As such, the results tend to be relatively volatile. The reaction to the terrorist attacks on September 11, 2001 is a prime example of this. The surveys taken in the aftermath of this tragic event showed a huge collapse in consumer confidence. Much of this collapse was restored within a few months.

Confidence then feeds into other indicators within the economy. If confidence is high, this will often encourage spending and other potentially inflationary forces. Though, of itself, confidence is a reflection of other factors.

8.5 Retail sales

Another important indicator of the level of activity in the UK economy is the retail sales figure. This measures the amount of consumer expenditure activity taking place in the shops. Once again, the level of demand is important, since this too links into the rate of inflation. If the rate of demand is too high and there are too few goods, this will almost inevitably result in an overheating of the economy and inflation – 'too much money chasing too few goods'.

Obviously, it is critically linked to other indicators. If consumer confidence is high, spending is likely to increase. Equally, if asset prices rise, then this will again, via the wealth effect, encourage greater confidence and more spending.

Within these statistics, there are clear feedback loops that can be observed. For example, rising house prices can make consumers feel more confident about the future. If consumers are more confident, then they are more likely to take on major purchases such as property. This will further stimulate the housing market, thereby forcing prices higher. In this way, asset price 'bubbles' are formed. A bubble is where a market rises too quickly and in effect overshoots its real value. This was the case in the housing markets of the late 1980s and the stock market at the end of the 1990s. The dilemma for policy makers is whether it is a real value or overheated. Equally, there is then the timing and strength of any move to reduce the market.

If the authorities fail to act, then there is a risk of severe economic distortion. In the 1980s, when the house price bubble burst, it left many homeowners with negative equity. Negative equity is where the outstanding loan on a property is greater than the value of the property. This is quite clearly a huge drag on economic activity. A similar problem was encountered with the technology stock boom of the 1990s. The more that the values of these stocks rose, the greater the number of buyers drawn in. When the market normalised, significant value was lost.

8.6 Labour market indicators

The key labour market indicators are the level of unemployment and the rate of change in earnings.

Unemployment measures are many and varied but generally try to measure the number of individuals who are available to work, but who cannot find employment. Average earnings measures seek to measure the rate at which payroll costs are rising in the economy. Historically, these indicators have been linked inversely in that, as unemployment fell, earnings rose. In this situation, the labour market would be described as 'tight'.

Supply-side reforms introduced into the labour market over the last 20 years have made the market much more competitive. These reforms have included the restriction of union power, the reduction in benefits and the limitation of employee rights. This has made it harder for workers to force up their wage rates in response to inflationary pressure. It has also meant that the historical relationship between low levels of unemployment and wage inflation is weaker.

Once again, these indicators will interact with the other measures we have considered. On its own, a rise in earnings might not trigger an overexpansion of activity. However, if it were coupled with an increase in asset prices, a buoyant economy and a high level of consumer confidence, it would be more likely that this would trigger an overexpansion of consumer spending.

8.7 Public Sector Net Cash Requirement

Every year, the government tends to spend more money than it raises in tax and somehow, must fund the difference. This funding is achieved through the **Public Sector Net Cash Requirement (PSNCR)**, formerly known as the Public Sector Borrowing Requirement (PSBR). The requirement is either expressed as the set amount of money that is being raised by the government, or the percentage it represents of the Gross National Product. Each year in the Budget, the Chancellor sets the PSNCR for the following year and it is then the responsibility of the Debt Management Office (DMO) to issue gilts, or use other measures, to achieve the borrowing required.

The City closely follows the PSNCR figure, as it indicates the amount of money the government is obliged to raise through the markets, which is important as it acts as a drain on available funds. It also indicates how much control the government has over its levels of expenditure.

The PSNCR tends to move in line with the economic cycle.

Boom	Revenue high	Expenditure low	PSNCR falls or is negative
Slump	Revenue low	Expenditure high	PSNCR rises

8.8 Retail Price Index

Historically, the main inflation index used in the UK has been the **Retail Price Index (RPI)**. The RPI is calculated by looking at the prices of a basket of over 300 goods. The prices are then weighted to reflect the average household's consumption patterns, so those important items on which a lot of money is spent get a higher weighting than peripheral items.

The index itself is based on movements in prices since a base period (the current series runs from January 1987 = 100). The markets concentrate on the RPI figure, as it is a good indicator of the level of inflation and consequently, government reaction to it. It also signals the need for potential increases in the yield on bonds in order to compensate for the erosion of real returns.

Two more refined measures were introduced in the 1990s.

RPIX	This excludes the impact of **mortgages**
RPIY	This excludes **mortgages and indirect (VAT) and local authority taxes**

Historically, the RPIX was used by the government in specifying its inflation target at a level of 2.5%.

8.9 Consumer Price Index

In his Pre-Budget Report statement on 10 December 2003, the Chancellor of the Exchequer changed the UK inflation target to a new base, the Harmonised Index of Consumer Prices (HICP), which was renamed the Consumer Price Index (CPI) in the UK. The level of the new CPI inflation target for the Bank of England's Monetary Policy Committee was set at 2% from 10 December 2003. Note that pensions, benefits and index-linked gilts continue to be calculated on exactly the same basis as in the past, with reference to the Retail Prices Index (RPI).

The CPI is calculated each month by taking a sample of goods and services that a typical household might buy, including food, heating, household goods, travel costs.

HICPs were originally developed in the EU to assess whether prospective members of European Monetary Union would pass the required inflation convergence criterion, and then to acting as the measure of inflation used by the European Central Bank to assess price stability in the euro area.

There are significant differences between the CPI and the RPI. The CPI excludes a number of items that are included in RPIX, mainly related to housing. These include council tax and a range of owner-occupier housing costs such as mortgage interest payments, house depreciation, buildings insurance, estate agents and conveyancing fees.

The CPI covers all private households, whereas RPIX excludes the top 4% by income and pensioner households who derive at least three quarters of their income from state benefits. The CPI also includes the residents of institutional households such as student hostels and also foreign visitors to the UK. This means that it covers some items that are not in the RPI, such as unit trust and stockbrokers fees, university accommodation fees and foreign students' university tuition fees.

Although, in most cases, the same underlying price data is used to calculate the two indices, there are some specific differences in price measurement. For example, different methods are used in the CPI and RPI to adjust prices for quality improvements in new cars and personal computers.

The two indices are also calculated differently. The CPI uses the geometric mean to combine prices within each expenditure category, whereas the RPI uses arithmetic means. The different techniques used to combine individual prices in the two indices tend to reduce CPI inflation relative to RPIX, this is known as the formula effect. When the Chancellor announced the changeover in target measure, the annual rate of RPI-X exceeded the CPI by more than 1%.

As a consequence, the main measures of inflation published in the UK are

- **The Consumer Price Index (CPI)** – based on an EU-wide formula allowing direct comparison of the inflation rate in the UK against that in the rest of Europe.
- **The Retail Price Index (RPI)** – an average measure of change in the prices of goods and services. Once published, it is never revised.
- **RPI-X** – this is RPI excluding mortgage costs. It was previously the target measure for the MPC with a target of 2.5%
- **RPI-Y** – this is RPI with both mortgage costs and the impact of changes in taxation removed.

A key advantage of RPI and RPIX is their familiarity and credibility based on their longer history. Inevitably, it will be some time before the CPI becomes as widely recognised. The CPI's exclusion of most elements of owner-occupier housing costs lessens its relevance for some users, but this must be weighed against the significant difficulties encountered in measuring such costs appropriately, reflected in the absence of any international consensus in this area.

8.10 Producer prices indices (PPI)

Producer price indices measure inflationary pressures at an earlier stage in the production process.

8.10.1 Input prices

Input prices measure the change in prices going into the production process. This will include raw materials and other inputs. Changes in commodity prices will directly affect this number.

8.10.2 Output prices

Output or factory gate prices measure the changes in the price on goods as they leave the production process and enter the retail sector. There is obviously a very strong relationship with input price variation.

Historically, any changes in raw material prices have tended to pass on through the productive process and resulted in higher retail prices. In recent years, the generally low level of inflation coupled with the more competitive nature of the labour market has made it increasingly difficult for producers to pass on price increases. Consumers are now used to stable prices and are unable to force their wages up in order to compensate for the higher prices.

Now, due to this intolerance of consumers to price increases, the productive and retail sectors have to act as a buffer to inflationary forces. Many price increases are not passed on, but are simply absorbed within the firm's margins. To compensate for this, beneficial price falls are also not always passed through to the consumers.

8.11 The balance of payments

The UK is an international economy and deals and transacts business all around the world. The balance of payments account simply summarises this position in one statement, showing inflows and outflows to the UK economy.

The flows are divided into two – the short-term flows (the current account), and the longer term transactions (the capital account).

8.11.1 Current account balance

The current account is often referred to as the balance of trade. It looks at the short-term flows in and out of the UK. Trade itself is divided into two blocks – visible and invisible.

Visible trade

Visible trade is trading conducted in physical goods. Over the past 20 or 30 years, the UK has had a deficit on its visible trade balance with the rest of the world. That is to say, the UK has imported more physical goods than it has exported. This situation would be impossible to maintain long term, were it not for the surplus the UK maintains on the invisible account.

A deficit on the current account is often seen as a sign of overheating within the economy. In essence, the households overspend and this draws in overseas goods.

Invisible trade

Invisibles are trades in services and income flows. It is here that the UK has been strong over the last 20 years. Included in the invisible earnings of the UK are the activities of the City of London, tourism and other services provided from the UK to overseas individuals. It is the surplus on the invisible trade that offsets the deficit the UK runs on visible trade and which occasionally results in a positive balance of trade overall.

Also included within the invisible earnings of the UK are flows resulting from income on overseas investments, dividends and interest payments. The UK is one of the world's largest investors overseas, with particularly large stakes in the US.

8.11.2 Transactions in long-term assets and liabilities

This is the longer term aspect of the balance of payments. Long-term investment flows either into or out of the UK. In the past, this statement has been referred to as the capital account.

It is impossible to give a general direction to the long-term flows. Much depends on the level of interest expressed by overseas investors in the UK and the opportunities to invest in the UK, which present themselves to UK investors, such as pensions funds, which may, in the absence of a viable UK alternative, invest overseas. Obviously, one key determinant of the level of inward investment is the interest rate and, in particular, the real interest rate.

When interest rates are high, they attract investment and thereby support the exchange rate through the balance of payments.

Overall, the balance of payments is again an important economic statistic and is followed closely by the markets. If the balance of payments is in deficit, it will eventually have to be corrected. One way of doing this where a country is importing more than it exports is for its exchange rate to fall or devalue.

At that point, imports become more expensive and exports become relatively cheaper. This automatic mechanism should bring the balance of trade back into line. In reality, economic systems seldom work this efficiently, and the UK has maintained a deficit on the balance of payments for a number of years.

The statistics themselves are notoriously unreliable, mainly due to the fact that they are based on a series of estimates. There will always be a number known as the **balancing item** in the balance of payment accounts, which simply ensures that the balance of payments itself balances.

8.12 Automatic stabilisers

Automatic stabilisers are factors within an economy that tend to counteract cyclical forces. For example, when the economy turns down, benefit payments restrict the level to which incomes can fall and, therefore, limits the fall in domestic demand. On the other hand, progressive taxes will have the effect of removing the upside overshoot by reducing disposable income during periods of economic boom.

8.12.1 A Summary of the key interactions of economic indicators

The following diagram endeavours to link the key economic indicators together and to suggest a form of interaction. In reality the economy is clearly much more complex than this simplistic structure. In many situation there are first and second order effects. However, some of the most important interactions are brought out.

Leading Indicators

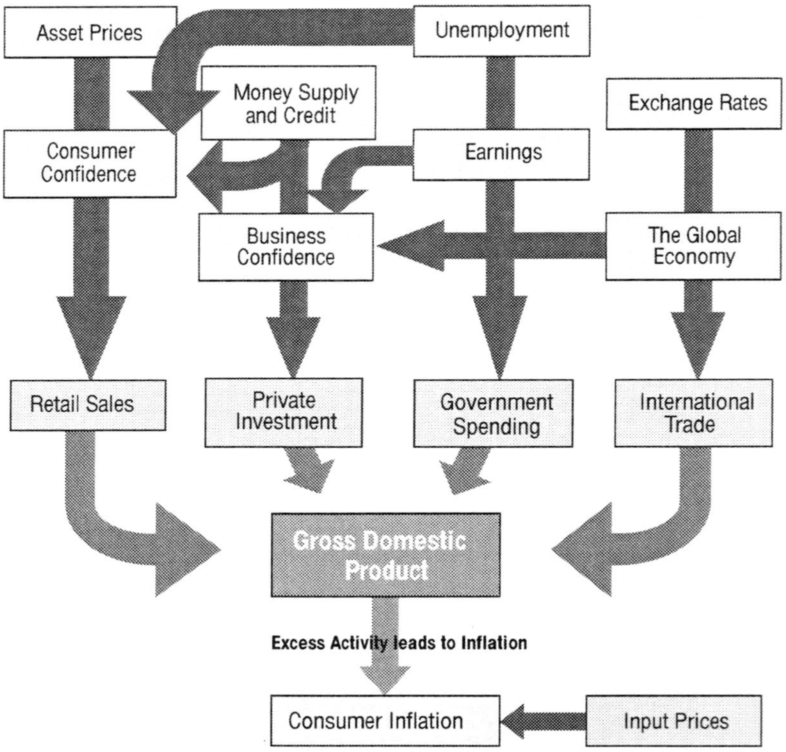

Lagging Indicators

9 The Economics of Business

9.1 The economic cycle

9.1.1 Peaks, recessions and depression

The economic cycle could be defined as fluctuations in the general level of economic activity. It has been an observed phenomenon in economies for a long period of time. This can be seen from observing a fairly typical pattern of boom and bust exhibited by the US economy.

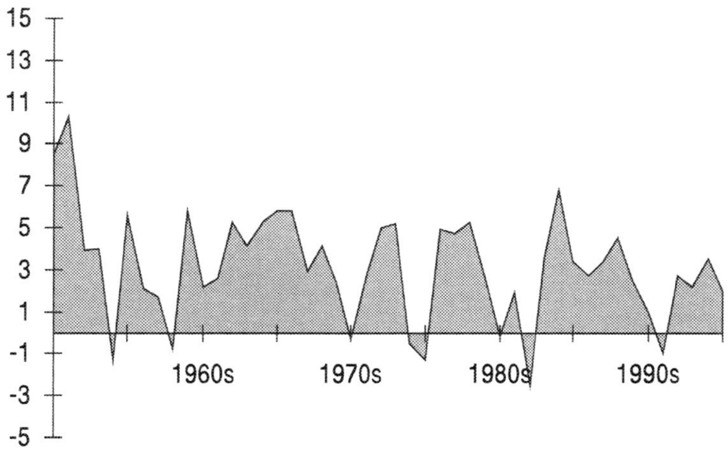

The business cycle is made up of an **expansion** phase that culminates in a **peak or boom** period, when GDP grows rapidly and there are high levels of activity.

The economy then **contracts**, GDP grows at a slower rate (or even contracts) and unemployment increases. The bottom of the contraction phase is referred to as the recessionary trough. If GDP contracts for two consecutive quarters and unemployment rises, this will be referred to as a **recession**. Where a recession continues for a prolonged period of time, this would be referred to as a **depression**.

Generally, there is an upward trend to the GDP through time.

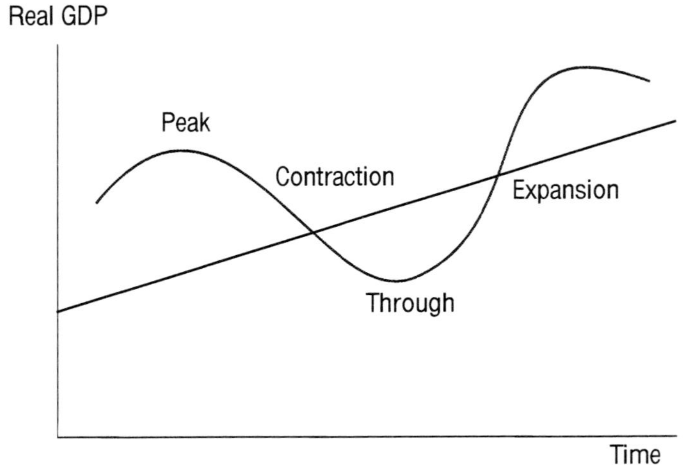

The level of economic activity is measured by variables such as the rate of unemployment and changes in real GDP.

Chapter Roundup

Economics is a vast area of study, however, in the context of the exam it is of fairly minor relevance and exam questions have been confined to short definitions or optional essays on topical areas.

You need to be able to

- Describe the problem of and possible cures for inflation.
- Define various economic growth measures such as GDP/GNP.
- Discuss the PSNCR.
- Discuss the role of the independent central bank.
- Describe and contrast the inflation measures of the RPI and CPI.

Test Your Knowledge

Check your knowledge of the Chapter here, without referring back to the text.

1. (a) Set out the four main expenditure generating components of Gross Domestic Product (GDP) and give broad definitions of each one.

   (b) How important is the publication of data relating to the components of GDP to investors?

   (c) Explain how Gross National Product (GNP) differs from Gross Domestic Product (GDP).

2. Distinguish between monetary policy and fiscal policy.

3 Explain what is meant by the term 'Public Sector Net Cash Requirement' (PSNCR). Describe briefly the potential impact that a rise (fall) in PSNCR may have on investment returns.

4. Explain what definition of inflation is used by the Monetary Policy Committee and why that particular definition has been selected.

Test Your Knowledge: Answers

1. (a) **Gross domestic product** is a measure of the overall economic activity in a country, regardless of who it belongs to. It is calculated by adding together the total value of the annual outputs of goods and services.

   The four components are as follows.

   Private consumption – the percentage of GDP expenditure made up of consumer spending on final goods and services such as food, clothing and transport. Also included is imputed rent on owner occupied housing.

   Total investment – the percentage of GDP expenditure on fixed capital investment, as opposed to financial investment by both the private and public sectors.

   Government consumption – the percentages of GDP made up of consumer spending by the public sector.

   Net exports – the percentages of GDP made up of the difference between the value of national exports of goods and services and that of imports.

   (b) **Investors**

   It is often the first estimate that is the one that most affects financial markets, given their demand for rapid and accessible information. It will give an indication of where the economy is heading and, if it is in recovery for example, whether this is being driven by industry or consumers. Faster and fairly broad based growth will usually be taken as a good sign, though if the economy is perceived to be near its productive potential it may lead to fears of inflationary pressures.

   Company Managers

   Economic growth usually suggests an expanding market. The extent of the market expansion will depend on how responsive sales are to changes in demand.

   (c) Gross National Product is the value of outputs of participants in that economy and therefore includes net income from abroad. That is GNP is made up of two main elements

   - Gross Domestic Product.
   - The difference between income arising on overseas investments by UK residents and that arising on UK investments by overseas residents.

2. **Monetary policy** is the way the government controls monetary stability. Experts differ as to the actual statistic to control: according to some it should be monetary aggregates. (M0, M3) as is the view of the Bundesbank; according to others it should be the rate of inflation as is the view of the Bank of England. Stability is ensured partly by the central bank changing interest rates periodically and partly by operations in the money market. In the UK monetary policy became important under the Thatcher years.

   Fiscal policy is the government's decision about the balance of spending and taxes, which according to Keynes was the way to control unemployment. The main method of control is through the annual budget. This method became generally accepted after the war, but went out of fashion as a main control when it no longer seemed to work in the 1970s as unemployment rose regardless.

   In the UK at present both methods are used in conjunction with each other. Should a single currency be introduced, it will be interesting to see monetary policy under the control of the European Central Bank while fiscal policy would still be under national control.

3. PSNCR represents the difference between the amount of money raised by the government in taxation and the amount it spends. Funding for the difference is obtained through borrowings with a consequent impact on the money supply. A high level of PSNCR is likely to provide inflationary pressure on the economy, raise interest rates and possibly reduce the value of Ordinary shares.

4. The target rate of inflation 2.0% as measured by the CPI. The CPI is an EU wide measure that was adopted in the UK in 2003. It represents a basket of goods and services that a typical EU household is expected to spend its income on.

14 Interest Rates and Interest Rate Forecasting

INTRODUCTION

As we have seen in looking through the various fixed income investments available to us, the value of these investments is heavily influenced by economic circumstances and economic changes. If we are thinking of investing in these securities we must be aware of the current economic circumstances that may impact upon us and how those circumstances may change. At the very least we will need to know the current shape of the yield curve and be able to forecast where it is going. The shape of the yield curve has already been covered, this section concentrates on the aspect of economic forecasting and particularly forecasting the yield curve.

CHAPTER CONTENTS

Chapter Learning Objectives

Analysis

Students should possess a broad understanding of both static and dynamic methods for the analysis and construction of fixed income securities containing both certain and contingent cashflows. Variable rate securities will be included. Students should be aware of the limitations of assumptions and mathematical techniques upon results. Although analysis will be concerned principally with 'risk–free' securities, students should be aware of the further considerations for 'risky' securities and the effect they may have on expected return. Students should possess a thorough comprehension of single–period and multi–period, single currency and multi–currency portfolio management theory.

Forecasting techniques

- Simulation and simple time series modelling (with an awareness of the limitations imposed by the assumptions and mathematical techniques employed)

1 Economic Forecasts

1.1 Definition

An economic forecast is a prediction of future economic events. It may represent a complete guess based purely on opinion, as is probably the case with many politically inspired forecasts. Alternatively, it may be based on an econometric model which has been established through the quantitative analysis of past economic data in conjunction with economic theory. It is the latter of these two methods that we are concerned with in this session.

1.2 The need for forecasts

Almost all organisations and individuals make plans, which involve some assessment of the current and likely future state of the economy.

- From a personal viewpoint, the scale of mortgage that you may be prepared to take on will undoubtedly be influenced by current interest rates and how you expect them to move.
- From a corporate viewpoint, major investment programmes may be dependent upon demand for the ultimate product which may, in turn, be dependent on anticipated exchange rates.
- From an employee viewpoint, pay claims will be, to an extent, determined by levels of inflation experienced and expected in the future.
- From a government viewpoint, economic forecasting is central to policy decision making in almost all major industrialised nations.

Although the required levels of economic detail may vary from user to user, economic forecasts have their uses to everyone.

1.3 Forecasting models

1.3.1 Theoretical models

Economic theory is derived from a consideration of common sense/human behaviour. It describes a part of the economy (microeconomics) or the economy as a whole (macroeconomics) in the form of words, diagrams or mathematical expressions. The theories indicate which of the major economic variables influences others.

Mathematical expressions of economic theory often predict the sign or direction of movement of an economic variable to a change in economic circumstances, or take the form of an inequality, although in general they are unable to predict the magnitude of the response.

For example, it is generally accepted that demand will fall as prices rise (one variable influences another), however, this microeconomics theory does not enable us to determine immediately the fall in demand that will occur as a result of, say, a 10% increase in the price of wood. The theory itself does not quantify the relationship, this needs to be separately assessed.

1.3.2 Econometric models

Econometric models are concerned with *quantifying* these theoretical relationships between economic variables. The models are derived using statistical techniques applied to historical data in order to measure the relationships indicated by the theoretical models.

Such models can then be used for economic forecasting assuming that the relationships that have been established are relatively stable.

2 Construction of Econometric Models

2.1 Introduction

Econometric models may be considered as being developed in a series of stages, specifically

- *Specification* – the determination and practical extension of the various underlying economic theories.
- *Estimation* – the statistical quantification/measurement of the relationship;
- *Testing and final model selection* – checking the accuracy of the various alternative models based on past data, and the selection of the most appropriate.
- *Forecasting with the model* – using the selected model to make future economic predictions.

Although it is easier to describe these stages as discrete steps, in truth they may be undertaken simultaneously.

Each of these stages has some associated problems, or requires an element of judgement which may translate into forecasting errors and differences between differing forecasting groups. This last factor always needs to be appreciated, macroeconomic modelling is *not* a precise science.

2.2 Specification of the model

Initial model specification will be based on the various economic theories that exist governing the areas in question, with a view to establishing the relevant equations and variables involved. Specification involves the extension and modification of these theoretical equations to make allowances for the complexities of the real world.

A complete macroeconometric model will consist of a number of interrelated equations representing the various macroeconomic relationships explaining the economy as a whole. The choice of the theories considered and tested will clearly have an impact on the effectiveness and usefulness of the final model or forecasting purposes.

In constructing an econometric model we must allow for *all* the various economic theories, since testing the theories with historical data may provide evidence to determine which is more appropriate.

We also need to give consideration to the form of the relationships. Frequently in economic theory, equations are described in a simple linear form. This tends to be more for simple convenience of understanding rather than an assertion as to the true relationship.

When constructing an econometric model we need to determine the true form of the relationship, i.e. linear, exponential or polynomial. If the economic theory is inconclusive, we may need to try various alternatives to see if one proves to be more accurate and reliable than the others.

2.3 Estimation of model coefficients

2.3.1 Modelling techniques

Once the models have been specified, the relationship between the variables needs to be measured. Estimation is the application of statistical techniques to historical data to quantify and test the effects specified in the equations. Estimation or measurement may involve the use of either

- Regression analysis (probably multiple regression); or
- Time series analysis.

Tests applied during estimation may allow the model to be simplified if the effects of particular variables prove to be either irrelevant or directly related. The estimation may alternatively show that the model is inconsistent with the historical data.

As a result, the model will need to be re-specified and re-estimated. As noted earlier, these stages, strictly speaking, are not distinct.

When all the model coefficients have been measured, the model is often referred to as a structure. Models that are structurally stable are clearly the most useful to forecasters, models that are subject to periodic structural change are less so unless this change can somehow be predicted and incorporated as, say, a seasonal fluctuation.

2.3.2 Regression analysis

The use of regression analysis for the estimation of model coefficients is appropriate if we believe all variations are independent of time.

Where, as is likely, the proposed models include several input variables, multiple regression analysis would need to be undertaken to determine the various coefficients.

One statistic that is automatically produced as a result of regression analysis is an assessment of the goodness of fit of the resultant regression line in the form of either the correlation coefficient or R^2 coefficient. These will be important in helping us to select the final model where several potential alternatives exist.

2.3.3 Time series analysis

This is appropriate if we believe that the value of the output variable varies with time and that there may be some relationship from one period to the next.

We can use time series analysis to establish the following.

- *Basic trend* – underlying general long-term movement in the value of the observed variable over time.
- *Cyclical variations* – long-term regular fluctuations that may take several years to complete a full cycle.
- *Seasonal variations* – regular repeating short-term fluctuations that complete a full cycle within a given period, typically one year.
- *Random variation* – random fluctuations arising as a result of unpredictable factors such as floods, strikes, elections.

Time series analysis assumes that there is only one input variable, time. Most economic theories require more input variables, hence this may be oversimplistic. It may well be, however, that the variables in question do demonstrate a strong time dependency, e.g. GDP growth, in which case the method may have some merit.

The basic approach to time series analysis is

- Identify the basic trend – The idea of time series analysis is that if we average over a sufficiently long period of time we will cancel out the effects of any regular (seasonal and cyclical) variations and the effects of any truly random events leaving us with just the underlying trend.
- Identify the variations – by comparing the actual readings to this trend.
- Split out the variations – for example by averaging the same season each year we should be able to remove the effects of random factors leaving just the seasonal variation.

There are a number of problems with this technique, specifically

- It can only deal with known regular cycles.
- It can only deal with small random events, large random events (e.g. the effects of an earthquake) are unlikely to be cancelled out by other more favourable ones.
- Data is effectively 'lost' as a result of the averaging process.
- It does not automatically produce measures indicating the goodness of fit of the model, that do result from linear regression. It is possible, however, to calculate the standard deviations of the residual error terms (the random variations) for the various alternative models and use these to assess the relative goodness of fit of these various models.
- There may be issues with the data availability, volumes, accuracy and timeliness, discussed below.

2.3.4 Problems associated with estimation

Data volumes

As a result of the need to test a variety of different potential models, each with several variables and coefficients that need to be established, the volumes of data and data processing requirements may become immense, requiring very powerful and expensive computing equipment whose expense is out of proportion to the benefit that may be derived from the use of the results.

The cost-effectiveness of the modelling may then be brought into question. The only solution, if this is the case, is to simplify the model specifications to reduce the data volumes and processing requirements. The obvious downside of this is that there is likely to be a consequent reduction in forecasting accuracy, once again bringing into question its cost-effectiveness.

Alternatively, a lack of data, i.e. incomplete data or data only gathered over the very recent past, may prove inadequate for our estimation purpose as the resultant coefficients that we establish may not be statistically significant.

Data collection timescales

In order to measure the model coefficients within acceptable error levels, a reasonable volume of data will be required. For example, monthly figures for the last five years would give us only 60 values which may be inadequate to show that the calculated coefficients are statistically significant, i.e. we are suffering from a lack of data. We may therefore wish to consider longer timescales.

There is, however, a trade-off that needs to be accepted when using longer run data rather than short run data to determine the various coefficients, specifically a longer measurement period will result in

- More measurements and hence a potentially more accurate regression result than would be the case over a shorter time frame.
- Greater potential for variations to occur in the values of the coefficients than would be the case over a shorter time frame.
- Greater impacts of genuinely unusual events, such as catastrophes or war, distorting the calculations.

To test for stability of the coefficients or effects of unusual events, we could examine a number of sub-periods and measure the coefficients within these sub-periods to see if they are reasonably stable, i.e. if there is structural stability within the model.

If this is not the case, then we should only include in our analysis the data over the more recent past, during which there does appear to have been some stability, although we would need to accept the resulting loss in statistical validity. We may also consider weighting the measurements such that the most recent ones, being most representative of current events, are given more emphasis.

Data availability and timeliness

A lot of the data we may wish to use in our econometric model will be monthly, quarterly or annual government/official statistics, all of which is subject to a time delay in publishing.

Monthly statistics such as PSBR, trade statistics, retail sales, CPI statistics and monetary measures are frequently subject to a delay of three or more weeks before publishing. Quarterly statistics such as GDP or balance of payment estimates are frequently subject to a delay in excess of two months. Annual statistics such as Inland Revenue income distribution statistics are frequently subject to a delay of a year or more.

As we can see, the data may well be one period out of date when it is published, hence our forecasts for the next period cannot be based on the most recent data but must be based on earlier periods, reducing their accuracy.

Data measurement

In addition to the time delay for the initial publishing of data, many government economic statistics are subject to longer term (often significant) revisions as more accurate information becomes available later. For example, the average revision in the figure for GDP is approximately 0.8%, which is quite large considering that GDP growth is generally of the order of 2% to 3%. Information from other independent research organisations, e.g. the CBI, also suffers the same problems.

If the data represent either input or output variables used to test the model, it will result in mis-estimation of the various coefficients. If used as the input to a model for forecasting purposes, this sort of mis-statement could clearly lead to significant forecasting errors.

To compound the problem, initial official statistics/forecasts may deliberately give incorrect measures in an attempt to induce some change in private sector behaviour.

2.4 Testing and selecting the final model

2.4.1 Testing

Once the models have been specified and fully estimated they need to be tested to determine their accuracy/usefulness so that a final model may be selected. Once more, strictly speaking, testing is not a separate phase, but is part of the overall model development process.

2.4.2 Selection of the final model

We may now have produced two or more alternative models that are as well specified and estimated as possible and both of which have produced reasonable results following testing. The question is how do we select the final model to use?

The selection of the final model will depend on the accuracy demonstrated by the model based on the past data, i.e. the goodness of fit. Our aim is to find a model that explains as much of the observed variation as possible, or leaves as little as possible unexplained. As a result, we will select the model that demonstrates

- The highest correlation or R^2 coefficient if we have used regression analysis.
- The lowest standard deviation of random fluctuations if we have used time series analysis.

3 Interest Rate and Yield Curve Forecasting

So far, we have seen how to compute the value of the yield – the implied interest rate in a bond. We have seen how these yields fit together to form a picture of the market at a point in time (the yield curve) and how this yield curve itself is dominated by the influences of liquidity preference and the expectation of future yields (though this picture is distorted by supply and demand effect of government issues and preferred habitat).

Implicitly within this analysis we have considered what makes up interest rates and yields and how they are affected by forces such as inflation and economic policy. We now need to consider more formally how interest rates are arrived at within the economy and the forces that work on them, and from this point consider how to develop a model for forecasting interest rates and yields into the future.

The commercial rationale behind such forecasting is obvious, for if the market says one thing and our expectation is something else, then provided that the market moves to our expectations, there are considerable profits to be made.

4 The Composition of the Yield

From the section on discounted cash flows we saw that the interest rate (r) may be determined as follows

$(1 + r) = (1 + i)(1 + R)$

where

i = rate of inflation
R = real rate of return

From our study of yield we saw that the factors affecting the yield of a government bond are

- r – interest rate which drives the yield on short dated gilts.
- Liquidity preference.
- Expectations of future interest rate and inflationary changes.
- Supply of new issues.
- Demand for bonds.

For corporate bonds we would expect a higher yield than for government issues to cover for

- Credit/default risk.
- Liquidity risk.
- Issue specific risks.
- Fiscal risk (e.g. tax changes).
- Foreign currency risk (if not sterling bonds).

From our study of foreign currency we saw that

$$\text{Forward rate} = \frac{1+r_s}{1+r_p} \times \text{Spot rate}$$

This is that interest rate differentials between economies influence foreign exchange rates, impacting on factors such as UK economic growth and inflation. Hence even if UK interest rates remain steady a change in overseas interest rates may well have an impact on the required yields of UK bonds.

Finally we know from our study of the money markets that the role of the Monetary Policy Committee is to control inflation and that its only tool in this respect is the setting of interest rates.

It is clear, therefore, that there are many factors that influence the yield on a specific bond and if we wish to forecast yields or yield curves for a certain class of bonds we will need to consider all of these factors.

5 THE REAL RATE OF RETURN

Any household has a simple choice with regard to the income that they earn. They can either spend that money (consumption) or they can save it. The principal motivation to save will be interest, in that if a household does defer its consumption it will earn an extra return on its savings enabling a greater level of consumption in the future.

Arguably, the real rate of return is the same for all investment products. The only reason that yields themselves differ would be the different risks attached to different investment products.

5.1 How is the real rate established?

There are a number of theories concerning the establishment of real rates of interest. As a start we will look at the simplest. Note, we are looking at some basic economic theories. Whilst these will provide some background knowledge, it is extremely unlikely that they will be examined in any detail.

5.2 Classical loanable funds theory

Loanable funds theory suggests that the interest rate is the product of demand and supply. Demand in this sense is the demand for loanable funds driven by the desire for investment (and other uses) and supply is the supply of loanable funds, i.e. savings.

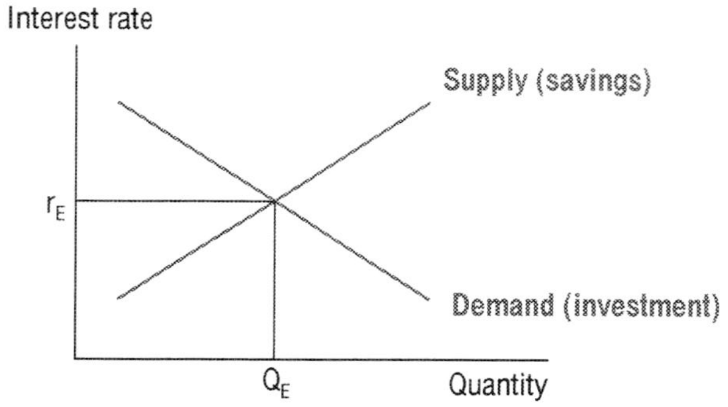

These two forces of demand and supply will find their balance point and that balance will give an equilibrium rate of interest. This equilibrium rate of interest reflects the forces in the economy at that point in time and is the point at which they will balance.

Loanable funds theory is a small element of the overall classical general equilibrium model, and as such it contains the same basic assumptions. The model works within the parameters of Say's Law, in that the market will always move to equilibrium, adjusting through the price mechanism, in this case the interest rate. For example, if demand for investment exceeded supply in savings, this would lead to upward pressure on real rates. As real rates rise, this encourages the households to save rather than consume and consequently savings rise in order to meet the demand from investment.

Whilst this is undoubtedly a simple model, it is the foundation for many studies on interest rate behaviour in the economy and is the theoretical backing to funds flow analysis.

5.3 Funds flow analysis

Funds flow analysis breaks down the economy into its key component parts. The private sector which would include households and businesses, the public sector, the government, the financial sector, banks and securities houses and the international sector.

Each of these segments of the economy has its own role to play in either the creation or the absorption of funds generated during a year. For example, the households and non-financial businesses will be the key generators of savings. These savings will then be allocated potentially to their own requirements (expenditure) with the remainder (saving) being available for other uses, in particular government and international financing.

5.3.1 Private net saving

Private net saving in this analysis will cover both the households and the corporate sector.

The households

Household savings will be driven by a number of factors and will certainly change as the economy cycles between booms and busts. Savings will tend to fall in the boom period when people are less concerned about what the future might hold.

Even behind this though there are some longer term themes. Looking at the US data would suggest (and this is not uncommon for most of the G7 nations) that savings ratios have been falling progressively since the 1950s. This data would tie in with certain economic models that have attempted to analyse consumption and saving patterns. Perhaps most importantly, they would tie in fairly strongly with the life cycle hypothesis.

The life cycle hypothesis is driven by the belief that consumers go through three stages of development. In the initial stage, youth, consumers tend to spend all of, if not more than, their earnings, making up for the excess expenditure by borrowing. This phase of expenditure would be the early stage of an individual's life when they are building up all of the consumer goods which they require. Subsequently, consumers would then move into a more savings orientated phase as they begin to consider the prospect of retirement. Finally, consumers revert back to a more consumption orientated philosophy spending more than they earn as they actually enter retirement. At this stage, they are using their capital to cover the excess of their expenditure over their income.

This theory also ties in with Milton Friedman's theory of the permanent income hypothesis, which suggests that consumers have a view of their own long-term permanent income and spend according to this view. Of course, tied up with the whole life cycle hypothesis is the concept that income increases over life, in line with career seniority, building up to retirement.

Corporate sector savings

The households are, of course, only one element of the savings matrix. Corporations will also have surplus cash. However, it should be noted that corporations may also be significant drains upon the system and consequently, their net contribution may be not particularly significant. As with consumers, the corporate sector's ability to generate savings will again often link in to the economic cycle.

5.3.2 The financial sector

This sector may be either explicitly dealt with in the matrix or implicitly left in the corporate sector. Financial institutions are important in that they act as generators of savings by recycling money through the financial system.

The ability of the financial sector to create investable funds out of a limited savings pool through the credit creation multiplier has been reduced over the last decade by the imposition of greater regulatory control. On an international level, the Bank of International Settlements (BIS) in Basel introduced more stringent controls on the use of capital and exposure levels. These controls were introduced in the wake of the Latin American debt crisis of the early 1980s. The consequence of this is that the banking industry is unable to expand its balance sheet to the same degree as before and therefore there is less credit available.

Within the EU, this has been reinforced by the introduction of the Capital Requirements Directives. The introduction of these new controls once again limits the freedom of the banking markets to extend credit.

The importance of a solvent and successful financial system was demonstrated by the Japanese economy where, in the wake of the collapse of both property and share prices in the early 1990s, the Japanese banking market was undermined. Consequently, the banking sector's ability to extend credit to the industrial sector was limited. This led to a fairly dramatic decline in the economy and recovery is heavily dependent on the banking sector being able to provide the finance required.

5.3.3 Public sector

It has been an increasing feature of many markets, demonstrated by the American data above, that growth of government has been particularly significant in the last decades of the twentieth century. In the 1950s and 1960s, the government's financing tended to oscillate from mild deficit to surpluses on a regular basis. However, since the 1960s, it has tended to be deficit financing on a more consistent basis.

The growth of a large government deficit obviously has huge implications for the funds flow analysis. In essence, the government will be the priority borrower representing the safest, most secure bet, and therefore most attractive to relatively risk-averse investors. If the government is borrowing heavily from the system, this will tend to drain down available liquidity for other projects and, consequently, force up the interest rates that they have to offer in order to obtain financing.

In this way, we are beginning to move away from the single interest rate that loanable funds would suggest to different interest rates for different segments of the economy, representing the different supply and demand functions appropriate for private and public sector.

This phenomenon of high public sector borrowing forcing out the private sector is referred to as 'crowding out' and has long been cited as one of the problems of Keynesian economics by monetarist and neo-classical economists.

More recently, fiscal responsibility on the part of the government has brought the level of borrowing down. At present, many governments are working to reduce their deficits. In part, it is hoped that this will encourage 'crowding in' so as to free up resources for the private sector.

In a simple closed economy, these would be the only real sources and uses of funds. However, we live in a globalised economy and it is now impossible to ignore the impact of the international sector both as a source and as a use of funds.

BPP LEARNING MEDIA

5.3.4 The international sector

As we can see from the above data, such was the size of the American deficit during the 1980s and 1990s that it would have been impossible to finance it from domestic savings alone without forcing real interest rates to unpleasantly high levels. The saving grace of the economy was the ability to attract funding in from outside, albeit through an increase in real interest rates.

It must be remembered that it is not simply an inflow which is an issue here for the US economy, there are substantial outflows of investment capital being made from the US, particularly into the emerging markets.

Many commentators are currently arguing that the increasing pressures on the developed economies' capital markets, both from falling savings ratios and from rising demand, from both the public sector and the emerging markets, will lead to a further increase in real interest rates. As mentioned before, real interest rates have generally risen since the 1950s, only beginning to fall back in the late 1990s.

On its own, loanable funds theory explains the general rate of interest. What funds flow analysis does is to segment the macroeconomy down into smaller sub-divisions. Within these divisions, we can see where the money is being either created or utilised and in this way we will begin to see the variety of interest rates which are apparent in the economy.

5.3.5 Links to other theories of the yield curve

This segmentation links into some of the theories that we looked at when we considered the shape of the yield curve. Within the yield curve itself, we effectively looked at a limited version of loanable funds theory and funds flow analysis by considering the segmentation approach. Under segmentation theory, there are different users and providers of funds operating within their preferred habitats. The interplay of these two forces of supply and demand leads to different interest rates along the yield curve.

Loanable funds theory and funds flow analysis can also be applied to explaining liquidity preference. Liquidity preference was another feature of the yield curve whereby investors were tempted to go further along the yield curve and, therefore, take greater risk by being offered slightly higher rates of interest. Again, one could simply argue this is a supply and demand relationship driven by rational investors requiring appropriate real returns on their money.

5.4 The Keynesian view of the determination of interest rates

5.4.1 Introduction

Keynesian analysis is fundamentally different from the classical school. In the loanable funds approach that we have developed thus far, our assumption has been that savings are automatically invested. Any excess of supply or demand is then remedied by the interest rate, which will adjust to bring about equilibrium.

This view of the world accords with the classical model's innate belief in long-run full employment equilibrium. Perhaps this theory was relevant in the nineteenth century when the savers and investors were more often than not the same people, with entrepreneurs saving to finance their own investment.

Once the supply of savings and the demand for investment come from different motivations, then Keynes argues that there is no natural rationale for balance. Savings in the Keynesian model is the other side of consumption and is therefore linked to income. Investment is driven partly by interest rates and partly by the rate of growth of national income – the accelerator principle.

Therefore, in the Keynesian model there is no natural reason why the planned level of savings should equate with the rate of planned investment at the full employment level.

If the households increase their planned savings, this will have the impact of reducing consumption. A reduction in the level of consumption will reduce demand and therefore national income. A reduction in national income is unlikely to stimulate an increase in investment. In the classical loanable funds theory it was assumed that the increase in savings automatically led to an increase in investment demand through the operation of the interest rate. What then generates the interest rate in the Keynesian model?

In the Keynesian model interest rates are determined by the supply and demand for money. The demand for money is made up of three elements.

The first two elements of the demand for money are not particularly sensitive to the interest rate. Transactions demand is the amount of cash required to allow the individual to complete their desired transactions. Precautionary demand is the cash required in case of unexpected purchases.

The third element of demand is the speculative demand. This is related to the bond market. If the interest rate is low, then the price of bonds will be high. If bond prices are perceived to be high, then it is logical to expect them to fall. Consequently, rational investors will choose to hold their speculative assets in the form of cash, which will be safer than the bonds that are likely to fall in value, therefore, increasing the demand for cash balances.

Conversely, if rates are high and bond prices are felt to be low, the expectation will be that prices will rise. Once again, the rational consumer will choose at this stage to hold his/her speculative assets in the form of bonds. Therefore, at this stage the demand for speculative cash balances will be low.

It is this speculative demand for cash that is at the heart of the debate between the classical economists and Keynes. Classical theory suggests that if savings increase, then the interest rate will fall, therefore inducing an increase in investment. However, as interest rates begin to fall, bond prices will rise. At this stage, bearish speculators will start to believe that the price has risen as far as it can go and will sell bonds (and consequently hold cash) in response. The actions of these speculators will therefore ensure that prices cannot rise (or rates fall below) a certain level. This cut off in the fall of interest rates therefore prevents the pure classical model from working.

The combination of the three demands for money gives the total money demand function referred to as the **Liquidity Preference Schedule**.

The Keynesian Demand for Money

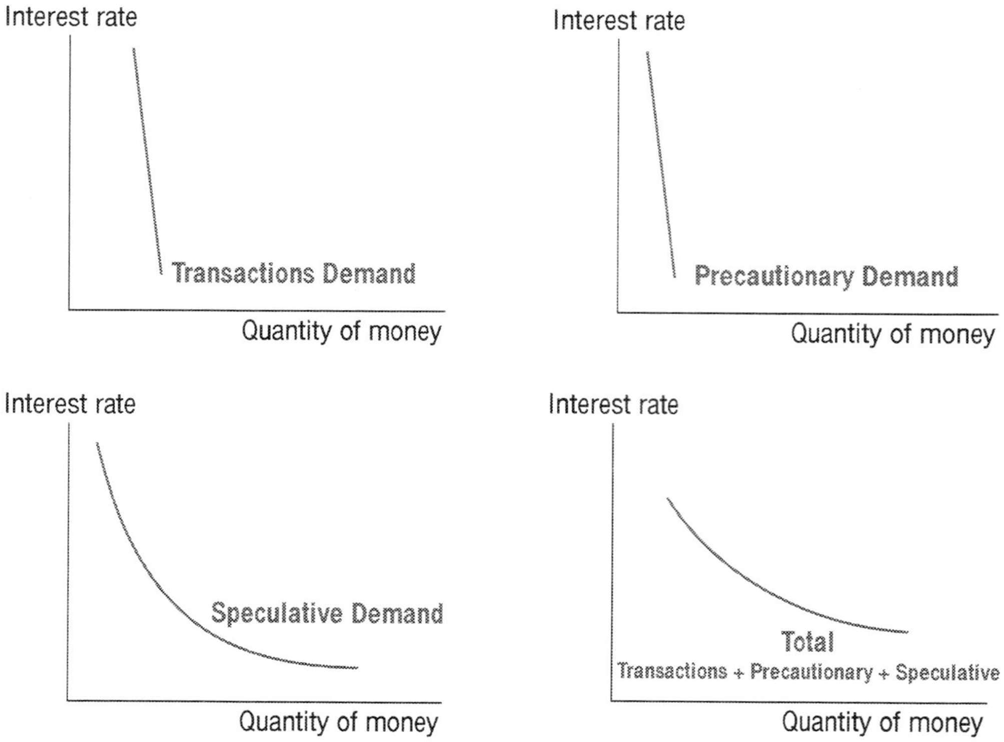

The interest rate is then determined by the interplay between money supply (set by the government) and the money demand.

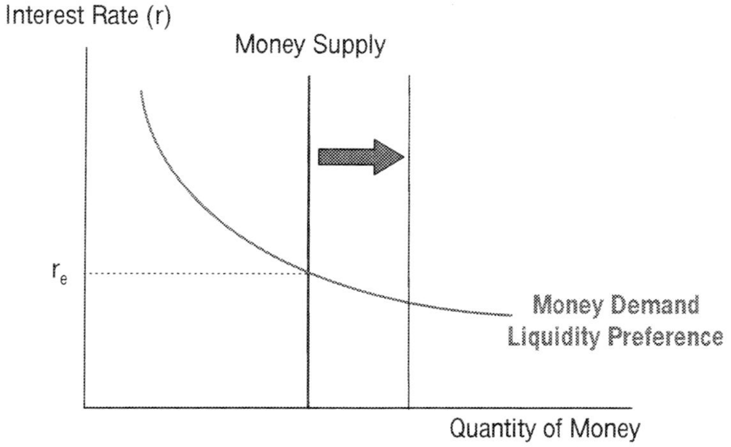

If money supply were to be increased, then this would lead to excess money balances. These would be absorbed by financial assets such as bonds and deposit accounts, thereby leading to an increase in demand and a consequent increase in price/reduction in yield. However, as constrained by the speculative demand for money rates it will not fall below a certain level. This demonstrates the ineffectiveness of monetary policy within the Keynesian model.

5.4.2 Reconciliation of the Keynesian and classical view

Whilst the models would appear to have diametrically opposed theoretical foundations, it is possible to reconcile them by arguing that the Keynesian model is only relevant for the short term with longer term rates being determined in line with the classical loanable funds theory.

6 INFLATION

So far we have been considering real rates of return. The rates of interest that are quoted in the market are nominal rates of interest. The difference between the two is crucial. For example, if nominal rates of interest are 10%, an investor who puts £100 on deposit will at the end of the year receive £10 in interest. So far, so good. However, inflation acts effectively as negative interest. What inflation does is to raise the price of goods that the consumer could buy. Therefore, to be able to buy the same number of goods at the end of the year as at the start of the year, they would actually need more money. If over the course of the same year, inflation had been running at the level of 8%, the real return to the investor would be of the order of 2%, since whilst their money has risen in nominal terms by 10%, its purchasing power has declined by 8% leaving them with a net return of 2%.

This relationship can be mathematically demonstrated using the Fisher relationship.

Formula to learn

$$(1 + r) = (1 + r)(1 + i)$$

where

r = nominal yield
R = Real yield
i = anticipated inflation

This formula provides the direct link between inflation, real rates and nominal rates. The nominal rates required by a bondholder reflect the real rate required by investors and protection against their expectation of inflation. It should be noted here that the inflation is not actual inflation at present, but expected inflation into the future. For example, if an investor required a real rate return of 3% and he had an expectation that inflation over the course of the life of the bond would average 5%, then he would require a nominal return of 3% real plus 5% inflation, i.e. roughly 8%. In this example, a simple additive approach has been used. It would be technically more correct to use the multiplicative approach, as laid down in the formula above.

More sophisticated versions of the Fisher relationship introduced a third term, leading to the construction of nominal rates. This third term is the risk premium.

Formula to learn

Fisher relationship – Risk premium = $(1 + r) = (1 + r)(1 + i)(1 + Pr)$

where

Pr = Risk premium

As mentioned earlier in this chapter, the risk premium is an adjustment to reflect the risk of our expectation of inflation being wrong. It is, of course, relatively difficult to differentiate between straight inflation and premium and the risk premium for errors in forecast. However, this would explain the difference between the implicit inflation expectations in bond prices (derived from the difference between the real yield on index-linked gilts and the yield on conventional issues) and the consensus economic forecast of both the government and City analysts.

Arguably, these risk premiums only became relevant during the 1970s when investors were caught out several times by inflation rates exceeding expectations leading to low or even negative real rates of return.

Equally, much of the correction which took place in 1994 after the bond bull run overheated in 1993 was to restore a risk premium in those markets in which it had been eroded beyond rational boundaries. Since then the emergence of the 'new paradigm' has further reduced the uncertainty premium.

Regardless of semantics as to whether it is inflation expectations and risk premium or pure inflation expectations, we can see that inflation has a crucial role in determining the level of yields appropriate for the market. It is crucial, therefore, to understand what leads to inflation and perhaps, more importantly, leads to changes in the expectation of future inflation.

6.1 Economic policy

Crucial to expectations of future inflation will be the credibility and focus of economic policy.

6.1.1 Focus of policy

Over the past 35 years, government economic policy has changed in focus fundamentally. Initially, in the post-war environment, most, if not all, governments were committed to an anti-unemployment policy, with an unequivocal commitment to full employment and a limited focus on inflation. The principal exception to this was Germany where, for historical reasons, there had always been a relatively strong fear of inflationary pressures.

The anti-unemployment commitments of the 1950s and early 1960s switched within the framework of Keynesian demand management to a commitment to achieving economic growth. Once again, inflation was at this stage a secondary consideration with regard to the framing of economic policy.

Since the mid-1970s, the focus has shifted and now, arguably, all of the major industrialised nations have a primary focus of policy towards inflation. Indeed, in most nations, inflation is regarded as being the only economic variable that the government has any control over. The argument used is that inflation is the key disrupter of economic activity through the creation of uncertainty and the control of inflation will bring with it key benefits such as a reduction in uncertainty premiums and a natural tendency for the economy to grow. This growth in turn will resolve any unemployment issues that may have been created in the initial control of inflation.

Since the 1970s, the UK government has been committed to an anti-inflationary policy. This has not, however, prevented inflation from frequently recurring in the UK and, in addition to the primary focus of policy, one would have to address the issue of credibility. Going back to our earlier analysis of the breakdown of nominal rates into real inflation premiums and risk premiums, the lack of credibility of a government would certainly tend to increase the risk premiums attached to their government bond market.

6.1.2 Credibility

Whilst governments may well espouse inflation control as a primary focus of economic policy, the inflationary expectations factored into the market will reflect the market's belief in this commitment to low inflation.

As we saw in the previous chapter, the UK government initially espoused a hard-line monetarist approach arguing on theoretical and dogmatic grounds that this should control inflation. This was linked in with a relatively long-term view of economic policy laid down in the medium-term financial strategy (MTFS). Combined with a doctrine of rational expectations this was supposed to lead to a benign return to government economic policy.

The logic here is that the government espouses a long-term commitment theoretically supported by monetary economics that control of the money supply will lead to control of inflation. The government lays down criteria for judging policy as a basis for this in order to test its own credibility and sets these criteria into the future. As the government begins to achieve its targets, the logic is that the market should begin to believe the government's credibility and as a benign return, implicitly factor out future expectations in inflation.

The rationale behind this is that the government commits itself to a plan of action and 'come hell or high water' sticks to it, therefore showing its credibility. This is all well and good if the policy is likely to be successful and is theoretically founded on strong grounds. However, it is politically and economically damaging if the opposite is true.

Monetarism foundered in the early 1980s because the theoretical link between money supply and inflation proved, in practice, less than strong. In the early 1980s, as the government attempted to control money supply, money supply grew. The only positive aspect of this was that inflation itself actually fell.

Towards the mid/late 1980s, the government turned to a second benchmark of credibility, the exchange rate.

Initially, the government adopted an informal policy of shadowing the DM, which was ultimately abandoned due to the government choosing an exchange rate that was too low given the economic circumstances at that time. In October 1990, the government revisited the idea of exchange rate targeting, but this time in a more formal and rigid way by joining the ERM. This mechanism tied sterling to our major trading competitors in continental Europe, thereby ensuring that if the UK were to remain within its currency bands, inflation rates could not rise above the lowest or benchmark inflation rates within the ERM system (implicitly assumed to be Germany).

This rigid currency link with a country with a proven track record of low inflation was supposed to act as a credibility signal for the UK government's anti-inflationary policy. Once the benefits of this policy had begun to flow through, the expectation was that the UK yield curve would converge with that of Germany, a situation that had already taken place with regard to French yield curves.

Unfortunately for the UK economic policy, sterling could sustain the agreed exchange rate against wave after wave of selling in the forex market. In September 1992, sterling was forced out of the ERM and the second attempt to target the exchange rate failed – ironically this time it was because the government chose a rate that was too high given the economic circumstances of the day.

6.1.3 Inflation targets – Independent Central Bank

With sterling's exit from the ERM in 1992 and the collapse of the system in 1993, the government had to look for a new way of guaranteeing credibility with regard to anti-inflation performance. The government felt that the introduction of inflation targets might be a way of achieving this and in 1993, the government established clear inflation targets that inflation should lie between 1% and 4% and fall to the range 1% to 2½% by the end of the Parliament.

Arguably, inflation targets established by politicians, who will always be conscious of the need for re-election, do not guarantee much stability of policy or credibility of commitment. Consequently, many commentators called for additional controls to ensure the targets were met.

One of the most often called-for controls was the introduction of an Independent Central Bank with prime responsibility for the maintenance of the inflation target and the control of monetary policy. In this way, the key aspect of economic policy, inflation, would be taken away from politicians and handed to the Central Bank.

In May 1997, Chancellor Brown announced the operational independence of the Bank of England, thereby bringing the UK into line with both the US and Euroland, where both the ECB and the Federal Reserve have considerable degrees of autonomy.

The immediate impact of his surprise announcement was that yields on the longer dated issues fell by around 50 basis points. This fall in yields reflected the market's revised expectations of future inflation in the UK under an independent central bank.

The initial inflation targets have been refined to require the Bank to generate long-term price inflation of around 2% as measured using the CPI. In order to avoid any potential deflationary bias which could arise from a single target, the range of acceptable outcomes is 1% either side of this 2% goal.

6.1.4 The role of the International Capital Markets

Arguably, the importance of an Independent Central Bank has been supplanted by the globalisation of international financial markets. Many commentators would argue that the power of these markets is now so substantial in the framing of economic policy that the mere independence of a central bank is no longer a requirement for a credible approach to inflation.

The logic here is that if a government were to attempt to stimulate the economy beyond its stable level, the markets would act in such a way as to immediately eradicate the impact of that move. For example, if the UK government were to introduce a massive fiscal reflationary package in order to resolve an unemployment crisis, then the result of this would be an uncertainty by international holders of sterling as to its long-term value. This would lead, in turn, to a sell-off in the gilts market, which would force yields along the yield curve to rise.

As assets in sterling were sold and sterling converted in the foreign exchange markets into more acceptable international investment currencies, this would lead to a downward pressure on sterling, which, if it reached significant levels, would require the government to take action or to support the currency. The primary vehicle they would have for supporting the currency would, of course, be to increase short-term interest rates and, therefore, invalidate any expansionary fiscal package.

The end result of such an over-expansion would simply be that the inflation risk premium has been increased slightly but, overall, government policy had been overruled by the financial markets.

The one key flaw in this argument is that it does assume that the international capital markets are perfectly logical in their approach to the regulation of policy and have perfect knowledge. It would be entirely plausible that a government could take a number of actions which, in retrospect would appear to be profligate, but which at the time appeared totally laudable to the financial markets. As such, the markets would only penalise the economy in question once the actions had already been taken and had effect and consequently, the policing power of the markets may not be all that we would wish.

6.2 Policy signals

As we have discussed above, governments have undoubtedly become more clearly associated with anti-inflation commitments over the past 20 years and by a number of means they have attempted to enhance the credibility of their policy.

Crucial to their effectiveness in terms of controlling inflation will be their ability to judge market signals appropriately. In New Zealand, the government introduced an Independent Central Bank with a strong commitment towards controlling inflation. However, the Central Bank missed key inflationary signals and as a consequence inflation breached the target ranges. This clearly illustrates that mere mechanics of independent central banks will not guarantee a long-run commitment to the control of inflation. What is perhaps slightly more important will be the experience of the implementers of policy, such as the Governor of the Central Bank, in judging the economic signals.

Obviously, for any trader in the bond markets, the ability to judge these signals is equally important, for this will determine the expectations of inflation that the market holds into the future. Let us now look at a number of the key economic indicators and the way in which they will be interpreted by the market.

6.2.1 Economic growth

The quarterly release of growth figures will of course have an important impact upon the market. The importance with regard to inflation is the rise in the level of output and its proximity to the full employment ceiling. The spare capacity of the economy is referred to as the output gap and is of course a relatively subjective measure since we will only really know when we have gone through the capacity constraint by the presence or otherwise of inflation.

The economic growth statistics will also shed light on the effectiveness of recent government policy, such as alteration in the level of interest rates.

6.2.2 Money supply

In the early 1980s, money supply was somewhat dogmatically regarded as a direct signal of inflationary pressures in the economy, the logic being that if money supply were to rise, then 9 to 24 months later inflation would follow. There are now very few governments who would dogmatically hold to this view. Many would undoubtedly espouse fundamentally monetarist convictions but on a pragmatic scale acknowledge that inflation is not always and everywhere a monetary phenomenon.

For example, the Bundesbank would closely monitor money supply and the market would wait for the release of the official statistics each month with the anticipation that the Bundesbank would respond to an untoward movement. However, the Bundesbank became less dogmatic and, if money supply were to rise in one month, would not automatically take action. There may be a number of economic justifications for such a shift in money supply and, as a consequence, policy would not necessarily change.

Money supply is, however, a good indicator of the level of activity in the economy and is undoubtedly important in monitoring inflationary pressures.

6.2.3 Aggregate demand

Aggregate demand, as we have already seen in the Keynesian model, can be broken down into a number of component elements, consumption, investment and government spending. Undoubtedly, these areas of demand will be closely monitored by the markets and the policy setters to estimate the inflationary pressures that may exist within the economy.

Many analysts have attempted to estimate the level of economic activity within each of the major economies, which would represent a non-inflationary, yet full employment position. They then attempt to measure the current position of the economy against this theoretical ceiling level, the gap in between being referred to as the output gap. As output gaps begin to narrow, then inflationary pressures begin to increase manifested in such items as skills shortages and wage level increases.

Therefore, all markets will closely monitor the quarterly release of figures regarding the output of the economy, judging these as an indicator of the narrowness or otherwise of the output gap and, therefore, the likelihood of inflationary pressures.

The market will also look for signs of collateral damage to inflationary prospects such as earnings increases and factory gate price increases, all often regarded as leading indicators of inflationary pressures. In some economies, even such unusual aspects as new car registrations can be seen as a symptom of expanding aggregate demand and as a leading indicator of potential inflationary pressures.

6.2.4 Commodity prices

All major industrialised economies are subject to potential inflationary pressures from increases in commodity prices. For example, the two major inflationary peaks of the 1970s were undoubtedly the direct result of the oil crises in 1973/74 and in 1979.

Whilst many economists argue that the direct link between commodity prices and retail prices is at best a weak link, if there were to be massive changes in import prices, then it is unlikely that output prices could remain totally unmoved, which is likely to feed through to retail prices.

These then are the key signals of economic policy. There are undoubtedly more indicators than the brief summary we have gone through above, but these are the most important. What is crucial, is how the government responds to the signals.

6.3 Policy weapons

6.3.1 Introduction

In direct opposition to the 1950s, 1960s and early 1970s, fiscal policy is regarded as a peripheral aspect of the government's armoury with regard to inflation. The focus is almost absolutely on the use of monetary policy in order to control the economy.

6.3.2 Imperfections of policy

The objectives of economic policy may be clear. The signals used to interpret the movement of the economy may be established over time and be consistent. The government's policy may be appropriate. It still may not all come together or perhaps more accurately may not all come together in time. Economic policy is dogged by a series of lags. There is a time lag between the economy changing and the government becoming aware of this through the official statistics.

Most official statistics are produced in excess of a month after the event and trends may take several months to emerge from what is often a chaotic picture. Consequently, the signals may be there, but the government may not see them until several months after the point at which they ought to have taken appropriate action. Even once action is taken, delays will again take place, lagging the introduction of the policy and its final end result.

A clear example of these lags can be seen in the UK in 1988 to 1990. In 1988, Chancellor Lawson increased interest rates from 7½% to 13% over the course of six months. Rates were further increased to 15% over the next 12 months. The objective of this policy was clearly to take the steam out of an economy that had grown too quickly.

Whilst it might be expected that such an increase in interest rates would slow the economy down, the actual slowdown itself did not begin to cut in until 1989 and the government could not be sure that the slowdown was sufficient until 1990. However, by this stage, the economy had moved into recession and by October 1990 monetary policy had to begin to reverse in order to alleviate the recessionary pressures which had begun to force the economy into negative growth.

However, since this point in time, the economy has become far more reactive to relatively small movements in policy. Historically, there has been a two-year lag between the implementation of policy and the economy's response. However, recent research by the Bank of England still indicates a two-year lag, but suggests that within this, the bulk of the impact is felt within a year.

This enhanced responsiveness has remained a feature of the UK and other major economies. Many commentators argue that at last we are seeing rational expectations theories at work. If key economic agents are more rational, then they will respond to policy more directly.

The variability of these time lags with regard to policy is obviously a hugely uncertain element within any expectation of inflation.

6.4 Interest rate policy and the economic cycle

6.4.1 Introduction

Interest rates are obviously crucial in determining the shape of the yield curve. Short-term rates are tied to money market rates, since effectively short-term bonds and money market instruments are the same risk, and, therefore, should also carry the same return. Longer yields are also sensitive to interest rates, this is because interest rates lead to inflation expectations and this is then reflected at the longer end of the yield curve.

Interest rate policy, as we have seen, tends to slightly lag the real economy in that the government tends to miss the turning points in the cycle. For example, in a typical economic cycle, as the economy begins to overheat, the government will respond to inflationary threats within the system, increasing interest rates as happened in 1988/89, 1994/95 and most recently in late 2006. The increase in interest rates will be designed to slow the economy down and to limit the inflationary pressures.

High interest rates in order to curb underlying growth and inflationary pressures will undoubtedly be successful. However, the problem is that the government will suffer information lags as we have already discussed, in that the government will not be able to see the economy turn before it is too late. This means that interest rates will remain too high for too long, inducing the economy to fall into a recession.

As the economy begins to go into recession, the government will respond by reducing interest rates in order to try and turn the economy round. Initially, their ability to reduce interest rates will undoubtedly be constrained by inflation performance only being able to reduce nominal interest rates as inflation begins to fall. As the economy and the government starts to reduce interest rates, the pressures will begin to abate and the economy's slowdown will begin to ease.

Interest rates will begin to fall, even as the economy reaches the absolute pit of the recession and indeed interest rates will continue to fall beyond that point in order to stimulate the recovery. In just the same way that interest rates remained at too high a level for too long at the peak of the economic cycle, interest rates will remain at too low a rate for too long at the depth of the recession. Logically, rates are low in order to encourage recovery and the early phases of any economic recovery are often extraordinarily fragile. However, the forces they then set in train within the recovery may well get out of control, leading to a surge in economic output and a return of the inflationary pressures that started this cycle off.

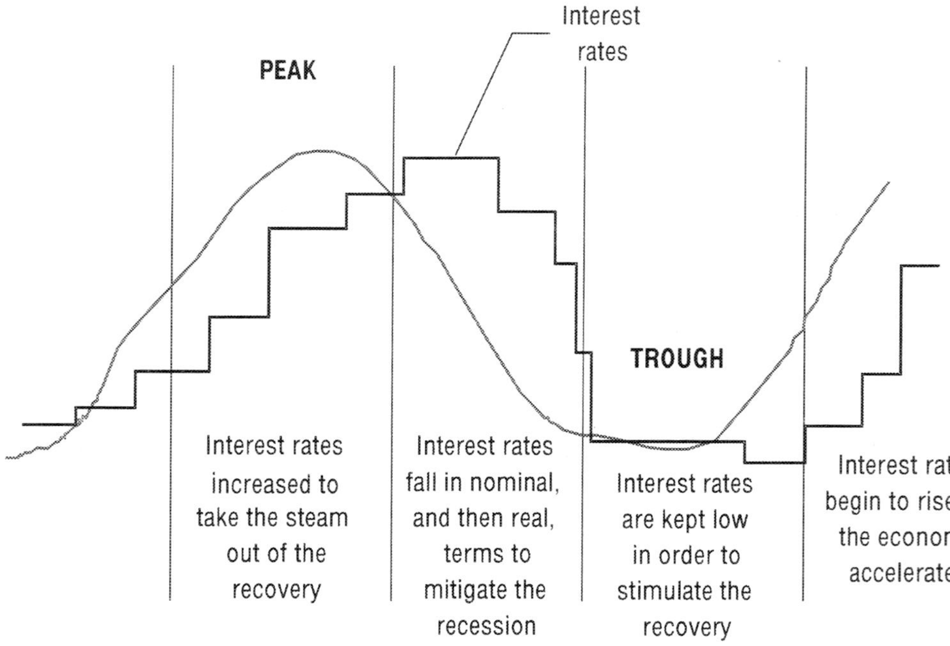

6.4.2 Is the cycle over?

At the turn of the century, many economists were beginning to argue that these lags in policy which lead to the interest rate driven economic cycle were no longer as extreme and, as a consequence, the cycle itself was coming to an end. This view has clearly been discredited by the credit crunch of 2008.

On the assumption that the economic cycle does, at least to some extent, reassert itself, despite the improvements in government economic policy, then there are certainly lessons to be drawn from the shape of the yield curve at different stages in the economic process.

For example, in the late phases of recovery as inflationary pressures begin to build and interest rates start to rise, the yield curve will tend to invert. This inversion reflects the fact that short-term rates increase beyond their normal level and long-term rates remain relatively stable, if not falling due to inflationary expectations being eased by tight monetary policy. This inversion will persist beyond the point at which the economic cycle has turned and the economy has begun to slow down. As the economy goes into recession, the inversion will begin to phase itself out.

Historically, the inversion of the yield curve has been seen as a good leading indicator of a recession. This is perhaps not too surprising. Inversions in this analysis represent situations where the policy makers have made mistakes. The turning point of the economy has been missed and interest rates have had to react strongly to bring it into line. The application of strong monetary policy will almost inevitably lead to a sharp slowdown in activity.

As short-term interest rates fall, the yield curve will move to a flat position and then gradually drift down as inflationary expectations are factored out of both the short and the long end of the yield curve.

As short-term rates continue to fall and are artificially reduced to relatively low levels to stimulate the recovery, the yield curve will steepen. This steepening will then continue into the recovery as inflation expectations begin to rise with the rise in the level of economic activity. In turn, short-term interest rates will begin to rise and as the economy overheats, rates will rise further going back to an inversion.

One interesting point to note is that the volatility evident within the UK yield curve has reduced markedly since 2000, which links in with the reduced volatility in the underlying economy.

It is clear that inflation is a crucial part of any yield and is difficult to forecast with any degree of accuracy due to the variety of influences at work. Crucial to understanding the role of inflation though is understanding the economic cycle and the way in which government policy is likely to respond and the consequent impacts of policy on the yield curve.

The short end of the yield curve is clearly reflective of the immediate expectations of policy. The longer end of the curve is more reflective of the background expectations within the economy.

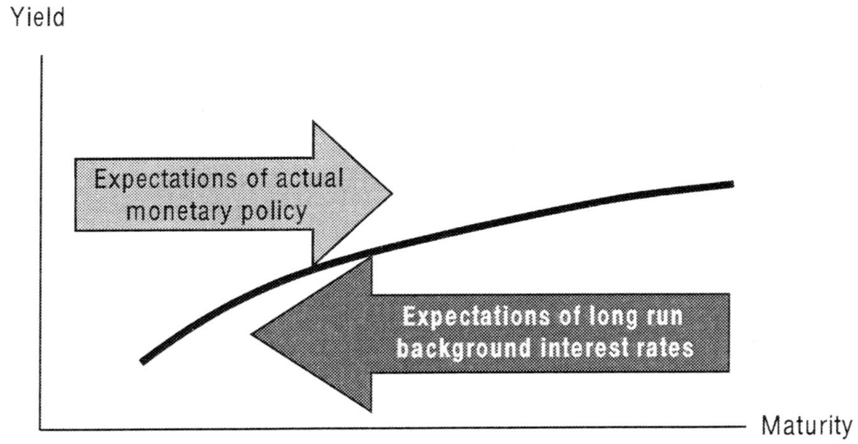

This is very evident if we look at the experience of the last few years. The long end of the curve has fluctuated within a relatively narrow range. This is reflective of the market's belief that, if real rates are around 2% – 2¼% and inflation will be delivered at 2%, then 4½% – 5% (allowing for some term premium) is not unfair. This view has not altered significantly in recent years. At short end, expectations of the next move in policy have varied as the economic picture has changed.

7 Credit Risk

7.1 Introduction

Another element in the construction of the yield would be a measure of return required to compensate the holder for credit risk inherent in holding a bond. Credit risk is obviously not particularly relevant for most developed government securities. However, it is obviously very significant with regard to the securities of corporates and certain supernational bodies.

That being said, any government issuing debt in a currency other than its own must have some form of credit risk and, indeed, with regard to certain emerging market debts, the government – even in its own base currency – would contain a significant credit risk, since its financial integrity would be far from certain.

However, the key risk must lie in the corporate sector and yields will endeavour to reflect the mark-ups required for credit risk. These mark-ups will vary with maturity and the innate creditworthiness of the firm.

It is conventional for corporate debt to price yields over the government bond yield curve as the following diagram shows with flows further into the future having a higher spread as a reflection of the greater uncertainty.

7.2 Yield curves

As the diagram below shows, the spread of an individual security against the appropriate benchmark will vary considerably. Once again for the corporate sector in particular, this will tie into the economic cycle since, as the economy expands, the credit risk will be diminished in the face of strong earnings flows. The opposite will tend to hold in recessions.

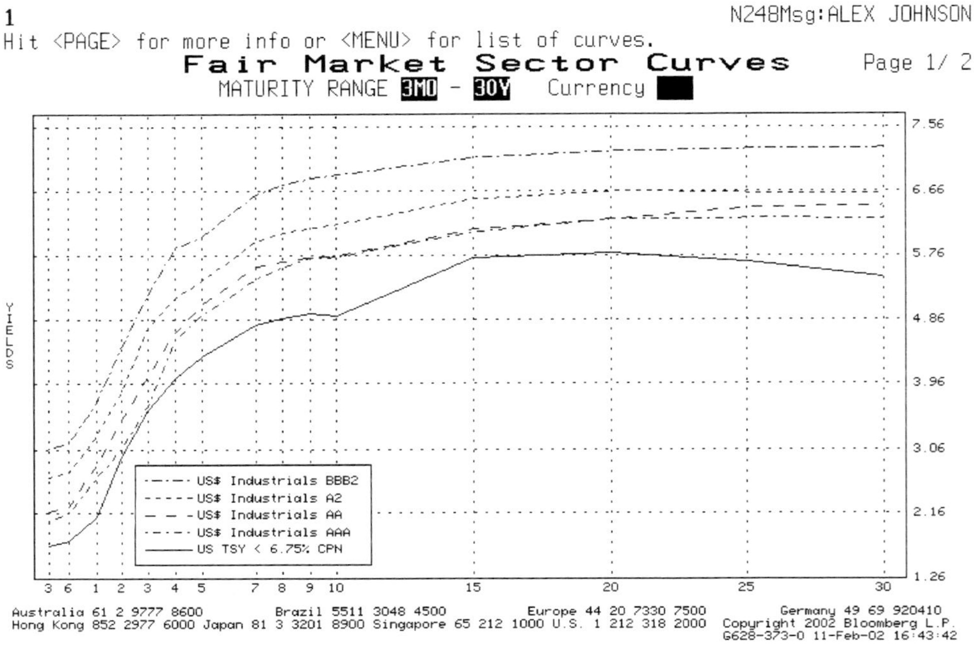

As you can see, the yield premia required on short-term debt are not particularly substantial, even for bonds of a much lower credit rating than AAA government. However, as maturities increase credit, risks also become greater as more uncertainties effect the ability of a company to repay its debt and consequently, the risk premia increase. These uncertainties will, of course, be exacerbated by the economic issues that we have already discussed regarding the inflation premium, for the creditworthiness of the corporate sector undoubtedly will be linked to its ability to earn income and is therefore driven by the economic cycle.

The following chart shows how this premia can change over time.

8 Relationships with Other Markets

The yields required from the government bond market will undoubtedly be affected by key relationships with other markets.

8.1 The money market

Obviously, the short-term anchor for the yield curve is the money market rates of interest. Short-term bonds are indistinguishable from government money market paper such as Treasury bills, which in turn are indistinguishable from CDs and eligible trade bills. Consequently, the rates of interest that the government manufactures through the money markets must be equivalent to the rates of interest offered in the bond markets and, as such, short-term money markets will obviously act as an anchor point for the yield curve.

Where this anchor point is perceived by the market to be unsustainable in the long run, then undoubtedly the market will exhibit a significantly steep short-term yield curve reflecting expectation of change.

8.2 The equity markets

In part, this analysis goes back to our analysis of loanable funds theory at the heart of real interest rates. The key flow of investable funds into the government bond market and, therefore, a very important impact on demand, will be institutional investment. Every year individuals within the economy save either consciously through unit trust investment or subconsciously through pensions and life assurance. These savings ratios will change over time and undoubtedly will be linked to economic growth and the economic cycle. Each year the institutions will benefit from an inflow of new investable funds.

The government bond market will only be one possible market into which these funds will be invested and the relative mix of investments will undoubtedly be driven by the returns on offer. It is certainly an argument to explain the upward shift of the yield curve during the recovery cycle of the economy by saying that at that stage, as the economy begins to recover, equity returns will be enhanced as dividend flows are increased and, consequently, equity markets will appear more attractive. As a result, investors will sell bonds and shift into equities and therefore the yield curve will shift up. Equally, this argument about the upward shift of the yield curve during the upward cycle of the economy can again be linked to expectations of inflation. In all of this analysis, nothing is certain and the breakdown of yields into real yields and inflation premiums is, at best, an estimate.

Equally, on the downside of the cycle as the economy goes into recession, the bond market will offer enhanced returns and consequently, funds will shift into bonds. This was evident during the crash of 1994. In 1992 and 1993, the bond market had been offering attractive returns and as a result, there was a substantial inflow of capital. When the market turned, these traditional holders of equity shifted back to their natural habitat. UBS estimates a withdrawal of some $750bn from the global bond market.

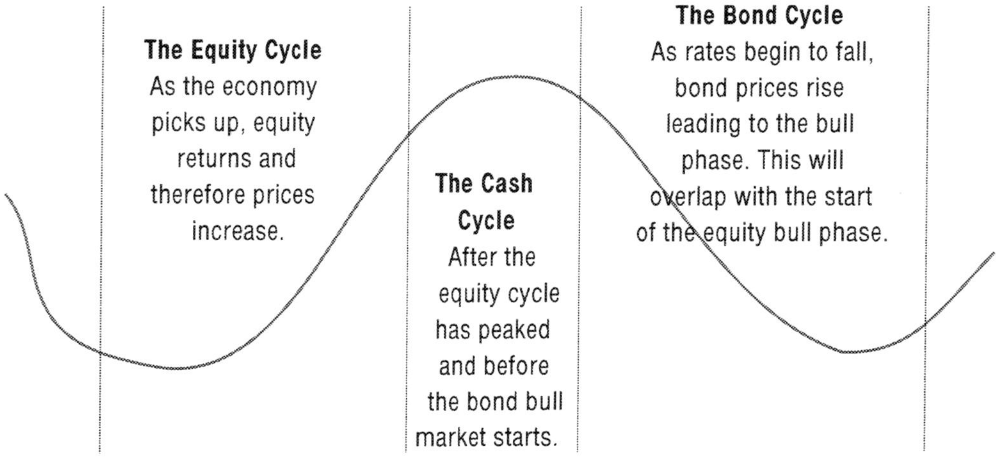

This competition with equity markets is not solely the UK equity market, but also, the international market for UK institutions are international investors currently holding 25% of their portfolio in non-UK invested assets.

8.3 The international markets

8.3.1 Introduction

Over the past 15 years, the government bond markets of the key G7 economies have been increasingly internationalised with greater and greater volumes of ownership from outside the domestic investor base. This process, which is far from complete, has led to a greater degree of correlation between the government bond markets than has been seen before.

This is perhaps particularly evident at present, because for the first time in perhaps 20 years the major developed economies are approaching the same point on the economic cycle (with perhaps an exception here for Japan) and background levels of inflation are relatively consistent.

8.3.2 The correlation of the markets

The yields on one government bond market are closely linked to the required yields in the international government bond market. This was demonstrated quite clearly during the crash of 1994 when the bond markets showed a frightening degree of correlation.

As the diagram below shows this correlation was an increasing theme of bond markets in the 1990s.

International Bond Yields 1986-2003

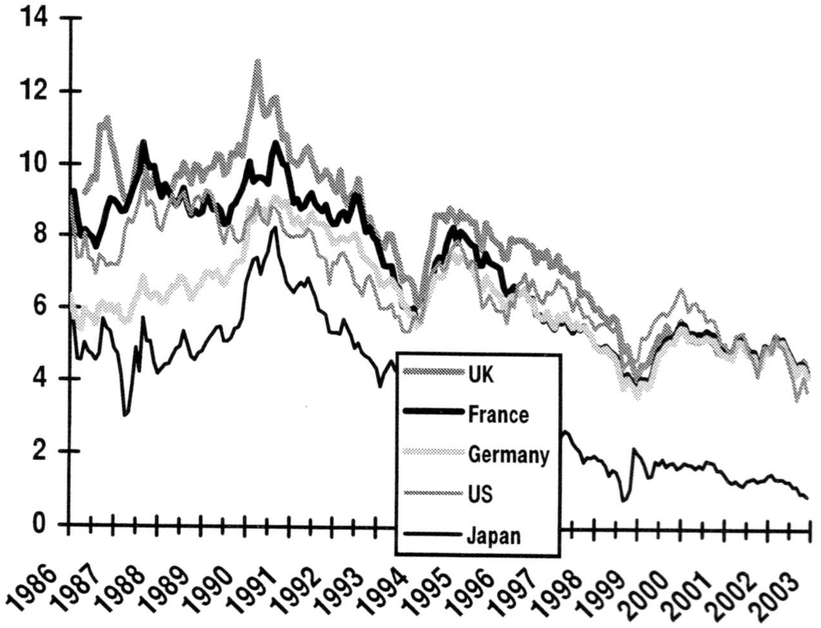

What has in part forced this correlation has been the internationalisation of the government bond markets with vast cross-border flows of capital. This competition for capital has meant that markets have had to offer equivalent yields in order to attract investment.

However, this could not take place without some logic behind it. Many economists are arguing that the age of inflation has gone and the big erratic of the 1970s and 1980s is no longer be relevant. Therefore, in the long term, inflation in all of the developed nations will tend to be of the same order. Ignoring the risk premiums, this would simply leave the real returns. Logically, real returns should not differ and therefore correlation of long yields will continue.

It is argued that the differing economic cycles will now be reflected not in the long bond yields, but in the short-term interest rates. Indeed, here there is a much closer link to the economic cycle.

As mentioned above, this process of globalisation is not yet complete, not only are there institutional barriers to the free flow of funds between different economies, there are also psychological barriers to be overcome in educating investors to be truly internationalised in their approach. However, this does seem to be taking place and consequently, one can expect a greater degree of correlation in the future than we have seen thus far.

9 Random Events

The final key driver of our yields would be random events, such as the commodity price shocks of the 1970s and political changes such as German reunification, which obviously had a profound impact upon the supply and demand conditions current in Germany and the German government bond markets.

Equally, the drive towards federalisation of the European Union and the commitment to EMU (European Monetary Union) again could not have been predicted 20 years ago and as such, represents a major and unexpected influencing factor on the yield curve creating instability.

Elections and political instability will also impact upon the required yield. It is conventional for the yield curve to rise in the prelude to an election as investors factor in an uncertainty premium. If the result of the election is a forgone conclusion and the policies of the incoming government are clear, then this premium may be factored out prior to the actual election.

Global political instability will have a particularly profound impact upon the dollar, with many investors regarding the dollar as a 'safe haven' currency. The Asian crisis of 1997/98 was a prime example of the impact that a 'flight to quality' can have. Whilst the yields in the emerging markets rose significantly, the developed markets and the US in particular saw yields forced down to historically low levels.

Equally, the events of 11 September 2001 had a profound impact on the global economy and were completely unforeseen.

10 Forecasting the Yield Curve

We have now analysed theoretically and practically what lies behind the yield. From the basis of our understanding, we can then extrapolate into the future to estimate an expectation of the yield curve. As we have already seen, markets' consensus expectation of yields is implicit in the current yield curve structure in the form of forward rates. The key thing here would be to model our own expectations of the future and to see whether we believe on fundamental grounds that the yield curve will be different from the consensus expectation.

This must be seen as something of a 'mug's game', since the forecasts that we make will be judged against actuality as it turns up, and forecasts made on the basis of a series of assumptions, which at the time were perfectly logical, will seem ludicrous in the cold light of day several years later. Indeed, one may not have to wait several years to realise that the assumptions made were inappropriate.

In the summer of 2004, it seemed inevitable that UK rates would continue to rise. The consensus market forecasts suggested that rates would rise well above 5% by the middle of 2005. However, by the autumn, with the housing market showing some signs of decline, the consensus was that rates would remain at 4.75%. In a matter of months expectations had been revised dramatically.

10.1 How to forecast

Obviously, there are a variety of techniques that one can use, including the sophisticated computerised econometric models that attempt to factor in all the understanding we have of the economy into a complex series of equations as discussed at the start of this section. The end result will be a composite prediction of the yield to a more 'back of the envelope' calculation driven by gut reaction and feel.

With regard to econometric modelling that can be undertaken, many economists will approach this with a due sense of scepticism, feeling that the models we devise now will reflect the world as we understand it at present and will be incapable of change.

To overcome this problem of the rigidity of models, many advanced modelling firms are attempting to create more interactive models that expand and change with time. These in many ways attempt to replicate the workings of the human mind in the form of a neural network.

Other models are constructed from a series of constantly mutating equations (genetic algorithms) linked to actual performance. In these models, relationships that explain how the real world works are built into the model until they fail. At the same time the basic relationships are mathematically mutated into alternative relationships and to the extent that one of these offers a more complete picture of the market it is included within the model.

A far more simplistic approach would attempt to plot the relationships over time and through perhaps even simple time series analysis try to predict from what we have seen, what we will see in the future.

When all is said and done, even the most complicated econometric model will only be as good as the information going into it and the complexity of the relationships within it.

Simple forecasting models would only take into account the absolutely key factors that are at work.

	Short-Term Rates	Long-Term Rates
Short-Term Forecasts	Monetary policy Demand and supply Market expectations (implicit in the forward rates)	Demand and supply Market expectations of inflation trends
Long-Term Forecasts	Inflation Monetary policy Demand and supply Economic cycle	Inflation Demand and supply factors Economic cycle

Source: Kern and Gutmann

At the end of the day, all forecasts are estimates and greater complexity may only lead to more confusion. Focusing on the key forces at work is perhaps the simplest and best approach.

Chapter Roundup

You need to be able to describe and discuss the limitations of

- Econometric modelling.
- Regression analysis.
- Time series analysis.

You needs to be able to describe

- The determinants of interest rates and inflation rates.
- The link between interest rates and the economic cycle.
- The link between interest rates and the economic cycle.

TEST YOUR KNOWLEDGE

Check your knowledge of the Chapter here, without referring back to the text.

1. Outline the problems of time series analysis.

2 Describe the link between interest rates and the economic cycle.

TEST YOUR KNOWLEDGE: ANSWERS

1. See 2.3.3
2. See 6.4

15 Bond Fund Management

INTRODUCTION

Having studied all of the fixed income investment vehicles available to the fund manager, we can now consider the fund management process in some detail. The ideas detailed in this section assume a complete understanding of the contents of all previous sections, and this section should not be studied unless or until that is the case.

Discussion questions from the ideas in this chapter are very common.

CHAPTER CONTENTS

CHAPTER LEARNING OBJECTIVES

Analysis

Students should possess a broad understanding of both static and dynamic methods for the analysis and construction of fixed income securities containing both certain and contingent cashflows. Variable rate securities will be included. Students should be aware of the limitations of assumptions and mathematical techniques upon results. Although analysis will be concerned principally with 'risk-free' securities, students should be aware of the further considerations for 'risky' securities and the effect they may have on expected return. Students should possess a thorough comprehension of single-period and multi-period, single currency and multi-currency through comprehension of single-period and multi-period, single currency and multi-currency portfolio management theory.

Security and portfolio management techniques.

Exam tip

> Questions from this section arise as basic definitions/descriptions in Section A, as applications to given scenarios in Section B (eg Summer 2008 Question 9) and as in-depth discussions in Section C (eg Winter, 2008 Questions 11 and 13, Summer 2008 Question 11). This must be regarded as a key session.

1 INVESTMENT STRATEGY

1.1 Introduction

Exam tip

> This is examined by reference to a case study requiring you to prepare a strategy, e.g. Winter 2007 Questions 8,9, Summer 2007 Questions 9, 10, Winter 2006 Question 10, Summer 2005 Question 9.

Fund management involves the investment of a client's assets in order to meet a number of key objectives. The objectives will vary from investor to investor and consequently the process of fund management must start with a detailed consideration of the fund's objectives and the development of a suitable investment strategy.

To satisfy the funds' objectives, the fund manager also needs to appreciate the constraints that he must operate within, i.e. he must know such factors about his client as

- Time horizons.
- Liabilities to match.
- Liquidity needs.
- Risk aversion/risk tolerances.
- Tax status.
- Other preferences and legal constraints, e.g. ethical considerations.

This is needed as

- It is a prerequisite to the initial portfolio structure.
- It influences the kinds of portfolio adjustment that can be made.
- It consequently influences portfolio performance.

1.2 Objectives of the fund

1.2.1 Introduction

Broadly speaking, the fund objectives fall into one of two categories, those who seek

- To maximise their returns, i.e. positive net worth individuals looking for a portfolio to match their risk/return preferences.
- To match liabilities, e.g. pension funds where the aim is to match asset and liabilities or minimise any mismatch.

1.2.2 Return maximisation

Risk/Reward profile

When adopting a policy of return maximisation, each fund will have specific objectives and targets to achieve. Within this, there will be specific limits on the degree of risk that the managers are able to take in achieving these returns. Understanding this **risk/reward trade-off** is crucial to understanding the overall objectives and then establishing the policy of a fund.

Given the choice, most investors would elect to have a high performance fund with minimal risk. However, this is not achievable and some trade-off between the two will have to take place.

Lower risk aversion or greater risk tolerance(Risk tolerance) results in

- Greater allowable portfolio risk.
- Greater potential gains (and losses).

Establishing client risk preferences or risk tolerances is clearly very difficult. The standard procedure is to ask the client to select his preferred mix of, say, equities and bonds, to give an idea of the normal mix desired. The client will then be asked to specify limits of different assets, i.e. maximum and minimum holdings of the different types of assets available.

1.2.3 Liability matching

The only way to achieve full liability matching, i.e. guarantee the matching of any liability, is through investment in government bonds where the income and capital inflows exactly match those liabilities, cash flow matching.

If the return from bonds is insufficient to achieve this required return, then we must use other assets. The result of the use of other assets is that we may achieve the higher return required, however, the risk associated with the use of these other assets means that the liabilities may not be exactly met – there may be a mismatch.

1.3 Constraints on the fund

1.3.1 Introduction

Given the fund requirements, the key to understanding the fund strategy is to appreciate the various fund constraints that operate on the fund itself.

1.3.2 Time horizons

The time horizons for the attainment of the return or the matching of the liabilities will clearly influence the types of investments that will be worthwhile for the fund.

A fund whose purpose is to meet some liabilities in, say, two years' time, may find that the investment vehicle is a two-year low-coupon gilt. This will especially be the case if the client is a high rate taxpayer as he will be able to benefit from a tax-free capital gain on these gilts at redemption.

For a fund that has liabilities to meet in 20 years' time, such investments would be inappropriate.

The time horizon will also influence the level of risk that can be taken in order to achieve the objectives. A fund with a long-term time horizon can probably stand a higher risk, as any poor returns in one year will be cancelled by high returns in subsequent years before the fund expires. This sort of risk clearly cannot be taken in a very short-term fund which may only span a couple of years and, therefore, may not have counter-balancing good and bad years.

1.3.3 Liabilities

As mentioned above, certain funds have fund liabilities that they are obliged to meet and the fund manager's objective must take these into consideration. For example, pension funds and life assurance companies will have statistical projections of their liabilities into the future and the fund must attempt to achieve these.

A further consideration is the exposure to currency risk. A pension fund may have all its liabilities denominated in sterling. If the fund were to invest heavily in overseas assets, this would expose it to an additional risk other than the risk inherent in the assets themselves. However, if the pension fund itself has liabilities in, say, dollars, then buying US investments matches their currency exposure and therefore minimises risk as well as taking on board an acceptable investment.

1.3.4 Liquidity needs

Within any fund, there must be the ability to respond to changing circumstances and consequently, there needs to be a degree of liquidity. Many investments may satisfy these liquidity needs, for example, fixed interest instruments can guarantee a tranche of the investment portfolio that will give easy access to cash, should the fund need it. However, other investments such as certain corporate bonds can be highly illiquid.

1.3.5 Risk aversion and risktolerances

We commented above on the risk/reward trade-off and how it impacts on the ways in which the fund's requirements can be achieved.

1.3.6 Tax status

Taxation is a consideration for all fund managers. The investment portfolio and the strategy adopted must be consistent with the fund's tax position. In some cases, such as pension funds, the fund does not suffer taxation. For these gross funds, the manager should normally avoid those stocks that involve the deduction of tax at source. For, even though it may be possible to reclaim any tax suffered, the fund will have incurred the opportunity cost of the lost interest on the tax deducted.

1.3.7 Other preferences and legal constraints

Obviously, when constructing a portfolio for any investor, the manager should consider the legal constraints that may exist. The regulatory framework adopted in the market needs to be adhered to. For collective investment schemes in the UK, there are certain investments into which the fund may not invest, such as derivatives, without seeking specific fund status.

Equally, a trust deed may exist which binds the fund manager to invest in certain securities and consequently, the manager must abide by this trust document. Where there is no trust deed, the provisions of the Trustee Act 2000 come in to force.

Finally, there may be ethical constraints placed on the fund. Ethical investments are ones that take an active interest in ethical and environmental issues. This covers issues as diverse as GM foods, gambling, tobacco production, child labour and the erosion of rain forests. The criteria applied may be positive – activities that the fund seeks to support (such as community involvement or environmental products); or negative – activities that the funds seek to avoid (such as nuclear power and animal testing).

1.4 Types of client

1.4.1 Return maximising

Collective investment schemes

Collective investment schemes are operations where a large number of small investors pool their money together to achieve a large fund that is placed under professional fund management. These funds can be in the form of unit trusts, OEICs or investment trusts. In essence, there is not a great deal of difference between the two types of trust barring a degree of regulatory difference.

The overall objectives of each fund are determined in advance in the trust deed. This states the objective in terms of risk/reward profile and may indicate the appropriate markets in which to invest. For example, it may be felt worthwhile for a fund manager to establish a unit trust investing in highly speculative fixed interest instruments, such as bonds with very high durations, in order to maximise returns for its investors.

On the other hand, other groups of investors may wish to have their money placed into reasonably secure short-term liquid issues generating a reasonable income flow. Each scheme will have its own particular emphasis and a selection of stocks and a strategy will be determined by this emphasis.

Discretionary customers

Discretionary customers are, generally speaking, high net worth individuals who place their funds under management with a broker. As with collective investment schemes, the objectives of these individuals vary. Some customers may be looking for rapid capital appreciation with minimal income flows, whilst others may be looking for a secure portfolio with a guaranteed flow of income.

Once again, it is the duty of the fund manager to ensure that he understands the objectives of the individual customer and that the objectives are consistent with the customer's circumstances. With regard to discretionary agreements for individual customers, there are a number of important rulebook procedures under the FSA's rules that need to be adhered to.

1.4.2 Liability matching

The objective of such a fund is that the return on the assets should not be less than the payout on the liabilities. Equivalently, this means that the present value of the portfolio assets should not be less than the present value of the liabilities.

Pension funds

A pension fund is exactly the type of client that will have such requirements. A pension fund represents a pool of money to be invested now to achieve either a specific return (final salary schemes) over a number of years; or a general increase in value (money purchase schemes). Hence, a pension fund has a future stream of pension payments to make and must always generate the right amount of cash at the right time to meet these payments.

In addition, a pension fund is not allowed to make a profit or loss. This implies that a pension fund has an obligation to ensure that the present value of liabilities equals the present value of assets. Furthermore, the stream of future pension liabilities is reasonably predictable by actuaries. This suggests that it is desirable to ensure the future cash flows from assets required to meet those pension payments are also reasonably predictable. This, in turn, suggests that bonds should play a significant role in the portfolios of pension funds.

In the past, when pensioners were not indexed at all, fixed coupon bonds were the ideal vehicle for meeting pension fund needs. Today, when there is some indexation of pensions, pensions funds will need to have indexed bonds and shares in their portfolios as well.

Generally speaking, pension funds have fairly **long-term** time horizons and as such are prepared to take on board a higher degree of risk, since any shortfall in the fund can be made up in future investment performance. Pension funds also have to keep control over the real rate of return that they earn, since their liabilities, the pension payments, will be expanding in line with inflation.

As a consequence, pension funds tend to invest in slightly more speculative assets, such as equities and property, with only a small proportion of the fund in fixed interest instruments. They will tend to be substantial holders of index-linked stocks, partly because these guarantee real returns over a period of time but also because the bonds themselves tend to have fairly high durations and are therefore sensitive to movement in real interest rates.

Life assurance companies

In common with pension funds, life assurance companies tend to have reasonably **long-term** liabilities and are, once again, able to take on board a higher degree of risk. Again, this tends to involve a high proportion of their assets being invested in equities and property with only a smaller proportion being invested into the fixed interest markets.

As a **long-term** fund, life assurance companies are able to take reasonably higher degrees of risk and again may be tempted towards bonds of higher duration.

General insurance companies

General insurance companies have a much **shorter liability profile** than life funds. In essence, insurance is like taking a bet. The insured person pays the company the premium. The insurance company makes money if they are able to take in this premium and earn investment income on it that exceeds the amounts of any claims arising on the policy. Since claims are likely to arise in the immediate future, for example, let us say in the next five years, then they are unable to take substantial risks forcing them to invest a greater proportion of their fund into 'risk-free' government securities. Whilst the returns may not be as high, the fund simply cannot take any risk.

Both life assurance funds and general insurance funds are closely monitored to ensure that the solvency of the company is in no way called into question. Overall, this tends to make both of them more risk averse than pension funds, but there is a marked difference between life assurance companies and general insurance companies in the risk/reward profile they adopt.

Discretionary customers

Discretionary customers may also be seeking to match liabilities, for example, school fee planning or mortgage repayment planning. The same broad principles apply to liability-matching clients regardless of who they are.

1.5 Available assets

Fundamental to an understanding of fund management is an appreciation of the relationship between risk and reward, that is

High risk = Potentially high return

The available assets for fixed income investment offer a range of risk and return as summarised below.

Risk	Investments
Low Risk	■ National Savings Certificates
	■ Bank and Building Society Accounts (Including money market deposits)
	■ Gilts Held to Redemption
↑	■ Gilts Sold Before Redemption (Here, there is the risk of a fall in the value of the stock)
	■ Local Authority Issues
	■ Corporate Bonds (Dependent on the credit rating)
Medium Risk	■ Life Assurance Policies
↓	■ Unit and Investment Trusts
	■ Shares, Property and Junk Bonds
High Risk	■ Warrants, Futures and Options (However, there is only a limited risk in purchasing an option or a warrant since, here, only the premium can be lost)

Before offering any investment advice, it is vital to ensure that the risk and returns match the customer's criteria.

2 Approaches to Investment Management

2.1 Introduction

The investment management process involves the investment of a third party's assets in order to meet a number of key objectives. The objectives will vary from investor to investor and consequently, the process of fund management must start with a detailed consideration of the fund's objectives and associated constraints.

2.2 Investment policy or investment strategy statement

The objectives and constraints of the fund lead the fund manager to consider a variety of strategies and within these, to select specific stocks that meet the fund objectives. The fund manager will be judged by his performance with regard to the objectives of the fund, and in the highly competitive world of fund management, an underperforming manager will not be given many second chances.

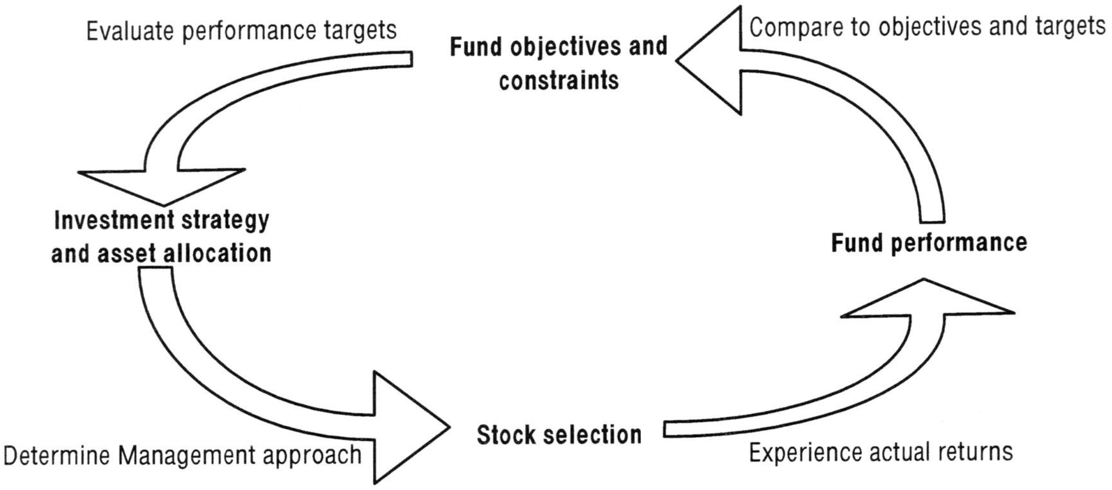

There are, however, a number of considerations that must be kept in mind in carrying out this fund management process. These include

- Should fund management be conducted on an active or a passive basis?
- Should fund management be conducted top down or bottom up?
- Should fund management be conducted on a global or specialised basis?
- How should currencies and exchange rates be considered in the fund management process?
- How much emphasis should be placed on analytical/quantitative analyses and how much should be given to judgmental/subjective assessments?
- Are there any ethical constraints to consider?

2.3 Active versus passive

There are three alternative investment management styles that may be adopted.

- Active investment management.
- Passive investment management.
- Mixed/hybrid approach combining elements of both active and passive management.

An active investment manager is one who intervenes in the portfolio on a regular basis, attempting to use individual expertise in order to enhance the overall return of the fund. An active fund manager believes that markets are not efficient and that mispriced securities exist. If this view is correct then there wil be a gain to be made from actively dealing in these stocks.

Passive investment management, on the other hand, establishes a strategy that aims to provide the appropriate level of return for the fund. A passive fund manager believes that markets are efficient and that no mispricing exists. If this is true then there is no benefit to be had from active trading. Any trade in these securities will simply incur dealing costs for no benefit.

These are perhaps two extreme versions of investment management – there are alternatives that represent hybrids between the two extremes. All these ideas are discussed further below.

2.4 Top-down versus bottom-up

Portfolio managers tend to use either a top-down or a bottom-up approach to the investment process.

2.4.1 Top-down approach

The fund manager using a top-down approach first allocates his assets based on the objectives and constraints of the fund, and then selects individual securities to satisfy that allocation. The most important decision in this approach is the choice of markets and currencies. Once these choices have been made, the manager then selects the best securities available.

2.4.2 Bottom-up approach

The manager using a bottom-up approach studies the fundamentals of many individual stocks and constructs a portfolio from the ones which he considers best satisfy the fund's objectives and constraints. The product of this approach is a portfolio with a market and currency allocation that is more or less the random result of the securities selected. This approach is appropriate when the manager is more concerned with risk exposure in various sectors than with either market or currency risk exposure.

2.4.3 Consequences of the choice of approach

The approach adopted will impact on the organisation of the department. A research department using a top-down approach focuses on country and currency analysis primarily. Such a department will therefore be specialised by country. Financial analysts using the bottom-up approach are specialised by worldwide industry sector.

When adopting a top-down approach, a fund manager will firstly consider the objectives of the fund, the constraints of the fund, and the available investments in order to determine a strategic asset allocation. The objectives and constraints of the fund will direct the fund manager towards certain asset classes and away from others, though a spread of asset classes should always be held to ensure the fund has the full benefits of diversification.

Empirical evidence has shown that securities within a single asset class tend to be more closely correlated than those in differing asset classes, providing some justification for the principle of diversification. Though it is clearly possible to select high risk or low risk securities within any asset class, a portfolio of securities from that class is likely to demonstrate the broad risk characteristics of that class (e.g. a bond portfolio will show the risk characteristics of bonds whether it is a low duration portfolio or a high duration portfolio).

Similarly, empirical evidence has also shown that securities within a single market tend to largely move together, but national markets and currencies do not provide justification for international diversification.

Where a top-down approach is adopted, this appears to demonstrate that the major factor contributing to portfolio performance is the choice of markets, currencies and asset classes, not the choice of individual securities.

The total risk of the portfolio will be a function of

- The risks of the various asset classes (a function of the stock selection decision, though probably representative of the risk of that asset class in general).
- The weighting of the various asset classes/markets/currencies.
- And perhaps most importantly, the correlations between those asset classes/ markets/ currencies leading to the diversification benefits.

The strategic asset allocation decision encompasses the second and third of these points, the weightings of and diversification between the asset classes/markets/currencies, and will therefore easily have the most significant impact on portfolio risk.

This, in turn, suggests that an international investment organisation should be organised along primarily top-down lines with its analysts specialised by country with possibly a few international sectors such as oil stocks.

Where a top-down approach is adopted, investment management involves three activities.

- Asset allocation.
- Stock selection.
- Market timing or tactical asset allocation.

This top-down approach is the one we concentrate on below.

2.5 Global versus specialised

A global fund manager is one who manages all the assets of a customer and determines both the asset allocation and the selection of each security for the portfolio. Specialised fund managers, as their name suggests, specialise in particular investment areas, such as Japanese bonds or Eurobonds. These specialised fund managers often handle specific funds that a client can buy into. The allocation decision is then made by the client, based on advice he receives from one or several managers. It is not unusual to find investors with the bulk of their portfolio in a passive, well-diversified fund and the remainder invested in few active specialised funds.

The trend towards specialised management is derived from the fact that no manager is a superior expert in all markets though some may be in a few markets. Since asset allocation is potentially the most profitable decision, a combination of global and specialised management is required. Global management is the only reasonable solution for the small investor, whereas large investors may afford both global and specialised management.

2.6 Currency

A manager adopting a bottom-up approach treats currencies only as residual variables; their currency breakdown is determined by the countries, industries and securities they selected for the portfolio. They argue that currency risk is a necessary evil, that currency movements are impossible to predict, and that in any event, they wash out in the long run.

Fund managers operating on a top-down basis will be aware of the level of currency exposure they have and will adopt one of two possible approaches.

- Hedge their foreign portfolios to remove the unpredictable risk they face.
- Attempt to utilise currency movements in such a way as to minimise the contribution they make to total risk and maximise the benefits they get from returns on currency movements.

2.7 Quantifiable or subjective

Quantification of the investment process is very useful as a result of the large number of parameters and decision variables involved. Quantification can be applied to various models or investment decision aids, including

- Dividend valuation models, duration, or option valuation models.
- Econometric or technical forecasting models of markets and currencies.

- Performance and risk analysis.
- Asset allocation optimisers.

Some investment managers base their investment decisions on the results of quantified analysis.

Other managers rely primarily on subjective judgements. They argue that models based on past data are not helpful due to the constant changes in the markets and the fact that such data is available to everyone. How can a fund manager outperform the market when all fund managers are basing their investment decisions on the same information?

In practice, many fund managers use fundamental and quantitative analysis to produce a shortlist of investment opportunities from which they make their own subjective selection.

2.8 Ethical and socially responsible investing

2.8.1 Introduction

Ethical investments are ones that take an active interest in ethical and environmental issues. This covers issues as diverse as GM foods, gambling, tobacco production, child labour and the erosion of rain forests.

The criteria applied may be

- **Positive** – investing in activities that the fund seeks to support (such as community involvement or environmental products);.
- **Negative** – not investing in activities that the funds seek to avoid (such as nuclear power and animal testing.
- **Socially responsible** – a broader, more pragmatic approach allowing investment in companies that are neither positively harmful nor positively beneficial.

Ethical fund management and socially responsible investment are now very popular and many funds publish an ethical/green policy and aim to invest only in companies involved in activities that satisfy the fund's policy.

2.8.2 Implications on risk and return

The big question about ethical and socially responsible investments is whether you have to suffer for your principles – in terms of lower returns and higher levels of risk.

Such investments currently tend to be in **smaller** companies, particularly those with stricter criteria, since large firms are more likely to break the negative screening tests due to the diversity of their operations. These small company shares can be more volatile, though the effects of this volatility can be mitigated through broad diversification.

Diversification, however, is often restricted by the fact that many industry sectors will be discounted by strict ethical funds due to the very nature of the business. Examples here include tobacco, mining and livestock. Funds leaving out key industry sectors can bear more risk than others – losing out, say, when those sectors boom. But on the other side of the argument, they will not lose out when these sectors slump.

Evidence suggests that ethical funds have performed much in line with their non-ethical equivalents over the last 15 years, albeit slightly less well.

2.8.3 Regulation

There is no specific regulation of ethical funds as such, but issues for the fund manager to consider would include

- Compliance with the trust deed (or similar).
- Providing adequate (and not misleading) information in the scheme particulars for the customer to make a balanced and informed decision.
- Advertisements are clear, fair and not misleading.

3 Asset Allocation

3.1 Introduction

Assuming that a top-down approach has been applied, the first stage in the investment management process will be the asset allocation decision.

Asset allocation is the allocation of the funds available between these various instruments or financial markets. At the asset allocation stage, the fund manager decides what proportion of the total portfolio to invest in broad asset categories such as government bonds, corporate bonds etc. Where a technical or quantitative analysis system has been used, this system may suggest the appropriate asset allocation.

Despite the existence of these techniques, all fund managers require knowledge of asset allocation according to more fundamental principles. This is perhaps the most subjective area of fund management, and one where there will never be a single correct answer. Given the same fund and client, it is unlikely that any two fund managers would produce exactly the same asset allocation and make exactly the same investment decisions. However, it would be reasonable to assume that any allocations would have a broadly similar effect. The justification for this last statement is that the fund manager has a legal and professional duty to base the asset allocation on the client's wishes with particular regard to the criteria discussed above, when identifying the client's objectives, specifically

- Matching liabilities.
- Meeting any ethical considerations.
- Remaining within risk tolerances.
- Maximising fund performance.

There are three basic rules the fund manager should bear in mind when trying to satisfy the client's investment objectives.

- The fund manager should take every step to diversify risk, a process requiring an understanding of the different risk factors affecting all the investments in which he may be investing as well as the impact of foreign exchange.
- The fund manager should be aware that the best way to match the client's liabilities if they are fixed in money terms is by investing in bonds (or similar nominal returning assets), since this will generate cash flows from interest and redemption proceeds, which will allow the liabilities to be met as they arise.
- Asset allocation is effectively a compromise between matching investments to client liabilities and investing assets in more attractive markets in order to maximise fund performance.

The optimal asset allocation should be based on the objectives and constraints of the fund and the fund manager's estimate of the risks and returns offered by the various securities.

The asset allocation decision is extremely important, since it dominates the performance of most portfolios. As we have already noted, this is because returns on securities within each asset category are usually highly correlated, i.e. they generally rise or fall together. This implies that selecting the best performing asset category is more important for performance than selecting the best performing securities within each asset category.

A fund manager should also be aware of the restrictions placed on them by the trustees, as these may mean that they are not completely free in making their asset allocation decisions.

3.2 Portfolio optimisers

Due to the large number of investments that are liable to be held within any portfolio and the complex interrelationships between them, the economy, etc. computerised portfolio optimisation techniques are frequently used to establish measures such as portfolio yield, total risk, maximum and minimum stock numbers, maximum levels in any one stock, etc.

These techniques all tend to be based on portfolio theory ideas, requiring the calculation and input of appropriate statistical measures.

3.3 Value at Risk

Exam tip

> Examined as a discussion in Summer 2000 Question 10.

3.3.1 The idea

Value at Risk (VAR) is the amount by which the value of an investment or portfolio may fall over a given period of time at a given level of probability. There are a few different ways to calculate value at risk. Regardless of how it is undertaken, the idea behind the calculation is how much value could be lost within a given period, i.e. what is the probable worst case loss over that time?

For example, if VAR is £1m at a probability level of 5% for one week, this indicates that there is a 5% probability that the value of a portfolio will fall by more than £1m over the next week. It therefore gives investors an idea of the amount of potential loss and the probability of that loss arising.

3.3.2 Required inputs

To calculate the Value at Risk, we need

- A unit of measurement, e.g. sterling.
- A specified time period. This is usually taken to be one day, one week or two weeks. It will depend on the liquidity of the assets concerned and the frequency of their trading. Longer holding periods are used for less liquid assets. The composition of the portfolio is assumed not to change over this period.
- A specified probability level. This is usually between 1% and 5%.

3.3.3 Methods

There are four main approaches to measuring VAR.

- Parametric.
- Historical.
- Historical simulation.
- Monte Carlo or stochastic simulation.

Parametric VAR

The parametric approach is also known as the correlation method, variance/covariance method or analytical method. It is the most popular of the various methods.

It assumes that the distribution of investment returns is Normal, meaning that it can be described by the returns and risks of the investments concerned.

It estimates the standard deviations of investments and their correlations with other investments, using historical data or future estimates. Given this information, it is possible to calculate the return and standard deviation of the overall portfolio as illustrated above.

Historical VAR

The problem with the parametric approach is that it assumes a Normal distribution, when there is much evidence that investment returns do not follow a Normal distribution. Empirical evidence suggests that generally

- Investment returns are more peaked towards the mean than a Normal distribution and have fatter tails, i.e. leptokurtic.
- They are negatively skewed, meaning that greater losses are possible than a Normal distribution would imply.

It is possible to overcome this problem by constructing a distribution of historical returns and establishing its actual shape.

Historical simulation

There may not be sufficient historical data available for particular instruments. This may be either because it is impracticable to hold historical data on a vast array of different instruments in which the company may invest, or the instrument itself might be relatively new.

In these circumstances we may adopt a historical simulation approach. Under this the data used to estimate VAR will not be the returns on the investments themselves, but the factors that drive those returns. For example, the major factors driving a foreign currency bond price will be exchange rates and foreign interest rates.

The historical performance of the current portfolio through time can be simulated by examining how it would have responded to the relevant factors over the period concerned. A distribution of returns can then be constructed.

Monte Carlo or stochastic simulation

The Monte Carlo or stochastic simulation method is an alternative to historical simulation having the benefit of additional flexibility. This method allows the consideration of different distributions and parameters (risks and returns) and through running a large number of simulations, typically 10,000, it aims to determine the potential distribution of returns and the potential for losses.

4 Market Timing – Tactical Asset Allocation

4.1 Introduction

Strategic asset allocation (discussed above) is the asset allocation that the fund should operate within the long term (on average) in order to satisfy its objectives and constraints. The strategic asset allocation is based on long-run estimates of capital market conditions – it ignores short-term fluctuations on the premise that markets are efficient in the long term.

Market timing (or tactical asset allocation) involves the short-term variation of the asset allocation of the fund in order to take advantage of market changes or fluctuations. Market timing implies that asset classes are mispriced, and looks to take advantage of this mis-pricing in order to enhance returns. As such, market timing assumes that markets are not efficient in the short term and may overreact to information.

Market timing is the variation of the asset allocation of the fund in anticipation of market movements. It involves adjusting the sensitivity of the portfolio to anticipated market changes. A fund manager engages in market timing when he does not agree with the consensus about the market, i.e. he is more bullish or more bearish than the market, and rebalances his portfolio to take advantage of this view.

The approach to market timing is to adjust the duration of the portfolio over time. If the fund manager is relatively bullish, he wants to increase the duration of the portfolio, i.e. make it more aggressive. If, on the other hand, the fund manager is more bearish, he will want to reduce the duration of the portfolio, making it more defensive.

One way of achieving this result would be to buy high duration bonds in a bull market and sell them in a bear market. However, the transaction costs involved would make this an expensive strategy. An alternative is to keep the portfolio of risky assets constant and raise or lower the duration through the use of derivative instruments, such as futures and options.

In summary, the action is

- **Falling market** – Reduce the sensitivity to the market fall, through
  - Switching from sensitive (high duration) stocks to less sensitive (low duration) stocks.
  - A derivatives overlay, such as selling futures or buying put options.
- **Rising market** – Increase the sensitivity to the market rise, through
  - Switching from insensitive (low duration) stocks to more sensitive (high duration) stocks.
  - A derivatives overlay, such as buying futures or buying call options (if these are permitted for the fund).

Many fund managers become involved in market timing. For example, pension funds have regular inflows from their clients that the investment manager may decide to

- Invest immediately, in which case the fund will benefit from pound cost averaging, i.e. the purchases are made at both the peaks and troughs throughout the year, hence the fund acquires the investments at the average cost for the year – a passive strategy; or
- Delay his investment (i.e. hold cash as an asset) and time his acquisitions in the hope that it will be the most favourable price – an active strategy.

4.2 Importance of market timing

As noted earlier, studies have shown that the asset allocation decision has a greater effect on performance than stock selection for most funds, especially international funds where the correlations between markets are low.

It follows that achieving the correct strategic allocation, and responding correctly to market movements with an appropriate tactical move should be the primary objective of most fund managers in order to maximise their funds' returns.

5 Stock Selection

Exam tip

The ideas in this section may be examined as brief definitions in Section A (e.g. Winter 2003 Question 5) but are more frequently asked as discussions in Section C comparing and contrasting alternative approaches (e.g. Winter 2001 Question 9) or applications to a case study in Section B (e.g. Summer 2004 Question 9).

5.1 Introduction

Having decided on the overall asset allocation (strategic and tactical), the fund manager must now select specific securities within each asset category. This is the stock selection decision. The various approaches to stock selection, either active or passive, depend on the specific asset category being considered.

5.2 Active stock selection strategies

5.2.1 Introduction

A bond portfolio will be actively managed whenever there are misvalued bonds around. Active bond portfolio management operates around the activities of security selection and market timing. However, there is a difference between active share selection and active bond selection. Most share managers engage in security selection, whereas most bond managers engage in market timing.

A bond picker will construct a portfolio of bonds that, in comparison with the market portfolio, has less than proportionate weightings in the overpriced bonds and more than proportionate weightings in the underpriced bonds.

A market timer engages in active management when he does not accept the consensus market portfolio and is either more bullish or more bearish than the market. Expectations of interest rate changes are therefore a crucial input into successful market timing. A bond market timer is interested in adjusting the relative duration of his portfolio over time. Market timing with bonds is sometimes called duration switching.

If the fund manager is expecting a bull market because he is expecting a fall in the general level of interest rates, he wants to increase the duration of his portfolio by replacing low-duration bonds with high-duration bonds. If the fund manager is expecting a bear market because he is expecting a rise in the level of interest rates, he wants to reduce the duration of his portfolio.

Active bond portfolio management is generally not as profitable as active share portfolio management. There are several reasons for this.

- There are more shares traded than bonds in the UK.
- The most liquid bonds are UK government bonds that have only certain maturities.
- The volatility of bond prices is generally much lower than that of shares, hence fewer opportunities for substantial mis-pricing of bonds exists.
- With only a few bonds suitable for active trading, the portfolio consisting of these bonds will be relatively undiversified.

The cost of active bond portfolio management can be reduced using futures and options.

5.2.2 Asset analysis

The starting point for the active fund manager is to analyse the available assets. There are broadly four approaches that are adopted to asset analysis.

- Fundamental analysis.
- Technical analysis.
- Quantitative analysis.
- A combination.

Fundamental analysis

Fundamental analysis concentrates on the economic strengths or weaknesses of the market in question or the individual features of a stock within a market. The basic idea behind this approach is that every market offers a return, and that every security has an intrinsic value that can be determined from a consideration of these factors.

With government bonds, this form of analysis entails reviewing the economic outlook for the economy and the funding requirement. This has already been looked at in detail in the forecasting section.

With corporate securities, fundamental corporate analysis involves economic analysis of markets and analysis of published corporate information with a view to forecasting future profits and hence, determining fair values and hence, the potential for mis-pricing. The stages in the preparation of such a profit forecast are as follows.

- Forecast economic growth in the UK and export markets derived from consensus surveys or own resources.
- Forecast market growth in the relevant sector, e.g. consumer, capital goods, etc.
- Consider special factors affecting demand like, say, VAT changes for consumer goods or seasonal order patterns for capital goods.
- Forecast sales growth for the company by combining market growth with changes in market share. Market share will depend on competition, innovation, price, etc. and hence, analysis will require knowledge of competing companies.
- Forecast margins. Usually, these depend on the state of the market and the strength of the competition. Cost cutting and productivity improvements can also be important. Operational gearing will also influence the result.
- Assess the risk to the corporate bondholder.

There is a lot of factual data and evaluative theory that fundamental analysis can be based upon. However, at the end of the day, it is a subjective exercise. Indeed, it is quite commonly the case that a company favoured by one analyst is not favoured by another.

Technical analysis

Technical analysts, rather than looking at the fundamentals of the economy, look to the pattern and trading history to determine the appropriate strategy to adopt.

There are two basic rules within technical analysis.

- All markets have trends.
- Trends remain in place until they are broken.

The intellectual justification for the use of technical analysis is based on the behaviour of crowds. Basically, the same group of people exposed to the same circumstances will react in the same way, i.e. 'history repeats itself'.

Frequently, through the use of charts, technical analysts develop patterns of market behaviour which they expect to be repeated time and time again. By charting the daily price movement in a market or stock, they believe they can predict the eventual outcome. To an extent, these predictions will be self-fulfilling, for if the charts predict that the price will fall and fund managers react to this sell signal, then undoubtedly the supply and demand factors will force the price down.

In the table below, we consider a number of the most important patterns and what they are purported to indicate about the state of the market. These are only broad patterns and in reality it will take some experience to be able to correctly interpret the data in the charts.

Bearish Patterns Reversals	Bullish Patterns Reversals	Continuation Patterns
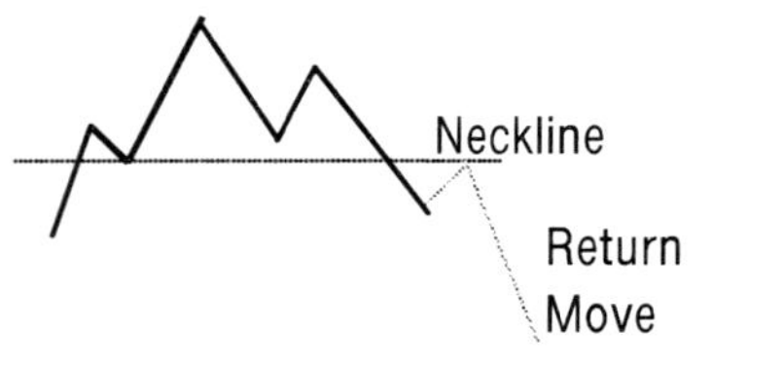		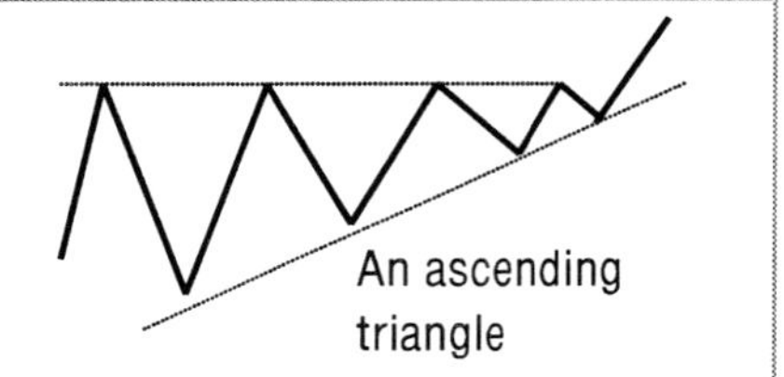
Head and Shoulders The final breakdown below the neckline is a very bearish indicator. There will frequently be a return move that temporarily restores the neckline.	**Inverse Head and Shoulders** Conversely, here the breakaway from the pattern is a positive indicator for the stock.	**Triangles** These continuation patterns give prices a chance to consolidate prior to continuing in their original direction. These can also take descending and symmetrical forms.
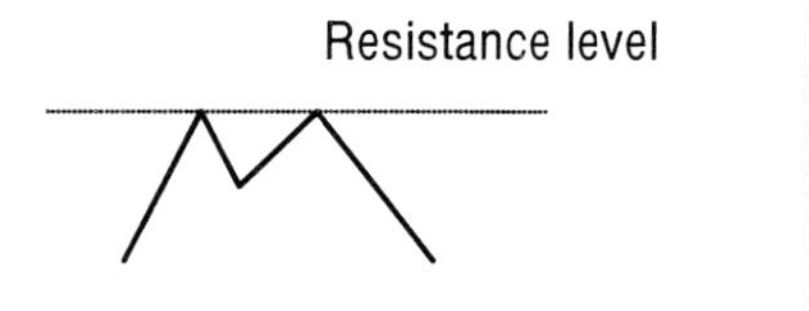	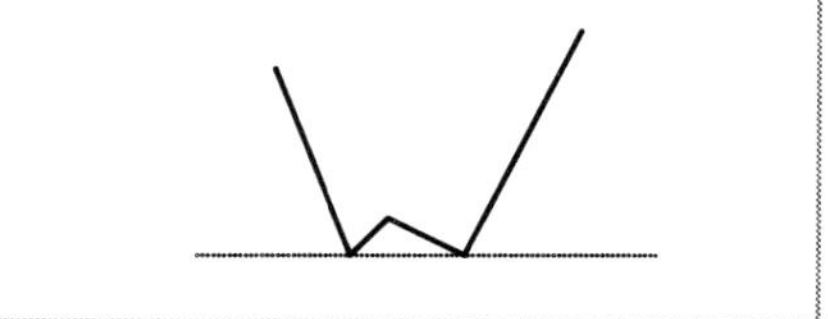	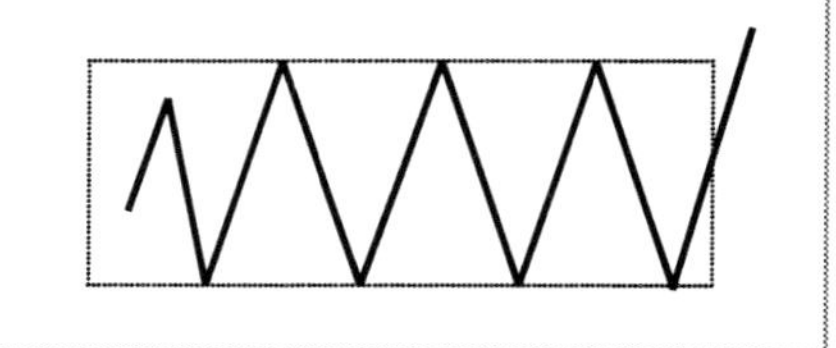
Double Top – M Patterns The rising price meets a resistance level and this is often followed by a trending down of the price.	**Double Bottom** Having found the floor level the stock will tend to trend upwards.	**Boxes and Rectangles** With prices trapped between resistance and support continuation is likely.
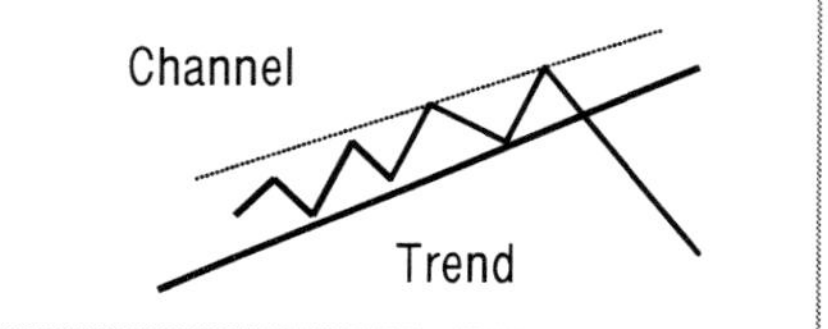	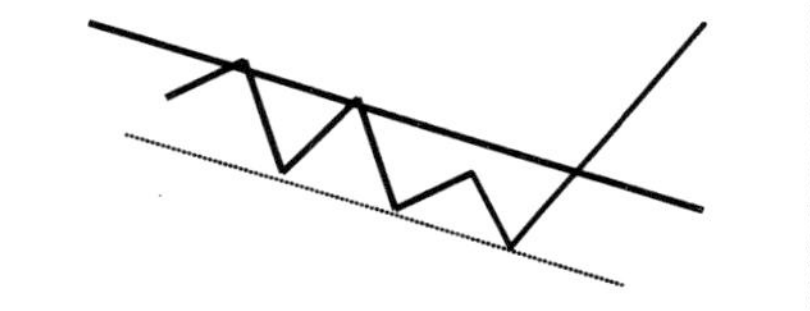	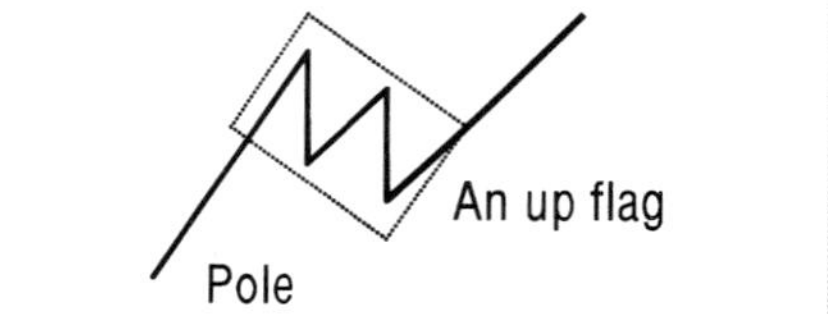
Breakout – Down The price breaking out of its current trend line again is regarded as a bearish indicator. The upward trend joins three or more lows and it is the reversal of this trend which is crucial.	**Breakout – Up** In this case, the upward break, which means a change in the pattern, represents a bullish signal.	**Flags** There are up and down flags. The pole is normally created by high volume and the flag is in the opposite direction to the trend.

Bearish Patterns Reversals	Bullish Patterns Reversals	Continuation Patterns

Topping Out – Saucer Top This is a more protracted pattern than a double top and again points to longer term price erosion.	**Bottoming Out – Saucer Bottom** Once again this longer term pattern indicates a more fundamental floor to the value.	**Diamonds** Uncertainty following a large swing will often lead to the creation of a diamond. The trend will then continue.

Gap analysis

A widely used form of chart analysis is to plot the daily high and low trading price on a graph, with a horizontal bar to indicate the closing price.

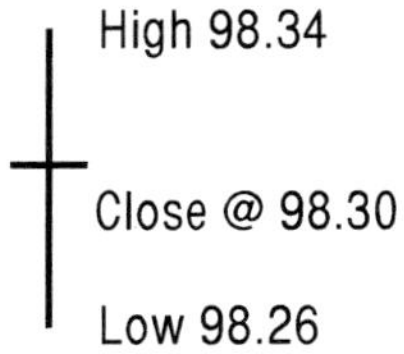

Whilst these charts may form the larger patterns that we examined above, there are also implications from the gaps which may emerge from the data.

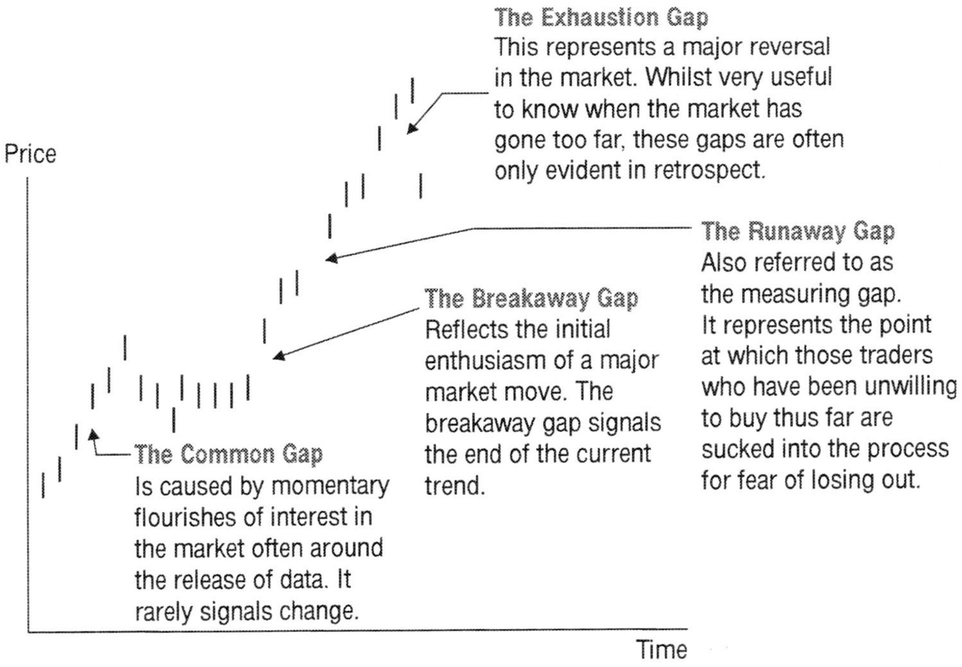

Momentum indicators

Momentum indicators measure the rate of change in prices and are used to indicate situations where the market has gone too far. These extremes are described as overbought and oversold.

The measure is calculated as the percentage price change based on the price a month ago (the period chosen can vary). Where prices rise (or fall) beyond thresholds demonstrated by the market's historical performance, then the market is likely to correct back, unless there has been some fundamental reason for a change in the general price level.

Moving averages

Moving averages are often used as signals of trends and reversals. A moving average is the average price over a preset period in the past. The period of calculation will vary considerably. Long-term moving averages are often regarded as the surest indicators of trends and reversals and are simple averages of the price over the past 30 to 40 weeks.

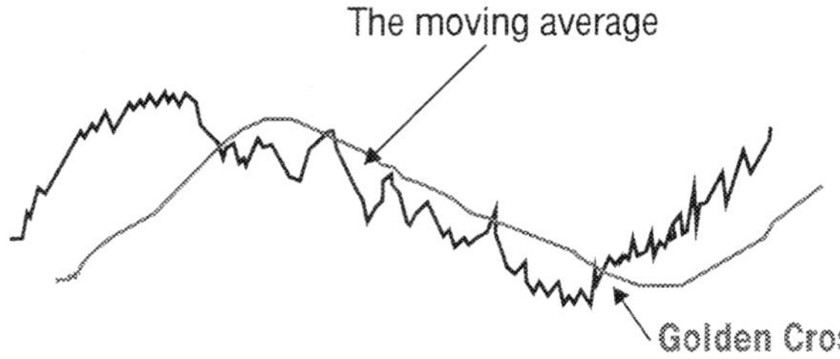

As illustrated above, it is the crossing point that is most important since this indicates a change in the overall direction of the market.

One problem with this is that by their nature moving averages tend to lag the market and consequently whilst they are useful to confirm reversals they may come too late for a trader to gain much reward. An alternative would be to use a shorter period moving average such as 15 to 20 weeks.

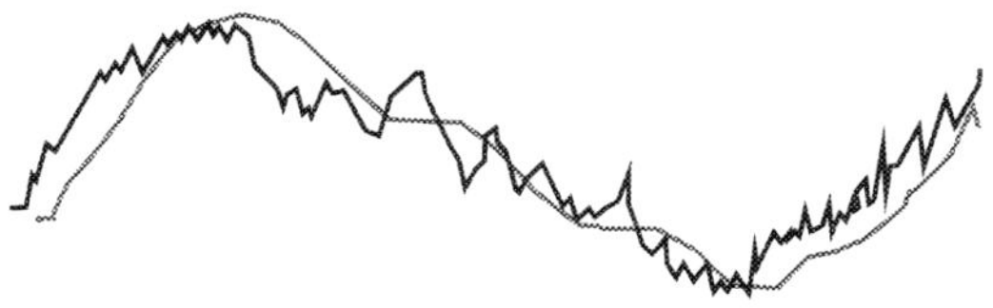

The principal problem with this is that a shorter period moving average will be strongly biased to recent movements and may trigger cross signals in error. An alternative is to use longer runs of data but to mathematically weight the data to the later periods.

Deeper trends

Beyond the immediacy of the price charts we have been looking at thus far, there are deeper more persistent movements. Many theorists have suggested that below the apparent confusion of the markets there is a longer term cycle. Perhaps the most accepted of these is the Elliot Wave theorem.

In 1939, Ralph Elliot advanced the idea that markets move in predetermined waves consistent with the Fibonacci series of numbers. That is to say, markets will tend to exhibit waves of five pulses in one direction and then three in the opposite direction. Inferring that if the general direction of the market is up, then there will be five pulses up followed by three pulses down.

This is obviously simplifying a much more academic argument, however, it does highlight the need to be aware of the underlying cycle.

Contrarian indicators

In any market, the trader who identifies the trend first will tend to make the most profit. Obviously, the charts that we have examined may point to reversals and changes. In addition, there are other somewhat cynical measures that can be used. Some analysts in the US measure the optimism of investment advisers on the belief that if they believe that things are positive, then the market must have gone too far.

These indicators can perhaps be seen as anecdotal overbought or oversold indicators.

Japanese candlestick charts

Regarded by many as one of the newest forms of technical analysis, Japanese candlestick charts are in fact one of the oldest forms of charting techniques. Advocates of their use regard them as much more sensitive than simple line charts.

The candlestick

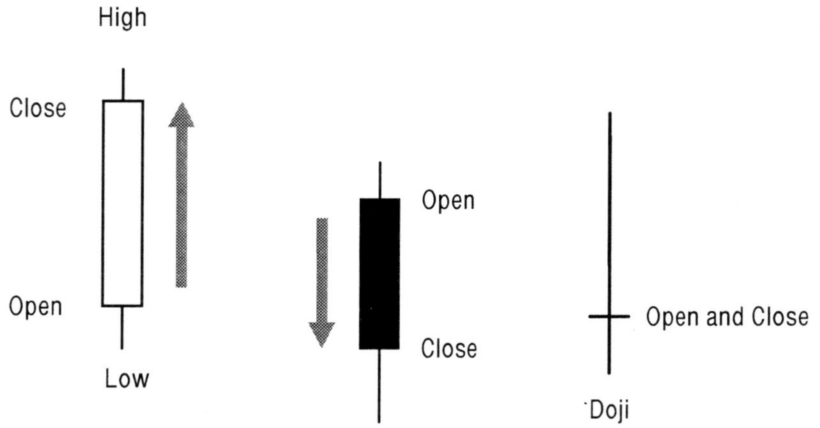

The broad part of the candlestick is called the body. When white, this indicates that the market closed above the open and indicates the dominance of bullish sentiment. Conversely, a black body indicates a close below the opening price and the dominance of bearish sentiment. The thin lines referred to as shadows represent the intra-day highs and lows of trading. Where open and close are the same, this is referred to as a doji. Dojis are often regarded as neutral signals indicating that the bullish and bearish sentiments are balanced. However, when they come at the end of a bull or bear run, they can signal a reversal.

It is argued that the combination of colour, shape and range make the candlestick a uniquely informative charting technique.

Timeframe

Candlestick charts can be developed on an hourly, daily, weekly or monthly basis and the interpretation remains broadly the same.

An example of conventional chart analysis

The following chart has been taken from the US T-bond market. Let us examine the patterns that emerge from it.

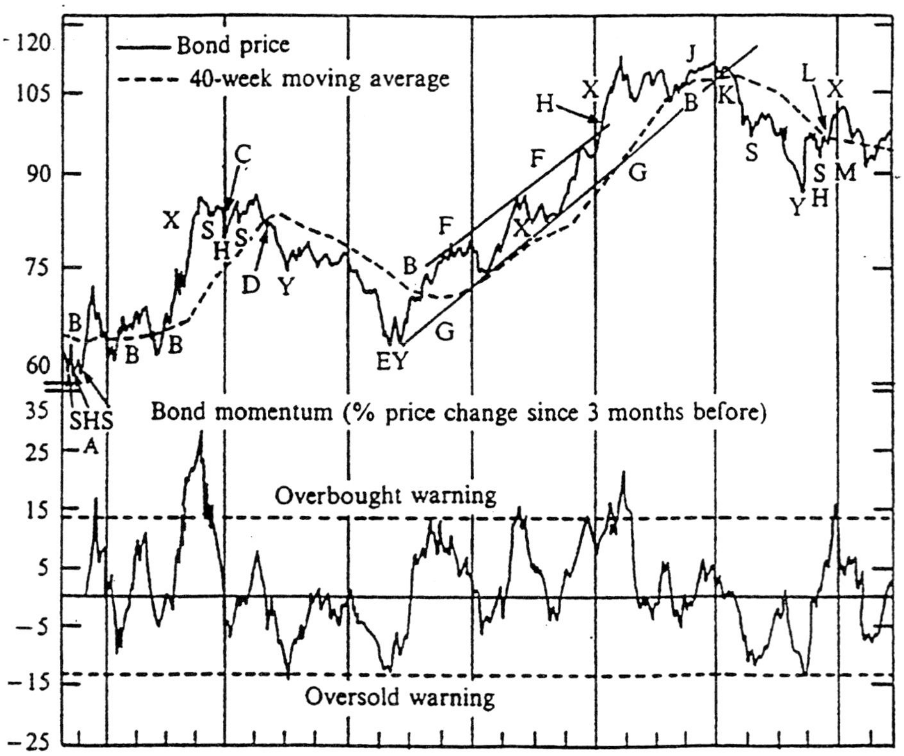

A An inverted head and shoulders pattern (SHS) points to the market moving upwards.

B A series of breakouts from the 40-week moving average and a double bottom again signal a bullish trend.

X An overbought indicator may warn of a slowdown or correction to come.

C A bullish inverted head and shoulders (SHS) again points to an upward trend in prices. However, this pattern fails and this leads to a reversal in the market.

D The fall in prices through the moving average is a bearish indicator reinforcing the breakdown of the head and shoulders.

Y Oversold indicators signal a slowdown or pause in the bear market.

E The double bottom pattern combined with an oversold signal (Y) pointing to a reversal of the bearish trend. This is then confirmed by the breakout above the trend at B.

F Bond prices now enter a bullish channel between lines GG and FF. The overbought warnings (X) trigger corrections within the trend but not a reversal.

H There is a breakout through the top of the channel, indicating a bullish move. This is then cut back by an overbought signal.

J The market would appear to be signalling that the bull phase is coming to an end with the topping out pattern that is emerging.

K This bearish aspect is confirmed by the double breakout from both the trend GG and the moving average. The bear market oversells and triggers an oversold warning (Y).

L An inverted head and shoulders triggers a bullish recovery and breakthrough of the moving average.

M The recovery leads to an overbought warning and the market corrects back through the moving average.

As with much technical analysis, analysing price trends in retrospect is always easier and patterns can clearly be identified. As the patterns are emerging, the data can be much harder to interpret.

Overview of technical analysis and its use

Whilst these are some of the basic patterns that traders may use, they have to be approached with caution. Successful traders are unlikely to rely on the simplistic patterns above. In reality, the patterns are not as clear as the portrait we have painted and a large amount of judgement will have to be exercised to separate the clear trends. Charts do, however, serve an important purpose in restraining the excesses of the market by clearly indicating extreme value beyond which the market should not go.

It is easy to ridicule charts and chartists, however, at the root of the whole process is the simple belief that trading is driven by individuals and individuals will tend, when faced with the same circumstances, to act in the same way. To this extent, the charts provide a valuable insight into the mind of the market. Equally, even if we do not believe in them, there are undoubtedly many houses that rely on nothing else in making their investment decisions.

Quantitative analysis

Exam tip

Examined in Winter 2007 Question 11.

Quantitative analysis involves analysing portfolio/investment instruments according to expected levels of return and risk. It is generally accepted that higher returns can only be obtained at the expense of higher risk, however, investment managers can use computers to generate strategies which allow them to invest at the most cost-effective and efficient trade-off between risk and return.

Quantitative funds

Introduction

A quant fund is an actively managed fund where the stock selection process is driven by computer models, and a pure quant fund relies solely on computer models to make this stock selection.

In a quant fund there is no place for manager's judgement based on fundamental analysis, instead they use pre-determined or pre-set models to undertake this stock selection process. Such models rely on ideas such as portfolio theory, CAPM, dividend valuation model, options pricing techniques etc, i.e. fundamental evaluation tools in order to determine which stocks to hold and in what proportions.

Characteristics and management

Quant funds tend to have fewer investment professionals than other funds due to this non-reliance on fundamental analysis. As a result they tend to have lower operating costs. Quantitative funds also avoid the behavioural aspects of fund management, reducing it to a purely objective process.

Quantitative funds mine through publicly available economic data and data on thousands of companies aiming to capture a company's 'fair value' in a set of computer programs. They can apply their models to virtually the entire universe of stocks in a matter of minutes, cheaply evaluating a very large number of companies – something that cannot be achieved through a more fundamental approach. This ability to evaluate such large numbers of stocks leads to them tending to hold more shares in their portfolios.

The idea is, however, that excess returns are available to such funds by analysing publicly available information. An assumption here then is that markets are not semi-strong form efficient.

The main strategies of quant funds are

- Growth Strategies
- Value Strategies
- Accounting Quality Strategies – or conservative accounting strategy which links future stock returns to specific accounting features and approaches such as how aggressive are their accounting principles (the more aggressive the less sustainable the future earnings).

As such, they are more commonly used for return maximising purposes rather than liability matching.

Performance

Returns from quant funds have been observed to be very similar to those of other funds, however they achieve these returns at lower risks and so offer higher Sharpe measures. It has been observed that quant funds tend to perform better in market downturns whereas more fundamental funds perform better in upswings. It has also been noted that quant funds tend to hold more small company stocks, potentially with higher trading costs and spreads.

Limitations

Quant funds rely on the accuracy and validity of any financial information that they analyse. Scandals such as Enron highlight the dangers of this reliance. Quant funds assume that the historical statistical relationships between stocks will continue into the future, which clearly may not hold true.

The combination approach

Many houses tend to use a combination approach, with fundamental and quantitative analysis dictating the markets and stocks which they wish to buy, and technical analysis being used to determine the timing of entry into the market place.

Regardless of whether the fund manager believes in technical analysis or not, they will have to keep an eye on the charts, since if sufficient numbers do believe the technical analysts, then the market will move in line with their predictions.

5.2.3 Riding the yield curve

Riding the yield curve is a valid strategy when the yield curve is upward sloping. If this is the case, then an investment manager can buy bonds with maturities in excess of his investment horizon. He proceeds to hold the bonds until the end of his investment period and then sells them. If the yield curve has not shifted during that period, the investment manager will have generated higher returns than if he had bought bonds with the same maturity as his investment horizon.

This follows because as the time to maturity declines, the yield to maturity falls and the price of the bond rises, thereby generating a capital gain (hence, the term yield curve ride). These gains will be higher than those available if bonds with the same maturity as the investment horizon are used, because the maturity value of the latter bonds is fixed.

Example

An investor has a liability due in one year. Two available bonds (both zero coupon) are

Bond	Maturity	Coupon %	Price £
A	1 year	6	$94.34 = \frac{100}{1.06}$
B	2 years	7	$87.34 = \frac{100}{1.06^2}$

Determine

- The return from a yield curve ride.
- The extra return from a yield curve ride.
- Comment on the risk of the position.

Solution

There are two alternative courses of action.

Alternative 1 – Invest in the one-year bond and hold to maturity

This is perhaps the most obvious course of action and would give the following.

Return

The return can be determined from the holding period return calculation, i.e.

$$r = \frac{100.00 - 94.34}{94.34} = 6\%$$

Alternatively, it can be taken as the yield on the bond of 6%, since the bond is a zero coupon held to maturity.

Risk

Again, since this is a zero coupon held to maturity, the risk is zero.

Alternative 2 – Invest in the two-year bond and hold for one year, selling as a one-year bond (The yield curve ride)

Return

The return can again be determined from the holding period return calculation, though an assumption is required regarding the selling price in one year. If we assume that the yield curve remains static, i.e. that in one year's time, bonds with one year to maturity are yielding 6% and those with two years to maturity are yielding 7%, then we will have

$$r = \frac{94.34 - 87.34}{87.34} = 8.01\%$$

Alternatively, this could have been calculated as the forward rate across from two to one year's maturity, i.e.

$$(1 + r_1)(1 + {}_1f_2) = (1 + r_1)^2$$

$$1.06 \times (1 + {}_1f_2) = 1.07^2$$

$$1 + {}_1f_2 = \frac{1.07^2}{1.06} = 1.0801$$

$${}_1f_2 = 0.0801 \text{ or } 8.01\%$$

Risk

The risk this time is not zero. Here, the investor is exposed to movements in the yield curve.

Conclusion

The yield curve ride is a strategy by which investors take on some risk in order to enhance returns.

5.2.4 Anomaly switching

Introduction

An anomaly switch is a switch between two bonds with very similar characteristics, but whose prices or yields are out of line with each other.

Substitution switching

The simplest example of an anomaly switch is a substitution switch. This involves the temporary exchange of two bonds that are similar in terms of maturity, coupon and quality rating and every other characteristic, but which differ in terms of price and yield. Since two similar bonds should trade at the same price and yield, this circumstance results in an arbitrage profit opportunity with the dear bond being sold and the cheap bond purchased initially.

If the coupon and maturity of the two bonds are similar, then a substitution swap involves a one-for-one exchange of bonds. However, if there are substantial differences in coupon or maturity, then the duration of the two bonds will differ. This will lead to different responses if the general level of interest rates changes during the life of the switch. It will therefore be necessary to weight the switch in such a way that it is hedged from changes in the level of interest rates, but is still exposed to changes in the anomalous yield differential between the bonds.

Pure yield pickup switch

Another type of anomaly switch is a pure yield pickup switch. This involves the sale of a bond that has a given yield to maturity and the purchase of a similar bond with a high yield to maturity. With this switch, there is no expectation of any yield or price correction, so no reverse transaction will need to take place at a later date, which may be the case with a substitution switch.

Identification of anomalies

Price differences and ratios

A price difference is simply the price of one bond less the price of the other. Here, the market plots the difference between the two bonds and establishes what it believes to be the normal difference. When the difference is greater or lesser than the normal difference then this represents a potential opportunity for a switch between the two bonds.

This is a very old and unsophisticated method of evaluating two bonds and the potential switch and has a number of important weaknesses. Firstly, it is not a proportionate measure and this can lead to erroneous decisions and secondly, due to the pull to redemption factor, it can only be used in stocks with a similar maturity and coupon.

The simple price difference was swiftly replaced by the price ratio. It is in essence the same idea of establishing a benchmark ratio and then appraising stocks by virtue of their difference away from this ratio. A price ratio has the advantage of being a proportionate measure. Here the price of one stock is divided by the price of the other.

Example

Stock	Price	Ratio	Historic Average
10% Trs	110½		
		0.961	0.94
11% Exch	115		

In this situation, the current ratio of the two prices is higher than the historic average and must be expected to fall, in the absence of any fundamental change in the relationship between the two stocks, back to its normal level. For that to happen, the price of the 11% Exch will have to rise or the price of the 10% Trs fall. This current ratio therefore suggests the switch out of the Trs into the Exch.

The crucial limitation of this analysis is that ratios are **historic** and there is the possibility that something may have taken place to distort the pattern of the two stocks.

A second limitation is that it ignores the dividend flows on the stocks.

Example

Stock	Price @ 1 January	Ratio	Price @ 1 July	Ratio
A 12% 8-yr bond	100		105	
		1.25		1.25
B 3% 5-yr bond	80		84	

Whilst the ratio between the two stocks has remained constant at 1.25, there would have been an advantage in the switch into the higher coupon stock. In terms of the return over the period

$$\text{Return from A} = \frac{\text{Coupon} + \text{Gain}}{\text{Initial price}} = \frac{6+5}{100} = 0.11 \text{ or } 11\%$$

For the 3% bond

$$\text{Return from B} = \frac{1.5+4}{80} = 0.06875 \text{ or } 6.875\%$$

Consequently, care must be taken to ensure that the price ratio is adjusted to reflect the differential coupon flows between the two stocks. The following formula neutralises the coupon disparity.

Δ Price ratio = $(F_b - F_a) \times R \times$ Time period in years

where

F_b = flat yield on Bond B

F_a = flat yield on Bond A

R = the initial ratio

Using the example from above

$(0.0375 - 0.12) \times 1.25 \times ½ = -5.15625\%$

The price ratio should fall by 5.15625% every six months. In effect, the ratio has remained constant suggesting that, all things being equal, it will be correct. Therefore, the price of the 12% bond will fall and/or the 3% rise, suggesting a switch out of the 12% and into the 3%.

Yield differences and ratios

More commonly, the market focuses on yield differences and yield ratios rather than price measures. As with the price measures however, these suffer from the drawback that they are historic measures and therefore only given a limited indication of what may happen in the future.

Example

Stock	Price	GRY	Modified Duration
12% 25-yr bond	76	15.90	6.3
12% 5-yr bond	85	16.52	3.5
	Difference	0.62	

By switching into the five-year bond, the investor picks up 62bp on the yield. However, if this switch were undertaken, the investor would be taking on a substantially reduced interest rate exposure (by switching into the lower duration stocks). Given that the yields are high at present and are likely to fall, then the stock with the lower modified duration will make the smaller gain.

It is possible to use duration-weighted switches in order to maintain the same level of exposure to the market.

One method of ensuring that the duration is taken into account is the use of switch profit projections.

Switch profit projections

A switch profit projection takes the proposed switch between two bonds and then evaluates it given a number of different yield assumptions. For example, we could take the illustration above with the 12% 25-year bond and the 12% five-year bond and look at the impact on overall gains if the yields rise by 1% and fall by 1%. The fund manager can then, based on their own assessment of the likely movement in interest rates, review the outcomes and look to the probable best return on the switch.

Moving one stage on from simple switch profit projections, fund managers can, if they wish, construct detailed **actuarial models** of the bond market to appraise the performances of various stocks and to assess the validity of certain switches.

The above analysis focused on a simple yield difference. Many fund managers, rather than using yield differences, use yield ratios in much the same way as a price ratio. Again, with a yield ratio, the key to interpreting the results will be the establishment of what is perceived as the norm, since this will, in effect, reflect the normal differences that you expect between the two stocks.

Yield curve comparisons

Whilst intra-stock comparisons are useful stock selection techniques, they are limited by virtue of the number of bonds in existence. A more general approach to evaluating an anomaly would be to look at the bond's position relative to the yield curve.

Obviously, in part, this is conditioned by the construction of the yield curve in the first place. However, once the fund manager has established the yield curve, he can then look to normal differences of stocks from that curve. For example, an eight-year, 7% bond may normally trade 25bp below the yield curve. If this difference becomes greater, it may represent a potential anomaly switch out of that stock and into a higher yielding security.

It is in the context of these comparisons of individual stocks against the yield curve that the yield surface becomes a useful investment tool and fund managers will appraise the stock by reference to its position against the yield surface.

Balance of term or breakeven yields

When purchasing stocks, the fund manager may have a choice between a short-dated stock and a longer dated stock. For example, the manager is investing money for two years. At present, the yield on a one-year bond is 10% and the yield on a two-year bond is 11%.

The choice that the fund manager faces is whether to invest in the one-year bond and on maturity roll that over into a second one-year bond, or whether to put the money into the two-year bond at the outset. The balance of term or breakeven yield indicates the return that will be required on the rollover in order to give them an equal return.

Two-year bond	11%	+ 11%	= 22%
One-year bond	10%	+ ?	= 22%

Using the example above, if the fund manager were to invest in the 11% bond, then in very simple terms over two years they would make a return of 22%. Consequently, if they were to invest in the one-year bond earning 10%, in order to break even the one-year rate in a year's time would need to be 12%.

This is obviously a very simplistic calculation and the creation of forward-forward rates would give a more accurate measure of the yield required. Once the breakeven yield has been calculated, the fund manager will then have to appraise whether it believes that 12% will be an achievable return in one year's time.

5.2.5 Policy switching

Introduction

A policy switch is a switch between two dissimilar bonds, which is designed to take advantage of an anticipated change in

- Interest rates.
- Structure of the yield curve.
- Bond quality rating.
- Sector relationships.

Such changes can be expected to lead to a change in the relative prices and yields of the two bonds. Policy switches involve greater expected returns, but also greater potential risks than anomaly switches.

Changes in interest rates

A market timer will always be on the lookout for changes in interest rates. Switching from low-duration to high-duration bonds if interest rates are expected to fall is an example of a policy switch.

Changes in the structure of the yield curve

Normally, the yield curve is a smooth relationship between yield and maturity. Occasionally, however, there may be humps or dips in the curve. If the humps or dips are expected to disappear, then the prices of the bonds on the hump can be expected to rise (and their yield fall correspondingly), and the prices of the bonds in the dips can be expected to fall (and their yields correspondingly rise). A policy switch would involve the purchase of the high-yield bond and the sale of the low-yield bond.

Another example of a policy switch resulting from changes in the structure of the yield curve is the bridge swap. This is illustrated in the diagram below, showing a rolling yield curve. The eight and ten-year bonds are selling at lower yields and higher prices than the nine-year bond. A bridge swap involves selling the eight and ten-year bonds and buying nine-year bonds, thereby selling bonds with an average yield of r_A and buying bonds with an average yield of r_B. The bridge swap gain is therefore $r_B - r_A$, and the duration of the portfolio will have been maintained.

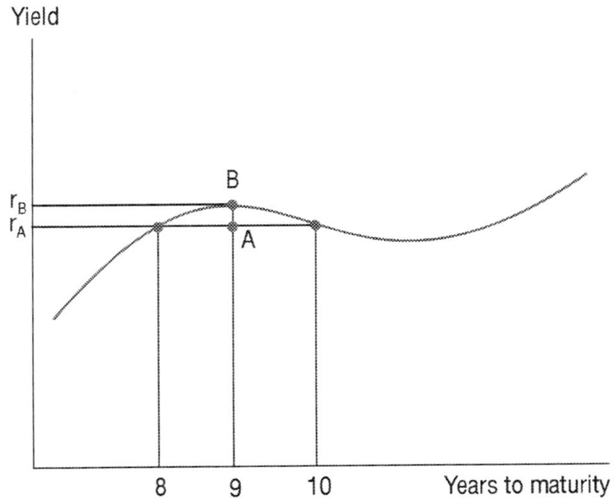

Changes in bond quality ratings

A bond whose quality rating is expected to fall will fall in price. To prevent a capital loss, it can be switched for a bond whose quality rating is expected to rise or remain unchanged.

Changes in sector relationships

An example of a change in sector relationships is a change in taxes between two sectors. For example, one sector may have withholding taxes on coupon payments, e.g. domestic bonds, whereas another, e.g. Eurobonds, may not. If it is anticipated that withholding tax will either be applied to all sectors or will be withdrawn from all sectors, then another switch is possible.

Spread trading

Policy switching is often conducted through the use of derivative instruments and indeed now, given the range of derivative instruments available on a variety of bond markets, the fund manager is able to spread one bond market yield curve against another – a form of policy switch.

For example, given the contacts currently available on Euronext.liffe, if the fund manager believed that the spread between the bund and the long gilt was likely to narrow then an appropriate spread trade might be to buy the long gilt and sell the bund future. It is also possible to trade one end of the yield curve against another and indeed the long end of one national yield curve against the short end of another, trading the long gilt against the three-month Euribor future.

5.2.6 Hedge funds

In a normal fund (pension fund, unit trust, etc.) the fund manager is constrained to taking long positions in assets/asset classes dictated by the trust deed/investment policy. Such funds will, therefore, gain in a rising market and lose in a falling one.

Losses in falling markets may be reduced through, if permitted

- Switching to cash.
- Hedging the fund, perhaps through the use of derivatives, though typically the manager would not be permitted to hedge more than the value of the fund

As a result, normal funds tend to either hold positive asset positions or a zero position (cash/fully hedged).

Hedge funds were originally intended to offer investments against falling markets using derivatives and short selling. However hedge funds have moved broadened from this and now there are many different hedge funds with a massive range of strategies. Some are geared and highly focussed, whilst others consider the macroeconomy and gamble on interest rates and currencies. The one thing that all hedge funds have in common is their desire to search for absolute returns.

The hedge fund manager is not concerned about performance compared to benchmarks and therefore has the freedom to try and generate high returns and hence high personal rewards. This may create the need for a risky portfolio, and therefore the name hedge fund is slightly misleading. A better name would probably be isolation fund, since the hedge fund manager looks for specific bets to try and generate high returns.

There are many different classes of hedge fund, hence it is difficult to give a general definition, however, the features of a hedge fund would generally include the following.

- The facility to take both long and short positions (i.e. no constraint to long positions only).
- The facility to gear up long or short exposure with borrowings and/or derivatives to gain a level of exposure (value at risk) significantly greater than the intrinsic value of the fund itself. The level of exposure gained
- May render arbitrage trades cost effective, that otherwise would not be.
- Produces geared performance, sometimes producing quite spectacular returns.

- The possibility of investing in any security from shares and bonds through to currencies and commodities, though many hedge funds specialise.
- Typically, a very high minimum investment level, often in excess of £1m, though this is now changing.
- Typically based offshore, where regulations and disclosure requirements are lower.

Regulation

Hedge funds are themselves not regulated by the FSA and so are not generally marketable investments. However, the fund managers are themselves FSA regulated firms.

Fees

Hedge fund managers will receive a fixed base management fee, which is a percentage (often between 1% and 2%) of the value of assets under management and an incentive fee which is related to profits. As this cannot be negative if losses are made, there will often be a clause stating that if losses are made, these losses have to be repaid in any subsequent profits before an incentive fee can be paid.

Example

A hedge fund has a base fee of 1%. The incentive fee is 25% for any returns made over and above the risk-free rate. Gross returns during the year were 38% and the risk-free rate is 6%. What is the net return?

Solution

Fee = 1% + 25% × (38% – 6%) = 9%

Net return = 38% – 9% = 29%

Types of hedge funds

As we have already noted, the name 'hedge fund' is a huge misnomer that is applied to many categories of fund, from very low risk to super-geared funds. These funds may be broadly classified as follows.

- **Global macro funds** bet on macroeconomic variables such as currencies or interest rates. They are often highly geared and use derivatives. Subgroups of macrofunds are **futures funds**, which use futures to bet on certain asset classes such as currency, fixed income and commodities and **emerging-market funds**. These can sometimes be referred to as speculative or tactical funds.
- **Directional long/short funds** take positions in stock and are often geared. They are not normally market neutral, but instead have a long or short bias.
- **Event-driven funds** but on events specific to a company or security. One example of this would be to invest in distressed securities or shares involved in a merger or acquisition.
- **Market-neutral funds** take long positions in stocks that are considered undervalued and short positions in stocks that are considered overvalued. The fund is neutral, in that the value of short positions is equal to the value of long positions and the sensitivity of long and short positions is the same. Other strategies of a market neutral portfolio are to look for arbitrage opportunities in warrants or derivatives. They should therefore be relatively intuitive to changes in the underlying market.

And each of these broad classes can be further sub-analysed as follows.

Global macro funds

- **Macro** – Looking to capitalise on economic change in certain countries, typically brought about by shifts in government policy that impact on interest rates, exchange rates, stock, and bond markets. They typically use gearing and derivatives to accentuate the impact of market moves. Typical risk = Very High.
- **Emerging Markets** – Invests in equity or debt of emerging markets that tend to have higher inflation and volatile growth. Short selling is not permitted in many emerging markets, and, therefore, effective hedging is often not available. Typical risk = Very High.

Directional long/short funds

- **Short Selling** – Short selling stocks assessed by the manager to be overpriced in anticipation of buying them back in the future at a lower price. Typical risk = Very High.
- **Aggressive Growth** – Invests in equities expected to experience acceleration in growth of earnings per share. The investments are often in smaller and micro cap stocks which are expected to experience rapid growth, though they may includes sector specialist funds such as technology, banking, or biotechnology. Typical risk = High.
- **Market Timing** – Allocate assets between different asset classes depending on the manager's view on the economy or market. The portfolio may swing widely between asset classes. The unpredictability of market movements and the difficulty of timing entry and exit from markets add to the volatility of this strategy. Typical risk = High.
- **Value** – Invests in securities perceived to be selling at deep discounts to their intrinsic or potential worth. Such securities may be out of favour or not well followed by analysts. Such strategies typically require a long-term holding and substantial until the ultimate value is recognised by the market. Typical risk = Low - Moderate.
- **Income** – Invests with primary focus on yield or current income rather than solely on capital gains. Such funds may utilise gearing to buy bonds and sometimes fixed income derivatives in order to profit from principal appreciation and interest income. Typical risk = Low.

Event driven funds

- **Opportunistic** – Aim to profit from events such as IPOs, sudden price changes caused by an interim earnings disappointment, hostile bids, and other event-driven opportunities. Such funds may utilise several of these investment styles at a given time and are not restricted to any particular investment approach or asset class. Typical risk = Variable.
- **Special Situations** – Invests in event-driven situations such as mergers, hostile takeovers, reorganisations, or leveraged buyouts. Strategies may involve the simultaneous purchase of stock in companies being acquired, and the sale of stock in its acquirer, hoping to profit from the spread between the current market price and the ultimate purchase price of the company. Such funds may also utilise derivatives to leverage returns and to hedge out interest rate and/or market risk. Typical risk = Moderate.
- **Distressed Securities** – Buying the shares, bonds or trade assets of companies in financial distress (and therefore at a deep discount), looking to profit from the market's lack of understanding of the true value of these deeply discounted securities and take advantage of the fact that the majority of institutional investors cannot own below investment grade securities. Typical risk = Low – Moderate.

Market neutral funds

- **Market Neutral - Arbitrage** – Attempts to hedge out almost all market risk by taking offsetting positions, often in different securities of the same company. For example, the fund can be long convertible bonds and short the underlying shares of the company. These funds may also use futures or interest rate swaps to hedge out interest rate risk. The focuses of these funds is on generating returns with low or no correlation to both the equity and bond markets.
  - *Convertibles arbitrage* – where a position is taken in convertibles and an opposite position is taken in the equities of a company to hedge out the equity risk of the convertibles and take advantage of any mispricing of that equity risk.
  - *Fixed income arbitrage* – where a position is taken in a fixed income product and an opposite position is taken with swaps or futures.
  - *Mortgage backed securities arbitrage* – as for fixed income arbitrage
  - *Capital structure arbitrage* – going long the high-yield bonds and short the equities of a company to hedge out the equity risk in the bonds in a similar manner to convertible arbitrage
  - *Closed-end fund arbitrage* – where a position is taken in a closed-end fund and an opposite position in the underlying stock, effectively trading on the premium or discount on the fund.

  Typical risk = Low.
- **Market Neutral - Securities Hedging** – Invests equally in long and short equity portfolios generally in the same sectors of the market. The aim is to reduce market risk and to generate a return from relative mispricing between the stocks. One technique is **pairs trading** which can be used for pairs of stocks whose prices are closely correlated and tend to move together. If the historical price relationship between them is ever breaks down, a long-short position is established in the two stocks in anticipation of the relationship being re-established. These funds usually have low or no correlation to the market and may uses market index futures to hedge out any residual market (systematic) risk. Typical risk = Low .

Others

- **Multi Strategy** – Adopt a variety of investment strategies in order to achieve positive returns. Typical risk = Variable.

Summarising

Hence at one extreme there are aggressive hedge funds that take a view on a market and heavily back that view. In these funds the money may not be protected by either a trustee or custodian, and the management fees may be very high as a percentage of the fund growth. It is these aggressive funds that get into difficulties if their hunches are wrong. Given the geared nature of many such funds, their trading stance can have a significant effect on markets. These effects have been further amplified by the time-zone arbitrages (or market-timing activities) of certain funds.

At the other end of the spectrum there are funds which do not gear up and use hedging to control risk. These more cautious funds have typically returned around 10% each year at very low levels of risk, due to extreme levels of international diversification not normally available to fund managers.

5.3 Passive stock selection strategies

5.3.1 Introduction

There are a number of very important approaches to passive bond fund management that we detail below. Passive management will be adopted if we believe that markets are efficient and that no mispricing exists (or more pragmatically that the benefit to be derived from any mispricing does not outweight the costs). Though this may possibly be the case in major developed markets it is unlikely to be the case in all markets.

5.3.2 Buy and hold

A buy and hold strategy involves buying a portfolio of securities and holding them for a long period of time, with only minor and infrequent adjustments to the portfolio over time. Under this strategy, investments bought now are held indefinitely, or if they have fixed maturities, held until maturity and then replaced with similar ones. The returns from a buy and hold strategy will be dominated by income flows, i.e. dividends and coupons and, for shares, long-term capital growth. Short-term capital movements are irrelevant for this strategy.

Since there is a consensus view when adopting a passive stock selection strategy that all securities are fairly priced at all times, it does not really matter which securities are bought and held. However, by buying and holding only a few securities, a substantial amount of diversifiable risk may remain in the portfolio. Hence, a reasonable number of securities must be held within the portfolio.

5.3.3 Indexation

Introduction

A version of buy and hold that eliminates diversifiable risk is index matching or indexation. Indexation involves the construction of an index fund that is designed to replicate the performance of a market index.

With indexation, the fund manager selects an appropriate index quoted in the market place. Having established the index, the fund manager builds a portfolio that mimics the index, the belief being that this portfolio will then perform in line with the index numbers.

Approach to indexation

The first stage in the indexation process must be to establish the appropriate market index that you are going to track. Once the appropriate index has been established, the portfolio must be constructed which, in some way, mimics that index. There are several possible approaches that could be adopted.

It should be noted that indexation itself is not a totally passive form of fund management since the constitution of each index will, over time, change and as such the portfolio will also be required to change.

Complete indexation

Complete indexation involves the construction of an index fund that exactly matches the underlying market portfolio. In the case of shares, this could be the FTA All Shares Index; in the case of bonds, it could be the Salomon Brothers Bond Index; in the case of an international portfolio, it could be the Morgan Stanley Capital International Index.

Complete indexation is very expensive. For example, the FTA All Shares Index contains several hundred securities weighted according to their relative market proportions. To construct a portfolio of all these securities with the same proportions as the index would involve extremely high commissions and dealing costs.

In addition, the constituents of the index change quite frequently and so, rebalancing the index fund would again involve dealing costs and commissions as well as dealing spreads.

A bond index fund is even more expensive to construct. Over time, the average maturity of a bond index will decline unless new long maturing bonds are added to replace those that have matured and automatically dropped out of the index.

All of this shows that complete indexation is not practical and that one of the following three alternatives must be adopted.

Stratified sampling

Stratified sampling involves the construction of an index fund based on a sample of securities from the total population comprising the index.

Obviously the more bonds that are selected to be part of the portfolio, the less the risk of sampling error, but the greater the overall cost that the fund will incur.

An appropriate methodology might be to begin by defining the classes into which the index is to be divided. The classes will be established by various maturity intervals.

- One to two years.
- Two to three years.
- Three to four years.
- Four to six years.
- Six to eight years.
- Eight to ten years.

Within each maturity level, coupon levels should be established.

- Under 10% coupons.
- Over 10% coupons.

Once these basic stratifications have been established, a computer programme is normally used to establish the number of stocks or the value of the fund to be invested within each band.

Once the basic criteria have been established, it then falls to the fund manager to select specific stocks from the market which meet the criteria for each band. At this stage, an element of active management comes into the indexation process as the fund manager attempts to pick those stocks which he believes will outperform all others in that particular sector of the market.

When selecting the value to be invested within each segment, the fund manager will also have regard to the size of each deal to ensure that all deals are economic in value. It is conventional to deal in round lots, which the market tends to regard as better bargains and therefore, offers finer prices. Once the index has been mimicked and the stocks selected, the fund manager will then have to reappraise the performance of the fund on a frequent (monthly) basis and, where necessary, take steps to rebalance as the constitution of the index itself alters.

Factor matching

Factor matching involves the construction of an index fund using securities selected on the basis of a number of factors or risk indices. The first risk factor may be the duration, so the selected portfolio may be chosen to have the same duration as the market. Other factors may be credit risk, coupon pattern etc. The selected index fund would be a portfolio of, say, 50 securities that matched the market in terms of the above factors and have the highest correlation with the market.

Co-mingling

Co-mingling involves the use of co-mingled funds, such as unit trusts or investment trusts, rather than the explicit formation of an index fund. Co-mingling may be especially suitable for clients with relatively small portfolios and may provide an acceptable compromise between the transaction costs of complete indexation and the tracking error of stratified sampling.

Results of indexation

Apart from the transaction costs involved in setting up and rebalancing, there are other problems associated with running an index fund. The most important of these concerns income payments on the securities.

The total return on an index may include not only capital gains but also income in the form of coupon payments. In order to match the performance of the index in terms of income, the index fund would have to have the same pattern of income payments as the index. It would also have to make the same reinvestment assumptions. Unless complete indexation had been undertaken, it would be unlikely that an index fund would exactly replicate the income pattern of the index.

In addition, the index may assume that gross income payments are reinvested costlessly back into the index on the day each security becomes ex-div. In practice, however, this assumption is violated in four ways.

- The coupon payment is not made until an average of six weeks after the ex-div date.
- The payment is received net of tax.
- There are dealing costs of reinvesting income payments.
- The income payments on different securities may be fairly small and it may not be worthwhile investing such small sums on the days they are received.

Another problem concerns the effect of changing the constituents of the index. When the announcement of a change is made, the price of the security being deleted tends to fall, while the price of the security being added tends to rise. These effects can cause major tracking errors between index funds and the index itself.

Overall, the likelihood is that the fund will underperform the index, i.e. suffer a tracking error, for a number of reasons.

Indexation is, however, a popular form of fund management. It attempts to avoid, as far as possible, decisions about selection and timing of investment. As already noted, however, it is not purely passive. At the very least, the choice of index and the reinvestment of income involve active intervention.

Indexation is normally used in conjunction with other active methods whereby there is an indexed core fund with actively managed peripheral funds, again with the objective of enhancing the overall return of the fund.

Exchange Traded Funds

Exchange Traded Funds (ETFs) are open-ended collective investment vehicles that are UCITS compliant. They allow exposure to an index through the purchase of shares which must be listed and tradable on a stock exchange. In the UK, ETFs are listed on the extraMark market of the LSE and their shares are traded through the SETS order book and settle through CREST.

ETFs are shares that afford the legal right of ownership over part of a basket of individual shares held by the fund. These ETF shares trade at prices that very closely match their underlying assets, hence very closely match the index.

To create an ETF a fund manager firstly needs to describe precisely the composition of the ETF, usually an index whose constituents change infrequently. They then assemble the appropriate basket of stocks and send them to a custodian bank for safekeeping. This basket of securities may have been purchased by the fund manager for the purposes of establishing the ETF, alternatively they may have been borrowed from other investors such as pension funds. On receipt of the appropriate stocks, the custodian issues the appropriate number of ETF shares. The ETFs can then be freely sold into the open market and from then on they can be freely traded between investors.

Redemption of ETFs is simply the reverse of the above creation process. The manager buys a large block of ETFs on the open market and sends it to the custodian bank and in return receives back an equivalent basket of individual stocks which are then sold on the open market or returned to their lenders.

In practice only the very biggest institutional money management firms with experience in indexing tend to play the role of managing an ETF. They direct pension funds with enormous baskets of stocks in markets all over the world to loan stocks necessary for the creation process. They also create demand by lining up customers, either institutional or retail, to buy a newly introduced ETF.

Because ETFs are based on indices that tend to be quite stable, the fund management costs tend to be very low. The manager looks to make money on the bid-offer spread and from any price anomalies between the ETF and the underlying shares. Whenever there is an opportunity to earn a little by buying one and selling the other, the manager will do so. This activity will have the effect of keeping the price of the ETF in line with the price of the underlying shares since it will involve buying the relatively underpriced asset (driving its price up) and selling the relatively overpriced asset (driving its price down).

Though a little cumbersome, this process achieves transparency and liquidity at modest cost. Everyone can see what goes into an ETF, investor fees are clearly laid out, investors can be confident that they can exit at any time, and the manager's fees are guaranteed to be modest.

ETFs are available in the UK over a wide variety of indices providing an easy and low cost route to investing in the main index, in high yield stocks, in growth stocks, in value stocks etc.

They allow investors to adopt an investment style even with low levels of investment.

5.3.4 Immunisation

Exam tip

> A key bond fund management idea, see Winter 2007 Question 6.

Introduction

Using immunisation (bond duration matching), it is possible to create a portfolio to have an assured return over a specific time horizon, irrespective of any changes in the interest rate. Hence, if we need to match a liability, we should select a bond portfolio with the same duration as the liability it is intended to meet.

The concept of immunisation

A bond is purchased with a yield of 10%. Interest rates fall to 8%. Consequently, the price of the bond will rise. However, the overall return on the bond will fall, as it is now only possible to reinvest the coupons received at the rate of 8%. As the bond approaches maturity, this fall in the return will become greater as the reinvestment loss outweighs the gain (which will fall as the bond moves to redemption and the price pulls to redemption at par). Overall, the investor will not receive a return of 10% (the yield).

The same is true of the opposite situation where interest rates rise and bond prices fall. Again, the fall in the bond's price will gradually be repaired as the bond approaches maturity and the bond pulls to redemption. The coupons, however, will have been reinvested at a higher rate, therefore generating greater returns. Under this scenario, the overall return from the investment will have outperformed the quoted yield of 10%.

As we saw earlier, the yield is not an effective measure of the anticipated return on a bond if it is held to maturity precisely because it assumes reinvestment at the same rate as the yield.

The concept of **immunisation** relies on the fact that these two effects (price and reinvestment) are balanced at the point of duration, the weighted average life of the bond. Therefore, by holding a bond to its duration and not its maturity, the return can be guaranteed.

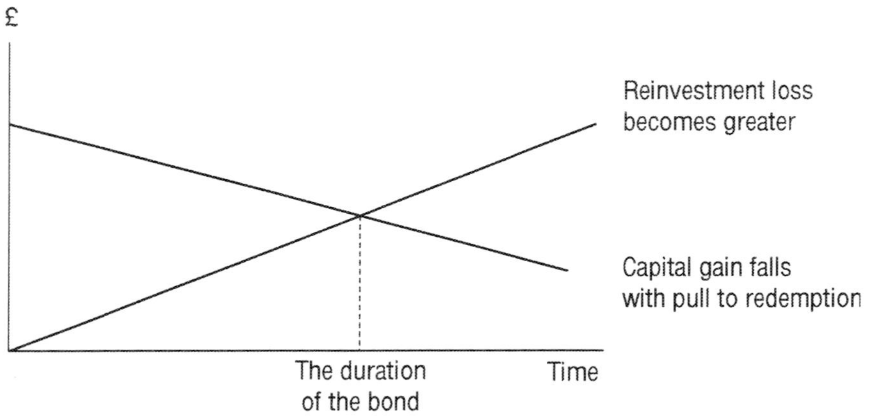

Immunisation is a process whereby the fund manager purchases a bond or portfolio of bonds with a duration equal to the liability. If the manager is able to do this, then he is guaranteeing that the fund will earn the gross redemption yield, since any alteration in capital value will be balanced by the reinvestment gain or loss.

Example

A 13.77% gilt with five years to maturity is currently yielding 10%. Its market value and duration can therefore be shown to be as follows.

Time	Cash Flow (£)	DF (10%)	PV (£)	tPV (£)
1	13.77	0.9091	12.52	12.52
2	13.77	0.8264	11.38	22.76
3	13.77	0.7513	10.35	31.04
4	13.77	0.6830	9.40	37.62
5	113.77	0.6209	70.64	353.22
			114.29	457.16

Market value = £114. 29

$$\text{Duration} = \frac{457.16}{114.29} = 4 \text{ years}$$

If this bond is held for four years (its duration) with income reinvested, the value of the fund at the end of that time (its terminal value) for three possible interest rates (9%, 10%, 11%) will be

Time	Cash Flow	Comp. Fact. (9%)	Terminal Value (9%)	Comp. Fact. (10%)	Terminal Value (10%)	Comp. Fact. (11%)	Terminal Value (11%)
1	13.77	1.09^3	17.83	1.10^3	18.33	1.11^3	18.83
2	13.77	1.09^2	16.36	1.10^2	16.66	1.11^2	16.97
3	13.77	1.09	15.01	1.10	15.15	1.11	15.28
4	13.77	1.00	13.77	1.00	13.77	1.00	13.77
5	113.77	$\frac{1}{1.09}$	104.38	$\frac{1}{1.10}$	103.44	$\frac{1}{1.11}$	102.50
			167.35		167.35		167.35

Hence, whatever happens to reinvestment rates, the fund value at four years will always be £167.35, and the yield will have been

$$\text{Yield} = \sqrt[4]{\frac{167.35}{114.29}} - 1 = 10\%$$

Equal to the original yield on the bond. By holding a bond for its duration, it is possible to lock in the initial yield to maturity.

Immunisation of bond portfolio

The same principles apply to portfolios of bonds. The duration of a portfolio of bonds is simply the weighted average of the durations of individual bonds (weighting by values).

It is possible to construct a portfolio with the specified duration from a whole range of bonds with different durations. For example, a portfolio could be constructed from bonds with durations close to that of the liabilities, this would be a focused or bullet portfolio. Alternatively, it could be constructed from bonds with durations distant from that of the liability, a barbell portfolio.

Example

A fund has a liability due in ten years and a set of bonds with durations of four, nine, eleven and fifteen years.

A focused portfolio would contain the nine and eleven-year duration bonds in equal proportions, giving a portfolio of duration

$0.500 \times 9 + 0.500 \times 11 = 10$ years

A barbell portfolio would consist of the four and fifteen-year duration bonds with 45.5% of the fund invested in the shorter dated bond and 54.5% in the longer duration bond, giving a portfolio duration of

$0.455 \times 4 + 0.545 \times 15 = 10$ years

The advantage of the barbell strategy is that a much wider range of portfolios with different durations can be constructed, compared with the focused strategy. However, the disadvantage of the barbell strategy is that it has greater immunisation risk than the focused strategy.

Immunisation risk

Immunisation risk arises whenever there is a non-parallel shift in the yield curve. The above example of immunisation showed that it works for parallel shifts in the yield curve, i.e. the reinvestment rate fell from 10% to 9% for each coupon. If this does not happen, then matching the duration of the investment to the liability horizon no longer guarantees immunisation. Non-parallel shifts in the yield curve will lead to the income component and the capital component changing in value by differing amounts.

This risk is reduced if the durations and convexities of the individual bonds in the immunising portfolio are close to that of the liability, i.e. a focused portfolio. In this case, the non-parallel yield curve shift will affect the individual bonds and the liability in similar ways. This is unlikely to be the case if a barbell portfolio had been constructed, since the individual bonds within the portfolio would be affected in different ways.

Rebalancing

Immunisation is not a completely passive approach to fund management because the portfolio will require a continual **rebalancing**. The initial bonds are selected on the grounds of their portfolios' duration, but because duration erodes over time and due to the effects of immunisation risk, new bonds will have to be purchased in order to match the liability.

One possible way around this is to immunise the portfolio using zero-coupon bonds. The advantage of zero-coupon bonds would be that their duration will change in line with time and therefore, the portfolio will not require a constant **rebalancing**. However, without the existence of a strips market, there are unlikely to be the stocks that are required as straight zeros.

Multi-period immunisation

So far, we have been considering a fund with one liability and immunising that fund against changes in interest rates by selecting a bond with a duration that matches the maturity of that liability. If a fund has several liabilities, then immunisation is still a possibility. With multi-period immunisation, a general approach would be to match the duration of the liabilities against the duration of the portfolio of bonds.

Within this, however, a number of additional caveats need to be made.

- The present value of the assets should be greater than or equal to the present value of the liabilities.
- The dispersion of the assets should be greater than or equal to the dispersion of the liabilities.

Dispersion

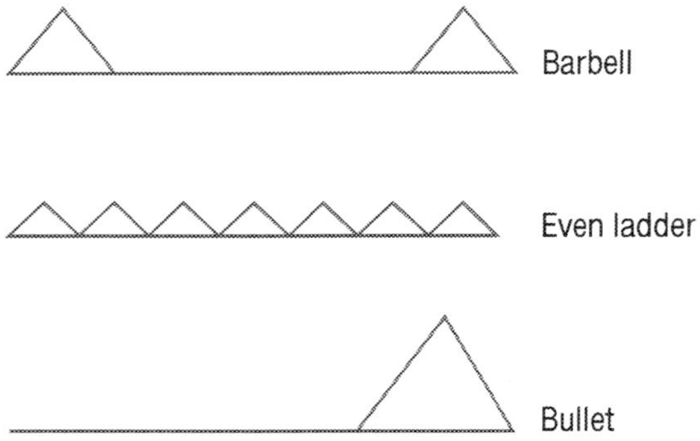

Dispersion refers to the need for assets to mature in order to meet liabilities and, for portfolios of equal duration, can be assessed by the convexity of the bond or portfolio. Note that the convexity of a bond portfolio is the weighted average of the convexities of the individual bonds.

With a barbell dispersion of liabilities, the weighting of assets must be matched to the need for liability funding. With an even ladder, the weighting of assets can be spread across the range of maturities. With a bullet, obviously there is only one liability to be matched.

Broadly speaking, these conditions are only relevant for parallel shifts in the yield curve. For other shifts, alternative approaches to immunising a portfolio need to be considered involving complex actuarial models of how the bond market may develop.

When selecting bonds to include as part of the immunised portfolio another factor to be taken into consideration is double-dated bonds. With these, the risk of call is a factor that needs to be considered, since this will obviously affect the duration.

Contingent immunisation

With contingent immunisation, the fund manager actively manages the portfolio attempting to enhance returns subject to an absolute **floor rate of return** which the fund must generate. If active management fails to generate the floor level of return, at that stage, the portfolio is immunised, locking in the minimum rate of return. In this way, the liabilities of the fund are insured against risk, guaranteeing that the rate of return will be sufficient to meet the liabilities as and when they mature.

5.3.5 Cash flow matching or dedication

Introduction

Cash flow matching is a much simpler approach to fund management. The approach is simply to purchase bonds whose redemption proceeds will meet a liability of the fund as they fall due.

Under the concept of matching, bonds are purchased to match the liabilities of the fund. Starting with the final liability, a bond (Bond 1) is purchased whose final coupon and redemption proceeds will extinguish the liability.

Turning next to the penultimate liability, in part, this may be satisfied by the coupon flows arising from Bond 1, any remaining liability being matched against the final coupon and redemption value of a second bond (Bond 2).

This process is continued for each liability, ensuring that bonds are purchased whose final coupon and redemption values extinguish the net liabilities of the fund as and when they occur.

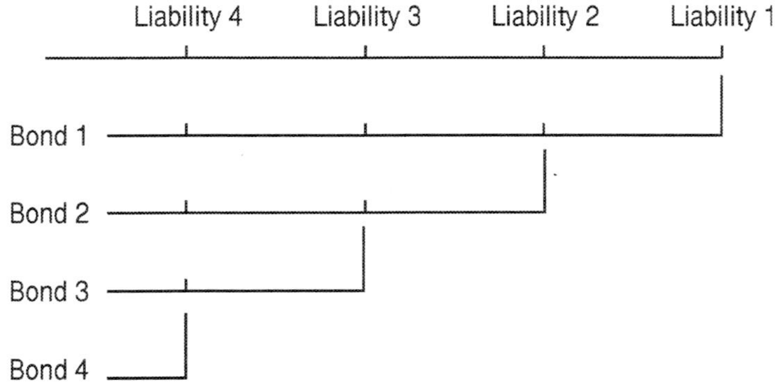

Example

A fund has to meet liabilities of £1,000 arising at the end of each of the next three years. There are three bonds available.

Maturity Years	Coupon %	Redemption Payment, Capital and Coupon £
1	14.29	114.29
2	12.50	112.50
3	11.11	111.11

Construct a portfolio to achieve cash matching.

Solution

Number of Bonds	Coupon (£)	Maturity (Years)	Cash Flows Year 1 (£)	Year 2 (£)	Year 3 (£)
9	11.11	3	100	100	1,000
8	12.50	2	100	900	–
7	14.29	1	800	–	–
			1,000	1,000	1,000

In effect, this policy is a simple **buy and hold** strategy and as such does not require a regular rebalancing. Technically, it is inferior to immunisation since, in practice, it is unlikely that bonds exist with appropriate maturity dates and coupons, it involves a greater initial capital outlay but, intuitively, it is easier to understand.

5.3.6 Combination matching or horizon matching

Combination matching is a mixture of the above two approaches to investment management. For example, we could construct a portfolio that cash flow matches the liabilities for the next four quarters but is immunised for the remaining investment horizon. At the end of the four quarters, the portfolio is rebalanced to cash flow match over the subsequent four quarters and is again immunised for the remaining period.

5.4 Mixed management

5.4.1 Introduction

We have considered active and passive strategies separately, but it is possible for fund mangers to use a mixed management style, mixing these two together. For example, the asset allocation decision can be passive, with active security selection. This is known as a security selection style of management. Alternatively, the fund manager may construct a passive portfolio of individual securities but make active allocation decisions. This is known as asset allocation style of management.

5.4.2 Core-satellite portfolio

Another mixed strategy is core-satellite portfolio management. Increasingly, fund managers are being requested to outperform indices rather than merely to track them. This inevitably requires a less passive/more interventionist approach, which could be achieved with an **indexed core fund** and a **peripheral fund**, which is more actively managed and potentially involves the use of derivatives in order to establish larger trading positions than the fund itself can obtain.

This is a management strategy often pursued by very large funds. The fund manager has a large core portfolio that is never traded because doing so would result in adverse market movement. The surrounding satellite portfolios are actively managed in order to generate superior returns.

5.4.3 Portfolio tilting

A fund manager may combine both active and passive fund management methods through portfolio tilting. That is holding all/a representative sample of the constituents of an index (like a passive tracker fund), but going slightly overweight in sectors he is bullish about, and underweight in others, this asset allocation decision constituting the active management component.

5.4.4 Derivatives

A third type of mixed active-passive strategy involves options and futures. Fund managers may have a passive portfolio of cash market securities that are not traded because of the high transaction costs involved. Instead, the fund managers trade individual stock options. Similarly, they can engage in market timing and shift the beta of their portfolio or the duration of their bond portfolios by buying or selling stock or guilt index options and futures. This is because transaction costs are low and liquidity is generally high in the derivatives markets.

An alternative version of this strategy is using equitised cash portfolios. The entire value of the portfolio is passively held in money market instruments, the active part of the strategy is performed entirely with derivatives.

CHAPTER ROUNDUP

General

Questions that get asked here are discursive and though we have used some numerical examples to illustrate ideas you should not expect to have to repeat them.

You need to be able to

- Detail the objectives and constraints of a fund, particularly in the context of a case study question.
- Discuss the various analysis approaches (fundamental, technical, quantitative).
- Contrast
  - Active and passive management outlining the beliefs underlying each.
  - Top-down and bottom-up approaches
- Discuss ethical or socially responsible investing.

Asset allocation

You need to be able to

- Outline the idea of portfolio optimisation.
- Discuss VAR in detail.

Stock selection

You need to be able to describe

- Active bond techniques
  - Fundamental analysis
  - Technical analysis
  - Quantitative funds
  - Riding the yield curve (calculations are possible here)
  - Bond switching
  - Hedge funds
- Passive bond techniques
  - Buy and hold
  - Indexation and ETFs
  - Immunisation – this is a major technique and may require the calculation and/or discussion of duration, modified duration and convexity
  - Cash flow matching
- Mixed management
  - Core and satellite
  - Portfolio tilting

Market timing

You need to be able to discuss the idea of market timing

TEST YOUR KNOWLEDGE

Without referring back through the chapter make brief notes on the following.

1. Fund objectives and constraints.

2. Pros and cons of socially responsible investing.

3. Contrast the approaches of top-down management to bottom-up management.

4. The principal of VAR.

5. The functioning of quantitative funds.

6. Reasons for the rise in popularity of tracker funds.

7. The risks of immunisation and the idea of contingent immunisation.

8. (a) You are responsible for a portfolio of international corporate and government bonds which you manage on behalf of a UK pension fund. Write a brief note designed for the senior management of your fund management company explaining the role of convexity in managing a portfolio and how you use it in order to manage your portfolio.

   (b) A portfolio consists of the following two US Treasury bonds.

Bond	Price ($)	Coupon	Maturity	GRY	Duration	Convexity
A	106.367	7.75	2006	7.375	8.053	83.351
B	104.584	8.25	2016	8.152	10.275	157.456

   Estimate the duration and convexity of a portfolio with $2.5 million nominal of each bond in it.

9. You have been given the following information on two US Treasuries obtained from Bloomberg. You hold $5m nominal of Bond A.

Bond	Coupon	Maturity	Modified Duration	Clean Price (in 32nds)	Accrued Interest
A	$7\frac{1}{4}$	30/3/08	3.00	$96-01	$0.0993
B	$7\frac{3}{4}$	26/01/25	9.51	$90-25	$1.5075

   (a) Determine the relevant amounts of each bond that you would buy/sell in order to carry out

   (i) A par for par switch.
   (ii) A modified duration-adjusted switch.

   (b) In the case of (i), if the yield on Bond A remains unchanged and the yield on Bond B falls 50 bp, estimate the profit you would make on the transaction.

   (c) Describe briefly the factors you would consider before carrying out a yield pick-up switch such as outlined in (a) (i) and (a) (ii).

10. You have a portfolio of bonds with the following characteristics.

Bond	Duration	Yield to Maturity	Price (in 32nds)	Nominal Amount $m
A	6.7	5.65	97-28	5.6
B	4.3	5.45	99-02	4.4

(a) What is the market value of the portfolio?
(b) Calculate the duration of the portfolio.
(c) What profit would the portfolio make for a 20 bp fall in yield to maturity on both bonds?
(d) What factors should you take account of when carrying out a risk neutral bond switch?

11. A two bond portfolio has been set up to meet a liability that will occur in three years' time. Bond A is redeemable at par at the end of two years and has a coupon rate of 8%; Bond B has a coupon rate of 7% and is redeemable at a premium to par of 3% in five years' time. The yield curve is flat, with yields to maturity of 10%. Both bonds have just paid their annual coupon.

Requirements

(a) Calculate the proportions to invest in the two bonds at the present time in order to immunise the portfolio relative to the liability.

(b) Compute the corresponding proportions at the end of the current year, assuming the yield curve has not shifted, and comment upon your result.

(c) Outline what other precautions are necessary in order to protect the portfolio against large shifts in interest rates (no further calculations are required.)

12. The present composition of a bond portfolio is summarised in the table below.

Bond	Current Price	Proportion in Portfolio
One-year, zero coupon	90.90	10%
Four-year, zero coupon	68.30	20%
Six-year, zero coupon	56.45	10%
Two-year, 10% coupon	100.0	30%
Three-year, 6% coupon	90.06	30%

All bonds are redeemable at par and the term structure is flat over the range of one to ten years. The coupon has just been paid on each of the coupon bonds.

Requirements

(a) Calculate the unanticipated change in the value of the bond portfolio that will arise with a 1% increase in yields across the whole term structure (you may assume that the interest rate change is sufficiently small to ensure that the relationship between price changes and yield changes is linear).

(b) Discuss briefly how you would immunise a bond portfolio linked to a multiple stream of liabilities.

TEST YOUR KNOWLEDGE: ANSWERS

The answers below simply refer you to the relevant section in this chapter.

1. 1.2, 1.3
2. 2.8
3. 2.4
4. 3.3
5. 4.2.2
6. 4.3.3
7. 4.3.4
8. (a) Whilst the duration of a bond will indicate its relative sensitivity to movements in the interest rate and the modified duration can be used to predict the change in price given a change in market rates both of these measures are prone to inaccuracy. Convexity is an attempt to measure this inaccuracy of the duration calculation.

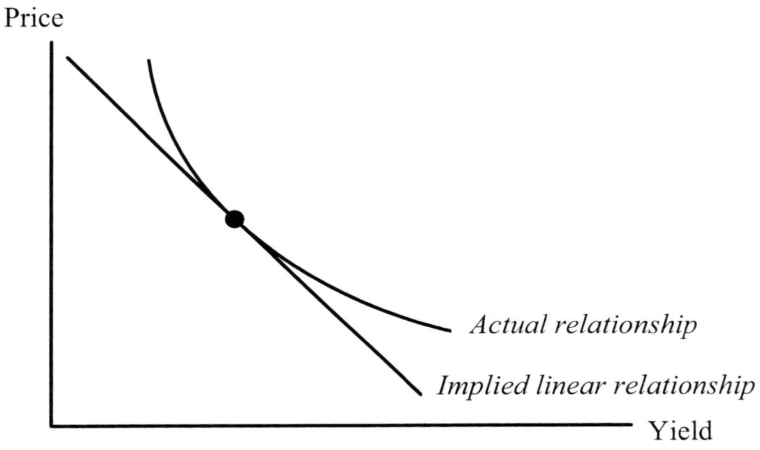

The principal impact of convexity will be that the bond with higher convexity will outperform other bonds with the same duration. In the market this will normally be implicit in the price of the bond reflecting the greater potential of the bond.

In order to gain the maximum exposure to the market, within a duration constraint, it would make sense to select those bonds with the highest convexities.

(b) This will require a weighted average (weighted by market value).

A $2,500,000 × $106.367 =	$2,659,175
B $2,500,000 × $104.584 =	$2,614,600
	$5,273,775

$$\frac{(\$2{,}659{,}175 \times 8.053) + (\$2{,}614{,}600 \times 10.275)}{5{,}273{,}775} = 9.1546 \textbf{ Duration}$$

$$\frac{(\$2{,}659{,}175 \times 83.351) + (\$2{,}614{,}600 \times 157.456)}{5{,}273{,}775} = 120.0903 \textbf{ Convexity}$$

9. (a) (i) \$5 million par

$$\$5m \times (90 \tfrac{25}{32} + 1.5075) = \$4{,}614{,}437.50$$

(ii) $$\$5m \times (96 \tfrac{1}{32} + 0.0993) = \$4{,}806{,}527.50$$

$$\$4{,}806{,}527.50 \times \frac{3}{9.51} = \$1{,}516{,}254.73$$

Value of Bond B

Dirty price of Bond B $(90 \tfrac{25}{32} + 1.5075) = 92.28875$

$$\frac{\$1{,}517{,}821}{92.28875} = \underline{\underline{\$1{,}642{,}946.44}}$$

Nominal of Bond B

(b) $Y \times P \times MD = P$

$-0.0050 \times \$4{,}614{,}437.5 \times -9.51 = \$219{,}416.50$

(c) In the case of (i) the impact of changing the duration of the holding from 3 to 9.51 increases sensitivity to rate changes, whereas (ii) has adjusted for this risk.

In effect, the switch is not just a simple anomaly yield pick-up switch since it involves a move along the yield curve and therefore the trade is exposed to changes in the shape of the yield curve.

One way of attempting to address these issues is to perform a switch profit projection that would assess the trade under a variety of scenarios.

10. (a) $97 \tfrac{28}{32} \times 5.6m = \$5{,}481{,}000$

$99 \tfrac{2}{32} \times 4.4m = \$4{,}358{,}750$

\$9,839,750

(b) $\frac{5.481}{9.83975} \times 6.7 = 3.732$

$\frac{4.35875}{9.83975} \times 4.3 = 1.905$

5.637

(c) $$97 \tfrac{28}{32} \times \frac{-6.7}{1.0565} \times -0.0020 \times \frac{\$5.6m}{100} = \$69{,}517.65$$

$$99 \tfrac{2}{32} \times \frac{-4.3}{1.0545} \times -0.0020 \times \frac{\$4.4m}{100} = \$35{,}547.89$$

$\$69{,}517.65 + \$35{,}547.89 = \$105{,}065.54$

(d) To create a risk neutral switch the positions switched will have to have an equal interest rate exposure. This can be achieved through the use of a hedge ratio.

$$\frac{\text{Modified duration} \times \text{price of Bond A}}{\text{Modified duration} \times \text{price of Bond B}}$$

Whilst this will ensure that the initial position is equal in risk, it will not protect against non-parallel shifts in the yield curve.

The rationale behind such a switch will have been to gain a pick up on yield without increasing risk. Before switching it would be important to consider dealing costs. Yield pick-up must exceed dealing costs.

4. (a) **Immunisation**

Duration of Bond A

Time	Cash Flow	DF (10%)	PV	tPV
1	8.00	$\frac{1}{1.10}$	7.27	7.27
2	108.00	$\frac{1}{1.10^2}$	89.26	178.52
			96.53	185.79

$$\text{Duration} = \frac{185.79}{96.53} = 1.925 \text{ years}$$

Duration of Bond B

Time	Cash Flow	DF (10%)	PV	tPV
1	7.00	$\frac{1}{1.10}$	6.36	6.36
2	7.00	$\frac{1}{1.10^2}$	5.79	11.58
3	7.00	$\frac{1}{1.10^3}$	5.26	15.78
4	7.00	$\frac{1}{1.10^4}$	4.78	19.12
5	110.00	$\frac{1}{1.10^5}$	68.30	341.50
			90.49	394.34

$$\text{Duration} = \frac{394.34}{90.49} = 4.358 \text{ years}$$

Portfolio Weighting

If p represents the proportion invested in Bond B, then (1 – p) will be invested in Bond A, giving

$$\begin{aligned} 3.000 &= 1.925(1-p) + 4.358p \\ &= 1.925 - 1.925p + 4.358p \\ 1.075 &= 2.433p \\ p &= 0.442 \\ (1-p) &= 0.558 \end{aligned}$$

i.e. invest 55.8% in A and 44.2% in B.

(b) **One Year Later**

Duration of Bond A

A is now effectively a pure discount bond paying one cash flow in one year. Its duration will, therefore, be one year.

Duration of Bond B

Time	Cash Flow	DF (10%)	PV	tPV
1	7.00	$\frac{1}{1.10}$	6.36	6.36
2	7.00	$\frac{1}{1.10^2}$	5.79	11.58
3	7.00	$\frac{1}{1.10^3}$	5.26	15.78
4	110.00	$\frac{1}{1.10^4}$	75.13	300.52
			92.54	334.24

$$\text{Duration} = \frac{334.24}{92.54} = 3.612 \text{ years.}$$

Portfolio Weighting

If p represents the proportion invested in Bond B, then (1 – p) will be invested in Bond A, and to satisfy a liability that is now due in two years we need

$$\begin{aligned} 2.000 &= 1.000(1 - p) + 3.612p \\ &= 1.000 - 1.000p + 3.612p \\ 1.000 &= 2.612p \\ p &= 0.383 \\ (1 - p) &= 0.617 \end{aligned}$$

i.e. invest 61.7% in A and 38.3% in B.

The weighting scheme must change through time in order to keep the portfolio immunised, since the durations of bonds change in a non-linear fashion through time. As the duration of the longer dated bond, B, declines by the smaller proportion, the weight attributed to this bond will decline.

(c) **Further Precautions**

With large shifts in interest rates, convexity needs to be considered. Ideally, the convexity of the portfolio should be set equal to, or greater than, the convexity of the liability, which can be approximated for a bullet liability as $\frac{1}{2}n(n + 1)$, where n = time to maturity of the liability (from the convexity formula applied to a zero coupon bond). In addition, the portfolio needs duration matching.

12. (a) **Change in Value**

This can be calculated from the modified durations of the bonds, for which we firstly need their durations.

For the first three zero coupon bonds their duration is their maturity.

2 Year 10% Bond

Time	Cash	DF	PV	tPV
1	10	$\frac{1}{1.10}$	9.09	9.09
2	110	$\frac{1}{1.10^2}$	90.91	181.82
			100.00	190.91

$$\text{Duration} = \frac{190.91}{100.00} = 1.9091.$$

3 Year 6% Bond

Time	Cash	DF	PV	tPV
1	6	$\frac{1}{1.10}$	5.46	5.46
2	6	$\frac{1}{1.10^2}$	4.96	9.92
3	106	$\frac{1}{1.10^3}$	79.64	238.92
			90.06	254.30

$$\text{Duration} = \frac{254.30}{90.06} = 2.8237.$$

Portfolio Duration

Maturity	Coupon	Proportion	Duration	Weighted
1	0	0.1	1	0.1000
4	0	0.2	4	0.8000
6	0	0.1	6	0.6000
2	10	0.3	1.0901	0.5727
3	6	0.3	2.8237	0.8471
				2.9198

$$\text{Modified duration} = \frac{2.9198}{1.10} = 2.6544$$

Hence if yields rise 1%, the portfolio will fall by 2.6544%.

(b) **Multi-Period Immunisation**

- Match duration of the bond portfolio to the duration of the liabilities.
- Ensure the PV of the bonds is greater than, or equal to, the PV of the liabilities.
- Ensure the dispersion of the assets (hence the convexity) is greater than, or equal to, that of the liabilities.

16 Performance Measurement and Appraisal

INTRODUCTION

To complete the bond fund management process we must be able to assess the performance of the selected strategy in order to take any corrective action. The techniques examined in this section are

- What techniques do we have for measuring returns
- What techniques are available for assessing the adequacy of those returns
- How can we sub-analyse or attribute those returns to the various decisions that the investor or fund manager has made

CHAPTER CONTENTS

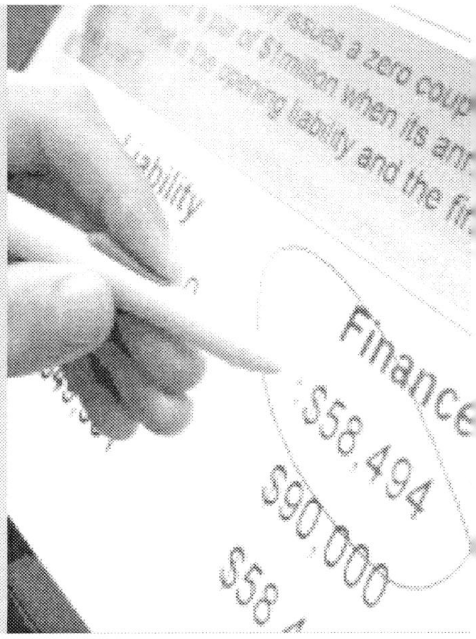

Chapter Learning Objectives

The syllabus areas covered by this section are

Analysis

Students should possess a broad understanding of both static and dynamic methods for the analysis and construction of fixed income securities containing both certain and contingent cashflows. Variable rate securities will be included. Students should be aware of the limitations of assumptions and mathematical techniques upon results. Although analysis will be concerned principally with 'risk–free' securities, students should be aware of the further considerations for 'risky' securities and the effect they may have on expected return. Students should possess a thorough comprehension of single–period and multi–period, single currency and multi–currency portfolio management theory.

- Performance Measurement
- Performance Attribution

Students will not be required to perform higher mathematical calculations, to derive any theoretical proofs, or to know any formulae other than for the topics marked (*) above to satisfy the requirements of the paper. Should other formulae be necessary they will be given. An awareness of the limitations of the mathematical techniques is necessary. Students may expect applications of analytic techniques in practical examples.

1 Introduction

An investor who has been paying someone to actively manage their portfolio will clearly wish to monitor how well the fund manager is doing his job. Such information can then be used to

- Alter or update the portfolio investment constraints in order to achieve a particular objective.
- Communicate investment objectives to the fund manager, which should affect how the fund is managed.
- Identify strengths and weaknesses of particular fund managers.

When measuring a fund's performance we have three objectives to establish.

- What was the performance achieved? That is, we need to be able to **measure performance.**
- Was the fund performance relatively good or bad? That is, we need to **appraise performance.**
- Did this situation arise due to skill (or lack thereof) or just fortune? That is, we need to be able to **attribute performance**.

2 Measurement of Performance

2.1 Introduction

In order to reflect all the actions of our fund managers, any performance measures must include both dividends and capital growth. As such, we must always be looking at the market values of any securities held in the fund as opposed to their historical costs.

Example 1

Investment A costs £100 and at the end of six months returns £10, before being sold for £110. How can it be compared with investment B, bought at £50, held for one year and then sold for £70 with no income paid out? Obviously the different cost must be taken into account, as well as the different returns and time periods involved.

2.2 Holding period return

2.2.1 Introduction

Each investment is characterised by a cost and a pattern of cash flows. We could describe a fund's performance by stating the dividends plus capital growth (final market value less initial value) as a percentage of the initial amount invested.

2.2.2 Calculation

Calculating the percentage holding period return for each investment avoids the problem of comparing different size investments. This return is simply the gain during the period held (money received less cost) divided by the initial cost, i.e.

Formula to learn

$$r_p = \frac{(D + V_e) - V_s}{V_s} \times 100\%$$

where

r_p = holding period return.
D = any returns paid out from the investment/fund at the end of the period.
V_s = is the initial cost at the start of the holding period.
V_e = the value of the investment at the end of the holding period.

Solution 1a

Using this equation the holding period returns for Investments A and B can be calculated as follows.

Investment A

$$r_a = \frac{(D + V_e) - V_s}{V_s} \times 100\%$$

$$r_a = \frac{(10 + 110) - 100}{100} \times 100\% = 20\% \text{ in six months}$$

Investment B

$$r_b = \frac{(D + V_e) - V_s}{V_s} \times 100\%$$

$$r_b = \frac{(0 + 70) - 50}{50} \times 100\% = 40\% \text{ in a year}$$

2.2.3 Results

The holding period returns of A and B are not yet directly comparable, since B was invested for twice as long as A. When A was sold, the proceeds could have been reinvested for another six months, but we do not know what return would have been available to the investor at that time. To compare the returns they must be for a standard period. This is achieved by using the equivalent period interest rate formula to annualise the returns as follows.

Solution 1b

Investment A

r_a = 20% in six months

Hence, annualising this return we get

$$1 + r = (1 + R)^n$$

$$1 + r = 1.2^2 = 1.44$$

r = 0.44 or 44% p.a.

Investment B

r_b = 40% p.a.

We have now got a standardised measure of return, the annualised holding period return.

The problem that arises with this measure, however, is what if there have been significant cash inflows to/outflows from the fund during the period other than the period end dividend. These could significantly distort the results.

Example 2

A fund has a start value of £10m, and halfway through the period it has the same value and a further £10m is deposited. At the end of the period it is worth £20m, no dividends having been paid.

What is the fund's performance?

Solution 2a

Using our equation above we have

$$r_p = \frac{D + V_e - V_s}{V_s} \times 100\%$$

$$r_p = \frac{£0 + £20m - £10m}{£10m} \times 100\% = +100\%$$

But has the fund really generated a 100% return? In truth, it has generated no return whatsoever. Its terminal value is simply the sum of what was initially held, plus the funds added. No return or growth has been generated.

This simple approach is, therefore, inadequate. We must in some way account for the deposits and withdrawals that occur during the period over which we are determining the performance.

2.3 Money-weighted returns

2.3.1 Introduction/calculation

A money-weighted return (MWR) is the internal rate of return (IRR) of the fund opening and closing values along with any deposits into/withdrawals from the fund.

If r is the money-weighted return then, using present value ideas, the current fund market value must be equal to the future fund cash payouts discounted at this rate, i.e.

Formula to learn

$$V_S = \frac{CF_1}{(1+r)^{t_1}} + \frac{CF_2}{(1+r)^{t_2}} + \cdots + \frac{CF_n}{(1+r)^{t_n}} + \frac{V_e}{(1+r)}$$

where

V_S = current fund value

CF_1 = cash (inflow to)/outflow from the fund at the Time t_1 during the period, including dividends paid out by the fund

V_e = fund value at the end of the period

r = money-weighted return

This has the advantage over our simple holding period return calculation above of considering all the relevant cash flows **and** their timings.

Note that this formula cannot be solved, the money-weighted return (or IRR) must be found through trial and error/interpolation in a normal DCF tabular calculation. Furthermore, in applying this approach we must assume we buy the fund at the start and sell it at the end.

Solution 2b

Applying this to example 2 above, we get

Time	Comment	Cash Flow (£m)	Discount Factor	Present Value (£m)
0	'Buy' the fund	(10)	1	(10)
$^1/_2$	Further investment	(10)	$\frac{1}{1.00^{½}}$	(10)
1	'Sell' the fund	20	$\frac{1}{1.00}$	20
				0

Giving a money-weighted return of 0%, the solution we wanted.

Unfortunately, this method does not always give the expected results.

Example 3

Our fund starts the year with a value of £20m. It falls to £10m by the middle of the year when a further £10m is invested bringing the fund back up to £20m in total. It then rises to £40m at the year-end. Calculate the money-weighted return.

Solution 3a

Before we calculate the money-weighted return, let us consider what we expect. Each £1 we held at the start of the period fell in value to 50p by the middle of the period but rose back to £1 by the end. Once more our overall performance has been zero.

Time	Comment	Cash Flow (£m)	Discount Factor	Present Value (£m)
0	'Buy' the fund	(20)	1	(20.00)
$^1/_2$	Further investment	(10)	$\frac{1}{1.40693^{1/2}}$	(8.43)
1	'Sell' the fund	40	$\frac{1}{1.40693}$	28.43
				0.00

The money-weighted return is 40.693%, clearly not what we expected.

2.3.2 Results

The performance appears good because there was more money invested in the second half of the period when the fund was performing well. The performance has been **money-weighted**, biasing this measure towards the performance during the period when money invested was at its peak.

What is needed is a measure that is unaffected by cash inflows to and outflows from the fund (deposits and withdrawals) over which the fund manager has no control.

2.4 Time weighted returns

Exam tip

Most recently examined in Winter 2008 Question 4.

2.4.1 Introduction/calculation

The time-weighted return achieves this objective. The method is to calculate the returns between any cash flow dates using our original holding period formula, then combine them in a similar fashion to compound interest to establish the return for the full period.

When calculating the returns between each cash flow (deposits, withdrawals, dividends), we will take

V_s = fund value immediately **after** the cash flow that marked the **start** of the sub-period (or start of the period if it is the first sub-period)

V_e = fund value immediately **before** the cash flow that marked the **end** of the sub-period (or end of the period if it is the last sub-period)

For the purposes of clarity of calculations, it is always useful to draw a graphical representation of how the value of the fund has changed over time. This helps to clarify the numbers to use.

Solution 2b

In relation to example above, we had a mid-period deposit and hence we need to evaluate two sub-periods, the sub-period before that date and the subsequent one.

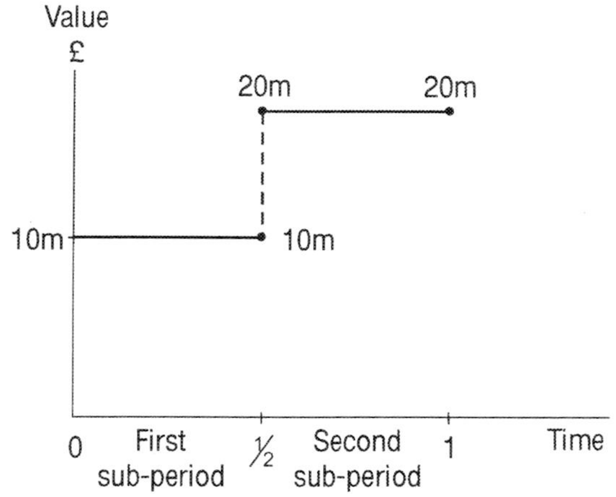

The idea here is that the fund manager controls the change in the fund value over time (i.e. the solid horizontal lines above). He does not control the timing and scale of any cash inflows or outflows (the vertical dotted line). The fund manager should only be assessed on the factors he controls, which is the aim of the time-weighted return.

First sub-period

Using

$$r_1 = \frac{(D + V_e) - V_s}{V_s} \times 100\%$$

We get

$$r_1 = \frac{(0 + £10m) - £10m}{£10m} \times 100\% = 0\%$$

Second sub-period

V_s is now £20m following the £10m deposit marking the start of this sub-period, hence

$$r_2 = \frac{(D + V_e) - V_s}{V_s} \times 100\%$$

Gives

$$r_2 = \frac{(0 + £20m) - £20m}{£20m} \times 100\% = 0\%$$

Combining

Clearly, if there is no return during either sub-period the combined periods return is zero. Demonstrating this formally to give the full period return r_p

$$1 + r_p = (1 + r_1) \times (1 + r_2)$$

$$1 + r_p = (1 + 0) \times (1 + 0) = 1$$

$$r_p = 0$$

Solution 3b

In relation to example above, again we have two sub-periods to evaluate.

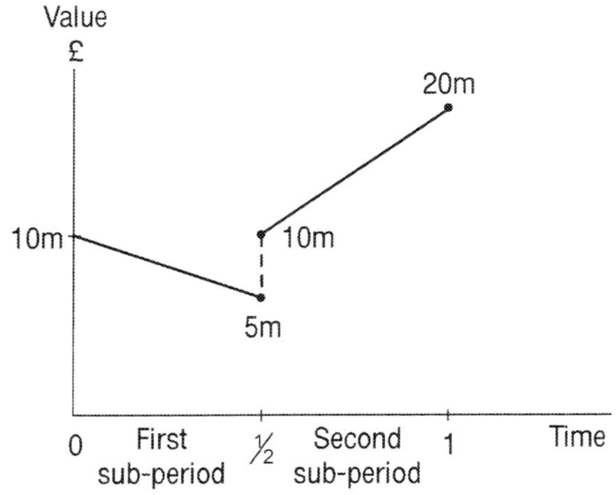

Once again, the fund manager controls the change in value over time (i.e. the solid diagonals), and it is this change in value over this time period that he should be appraised on.

First sub-period

The fund starts with a value of £20m which falls to £10m, hence

$$r_1 = \frac{(D + V_e) - V_s}{V_s} \times 100\%$$

Gives

$$r_1 = \frac{(0 + £10m) - £20m}{£20m} \times 100\% = -50\%$$

Second sub-period

Following the deposit of a further £10m the fund value starts this sub-period with a value of £20m which rises to £40m, hence

$$r_2 = \frac{(D + V_e) - V_s}{V_s} \times 100\%$$

Gives

$$r_2 = \frac{(0 + £40m) - £20m}{£20m} \times 100\% = +100\%$$

Combining

Combining these two sub-periods to give a full period return r_p using

$$1 + r_p = (1 + r_1) \times (1 + r_2)$$

Gives

$$1 + r_p = (1 - 0.5) \times (1 + 1) = 1$$

$$1 + r_p = 0.5 \times 2 = 1$$

$$r_p = 0$$

Hence, the overall periodic return is reported as zero as we felt it should be.

By combining the returns as effectively compound interest in each sub-period we are **time-weighting** the returns.

2.4.2 Results

The time-weighted return is unaffected by either the timing of cash inflows/outflows or the value of funds invested in the period. It therefore represents a good measure of the manager's performance.

Example 4

A fund starts the year with a value of £100m. The value of the fund at the end of each quarter and the cash inflows/(outflows) following those valuations are

	Q1	Q2	Q3	Q4
Value	105	107	116	117
In/(Out)	(2)	3	(4)	(2)

Calculate the time-weighted return for the year and the average quarterly return.

Solution

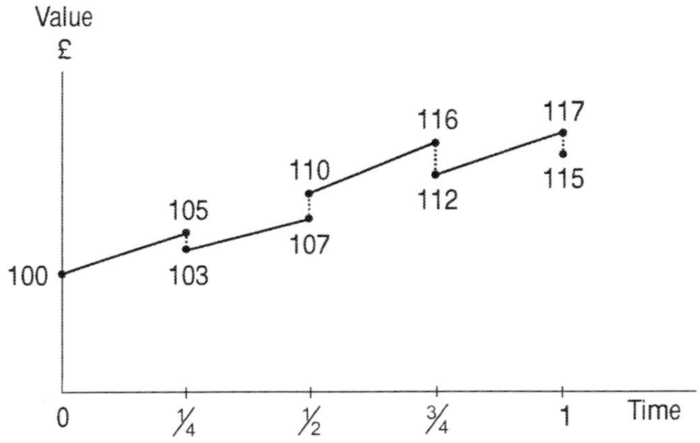

$r_1 = \frac{105 - 100}{100} = 0.05$ or 5%

$r_2 = \frac{107 - 103}{103} = 0.0388$ or 3.88%

$r_3 = \frac{116 - 110}{110} = 0.0545$ or 5.45%

$r_4 = \frac{117 - 112}{112} = 0.0446$ or 4.46%

Annual return

$$1 + r_{yr} = (1 + r_1)(1 + r_2)(1 + r_3)(1 + r_4)$$

$$= 1.05 \times 1.0388 \times 1.0545 \times 1.0446 = 1.2015$$

$$r_{yr} = 0.2015 \text{ or } 20.15\%$$

Average quarterly return

The average quarterly return can be best calculated as the geometric mean of the individual quarters, since this is a compounding relationship, i.e.

$$(1 + r_{qtr})^4 = (1 + r_1)(1 + r_2)(1 + r_3)(1 + r_4)$$

$$= 1.2015$$

$$(1 + r_{qtr}) = 1.04696$$

$$r_{qtr} = 0.04696 \text{ or } 4.696\%$$

19.2.5 Conclusion

In general, the **money-weighted method** of measuring returns for the purposes of evaluation is considered **inappropriate,** since this measure is strongly influenced by the size and timing of cash flows outside the control of the fund manager.

The **time-weighted** return does not suffer from this problem and must be considered **more appropriate**.

3 Appraisal of Performance

Exam tip

> This area has been examined as a discussion in both the compulsory Section B an d optional Section C, see Winter 2004 Question 11

3.1 Introduction

We have now established a way of assessing the return achieved, but how can we tell whether this is good or bad, e.g. is a return of 5% good? Clearly, we cannot answer this question unless we have a yardstick to measure against, such as interest rates or general market performance.

Furthermore, there are two different performance appraisal criteria that could be utilised depending on the circumstances, absolute performance and relative performance.

Absolute performance measures aim to establish whether the total return is at a suitable level given the total risk experienced. Given that the basis of most finance theory is that investors are rational and risk averse, it is appropriate to determine whether they are being adequately compensated by way of absolute return for that absolute risk. Methods that we can utilise for this purpose include

- Comparison of total returns to a customised benchmark index.
- Excess return per unit risk measures, determining how well the excess absolute return over the risk-free rate compensates for the total risk.

Relative performance measures may be appropriate when the investment strategy is to outperform a specific index. In this case, it will be the excess return and risk in comparison to the index that will be relevant. Almost by definition, this is best achieved by considering excess return per unit risk measures.

3.2 Peer group benchmarking

3.2.1 Introduction

Peer group benchmarking may be appropriate where the fund manager is responsible for both the strategic asset allocation and stock selection for the fund. In this situation it is unlikely that there will be a suitable index that reflects any possible realistic asset allocation so management performance may be most conveniently measured by reference to the relevant peer group.

The peer group would be fund managers who are also responsible for the full range of management decisions (asset allocation and stock selection) for a fund with similar objectives and constraints. With peer group benchmarking the fund management objectives will probably be defined as, say, outperform the peer group median performance.

One potential problem with this approach, however, is that these objectives for the fund manager may not tie in well to the objectives of the fund (i.e. match the fund liabilities).

Peer group benchmarking has also been criticised as tending to produce asset allocation decisions based simply on what other funds are doing, rather than the needs of the fund involved.

Additionally, a peer group benchmark does not show whether a fund manager is performing well in absolute terms. If all of the peer group are poor fund managers, he may be top of the peer group but still be showing poor absolute performance.

An alternative to peer group benchmarking is customised benchmarking. This is appropriate where the asset allocation decision and stock selection decisions are separated, the asset allocation decision taken by the trustee, say, with the stock selection decisions being taken by the fund manager/managers.

The manager's performance can then be assessed by reference to an appropriate index or customised benchmark based on the assets under his management. Using this approach, the selection of the precise index is an important decision – is that index suitable for satisfying the fund's liability matching objectives? In addition, setting the limits for any permitted divergence from that index is also highly important. If these limits are tight then the fund becomes a pseudo-tracker, and the fund is paying active management fees when the true style is passive.

3.2.2 Myner's review

The Myner's review of 2001 examine these benchmarking issues, among others, especially in the context of assessing pension fund performance. As a result of the weaknesses of the peer group approach, the review concluded that this was inappropriate for managing pension funds and recommended a customised benchmarking approach under which the fund should

- Consider the suitability of any index benchmarks in achieving the fund objectives.
- Consider for each asset class whether active or passive management is most appropriate.
- Where they believe that active management has the potential to achieve higher returns
  - Set divergence limits for fund managers to operate within.
  - Set challenging targets and risk controls for out-performance against the index, allowing sufficient freedom for genuine active management to occur.
  - Encourage an active management approach to be undertaken with conviction.

3.3 Comparison to a benchmark index

3.3.1 Introduction

In order to assess how well a fund manager is performing, we need a yardstick for comparison. One such suitable yardstick may be a benchmark index. Once we have determined an appropriate benchmark, we can then compare whether the fund manager outperformed, matched, or underperformed.

The appropriate benchmark is one that is consistent with the preferences of the funds' trustees and the funds' tax status. For example, a different benchmark is appropriate if the fund is a gross fund and does not pay taxes (e.g. a pension fund), than if it is a net fund and does pay taxes (e.g. a general insurance fund).

Similarly, a general market index will not be appropriate as a benchmark if the trustee has a preference for high-income securities or an aversion to certain securities, e.g. rival companies. The FTSE UK Gilt Index would not be an appropriate benchmark if half the securities were held overseas.

There will therefore be different benchmarks for different funds and different fund managers. If the benchmark is an index of one kind or another it is important to understand the structure of the relevant index. The structure of indices has been discussed in an earlier chapter.

The characteristics that are required to render an index suitable as a benchmark are that it is

- Specified and unambiguous.
- Appropriate to the preferences of the fund (e.g. a government bond fund may utilise the FTSE UK Gilt index).
- Appropriate to the currency of the fund.

- Investable, i.e. composed of investments that could conceivably be held in the fund.
- Measurable, i.e. the return can be calculated on a frequent basis as required.
- Representative of achievable performance, i.e. it has an arithmetic weighted composition (remember that the return of a portfolio is an arithmetic weighted average of the individual stock returns).
- Measures the relevant component of performance, i.e. total return indices for total return performance and capital value indices for capital growth.

3.3.2 Performance appraisal

Once we have established a suitable benchmark we can appraise the fund manager's performance by reference to it. The benchmark performance can be quite simply calculated as the weighted average of the holding period returns on the relevant benchmark indices.

Example

A pension fund manager has a portfolio with an initial value of £100m. The company for whom the fund is run is internationally based with 80% of its employees in the UK and 20% in the US. As such, it requires a corresponding international investment strategy concentrating on a diversified spread of shares.

The company feels that the fund manager should be able to at least match the following two indices on the relevant portions of the fund.

- FTSE UK Gilt index (over 15 years) on the UK portion.
- Lehman Brothers US Government Bond Index.

The values on these indices at the start and end of the year were

	FTSE Gilt	US Bond
End of Year	226	1500
Start of Year	200	1380

The fund had a capital value of £113m at the end of the year, there having been no cash inflows and outflows during the year. What return has the fund manager achieved, what return has the benchmark portfolio achieved and has the fund manager achieved his target of at least matching the benchmark?

Solution

Fund performance

Since there have been no cash inflows/outflows during the year, we can use the simple holding period return formula to assess the fund performance, giving

$$r = \frac{(D + V_e) - V_s}{V_s} \times 100\%$$

Gives

$$r = \frac{(0 + £113m) - £100m}{£100m} \times 100\% = +13\%$$

Benchmark performance

FTSE Gilt

$$r = \frac{226 - 200}{200} = 0.13 \text{ or } 13\%$$

US Bond

$$r = \frac{1{,}500 - 1{,}380}{1{,}380} = 0.087 \text{ or } 8.7\%$$

Weighted average

$r = 0.8 \times 13\% + 0.2 \times 8.7\% = 12.14\%$

Appraisal

Actual Performance	+13.00%	+0.86%	**Outperformance**
Original Benchmark	+12.14%		

The fund manager has achieved a return of 13% against the benchmark portfolio return of 12.14%. Hence, the fund manager has achieved his target of outperforming the benchmark.

Note, however, that this conclusion is only valid so long as the total return achieved was at no higher a level of risk than that of the underlying index. If this actual return has been achieved at a significantly elevated level of risk, this conclusion would be invalid.

In addition, no account has been taken of currency effects in this example – this is dealt with later.

3.3.3 Performance attribution/decomposition

The above performance appraisal assumed that the fund manager made no decisions regarding asset allocation, rather he simply took the 80:20 split proposed by the company and concentrated on selecting stocks within those sectors. Thus, we have established in the above example that the fund manager is good at stock selection.

The fund manager may, however, be free to determine his own asset allocation. If this is the case, then we may wish to appraise his performance in the two key investment management areas of

- Asset allocation.
- Stock selection.

To achieve this performance attribution or performance decomposition, we need to consider the actual performance and the performance of the following two benchmark portfolios.

- A portfolio with the asset allocation determined by the fund manager – a revised benchmark.
- A portfolio with the asset allocation as proposed by the client – the original benchmark.

Example

Based on the above data, but now assuming that the fund manager has decided on a different asset allocation, investing 85% in UK bonds and 15% in the US, establish how the fund manager has performed.

Solution

Fund performance

As before the fund performance is +13%.

Revised benchmark

The performance of the revised benchmark can be calculated in exactly the same way as for the original benchmark.

FTSE Gilt

$$r = \frac{226 - 200}{200} = 0.13 \text{ or } 13\%$$

US Bond

$$r = \frac{1,500 - 1,380}{1,380} = 0.087 \text{ or } 8.7\%$$

Weighted average

$r = 0.85 \times 13\% + 0.15 \times 8.7\% = 12.35\%$

Original benchmark

The original benchmark performance is unaltered at +12.14%.

Appraisal

Fund Managers's Performance vs Benchmark

Actual Performance	+13.00%		
		+0.65%	**Stock Selection Gain**
Revised Benchmark	+12.35%		
		+0.21%	**Asset Allocation Gain**
Original Benchmark	+12.14%		

The actual performance has exceeded both benchmarks, but what does this tell us?

The actual fund and revised benchmark have the same asset allocation (85% UK, 15% US), hence any difference in performance must be attributable to **stock selection**. As a result, we can say that the fund manager has boosted fund performance by 0.65% (13.00% – 12.35%) as a result of superior stock selection, or £650,000 based on our original fund size of £100m (£100m × 0.65%).

The revised benchmark and original benchmark are based on the same indices (same stocks), hence any difference between them must be due to **asset allocation**. As a result, we can say that the fund manager has boosted fund performance by 0.21% (12.35% – 12.14%) as a result of superior asset allocation, or £210,000 based on our original fund size of £100m (£100m × 0.21%).

3.3.4 Dealing with foreign currency

Introduction

When undertaking international investment, the fund manager has two decisions to make.

- Which broad markets/geographic areas should he invest in (e.g. Europe, Far East, America, etc.)?
- Which specific countries should he invest in within those areas?

This is very similar to the asset allocation/stock selection decision above, which considered

- Which countries should he invest in?
- Which specific securities within those countries should he invest in?

The approach adopted is, therefore, very similar.

Approach

The approach to international investment appraisal is to isolate out asset performance and currency influences and deal with each separately using the above ideas.

Example

An international portfolio is being assessed against a benchmark with a 60:40 allocation between Latin America and the Far East. The actual allocation adopted by the fund manager is 70:30. The performances of the fund and benchmark have been decomposed into asset and currency components as follows.

	Actual		Benchmark	
	Asset %	Currency %	Asset %	Currency %
Latin America	10.0	6.0	10.0	5.0
Far East	12.0	3.0	11.0	4.0

Decompose the returns into asset allocation, stock selection and currency components.

Solution

	Actual		Benchmark	
	Asset %	Currency %	Asset %	Currency %
Latin America	10.0	6.0	10.0	5.0
Far East	12.0	3.0	11.0	4.0
70:30 Portfolio	10.6	5.1	10.3	4.7
60:40 Portfolio			10.4	4.6

Asset performance

Actual (70:30)	10.6%		
		+0.3%	**Stock Selection Gain**
70:30 Benchmark	10.3%		
		−0.1%	**Market Allocation Gain**
60:40 Benchmark	10.4%		

Currency performance

Actual (70:30)	5.1%		
		+0.4%	**Currency Selection Gain**
70:30 Benchmark	4.7%		
		+0.1%	**Market Allocation Gain**
60:40 Benchmark	4.6%		

3.4 Excess return per unit risk

3.4.1 Introduction

One of the basic ideas running throughout has been that risk and return tend to go hand in hand, i.e. a higher expected risk will need to be compensated by a higher return.

What this measure does is assess the extra return we are getting per unit of extra risk. The higher the figure, the better.

Excess return to relative duration

The excess return to relative duration measure is suitable for bond portfolios where the measure of risk is the duration. The measure can be calculated as

Formula to learn

$$\text{Excess return to relative duration} = \frac{r_p - r_f}{d_p/d_m}$$

where

r_p = portfolio return
r_f = risk-free return over the same period
d_p/d_m = duration of portfolio (d_p) relative to that of the market (d_m)

The higher the measure, the better the performance and the calculation of this measure is very similar to the above.

Example

Two fund managers are employed to manage portions of a large pension fund. They both have the same objectives etc. Details about their portfolios are given below.

Fund	Return %	Relative duration
A	9.5	1.05
B	12	1.20

Over the same period the risk-free rate was 8% and the FTSE Gilt index showed a return of 10%.

Solution

$$\text{Excess return to relative duration} = \frac{r_p - r_f}{d_p/d_m}$$

Gives

$$\text{Fund A} = \frac{9.5 - 8}{1.05} = 1.43\%$$

$$\text{Fund B} = \frac{12 - 8}{1.20} = 3.33\%$$

$$\text{Gilt Index} = \frac{10 - 8}{1} = 2.00\%$$

Hence, we can say that on a risk-adjusted basis fund manager B has outperformed both fund manager A and the index. Fund manager A has underperformed the index.

CHAPTER ROUNDUP

Return measures

- Holding period return

$$r_p = \frac{(D + V_e) - V_s}{V_s} \times 100\%$$

- Money weighted return is IRR calculation.
- Time weighted return – Plot a chart of the changes in fund values and use this to assess the return.

Appraisal

You need to be able to decompose or attribute performance

- Between stock selection and asset allocation.
- Between asset and currency returns.

You must be able to calculate and comment on

- Excess return to relative duration

$$\text{Excess return to relative duration} = \frac{r_p - r_f}{d_p/d_m}$$

TEST YOUR KNOWLEDGE

Check your knowledge of the Chapter here, without referring back to the text.

1. A US investor buys 1 million yen at 105 to the dollar to hold for six months in a euro-yen account yielding 4 1/2% p.a. If the yen are sold at the end of the period for 99 to the dollar, what is the dollar holding period return?

2. £20m is invested in a fund that pays on annual coupon. The year end dividend and fund value prior to the payment are.

Year End Value	23	25	26
Dividend	2	3	3

What is the average annual time weighted return?

3. A fund manager invests 80% of his portfolio in the UK and 20% in the US. The fund has a value of £50m at the start of the year and £57m by the year end. Comparison benchmark indices for each part of the portfolio had the following values.

	UK	US
Start of year	3,000	500
End of year	3,400	580

Based on the above portfolio details, but given that the fund managers asset allocation differs from that suggested by the client of 75% UK, 25% US, what gain or loss has the fund manager generated through the activities of stock selection and asset allocation?

4 The FTSE Gilt index has returned 5.3% and has a duration of 8.8 years. A bond portfolio has returned 5.45% and has a duration of 9.7 years. If the risk free rate was 4.75% calculate the excess return to relative duration for both the index and the portfolio and comment on your findings.

TEST YOUR KNOWLEDGE: ANSWERS

1 Value of \$1 end = $\frac{\$1 \times 105 \times \left(1 + \frac{4.5}{2}\right)}{99}$ = \$1.084 a gain of 8.4%

2

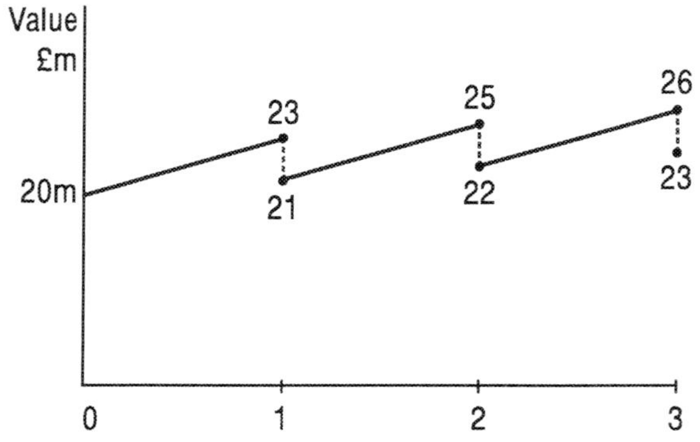

$r_1 = \frac{23-20}{20}$ $= 0.15$ or 15%

$r_2 = \frac{25-21}{21}$ $= 0.19$ or 19%

$r_3 = \frac{26-22}{22}$ $= 0.182$ or 18.2%

$(1 + r)^3 = 1.150 \times 1.190 \times 1.182 = 1.618$

$1 + r = 1.174$

$r = 0.174$ or 17.4%

3

Actual Performance	+14.0%		
		+0.1%	**Stock Selection Gain**
Revised Benchmark	+13.9%		
		–0.1%	**Asset Allocation Gain**
Original Benchmark	+14.0%		

$$\left(0.75 \times \left(\frac{3{,}400 - 3{,}000}{3{,}000}\right) + 0.25 \times \left(\frac{580 - 500}{500}\right)\right)$$

4 Excess return to relative duration

Index = $\frac{5.3 - 4.75}{1}$ = 0.55

Bond = $\frac{5.45 - 4.75}{9.7/8.8}$ = 0.64

With a higher excess return to relative duration the bond portfolio has outperformed the index.

BPP LEARNING MEDIA

INDEX